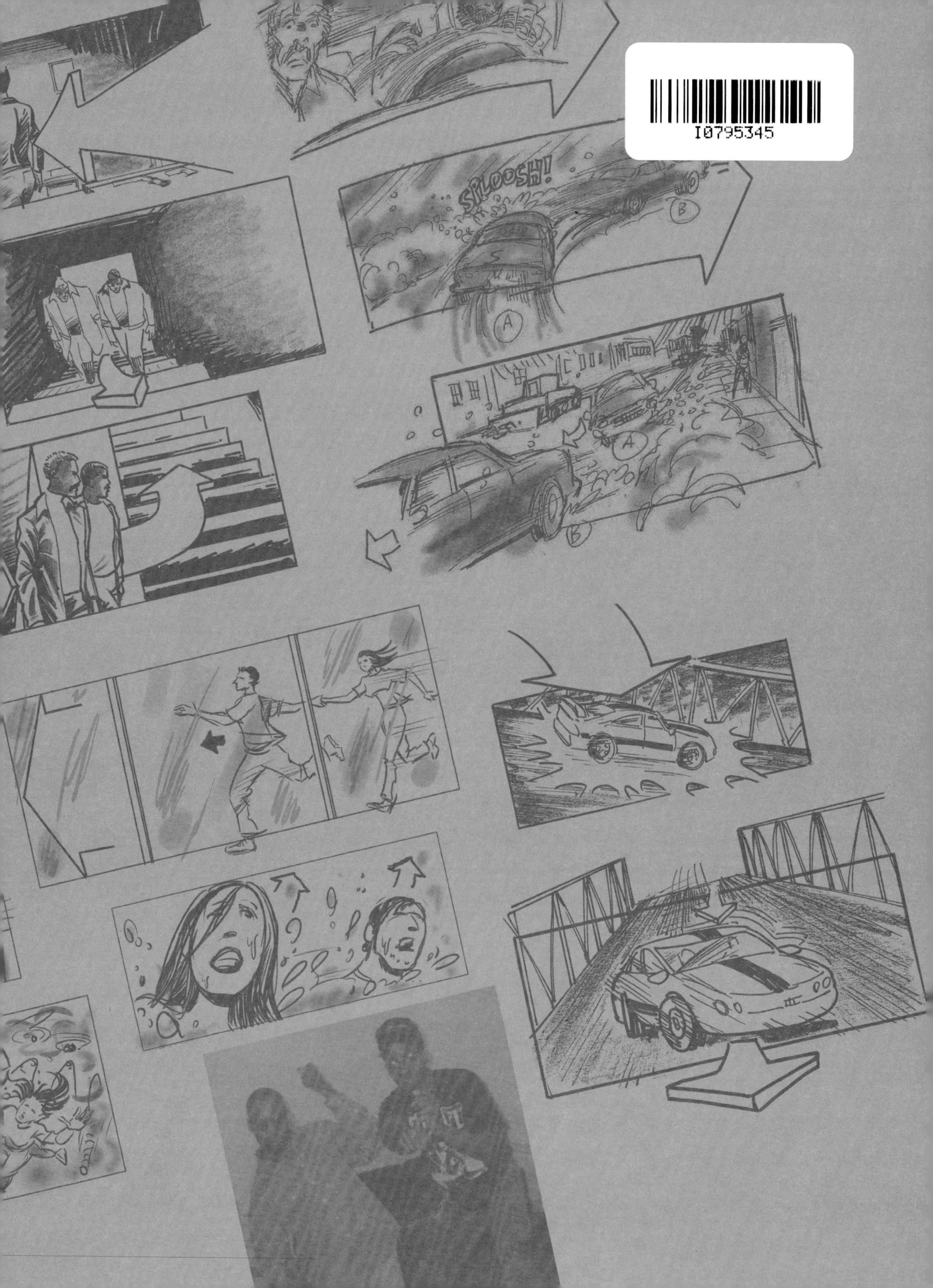
SPLOOSH!
B
A
A
B

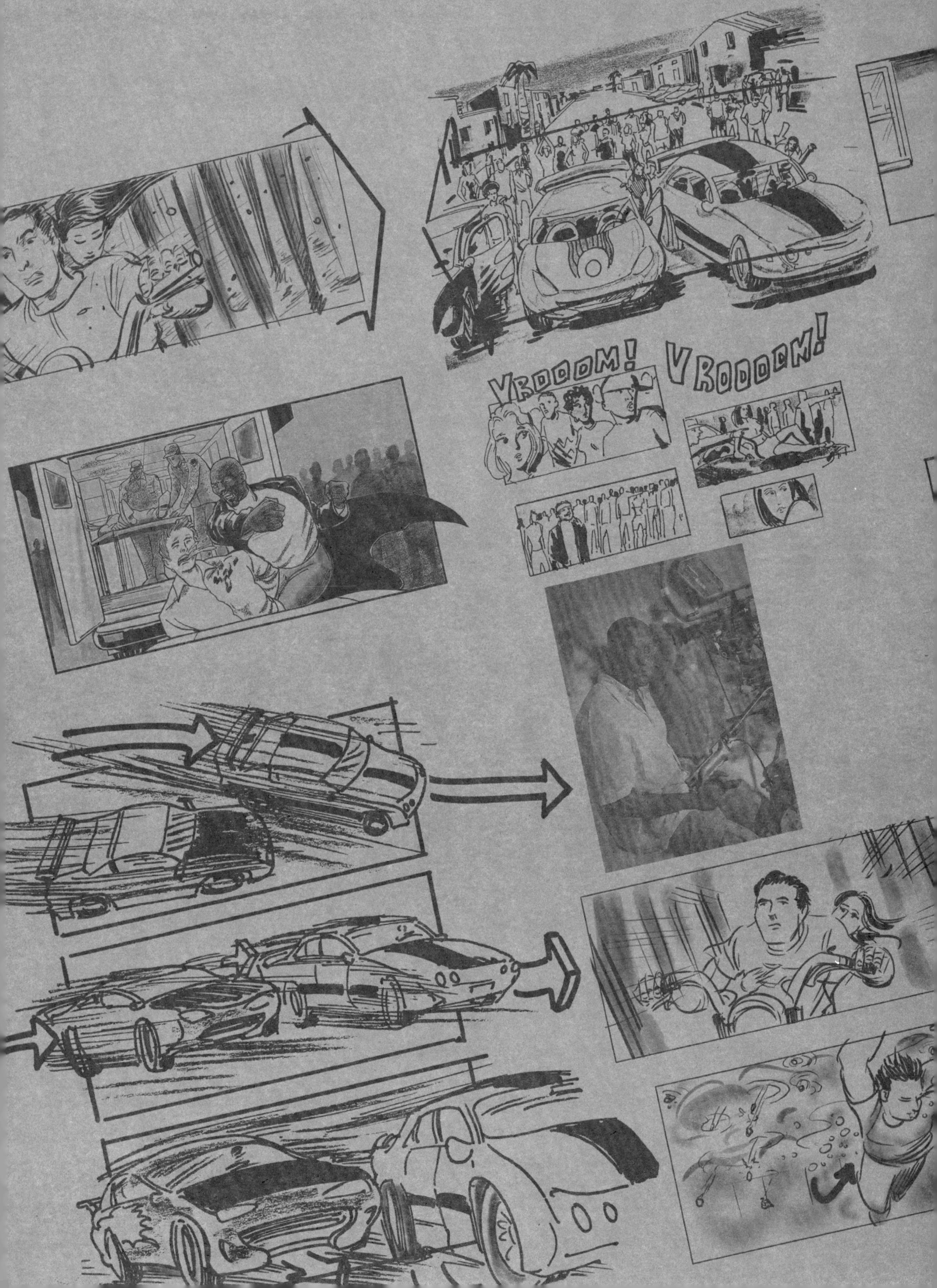
VROOOM!
VROOOOM!

A Hard Day's Work

STORYBOARDS AND STORIES OF 15 SELECT FILMS AND TELEVISION SHOWS

BY

WARREN DRUMMOND

Author: Warren Drummond
Book Concept / Art Director / Editor / Publisher: Betty K. Bynum
Art Layout Design / Graphic Design: Brian Boehm

ISBN HARDBACK: 978-0-578-3355-5-1

First Edition.
Printed in China.

Library of Congress Control Number: 2023937641

DREAMTITLE PUBLISHING, LLC
LOS ANGELES

A Hard Day's Work

STORYBOARDS AND STORIES OF 15 SELECT FILMS AND TELEVISION SHOWS

BY
WARREN DRUMMOND

Thank You

I wish to thank these studios for their support in granting permissions for this project:

Paramount Pictures Corp

Marvel Studios

20th Century Studios

Universal Studios

ABC Studios

New Line Cinema / Warner Consumer Products

Lions Gate Films Inc

Miramax

Dedication

This book is lovingly dedicated to my mother, Ruth.
She gave me wings to fly but always had a parachute of love and wisdom.
I miss you, Mom and will always love you.

—◆—

And to John Singleton,
whom I loved as my own brother.
John's light and love of cinema shines on me, still.

—◆—

"Because of her, I am."

This book is the result of the sincere love of my wife, Betty, the guiding light of my life. She had the singular vision to create this book as a legacy of my work to date and labored intensely to make this book happen. She edges me forward and inspires me to believe in my own talents by her tenacious and endearing care.

"My own Anakin..."

And our son Josh, a young man full of good character and gifted with talents, whom I am eternally proud of.

Thank you both for supporting me. You are my beating heart. I love you.

Acknowledgments

I wish to thank the following studios for their help in this endeavor:

UNIVERSAL STUDIOS

2 Fast 2 Furious 2003 © Universal Studios. License by Universal Studios Licensing LLC.
All Rights Reserved.

A Beautiful Mind 2001 © Universal Studios and DreamWorks LLC. All Rights Reserved.

One True Thing 1998 © Universal Studios. All Rights Reserved.

Halloween Kills 2021 © Universal Studios, Miramax. All Rights Reserved.

20TH CENTURY STUDIOS

Die Hard: With a Vengeance ©1995, Roll Bounce ©2005, Rise of the Planet of the Apes ©2011 Twentieth Century Fox.

Free Guy ©2021 20th Century Studios. All rights reserved.
New Line Cinema/Warner Consumer Products

Above The Rim and all related characters and elements © & ™ New Line Productions, Inc (s18)

ABC STUDIOS

Agents of S.H.I.E.L.D. material provides by ABC Studios
Lions Gate Films Inc

Abduction ©2011 courtesy of Lions Gate Films Inc

PARAMOUNT PICTURES CORP

Shaft courtesy of Paramount Pictures ©Paramount Pictures Corp. All Rights Reserved.

Four Brothers courtesy of Paramount Pictures ©Paramount Pictures Corp. All Rights Reserved.

Fences courtesy of Paramount Pictures ©Paramount Pictures Corp. All Rights Reserved.

Images of Marvel Characters Reproduced with permission © 2023 Marvel.

COLUMBIA PICTURES

The Devil's Own ©1997 Columbia Pictures

A very "special thanks" to Graphic Designer BRIAN BOEHM of iDesign Graphics for his superb talent and elegant character.

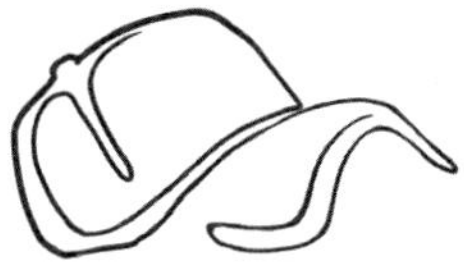

foreward

The best motion pictures simply tell a good story in a compelling way. A story begins with words on the page and then the filmmaker(s) shape and paint those words into the visual medium. That is where storyboards play a major role in inspiring the director to take the ideas suggested on the page and begin to design the visual style and shot selections that will engage and hopefully transport audiences in memorable cinematic ways.

Storyboards also serve a tremendous practical value as they become a tool of communication so that actors, cinematographers, production designers, stunt coordinators and special effects teams can explore and expand ideas and of course, figure out how in the world these visuals can be staged, shot and achieved.

The "boards" as we call them, play an ongoing role through the production as they inspire ideas for maintaining the budget, and even maintaining on-set safety for action scenes.

All that makes the storyboard artist a vitally important factor in the conceptualization of the project and therefore must themselves be strong and imaginative visual storytellers. Not easy to find these great artists who can help projects in the right direction.

I had the good fortune of working with Warren Drummond on *A BEAUTIFUL MIND* and I was very happy to have him as a crucial part of my storyboard team on the film.

I've always respected his talent, his creative instincts, his kindness and his professionalism. Kudos, Warren!

—Ron Howard, *Director*

STORYBOARDS AND STORIES OF 15 SELECT FILMS AND TELEVISION SHOWS

HARD DAY'S WORK

Chapter 1
SECRET ORIGINS

Secret Origins

It was the 1978 Christmas gift of The Art Of Star Wars book in that I became aware of storyboards.

I was born and raised in Jamaica, Queens to Ruth and John Drummond. I've always drawn, as have my older siblings, John Jr and Linda. John Jr, aka "Johnny" was the person I wanted to draw like, he had an amazing talent. As I was huge comic book enthusiast, my favorite artists were Marvel Comic's John Romita, Sr. and John Buscema.

Being accepted to The High School of Art & Design was a big deal for me. The school was legendary, as even John Romita, Sr. had attended many decades earlier when it was known as The High School Of Industrial Arts. I was reunited with my friend and upper-classman, Denys Cowan from middle school, who was one year older than me. Denys would later became a well known and respected comic book artist who now counts the Milestone comic book characters "Static" and "Hardware" as a co-creations. At A&D, I was in a school full of other artists like myself, with kids of all colors, so I started to find my way as a creative spirit.

I was selected to the renowned art and film college, The School Of Visual Arts upon graduation. At SVA, I had the opportunity to study with comic book legends, Will Eisner (creator of *The Spirit*), Harvey Kurtzman (co-creator of *Mad Magazine*), Art Spiegelman (creator of the Pulitzer Prize winning graphic novel *Mauz*) and Sam Viviano, who was a top magazine caricaturist. I mention these men as they were my first consistent connection with people who made art their career. I was shown it was indeed possible to make a living with what you loved if you put the work in.

My freelance work after graduating college was "sporadic" at best. I worked at New York's Bloomingdale's department store to support myself.

So let me explain how a series of events got me into the film industry. A Bloomingdale's friend and co-worker named Oscar Nunez—who's acting comedic talent later paid off US television version of *"THE OFFICE"*—got me into an organization called The Black Filmmaker Foundation.

The "BFF" was formed by The Hudlin Brothers, Warrington and Reginald who had a recent hit in the comedy movie *"House Party"*. Every third Saturday of the month the BFF workshops took place in NYU's Tisch School of the Arts. It was a place for Black film people to gather, learn and network with each other.

During this same time period, I made my way to Los Angeles for the first time, staying with my childhood friend, Greg Mays, who worked at a Columbia Pictures on the Sony lot. I also met Greg's buddy Hill Harper, who was then a struggling young actor along with some other friends.

One day Greg told me that a friend of his was doing a short film that needed storyboards. There wouldn't be any pay, but I could use the work as samples for future work.

After getting back to New York I got a call from my friend, Rodney Stringfellow, who was the executive assistant for The Hudlin Brothers. Rodney had friends who were going to do a movie called *THE DROP SQUAD*, which was to be executive produced by the one and only Spike Lee. Rodney said they needed a storyboard artist! Due to the short film I had previously done, I had the samples needed to get the job.

The point being, is to put yourself in the position to succeed. The hard work one puts in early can pay off later in ways you won't see until it happens.

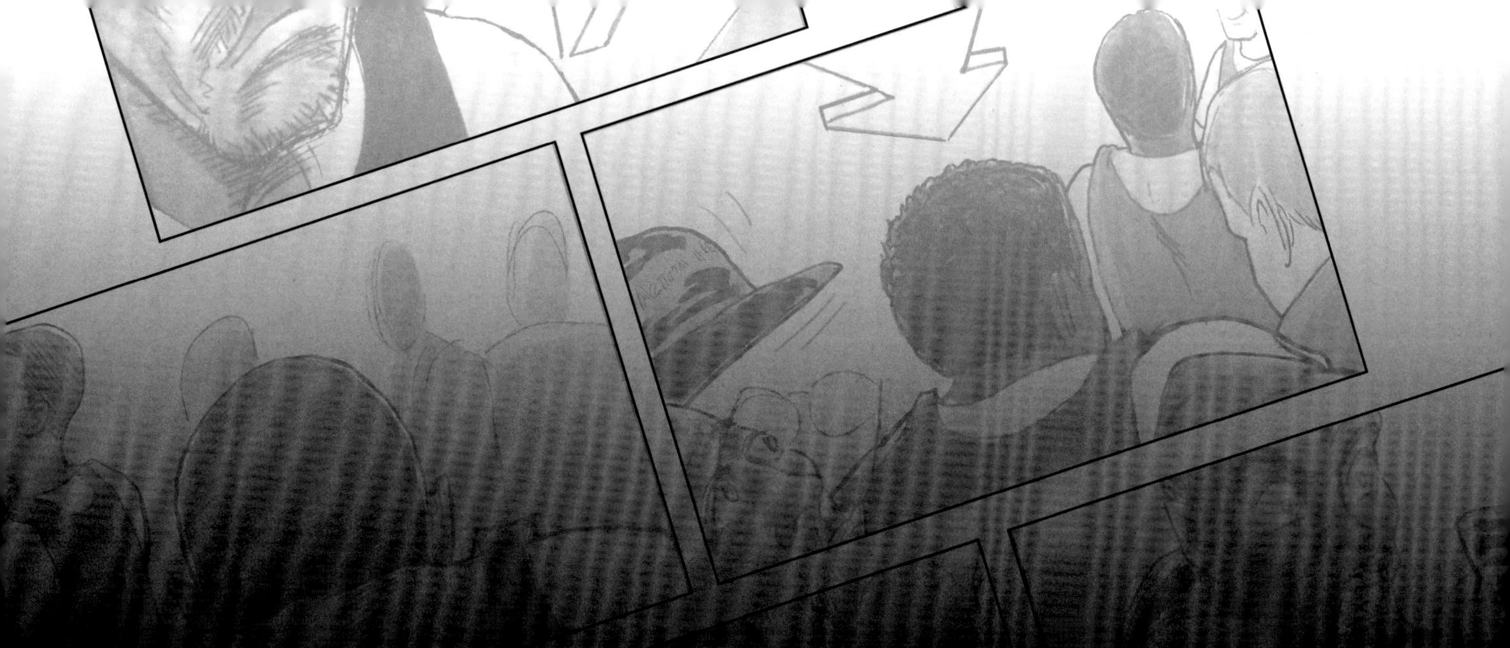

STORYBOARDS AND STORIES OF 15 SELECT FILMS AND TELEVISION SHOWS

HARD DAY'S WORK

Chapter 2

ABOVE THE RIM

FROM BELOW THE LINE

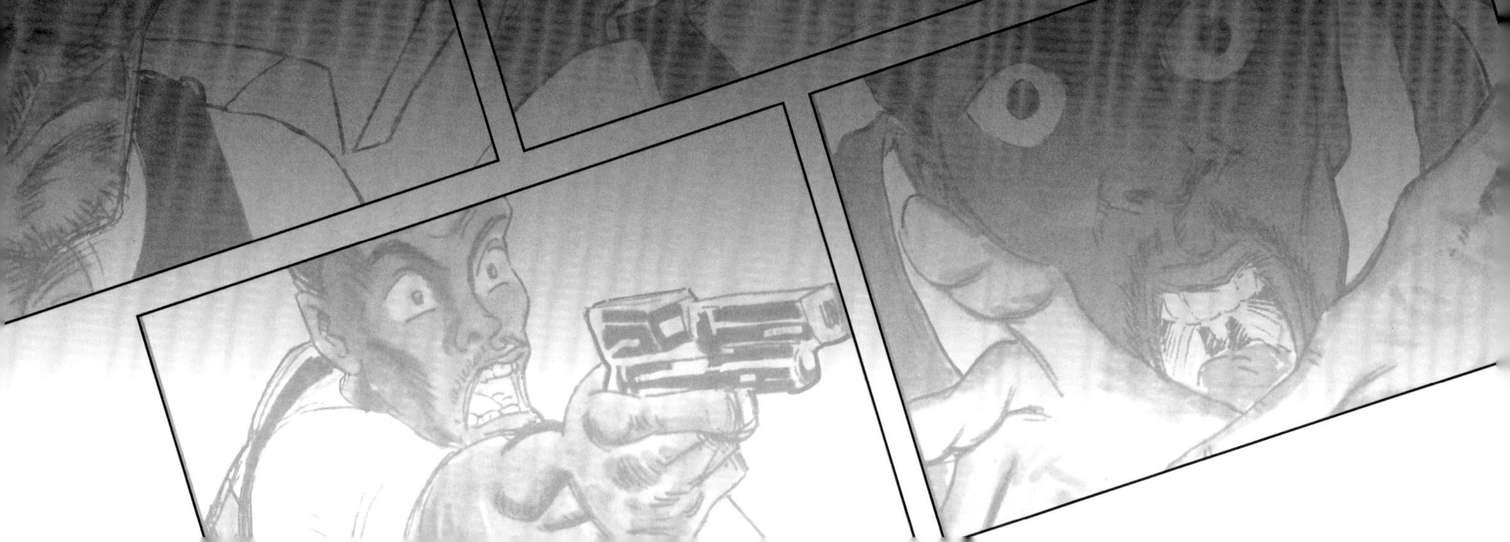

Above the Rim ... from below the line.

The film *Drop Squad* was my first professional job and my entry point into the world of cinema in June of 1993. I was scheduled for six weeks of work that also pivoted on the fun of being involved in the film industry while surrounded by cinema veterans as well as new talents. I was finally in the "movie biz." *Drop Squad* was shot in Atlanta but because it had a very limited budget, director David Johnson and I worked remotely through telephone calls and FedEx deliveries of my storyboards. It was a unique but pleasant experience. I was finally getting a taste of working in the film industry.

Above The Rim began pre-production in the fall of 1993. I was recommended by my cousin Maria Nelson, the film's casting director in partnership with Ellyn Marshall—both owners of Orpheus Group Casting. I also got a great "thumbs up" from Ina Mayhew, the production designer, who had also worked on *Drop Squad*. I arrived at the production office meet with the producer Jim Brubaker for an interview and I was soon employed on my second feature film.

Above The Rim was a basketball film with a strong element of crime set in a Black neighborhood. This film was riding the wave of the film industry's production slate of a bevy of "Hood" movies released in the early to mid-nineties. The movie starred relative newcomers, Duane Martin, Leon Robinson, Wood Harris, Tonya Pinkins, Henry Simmons, Marlon Wayans, Bernie Mac and legendary rapper and actor, Tupac Shakur as the villain, "Birdie." The story centered around a basketball tournament to be held at the legendary Rucker Courts in Harlem, NYC.

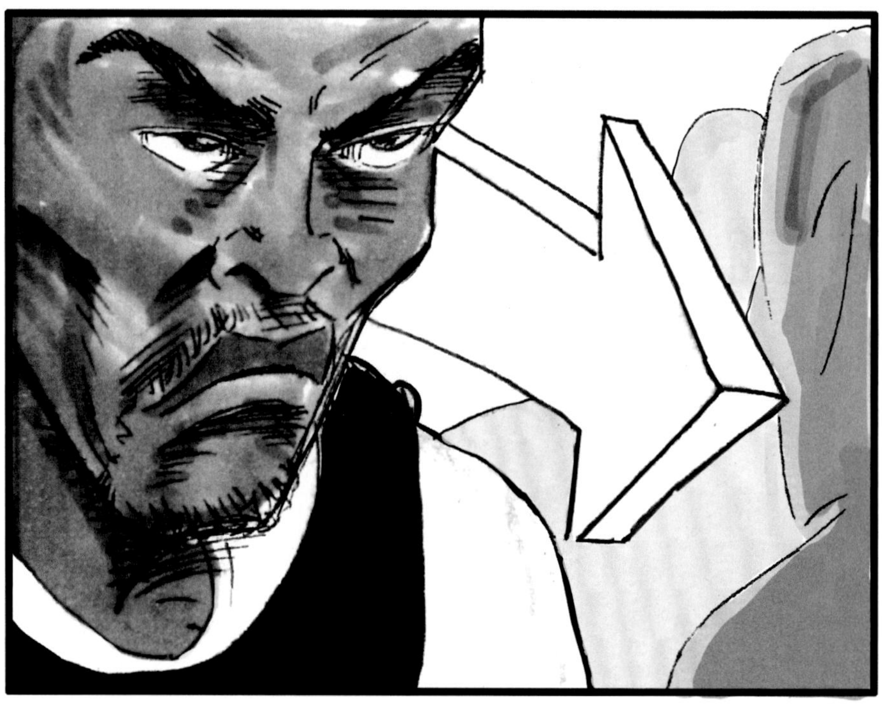

On *Drop Squad*, I was put to work as soon as I started, but the work process was not as how I envisioned it. Before a storyboard artist starts a new project, he or she needs to know what the locations and sets on the project will look like. Every movie, commercial and TV show has a location department. It is this department's responsibility to find all the practical interior and exterior locations for a project. Yet, this department's preliminary work does not even include the preparation for shoots to be done on a sound stage. Once the location for a scene is narrowed down from a few "A," "B," and "C" choices, the producer, director, and other department heads go to locations look at these final choices. This is called a "tech scout". The department heads consider all the technical issues for that location and address several key questions:

- Is the "look" of the location the right choice?
- Is the lighting conducive for good shots?
- Does the location look good from various angles?

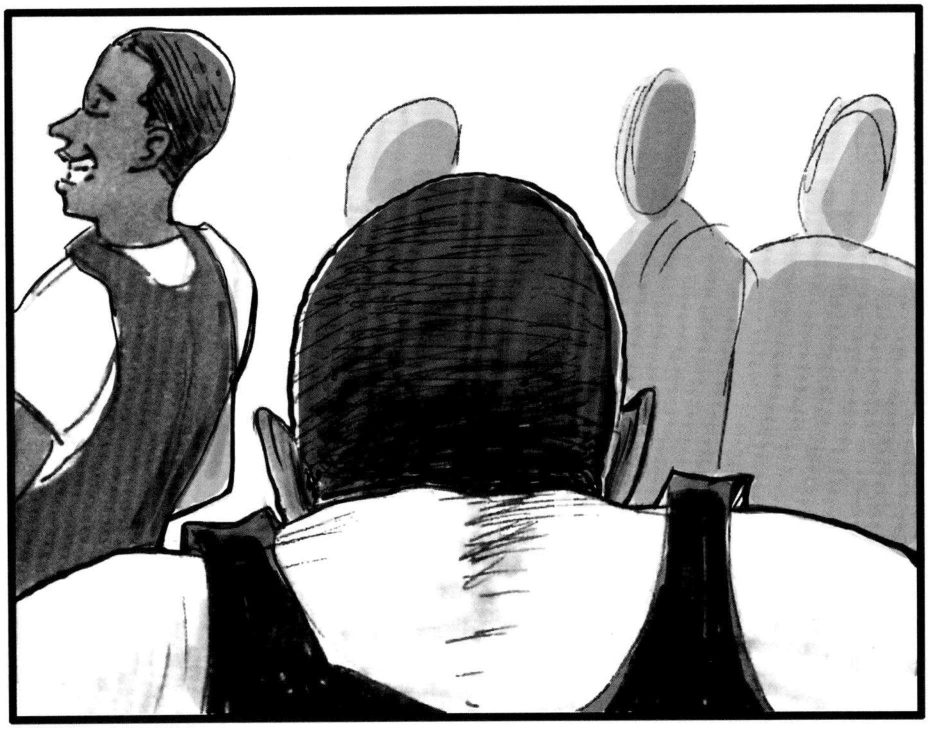

If a location is good for an interior shoot, are a location's hallways wide enough for cameras and cables to move through by going in and out of the location without complications? Are there nearby exterior locations for the crew to park trucks and trailers for a base camp — the crew and cast home base location? These procedures are contemplated in detail before and during the time before my storyboarding process begins. On *Above The Rim*, I joined the crew on a scout van for two weeks. This was my very first production scout experience. Admittedly, I usually dislike going on scouts. However, once a location is finalized it is very helpful to be present on a scout to block things out with the director. What I did see a lot of, were cell phones which in 1993 were still rare among the average person. Jim Brubaker would make his calls on the go wherever we were. I only had a "pager" device that clipped to my belt and alerted me with a beep that sent me to the nearest pay phone to respond to the phone number of the person that was alerting me. Jim had special requests to the scout van driver to stop by smoothie bars daily where he would order a wheat grass drink, which he swore by for the

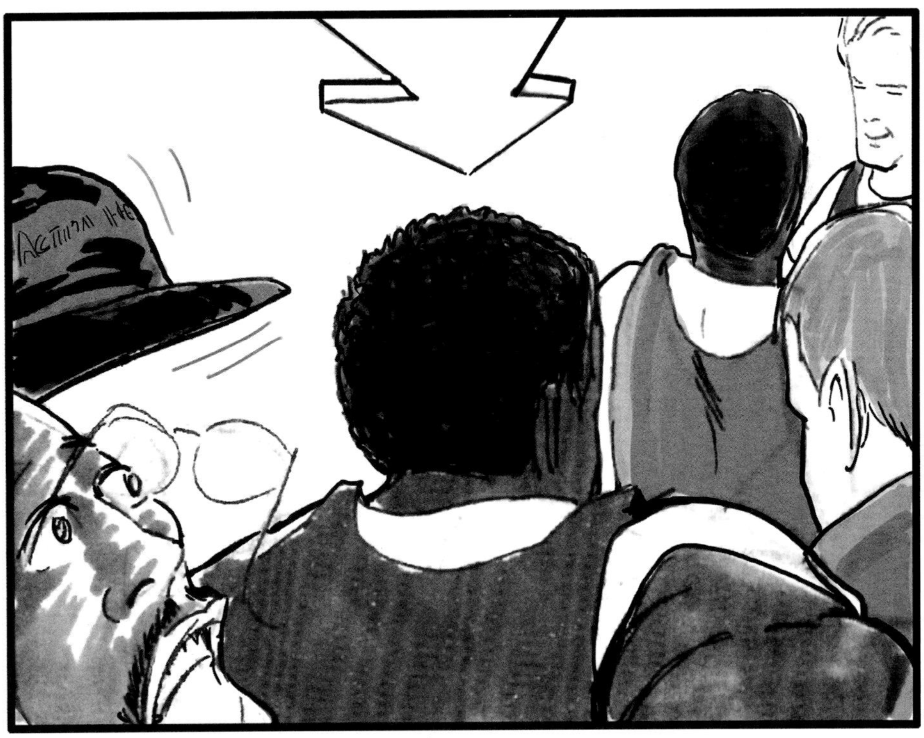

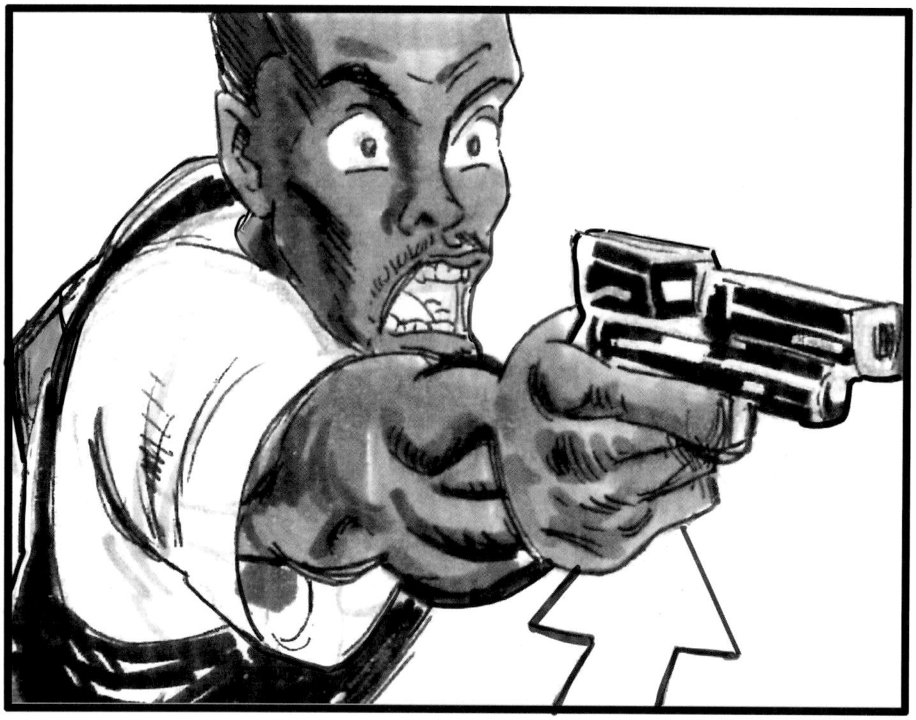

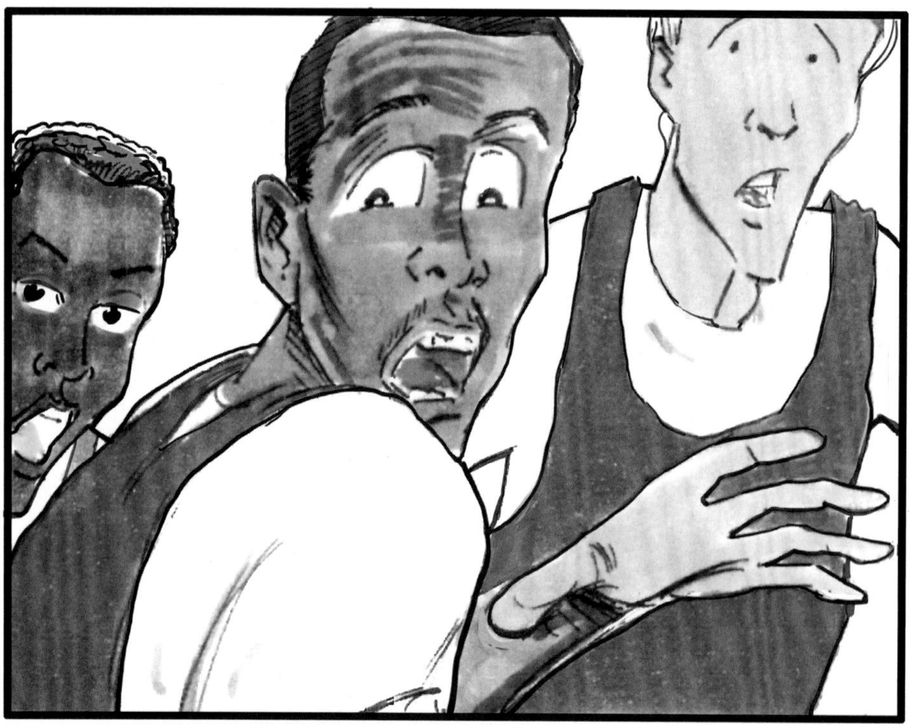

health benefits. More importantly, I picked up that Jim was a shrewd businessman. He was a former teamster and knew all the angles of getting a film made.

As for the director Jeff Pollack, *Above the Rim* was his first feature film. Jeff was already an executive producer on *The Fresh Prince of Bel-Air* but he was a novice to directing as well as being present in the mostly African-American populated area of Harlem. I fondly remember scouting a Harlem location with Jeff when he sent a P.A. (production assistant) on an errand to buy matzo ball soup for him from a local deli that only carried soul food! He would have been much better off looking for a Jamaican beef patty and a forty-ounce St. Ides bottle.

I was able to chat with cinematographer/director of photography (DP) Tom Priestley on shot composition. Tom was the first person to tell me that a frame should have a foreground, middle ground and background elements. This sense of composition was what John Singleton later keyed me into with Steven Spielberg's style of framing. When the cinematic frame is composed with all or most of these elements, it's a true work of art. Once my scouting tenure was completed, I was finally allowed to storyboard.

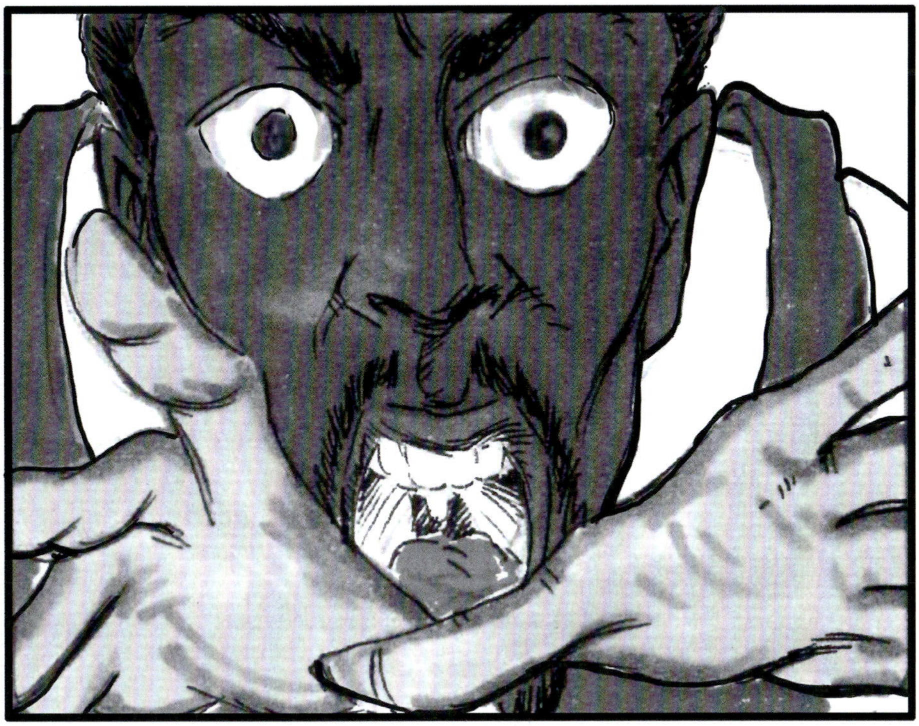

I learned a bit about set protocol from first assistant director (1st A.D.), Howard McMaster when Tom Priestly was blocking a scene and Tom backed into me accidentally. I didn't get out of his way quick enough. Howard said firmly, "The cinematographer's space is sacrosanct!" To this day, when a director or DP starts moving around a space, I evade them as I would a Kung Fu sparring partner.

The most frustrating thing for my work process was the always amicable Jeff, was rarely available to meet with me to give any actual direction. I'd get direction from Jeff to work on a particular scene but I never got a shot list or any indication on how he wanted to actually shoot it. I was pretty much left to storyboard the scenes on my own.

Looking back at my work, I'm thankful that with such little experience that a low budget film by studio standards actually took me on as their storyboard artist. I had no real sense of how many shots to create in any given scene, how many setups, i.e. camera placements that could be shot in one day. I didn't know what screen direction was, which is the direction that a character(s) appears or moves on-screen in relation to the camera or movie audience point of view (POV). I also used frames that were the wrong aspect ratio: the proportional relationship of the screen's width and height. The pre-made storyboards I bought at an art supply store had television proportions, not feature film proportions. My rookie mistakes continued.

The movie's basketball technical advisor was a gentleman named Richard "Pee Wee" Kirkland. Pee Wee was a true to life street ball legend. As a younger man, he had the skill set to make it into the NBA but Pee Wee realized that he could make a lot more money selling drugs. Pee Wee became a millionaire but he was eventually caught and sent to prison for several years. Upon being released, Pee Wee became a motivational speaker as well as a basketball technical advisor on film projects. Having talked with him a few times, Pee Wee was a gentleman who everyone treated with respect. He trained the actors so they looked like real streetball players.

There was in fact great basketball pedigree with the lead actors. Duane Martin had been an alternate for the New York Knicks, Wood Harris had great jumping and dunking ability, while Leon could ball as well. Marlon Wayans was the wild card. He was skinny as a rail and always "on" comedically. I strictly remember Marlon quickly getting out of the production van which transported the cast to the basketball court, running around the court like a ball of energy, grabbing a basketball and promptly shooting a perfect "swish" from behind the three-point line. Marlon was like the Tazmanian Devil after drinking a case of Red Bull.

The basketball sequences were something that I was able to sink my teeth into. Following the script, I tried to make the storyboards as dynamic as possible within my capabilities, which were still in their early stages. Being able to go to set for the very first time to watch the actual filming was the pivotal point that shifted my goals for me to seriously build a career in film. *Above The Rim* served as a great learning experience. I would later work on a large number of basketball sequences in commercials, television shows, and music videos.

Looking back, I was able to see the early work of future hip hop legend Tupac Shakur in all his glory. Who would have suspected that he would be taken from us within three years? "Pac" as he was called, was already having issues with the powers that be on the film's production. He didn't like studio execs or "suits", from what I heard. But what I did see, is that in between film takes he would love to interact with the extras who played roles as the basketball spectators in the Rucker Park's bleacher stands. Tupac would freestyle rap verses with folks or yell out a random "A'ight?!" and the extras in the bleachers would respond back to him in unison. I keenly remember standing outside his trailer when a teenaged girl who was crying, wanted to get a chance to see him. Tupac came out of his trailer moments later to meet the young lady, gave her a warm hug and said something kind to her that gave her a big smile.

In filming, there was a scene to be done where the "Motaw" character (played by Wood Harris) meets his end. The film's armorer (the person in charge of any and all firearms on the set) made sure that the entire crew and cast observed safety protocols because this was only months after the Brandon Lee tragedy on *The Crow*. Leon's character, "Shep" was originally killed in an act of self-sacrifice but was later brought back in reshoots. When I storyboarded the scene leading up to his character's demise I approached it as if I was doing a Terminator movie. I wanted to create a sense of unbearable tension as Motaw with gun in hand, stalks Duane Martin's character "Kyle" as Shep is trying to intercept Motaw.

What was additionally cool was that the production cast me in the film an extra in the conclusion of the final game and death scene. I was also one of the people standing over Shep's wounded body in a slow panning shot. But since the character was only wounded due to the reshoots, my close-up shot was cut. I'm still visible in a couple frames of wide shots after Duane Martin's "Kyle" makes the winning dunk —the stunt department having aided Duane with the boost of an off-screen springboard.

As with the crew of the *Drop Squad*, I made many friends on that show which I still have to this day. In the film cast as a small part as a high school baller, one of those current friends is Henry Simmons of *Marvel's Agents of S.H.I.E.L.D.*— the television show on which I worked on for six of its' seven seasons. The stunt coordinator Jeff Ward bonded with me in friendship by our mutual passion for martial arts. He went on to do stunt coordinate on the films *Blade* and *Blade 2* in addition to two films by Ron Howard, *The Paper* and *Ransom*. Jeff has remained a close friend to this day. Further connections from my start with Above the Rim include continued work with Jim Brubaker on several features. Twenty-five years later, I worked with his lovely daughter Marcei A. Brown who became a producer in her own right. At the time of this writing, Jim Brubaker passed at the age of 85. I will never forget him, nor shall anyone who knew him.

When A*bove The Rim* wrapped, it was the first time I had that little let down one gets at the end of a shoot. When I was told that they didn't need any more storyboards, the age-old question of "what next?" ran across my head.

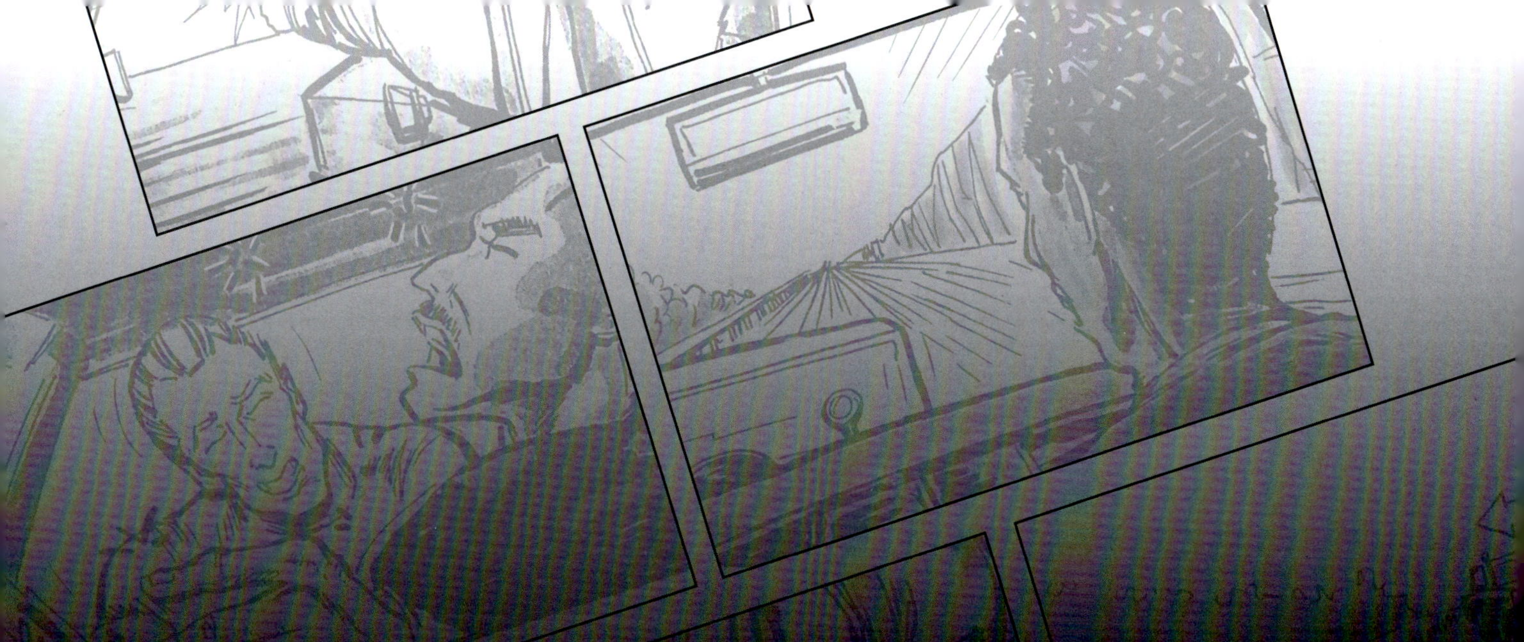

STORYBOARDS AND STORIES OF 15 SELECT FILMS AND TELEVISION SHOWS

HARD DAY'S WORK

Chapter 3

DIE HARD WITH A VENGEANCE

SURVIVING THE FILM LIFE

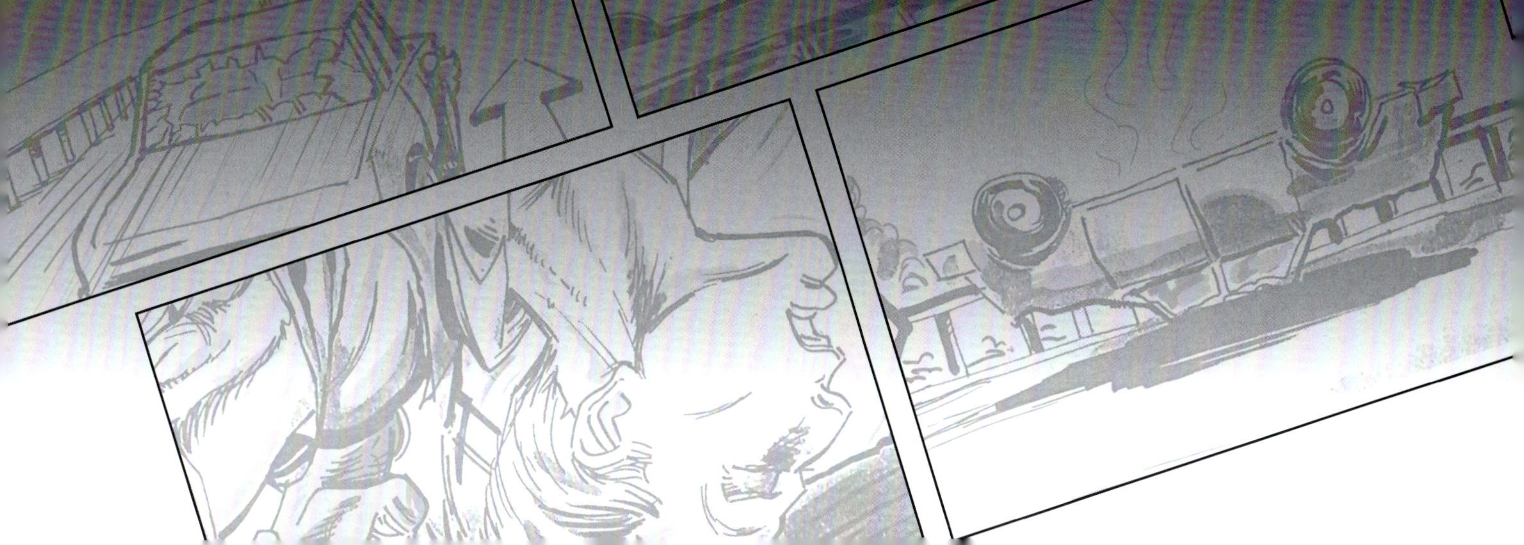

Die Hard with a Vengeance...surviving the film life

I had wrapped work on three films by the fall of 1993: the *Drop Squad*, *Above The Rim* and *Major Payne*. But at the end of that year, the winter was cold indeed. Even with all of the film work and a handful of freelance magazine illustration jobs for The Source, Glamour and Starlog—I was less than six months removed from leaving my stockperson job at Bloomingdale's. I only had a few remaining commercial clients that could provide any ongoing steady work and that was sporadic, at best.

Unemployed, I had no money coming in. I remember calling Jeff Ward in a bit of a panic and asking, "How do you get work in the winter?" Jeff, who was between jobs himself and was hanging at his place said, "I'm just staying warm by my fireplace, having a drink and waiting it out." Meaning there was really nothing one could do in the winter. This was the time of year that just sucked for work, so you had better made some money in the early part of the year and saved a lot of it. Somehow, I made it to the spring and I got a call to work on the next *Die Hard* movie, which at that stage was called *Die Hard 3: Simon Says, Die Hard*.

As a fan of the first two *Die Hard* movies, I was ecstatic to be a part of the crew on a big budget major film release. The other jobs I had gotten thus far were cool films individually but this would be my first "A" movie. M.J. Magbanua, who I had met on *Above The Rim* was the production secretary on this new Die Hard and had recommended me for the job. I learned very early, that this industry is about relationships. Much of the work I've booked has been through recommendations from co-workers and colleagues on previous film jobs. When I arrived at the Die Hard production office, the first person I met was Justin Moritt, the production supervisor. Justin was young, handsome and looked like an actor, himself. He told me that the show needed a storyboard artist to work with the second unit director, Terry Leonard.

My thoughts were twofold: I was disappointed that I wouldn't be working with director of the first *Die Hard*, John McTiernan and the main unit crew—but when Terry Leonard walked out to meet me I was overjoyed. I have long been a big fan of the talents of the stunt community and I recognized Terry as soon as I saw him. Over a decade earlier in

Second unit director Terry Leonard and his team were already shooting this sequence when I handed him the storyboards. I stayed around for a few hours to watch them shoot on the Saw Mill Parkway.

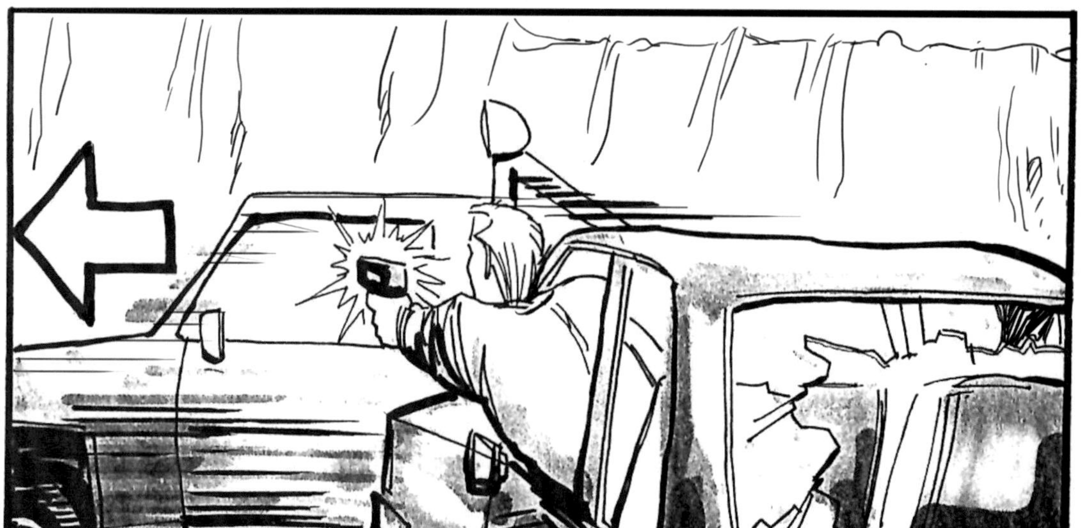

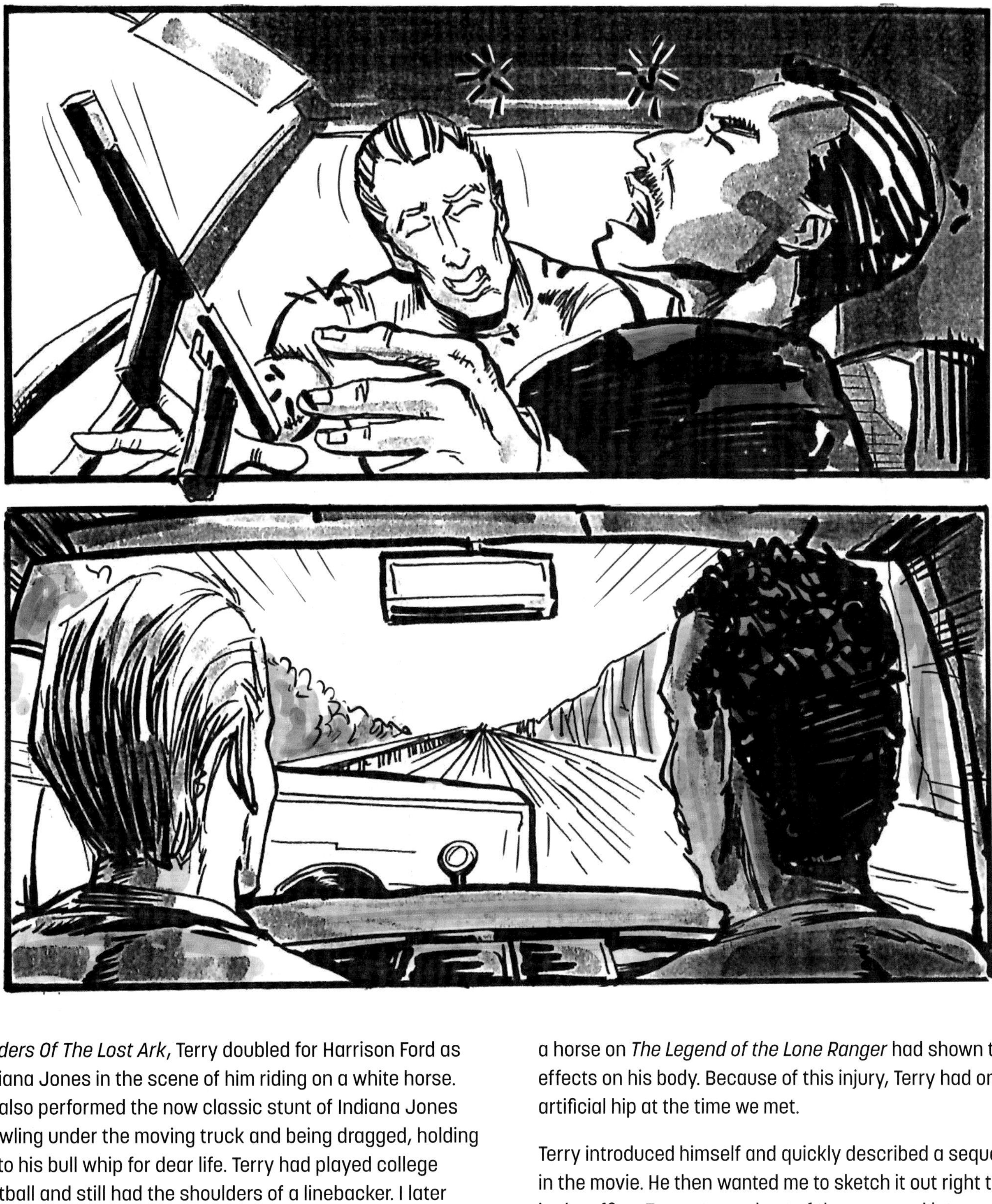

Raiders Of The Lost Ark, Terry doubled for Harrison Ford as Indiana Jones in the scene of him riding on a white horse. He also performed the now classic stunt of Indiana Jones crawling under the moving truck and being dragged, holding on to his bull whip for dear life. Terry had played college football and still had the shoulders of a linebacker. I later learned it had pained him that a bad injury kept him out of possibly playing in the NFL. I noticed Terry's unique walk. His years of stunt work, especially having been trampled by a horse on *The Legend of the Lone Ranger* had shown their effects on his body. Because of this injury, Terry had one artificial hip at the time we met.

Terry introduced himself and quickly described a sequence in the movie. He then wanted me to sketch it out right there in the office. Terry stepped out of the room and let me go to work. Fifteen minutes later, I had drawn a few action scene panels and given them to a P.A. who then gave them to Terry

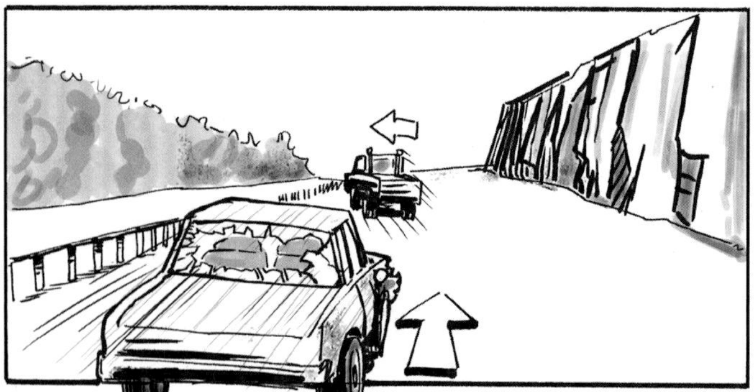

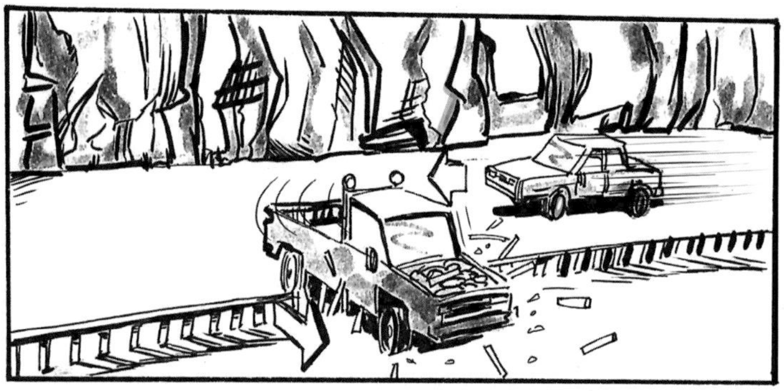

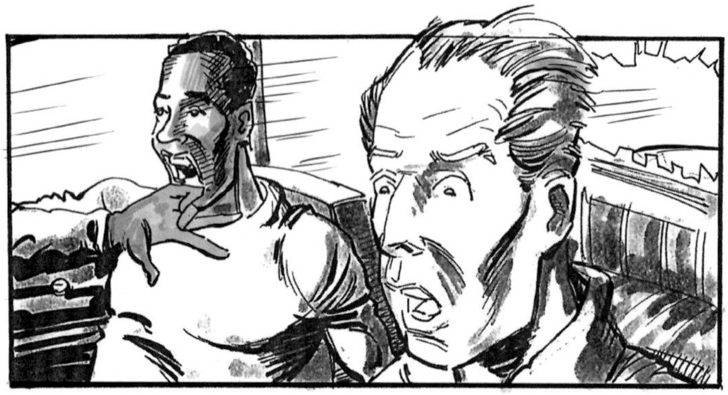

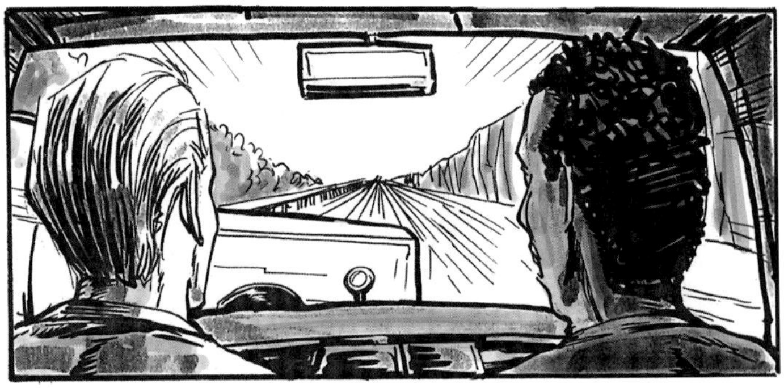

for his approval. More anxious moments later, Terry walked back into the waiting room and with his gruff western twang he said, "You're hired!"

I met up with Terry the following day at his hotel to join the crew van that would take us on a scout. I was a bit nervous. I didn't know how the temperament of the crew would be on a big film like this and especially with Terry. I was still relatively new to the business. I fondly remember that as we waited for the van to load, Terry was kneeling on one knee on the sidewalk with his cup of orange juice. I stood there beside him and the first thing he did was look up to me and to offer to drink from his cup. I took a sip, passed it back to him and he drank back out of it. I have to admit, I thought, well he isn't afraid of Black folks! This display of generosity was exactly who Terry was on the entire movie shoot. He is a man's man who is extremely friendly and respectful to everyone on the crew. Terry remains like family to me to this day.

If I remember correctly, I did my initial rough pass of this scene without location photos. I got a last minute call to do the scene and may have heard that there were 'a lot of trees' from and A.D. With more experience, I would have gotten location photos of the Saw Mill Parkway from the location department in advance. Nowadays, film and television location departments put the scene locations on a website, usually the 'SmugMug.com' site where any crew member has access. And in a pinch, if I get a location address, I can use Google Maps, which I have used to great results.

Terry is a master storyteller. His exploits in the business are Hemingway worthy. He did five movies with John Wayne. Despite my feelings on Wayne's political or racial leanings, he was one of the greatest stars in film history and Terry got to work with him on a consistent basis. Terry's great enthusiasm, in addition to his cowboy charm and emotion, made hearing the stories of his colorful years in the industry a spellbinding experience. I worked with Terry on two action sequences. The first was a Central Park scene where the character John McClane and his new accomplice "Zeus" navigate the streets of New York City in a stolen taxi. McClane steers the taxi between two semi-trucks and then proceeds to race through Central Park while miraculously not killing or maiming any pedestrians in the process. The second scene was a car chase along the Sawtelle Parkway outside of New York City.

Terry had the duel job of being the second unit director as well as being the stunt coordinator. As second unit director, he was in charge of directing all of the exterior footage of the taxi (driven by Willis' stunt double, Terry Jackson) weaving in and around stunt people who were standing-in as park goers. This footage was intercut with what John McTiernan would shoot with Bruce Willis and Samuel L. Jackson as "Zeus". Everything was ultimately under the guidance of the director but the stunt-heavy second unit would shoot separately than the main unit. Second unit had its' own crew though it was smaller than main unit.

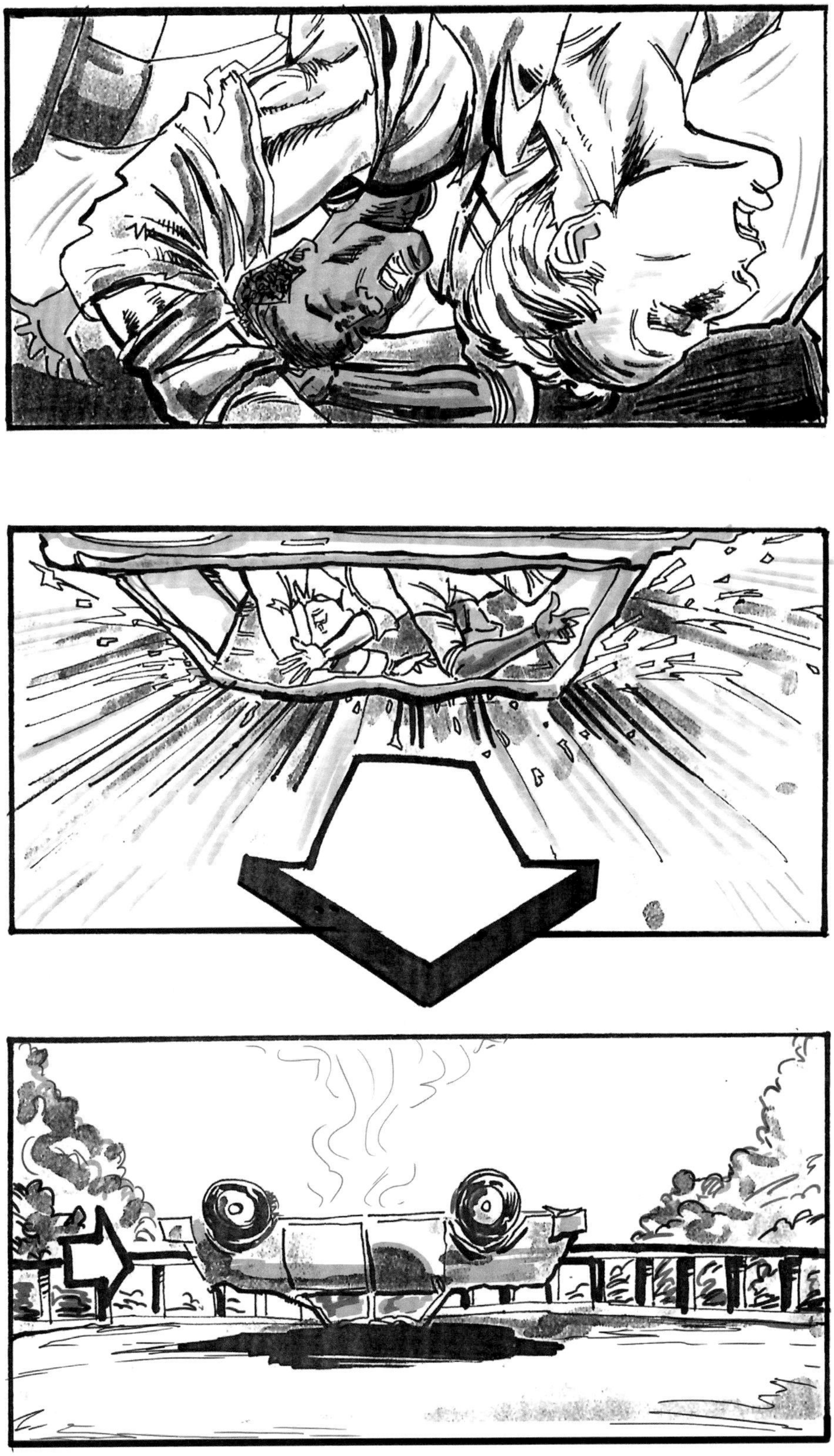

In prepping for Central Park, Terry and I separated on the scout and walked the path of where John McClane would drive the stolen cab. Terry taught me new terms like "S Curve" for how the car would skid and weave in a pattern. I remember telling Terry with enthusiasm in trying to impress him on how quickly I would complete the work. Terry looked at me and said with sage-like brilliance, "Never work your way out of a paying job." It was his way of telling me to not make myself obsolete. Terry was quite pleased with my boards as I captured what he wanted. Looking back on them with over twenty-five years' more experience, I'd kick myself in the teeth if I drew the same way now. Experience has taught me dynamics, composition and storytelling. I was also drawing everything by hand then with paper, pencils, and markers. Thankfully, my skills have increased and I work digitally with all of the bonuses that art technology and the Internet can provide. But I do marvel at the old storyboard masters that did amazing work with a number two pencil by sheer talent and craft.

I remember first meeting Samuel "Sam" L. Jackson. Sam had just come off Pulp Fiction and was a very hot commodity as an actor. Sam was dressed as his locksmith character Zeus, complete with eyeglasses and a torn short from previous scenes. He was kind and relaxed when we first met and he continued to be whenever I saw him. Sam was into comic books as I was, as well as martial art films. I was careful not to overstep my welcome but Sam was always cool with me. He talked with me as a peer and it was very appreciated.

As the supreme Bruce Lee fan, I also remember meeting actress Colleen Camp who played the role of a detective friend of McClane's. Fifteen years earlier, Ms. Camp had been in *Game of Death*, a Bruce Lee movie where most of the film features unknown actors filling in for Bruce who had passed away five years earlier. Colleen got a kick out of me recognizing her for her work in that classic genre film.

One of the cool things about a working on a movie is to be able to watch it being shot. I watched a scene where McClane has to pull open a street grating and jump on top of a subway train. Any New Yorker knows that you can't just pull up a street grating and jump on a subway train. Because the distance between the street above and the train tracks below is blocked by a concrete separation for safety.

The film production was shooting on Broadway and 8th Street in Greenwich Village. Arriving to the film set location, there were P.A.'s at the top of the subway stairs to check in all crew members. After checking in I turned and bumped right into Bruce Willis, who said "Hey" with a smile and went about his business. My novice eyes also noticed Bruce had on makeup, which was something else I wasn't used to.

The other action scene that I storyboarded was the Sawtelle Parkway car chase scene that entailed John McClane and Zeus driving a stolen Mercedes Benz while being pursued by the villain's henchmen. For this scene, I was only told at the last minute by a production person over the phone that the chase scene had to be storyboarded immediately. I panicked. I remember zipping through about seventy frames overnight! Terry Leonard took my boards my work was helpful for the remainder of the sequence. What I later found out is that Terry and the second unit crew were already shooting the sequence. I went to the set and indeed saw Terry and crew in action. Stuntman Terry Jackson was standing in for Bruce Willis and Tony Brubaker was doubling Sam Jackson. Meeting Tony was amazing as he was a pioneer for Black stuntmen along with Bob Minor in the 1970s.

One of the most incredible things I was able to witness was the first team shooting the store bomb explosion, which opens the film. The villains, led by Jeremy Irons' "Simon Peter Gruber" set off a bomb in a Manhattan Bonwit Teller store. The actual location was the Barnes & Noble on 6th Avenue and 22nd Street. The building took up half a block. It was a store and location I knew very well having attended college nearby at the School of Visual Arts (SVA).

Jeff Ward was one of the stuntmen hired to play one of the pedestrians in front of the store. Jeff's close friend and colleague, Manny Siverio, was also part of the stunt team monitoring the explosion scene. There were multiple cameras set up all over the block to catch the explosion from different angles. This was something that could only be done once. I even saw Tom Priestly, the DP from Above The Rim, as one of the additional camera operators. The shot had to be covered by multiple angles. Crewmembers, who were not a part of the stunt crew were relegated to remain indoors for safety measures. This wasn't a concussive explosion that would cause actual damage but the blast still sent lots of debris flying in the area.

I remember when the explosion was filmed, and there was a countdown and then, "KA-BOOM!" If you just saw the explosion with fake glass and debris blowing everywhere especially in a dense city like New York, you would have thought that an actual bomb had gone off. A huge dust cloud of debris kicked up, and the store was invisible for a few seconds. I heard cheers over the crew radios and I joined everyone in the cheering after the first AD yelled, "cut." It took a few moments for the dust to settle to see that all the blast "victims," like Jeff and the other stunt people were alive and unhurt. It was a fascinating film set experience to witness.

One of the cooler things that happened that day before shooting was meeting the guitarist Vernon Reid, of the group Living Colour. My friend Maurice Dwyer, who I had gotten to know during *Above The Rim*—who was also on this film—was walking around the area during a break and we spotted Vernon walking on the street. Living Colour was a groundbreaking rock group because like Fishbone, they were Black musicians who played rock and roll rather than R & B or funk. Maurice and I were both big fans, so we just approached Vernon to give a "what's up." Vernon was not only appreciative of fans but he was also very down to earth. He said, "Let's hang out," and so we did right there and then! Vernon, Maurice, and I went into a neighborhood Italian restaurant. They were open for business just after the lunch hour but there were no customers seated in the entire restaurant. The three of us stood patiently at the entrance waiting for someone to offer us a table.

The workers definitely saw us, but no one came up to us address our presence. Vernon remarked "I'm getting a funny vibe" in reference to Living Colour's song "Funny Vibe" on the projection of racial prejudice at the sight of a Black man. Disgusted by this treatment, we all turned and left. As post civil rights children living in New York City with a million other restaurants available to us, we couldn't give a damn. We, as the Black kings of dignity and talent that we bear refuse to spend our money where we ain't welcomed. That's their loss, not ours. Vernon and I still remain friends after all these years.

The next year, I was working in Los Angeles for several weeks due to getting a job with Max Kleven, a second unit director and close friend of Terry Leonard. It was a Disney movie called *The Jaguar*. It was to be helmed by a French director named Francis Veber. Hill Harper, who's acting career was heating up at the time let me stay with him for a while and then I stayed with Max. It was great seeing Hill's career beginning to grow.

While staying at Max's place I pulled a muscle in my lower back while working out with his home gym. The next day at the Disney lot on the way to a meeting with Francis, I got out of my rental car in sudden and extreme pain. By the time I got to Francis' office for a meeting, I was lying on the floor. I could barely move. Max recommended a masseuse he knew that worked on actor Gary Busey. Francis kindly paid for the masseuse out of his own pocket. Max and Francis were both great gentlemen to work with.

The trip ended when I interviewed with first-time director Kevin Spacey on a feature called *Albino Alligator*. I had to bow out after the job interview because I didn't have an ongoing place to stay in Los Angeles even if I was hired for that film. Looking back, I think I dodged a bullet by not getting that job because curious things related to this actor/director were revealed decades later. What I learned early, is depending on who is running the project, not every job is the job you need...or even want. Because all that shines isn't gold.

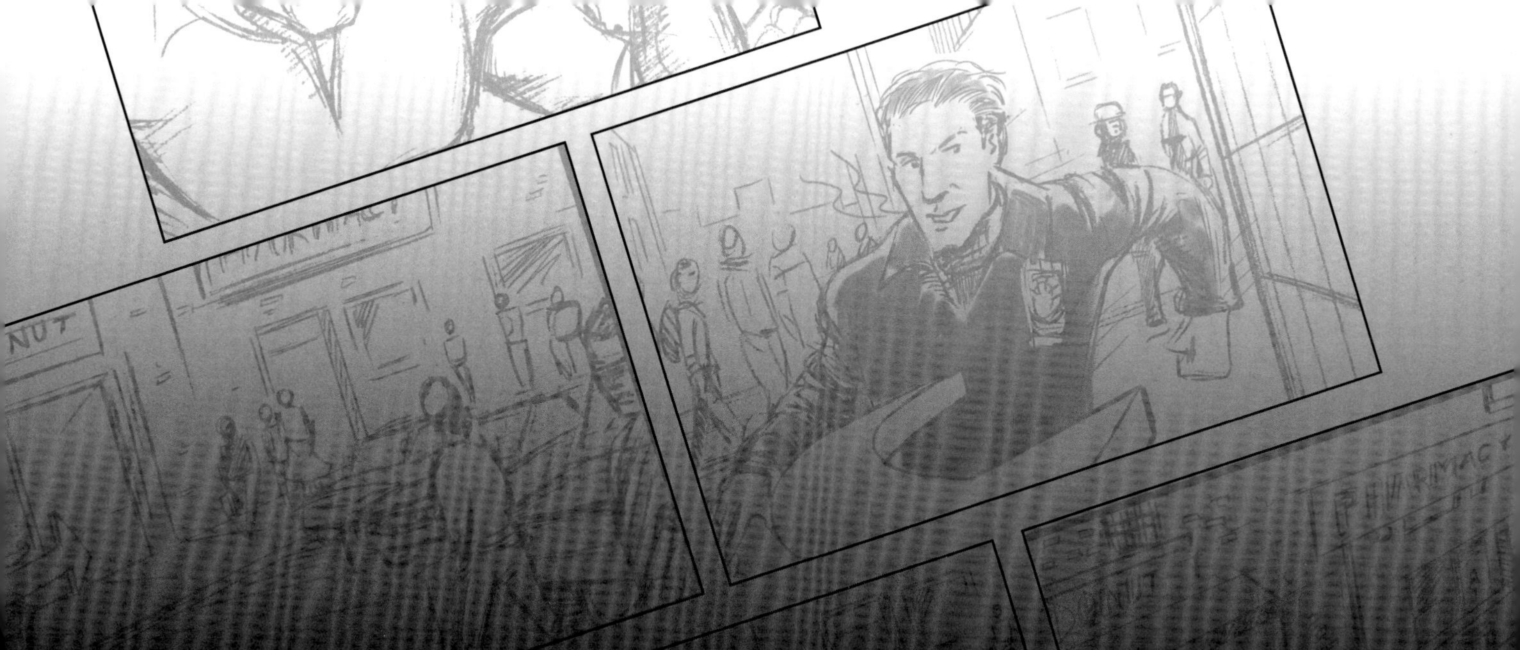

STORYBOARDS AND STORIES OF 15 SELECT FILMS AND TELEVISION SHOWS

HARD DAY'S WORK

Chapter 4

THE DEVIL'S OWN

FROM BELOW THE LINE

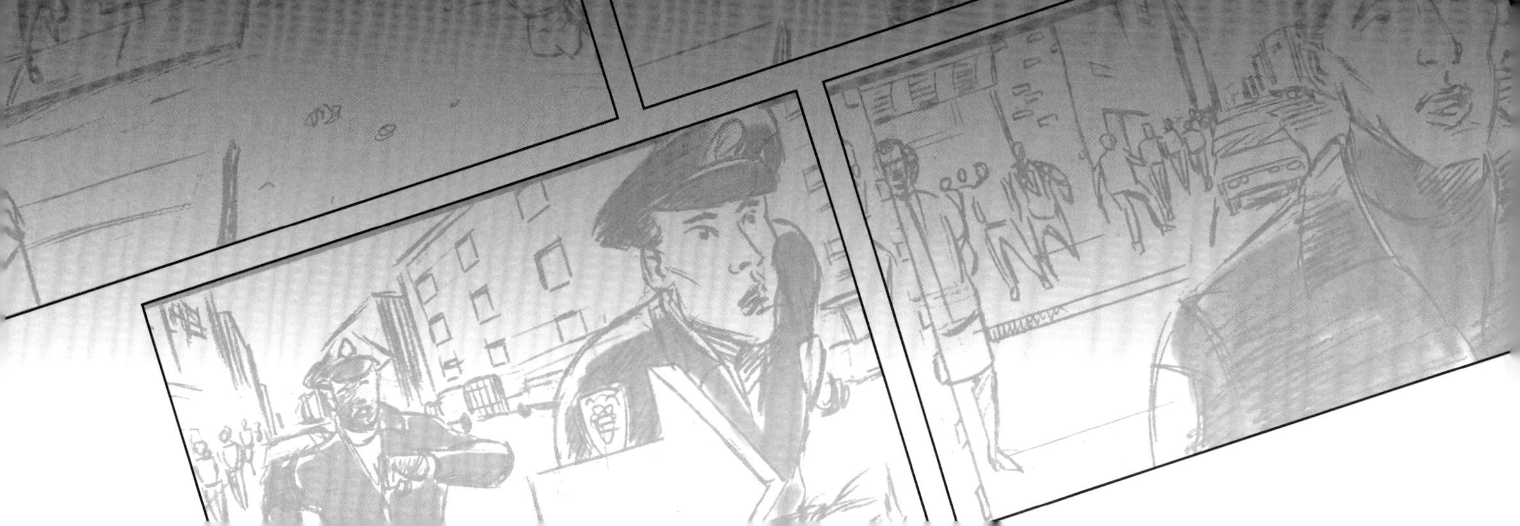

The Devil's Own... with a cross to bear

I remember getting a call to work on the Harrison Ford/Brad Pitt movie, *The Devil's Own* and being in shock. These were still my early years in the business and I couldn't believe I was actually *getting* work rather than expecting work. I would learn one's mindset is an important aspect of one's makeup. There were storyboard artists in the tri-state area that had been in the movie game a lot longer than I was at this point who could have been considered for the job. But hey, I got the call.

It was on the train ride into Manhattan where I had the chance to reflect just a bit. The opportunity on this film could be one of those career game changers. This job would upgrade my reputation as a professional storyboard artist just as doing *Die Hard with a Vengeance* had years earlier. This time, I would be with the main unit on a potential blockbuster.

As usual the production office was *not at all diverse*. There were no Black, Asian or brown crew members hired. This was in 1997. This noticeable distinction is only changed when there is a Black star or a director and miraculously, more people of color manage to get hired. This lack of diversity in hiring exists because people hire who they know and have worked with previously. Their comfort zone of hiring is also aided by the fact that they socialize with those same hired crewmembers at restaurants and bars after work while away from the office. In addition, other prejudices may—and do—exist. I get referred and hired all the time by people who know me and my work, many of them are in fact white. Among films with Black directors and crews, I'm even more known for my work as we deliberately refer and hire each other.

I think my first meeting for *The Devil's Own* may have been with the production manager, Jonathan Filley. Jonathan is a laid-back fellow with a quiet and friendly demeanor. It was later in the production when I found out that Jonathan started as an actor and portrayed "Cassidy" in my all-time favorite movie, *Jaws*. That tidbit blew me away and of course, I later drew Jonathan-Jaws cartoon as a whimsical gift to him.

The next and most important person I met was the legendary cinematographer, Gordon Willis of *The Godfather Trilogy*. *The Godfather* and *The Godfather: Part II* are movies that my wife Betty and I will just stop and watch every time they are on television no matter where the movie is in the run. Every shot is perfectly lit and composed.

When I got hired, Gordon told me that I was replacing their first storyboard artist who was "released". The details of that telling will stay with me, but the point is that I had the job and I couldn't make any mistakes due to what happened with my predecessor. Gordon was a bit of a friendly curmudgeon. He knew the shots he wanted and didn't want any deviation from his ideas. The director of *The Devil's Own* was Alan J. Pakula, who also directed *All The President's Men*, *Klute*, *Sophie's Choice*, *Parallax View*, and more. The sad thing was that I never had the chance to work directly with Alan because I worked directly with Gordon and as DP he set up the shots. Alan's relationship with Gordon was this: the DP set the shots up and then Alan would approve those shots later. This was the similar relationship that I had with DP, Stuart Dryburgh on *Analyze This* and how he had worked with the late and kind Harold Ramis, Director.

Immediately, I had a cross to bear: I had to prove that I could consistently do the job. The first thing that I was tasked to do was redraw the sequence that the previous storyboard artist had done. That was easy. The hard part was getting the approval of the legendary Gordon Willis and *not get fired*. The composition of the frames was already locked in. I just redrew the frames my own style. I finished with that work with baited breath and waited for the word from Gordon... and the word was "yes". My work passed the muster

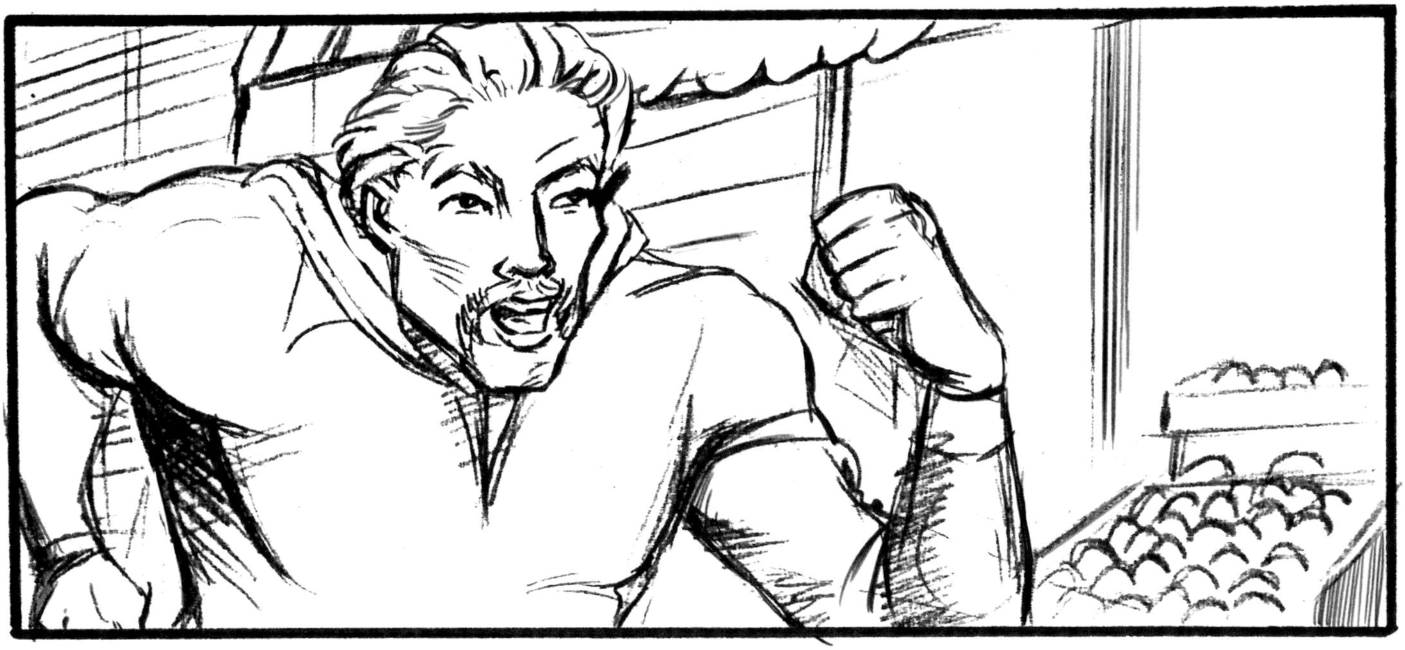

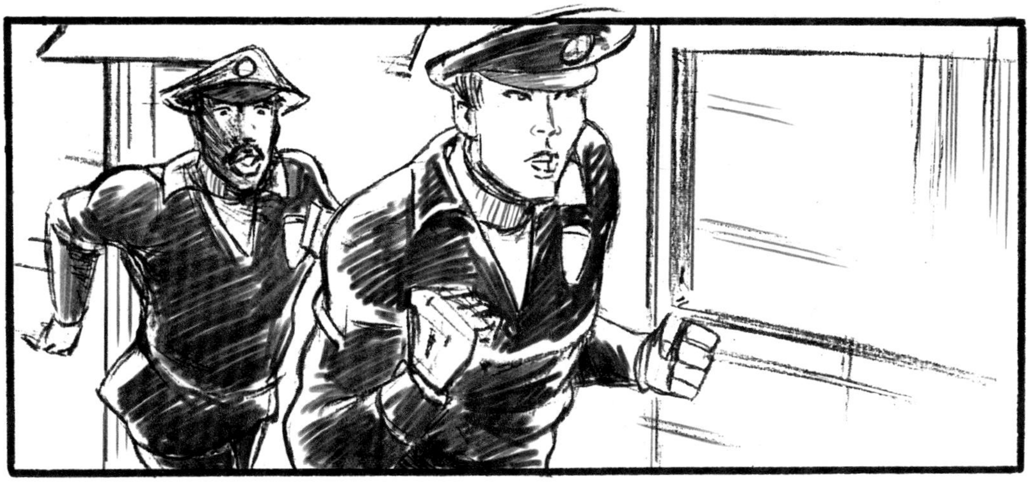

under Gordon's approval. Relieved that I was going to be employed on the film, I was directed to move on to storyboard another scene.

The office was run by production office coordinator, (POC) Ellen Gannon. Ellen was by-the-book and very professional. She didn't chitchat a lot. I remember thinking, "what's up with that?" I made it my humorous challenge to see if I could find another side to Ellen. I've often done caricatures of office co-workers in my paper and pencil days. After drawing a number of crewmembers on the film I decided to draw Ellen. This could have gone sideways, but I just decided to do it. When I have drawn people, I make a point to never make "fun" of a physical feature or to really go too far with the resemblance. I create a cartoony version of someone in a situation that is often an observational humor or I draw the person in a way that is the antithesis of how people see them. Ellen

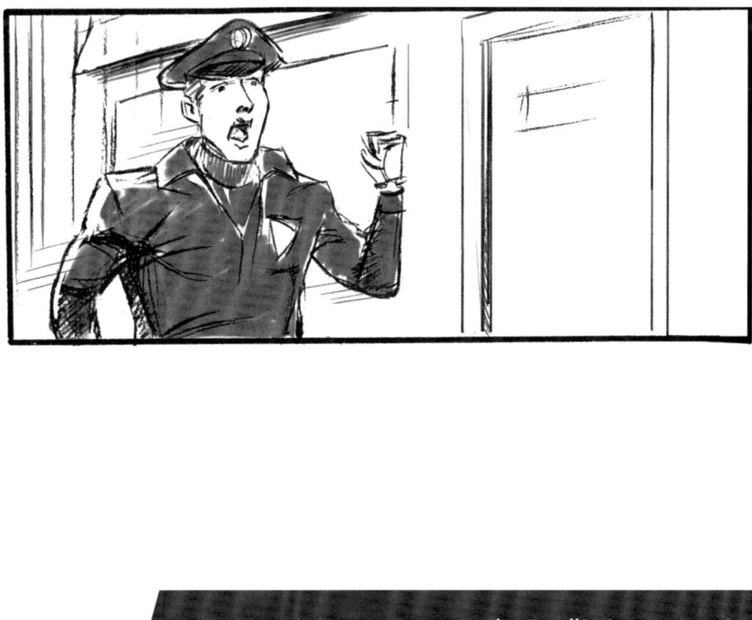

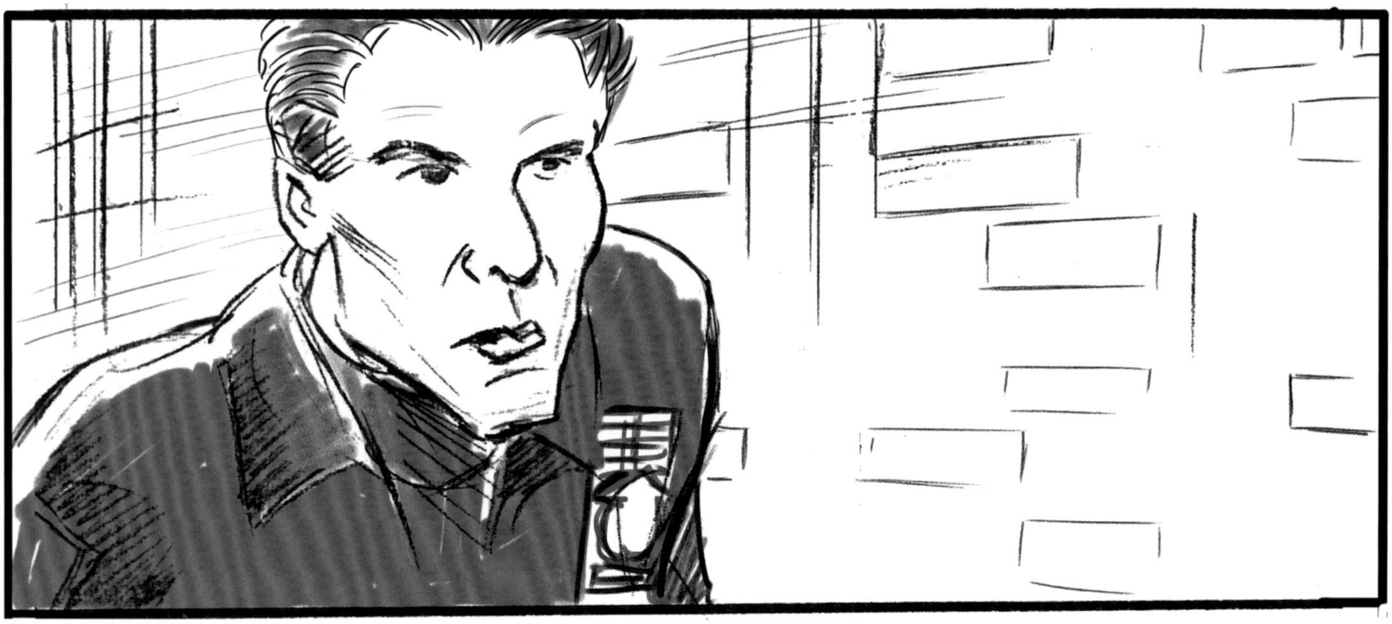

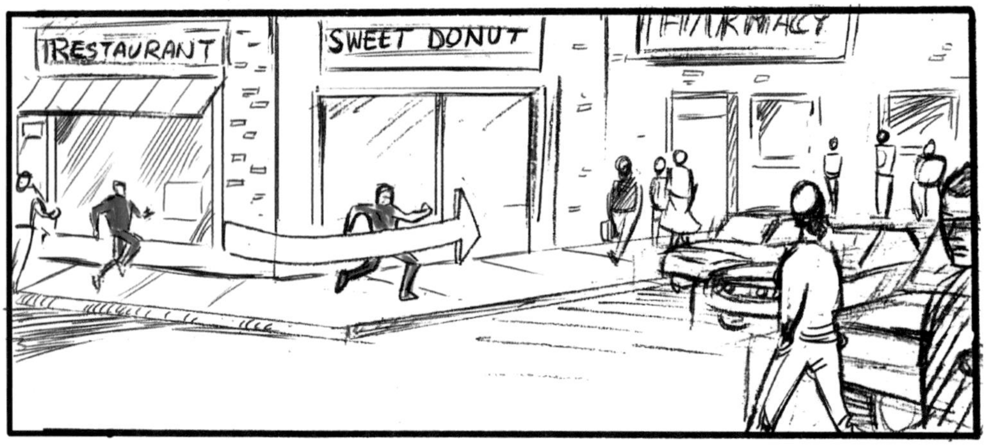

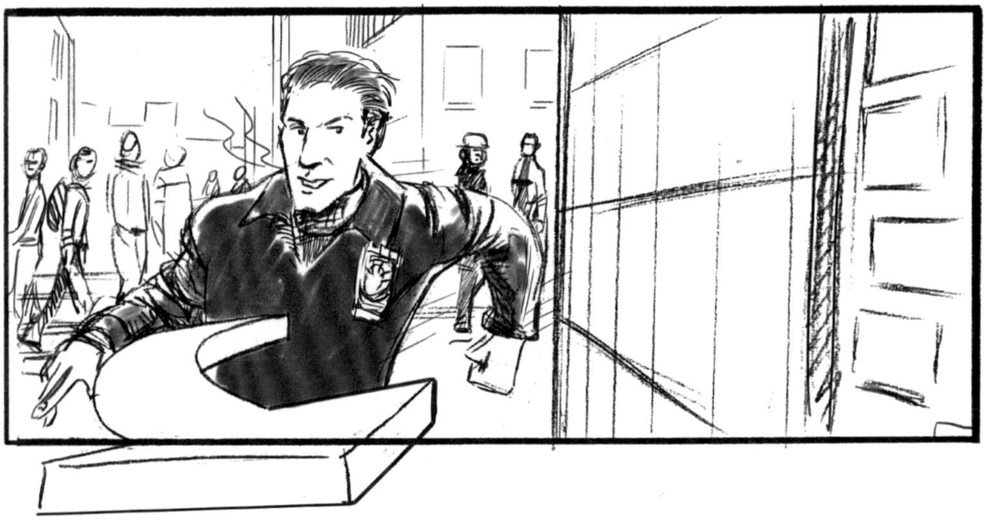

was a no-nonsense pro, so I drew her frolicking through a grassy field in a Julie-Andrews-esque joy. I then left it on her desk and waited to see what happened. Suffice it to say, Ellen loved it and gave me a hug. I have come to learn that women need to have professional barriers in order to gain respect for their positions that men don't have to deal with. They have to be professional, strong, but not too strong and be friendly, but not so friendly that a male might "get the wrong impression." I went on to draw Ellen a few more times, and we always smiled broadly when we saw each other.

Soon after, I had another crewmember to meet. Doug Coleman was the show's

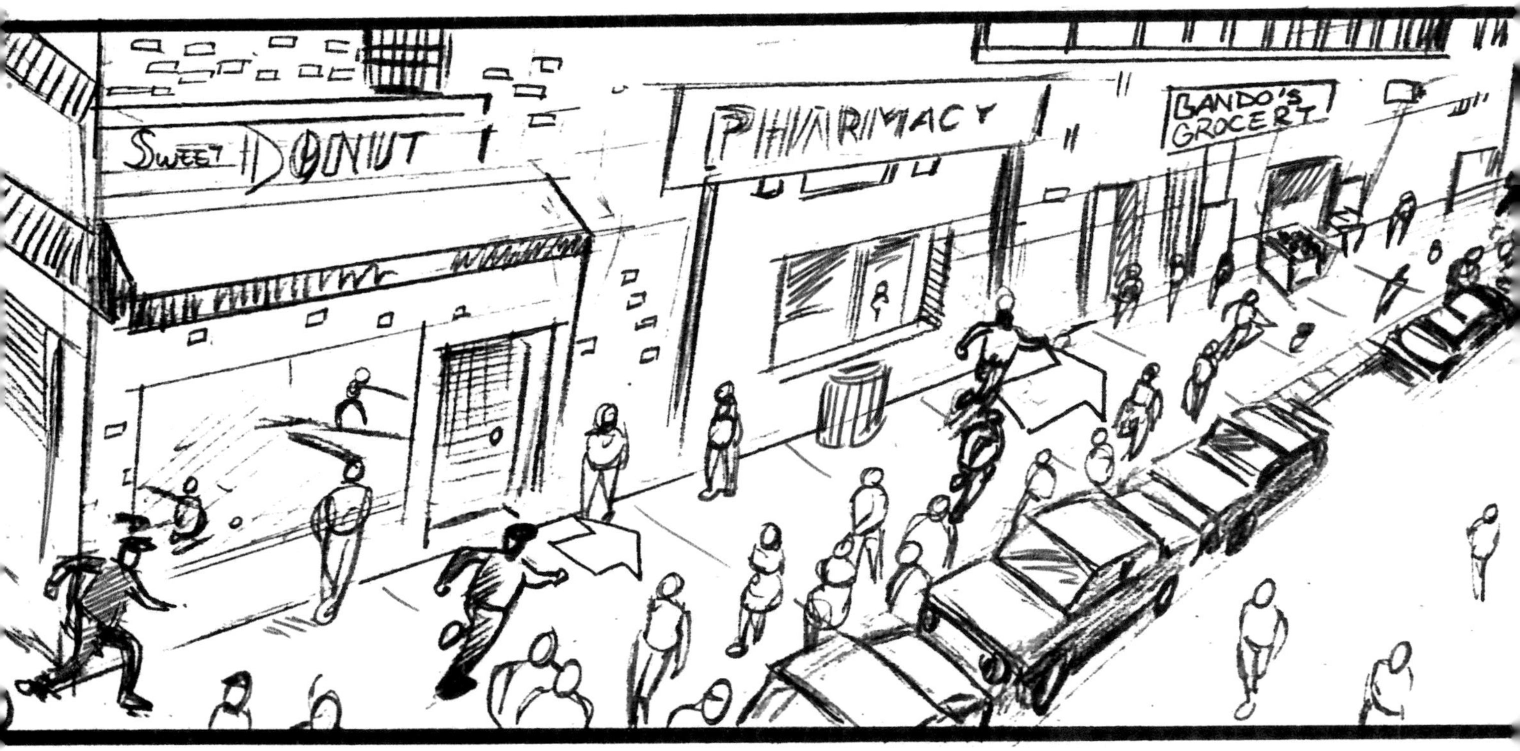

stunt coordinator. Stunt crews are perhaps my favorite people to meet and to work with on a job. Many of them are martial artists but even when not, they are dedicated professionals who work extremely hard to make sure an action sequence looks spectacular while making sure no one gets hurt. The stunt coordinator works with the director to fulfill their vision. They also work with the camera department in shooting the stunt a.k.a. "gag." Sometimes, the stunt coordinator will double as the second unit director as Terry Leonard did on *Die Hard with a Vengeance.* The other job of a stunt coordinator is to train or supervise the training of an actor when called upon to do a stunt. The actor has to feel confident that they will look good and not get hurt. Sometimes, stunt coordinators need to dial back an overanxious actor who wants to perform his or her own stunts. For safety, they will inform the actor and the director that it is best that a trained stunt person perform the gag.

I met Doug while he was wearing a full back brace from an accident months earlier on the sequel to *The Crow*, called *The Crow II: City of Angels.* Doug explained he was doing a high fall as a stunt performer from a building on a "descender"—a wire rig used in falls—and there was a malfunction where he had to use an emergency break. The sudden stop jerked his body so hard that the soles of his feet hit him in the back of the head. Doug had suffered a major back injury but there he was talking to me in a back brace. He healed enough later in the production to have the brace removed. Doug was tough and is one of the most fun people I have worked with. He always had a twinkle in his eye and was great at practical jokes. Doug would call me at home using the voice of a mysterious neighbor named "McClutsky" and tell me the city was cutting the power or there was a flood. I have since tried to pay him back and failed in the following twenty years. Doug and I also talked a lot about martial arts. He was very proficient in the Korean system called Tang Soo Do and I was studying Kung Fu. What caught my interest was when he told me that Harrison Ford wanted to work with the storyboard artist. This was a rare occurrence for an actor to be involved with storyboards, but it was fantastic news to me.

Then, the meet day came. Doug told me that he and I were going to meet Harrison in his "star bus," a hybrid movie trailer and bus. I walked in with Doug and there sat Harrison. He was very laid-back and cordial and had that low-key way

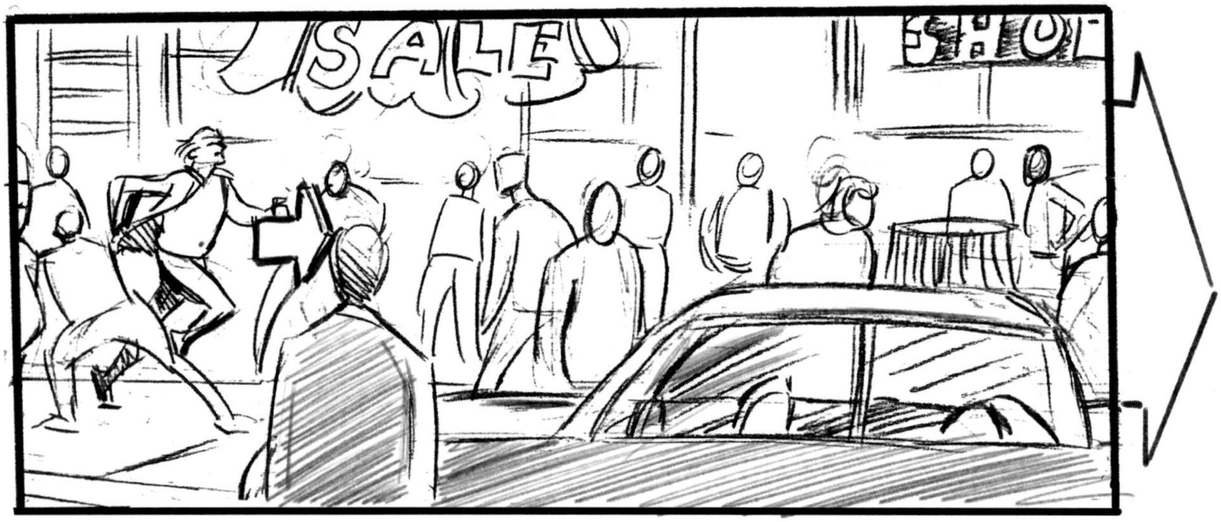

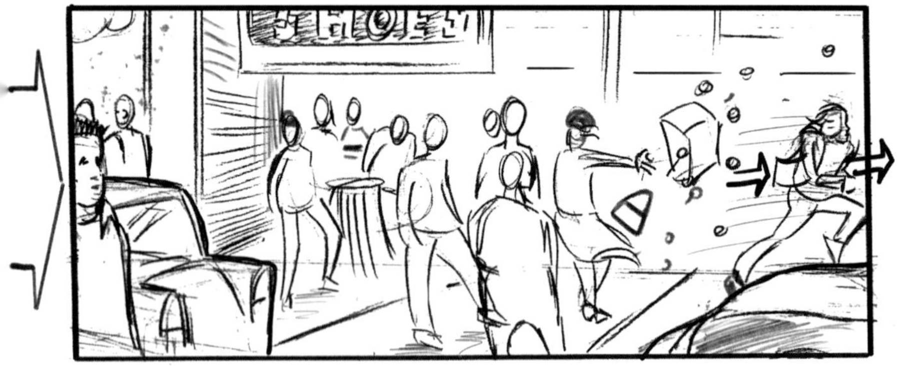

of speaking we have all come to know. All I was trying to do was not to freak out. This was Han Solo, Indiana Jones, and Rick Deckard right in front of me. I was able to utter, "Oh, nice bus" with a smile while spinning inside with a fan's internal combustion. A relatively new actor named Brad Pitt was co-starring in this film with Harrison Ford. Everyone spoke well of Brad on the show and since he was dating Gwyneth Paltrow at the time, I decided to do a color

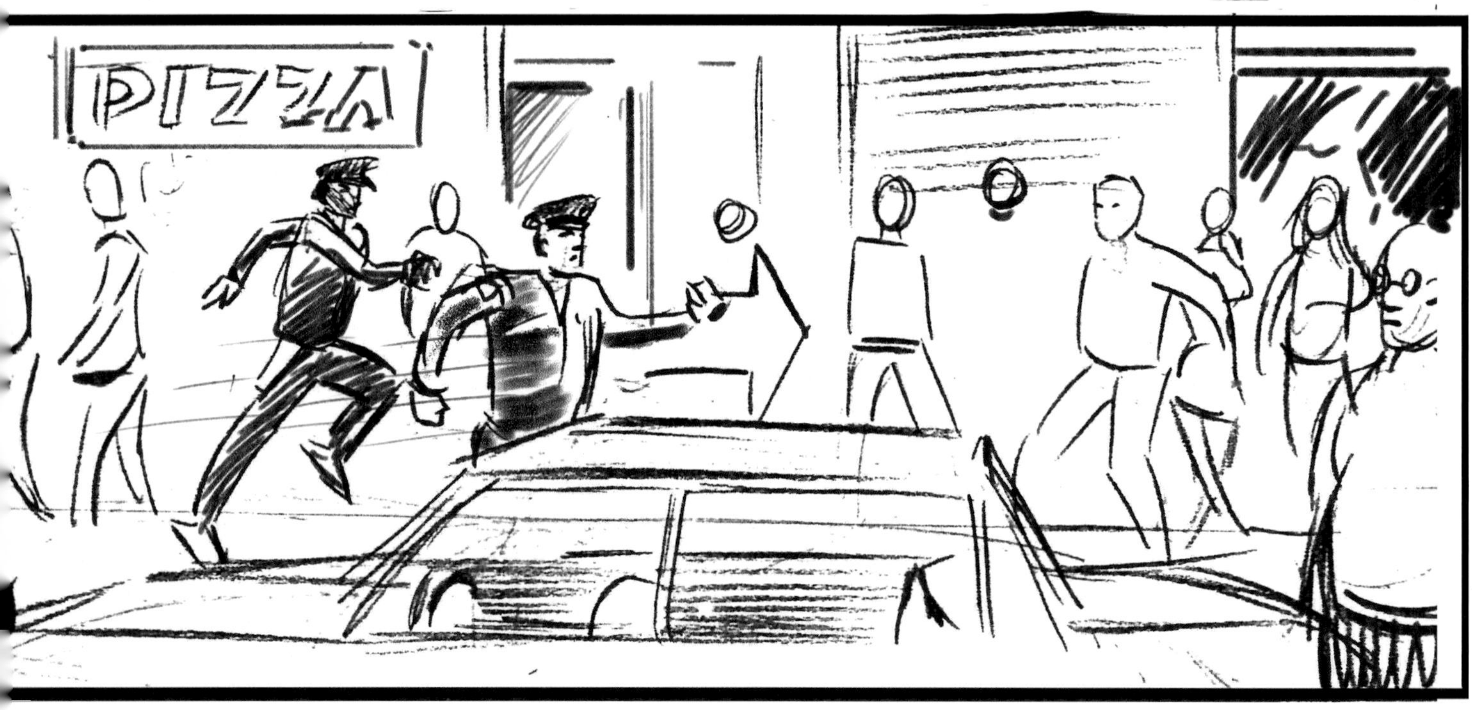

sketch of the two. I left it with a PA to slip the sketch to him in his trailer. Harrison was being paid about twenty million dollars for the movie while Brad's star was still ascending at this time. Ford wanted some creative input and had the star power and longevity to

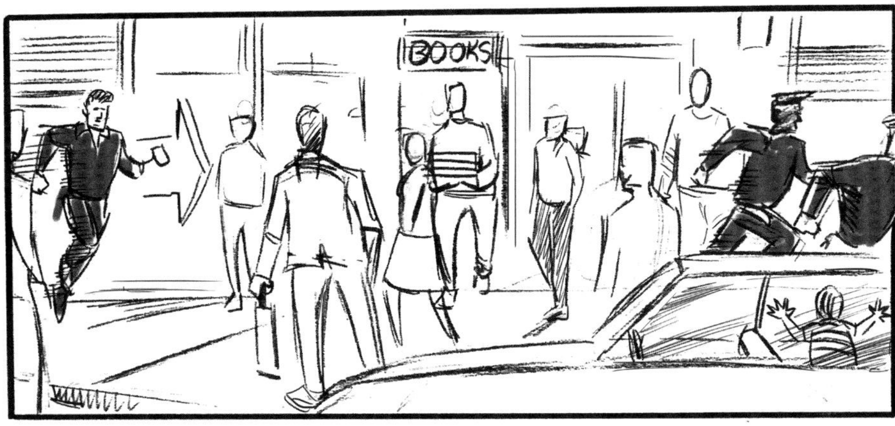

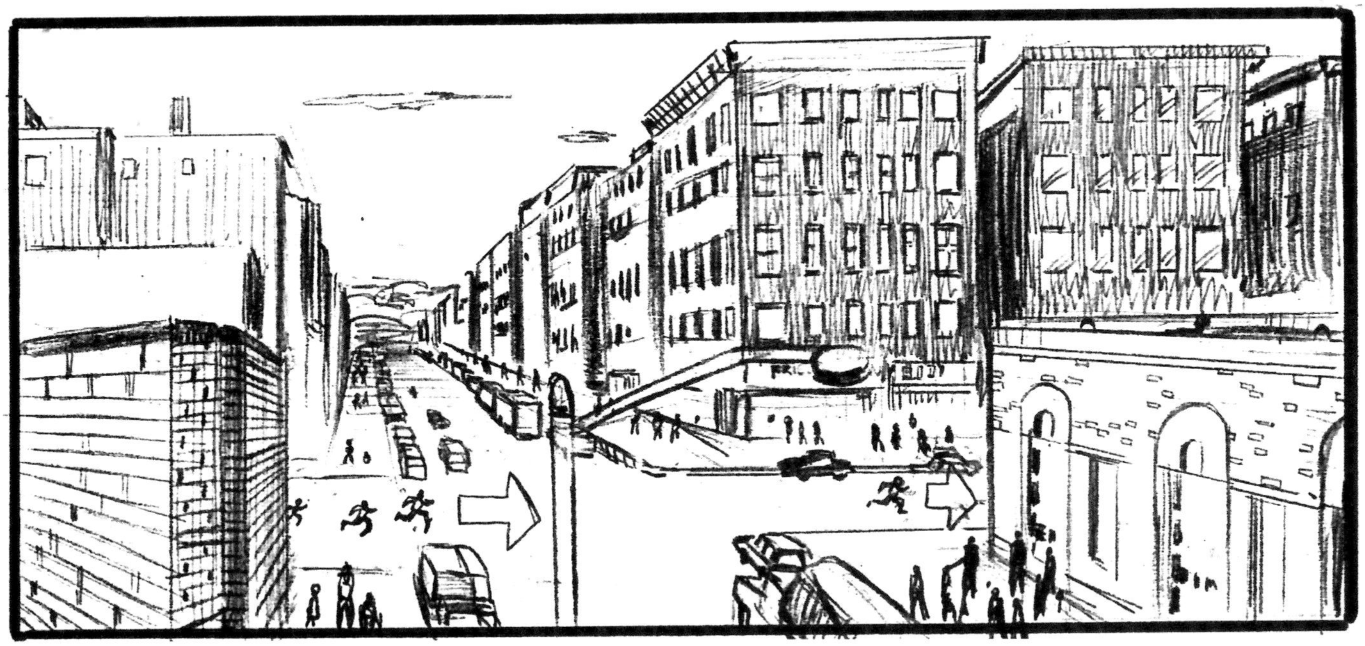

get it. The sequence that we worked on in star bus entailed Harrison Ford's character officer Tom O'Meara, chasing down a street criminal on foot. O'Meara is aided by his partner Diaz, played by singer/actor Rubén Blades, who later intercepts O'Meara and the suspect with their patrol car. I asked Harrison how he saw the "action" in this sequence. Doing his now famous Richard Kimble finger point, Harrison quickly said, "not action ... chaos." He wasn't looking for an over-the-top action movie scene

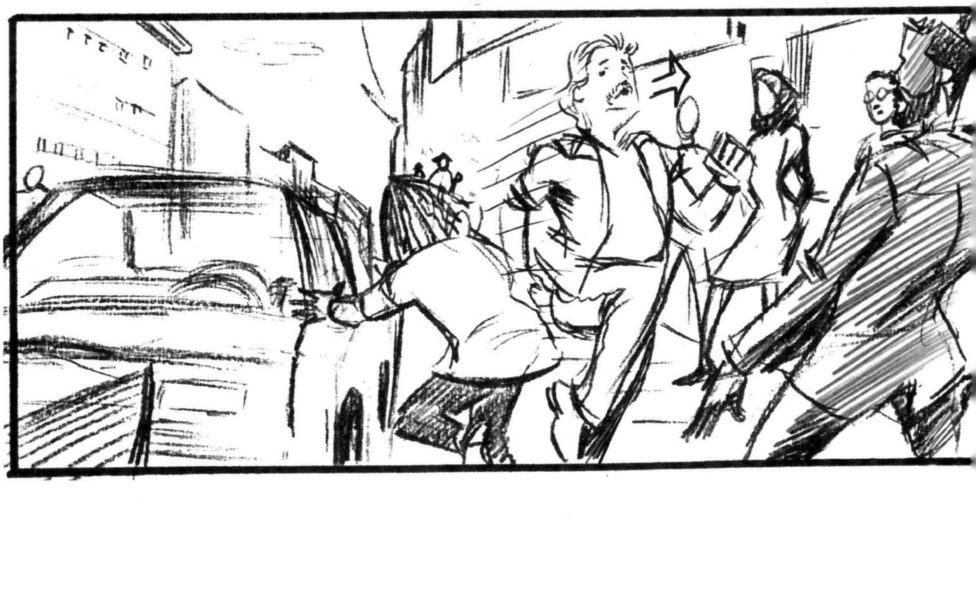

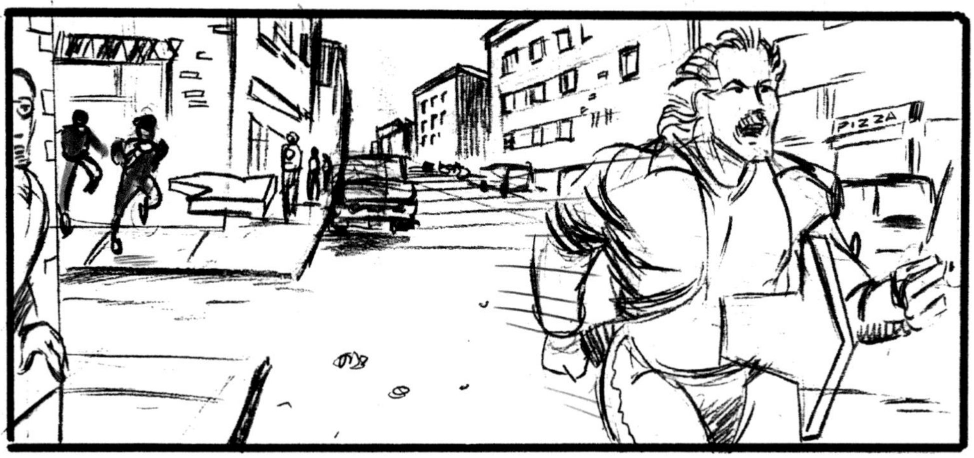

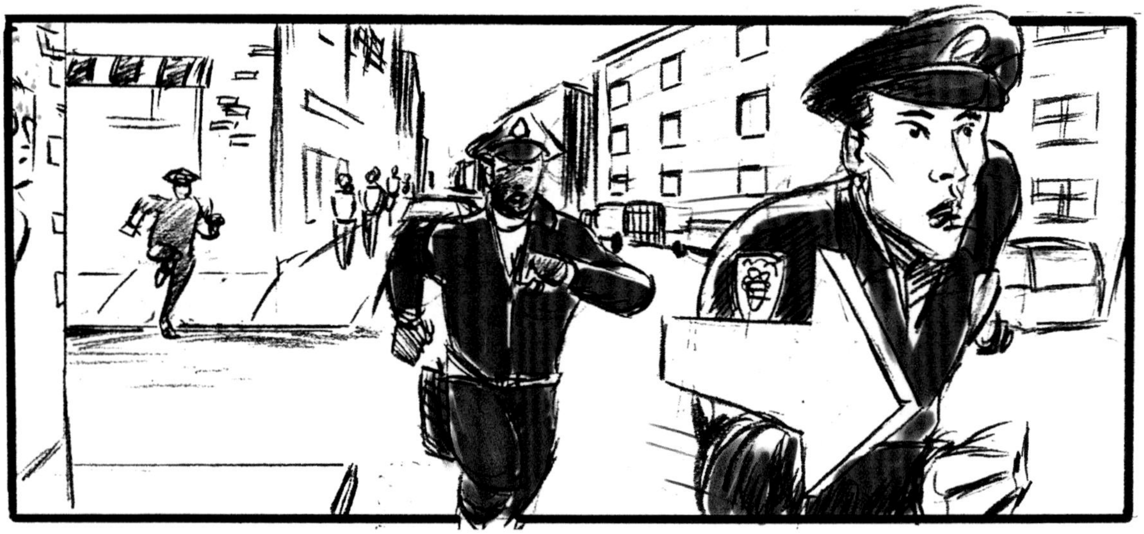

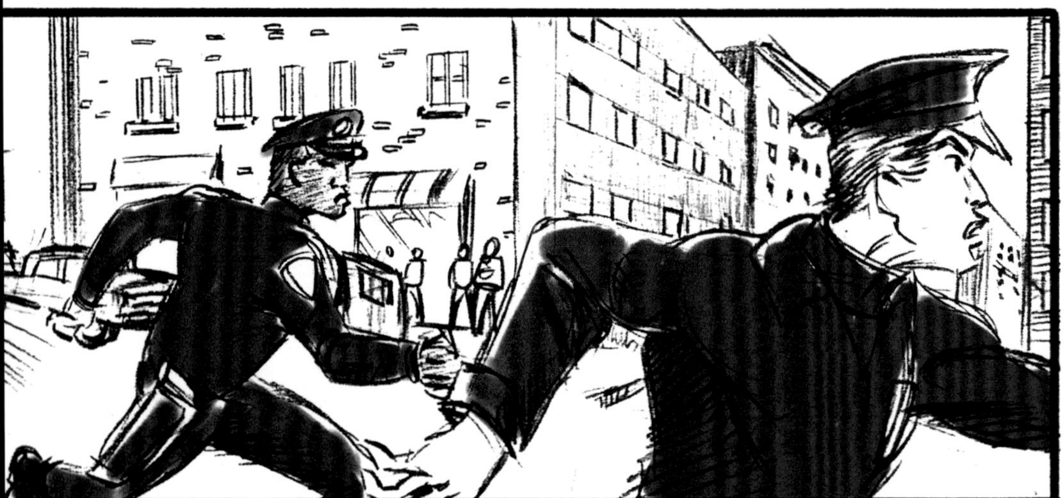

but a real-life situation where things go array that was more in the style of a Sydney Lumet than Steven Spielberg. After we chatted, Doug and Harrison started talking about preferred cigar brands. I believe that's when I exited the star bus to begin drawing the "chaos" sequence.

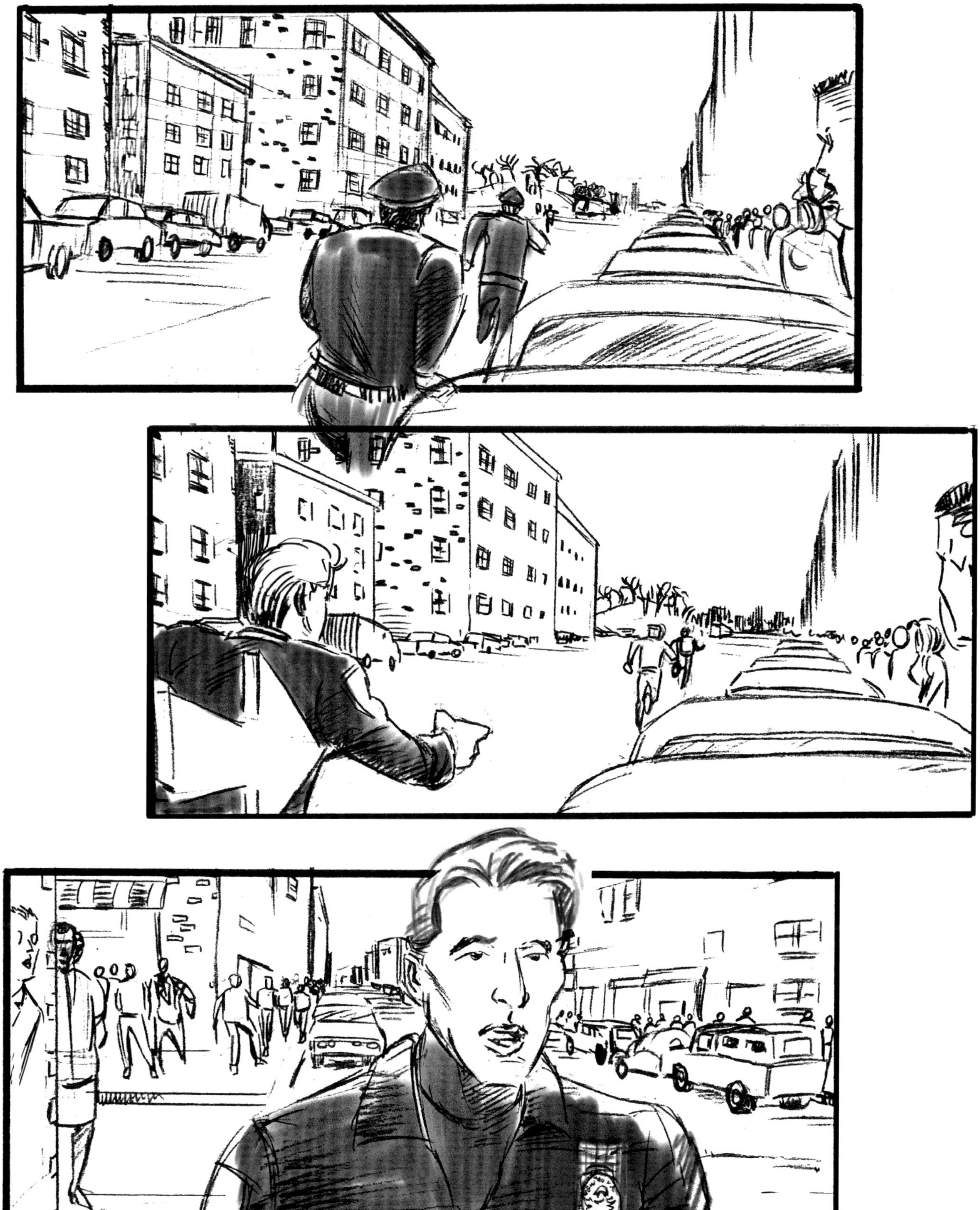

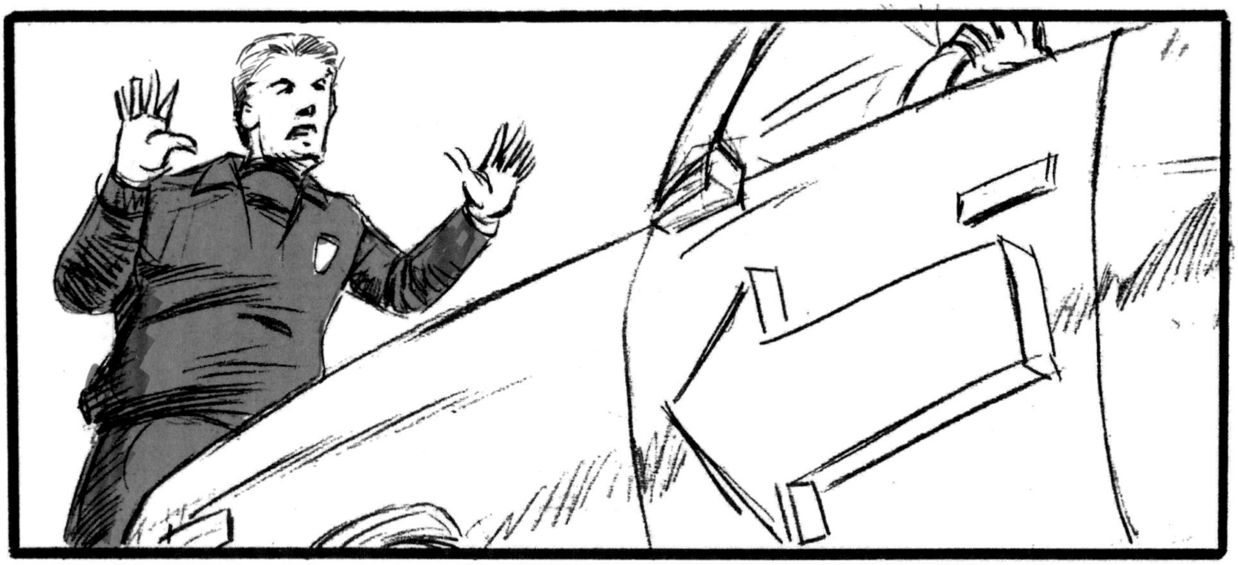

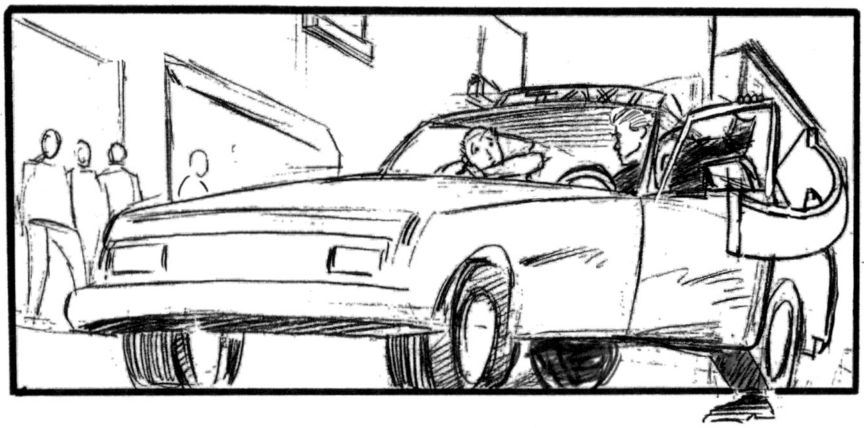

The movie was in a constant state of flux. Rewrites were being done all the time and I was asked to come up to Long Island where the climax of the film was being shot. There was still a section of the film to be shot in Ireland as well, but because the movie was not being shot in continuity, there I was. I went with my sketchpad and was ready to work with Doug and Gordon. I was able to watch Harrison Ford and Brad Pitt work on set. The climax of the film was still being worked out. I remember meeting *The Karate Kid* writer, Robert Mark Kamen on set. I think he said he was the fourth writer hired on this film. One time on set when Brad was done with a shot, I went up and asked if he had received the caricature of himself and Gwyneth. Brad smiled and said, "Yea, it was cool! Thanks!" I shook his hand and let him do his job, taking the lesson of leaving early rather than late in a conversation.

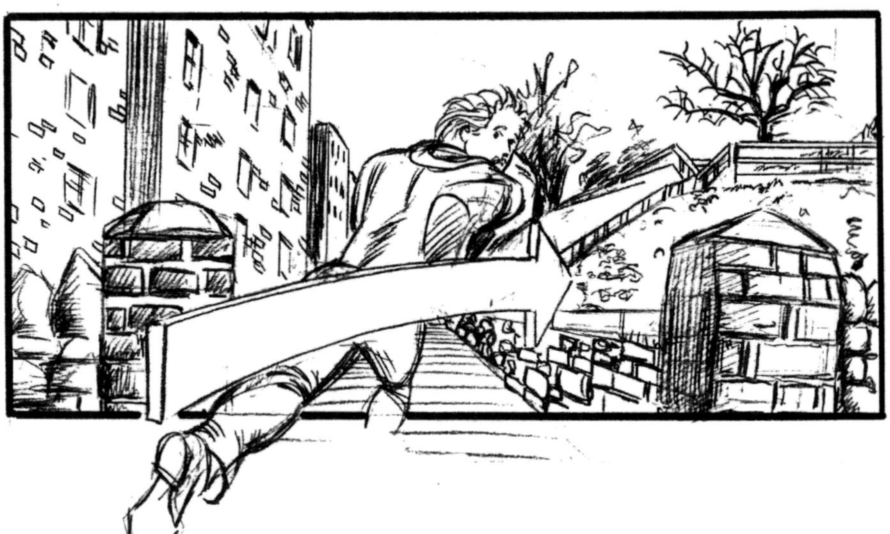

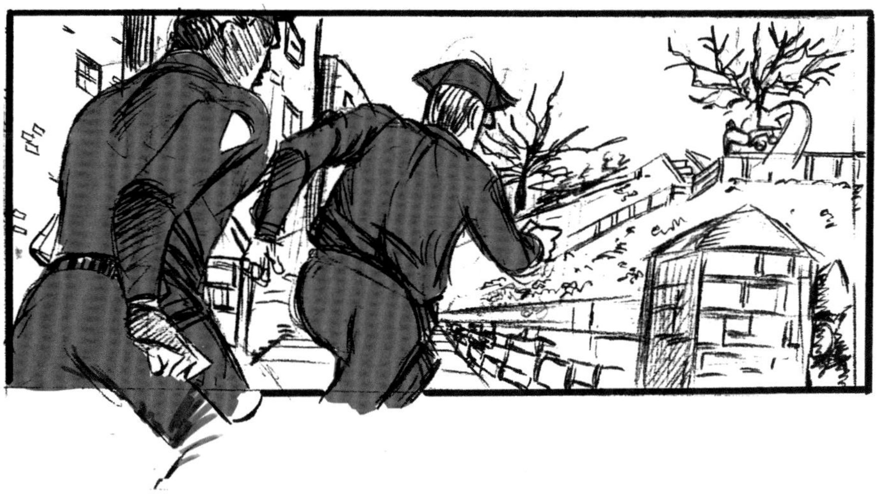

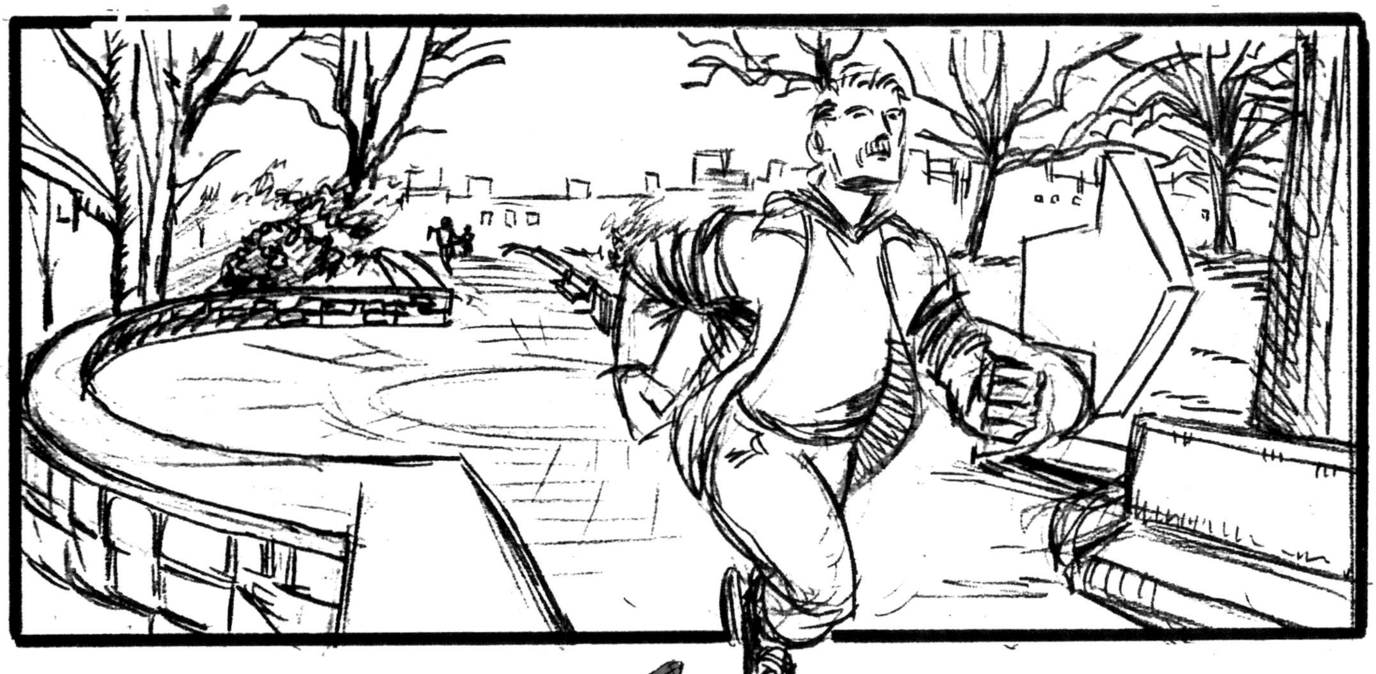

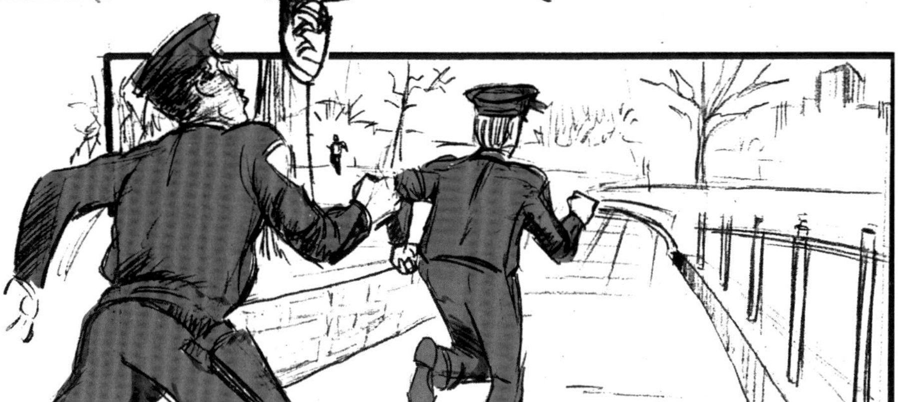

Soon afterwards, I was put on hold because again, the movie was in constant rewrites and created gaps in my work schedule. I would ask the producer, Robert "Bob" Colesberry (who later did the legendary show, *The Wire*), when I could get back to work and he had no idea. It was weeks later when I was on another television movie that I got a call to come back on

These incredible stairs are the 215st stairs in the neighborhood of Inwood in upper Manhattan. The stairs are comprised of ninety-four steps.

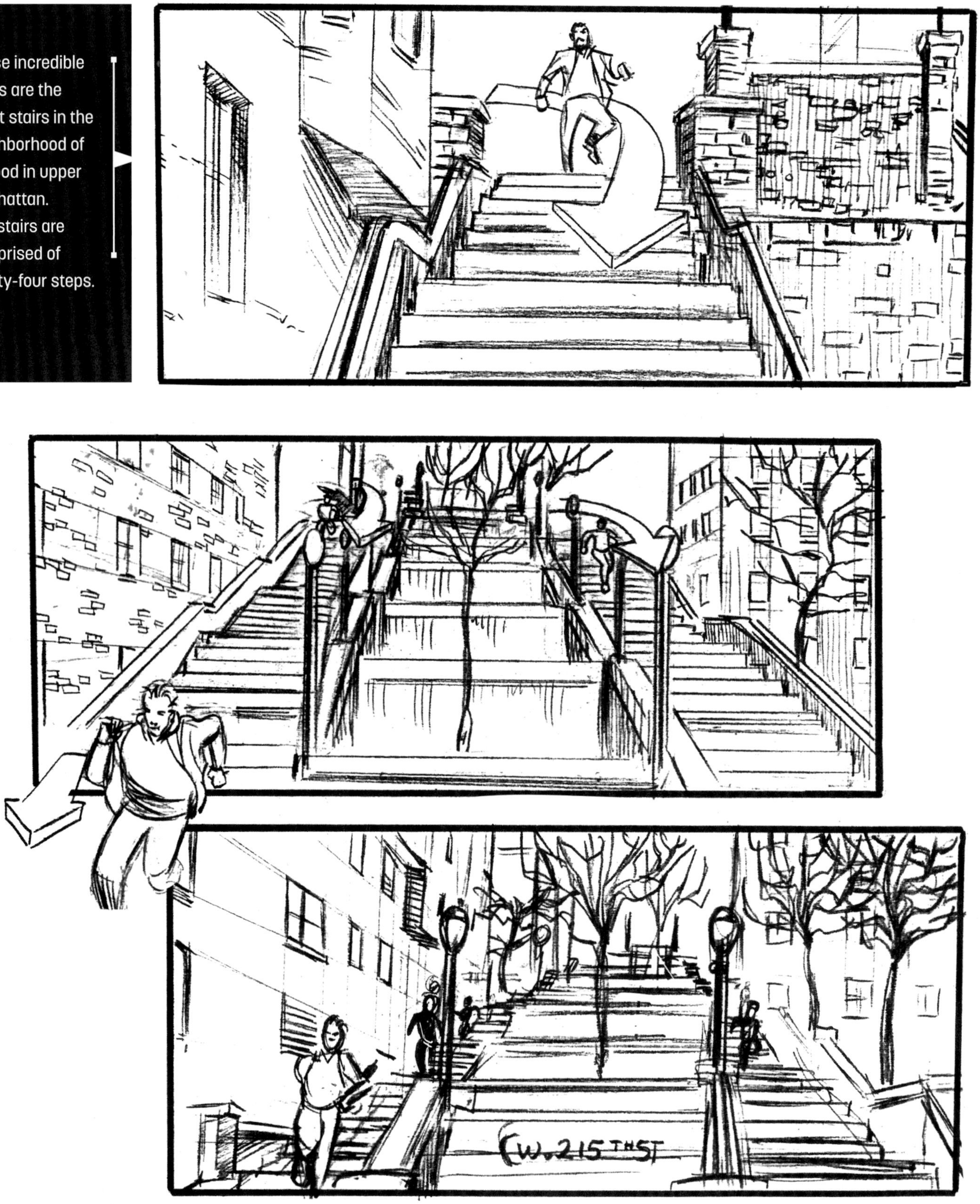

The Devil's Own. I told Bob that I was on a television show and that I could do two shows at once. That was crazy talk, of course.

The film ended up hiring Peter Ramsey on the storyboards. I believe this was one of my first times meeting Peter. Needless to say, I was upset that I was replaced by another storyboard artist on a film job that I originated. I love working with other artists, but it rankled me to think that I could be replaced. Peter was of course as nice as always when I visited the office but I saw him sitting in *my* seat. Yes, storyboard artists can have egos, too.

When the shoot went into the winter months, I ventured back to the film set just to visit the location on a Manhattan street. I remember that it was one of the coldest days I had ever felt. The already frigid temperature was made worse by the intense wind. Crewmembers were handed small pouches filled with some sort of heating crystals. Once shook, the pouches immediately grew warm. I watched Harrison do a scene of his character running on a NYC street and I was able to see Gordon in his full mode of work again. *The Devil's Own* turned out to be his last film. The incredible and legendary Gordon Willis retired from the industry after this movie.

Years later in 2017, Brad Pitt produced and starred in the film *Ad Astra*. I worked on this film with the second unit director, Dan Bradley to storyboard a lunar buggy action sequence. In 2019 (two years later) I was called back to the same film to do additional reshoot storyboards with the director, James Gray. In one of the daylong sessions I was in the editing room working with directly with Brad. Not only had the unshaven Brad managed to still be the best-looking man you would likely see, but he was also just as nice and humble as he had been twenty years earlier. He told me that he still had the drawing I had done of him and Gwyneth!

Brad and I talked a bit about the work on *The Devil's Own* all those years prior. So much had happened since then. One thing about being in the film industry is that your life seems to jump in quantum leaps. In the industry, so many people come and go and some are lost along the way. The Long Island location shoot was the only time I was able to meet

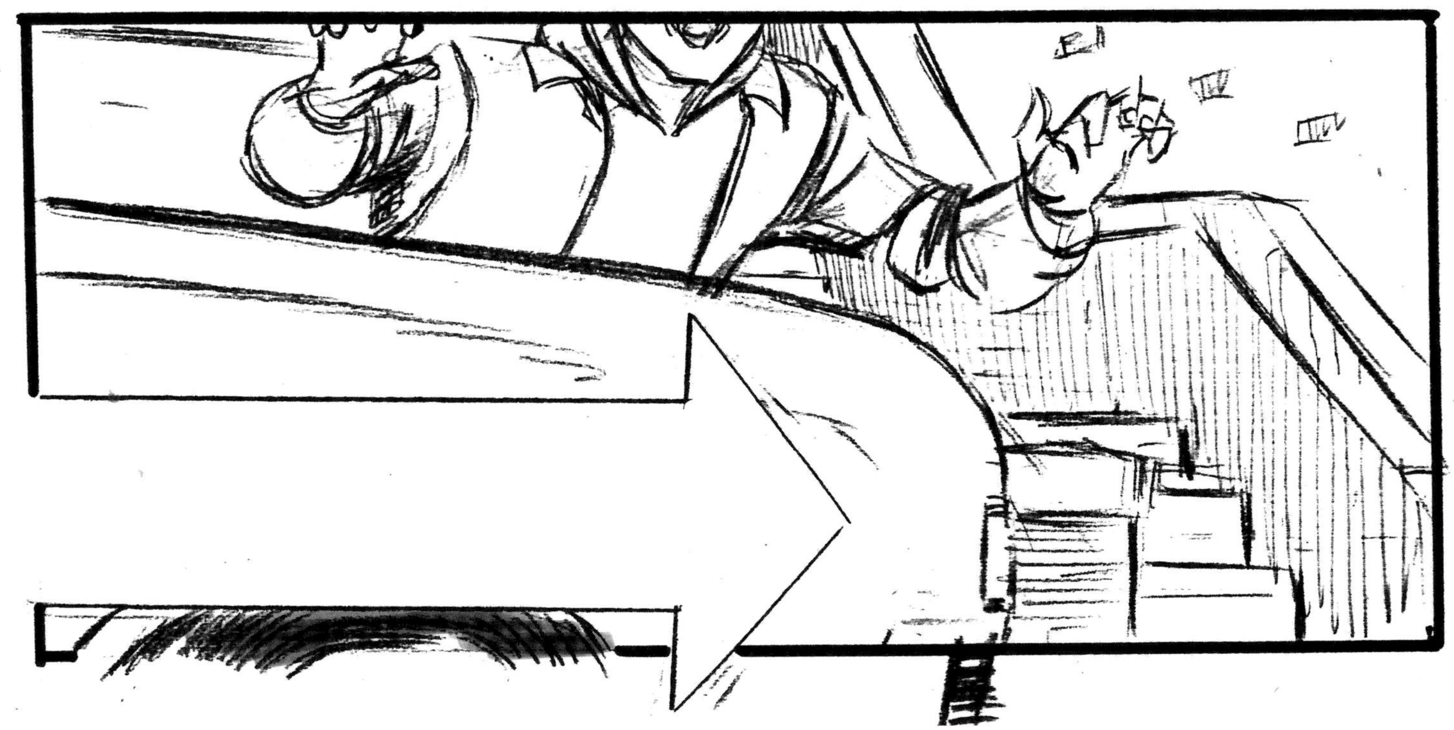

the director, Alan J. Pakula. My workday on location had fallen on his birthday and the production office asked me to do a drawing of Alan in a devil costume to reflect the title of the film. I remember finally introducing myself to the sincere and warm personage of Alan as he thanked me for my work on the film as the storyboard artist.

Within a year, Alan J. Pakula died in a freak car accident on the Long Island Expressway. We lost a dear and wonderful man.

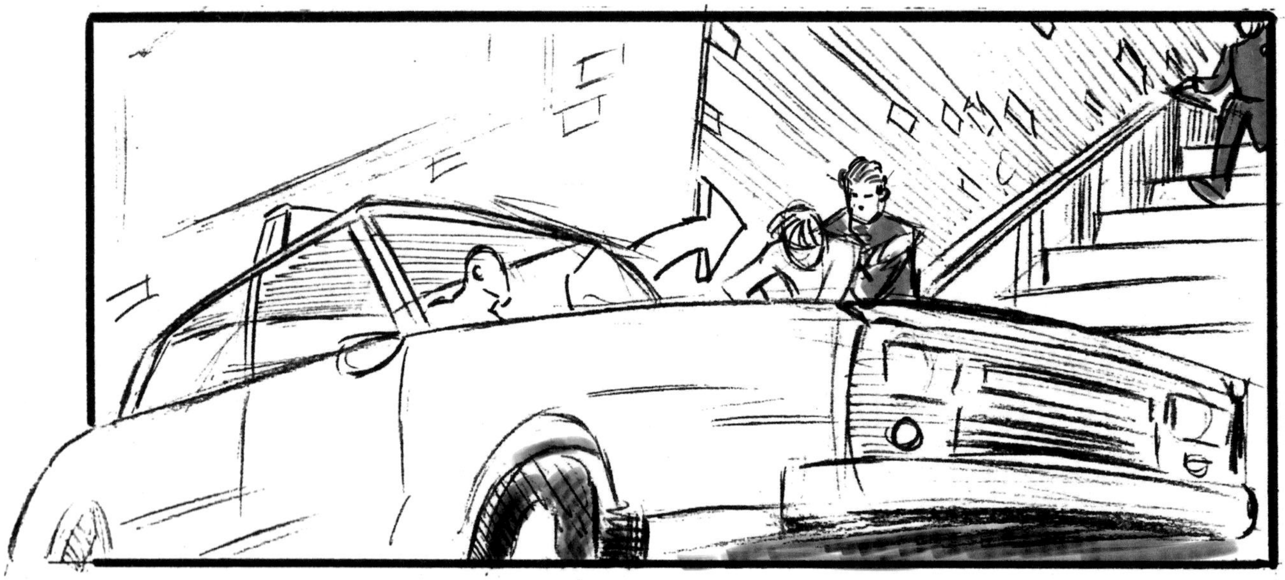

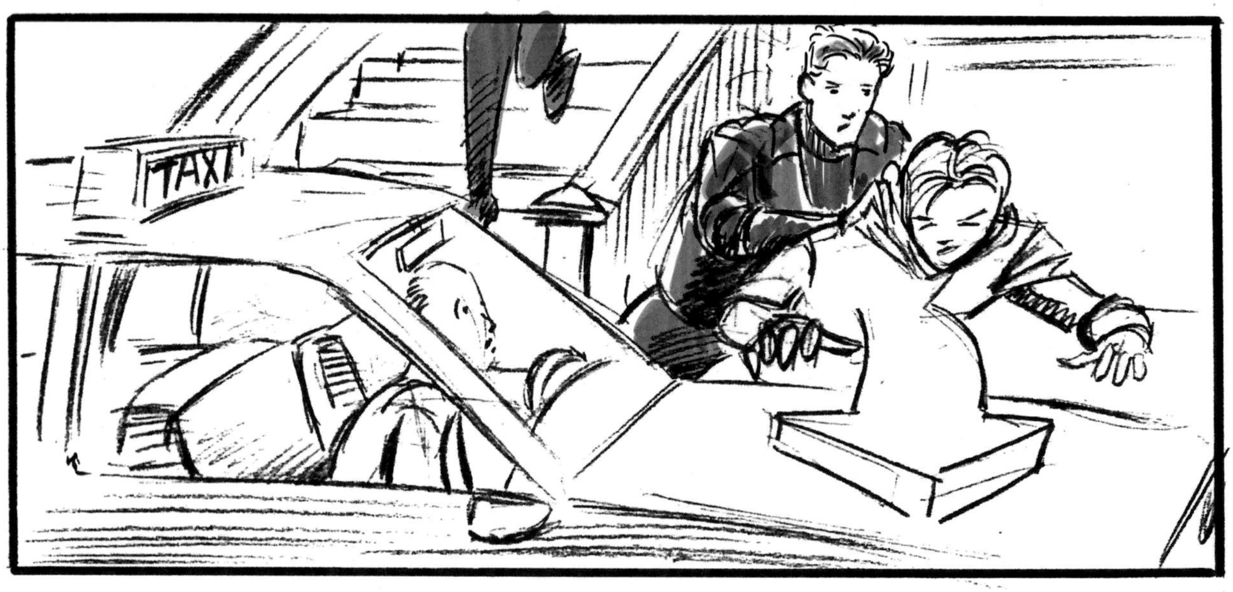

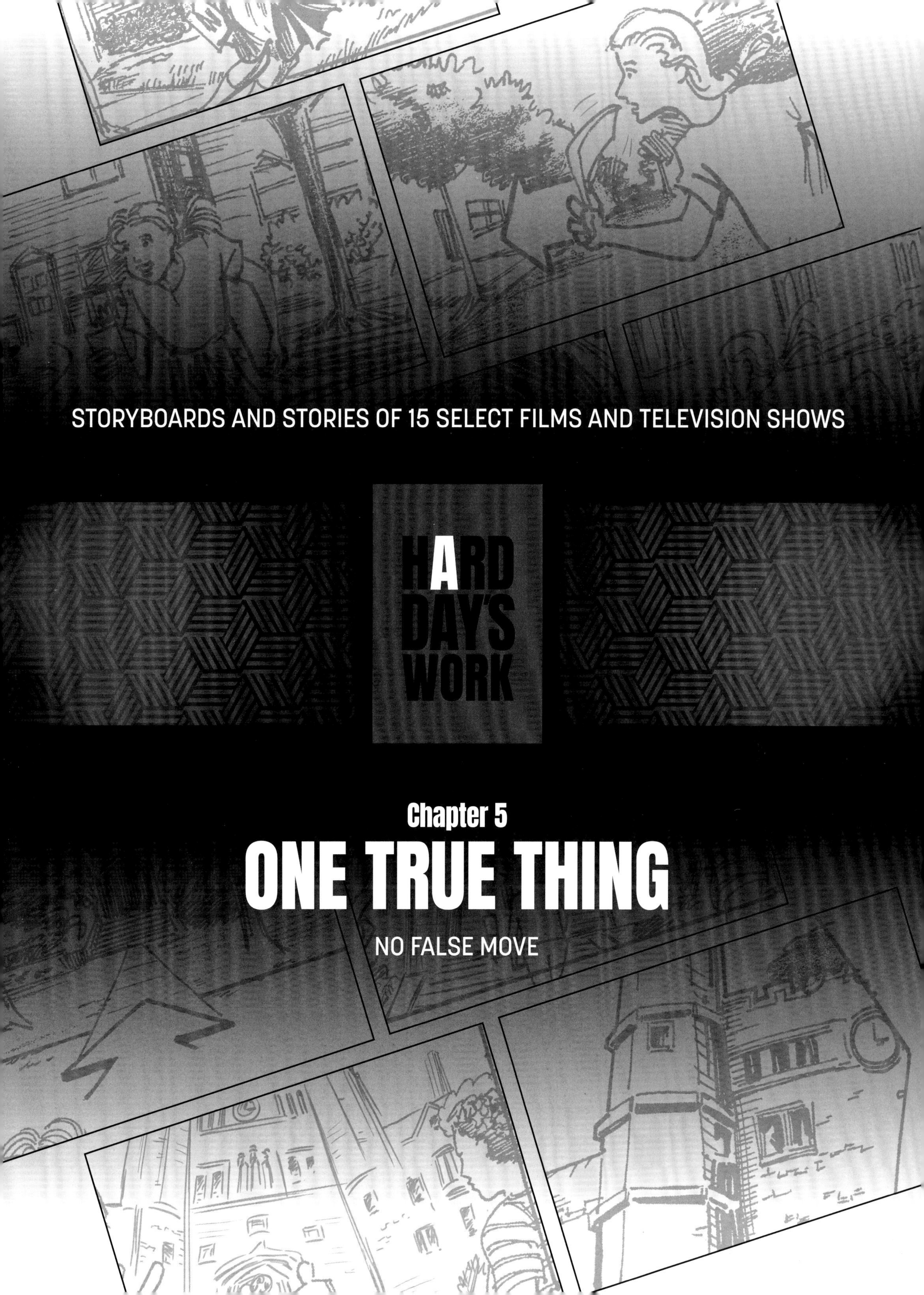

STORYBOARDS AND STORIES OF 15 SELECT FILMS AND TELEVISION SHOWS

HARD DAY'S WORK

Chapter 5

ONE TRUE THING

NO FALSE MOVE

One True Thing... no false move

In 1997, I was hired by producer William "Bill" W. Wilson to do storyboards for the Tim Allen movie, *Jungle 2 Jungle*. An LA based storyboard artist had worked on the movie during Los Angeles preproduction, but I was brought on when the film started shooting in New York City.

When I visited the set, I was able to see Tim Allen work and meet the amazing Martin Short of whom I had become a fan of during my college days while watching him on the show, SCTV. Months after *Jungle 2 Jungle* wrapped production, Bill Wilson contacted me to work on his next movie, *One True Thing*.

One True Thing was a drama starring Meryl Streep as the cancer-stricken wife of an emotionally distant Princeton professor played by the late William Hurt. Renee Zellweger was hired to portray their daughter fresh off her star making turn in *Jerry Maguire*. I strictly remember Renee greeting every crewmember with a warm 'hello'. And this was when many "hot" actors could easily ignore the crew and not think twice about it. Renee's reputation of warmth to film crews remains to this day.

Carl Franklin, a former actor who had directed the very memorable and great crime thriller film *One False Move*, was hired on as the director. Carl had also worked with Denzel Washington twice, having helmed the *Devil in a Blue Dress* and *Out of Time*.

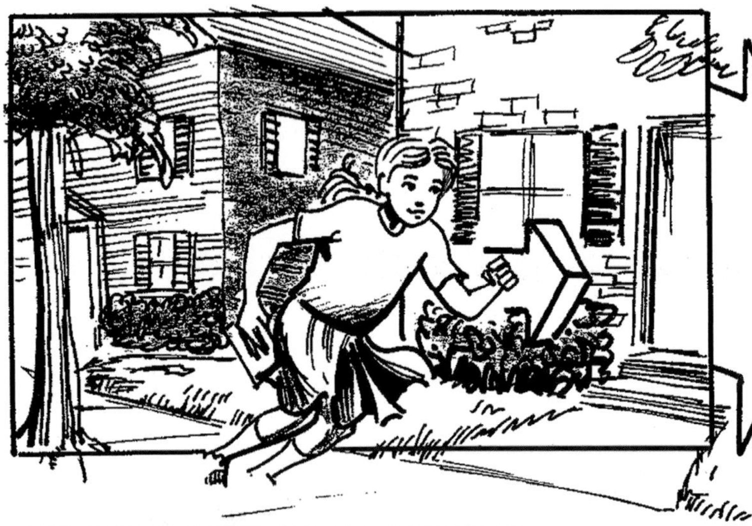

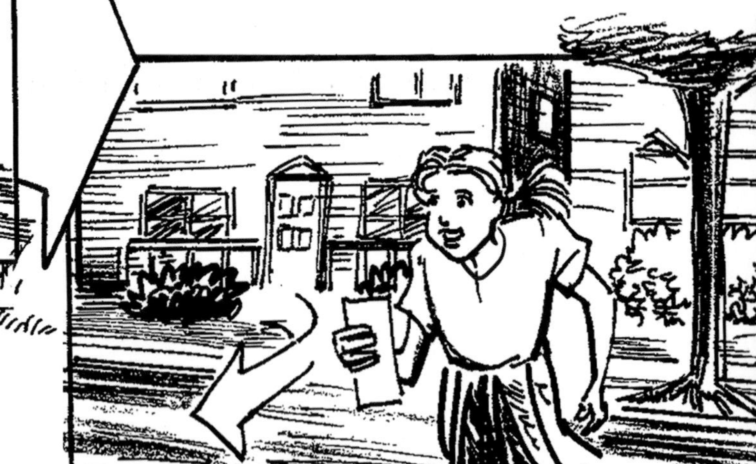

These storyboards have a somewhat pixelated look these are scanned from photocopies. In the pre-digital age, board artists had to give the original boards to the studio.

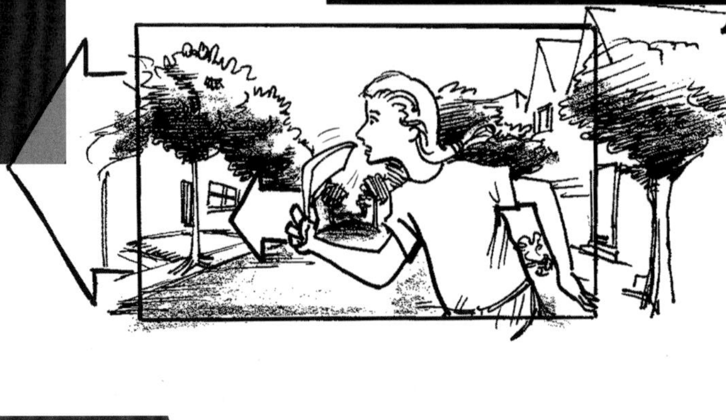

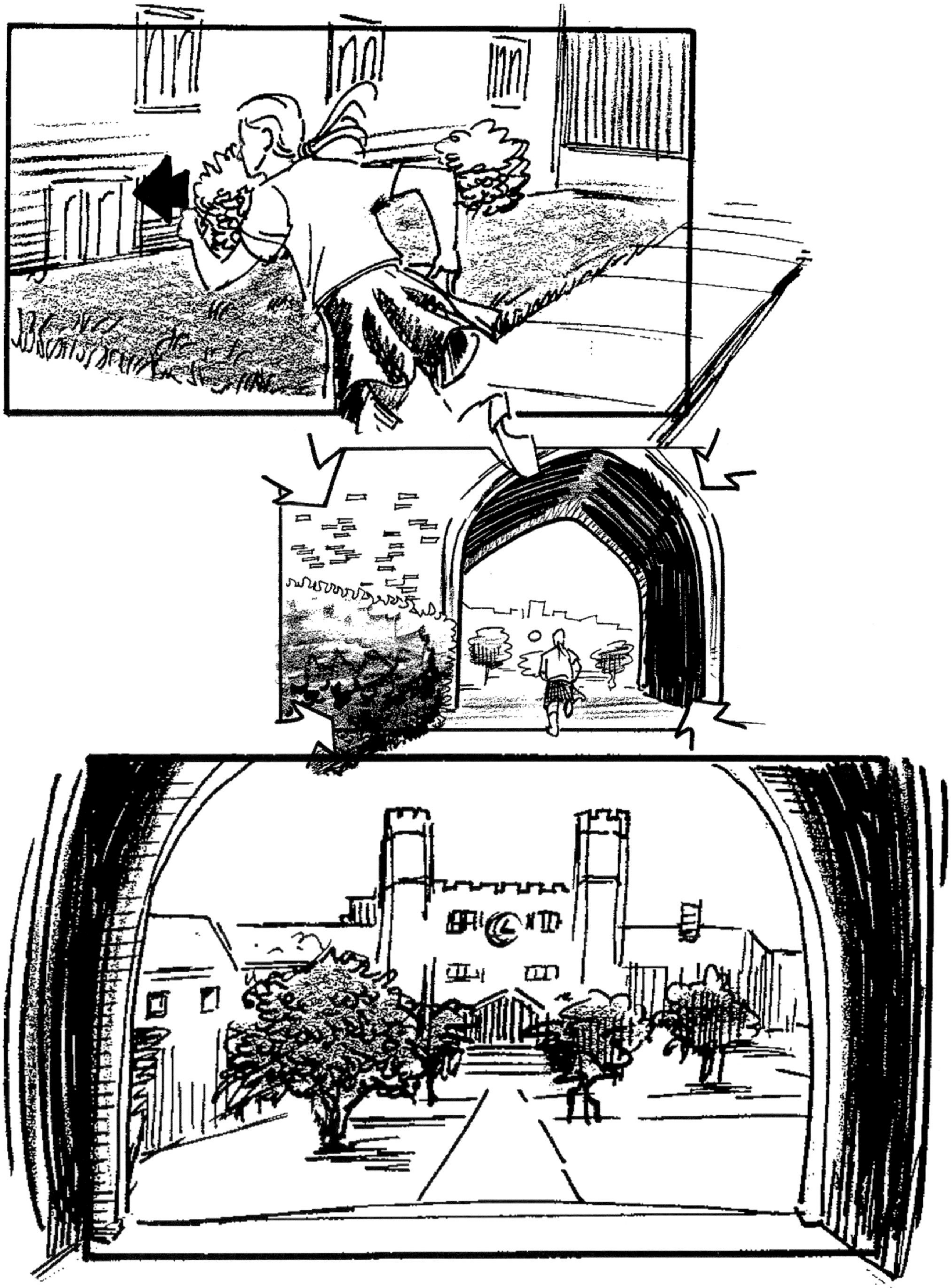

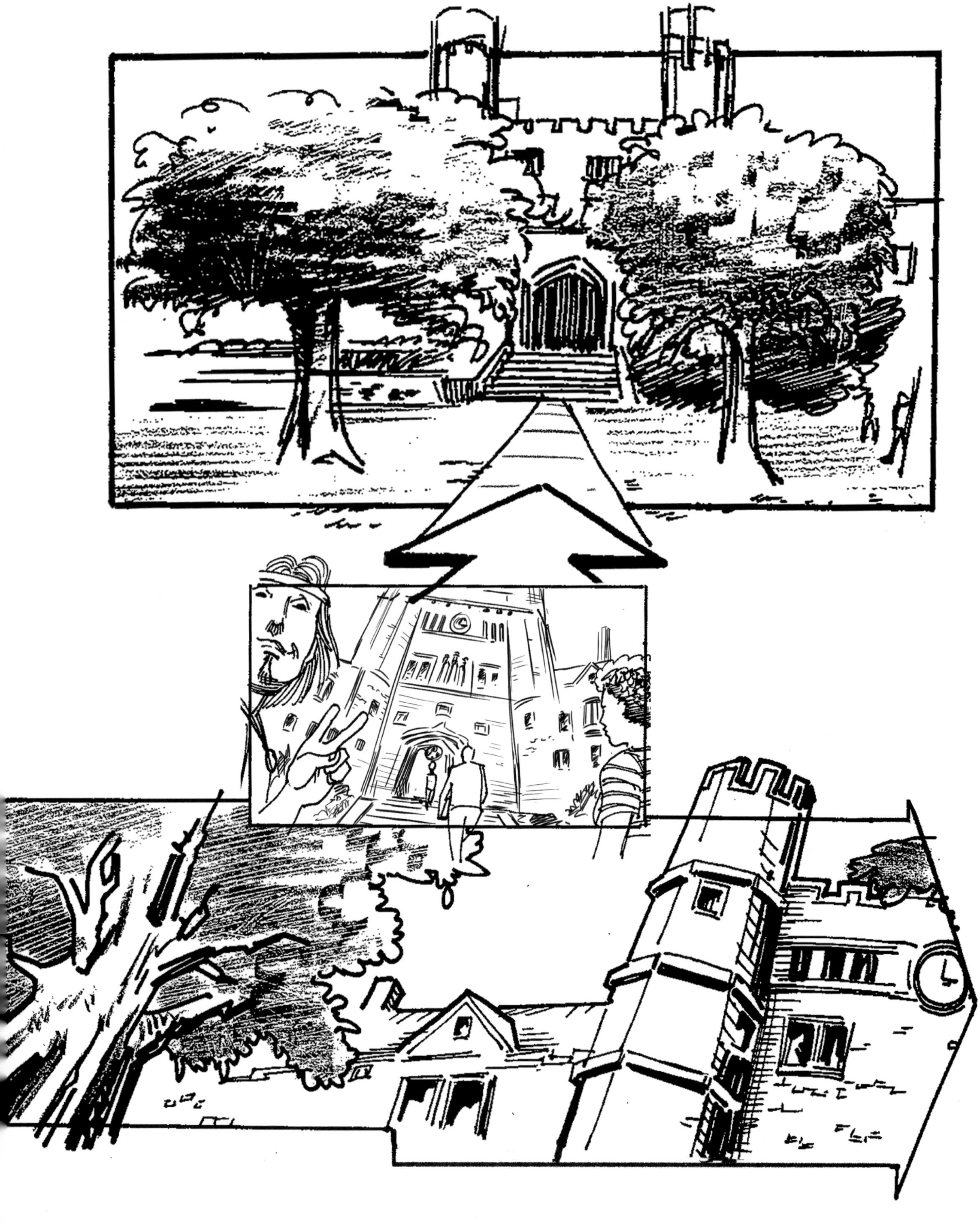

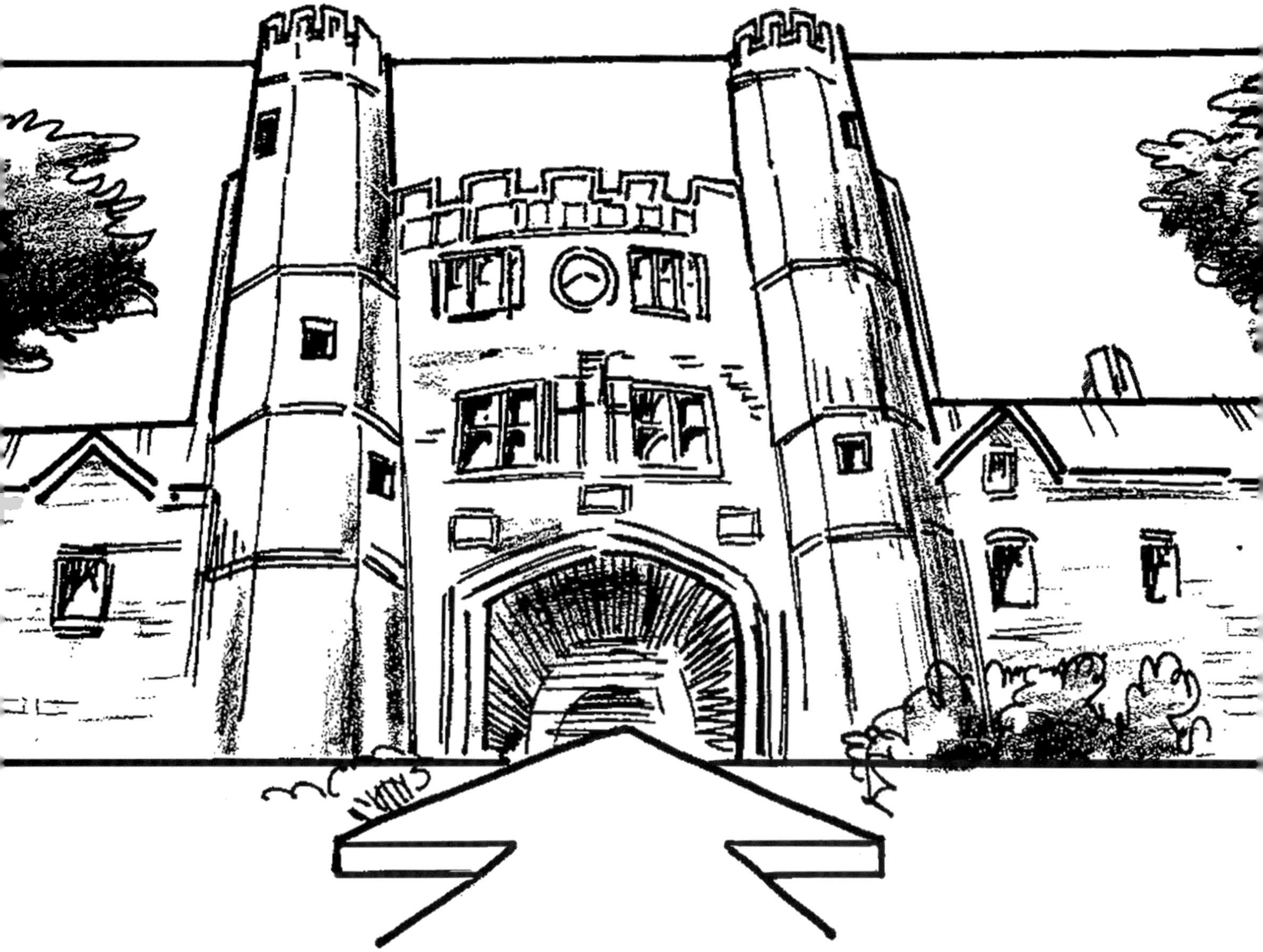

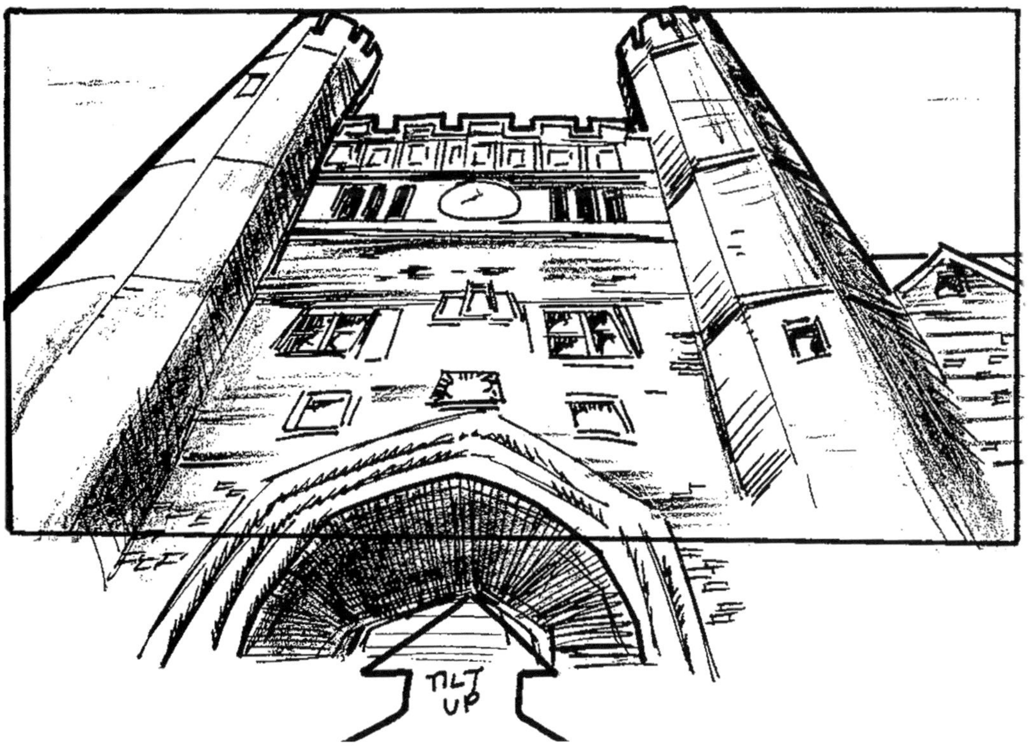

A product of California's Bay Area, Carl is an easygoing man. Carl's wife Jesse Beaton is his producing partner. Jesse was always an extension if not primary directive of Carl, with a collaborative and amicable personality that complimented her professional manner.

One True Thing was a drama without any action sequences, but there were some dramatic scenes and montages that Carl wanted me to storyboard. I worked with Carl and his DP, Declan Quinn, (who is the brother of actor Aidan Quinn). I was very familiar with Carl by the time we met, but it was not of his directing work, specifically. When I was in high school, one of the sci-fi shows I used to watch was *The Fantastic Journey*. It was a weekly NBC series about a small group of people plucked from various time periods who are sent on a mission where they ultimately ended up saving people in every episode. Carl was one of the lead actors. I found a *Fantastic Journey* cast photograph featuring Carl's image and I had it printed on to a porcelain cup. I presented it to Carl as a gift and he half-smiled, then said in a stealthy low whisper, "don't show *that to anyone*." This was Carl's way of saying that his acting days were in the past and that he was now singularly, a director.

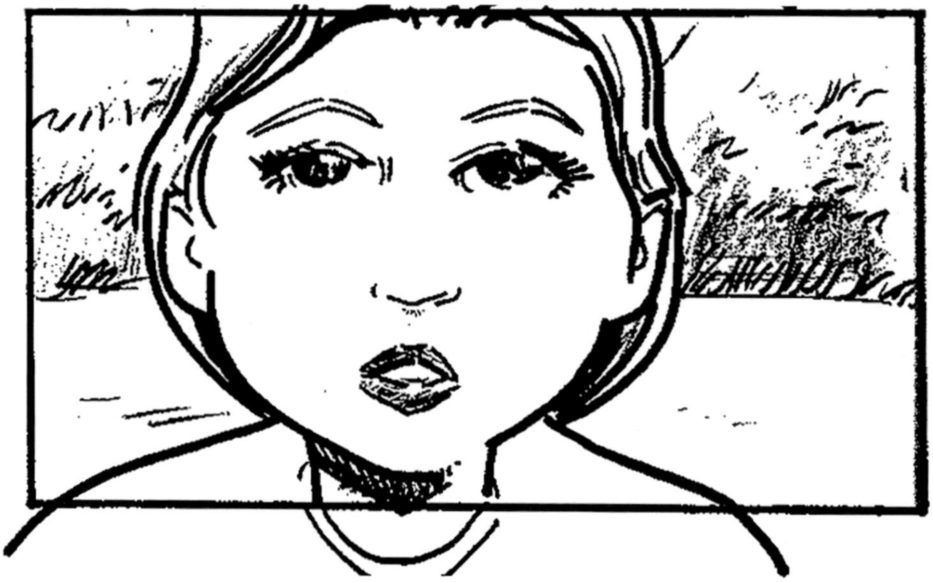

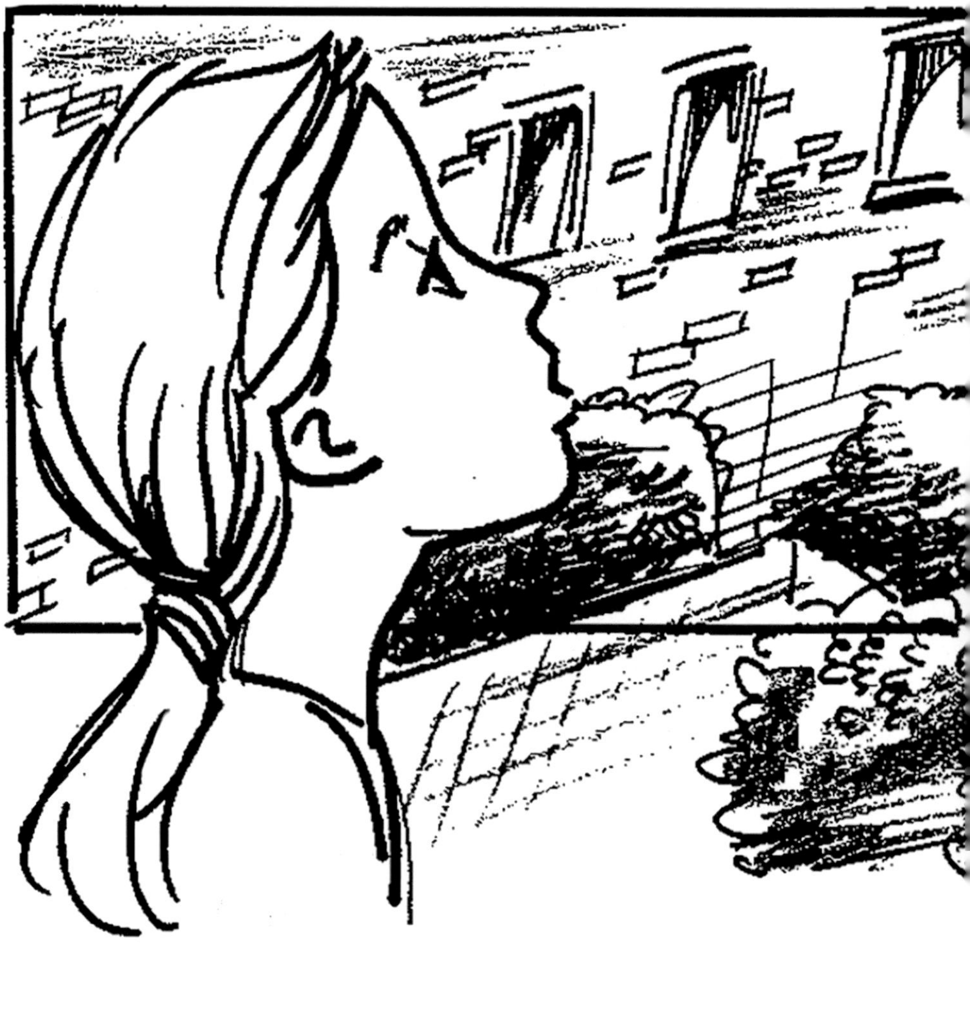

One True Thing had a sparing need for storyboards and there would be nothing overly dramatic about the camera work. I just had to listen to Carl's notes and draw the shots as such. The first scene that I worked on was a flashback/dream to Renee's "Ellen" character as a child. In the scene, young Ellen visits her father, a college professor as he teaches in Princeton. Carl laid the shots out clearly. Young Ellen happily walks through the Princeton campus where

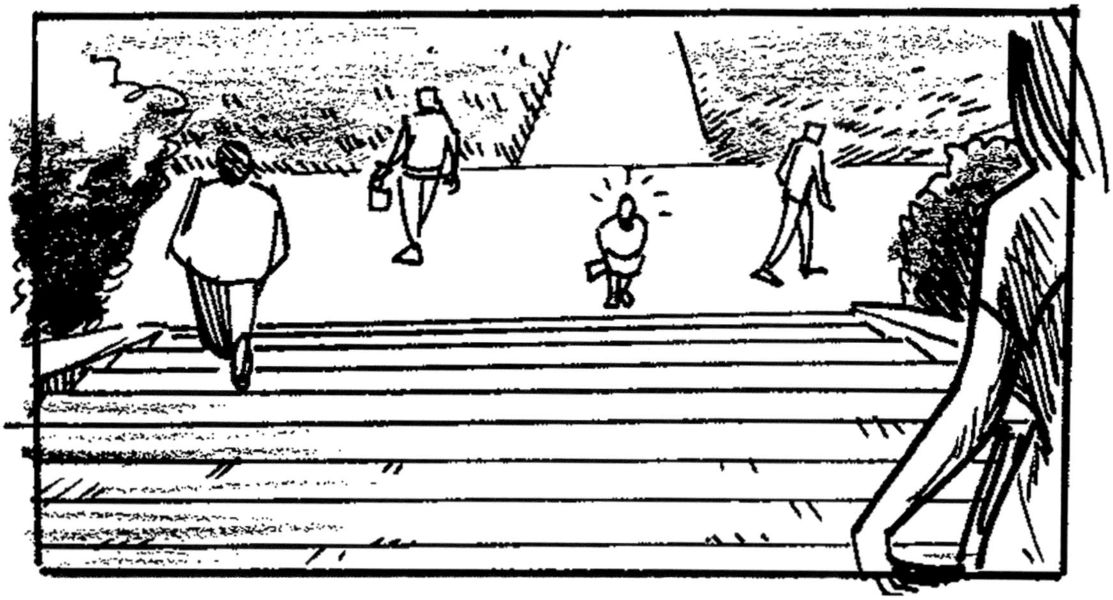

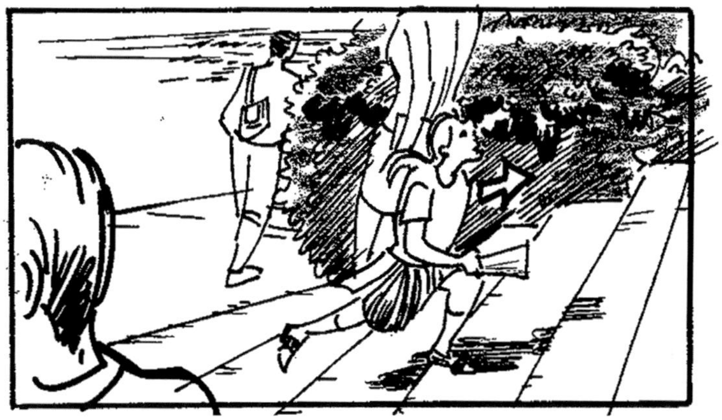

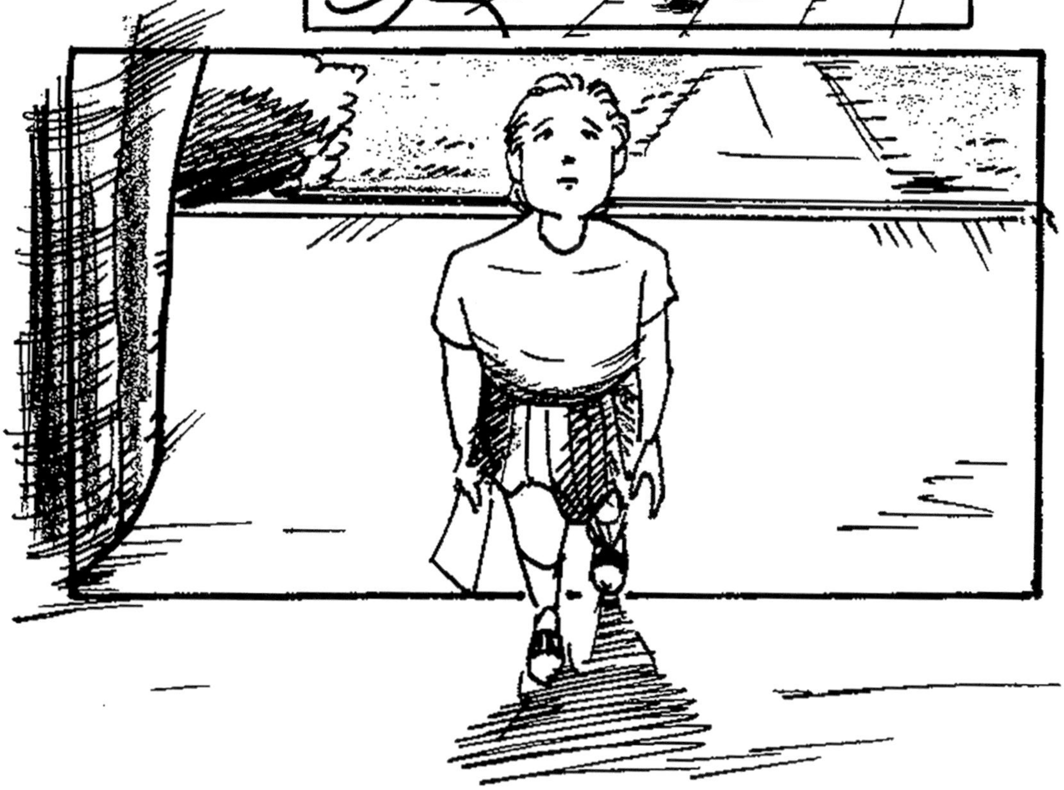

she comes upon the building in which her father teaches. For the campus grounds, I was given some nice photographs from the location department. I tried to be meticulous with the renderings of the buildings as I rarely get the chance to draw detailed architecture. Carl had some specific camera moves in mind, so I implemented them. The scene ends where young Ellen arrives in her father's classroom. The camera pans through the students, where I drew in one student that looked like a younger Carl Franklin, complete with the afro that he wore in *The Fantastic Journey* as my homage to his acting work.

In a later scene, I had to draw a wheelchair-bound Meryl Streep struggling in the kitchen but she needs to enlist her daughter's help to maneuver. In one spectacular moment, I was able to watch Meryl Streep act out the scene on set. Even then, it was an amazing once-in-a-lifetime experience.

Days later, a scheduled storyboard shot meeting was delayed when Carl was on a location scout and was late getting back to the production office. I waited patiently in Carl's office. Jesse as the film's producer and being singularly present in the office was totally fine with talking shop and other life things with me until Carl came back. I was often told to wait in reception when directors are late to a meeting, so this was different. While chatting, I mentioned my desire to make another trip to Los Angeles. In a beat, Jesse offered their home as a possibility. It was such a sweet gesture and I was blown away by her generosity. Though their home was under construction, Jesse and Carl connected me with a friend of theirs named Don, who lived in the guesthouse of a home they used to rent in Hancock Park. Don then contacted a young woman named Betty, who was a resident in the sprawling main estate house of eight huge rooms. Upon being invited to stay in her place on Carl's suggestion, Betty and I had a very friendly conversation over the phone. And *only because I came recommended by Carl Franklin* whom she knew and completely trusted, she agreed to let me stay for two weeks in a back spare bedroom with its' own entranceway.

After *One True Thing* wrapped, I went to Los Angeles and met Betty at the residence. When I heard her on the phone, her voice and laugh sounded like she was a large woman. When I rang her doorbell and she appeared I was talking to a tall, beautiful woman who as it turns out, was a former model among other things as well as a talented and established actress with a resume of professional theater and screen experiences as well as sensational singer. Betty and I would have never met without my work on this film with Carl and Jesse. It is my joy to report much has grown from that initial meeting: Betty and I were married years later. Our son Josh is an actor, writer and recording artist under the name of Josh D. King, also known as Joshua B. Drummond.

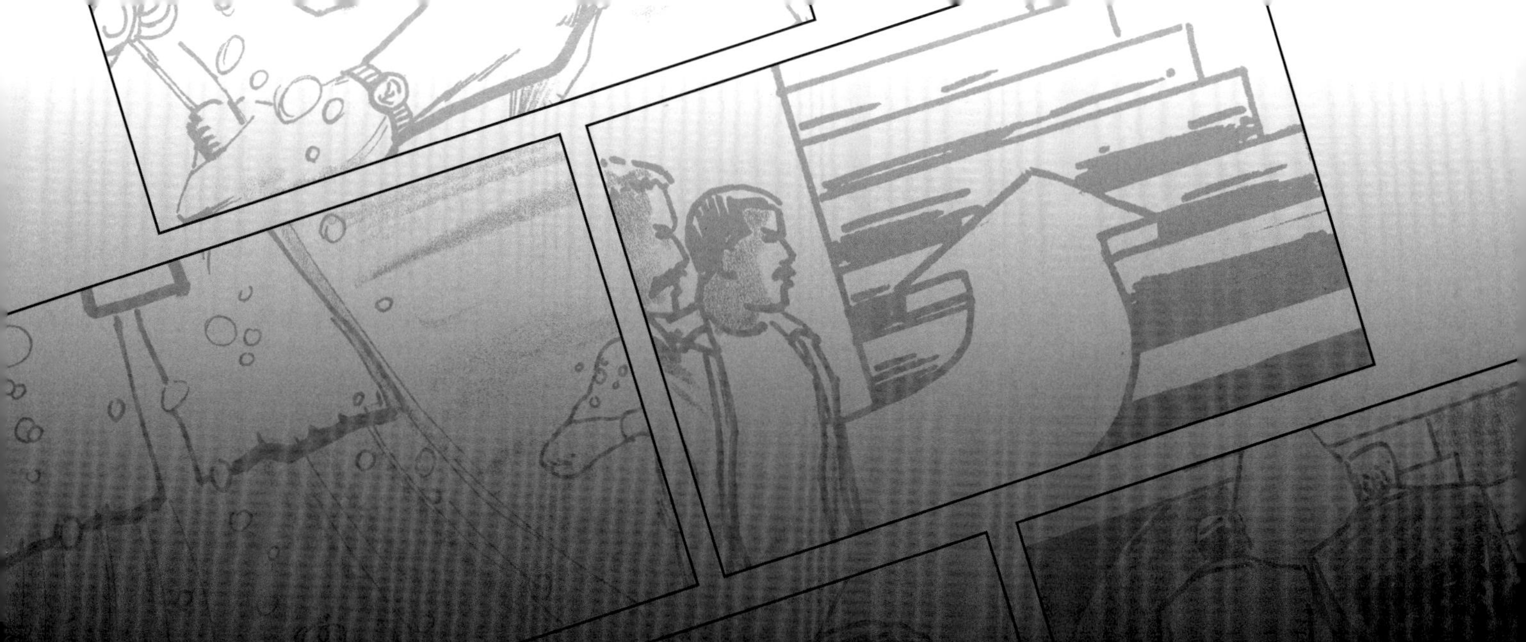

STORYBOARDS AND STORIES OF 15 SELECT FILMS AND TELEVISION SHOWS

HARD DAY'S WORK

Chapter 6

SHAFT

AND BROTHER, JOHN

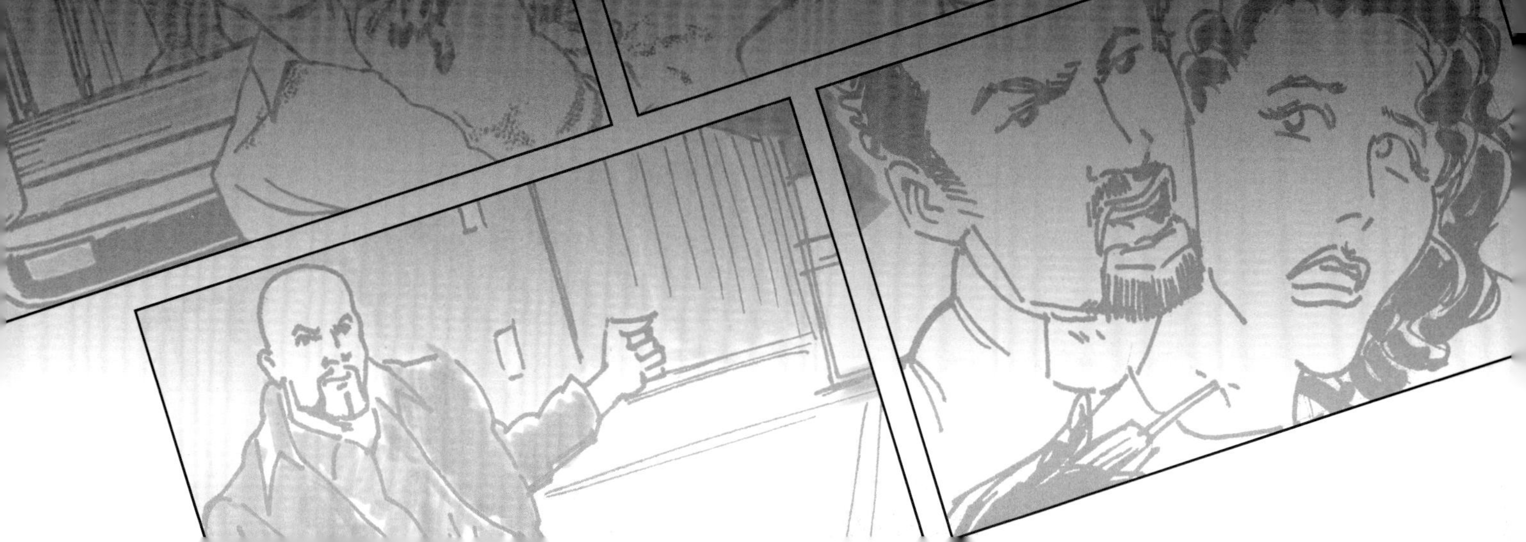

Shaft . . . and brother, John

John Singleton. That name alone lifts my soul.

The first time I met John Singleton was in 1994 at a Christmas party for *The Source* magazine. John was a contributing editor for that hip hop focused magazine, and I was still a freelance artist who did caricatures and spot illustrations for their articles from time to time. I had drawn a caricature illustration of John for the magazine and he dug it. Always on the lookout for gig with a working director, I asked him if he used storyboards. John said that he had a "guy" whom he used. John's "guy" turned out to be the aforementioned Peter Ramsey, who has gone on to become an Academy Award-winning director with *Spider-Man: Into the Spider-Verse* and also the director of the *Star Wars* shows, *The Mandalorian* and *Ahsoka*.

A few years passed and I was called in to work with John on his reboot/sequel to *Shaft* which was to be called *Shaft Returns*. Producer Roger Paradiso, who I had worked with on another project dropped my name in the hat when Peter was busy on another show. When I got the call to work on *Shaft Returns*, I was told that the movie would start early preproduction in Los Angeles, and then move to New York City where it would be shot. I was still living in Queens, New York and I needed a place to stay in Los Angeles. Part of my deal in taking this gig was that I would have to cover my own living expenses. There were plenty of storyboard artists in Los Angeles they could have hired. I knew I had to take a risk in order to achieve my ultimate goal of getting established in the industry and working with big directors like John.

I did some "sofa-surfing" in Los Angeles for a few weeks to get and keep the gig. Hill Harper put me up for a couple of weeks. Actor Shawn Michael Howard, who I met on *Above The Rim* was going out of town and allowed me to stay at his Hollywood apartment for two weeks. Shelley McLean,

These underwater frames were form John Singleton's original script which was never filmed. A yacht party were to be attacked by modern pirates as some of the partygoers scuba dived below. The original John Shaft rescues the yacht party in the opening of the film. It was a bad ass intro to Richard Rountree's Shaft. John wanted a James Bond style opening for the film.

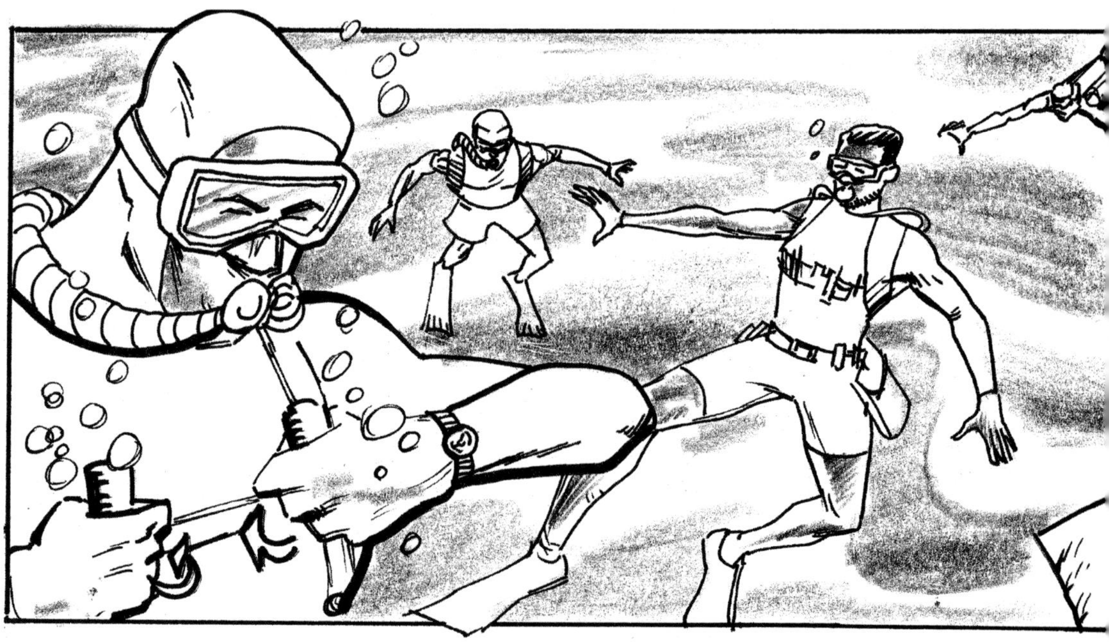

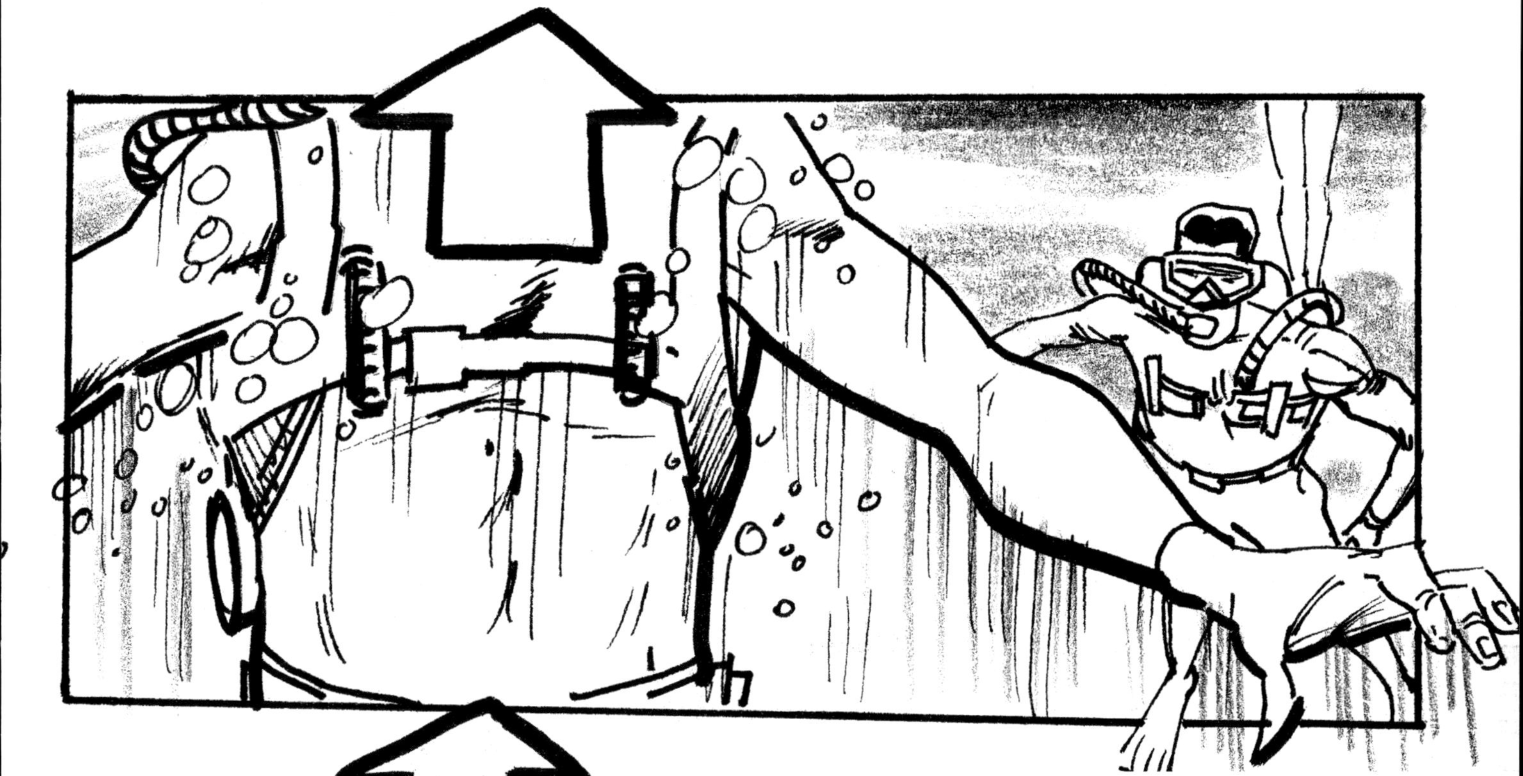

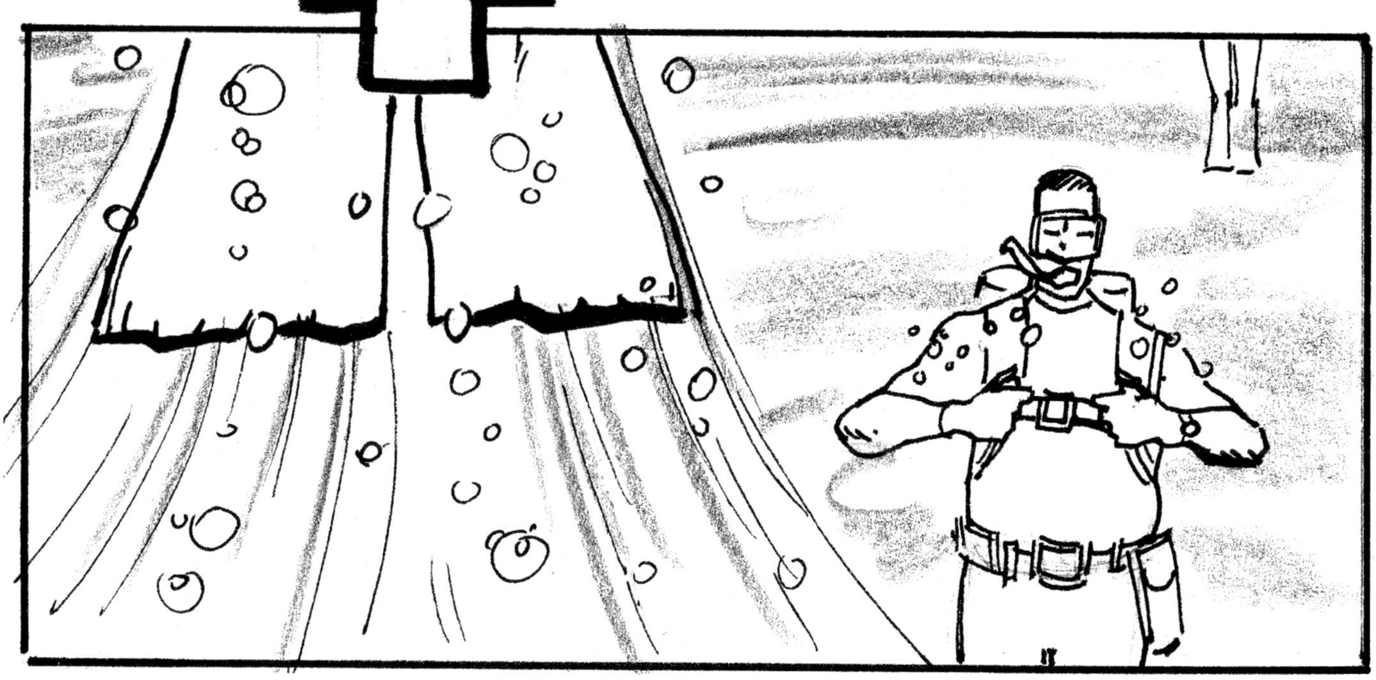

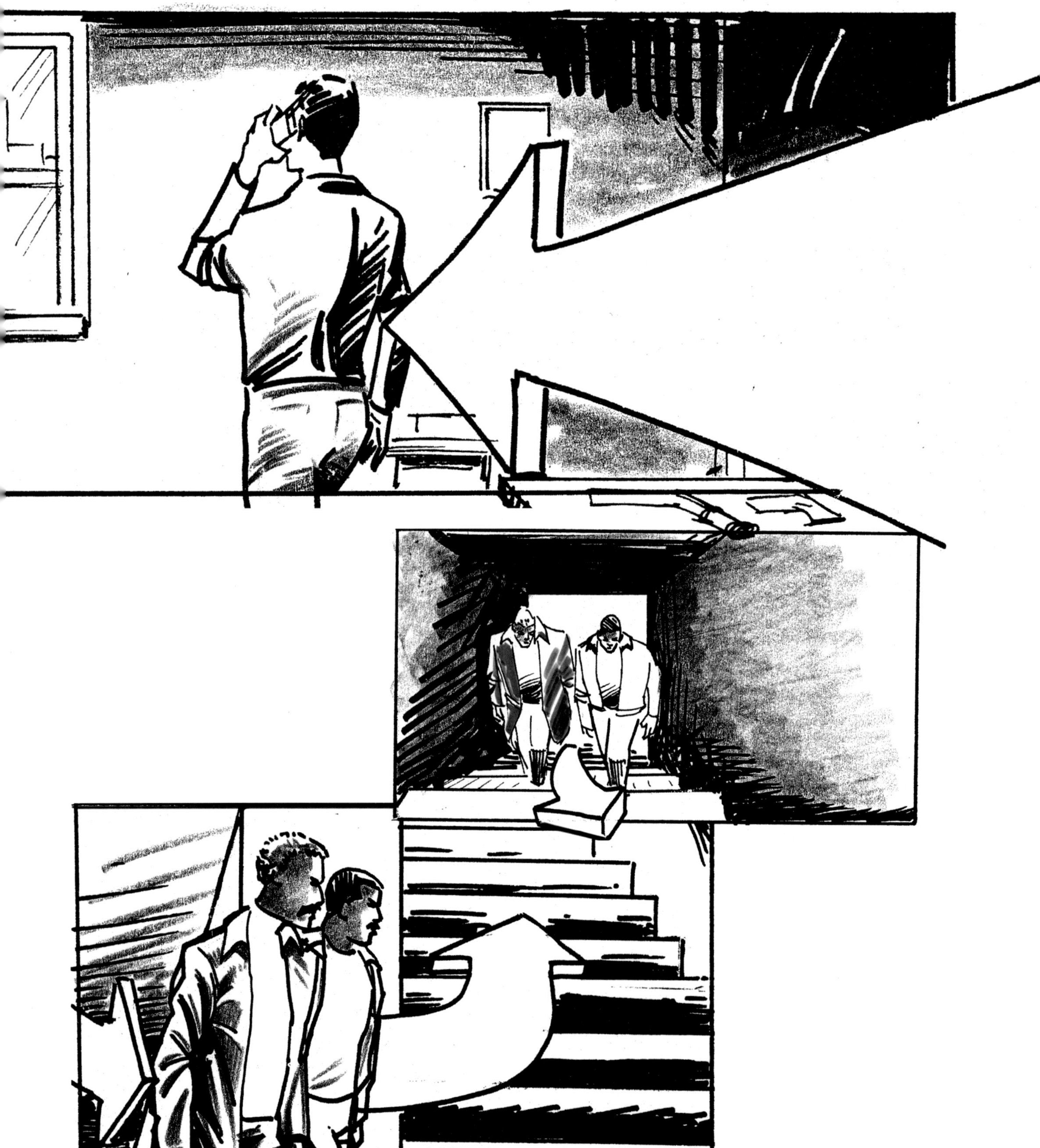

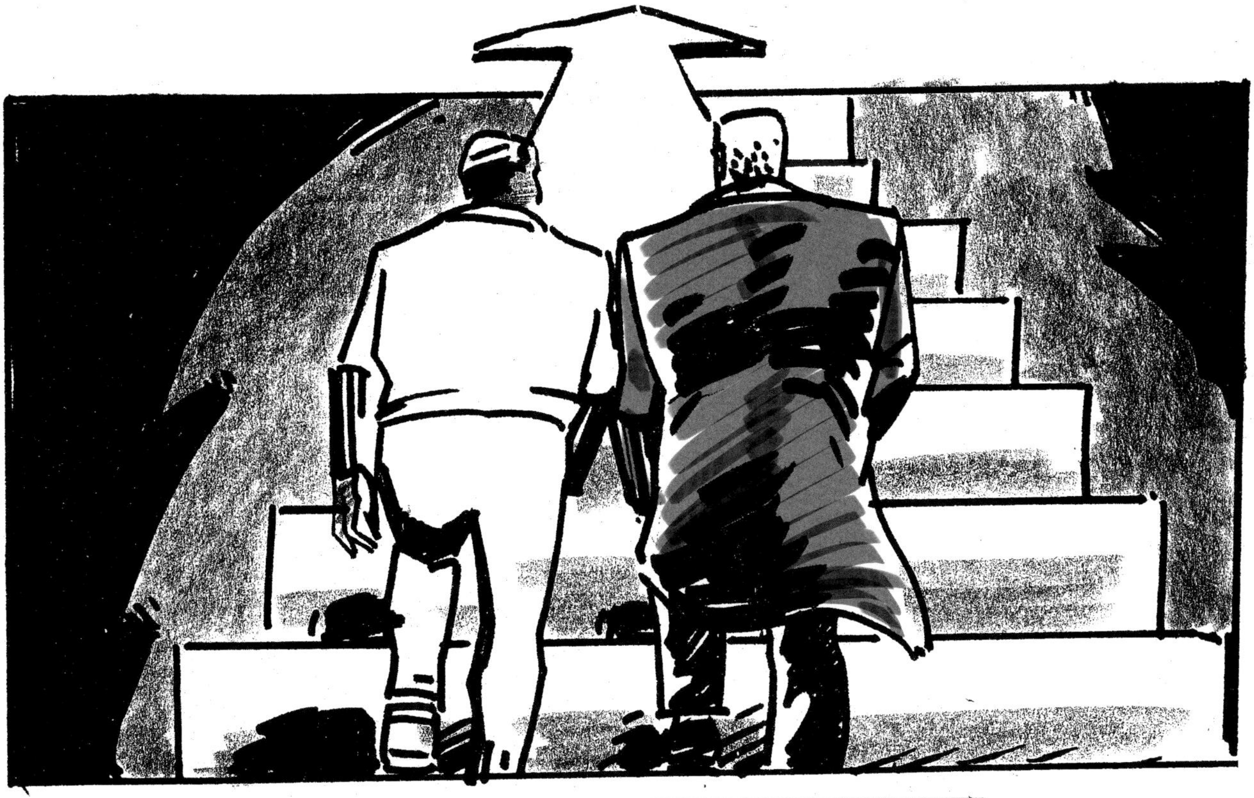

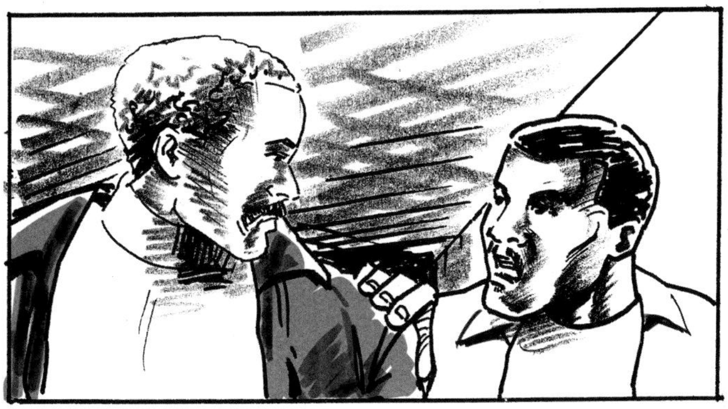

a friend from my early days as a retail stock worker in Bloomingdale's a decade earlier was now living in nearby Torrance, California and let me land at her place for a few days.

John was cordial in our first meeting at the *Shaft Returns* production office in the MGM building. I reminded him that we had met a few years earlier. As soon as John and I got to know each other we became fast friends. We both loved comic books and movies. We both idolized Steven Spielberg so that was an instant connection with the real difference being that John actually *knew* Steven. They had a "wunderkind connection" of two directors who were only in their twenties when they gained major success. On the first day of work John showed me a huge spiral notebook of Peter Ramsey's storyboards from his then current film, *Rosewood*. I have to admit to being more than a little intimidated by the work. The magic of Peter's style wasn't in the detail, but in his perfect shot selection as well as his knowing exactly where to throw shadows and to add line weight. With any good set of storyboards a viewer's eyes should bounce from frame to frame without confusion.

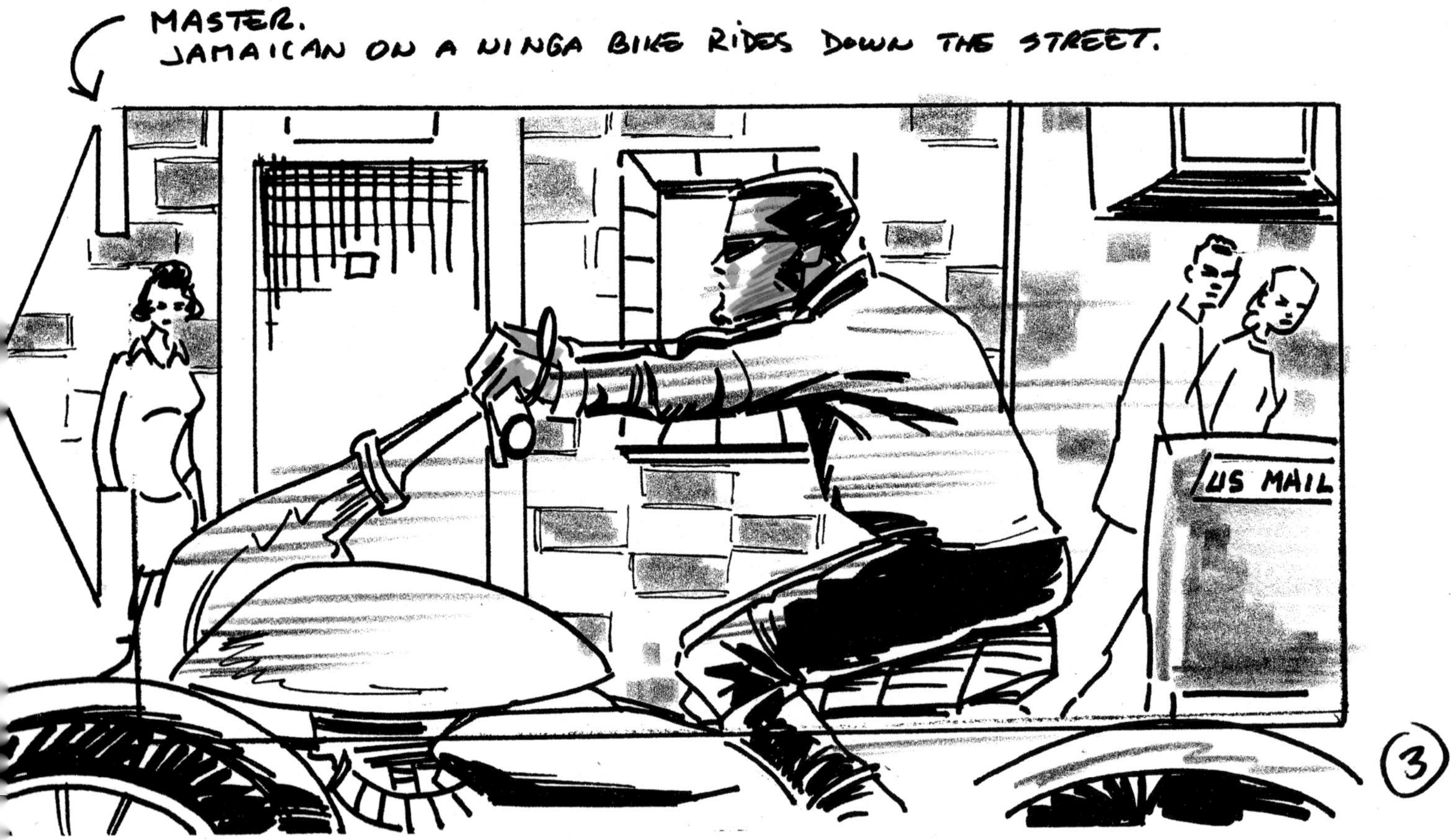

John was the most enthusiastic filmmaker anyone could dream of working with. He was always energetic and in good spirits. He even forgave the fact that I had yet to see *Rosewood*. "You didn't see my movie, man?!" So...I saw *Rosewood* that evening. John and I became the "go-to person" for each other to share our enthusiasms for the latest comic books. In that way, we were total geeks. On lunch breaks, we would drive over to Golden Apple Comics on Melrose Avenue where John would walk in and be treated like Hollywood royalty.

At the *Shaft* production office, John would get his mind into the perfect state to work. We would look at scenes from different movies including Seven, taking time to study David Fincher's shooting and editing style as well as the grittiness of the film. We would watch *Jaws* while John told me the shots he "borrowed" and used in *Boyz n the Hood*. John had a wide variety of cinematic influences but never copied anyone. He showed me by film scene comparisons how Spielberg was influenced by David Lean and Sergio Leone. While John was a cinephile and always inspired by these filmmakers, when he completed his work it was always a John Singleton film of his own singular vision. He was an artist of his own voice, period. For *Shaft Returns* as it was originally called, John had the idea for the audience to meet the original John Shaft in this new film now as an older man. The role was still to be played by Richard Roundtree and to acknowledge that many years had passed since the original film of 1971. This now older Shaft would have a police officer son named John Shaft Jr., as well as a martial arts daughter that John had me draw in the likeness of singer, Lauryn Hill.

John brought me into his long standing "film family" of people that he had used on his films since Boyz n the Hood. A number of these people were with him all the way to his last production of the hit television show *Snowfall*. I still work with many of my Singleton film family to this day. Working with John for so many people was the groundswell point of their careers. John and I would discuss scenes, then John would shot list the scene and have Liba Daniels, his assistant, type it up. Liba eventually progressed over the

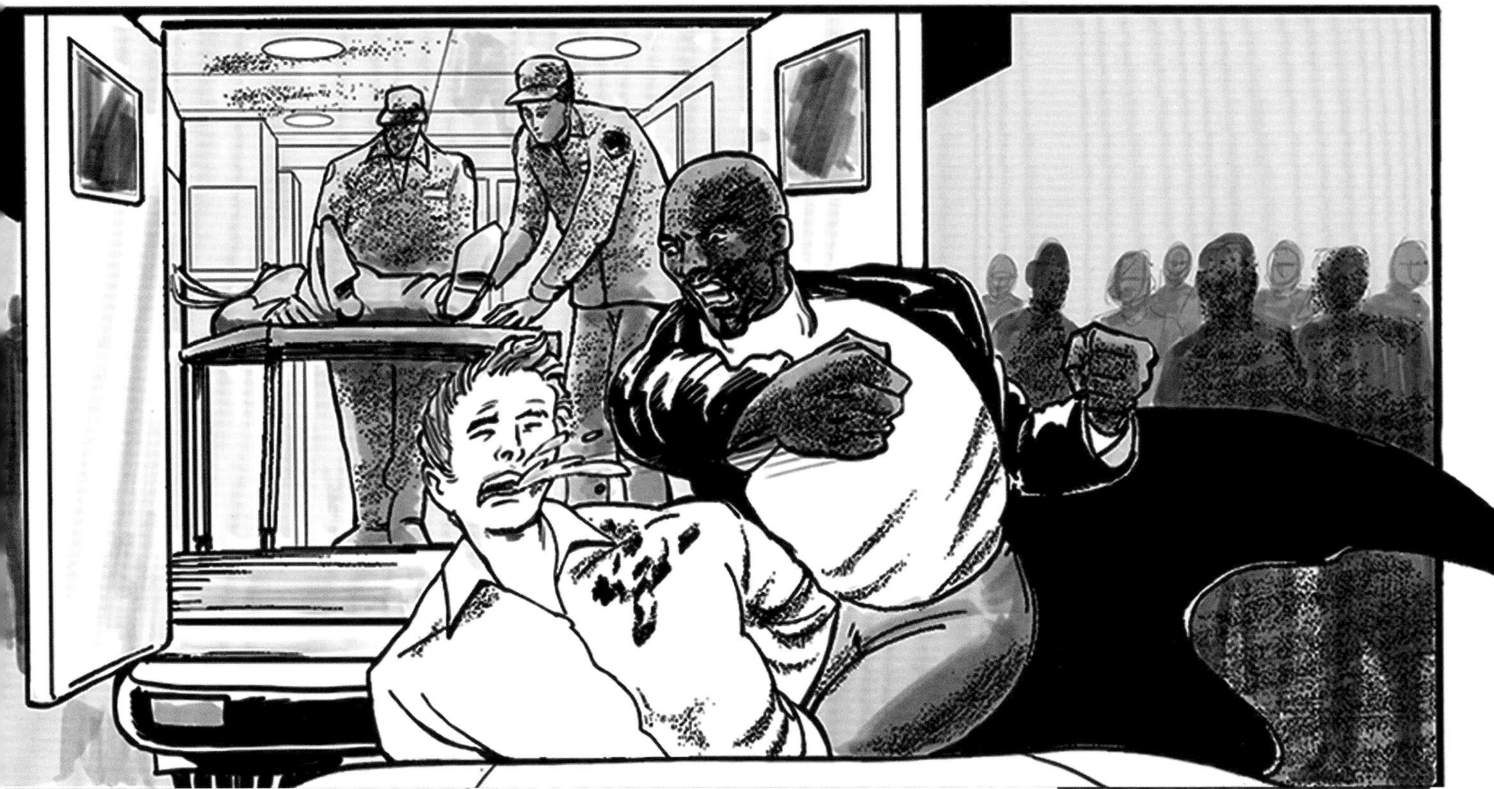

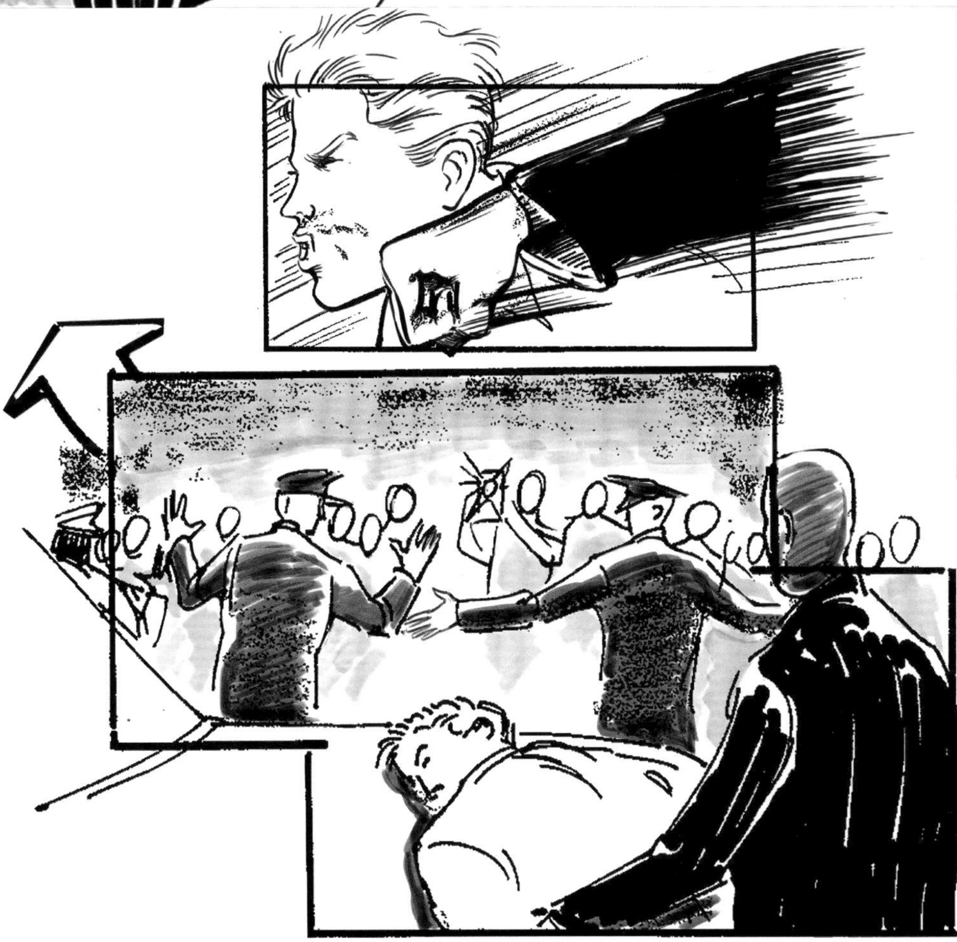

The following frames are from the filmed Samuel L. Jackson version of Shaft. I did love drawing Shaft decking the Walter character. I later boarded a another fist fight between the two which was sadly never shot.

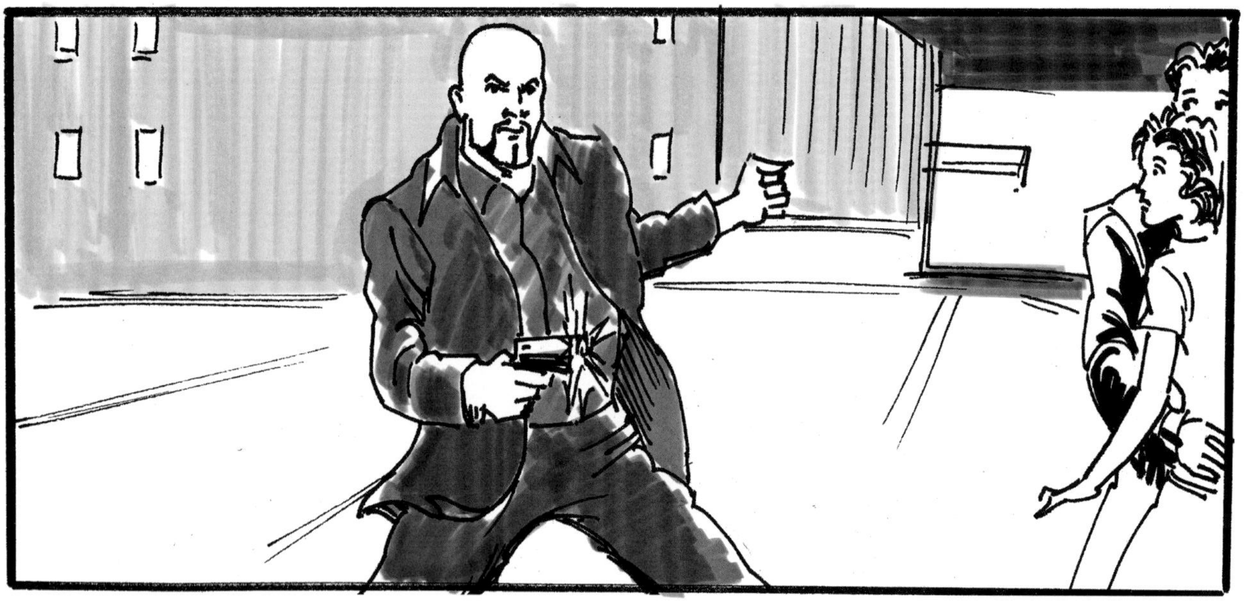

years to become John's art director then landing as art director on the hit television network show, *Blackish*. Cassandra Butcher, who I met on *Above The Rim* was John's publicist since *Boyz n the Hood* and went on to head up publicity at Fox Searchlight and later BRON Studios. His costume designer, Ruth E. Carter, later won the Academy Award for *Black Panther*. John always championed talented Black women.

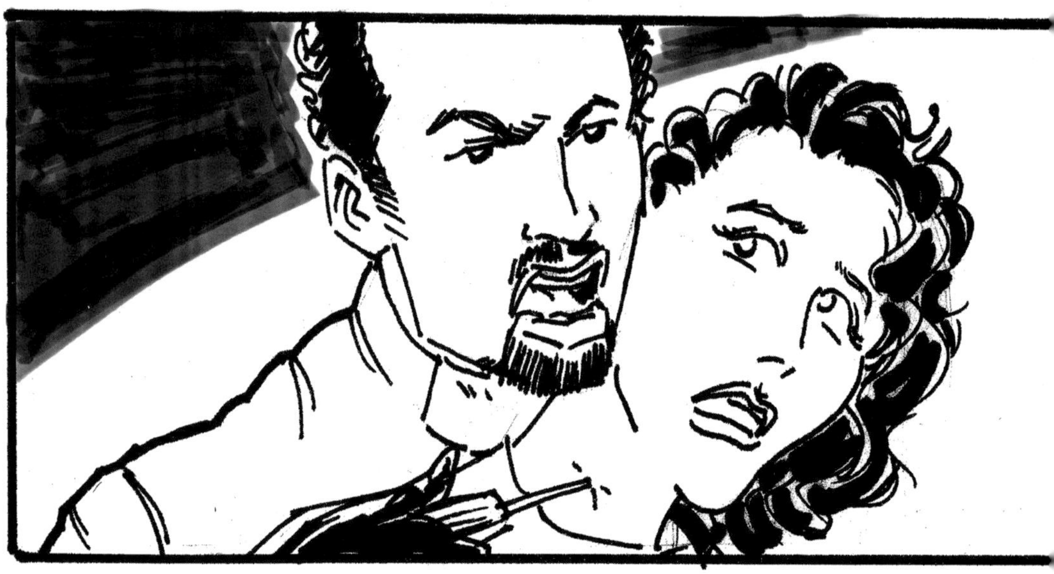

As for my storyboards, I focused on crisp storytelling and line work. I designed every frame to flow but to be powerful as well. John imagined a *James Bond* like opening scene for his movie including the elder *Shaft* foiling modern day pirates in Jamaica, who hold guests hostage on a party yacht. The scene was majestic for Mr. Roundtree, who John rightfully described as "our Sean Connery." John really wanted the film to feel "big" and not be held down to merely a "street movie." He also wanted the film to connect to the original trilogy, especially the film *Shaft in Africa*. John Shaft Jr. was to be similar in looks to Roundtree's original character and still in the police force as a man who "goes by the book". The father and son characters would also have a strained relationship.

I was thankfully winning John over with my work and having a good time as well. One time while coming back into his office at MGM, John and I came in right behind Denzel Washington whom I had never met. Denzel was sporting an afro for his upcoming film role in *He*

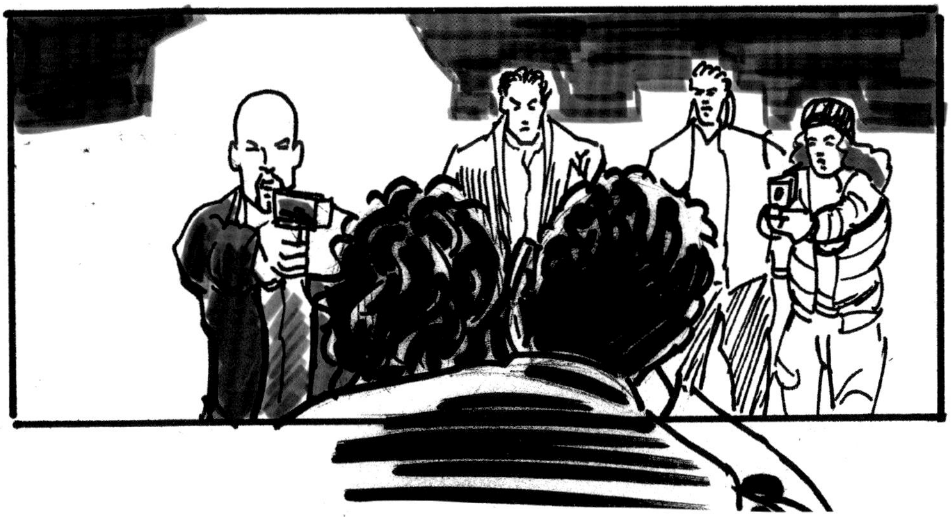

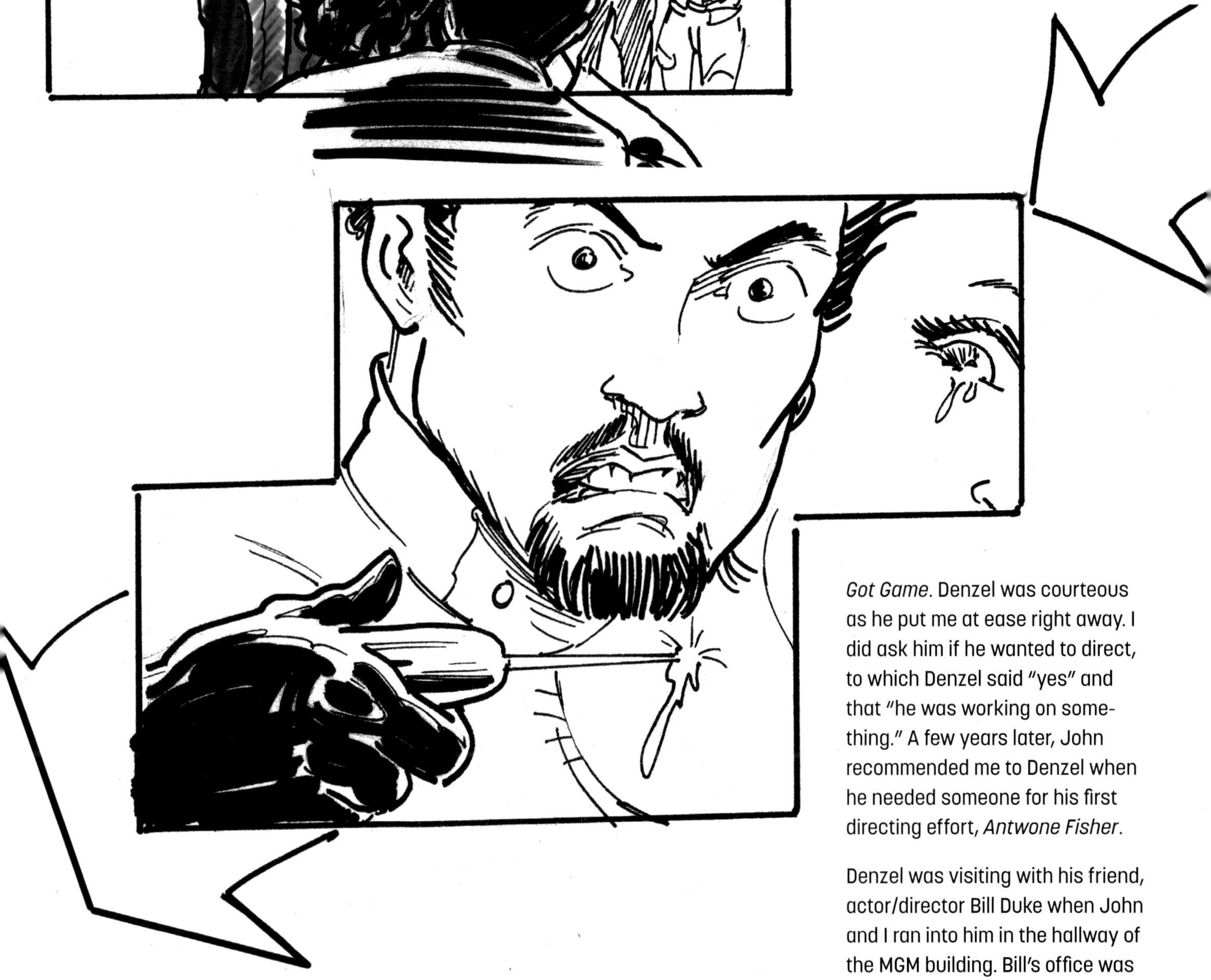

Got Game. Denzel was courteous as he put me at ease right away. I did ask him if he wanted to direct, to which Denzel said "yes" and that "he was working on something." A few years later, John recommended me to Denzel when he needed someone for his first directing effort, *Antwone Fisher*.

Denzel was visiting with his friend, actor/director Bill Duke when John and I ran into him in the hallway of the MGM building. Bill's office was next to John's. Most people know

Bill from his role in *Predator* but he is also an accomplished director having done the film, *Deep Cover*. Bill's latest film *Hoodlum* that starred John's frequent collaborator, Laurence Fishburne was about to be released at that time. Bill always wore a GQ worthy suit or traditional African attire every day he came into his office. It was Bill who opened my eyes to getting annual checkups for prostate cancer and he even personally drove me to a men's health seminar. Bill and I both lost our fathers to prostate cancer. So he was on a mission to educate his male friends on the importance of getting regular checkups. I now get a routine prostate cancer checkup every year thanks to Bill Duke.

Shaft Returns was a movie that went through several trials before production started. The first hurdle was getting a "bankable" actor as John Shaft, Jr. A top actor passed on the project which led to another big name to come in who was right for it, but there was an "artistic difference" causing the actor to leave. Unfortunately in the late nineties, there were only a finite amount of "bankable" young Black actors. Hollywood never tried to create Black actor stars but usually mined hip hop music for established names who could act. In the early 2000's, I could name thirty African American rapper/singers who became actors. I couldn't have done the same for their Caucasian counterparts.

With finding a star as an issue, the movie was "pushed" and I was sent home to New York. John later told me about the inner workings of the business operations and politics of the film industry that opened my eyes. When preproduction of *Shaft Returns* resumed a year later in 1998, the script was still going through a transition. John and the studio were also still seeking to land a star for the lead role. Though I had started in March, 1997, I returned to Los Angeles for another two weeks in July, 1998 but there was still no lead actor attached to the film. The rewrites pushed the movie back to a 1999 start. Then in a brilliant casting move, Samuel L. Jackson was signed to take over the role. The project was now mostly a reboot. Richard Price was hired to write an entirely new script, simply renamed *Shaft*. John was super excited that this famous author was hired and writing the new *Shaft* screenplay to add the feel of New York City's authenticity. The "son of Shaft" element was removed from the script and Sam was to play a modern and more hip incarnation of John Shaft, full of swagger. Sam later told the powers that be that he wanted Richard Roundtree back in the movie as well. So with this "request" Sam's role was rewritten as the nephew of the original John Shaft character and Richard Roundtree was cast as his uncle. It was great to be reunited with Sam who I had befriended when I did *Die Hard with a Vengeance*. While filming Shaft in New York, I would often spend some down time with John in Sam's trailer. Sam proudly showed me his formidable collection of Hong Kong action DVD's. Sam was as approachable as ever.

I fondly remember meeting Christian Bale, who was playing one of the films two villains. He had just finished portraying Jesus in a TV film and he walked into the production office to meet with John with shoulder length hair and a beard. John also cast rapper Busta Rhymes in the role of Shaft's sidekick, "Rasaan".

As far as the storyboards, John and I really clicked. Two years earlier when I worked on the initial version of the film, I studied everything Peter Ramsey did but added my own style as well. John loved comic books so I gave him a comic book style in my storyboards. I was making my own way and finding my own style as a storyboard artist. John and I had a system. He would hand write his shot list on a notepad and his new assistant Arnold Yanovich, would type it up and get it to me.

A shot list looks something like this:

1. Wide establishing on the street above bar
2. Mini master as Shaft gets out of his car and walks left to right
3. Close up on Shaft looking at the body

... and so on.

John would do this for dialogue scenes as well as the action beats. It was in no way robotic because John would let me add some cool twists to a scene and let me collaborate with new ideas. Unlike *Die Hard with a Vengeance* where I was the second unit storyboard artist or *The Devil's Own* where I had sporadic work, I would work constantly in storyboarding almost every scene of this big studio movie myself. The great thing for me was that I was based in New York while working on *Shaft*. When you are from New York, it's a treat to work at home in a film that really exploited the city's varied locations. Location manager Len Murach, was really detailed and specific so I was supplied with great references for places where the movie was shooting. My scouting was minimal, though I did visit some shooting locations.

One of the great friends I made on that film was the stunt coordinator, Nick Gillard. Nick is a tough-nosed Brit who always had a swagger to go along with an impish grin. He was the stunt coordinator on *Star Wars: Episode I—The Phantom Menace*. I loved the lightsaber fight choreography in the film. Nick and I got along famously. He respected my *Star Wars* fandom as well as my modest martial arts background. A year later, Nick contacted *Star Wars* producer Rick McCallum and landed me a week's work at George Lucas' famous Skywalker Ranch where I did some storyboards for *Star Wars: Episode II—Attack of the Clones*. That was the time of my life for which I am eternally grateful to Nick. We still get together when he comes to this side of the Atlantic.

Shaft is where I really started to hit my stride as a storyboard artist. My storytelling was getting better. My execution of images and strategy of how much detail I should create in the storyboards was better. I had evolved tremendously in a short amount of time.

John threw a great Watch Party for the Oscar De La Hoya versus Félix Trinidad fight in his downtown apartment for the movie shoot. I met Mary J. Blige who was shy but sweet. I also met Seth Green, as well as actor Barry Pepper who had a great respect for storyboards. I was also reacquainted with Vin Diesel whom I had known years earlier as Mark Vincent. We used to train at Better Bodies, a gym in the Chelsea district in New York City. Vin was totally cool to me and has always been himself even on the rare occasions that I have seen him after becoming an action movie star.

A big transition in my life happened during the making of *Shaft*. I was planning to move to Los Angeles. Betty and I had started our long-distance relationship. I knew that I had reached my zenith in New York doing storyboards. My best client in movies, John, was based in Los Angeles as were most directors. New York based filmmakers Spike Lee, Martin Scorsese and Woody Allen did not routinely use storyboards and I had no other regular feature film clients besides John. My other purpose as an artist is a screenwriter. All of the film industry professionals that I knew of and wanted to meet are based in Los Angeles. For all of you who have lived one place in your life and suddenly relocate, it is not the easiest thing. Most of the big movies that came to New York originated in Los Angeles and most often the cast and crew hiring was done there. Storyboards were also originated in L.A. while the main cast and crew were flown in to stay in New York during film shoots. I had to live in Los Angeles. So, I made the move. I was going to miss my old NYC haunts as well as NY pizza, real hip hop, my old church, reading on the train and other things one doesn't always appreciate when you have it available to you every day. I had close family that I would miss that I talked to on the phone because FaceTime and Zoom hadn't been invented at that point.

My work on *Shaft* was completed and the film was in full shooting mode in New York when I left for Los Angeles in December of 1999. Len Murach and I were hanging out at a *Shaft* crew party and he saw me dancing and having a great time. Len said, "You can't leave now! You love New York!" But I had to leave in order to grow as an artist. I felt like I was a little behind in life, like I should have had things figured out a bit more at that point. I certainly found my stride on that shoot. In retrospect, my growth would have been stunted had I stayed in New York. As my friend and SVA caricature teacher, Sam Viviano said after I got into the biz, "Warren, you've always thought big." So I had to *live* bigger.

With my work done, I left *Shaft* and New York. I took the leap into my life's new adventure to live in Los Angeles as I had always desired: to be a working professional in the circle and company of other professionals.

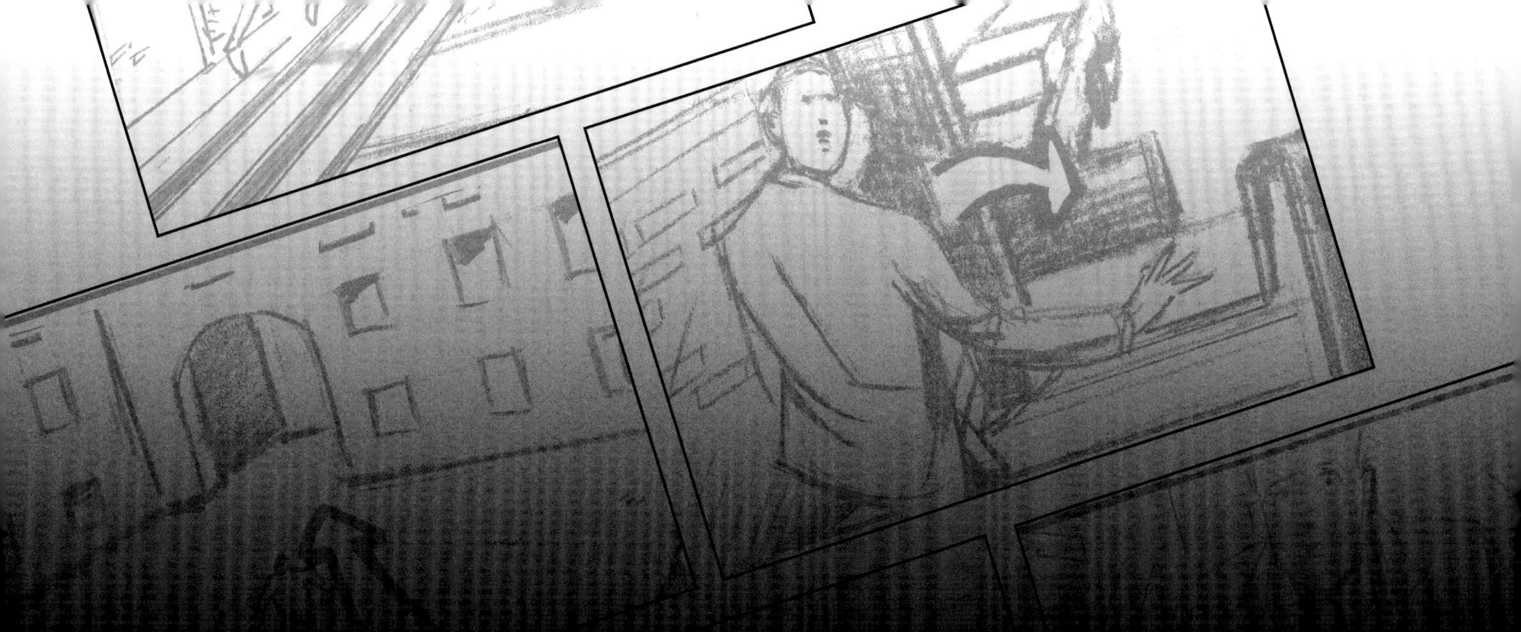

STORYBOARDS AND STORIES OF 15 SELECT FILMS AND TELEVISION SHOWS

A HARD DAY'S WORK

Chapter 7

A BEAUTIFUL MIND

A VERY COLD WINTER

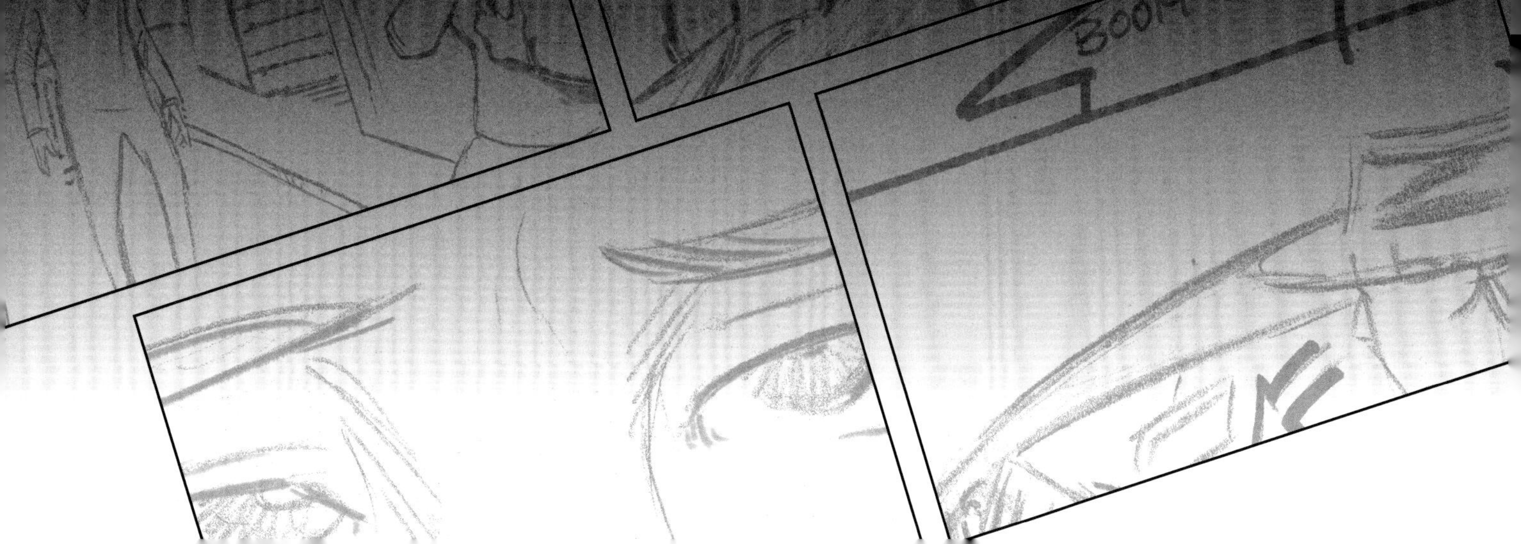

A Beautiful Mind...a very cold winter

I had worked hard for the last six years building up my "street cred" in the industry. Even though I was moving to someplace that would increase that, I still had the pains of giving up my New York clients that I had fought so hard to get. My mother always encouraged my move and never laid on any "Mom guilt." She was the best. The difference between New York and Los Angeles is both cosmetic and visceral. In New York, there are so many people always pressed together. In Los Angeles, everyone is separated by their individual home locations distanced by a sprawling county, always in their cars with no use of public transportation and of course, the seemingly never ending lengths of freeways. People of all economic classes and races travel together on the New York City public transportation. From Wall Street bankers to construction workers, mass transit buses and subways in New York are the arteries to the city and the life energy all around. Cars are seen mostly as an expensive nuisance, though still very desired by many to escape the crush of the city. Cars in Los Angeles are a way of life—as I soon found out by not having one.

I was just settling into my Los Angeles when I got a call. Brick Mason, a New York storyboard colleague recommended me for a job to help him on a big film. At that point, Brick and I had never met but knew of each other's storyboard work. The film was Ron Howard's new directorial effort, *A Beautiful Mind*. I nearly exploded with excitement but I had to figure out how to leave Los Angeles when I had only recently arrived to stay. As Betty told me of her acting experience, "They never want you where you are, it seems. But that's the life we chose."

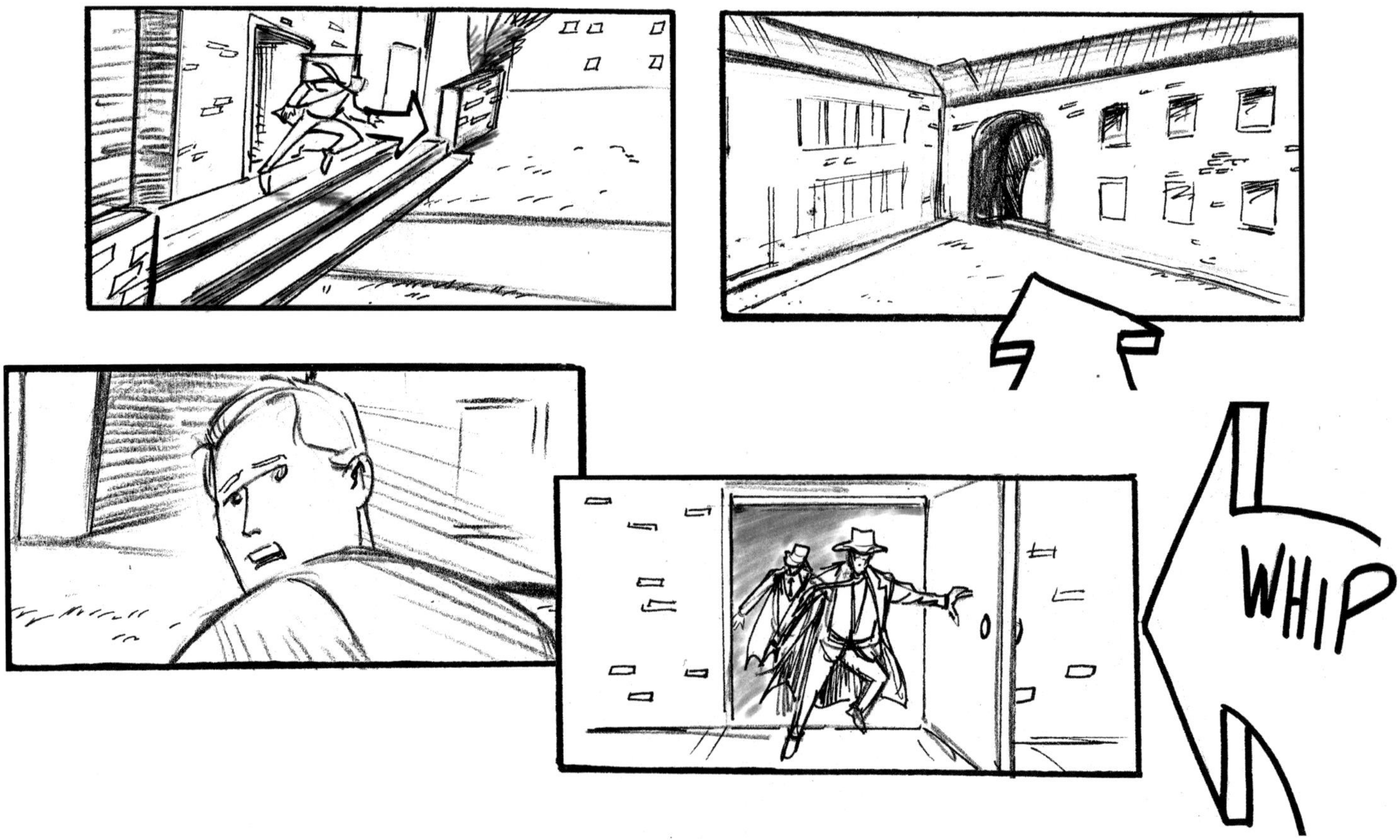

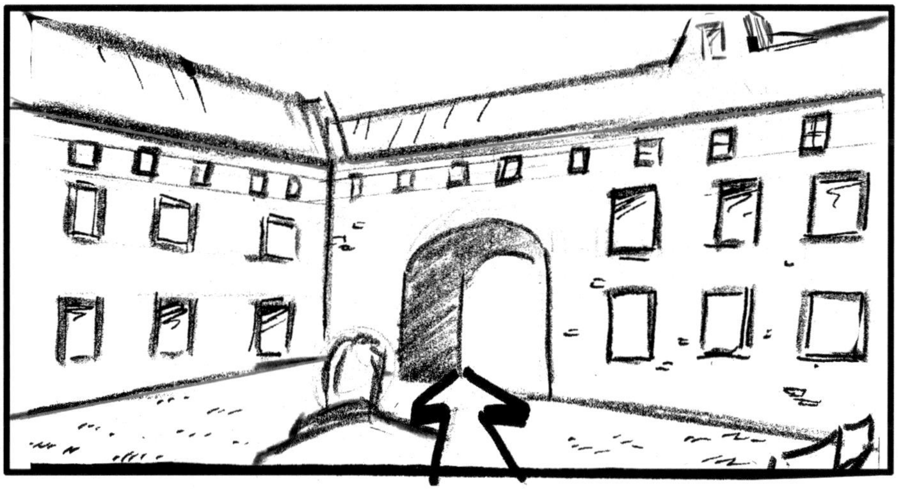

Like so many Americans growing up on television, I had been a fan of Ron's from his two most memorable series roles as an actor, *The Andy Griffith Show* and *Happy Days*. I had even actually watched Ron's little-known show with Henry Fonda, *The Smith Family*. Ron had pivoted in his career and had now made a name himself as a director. He earned a legion of fans with *Splash, Willow, Apollo 13* and *Ransom*. As soon as I was about to use some sun block for my LA life, I was on a plane back to NYC to work with Ron Howard. This is the randomness of life in the film industry. Jobs can happen at the last minute and you have to be prepared to travel if necessary.

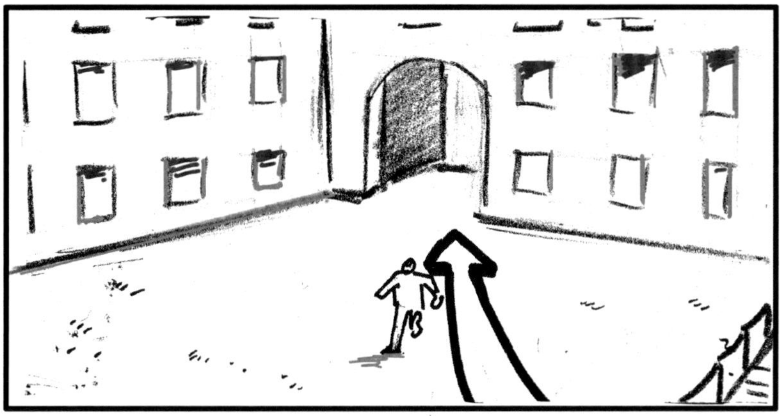

I went back to the Northeast in the dead of winter. I was staying in Jamaica, Queens with Mom but the production office for *A Beautiful Mind* was quite a distance away on a former military base in Bayonne, New Jersey. It was a daily two-hour trek just to get to the office by bus, subway and train. I no longer had the use of my car because I sold it just before I left for my new Los Angeles life. I had to hop on a bus, get on the subway, go to the World Trade Center and then hop a train to Bayonne, New Jersey. But to me, having

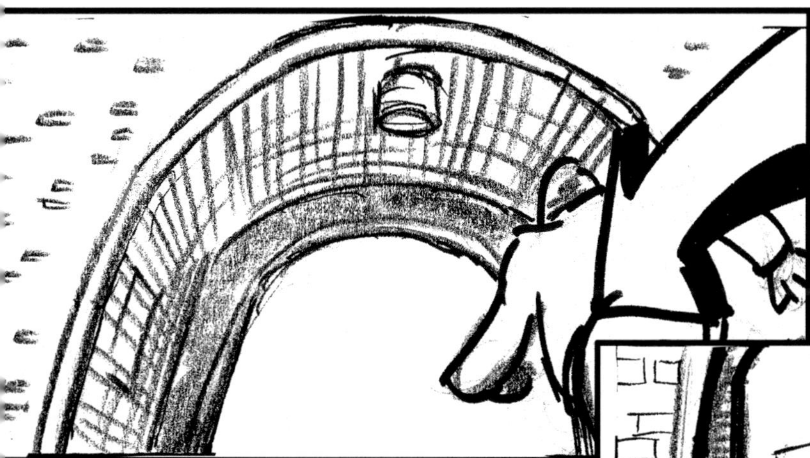

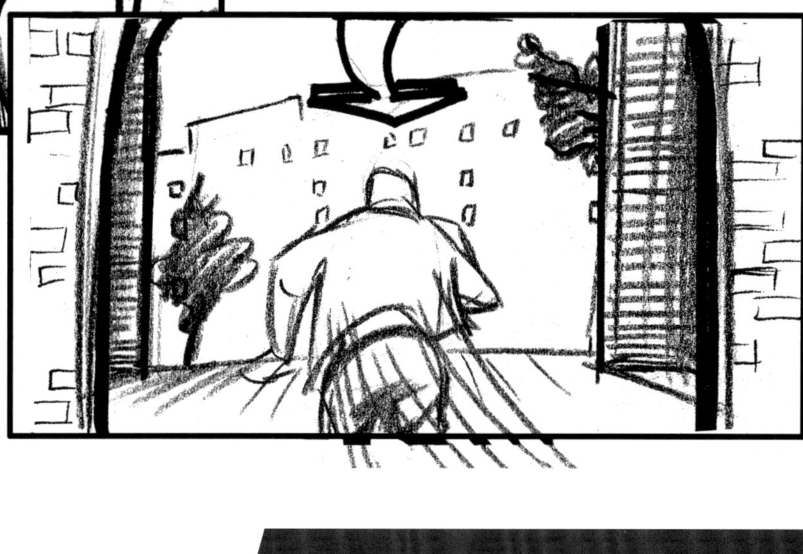

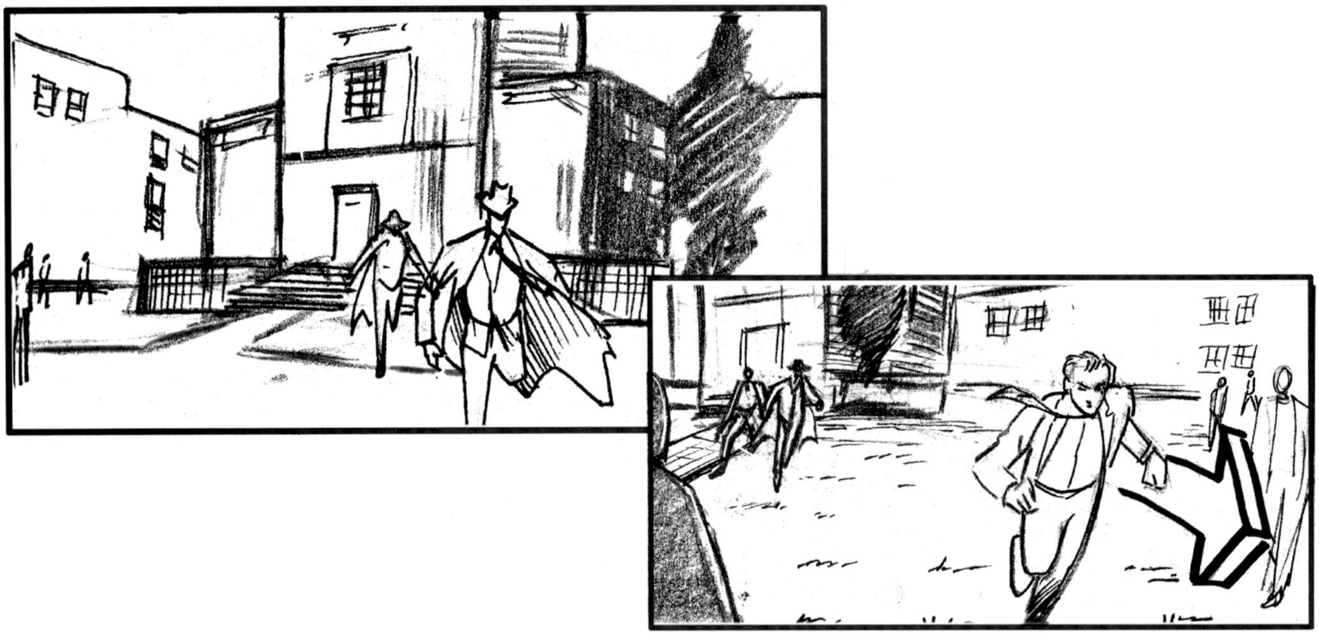

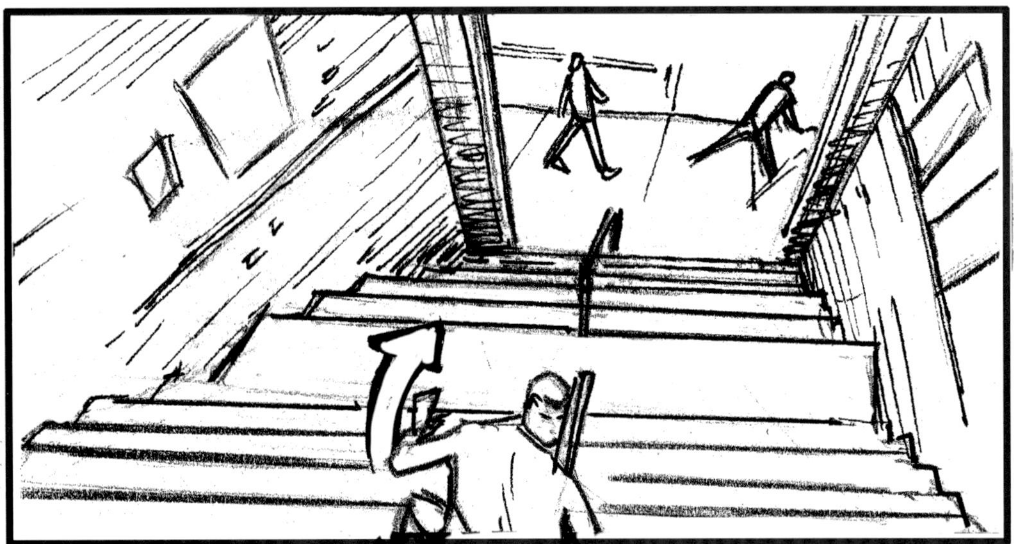

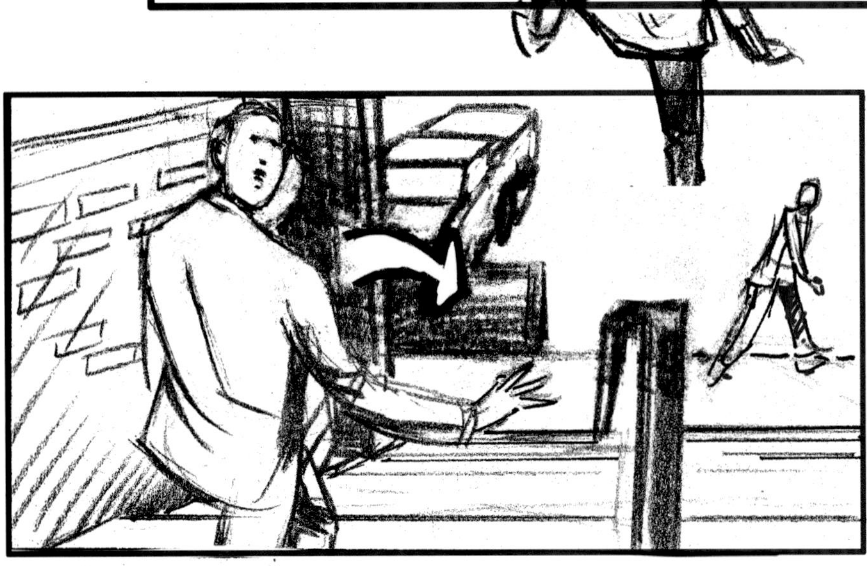

the opportunity to work with the legendary and visionary director, Ron Howard was more than worth every minute of the four-and a half hour round trip trek to the office every day. When I arrived at the office, the first person I met was Brick. Brick turned out to be a great guy with a sly sense of humor and was always good to be around. And even though this was our first time meeting in person, we felt an immediate sense of camaraderie. We shared an office space on *A Beautiful Mind* for seven weeks. I was also reunited with production designer Wynn Thomas with whom I met on *Analyze This*. Wynn came into prominence working with Spike Lee on films like *Malcolm X* and later did Tim Burton's *Mars Attacks!*, a sci-fi genre film. A trailblazer in the production design space, Wynn came up during a time in film where Black production designers on movies did not exist. To this day, I have only worked with a few other Black production designers.

Another important person I met on this job was the movie's producer, Todd Hallowell. Todd and Ron had worked together for over a decade going back to *Parenthood*. Todd had even started out as a production designer himself on films like *Back to the Future Part II*. He always had a great sense of humor about things and was

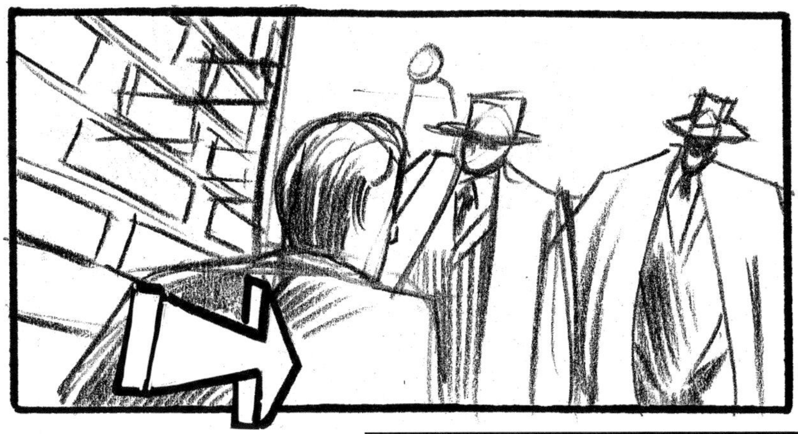

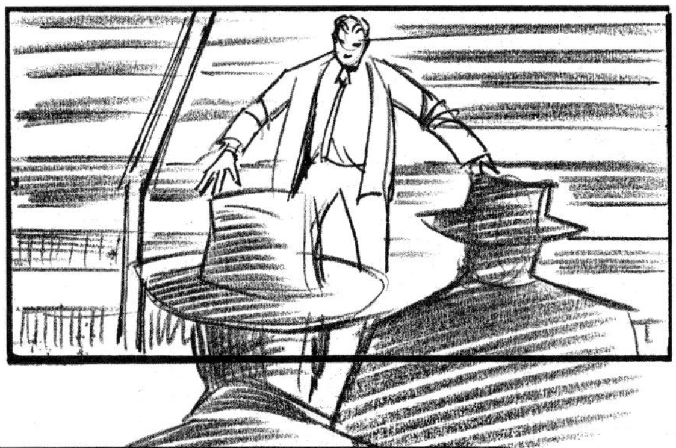

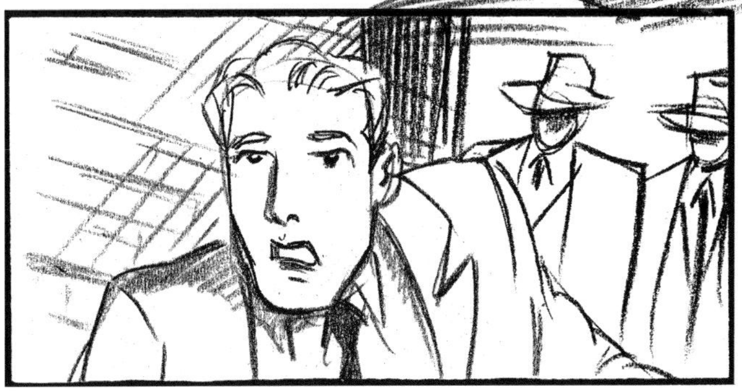

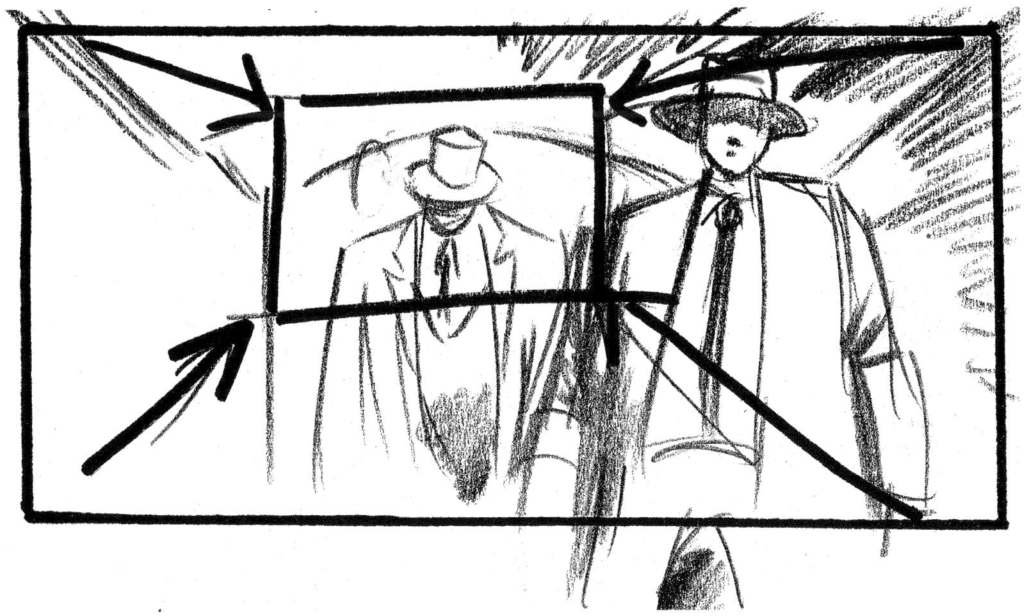

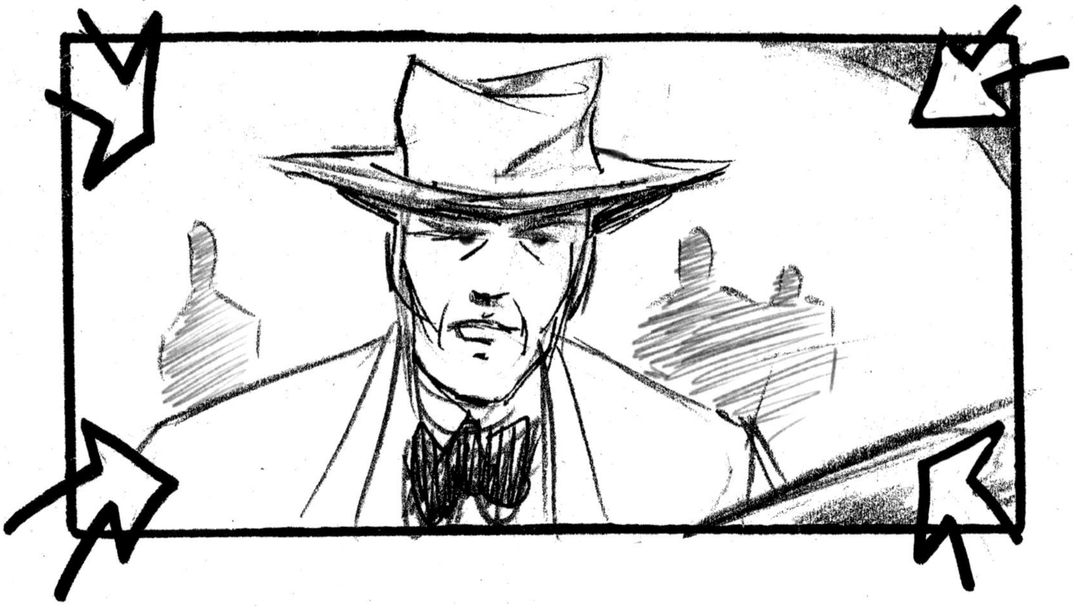

My mysterious reveal of Dr. Rosen was shot pretty close to how I imagined it. Other shots were totally the genius of Ron Howard and Roger Deakins.

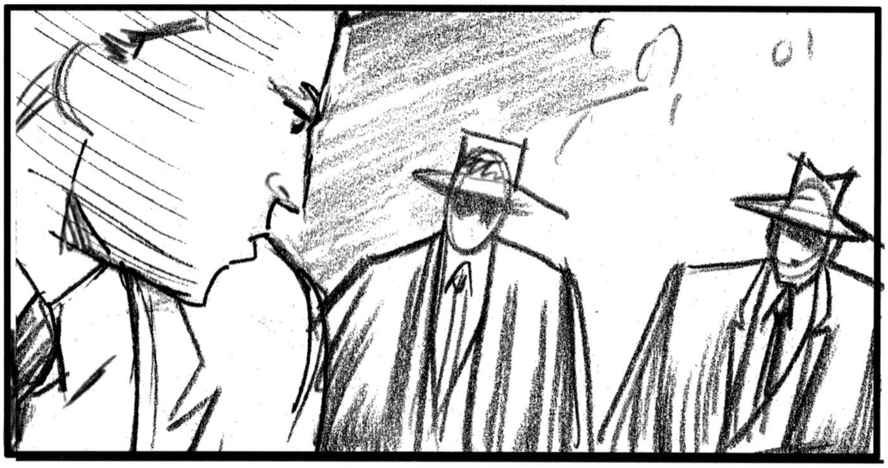

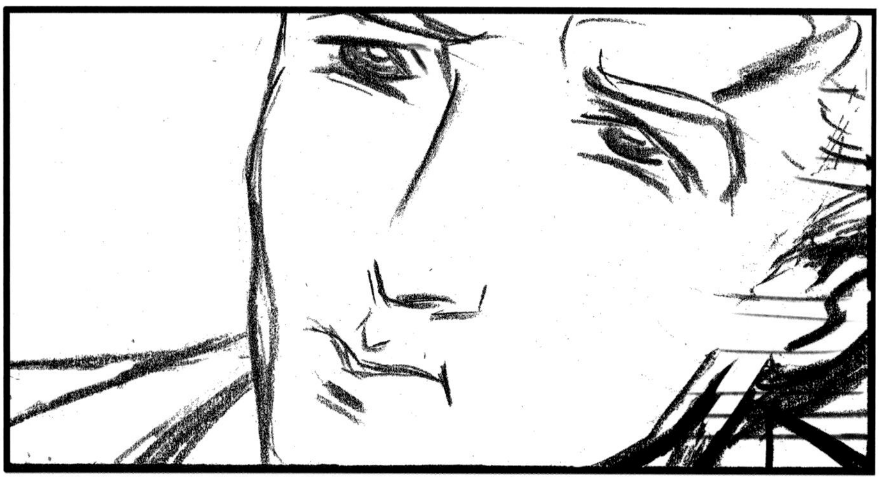

easy to talk to as well as being open to ideas. For Brick and I, Todd was our creative contact on the days Ron wasn't around.

It was somewhere during that first day of work that I finally met Ron: and to say this moment was a full circle moment of joy in my life is an understatement in so many ways. Ron is as friendly as his fictional characters Opie Taylor and Richie Cunningham were on their television shows. Ron is very intelligent and yet still inquisitive. He was humble in how he carried himself in the office but his underlying strength was always evident. In Imagine Entertainment, Ron co-owns one of the biggest production companies in the industry. I think the Oklahoma roots and earnestness of his parents permeates through him even though he has spent so much time in his life on sets

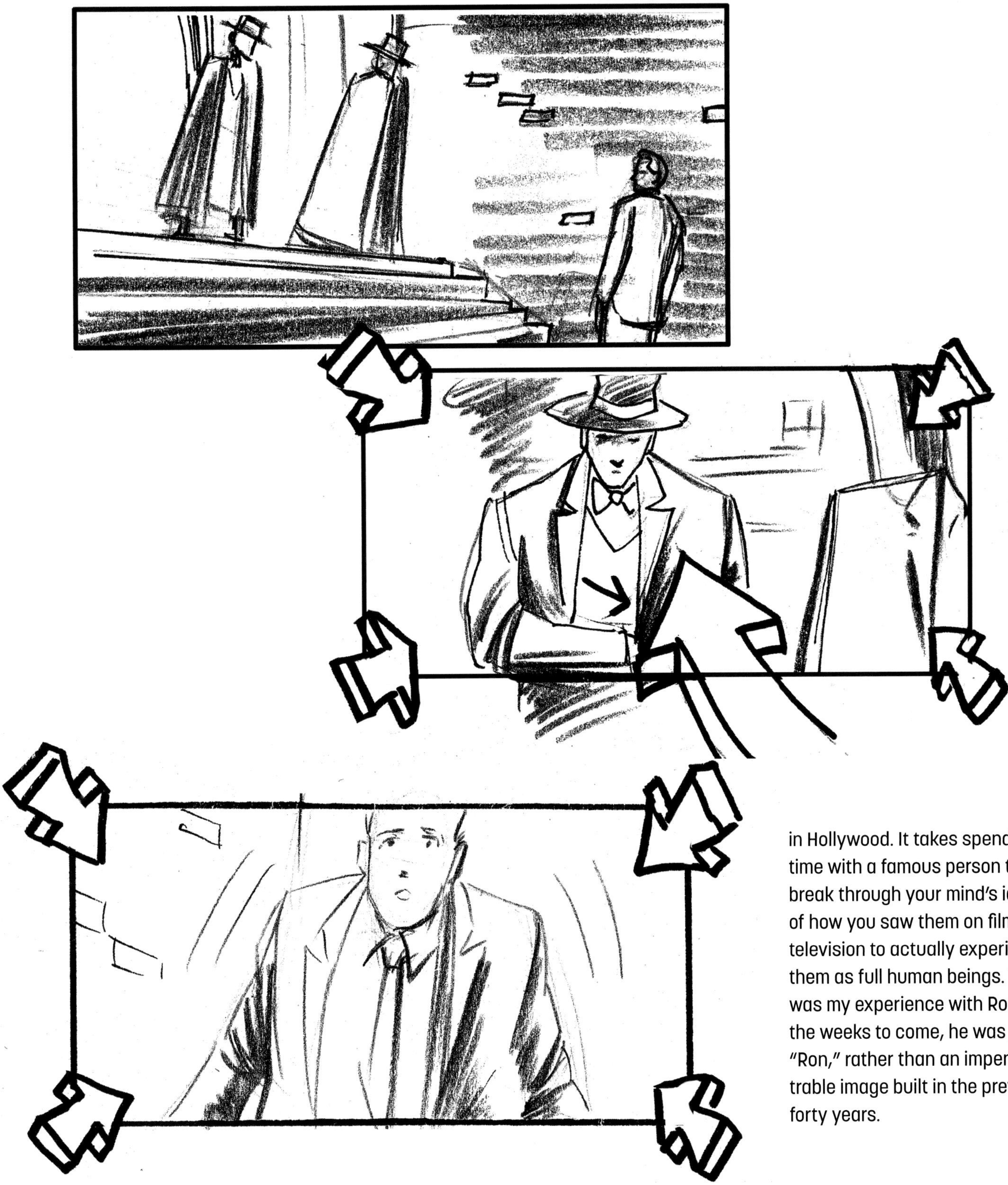

in Hollywood. It takes spending time with a famous person to break through your mind's idea of how you saw them on film or television to actually experience them as full human beings. This was my experience with Ron. In the weeks to come, he was just "Ron," rather than an impenetrable image built in the previous forty years.

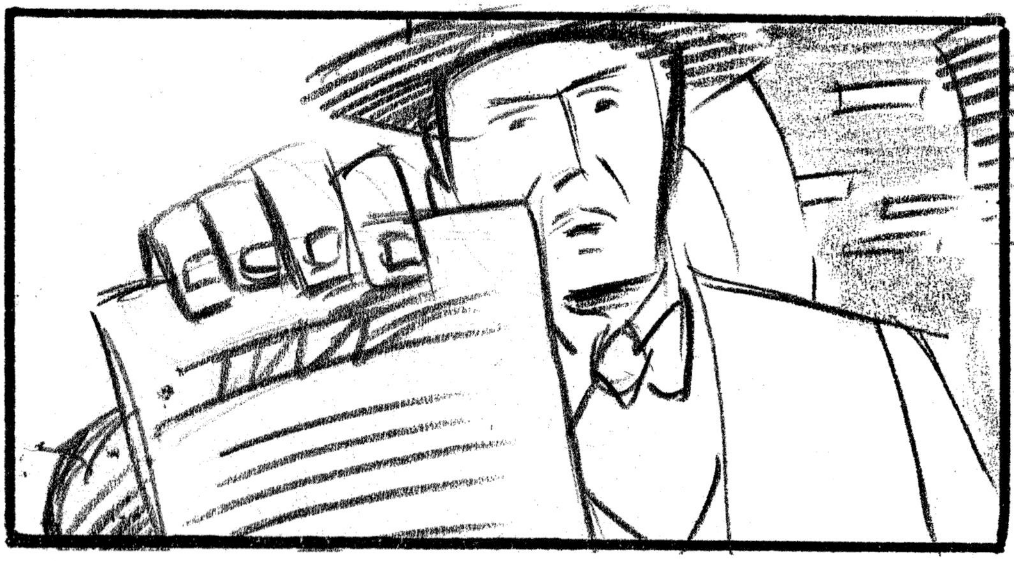

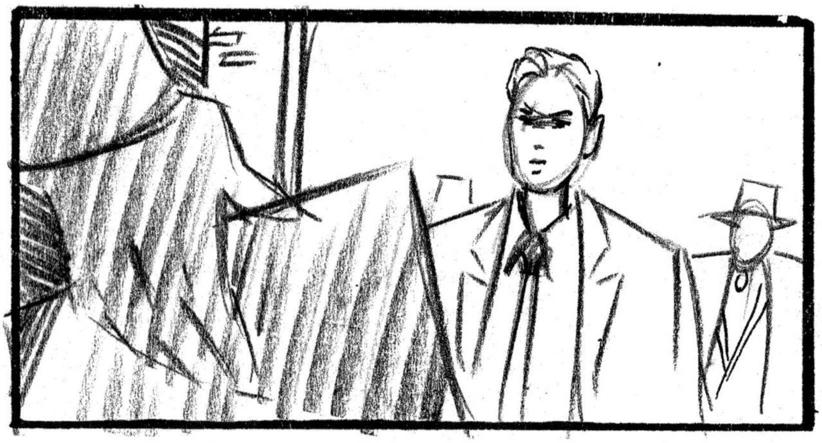

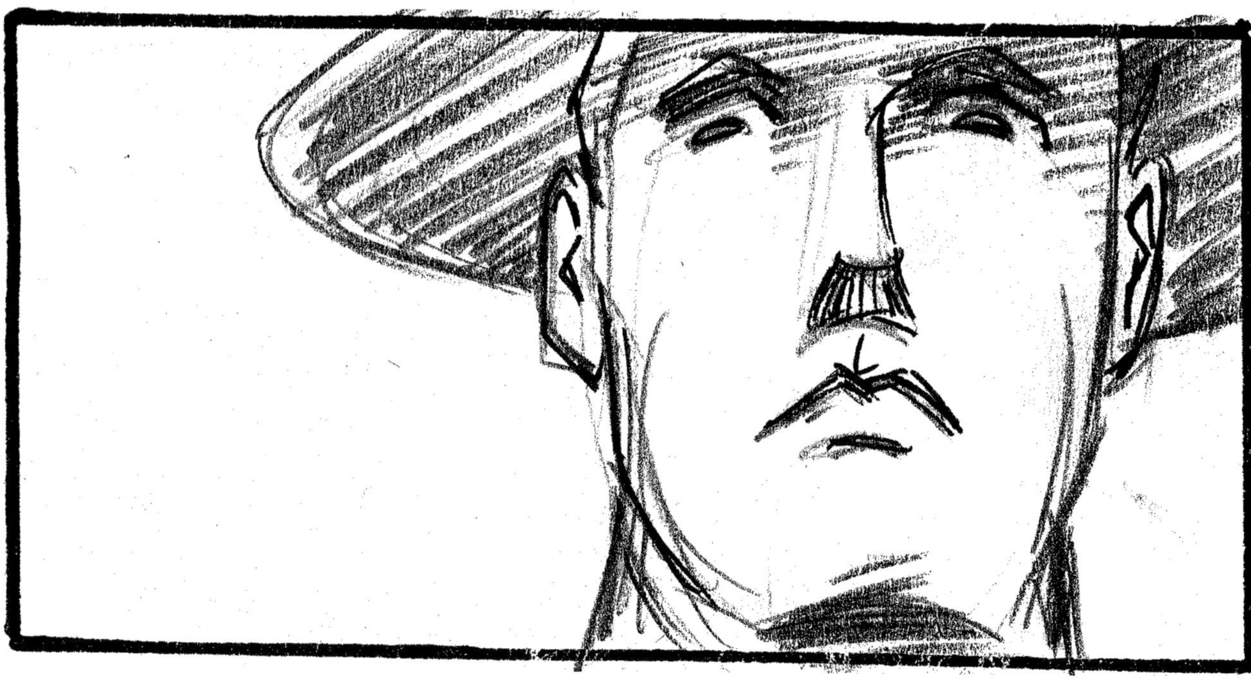

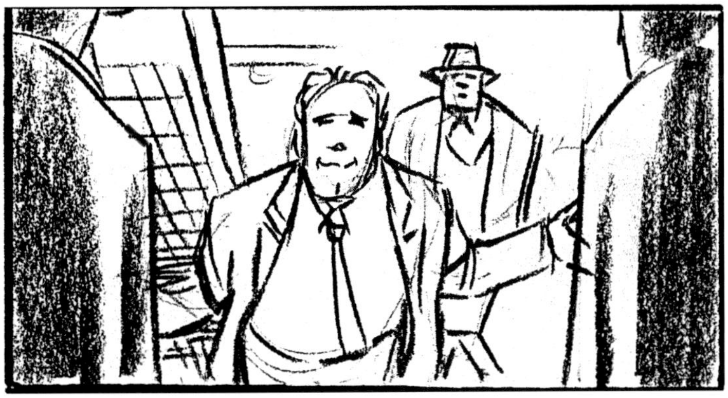

Ron's commitment to loyalty shows in the fact that his former executive assistant and associate producer, Louisa Veles, had worked with him since they were teenagers. In fact as I write this the two worked together until only a few years ago. Ron knows how to keep quality people like Louisa in his orbit.

Ron stopped by the storyboard office to tell me how he visually and thematically saw *A Beautiful Mind*. It was a biography of John Nash, a mathematician who battled paranoid schizophrenia in his adult life. Nash's mental illness would be crystallized in a story concept, where he sees a growing

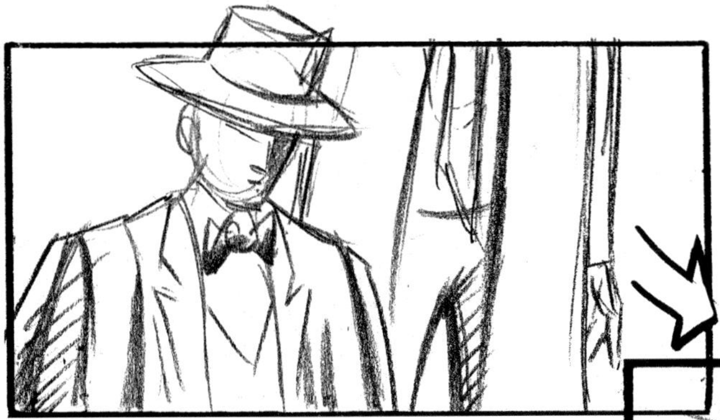

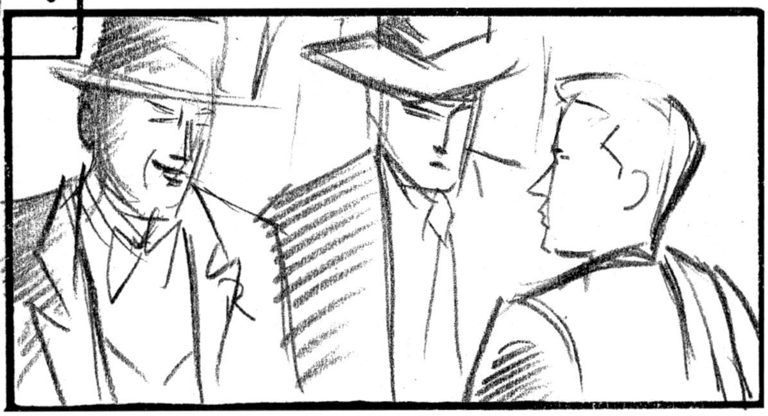

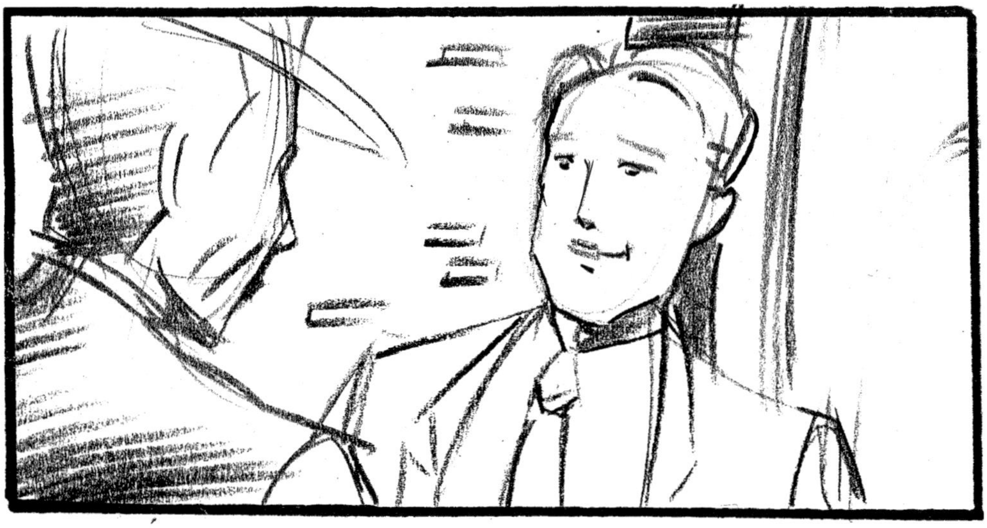

conspiracy against him with imaginary foreign spies. One of the first things I remember being told by Ron was how he wanted to shoot the movie. The big reveal of the script, written by Akiva Goldsman, was that the characters—the mysterious "William Parcher" played by Ed Harris, Nash's Princeton roommate "Charles" played by Paul Bettany, and Charles' niece "Marcee" played by Vivien Cardone—are later revealed to be hallucinations. Since they were all created in John Nash's head, Ron wanted to set this up subconsciously in the audience's mind, but not in a way to spoil the surprise. In a conversation scene in a normal shot, "point of view" (POV) is established from one character to another. The spatial and emotional relationship is often shown over one character's shoulder as we view the other character's face, or several characters, or the location. This standard cinematic coverage connects the characters to the audience on how the characters relate to each other and their environment. However, Ron told Brick and I that we should never see John Nash from the point of view of the imaginary characters because they would rightfully have no true point of view—because they did not really exist. We would not see Parcher, Charles or Marcee over Nash's shoulder nor would they see Nash in a POV of their own. Instead, most of the coverage would be from a third person or "God's eye" view of the characters interacting. Also none of the other main or background characters would react to these imaginary characters. After the

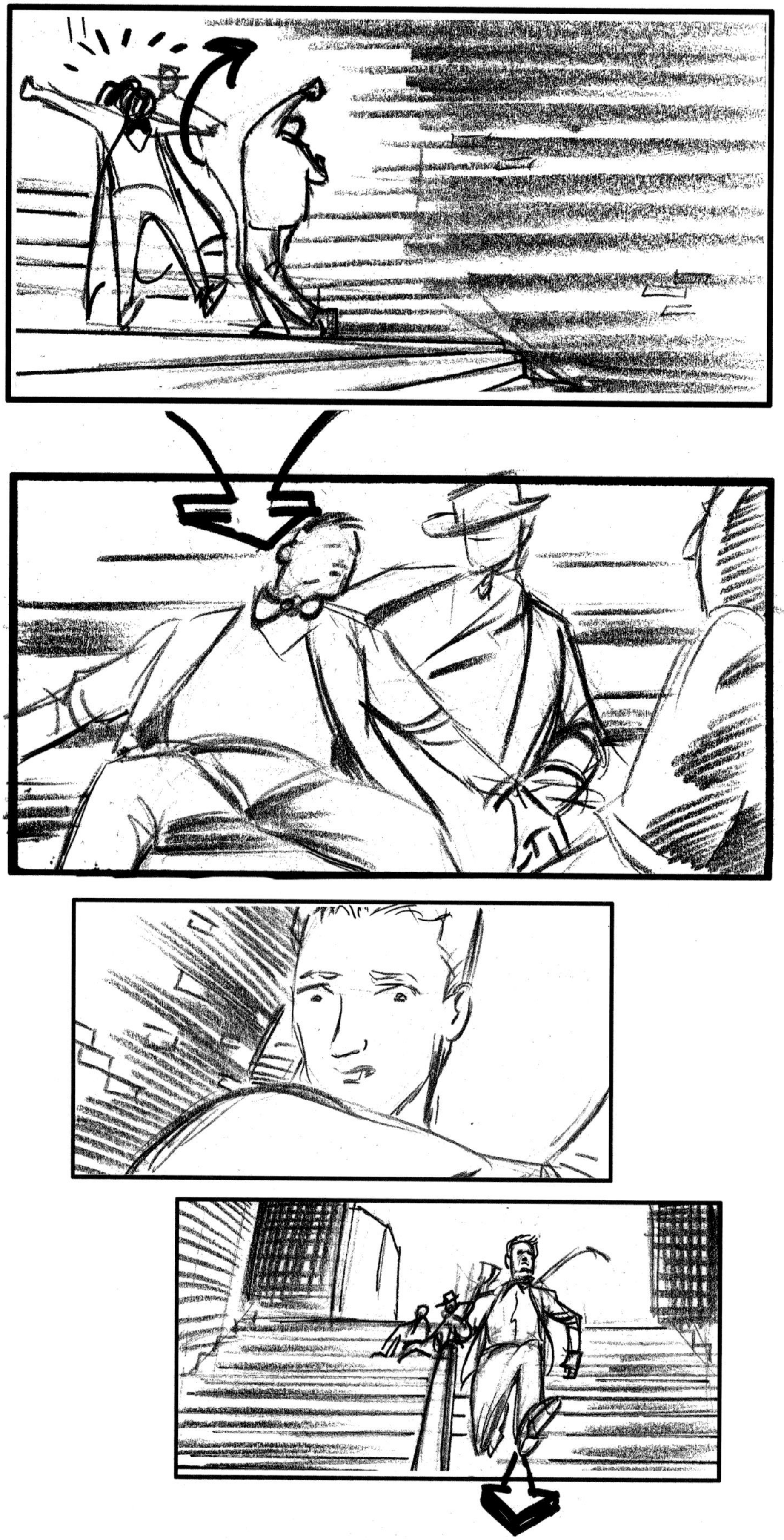

big reveal, the audience woul remember the clues that thes imaginary characters never shared space with Nash. This was a similar concept to how the Bruce Willis' role of the "dead" Malcolm Crowe was filmed in *The Sixth Sense*.

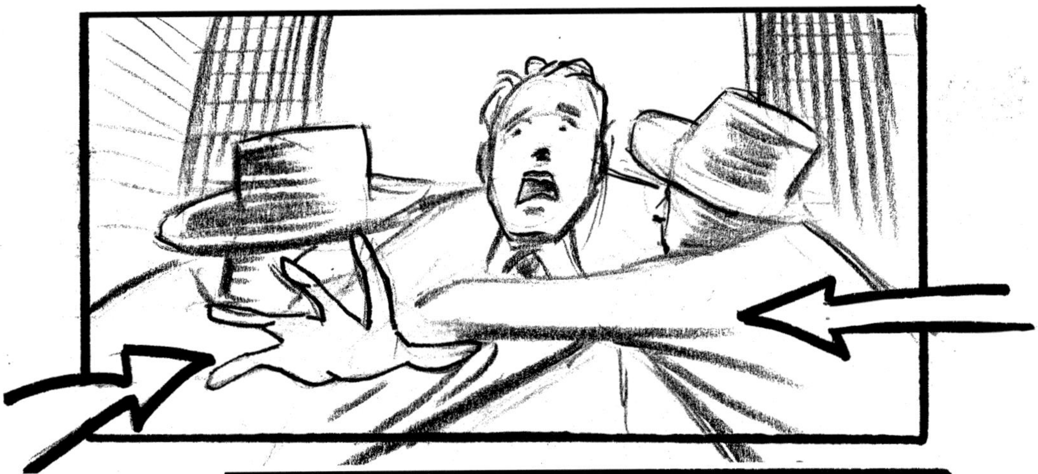

One interesting extra assignment Ron gave Brick and I was to come up with unique necktie patterns for certain characters. Conceptually, this was based on John Nash seeing numbers and mathematical symbols everywhere as a part of his brilliance. Nash would look at a necktie in a scene and numbers would appear to float up and out of the neckties in a three-dimensional style. In the end, this device for the neckties was not used in the film. However, the idea of numbers becoming three dimensional to Nash was saved for a decoding sequence in the final cut. Ron's method of working was that he never gave us a shot list. Ron wanted our full creative input. Ron merely discussed the scene details with Brick and I and told us his impression of the individual scene. Besides character goals within the scene and some camera ideas, Ron let us do our thing.

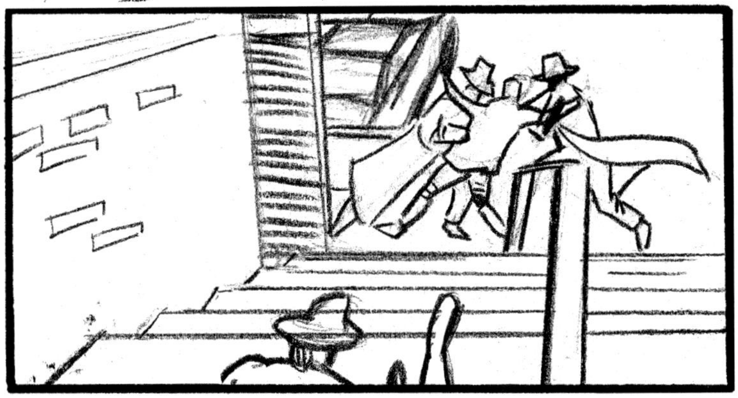

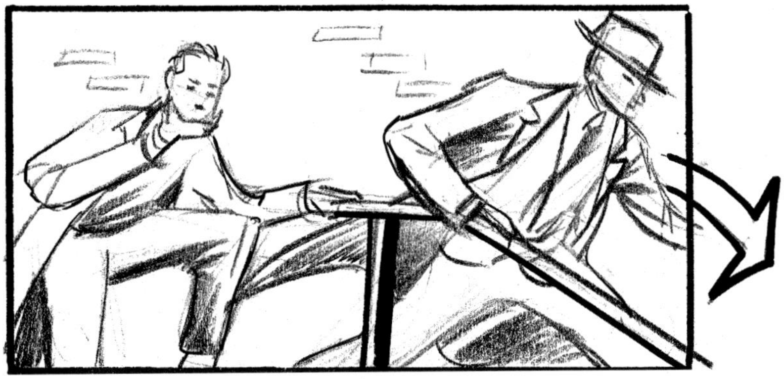

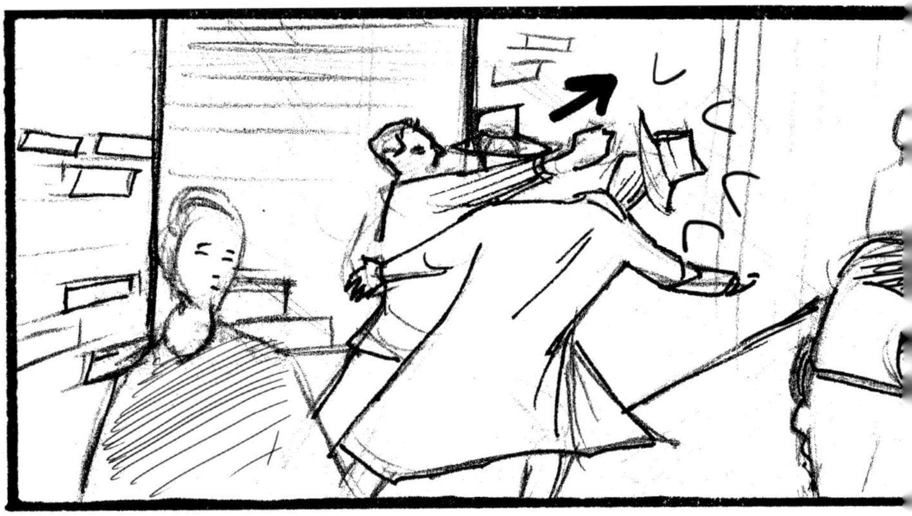

All in all, I had to approach the storytelling on *A Beautiful Mind* differently than I ever had to do before on a film. I had to think in terms of odd

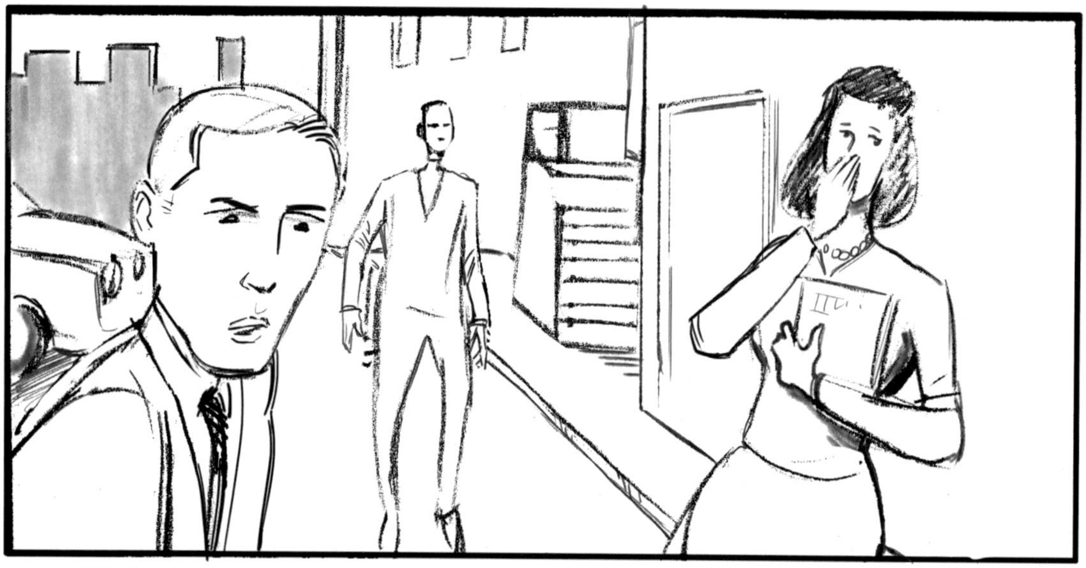

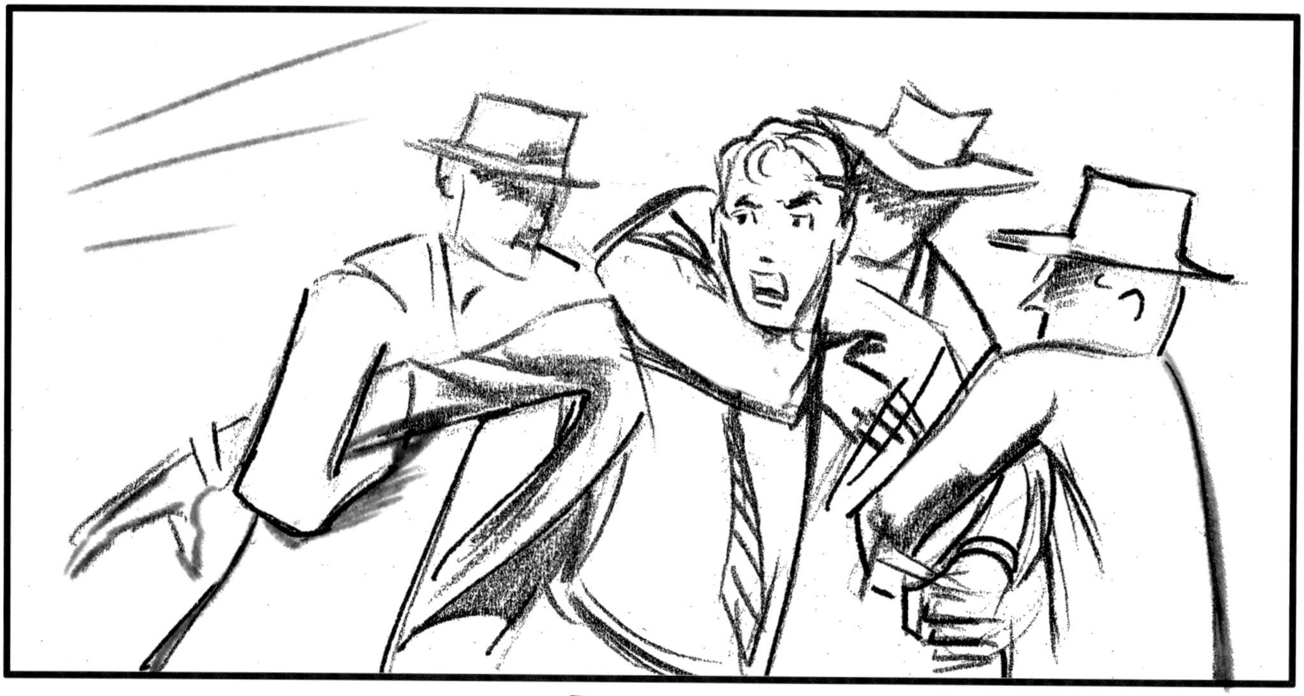

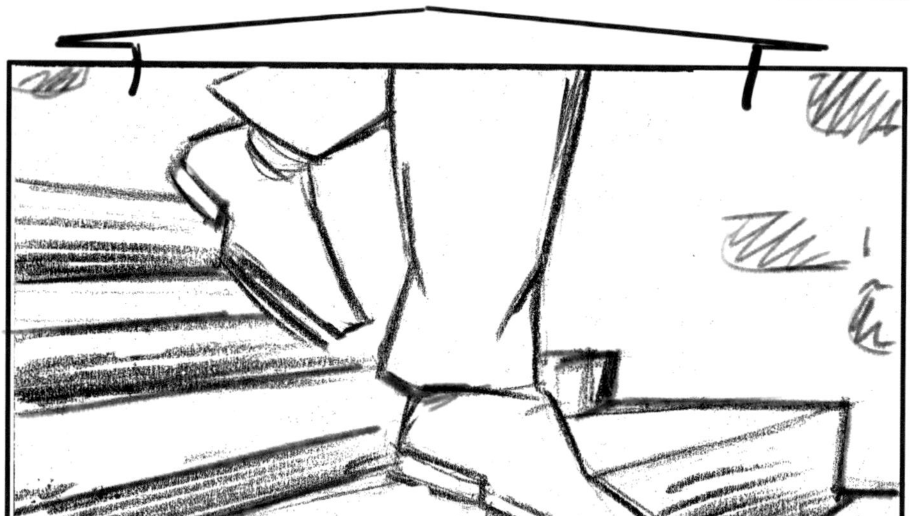

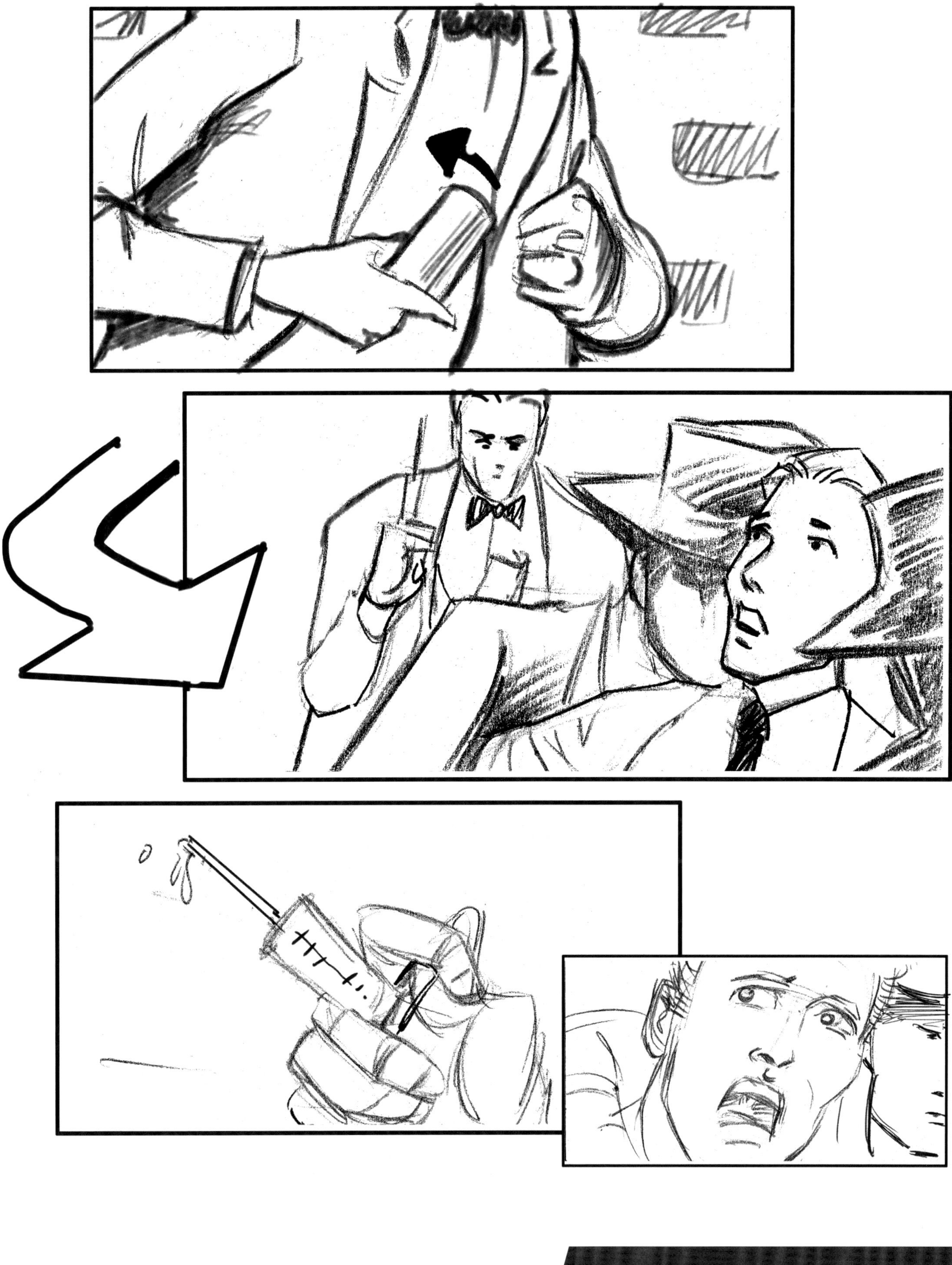

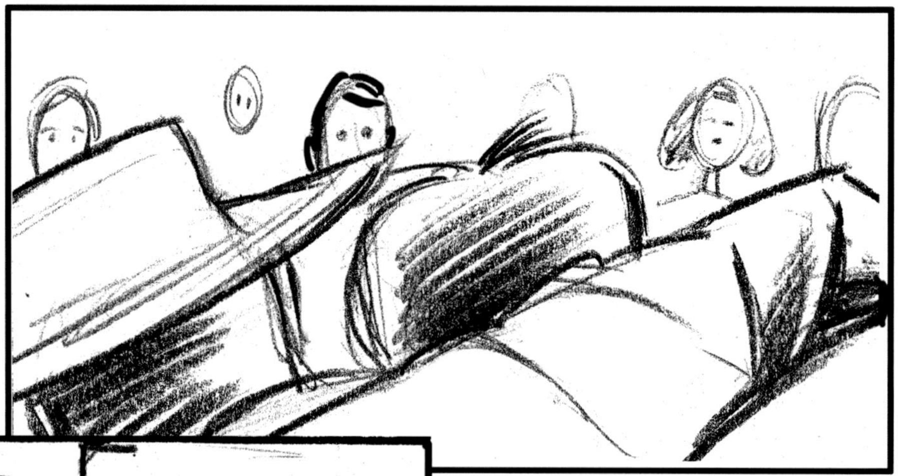

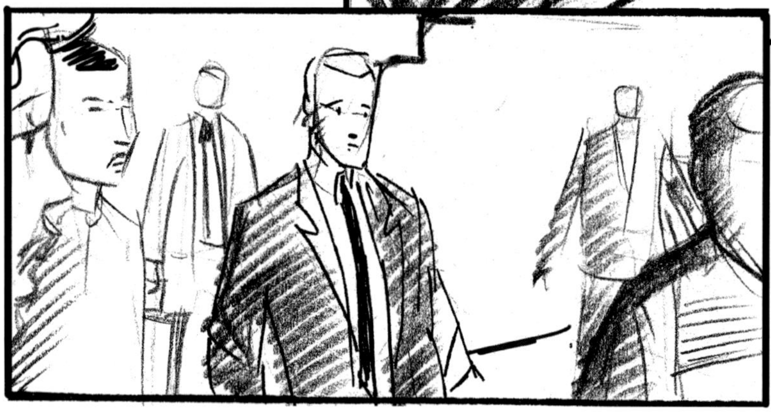

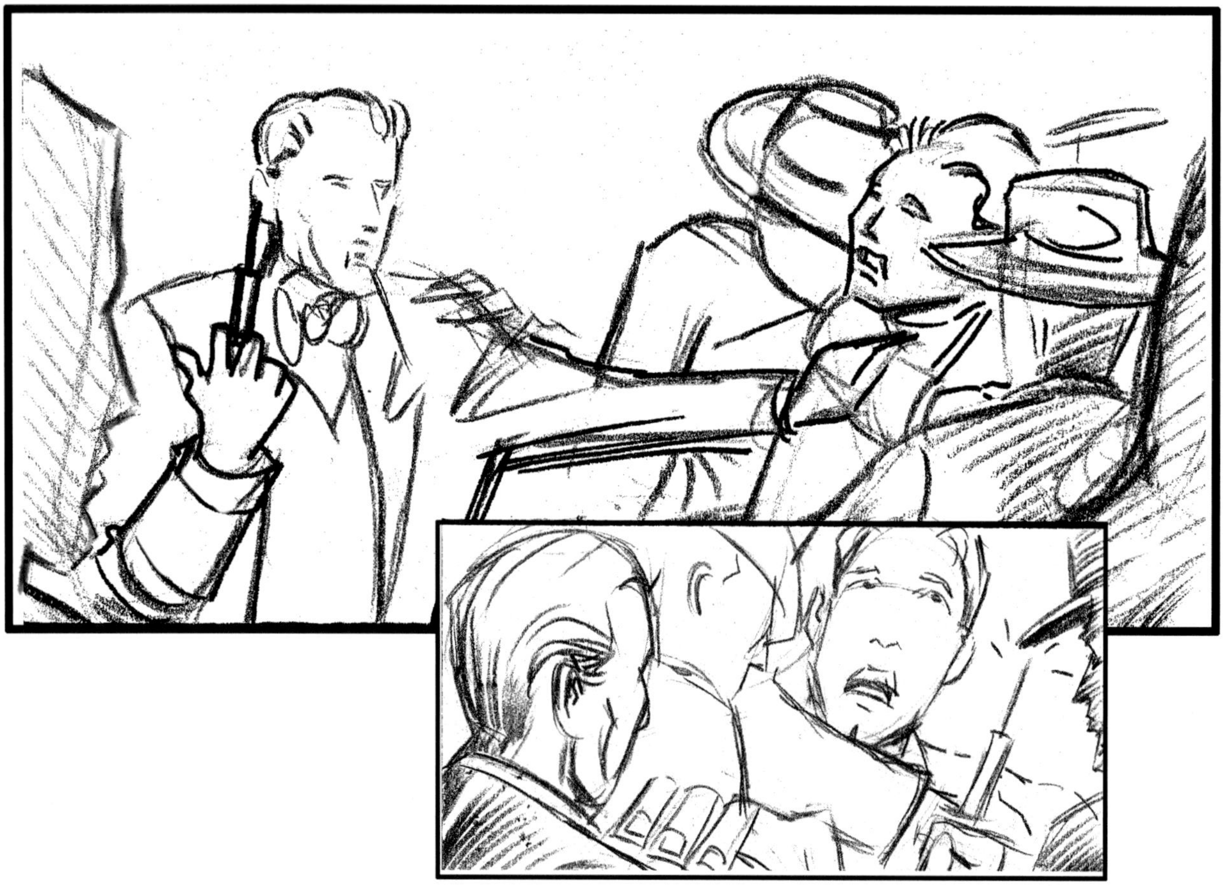

angles and particular lighting since this Ron's approach to this film was unique. I got a kick out of looking at what Brick would cook up. His storytelling was excellent but never flashy. Brick's style was simple in terms of line quality but you instantly knew who everyone was, especially when he broke down how to capture Russell Crowe's facial expressions. It was all in the slope of Russell's eyes.

Brick and I were both big fans of Seinfeld. A term we had for getting in a meeting with Ron was "Ron time." Our chatter would go as follows:

"Did you get in any Ron time?"

"Oh yea, we got in some great Ron time today."

"Love me some Ron time."

It was hilarious to us as a way of entertaining ourselves in the office. Sometimes, when Ron was out, Todd Hallowell would step in and we would run ideas past him as well. This was "Todd time" and it was fun for different reasons but we craved our "Ron time"!

As I said, preproduction was took place during the dead of winter. We had to deal with snow blizzards for stretches of time. The trek we endured to get to the office was made a little easier with a carpool made available to us that met us in Manhattan and then drove us directly to the Bayonne office. My one-way travel time was cut down to ninety minutes but going back to Queens was still a nightmare. When it was snowing — and it snowed hard that winter—we

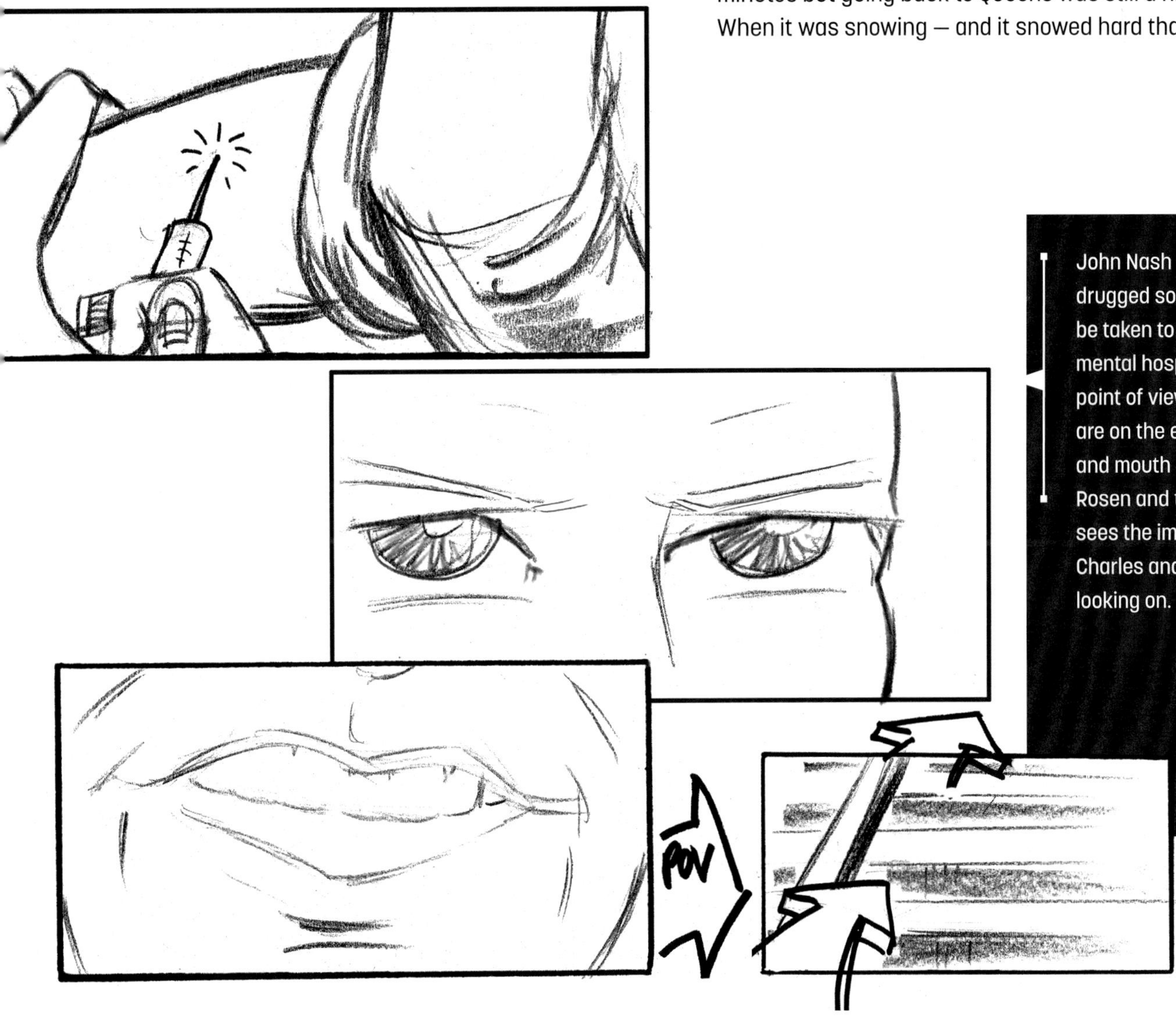

John Nash being drugged so he can be taken to the mental hospital. His point of view shots are on the eyes and mouth of Dr. Rosen and then he sees the imaginary Charles and Marcee looking on.

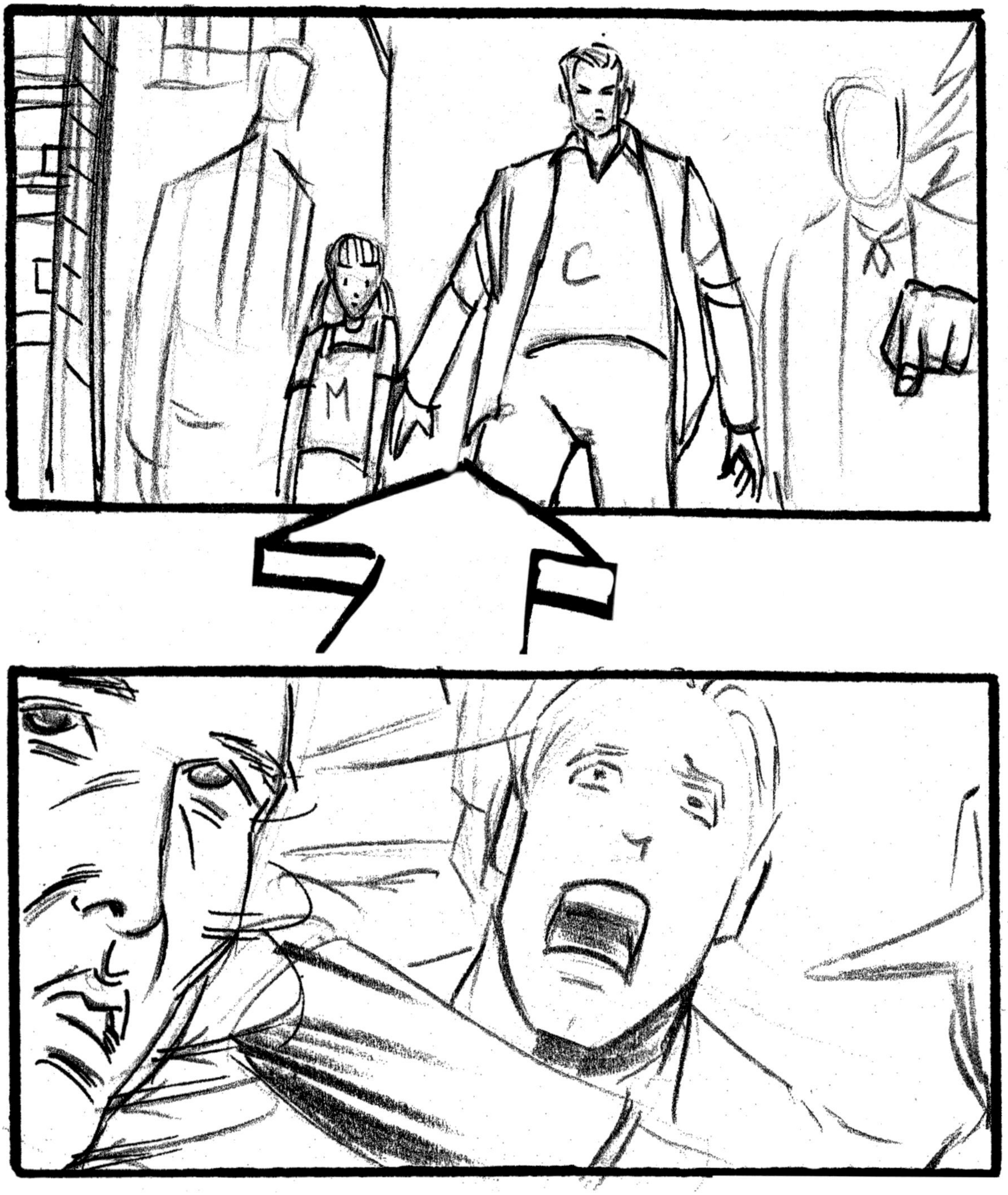

had to wait at the outside train station for the next train arrival. In the blowing snow and freezing temperatures, this was no small task. It would be a rare day that Todd's assistant, Eva Burkley would be leaving the same time as Brick and I. Eva had the ability to drive, talk on a cell and take notes from Ron or Todd at the same time. She was the ultimate multi-tasker. This split focus while driving would of course be frowned upon today. Once in freezing blizzard conditions, we tried to get a ride into Manhattan with Todd and Ron. But we were not invited to be a party to million-dollar business conversations in the production vehicle. Chilled to the bone, we the storyboard artists, were

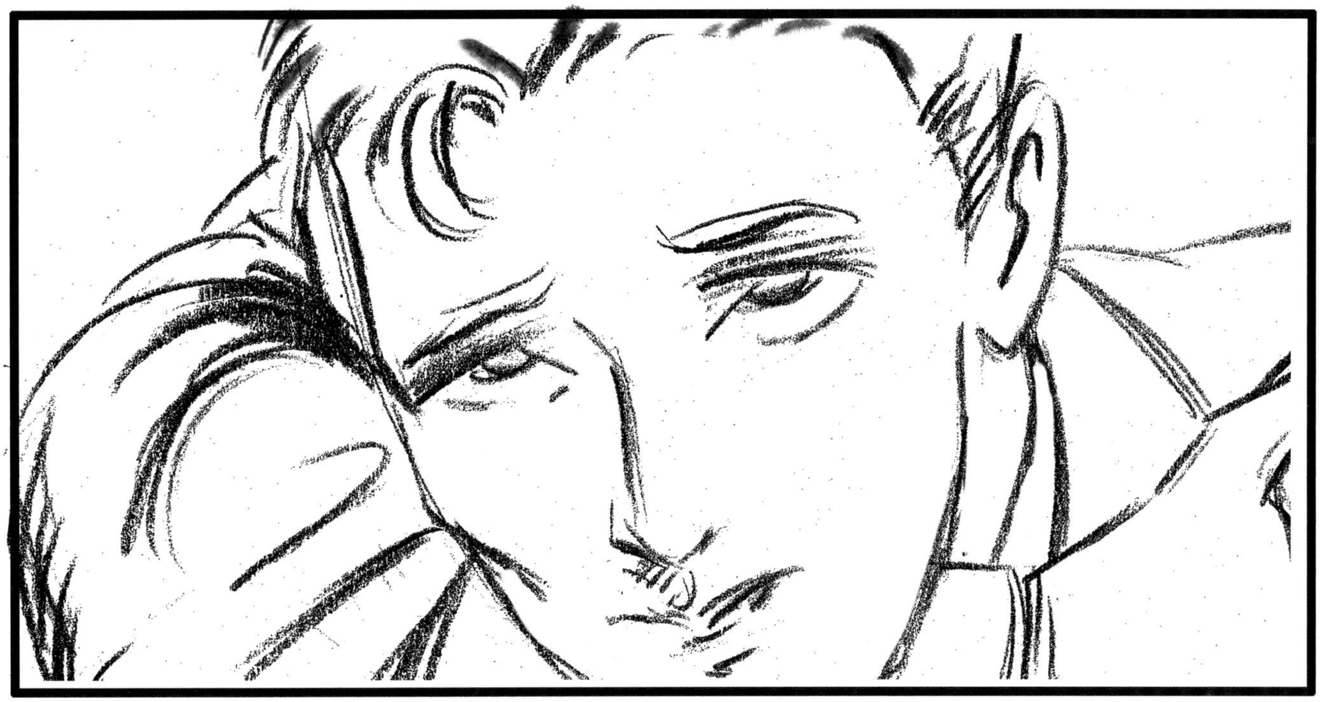

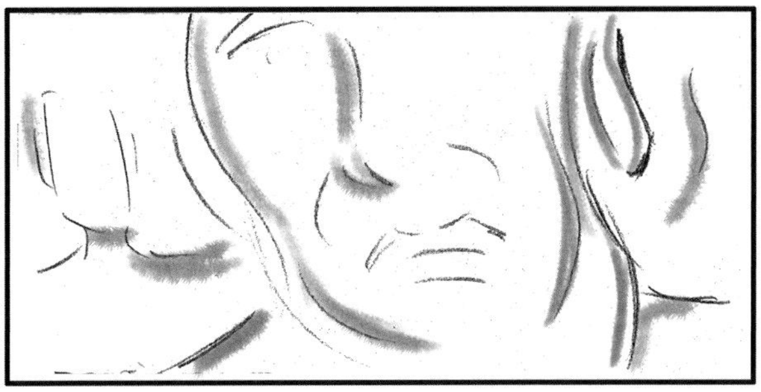

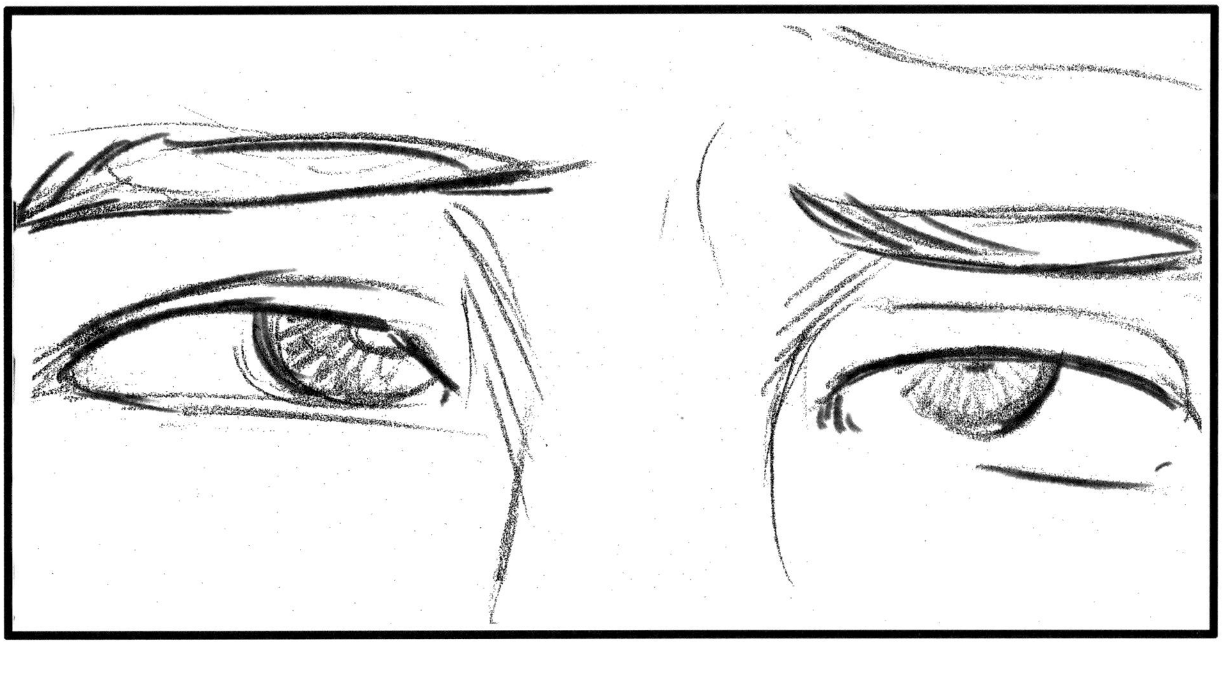

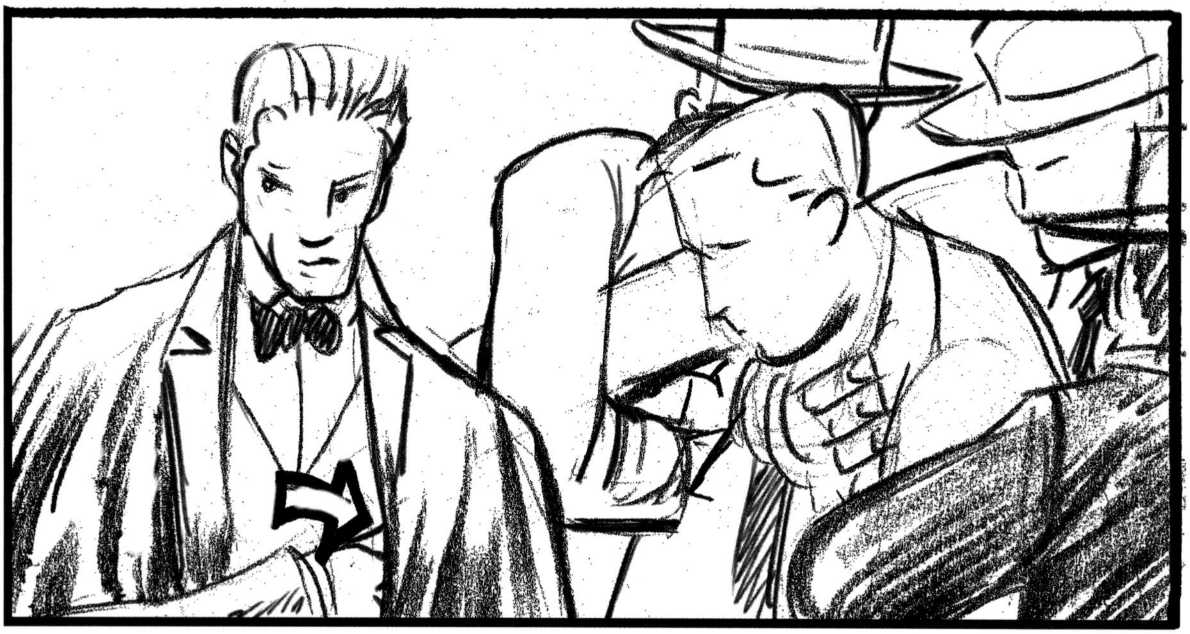

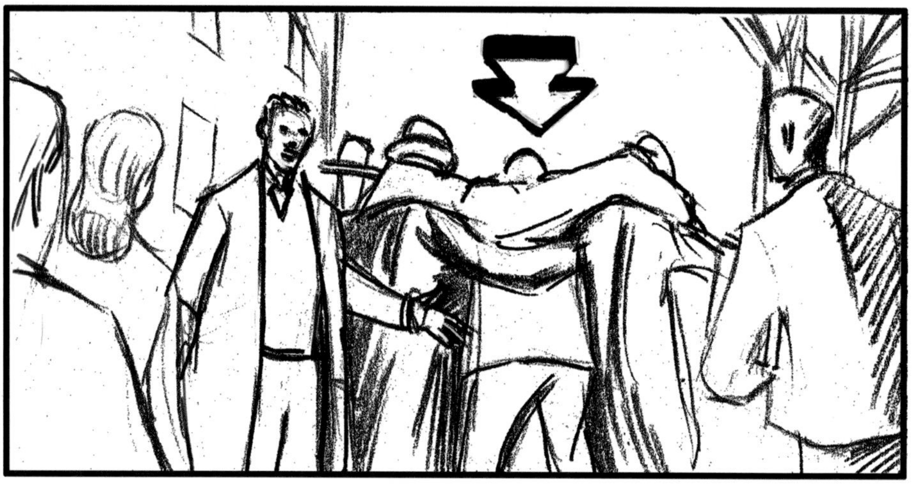

left standing in the cold snow and to our own travel devices. Ultimately, it was a small price to pay. We were on a great project that had multiple Academy Awards written all over it. Once they got closer to shooting, we would see Russell Crowe, Jennifer Connelly and Ed Harris at the production office from time to time.

While most shows had had wrap parties to mark the end of principal photography, *A Beautiful Mind* had a "start shooting party." The cast and crew met up at a nice bar in lower Manhattan. I brought my niece, Malaika Johnson who had recently graduated college and was looking for work in the business. As Ron was talking to some people, I waited for a break in the conversation to introduce Malaika. Once I introduced them and told him Malaika was looking for a job, Ron stopped what he was doing, warmly took Malaika by the arm and escorted her through the crowded room to his first AD, Aldric La'Auli Porter. Let's be clear: directors are not known to do this, especially major directors. This is simply who Ron is. Malaika was hired on the film as a PA in that very moment. She is currently one of the top location scouts in New York having worked on series such as *Elementary* and movies like *The Avengers* and *The Dark Knight Rises*.

Another scene in the movie was shot at my sister Linda's church on Queens Boulevard, where she was a music minister on Sundays. Ron got to meet her as well and took a photo with her. It was a strange coincidence. Years later at a Los Angeles event, I was able to introduce Ron to my son Josh, who was a young adult in his early twenties at this time. Again, Ron took the time to engage with Josh and to have an actual conversation. As timing worked out, I was in New York long enough to attend the Shaft production wrap party so this was a beginning and an end for me all at once.

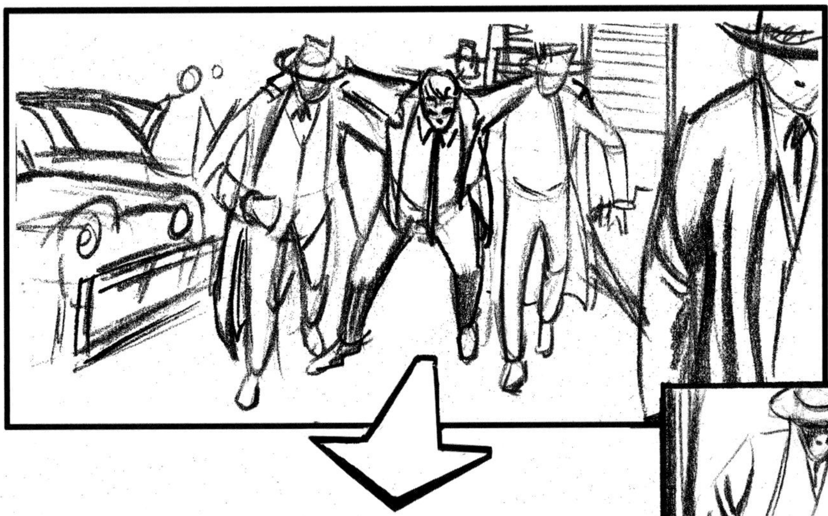

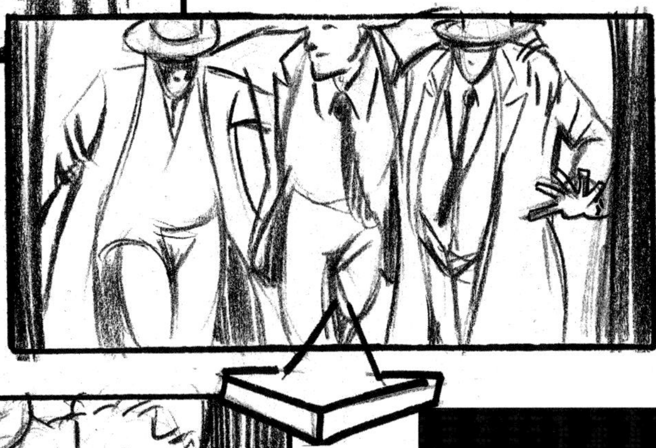

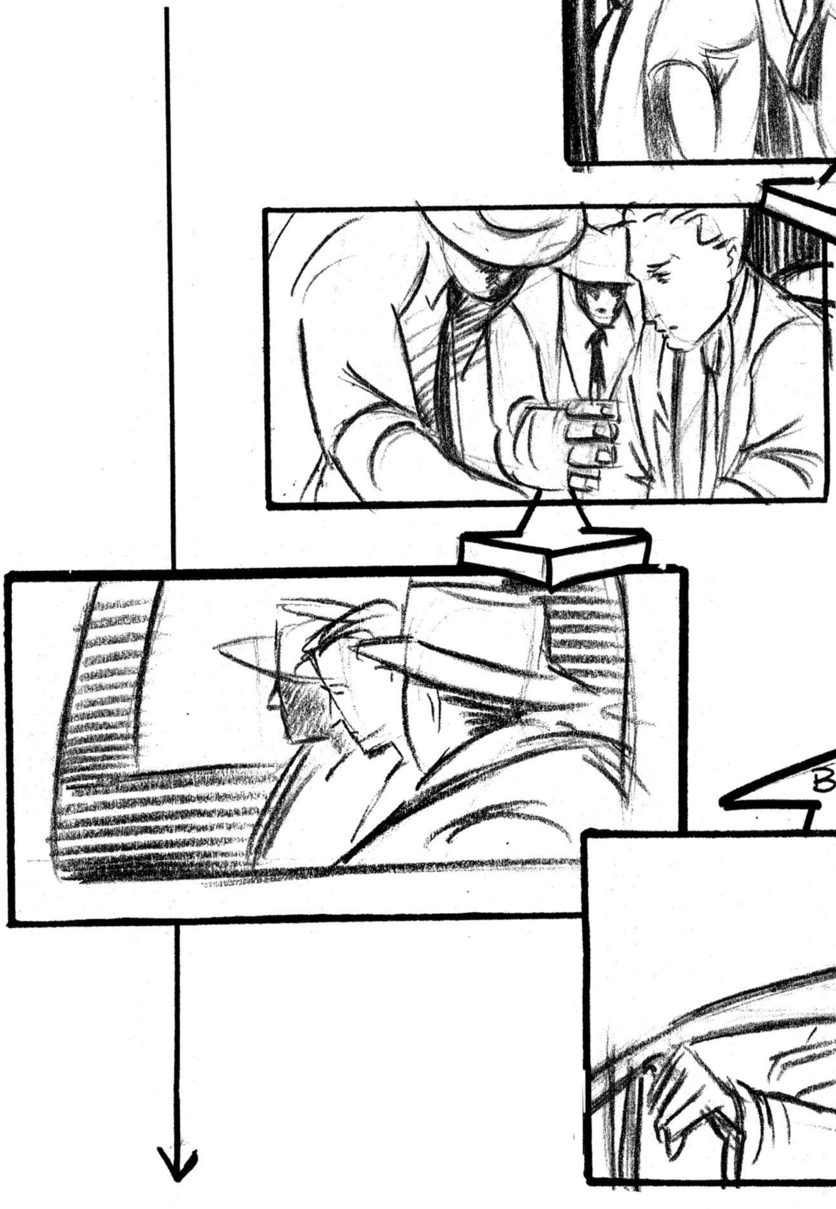

This was a shot that begins outside of the vehicle and precedes the semi-conscious Nash into the car. The shot was broken up in the final edit, but it was supposed to be one continuous shot.

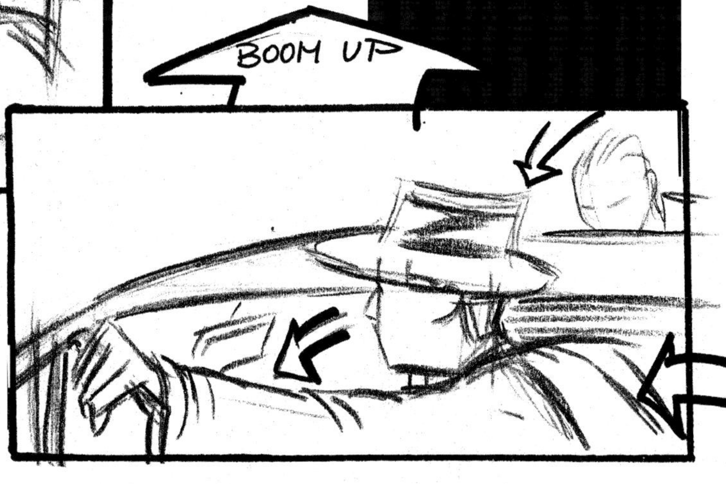

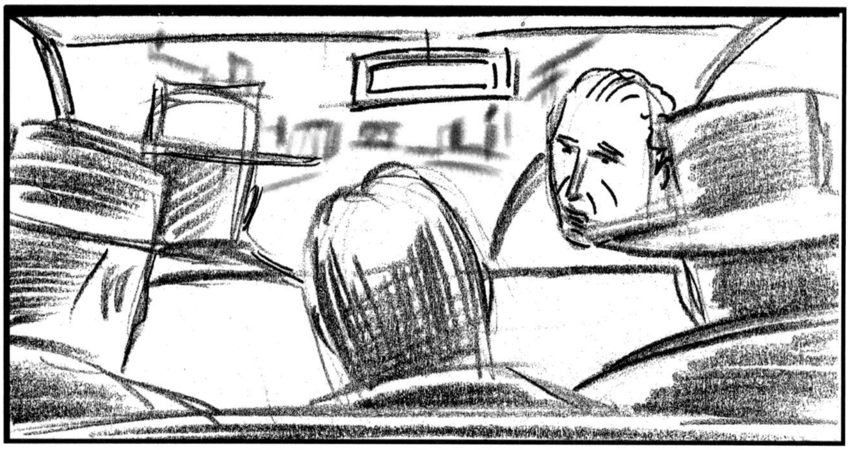

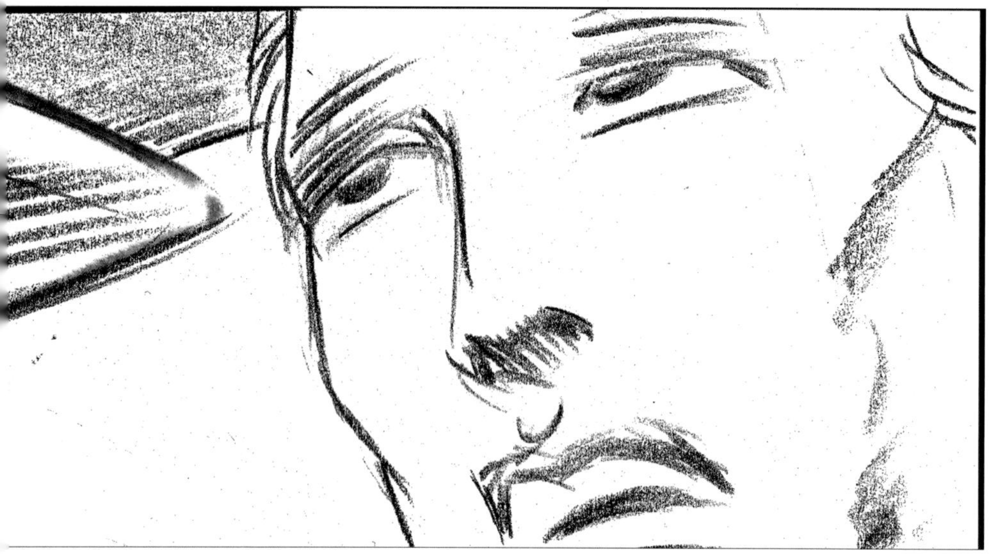

I never had to do any location scouting on *A Beautiful Mind*, but the location department did an excellent job of providing Brick and I with material as did the art department. We got to draw a lot of images of Princeton University as well as Harvard and MIT where much of the movie was filmed. Of all the scenes I worked on, the most notable for me was the one where Nash is lecturing at Harvard University and he sees what he believes to be Russian spies lurking in the classroom. Nash bolts from the classroom and cuts across the campus lawn with the men in pursuit. As he runs down the stairs, he stops because another possible "spy" is waiting for him to intercept him. It's in that moment where he meets Christopher Plummer's "Dr. Rosen" character. This scene was important as Ron had a firm concept of what he wanted to see and he gave me notes. However, Ron also gave me the freedom to come up with the visuals even as he pinpointed on the location photos where the characters needed to be in each part of the scene. As Nash is cornered on a campus stairwell, I wanted the opposing men to be in shadows with the brim of their hats

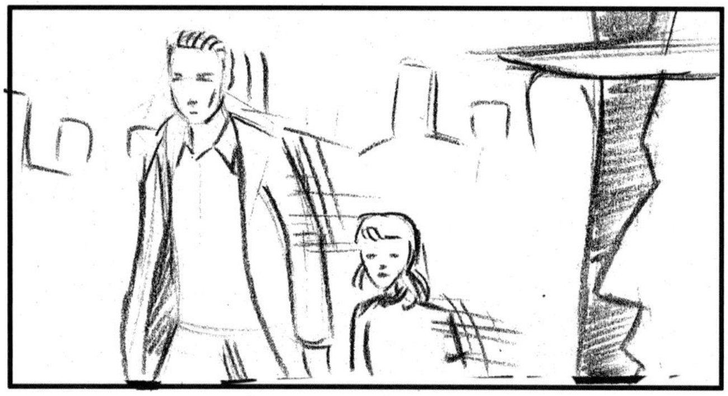

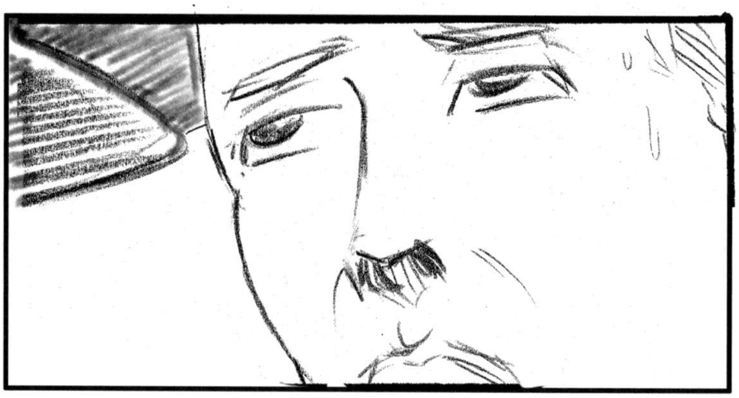

down to conceal their eyes and intentions. The low angle point of view from which Nash sees them would add mystery and danger. I drew a dramatic camera push into Dr. Rosen as a possibly nefarious introduction to his character. These shots I created were followed closely and used in the movie.

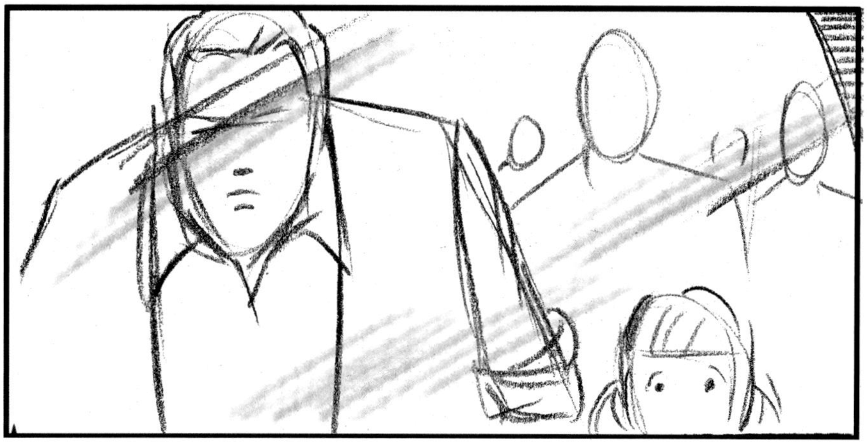

Even though I was allowed a lot of creative input from my work of the scenes in the storyboards, being the exquisite director that he is, Ron always gave us definitive shot ideas. After Nash is subdued by Rosen's men, drugged with a hypodermic needle and shoved into a car, Ron wanted the camera to lead Nash through Rosen's car as he is carried inside, then stop once outside the opposite door window as the door closes. Ron had a total understanding of how he wanted the sequences laid out.

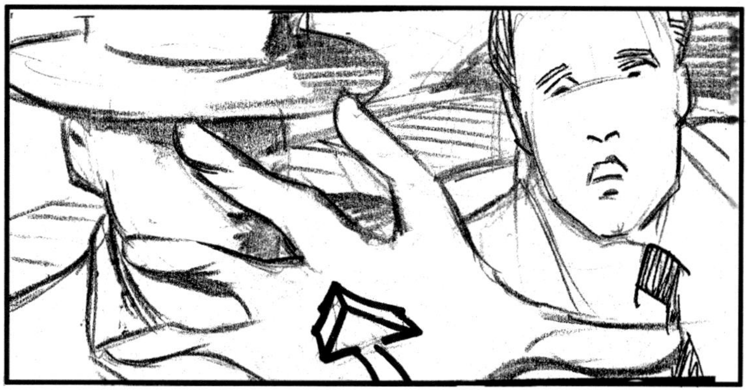

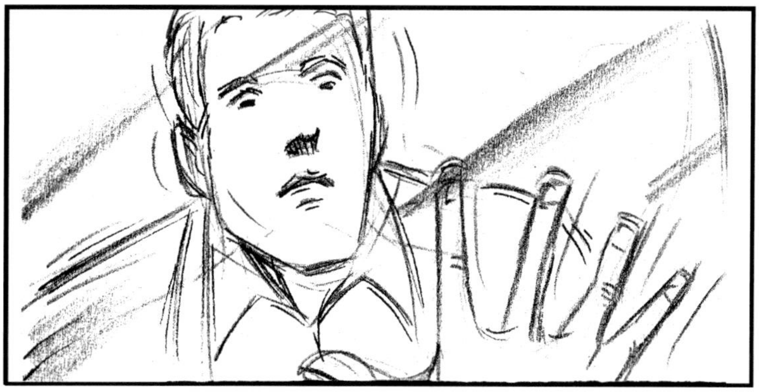

The director has his singular vision so not all of my ideas made it into the film. There was a later montage sequence during Nash's middle-aged years where we see he is no longer capable of teaching due to his mental illness and he is still trying to find his way in the world. I approached Todd with the idea of The Beatles' "Nowhere Man" being played in the montage as the song's release would match the years in the movie. Todd thought it was an interesting idea and I titled the storyboard scene "Nowhere Man." Ultimately, the song was

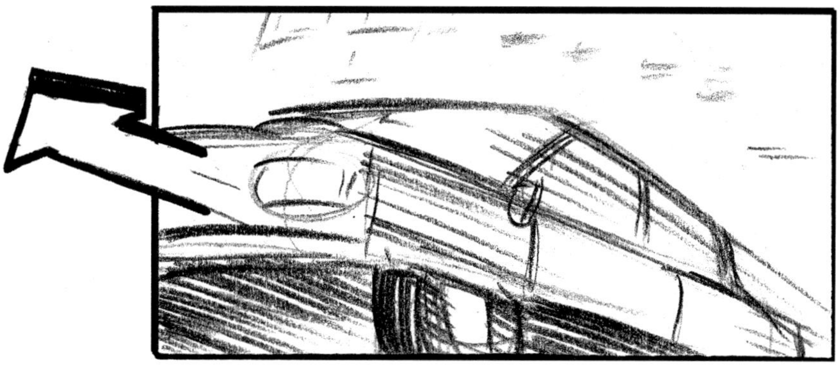

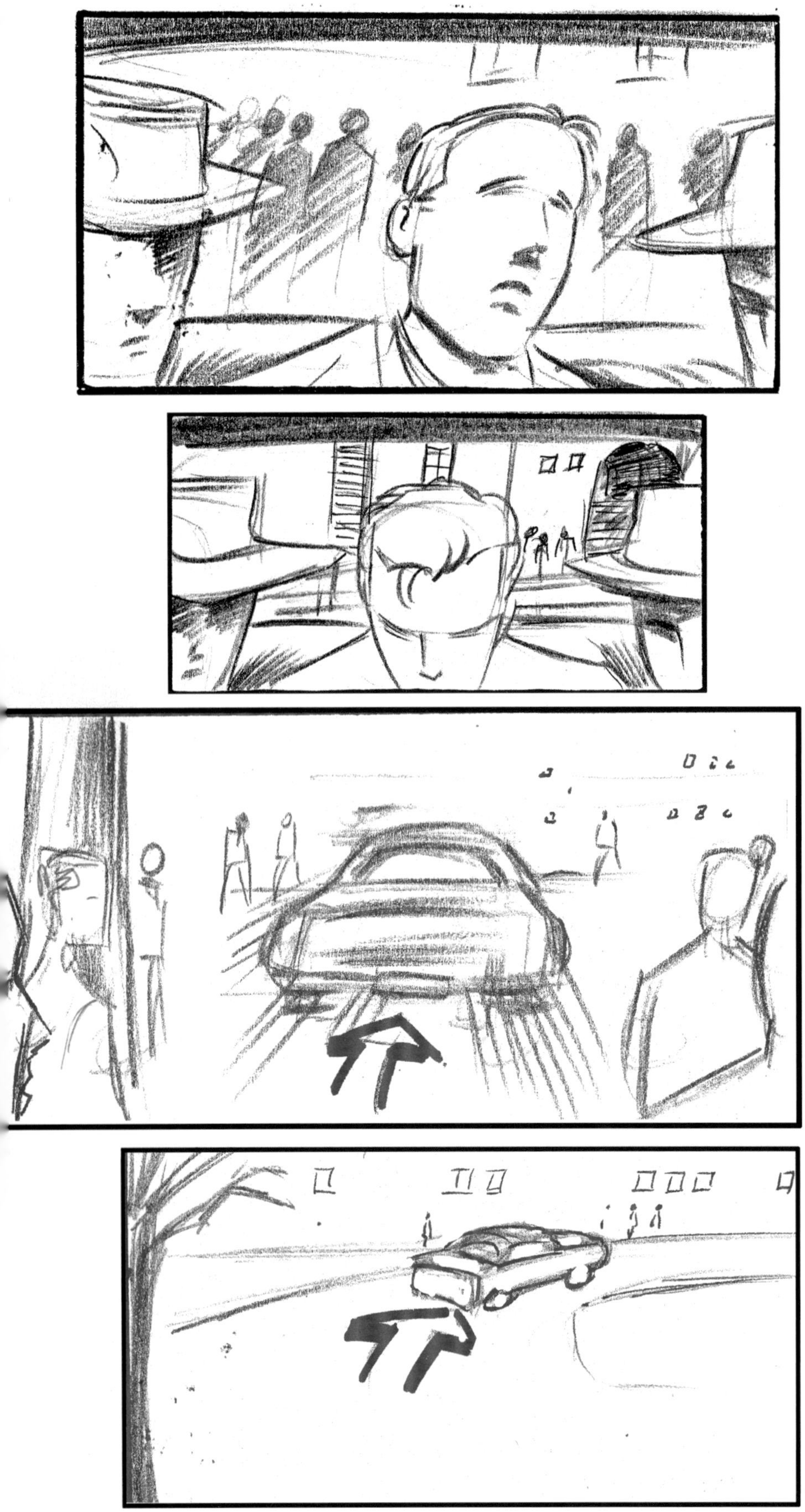

never used in the film but I tried to think out of the box as a storyboard artist. Eventually, my work time on the film came to an end. It was a great seven weeks by any measure. Brick went on for another month or so into principal photography and he kept me updated on shooting, as well as his "Ron time."

I was not at all surprised when *A Beautiful Mind* was nominated for Best Picture but when it won I was elated. I had in my small way, contributed to an Academy Award winning movie with a top director, cast, and crew. As I saw the movie, I regretted that I never had the chance to really work directly with the cinematographer, the extraordinary Roger Deakins. Roger was around the office and was always a gentleman but he was never part of the storyboarding process with Brick, Ron, Todd, and myself when I was there. Roger has since become one of the most legendary cinematographers of all time, finally winning an Oscar for Blade Runner 2049 and then again for the film, 1917. I still run into Roger from time to time in Los Angeles.

All the time that I was taking the train at the World Trade Center going to and from Bayonne, I could never have dreamed that the buildings would be taken away from us the following year with so many lives lost. We often take things and people for granted that they will always be there.

On a much lighter side, in 2000 during my first year away from New York, the Mets versus Yankees World Series that I had been waiting for my entire life finally happened. And there I was, living in Los Angeles. The recipe of comedy is of course, "timing."

STORYBOARDS AND STORIES OF 15 SELECT FILMS AND TELEVISION SHOWS

HARD DAY'S WORK

Chapter 8

ANTWONE FISHER

A MOMENT IN THE DIRECTOR'S CHAIR

Antwone Fisher... a moment in the director's chair

In September of 2001, I had been living in Los Angeles for just over a year. I was just getting the swing of things and the energy of the city when I got a call from a production office stating that I was in the running to work with Denzel Washington on his directorial debut. What? Denzel Washington??! The film was *Antwone Fisher*, a story written about the life of a first-time screenwriter of the same name.

When I entered the Sony lot and made my way to the Escape Artists offices of the film's Producer, Todd Black I was greeted by Gina White, the associate producer. I then met Todd for the first time. Todd is sincerely one of the nicest people I have ever met in the business, especially as a person in a position of power. When Todd asks, "How are you?" he is really asking that question from a true point of interest and not as a way to boomerang the conversation to himself.

The most intimidating person for me to meet was of course, Denzel. The first time we met was a chance meeting while I was with John Singleton and I had been caught by surprise, but this time I was prepared. My previous question to Denzel was asking him if he would direct and now that answer had come to pass. And with this *Antwone Fisher* script, Denzel had a fascinating life story to direct. I sat down with Denzel and Todd for what I assumed was an interview. I was told that this was the autobiography of a young man named Antwone Fisher who suffered from anger issues while in the Navy due to his emotional, physical and sexual abuse years earlier in foster care as a child in Cleveland. Apart from directing, Denzel would play the role of a naval psychologist who helps Antwone through his emotional issues.

I asked Denzel what his "visual paradigm" was for the movie and he said, *"Ordinary People,"* the Robert Redford classic from 1980. That was a perfect answer as the two films were thematically very similar with a troubled young man being helped with an older male psychologist about a traumatic experience. I was still in full interview mode until Todd started a sentence with, "And when you start working on the movie..." My reaction was, "Does that mean I'm hired?" Todd smiled and said, "Yes," which of course relaxed me immediately. Denzel and I then talked about some shot visuals, which set us up to go more in depth in our second meeting. Talking to him was amazing, not just because of who he is but his voice is amazing due to his theatrical training. Soon afterwards, the two of us had a meeting scheduled at his house and then on that tragic day, 9/11 happened. And the whole world seemed to stop.

On the morning of September 11, 2001, I was sleeping in during the late morning hours in Los Angeles when my mother called. Mom sounded rattled and asked me if I heard what had happened in New York? I replied that I hadn't and then Mom said, "The World Trade Center was destroyed!" It was one of the moments we all experience when time stops and one wonders if you heard things correctly. Relatedly in 1993, Hill Harper called me to inform me that Brandon Lee had been killed in an on set accident on the film *The Crow* and hearing that news totally devastated me. This particular news however, was an otherworldly experience and so much larger. And reading this, you most certainly know what I mean. I turned on the news and there were the Twin Towers—burning with smoke filling the screen. Thousands of lives were lost instantly. It was a helpless feeling to see my hometown attacked. I had no idea if I knew anyone in the buildings.

I was in a daze. After I got dressed, I walked to my local newsstand that was owned by Michael Martin, a good man around my age. Betty knew I had to get out of the house. When I got to the newsstand, folks were watching the events on the small television that Mike had set up. It was cathartic to just be out in the open air with other people to actually come to grips with what was happening that day. As far as Denzel, he is a New Yorker by birth. Both of our mothers were from Harlem and born within a year of each other. Being a New Yorker in his heart, he flew back to see what he could do and to be of any kind of support.

The *Antwone Fisher* preproduction work was pushed back a little as the entire country was in flux. Air traffic and security were about to morph into the current state we now experience of tightened x-ray scanning and shoes removal due to bomb threats. Three years earlier, I traveled back from a job in Morocco with a foot-long, Middle-Eastern knife in my bag to add to my martial arts collection. Airport security let me through without hesitation. That will never be possible again...and thankfully.

In October when things went back to some sense of normalcy, I was flown out to the film location in Cleveland to work with Denzel in preproduction. I met the real Antwone Fisher as well as the young actor, Derek Luke who had just nabbed his first role as "Antwone". Derek had been working as a sales clerk in the Sony Pictures' gift shop when he auditioned for the part and was hired. Denzel had his meetings arranged with one department head after another. Denzel and I are both avid sports fans so the first hour of our meeting was an enthusiastic exchange about teams and players. Just getting to know each other, we gleamed over talk about New York, baseball and boxing. When Denzel had his lunch brought in, he generously offered me one half of his chicken sandwich. The same manner of courtesy that Terry Leonard had done years earlier that gesture immediately reflected Denzel's character. In that simple moment, he was a superstar just hanging out and sharing his meal with someone he had just met. I took his offer and I must say that his chicken sandwich was delicious. Denzel saw my smile after I finished it and asked, "Are you straight?!" (Black folks talk for "are you good?"). I replied, "I'm so straight I have right angles!" That got the truest laugh from Denzel that I'd ever seen.

The rest of our meeting was spent going over shot ideas for some sequences. As a filmmaker, Denzel is not fancy by any means. He shoots clean, clear, stays true to the story and allows space for actors to breathe. He's very much like Redford and Eastwood in that manner. Denzel only wants to serve the story of the scene and make sure the actors shine. It's never about intricate camera moves. As a great actor himself, he never wants us to lose track of the character or performance.

Denzel is also the most singularly focused director I have ever worked with. When he is with you in a meeting, he is there 100 percent. There is no question that you may have about his film that he won't answer. When you are ready to leave his office, he will shake your hand and then you benignly cease to exist in his eyes as his attention shifts totally to the next person coming into the room. There is absolutely no malice in this, but it's his way to be as efficient and present as possible for each person. Like Ron Howard, Denzel gave me a lot of leeway in terms of shots. He was formulating what he wanted and we would have long talks on each scene. Ever so often, he would do a quick doodle of the layout of a set but would never draw frames or try storytelling. Denzel would describe very clearly how he wanted a scene to unfold.

As the film opens in a dreamlike sequence, Young Antwone has visions of the biological and loving family he has never had. Denzel wanted things from the child's point of view as his eyes move through a wheat field and then into a barn revealing family members of the past and ancestors of his past life about to engage in a sumptuous banquet. The visual key that would be echoed at the end of the film, would be a loving hand coming toward young Antwone in an offer towards him to join his family. I worked on this sequence in my hotel room and got the pencil roughs to Denzel's satisfaction. I would then create a tighter storyboard version of the scene.

While in Cleveland on one brisk evening, I visited the Rock & Roll Hall of Fame. I am a big-time fan of The Beatles as you may tell by the title of this book. The Beatles' collection in Hall of Fame was incredible. To actually see the handwritten lyrics of "Imagine" by John Lennon is pretty incredible to behold.

Once I got back to LA, I had a little downtime before I got back to work on to the movie. I had storyboarded a lot of the Cleveland section of the film. My next assignment was to storyboard some of Antwone's time in the Navy. I was assigned by Denzel and Todd to create an illustration of a cricket that appeared in a scene of the movie itself. In the script, Antwone spends some of his idle time while in his naval bunk sketching whatever comes to mind. In one scene, adult Antwone has a flashback childhood memory of holding a cricket and begins to draw the cricket. I was provided with photographic stills as well as young Antwone's direct POV of the cricket in his hand. Using the photo still as a guide, I did a pencil sketch version of it.

For my additional position on the film, I traveled to San Diego for a couple of weekends to work with actor Derek Luke in order to assist him in embodying the feel of an artist a work. He would be tracing over my original sketch that was used in the movie. I taught Derek the various ways an artist might hold a pencil while sketching. For example, holding a pencil straight on for a hard line, or tilted to the side to get shading techniques, etc. I even directed him on how to execute the type of facial expressions an artist might make while being focused on creating a drawing. Derek was fun to work with, a great listener and very open to my direction.

On the day the drawing scene was to be shot, I was called to set. In the movie, Antwone is laying in a bottom bunk as he sketches the cricket from memory. The camera couldn't achieve this visual if it was shot in a practical bunk bed so the bottom part of the bunk prop was laid on the floor of the set. A camera was placed directly overhead of this rigged bunk below, which was framed so none of the actual floor was shown. The lighting was also adjusted so the bunk in the camera frame actually looked like as though it was under another bunk against a wall of the ship.

I was sitting in "video village" where a monitor is set up for a director and others in the exact way a camera is filming a scene. I was there with Denzel, Todd Black, the script supervisor and others. Denzel calmly said, "Warren, why don't you go direct that shot?" In one of those slow-motion moments, I believe I said "Um ... sure." I soon was floating my way over to the active part of the set. I had spoken to Denzel some time ago about my writing screenplays but I don't believe I ever mentioned directing. Denzel saw something in me and was so amazingly giving in that moment. He truly wanted me to succeed.

To my surprise, the camera operator was Pam Rittelmeyer who I had met a decade earlier through a mutual industry friend, Al Valentine. Months after that initial meeting, I happened upon Pam in Times Square where she was working as a camera operator on Arnold Schwarzenegger's the *Last Action Hero*. I was a struggling artist at that point and I remember thinking how much I wanted to be working on a movie of that magnitude. It was a great turn of events that I was now about to direct a scene with Pam as a colleague all these years later. I looked through the camera viewfinder to make sure the shot was lined up. I even posed as Derek/Antwone to have Pam make sure that everything was composed well enough within the frame. When Derek came on set, we went over the sketching techniques for a quick tune-up. Minutes later, we were shooting. I called out sketching techniques off camera as the camera rolled. Derek remembered what I had showed him the past two weekends and repeated everything like a pro as he traced over my original sketch. It was a great and exhilarating experience that Denzel provided for me. My time on the *Antwone Fisher* shoot wrapped with the San Diego stint and I was on to the next thing. It was a great beginning to my working relationship with Denzel as well as Todd, who has remained a friend and colleague.

The great possibilities that come of working in this industry is of having dreams come true. A short time after *Antwone Fisher* had wrapped, Todd was kind enough to take a read of the first script that Betty had written which was a period piece based on a true story. He was so impressed by her talent as a writer that he requested to read her second script, a family comedy — and immediately optioned that script for *Escape Artists*. That comedy script was bought and set up with a deal at Searchlight Films, initiating Betty's entry into the film industry as a professional writer and full member of The Writer's Guild (WGA).

STORYBOARDS AND STORIES OF 15 SELECT FILMS AND TELEVISION SHOWS

HARD DAY'S WORK

Chapter 9

2 FAST 2 FURIOUS

AND THE MIAMI HEAT

2 Fast 2 Furious... and the Miami heat

I got a call from John Singleton and he sounded as giddy as a schoolboy. He had landed the directing job for *2 Fast 2 Furious*, the sequel to *The Fast and the Furious*. This would be the biggest film he had ever worked on in his career at this point. It would be his first project as a director-for-hire. John had always written or created the initial ideas for all of his previous films. He was a maverick *Shaft*, which morphed away from the father/son concept was an idea that John originated. It's fair to assume that the powers that be at Universal liked what they saw in how John handled action and delivery of his modern take in *Shaft* and knew they had their next director for the *Fast and Furious* sequel. However, the franchise's star, Vin Diesel would not be part of the project because he had become a big star in his own right having landed the potential franchise of *XXX*. His co-star, Paul Walker would be carrying this film along with John's new protégé, Tyrese Gibson. Tyrese was the lead in John's film, *Baby Boy* which we had worked on a year and a half earlier. John thought that Tyrese or "Reese" as he called him, could be an action star his own right.

For the second time, John would be alongside a hot producer. Neal Moritz produced the original *The Fast and the Furious*, brought the franchise to Universal and hired Vin Diesel. Neal was much hipper than producer Scott Rudin, who was on *Shaft*.

I had been working on the movie *Biker Boyz* with director Reggie Bythewood when John contacted me. Producer Stephanie Allain, who got me on the *Biker Boyz* project had discovered John in his early twenties when he wrote and directed his pivotal and now legendary film, *Boyz N The Hood*. In every way possible I would avail myself to work with John on this big budget film. John and I had become close friends by this time and where Butch went, Sundance followed.

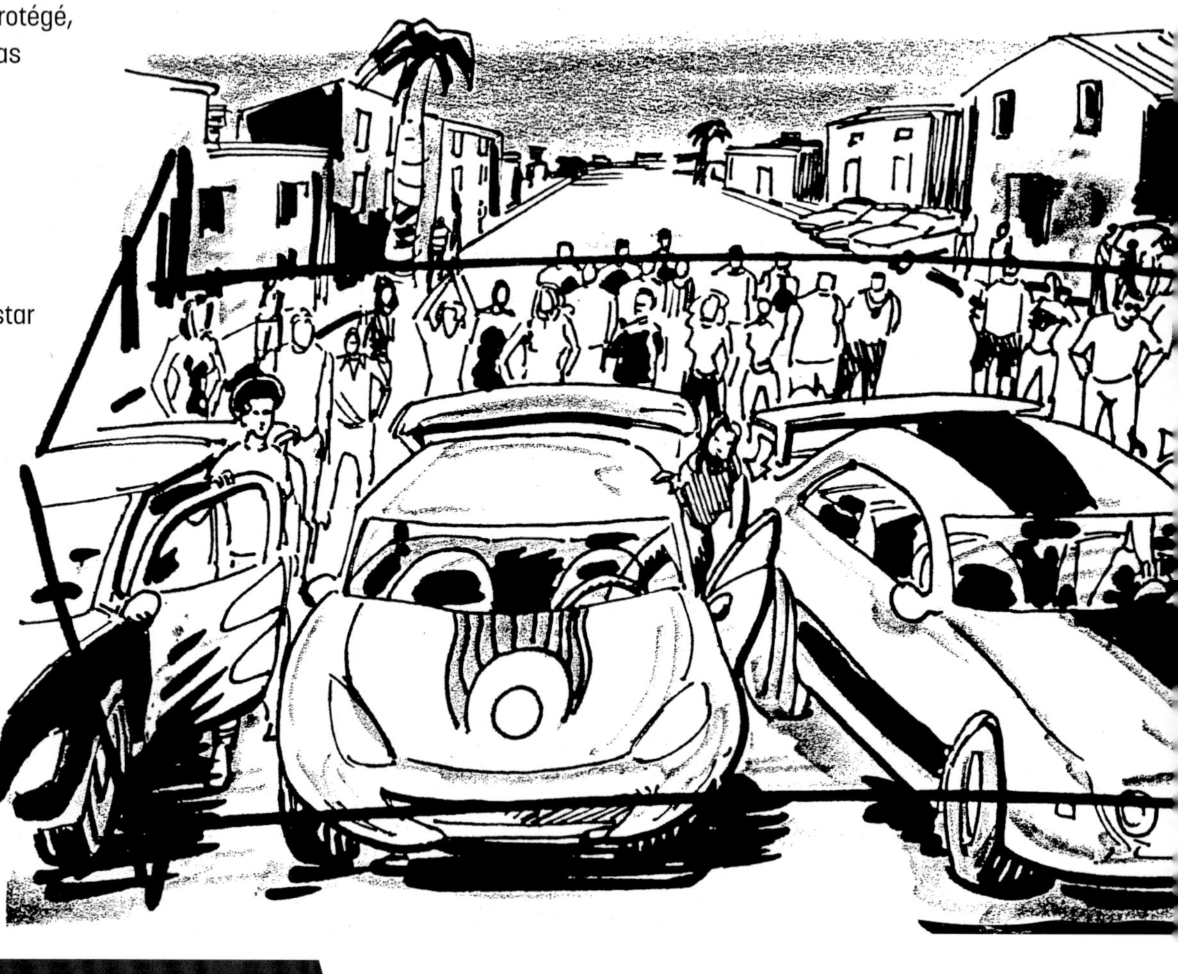

These 2 Fast 2 Furious story-boards are scanned from photocopies.

I informed Reggie that I had to leave *Biker Boyz* and he was totally cool with my decision. I instantly found a storyboard artist replacement for myself in my friend and "padawan," Brian McGee Our relationship dated back to New York and I knew he was an incredible colorist and artist. Brian had moved out to LA and wanted to break into storyboards because he had worked as a Disney artist up to that point. I would later guide Brian on storytelling elements in the boards and the rules of the industry. I handed over *Biker Boyz* to him and he aced the job.

Now that I was on *2 Fast 2 Furious*, one of the first things John and I did was to screen *Mad Max 2: The Road Warrior* in his cozy screening room at his South Central LA office. John wanted to get a real sense of cars and driving choreography. It was great to watch *The Road Warrior* on a big screen again. Director George Miller's shot selection was perfect and there was not a wasted frame of film.

John instantly started me on some scenes to create for his shots. However, my concern at the time was that I was not a member of the Los Angeles Illustrators Union for storyboard artists. I was in the New York United Scenic Artists Union that included storyboard artists in its membership I tried previously to get into the Los Angeles Illustrators Union (which represented storyboard artists) but the catch-22 was, a person could only get into the union by somehow being on a non-union movie that *became* a union movie. This was the strategy that earned the required thirty days of work to be admitted. The other caveat would be in the case where all the union artists were booked and working on other shows; or if the artist had a special standout skill that the filmmakers needed, then that artist would be hired and immediately admitted into the union. The latter variable to getting in the union was the case with the original *Jurassic Park*. A number of dinosaur artists were brought on to the movie and were given union status because of their unique skill in drawing these creatures. Admittedly, I had no such expertise in cars that would be my entry into the union in that manner.

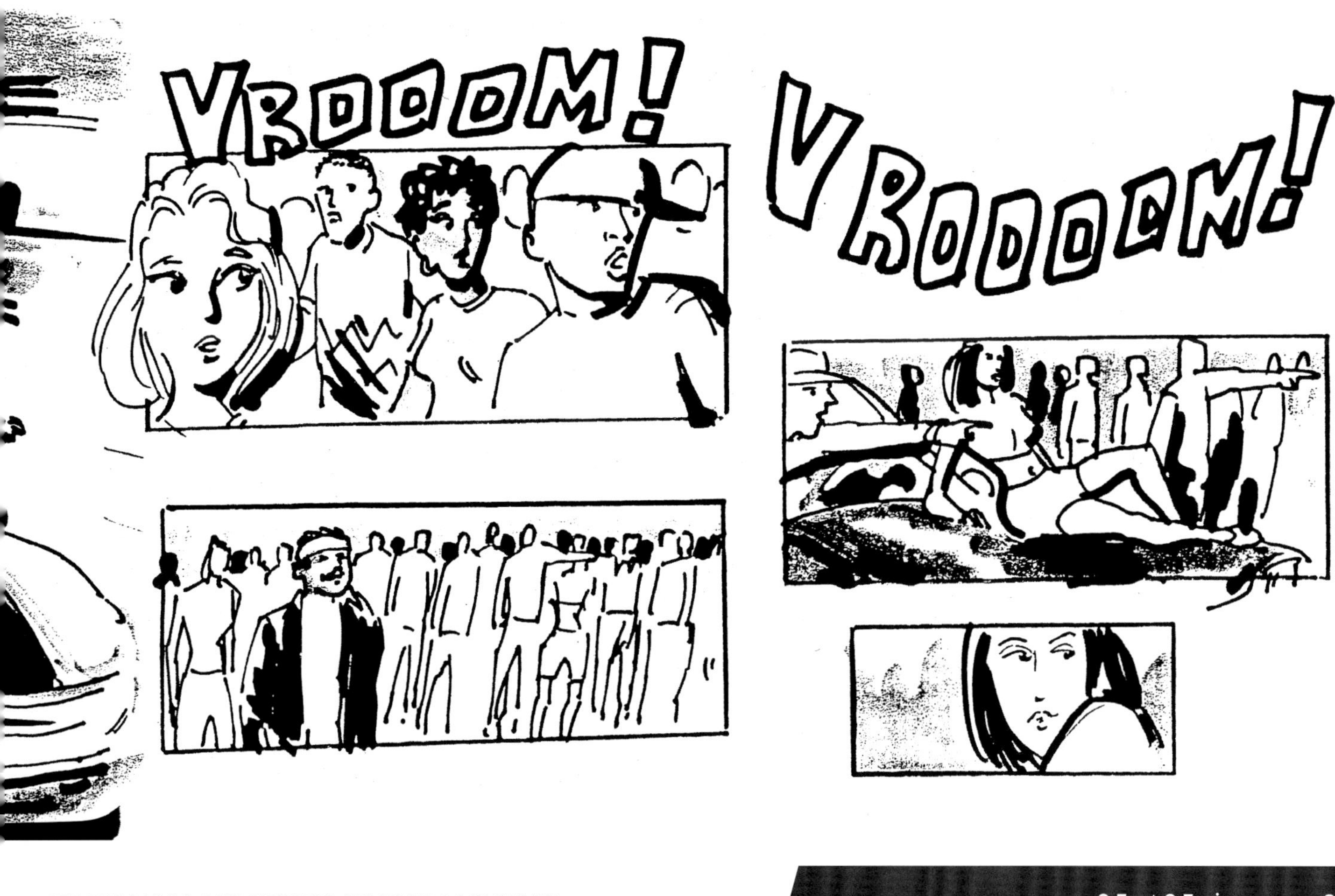

I remember John saying that he wanted steam coming out the front of Brian's car like a bull.

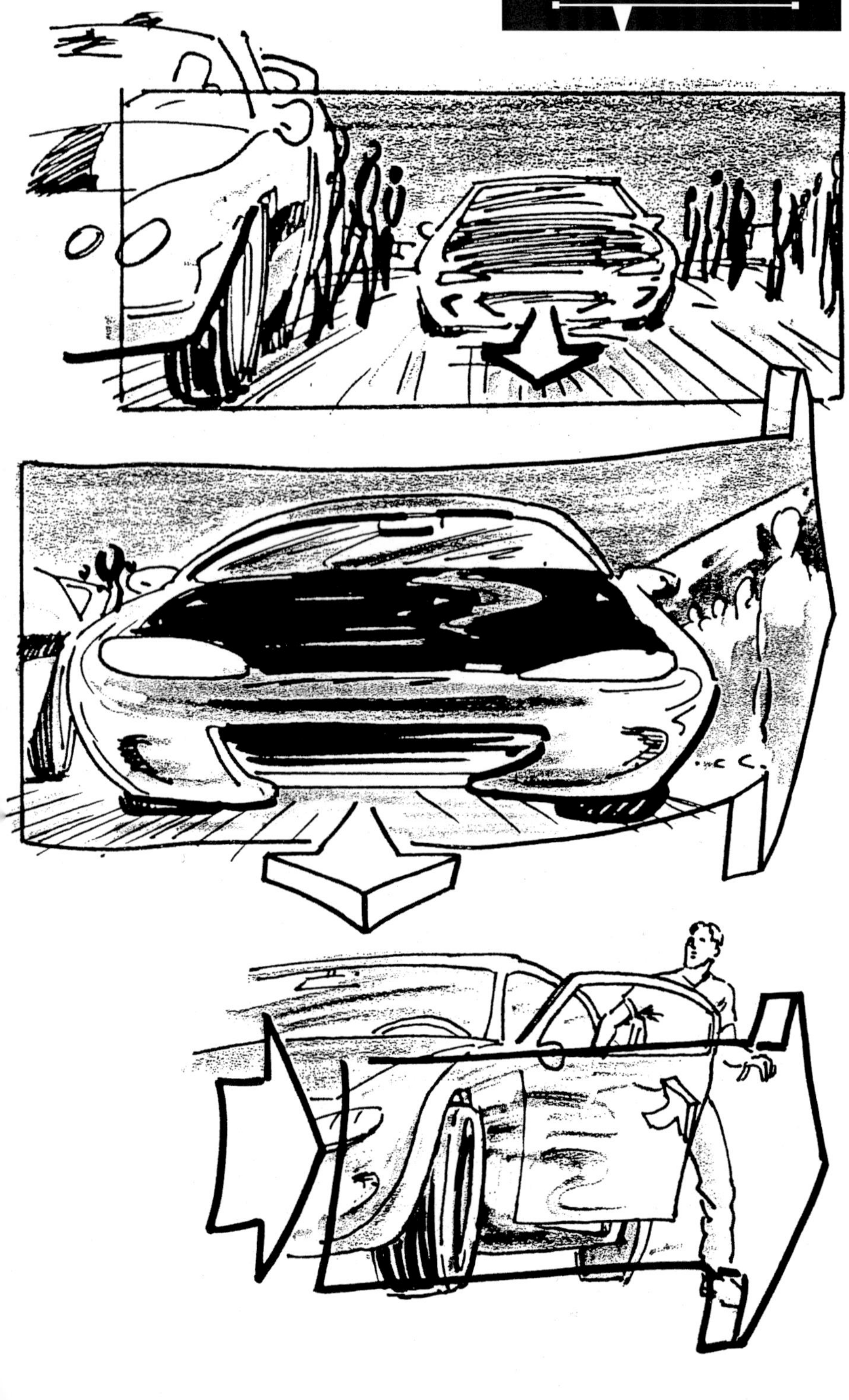

Until a work strategy was devised for me to be officially hired on the film, I worked as a freelance artist from my home and stayed out of the office. With union artists being hired on to assist John on this mammoth film, the last thing we needed was a union artist reporting me for violating any laws of employment. I eventually joined the Art Directors Guild in order to be technically credited as an assistant art director. Even with this approach working in my favor, I had to prove how many days I had worked in film and television since being a resident in Los Angeles. It took another two years for me to join the Illustrators Union and that was thanks to a job recommendation by my storyboard mentor, Darryl Henley. Struggling a bit financially at that time, I was supported by my lovely cousin Araceli Cabarcas who loaned me the very hefty sum of money for the initiation fee. Araceli's heartfelt gesture was an act of love that I will never forget. Once initiated into the Art Directors Guild I could attend the union's industry meetings. In the coming years, the Los Angeles Illustrators Union was absorbed into the Art Director's Union and that was a beneficial move for all members.

One of the unexpected occurrences working on this movie was that John and I were invited to participate in a multi-part documentary *Beyond The Color Line* by Harvard professor and documentarian, Henry Louis Gates. I wasn't used to being on-camera but I got through it. John and I were filmed for some behind-the-scenes film footage.

The movie *2 Fast 2 Furious* was to be set in Miami. John and I, along with several personnel made an initial location scout trip to Miami. The Miami heat in July is dense. As soon as I arrived and walked out of the airport in Miami, the air was so humid that my glasses fogged. We spent about a week on an initial scout. The crew went on to scout the various parts of Miami but spent most of the time searching locations in South Beach, the glamorous part of the city. While Miami is very much "the south" with working class Blacks and whites, South Beach is a haven for wealthy Europeans, college kids, athletes, models and people of Cuban descent. Miami is quite a mix of a lot of elements. I was set up at the South Beach Marriott, a great hotel and right off the beach. I could wake up and jog along the long walkway on the ocean, shower dress and then go on the scouts.

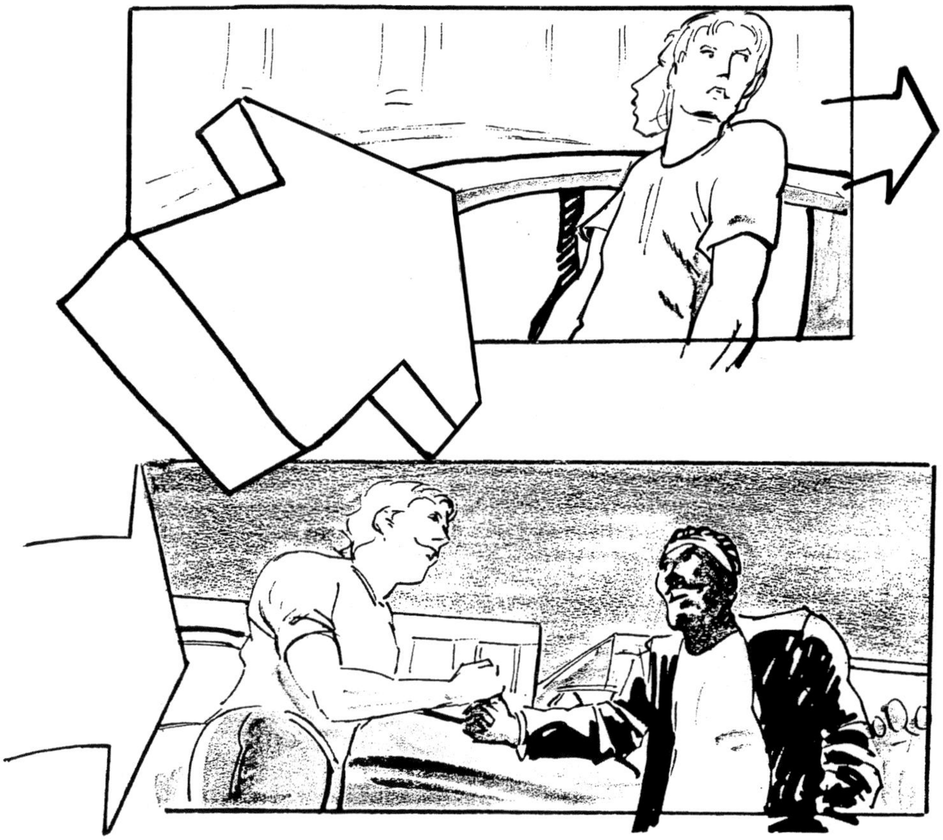

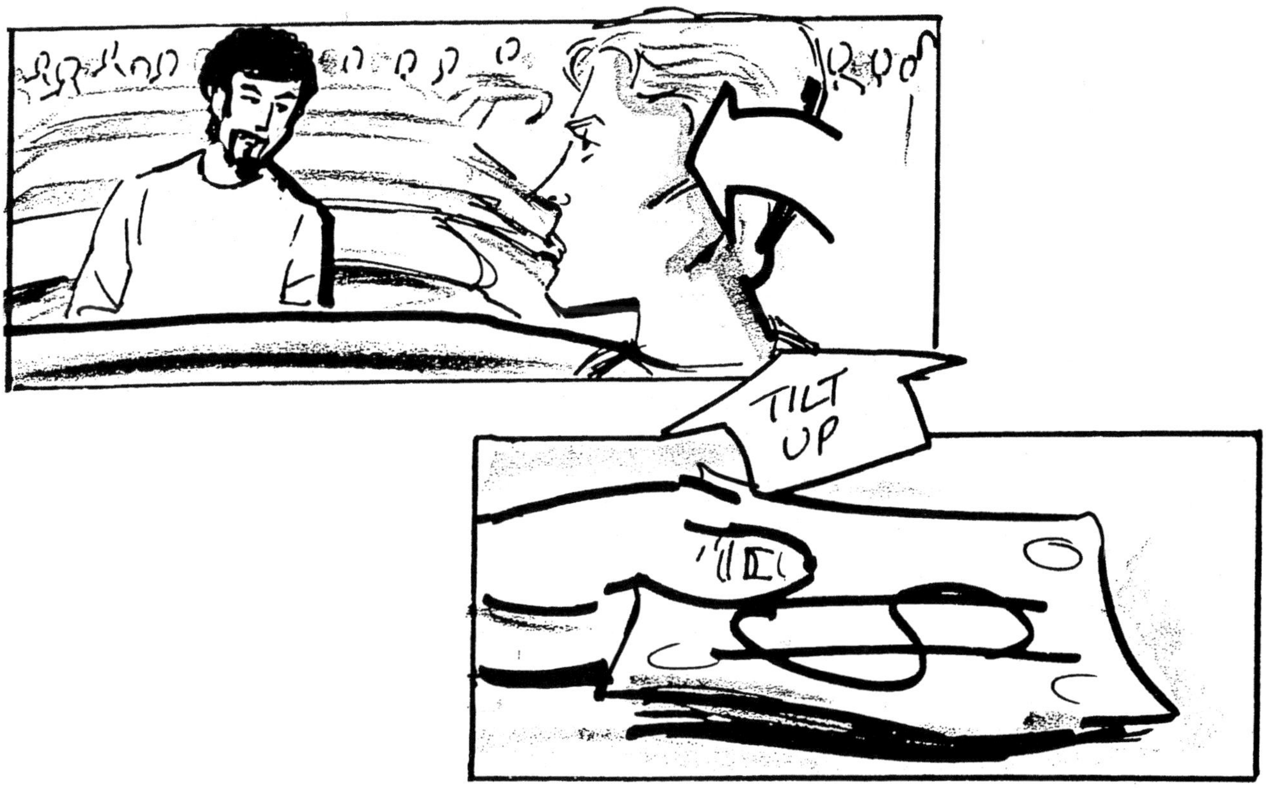

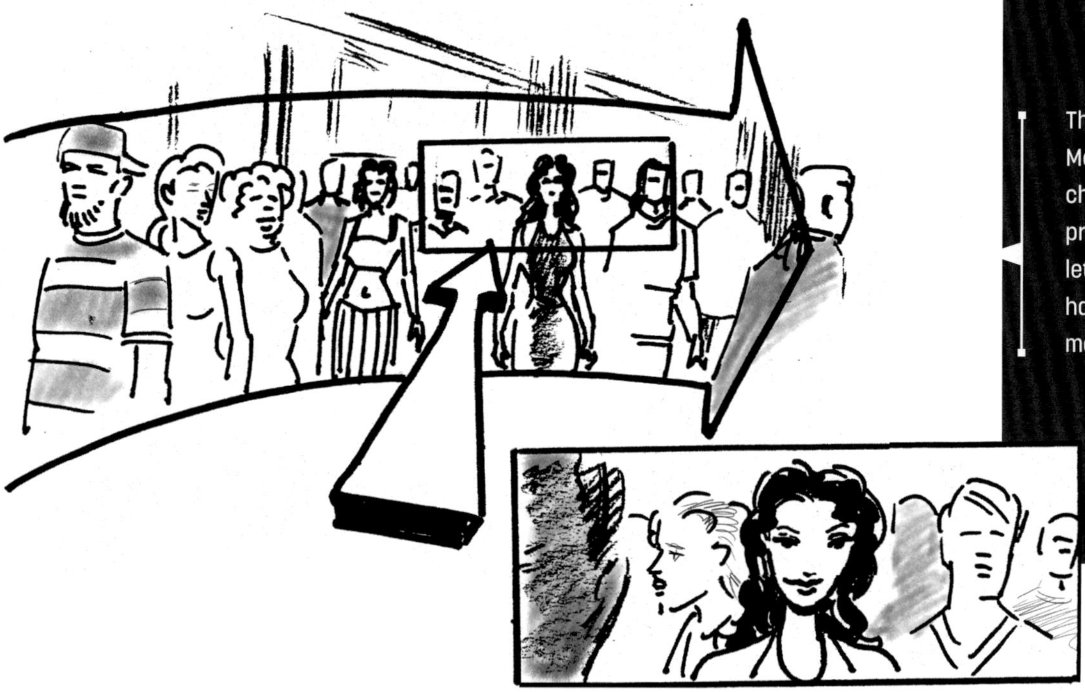

This reveal of the Monica Fuente character was pretty mush to the letter. John always had his camera moves well planned.

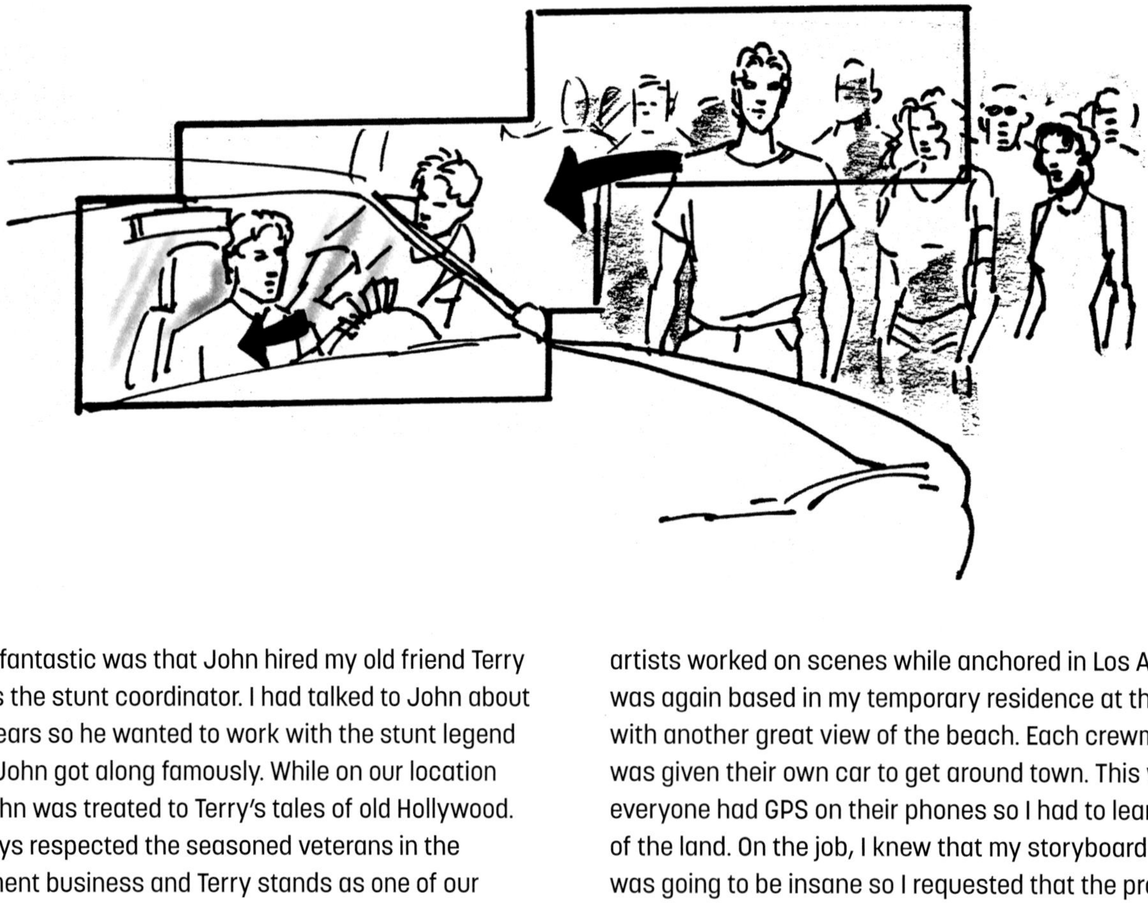

What was fantastic was that John hired my old friend Terry Leonard as the stunt coordinator. I had talked to John about Terry for years so he wanted to work with the stunt legend Terry and John got along famously. While on our location scouts, John was treated to Terry's tales of old Hollywood. John always respected the seasoned veterans in the entertainment business and Terry stands as one of our greatest. After the week of scouting ended I returned to Los Angeles. I was back in Miami a few weeks later for the long haul of a nearly three months' stint of preproduction. I was hired as the lead storyboard artist. The other storyboard artists worked on scenes while anchored in Los Angeles. I was again based in my temporary residence at the Marriott with another great view of the beach. Each crewmember was given their own car to get around town. This was before everyone had GPS on their phones so I had to learn the lay of the land. On the job, I knew that my storyboard workload was going to be insane so I requested that the production office hire Brian McGee to assist me. Brian came to Miami a few days later, worked in my office and we had things up and running quite quickly. John and Terry would come by the office and we would map out the scenes under their

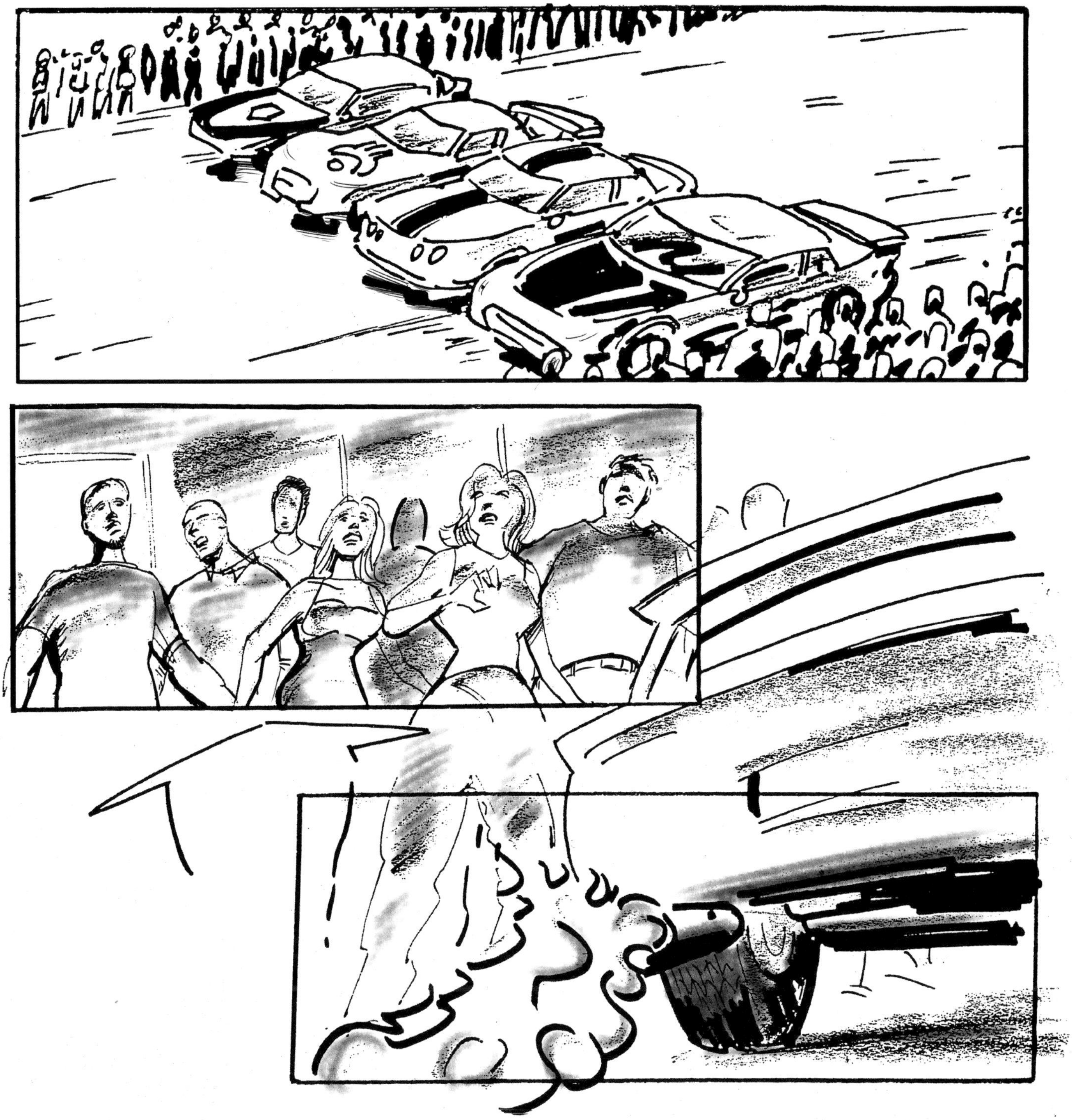

approval. This was during the time of pre-digital work on the Cintiq so everything was still drawn by hand with pencil and paper. Each frame of action was then hung on the walls to view and discuss the scenes ahead of production meetings. Panels would be cut out and moved around the wall as we figured out the order and flow of the shots.

The screenwriters, Derek Haas and Michael Brandt came down to Miami as the script was still being worked out and there were always rewrites. The big scene that I initially dived into was the first car race scene in the film. John and Terry worked out the action beats and I was given a massive shot list to work from. The car race scene took over a month to storyboard.

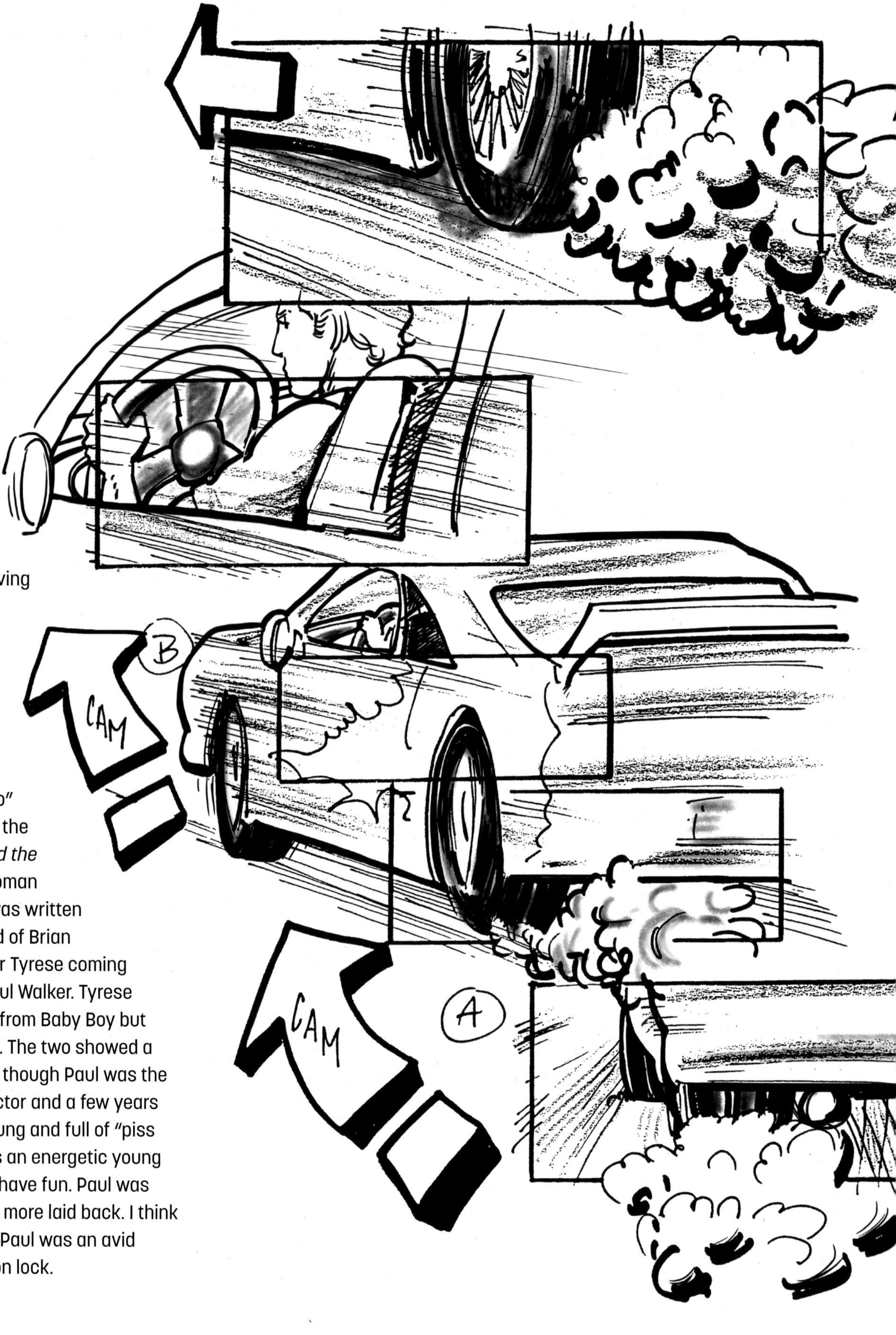

The actors were arriving to Miami as well. Paul Walker's "Brian O'Conner" character was supposed to be on the run due to him letting Vin Diesel's "Dom Torreto" go free at the end of the original, *The Fast and the Furious*. Tyrese's "Roman Pearce" character was written as a childhood friend of Brian O'Conner. I remember Tyrese coming by the office with Paul Walker. Tyrese knew me previously from Baby Boy but I had never met Paul. The two showed a natural kinship even though Paul was the more experienced actor and a few years older Tyrese was young and full of "piss and vinegar" He was an energetic young man who wanted to have fun. Paul was comparatively much more laid back. I think it's no accident that Paul was an avid surfer. He had chill on lock.

I will sometimes do a bird's eye view diagram so the director or DP knows where all of the elements are spatially. These diagrams are certainly great when directors and DPs give them to me.

I fondly remember a couple things that transpired in Miami with Paul. The first was that Paul volunteered to drive me in his demo-sports car on the test track. The actors all went to stunt driving school to prepare for the film and Paul was an old hand at it by this second movie. Like Paul Newman and Steve McQueen before him, Paul competed in car races in his personal life. With me in the backseat, Paul whipped around the test track. He aced every turn like a pro and I was flung from one side of the backseat to the other. It was glorious. In the movie when Brian O'Conner whips his car into a slide so that his face comes right up to the camera with a smile, that was all Paul's real skill as a driver. Another memorable time I had of Paul was when Brian McGee and I were having drinks in a restaurant as the De La Hoya versus Vargas fight was about to start. Paul walked in with John and Tyrese. Instead of sitting with his director and co-star, Paul sat with Brian and I to watch the fight. That's who Paul was. Paul Walker is dearly missed by all who knew him.

Brian and I were enjoying our stay at our hotel off the beach. I told him that we should go down to the beach to sit in the sun and work on storyboards. I figured we should live a little, if only in this modest way. A little later the two of us were sitting in our lounge chairs going over a scene when a beautiful young woman laid herself down on her towel five feet away. She took off her top fully bare-breasted and started her act of sunbathing. This seemed to happen frequently on South Beach. Minutes later, two male Europeans who had matching speedos, haircuts and nipple rings sat down with their towels right in front of us and totally destroyed our vibe of the bare-breasted woman. Brian and I took a last glance at the young woman as we walked back to the hotel.

I was having a great time on the movie. Brian and I worked our tails off and the bonded and had a great time hanging out every weekend. At the same time, while calling Betty and Joshua daily, I had to make calls to New York in helping to

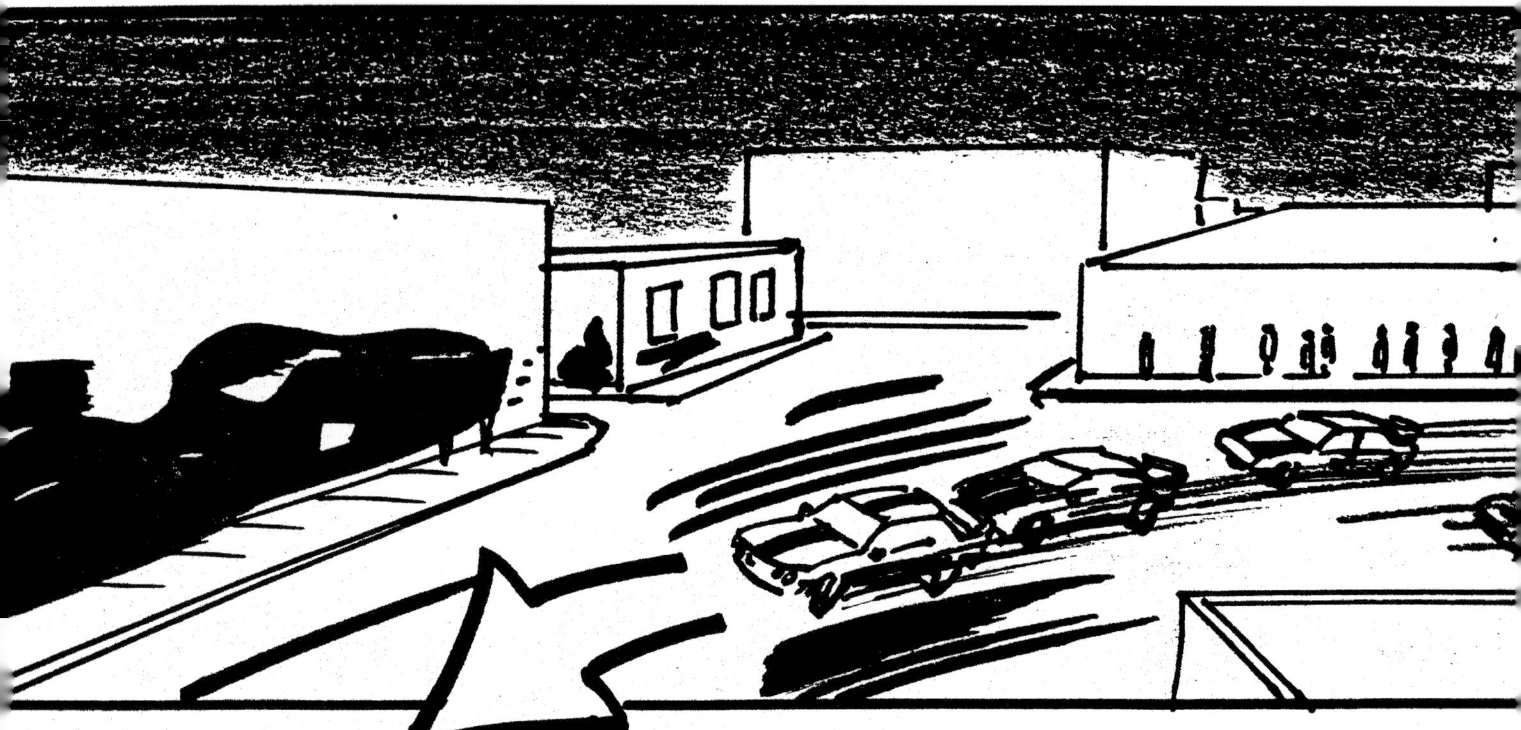

As a lot of the car shots were composites from being on a sound stage with the backgrounds added via green screen, a lot of the cars were drawn to pass very close to camera.

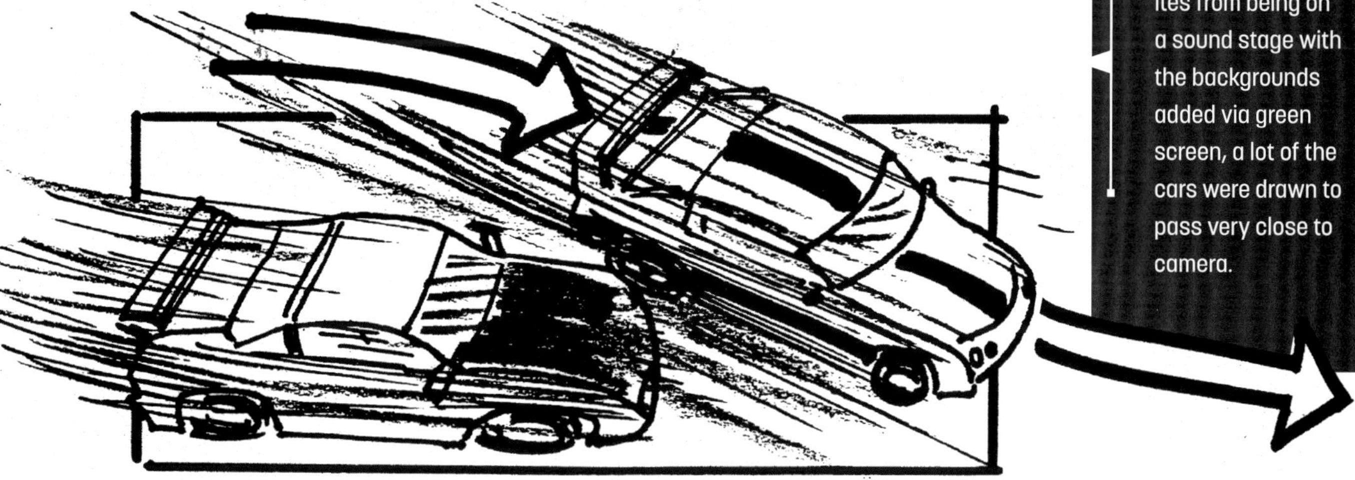

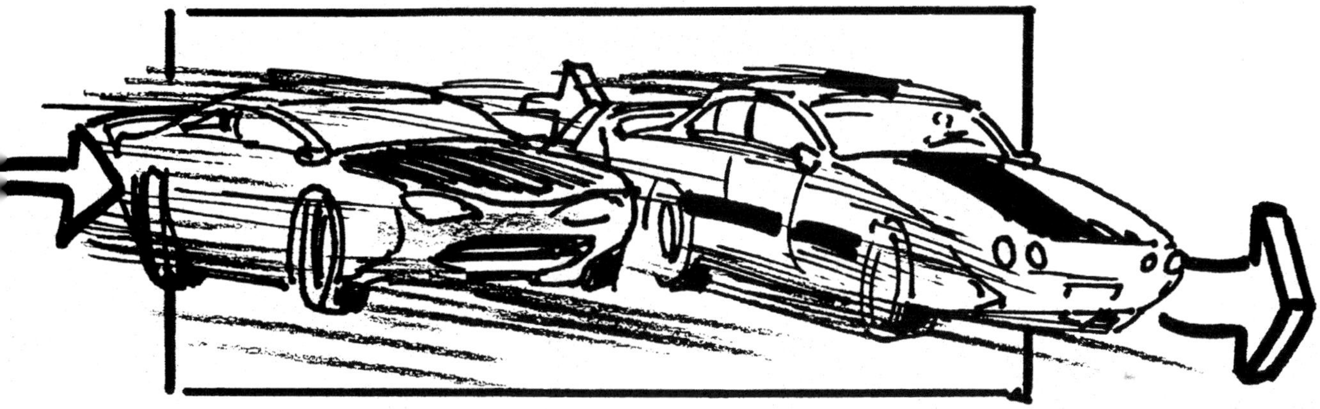

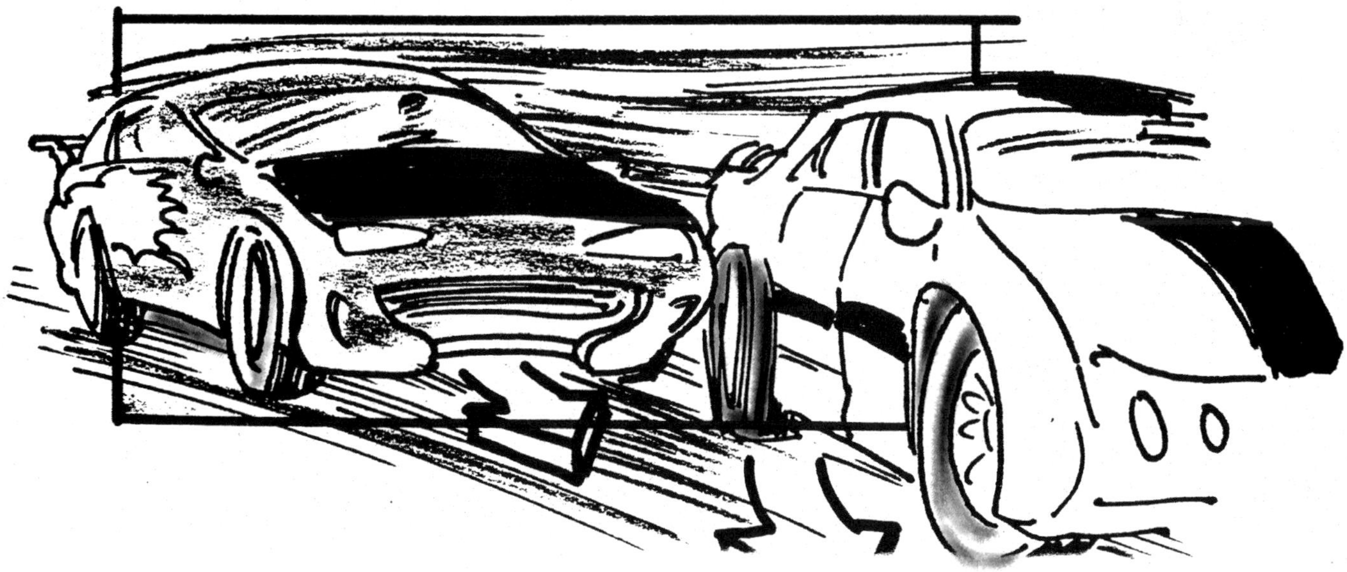

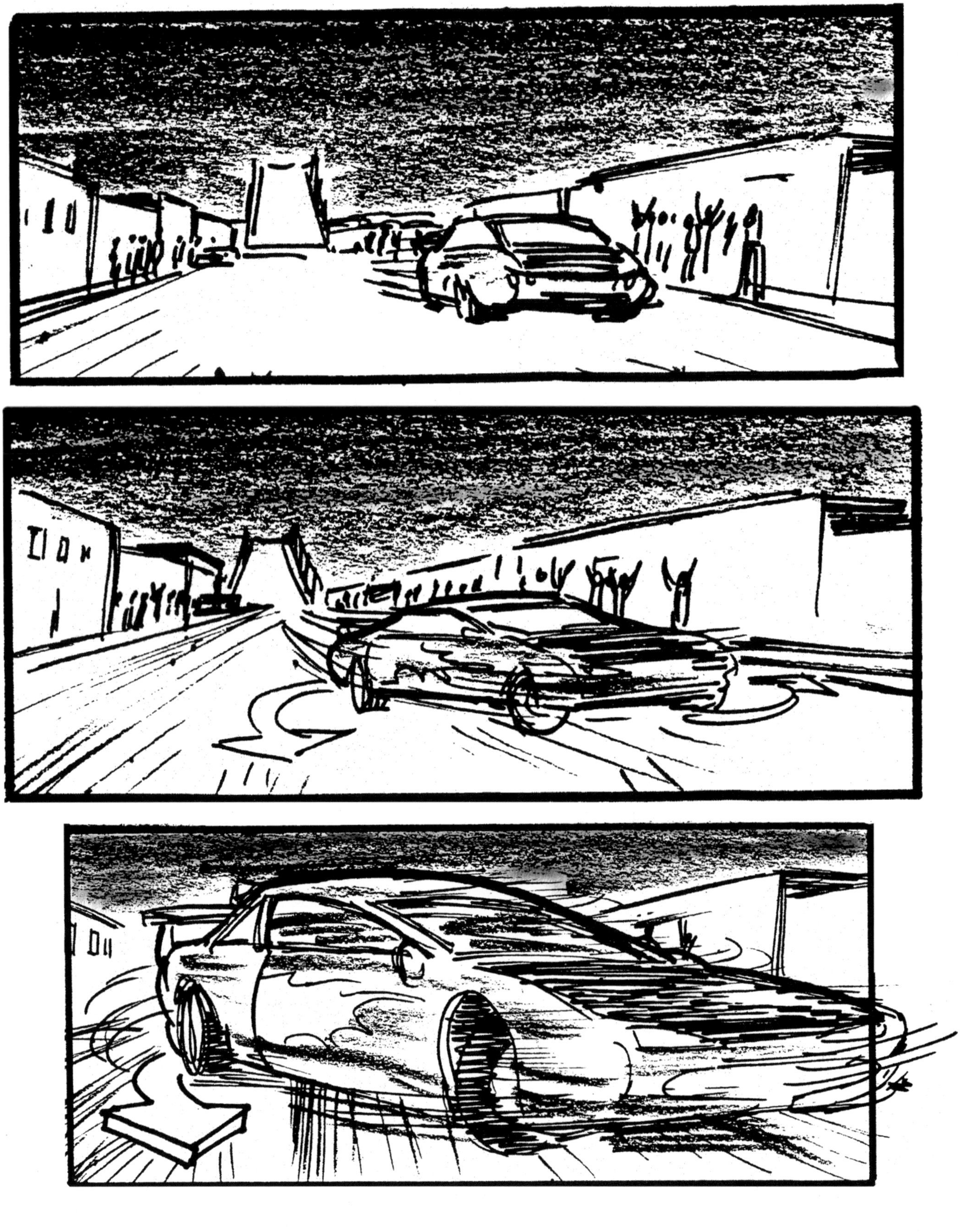

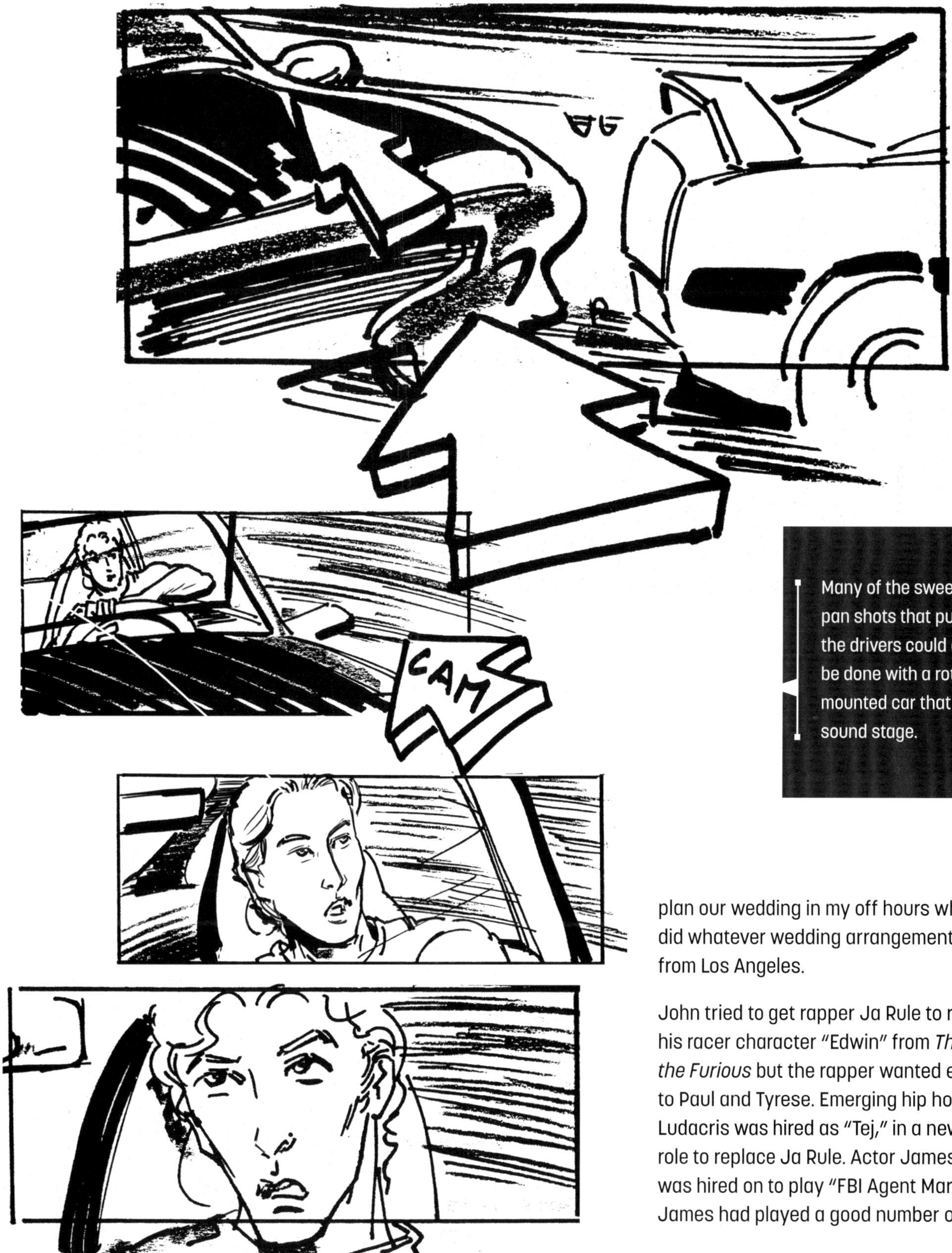

Many of the sweeping pan shots that push into the drivers could only be done with a rotating mounted car that is on a sound stage.

plan our wedding in my off hours while Betty did whatever wedding arrangements she could from Los Angeles.

John tried to get rapper Ja Rule to return as his racer character "Edwin" from *The Fast and the Furious* but the rapper wanted equal billing to Paul and Tyrese. Emerging hip hop star Ludacris was hired as "Tej," in a new character role to replace Ja Rule. Actor James Remar was hired on to play "FBI Agent Markham." James had played a good number of villains

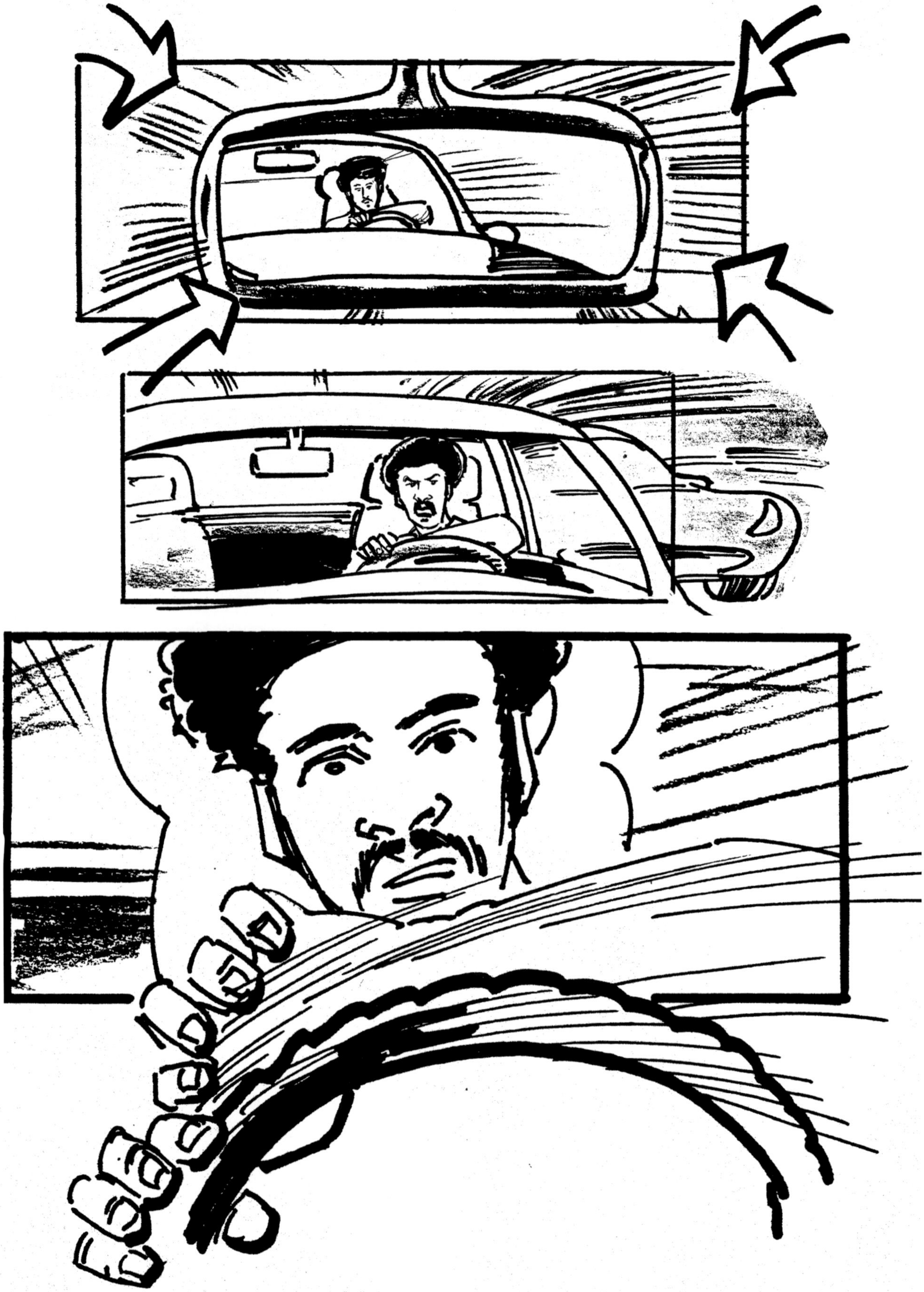

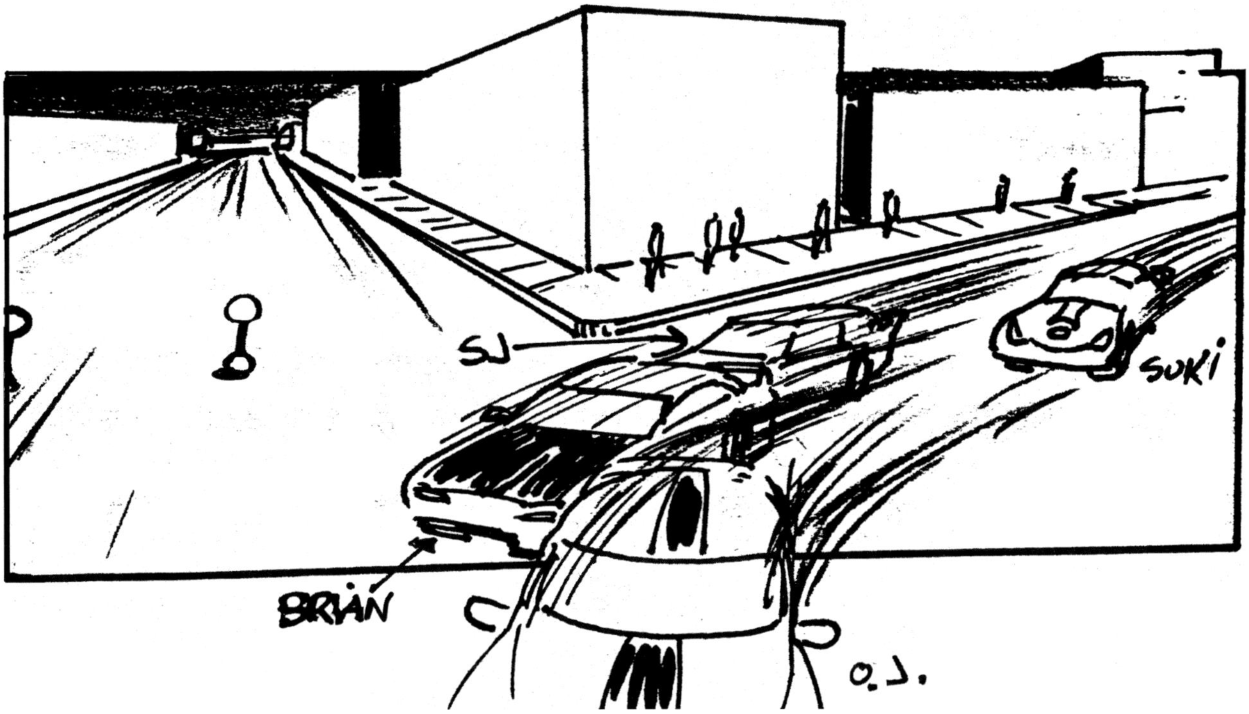

such as "Ganz" in *48 HRS.*, but had played varied roles later in his career. Because I was a fan and as he was older than me, I respectfully called him "Mr. Remar" when we met. He instantly said, "Call me James." To this day, James is one of several people from that film with whom I am still friends. Terry Leonard was grateful that my referral of him to John had gotten him the gig. I said it was only a form of reciprocity because he had hired me years earlier on *Die Hard with a Vengeance*. Terry never allowed me pay for a meal at anytime that I was with him in Miami.

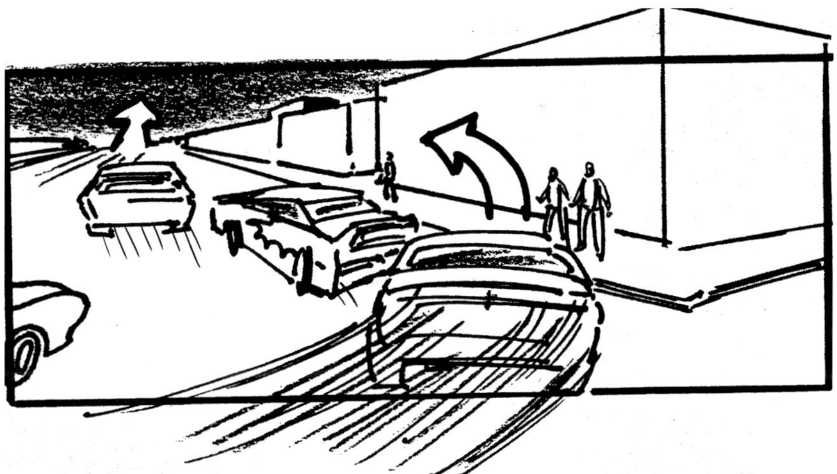

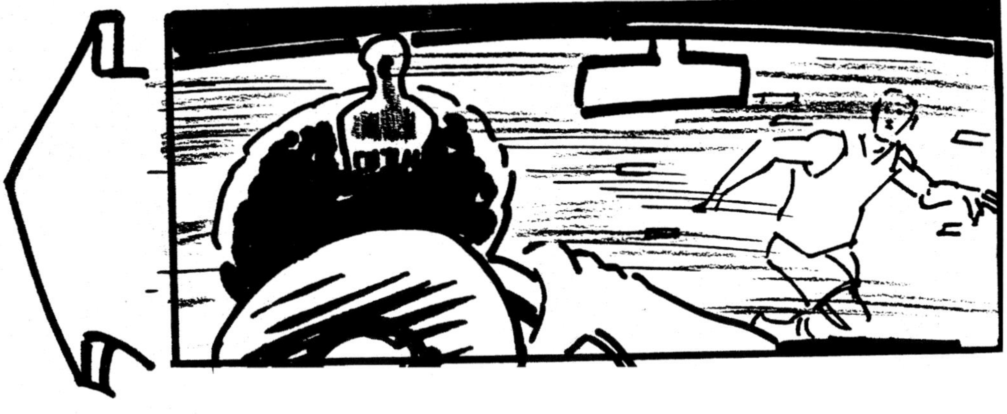

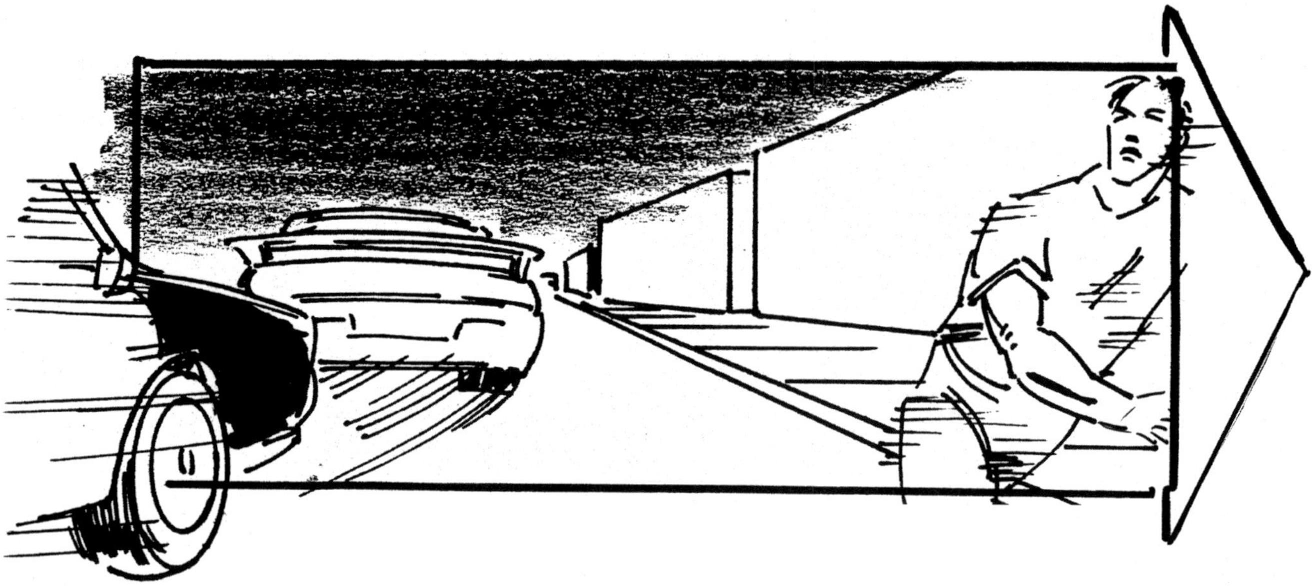

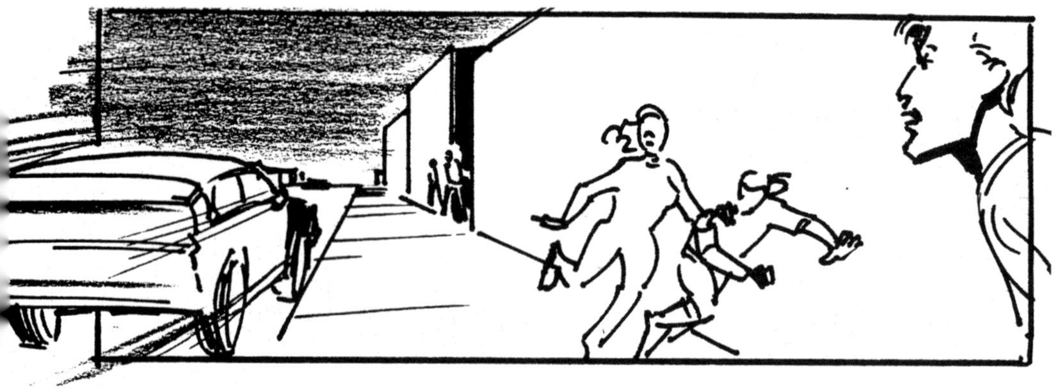

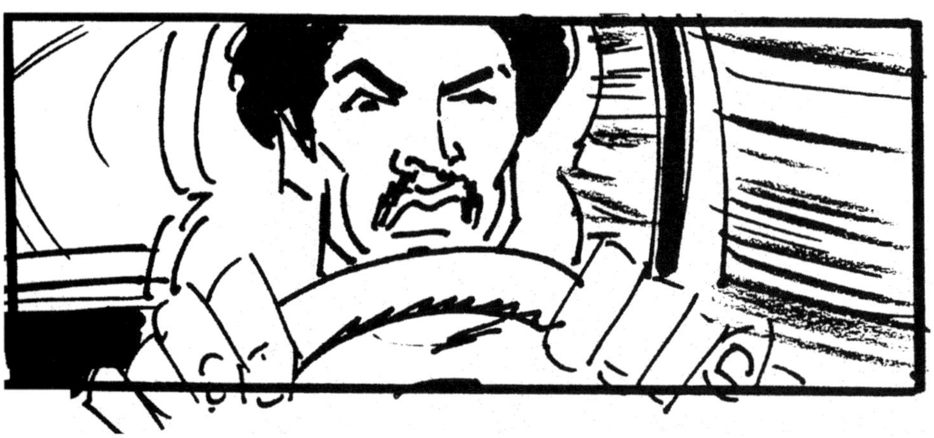

On *2 Fast 2 Furious*, the first storyboard period was rough. Brian and I were putting in long hours as the sequences were being refined. We pushed each other to do our very best. As storyboard artists we all have our strengths. I couldn't render the way Brian could but I had the superior storytelling skills. After several weeks, there came a time that I knew he was "there" as a storyboard artist. One day I had Brian bow his head and I lightly "crowned" him with a pencil. I told him that he was no longer my "padawan" and that he was a full-blown Jedi storyboard artist in his own right. It's this type of geeky fun that keeps the energy of production offices buoyant when there are plenty of stressful situations at any often and unpredictable time.

The stunt legend Terry Leonard directed the 2nd Unit photography of the car races. Terry knows cars as well as he does horses.

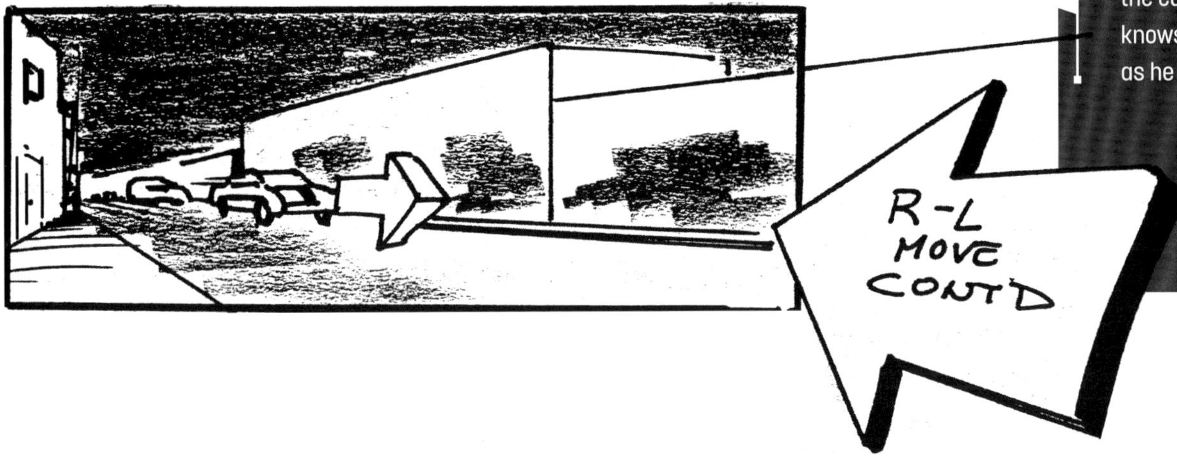

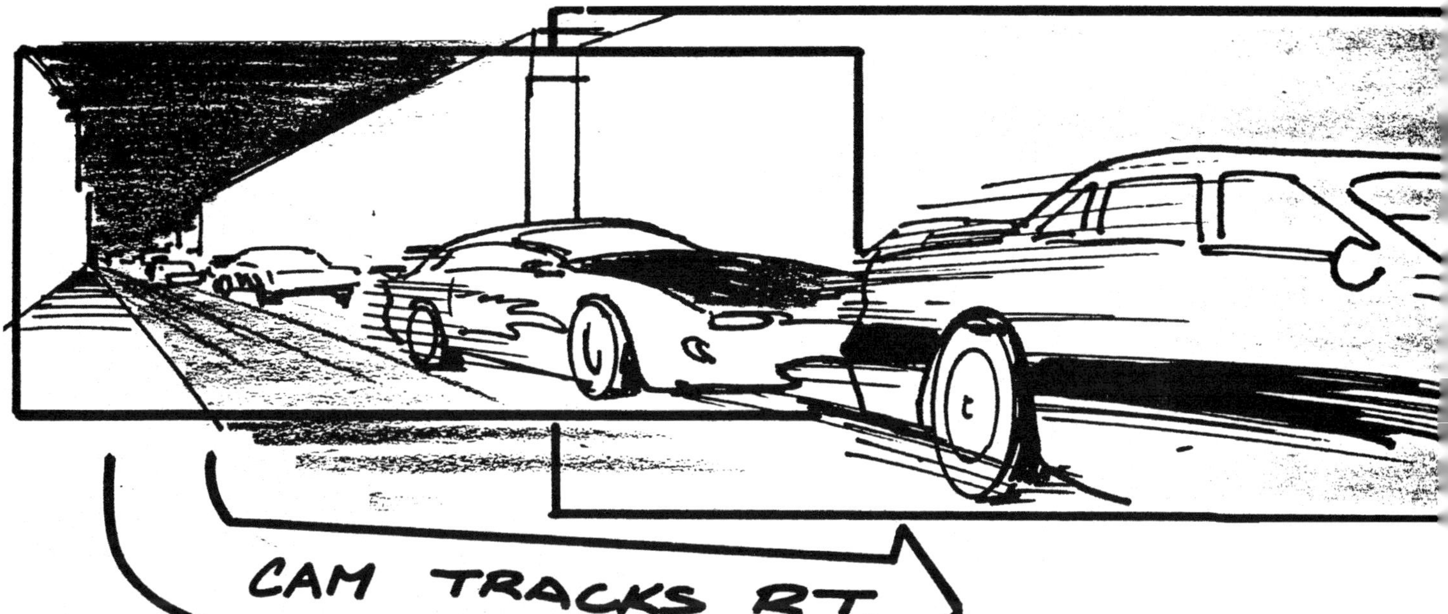

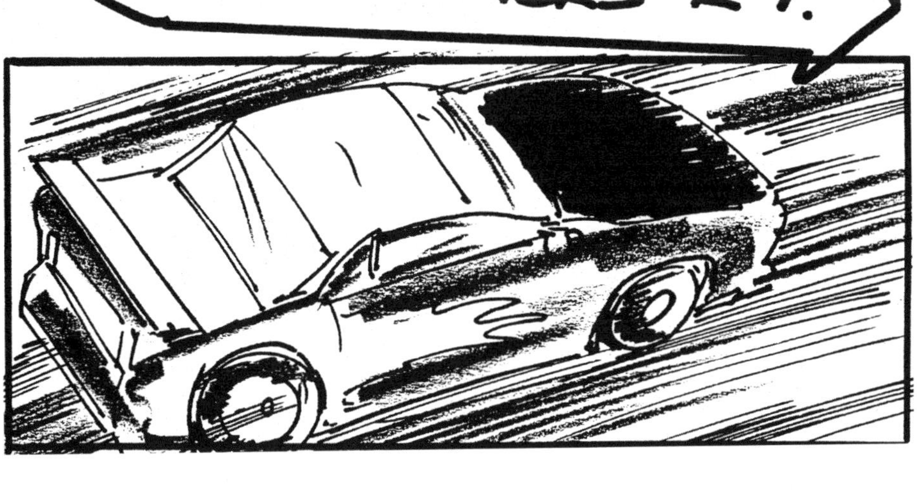

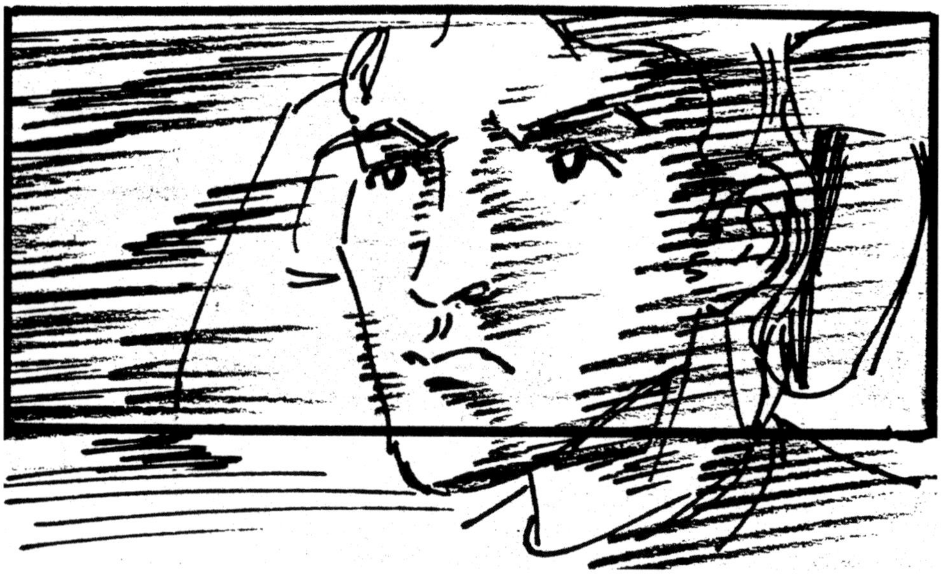

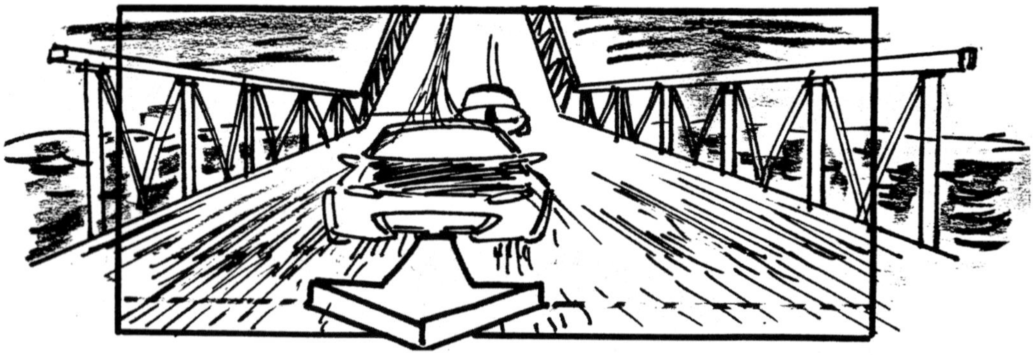

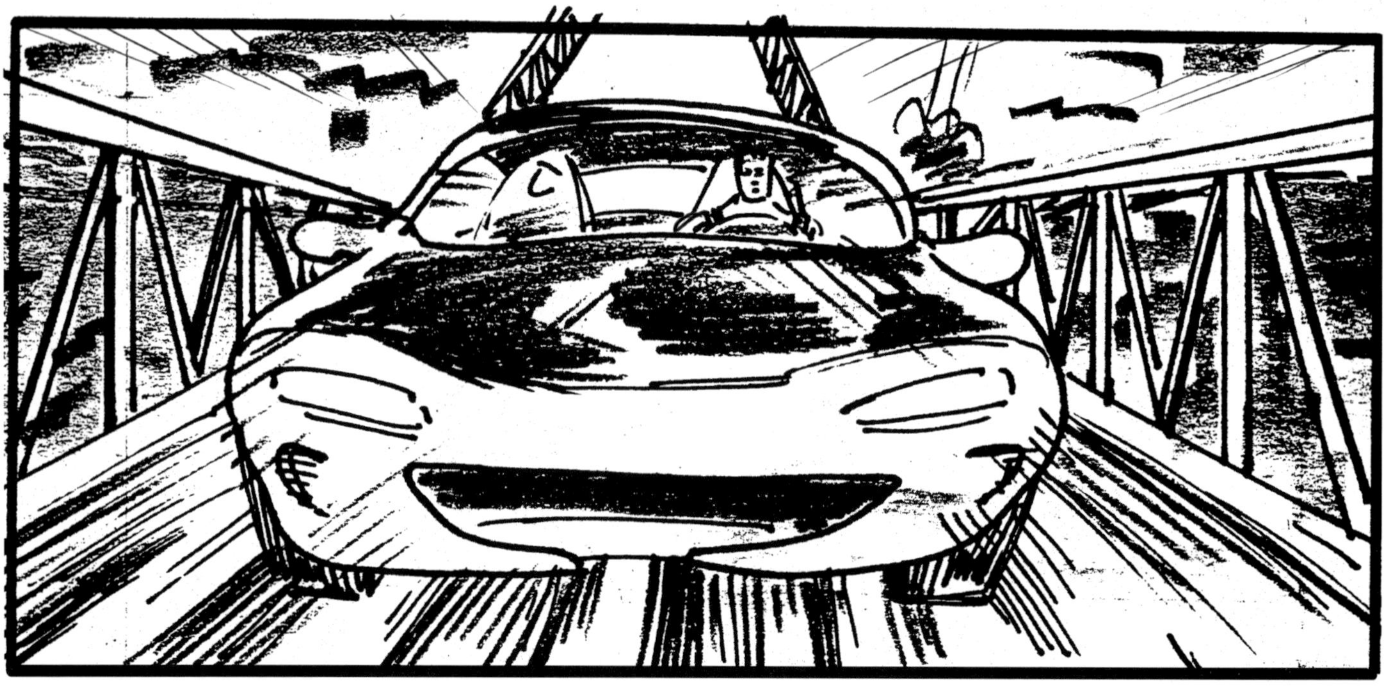

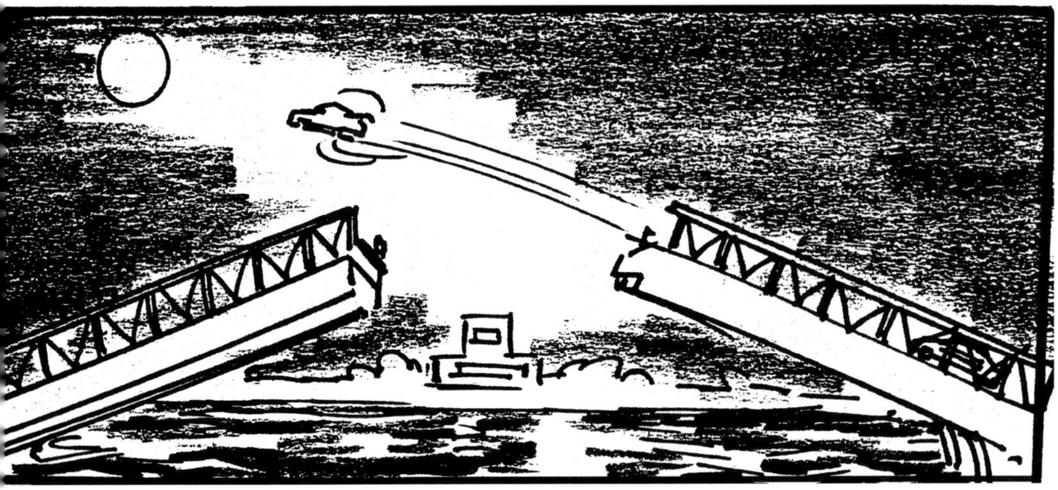

The bridge jump was fun to draw, via John's shot-list and amazing to see fulfilled on a big screen. Of course a lot of VFX was involved.

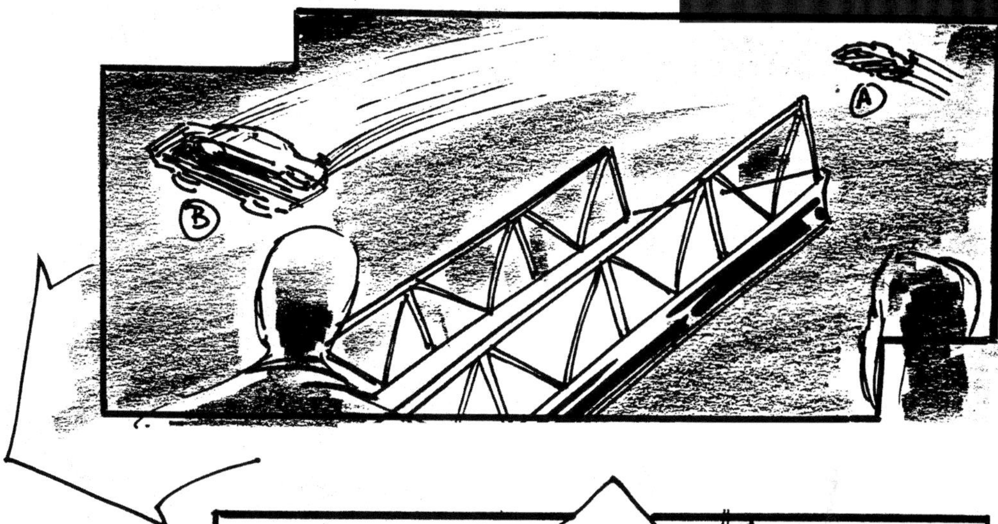

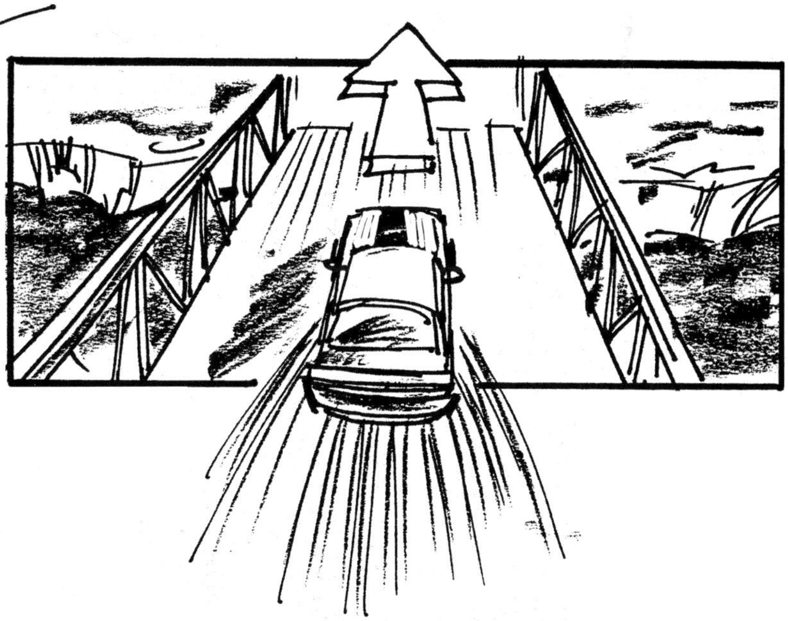

After a period of daily grinding on the film, things slowed down. Brian and I were able to throttle down on our workload and have time at the end of the day to relax into fun things like barbecues, pool parties, and boat rides.

John brought Brian and myself in to watch the dailies whenever we had time. It's a fascinating process to watch the raw footage of scenes before they are assembled and cut down. John's longtime editor, Bruce Cannon had the job of making the selected takes work seamlessly with the element of cinematic storytelling.

After more than two months in Miami, my time was wrapping up. I was getting married with a wedding at my childhood church in Queens, New York. Brian was going to have to handle everything as I was headed back to Los Angeles and then on to New York. Weeks later after being a newly married man, I was at the gym in Los Angeles when I got a call from the *2 Fast 2 Furious* unit production manager, Terry Miller asking if I could come back to Miami for two weeks.

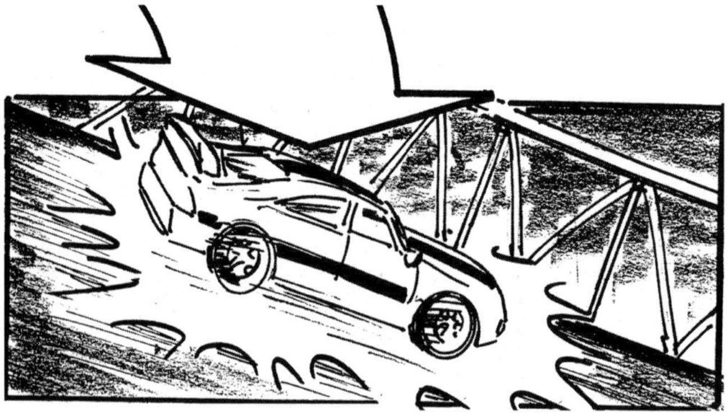

The ending was still being worked out and they needed my experience. I was, of course, elated. I hadn't been working since I had gotten back to LA and I was restless. My pride in my work ethic set in again and I felt that since I started the movie, I wanted to end it. I was back in Miami the next day or so and back in action. It was the final round up to work with John, Terry, Brian, and the crew.

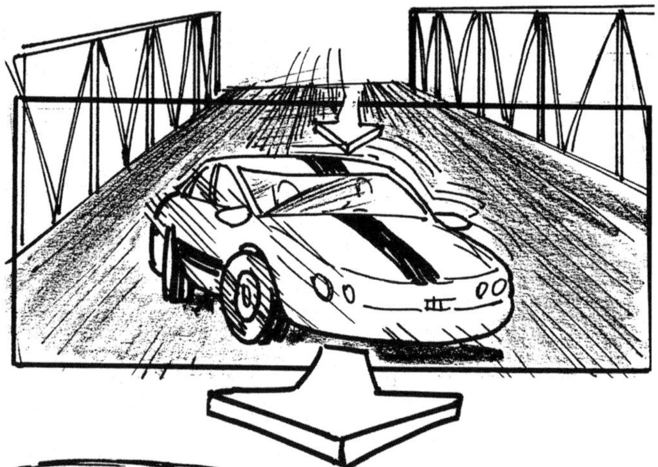

A touching story that Terry Leonard told me after John's passing was that when they started working together on the film, John said, "You're going to be my Mickey Moore." Michael "Mickey" Moore was a legendary second unit director who directed the stunt-oriented truck chase shots in *Raiders of the Lost*

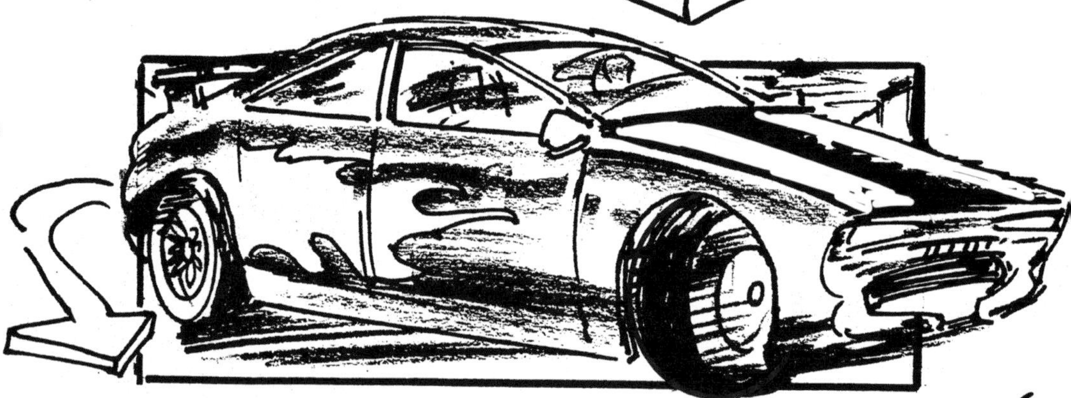

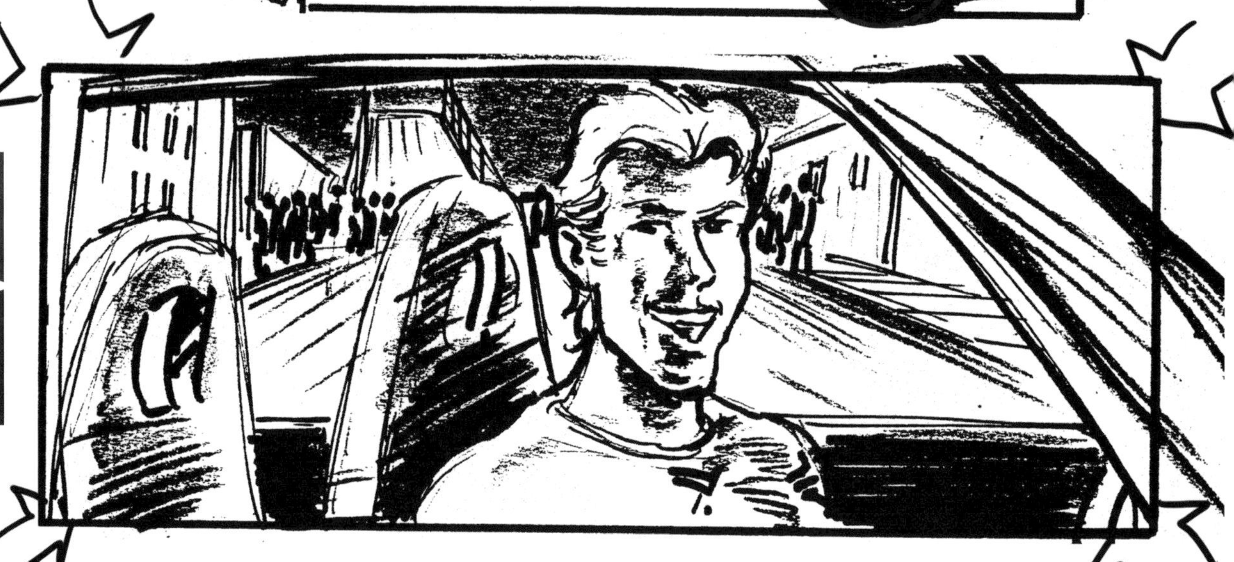

Paul Walker performed the car slide into camera for real.

Ark. When someone says "you're my so-and-so" in movie relationships when referring to a legend, it's a badge of honor. At the end of the shoot, Terry had directed a terrific stunt of Paul and Tyrese's characters making a high-speed jump and crash onto a mockup of the villain's boat. Terry told me that when the shot was done, John approached him as Terry was overseeing the stunt on a scaffold. John told Terry, "You're not my Mickey Moore, you're my Terry Leonard." Terry said those words almost brought him to tears—and Terry is one of the toughest people I know. Lightning is afraid to strike Terry! That's the effect that John could have on people. He was authentic in his love and respect for his friends and colleagues.

The next year, I took Betty to our *2 Fast 2 Furious* premiere at Universal. It was a huge event and I was able to introduce her to Paul Walker, who was as cordial as ever even at the film opening red carpet event. I think about that time now and remember the lovely human being we lost. On a happier note, 2 Fast writers Derek Haas and Michael Brant later created the *Chicago PD, Chicago Fire, Chicago Med* television universe. Under Neal Moritz, *The Fast & The Furious* became a global franchise.

In February of 2023, I was part of an after-screening Q&A panel celebrating *2 Fast 2 Furious*. John's alma mater, University of Southern California (USC) was presenting a showing of John's films in chronological order of release. The event was held at the Museum of the Academy of Motion Pictures Arts & Sciences in the David Geffen Theater. I was joined on stage by Greg Hedgepath and Bobbi Banks, John's long time supervising sound editor and supervising ADR editor respectively. Also in attendance was Derek Haas, the co-writer of the film and Tyrese, who stole the show on his sheer charisma. The panel's emotions ran from tears to laughter, telling fond stories on how John either began or impacted our careers. I was amazed in how much Tyrese had grown as a man. He was still full of fun, but he was now also a man of God who eloquently spoke about our dear departed brother, John. The years had added great maturity and wisdom to Tyrese, some of which I had seen when he spoke at John's funeral. This night was special, as it was all love between the large audience and the panelists.

When I was a college student at the School of Visual Arts, director Peter Hyams was a guest at the school and made a presentation on his upcoming film, *Outland*. At about nineteen years of age, I enthusiastically I went up to Mr. Hyams after his panel, and asked "How do you become a screenwriter?" Hyams calmly said "by *writing*." After the 2 Fast 2 Furious panel, I now found myself as the seasoned veteran among college kids who were now looking to me for sage advice. I now offer the same moments of consideration to young artists that Peter Hyams, James Cameron and Steven Spielberg graciously showed me in my fan moments when I met them at events.

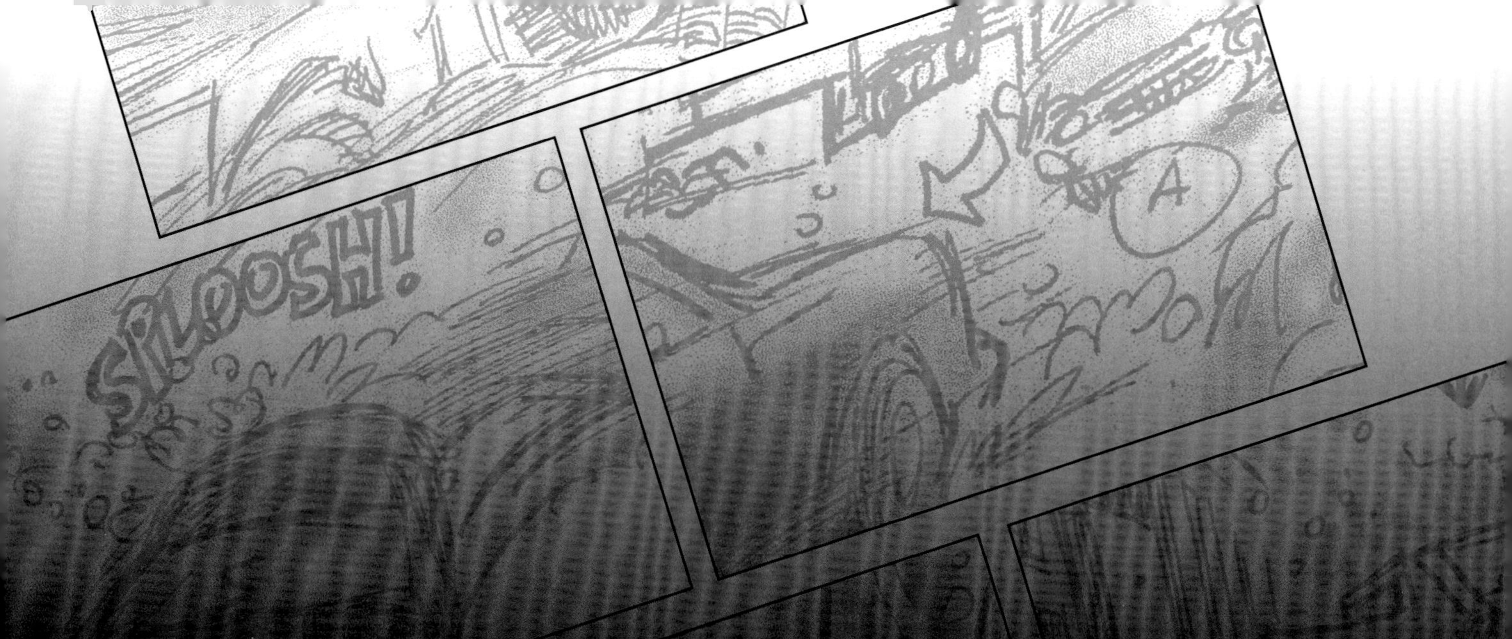

STORYBOARDS AND STORIES OF 15 SELECT FILMS AND TELEVISION SHOWS

HARD DAY'S WORK

Chapter 10

FOUR BROTHERS

CARS, GAMES AND THE DOUBLE DIP

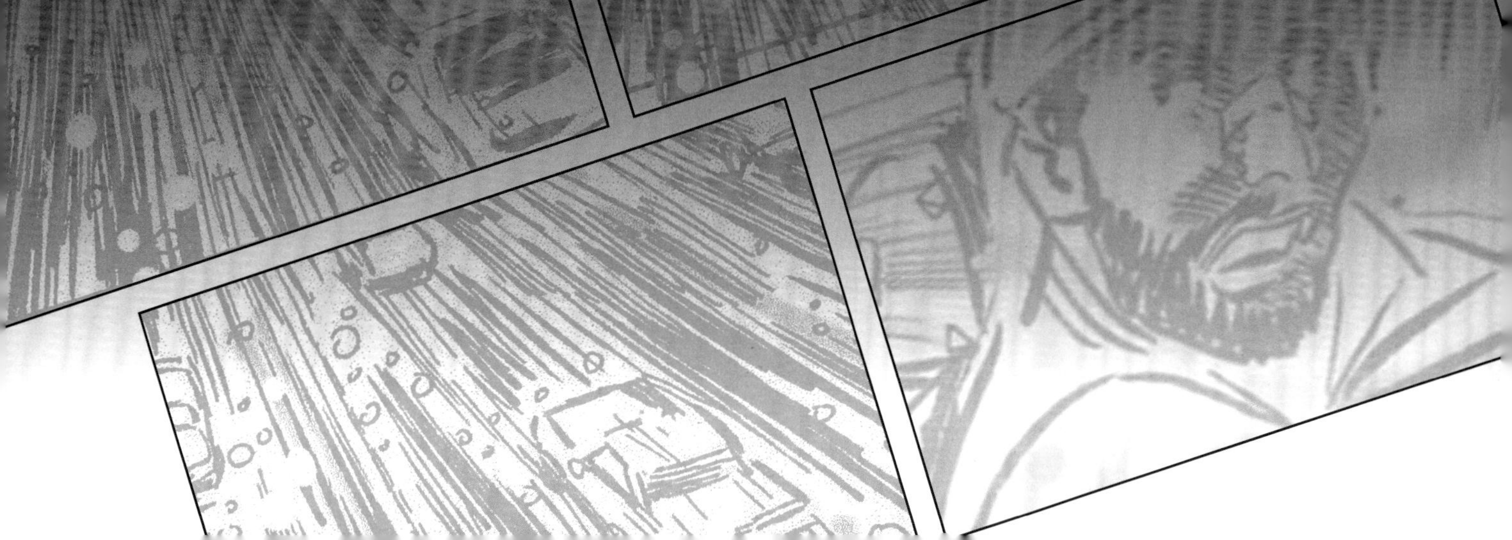

Four Brothers... cars, games and the double dip

A year after *2 Fast 2 Furious* was released, John was hired on to another studio assignment on a project called *Four Brothers*. This film told the story of four foster brothers who shared the last name of Mercer and banded together in their adulthood to reap vengeance for the murder of their foster mother. When I heard the concept my mind immediately went to the John Wayne/Dean Martin western vehicle, *The Sons of Katie Elder* that had the same premise but the sons in that film's storyline were biological brothers, not foster brothers. There are really no new ideas in film, but old ideas can always be reworked with new aspects for a new audience. John cast Tyrese in a role of one foster brother but the lead of the film would be Mark Wahlberg.

Unlike my last three films with John, the movie was going to be shot mostly in Toronto, Canada that stood in place for areas of Detroit, Michigan. Canadian film rules necessitated that most of the crew on location had to be Canadian hires, so I couldn't join the crew on location. John was limited to bringing his own crew hires of DP, production designer, and stunt coordinator. I storyboarded about half of the film from my home office in Los Angeles. John had his shot list typed up by his new assistant, Sueann Han. I was ready to get to work. John wanted to start with the very beginning of the film, which was the buildup to the mother's murder. He had me draw an interior of the car that the two killers drove with their motif dice hanging from their rearview mirror. That was the first image he wanted to establish as well as Marvin Gaye's "Trouble Man" the song playing over the scene. The scene was all about establishing the tone of the movie.

The set piece of the film was a car chase with Mercer brothers going after their mother's assassins. The scene starts in a casino and continues into a snowy nocturnal evening as the brothers frantically pursue the killers. Undeterred, the Mercers quickly follow in their car in a rapid chase. What would set this chase apart was that it would be happening during a full blizzard. John was proud that this unique angle to a car chase had never been done before.

The *Four Brothers* tent pole car chase scene was very elaborate. As usual, John had each shot planned out very detailed and with clear specifics. With me, however, he could mention shots in visual shortcut ways that I would instantly understand and deliver the images in the storyboards. There is a moving shot that starts on the Mercer brothers' vehicle and booms up into a high and wide angle with snow in the foreground. That particular shot was a borrowed shot from the Death Star battle at the end of *Star Wars*. John knew how to place creative homages in his shots that never directly looked like the original shot.

John had specific moves in choreography that he had mapped out. There were more exterior car shots in this film than there were in the car chase scene in *Shaft* and I was thankful for that because exterior images were visually more impactful. I wanted to recreate the inspirational classic car chases of *Bullitt* and *The Seven Ups* in the snow. It was important to establish some visual location geography for the audience as I created the storyboards for this film. I added a tasteful use of my comic book flair in the execution of the storyboards with my marker stokes because this was still in my days of using paper and markers. The second unit director was Doug Coleman, who I had worked with on *The Devil's Own*. Doug directed the shots so closely based on my

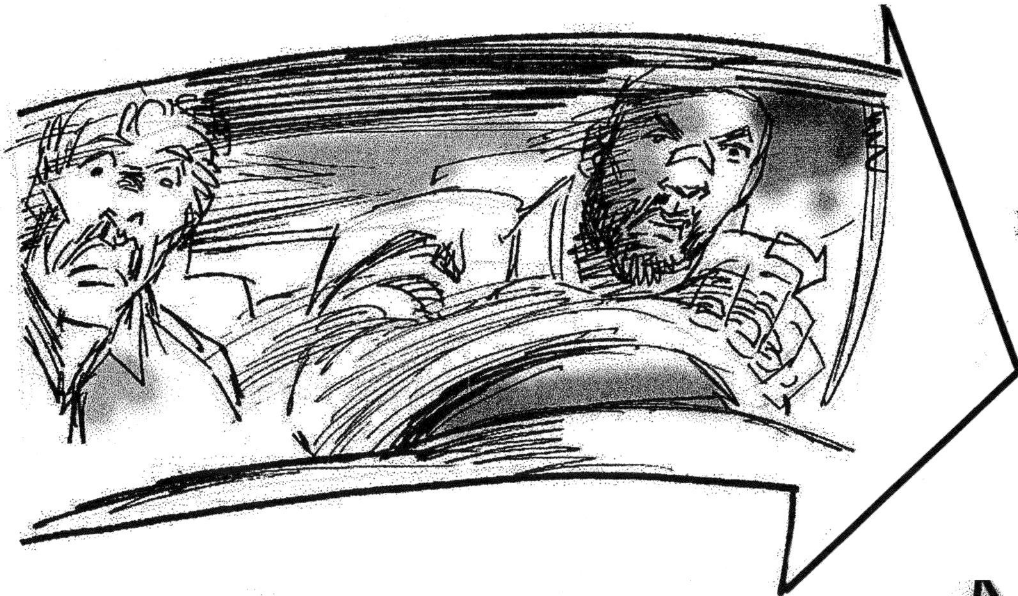

INT: SHOOTERS

DRIVER SWERVES RT

These *Four Brothers* story-boards were scanned from photocopies

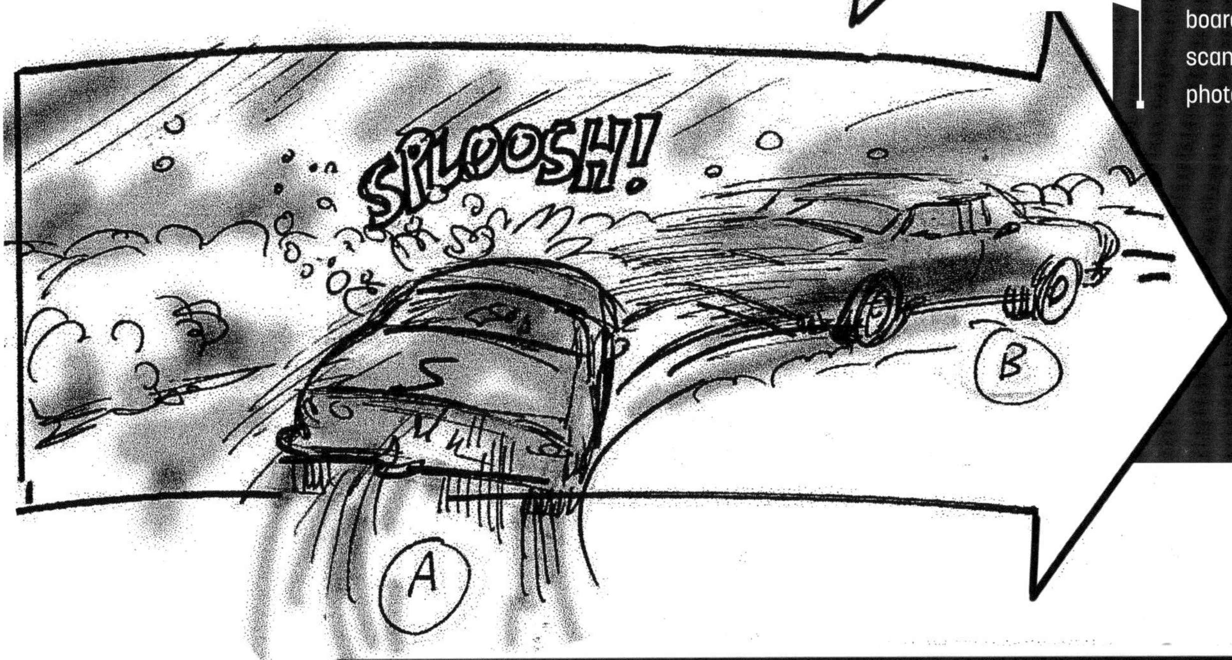

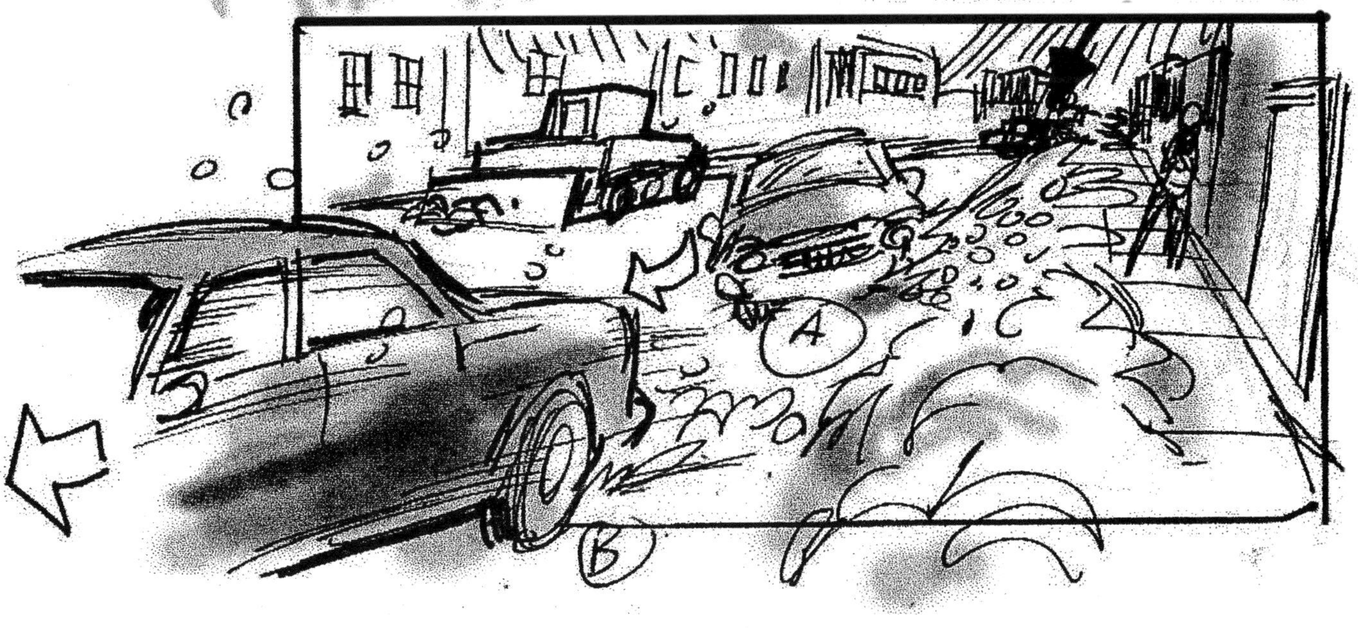

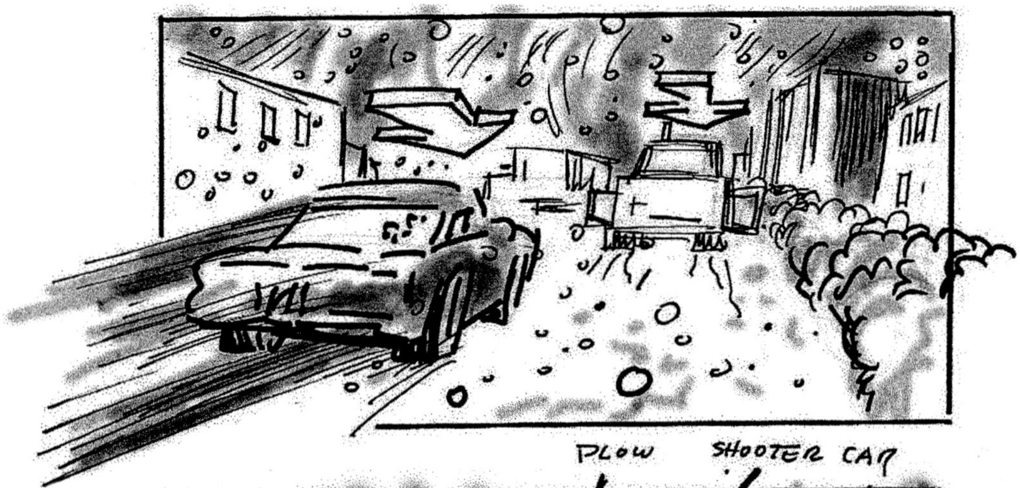

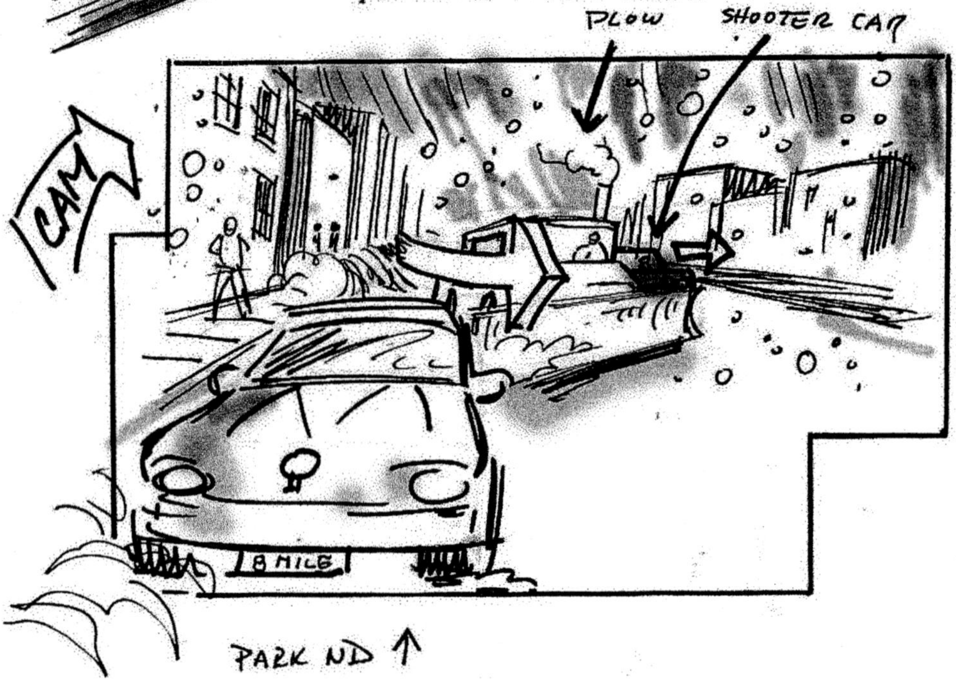
PLOW
SHOOTER CAR
CAM
8 MILE
PARK ND

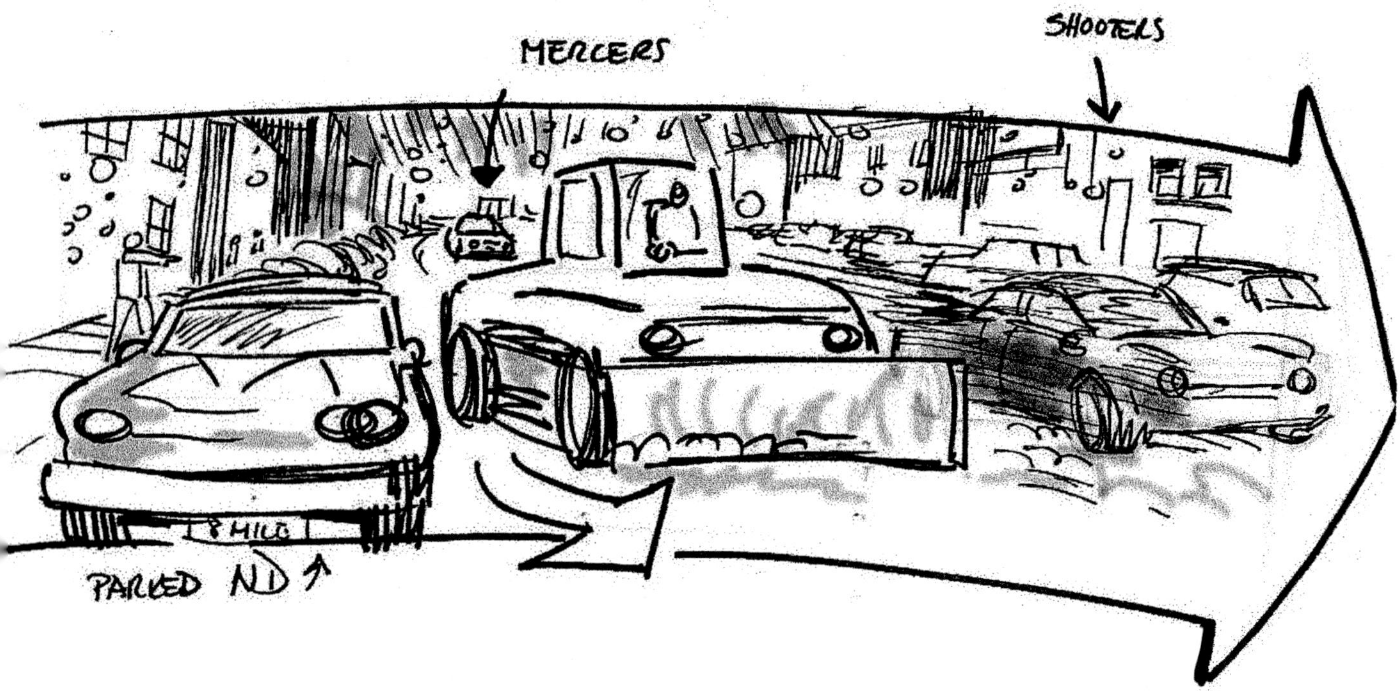
MERCERS
SHOOTERS
8 MILE
PARKED ND

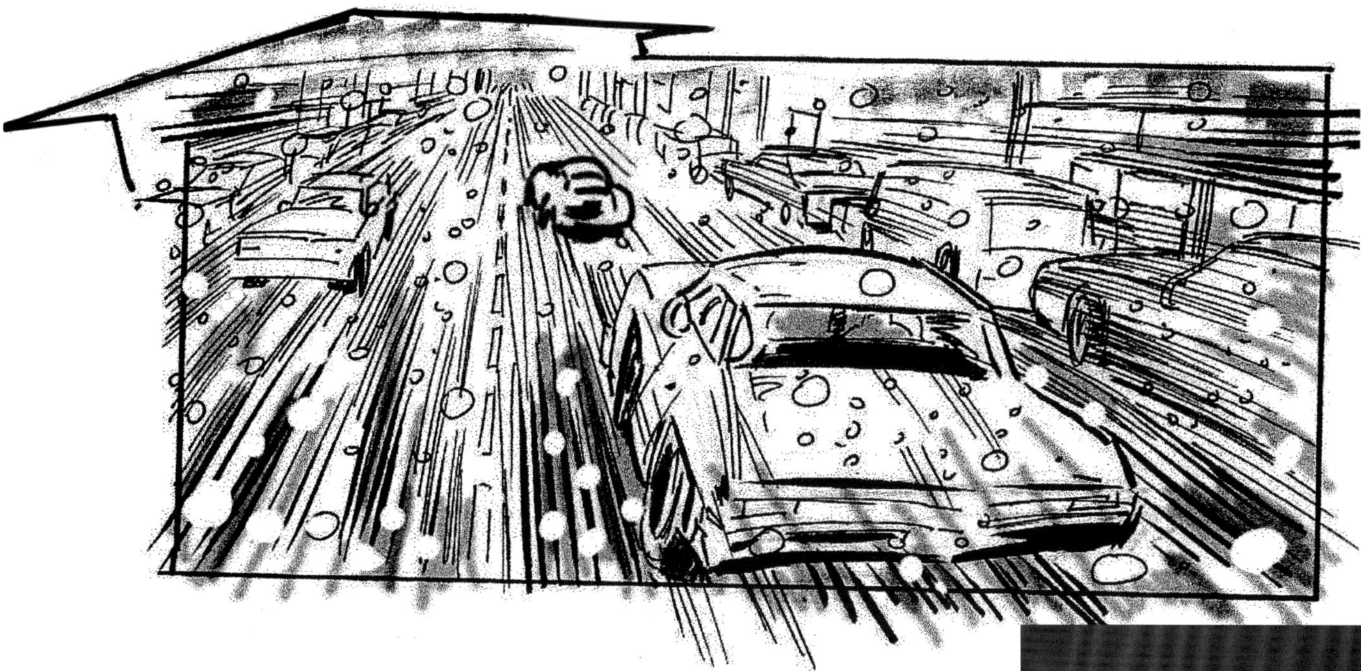

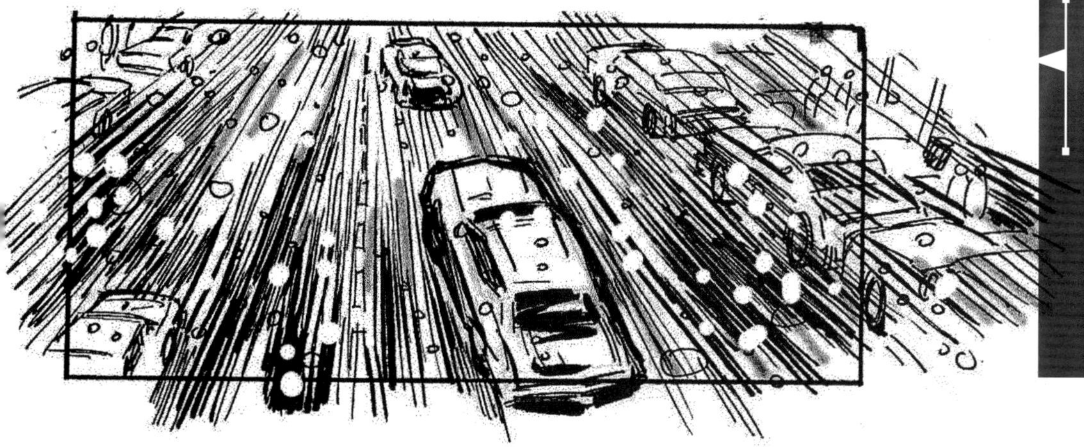

John Singleton explained this rising shot above the Mercer brothers car with calling out a shot in the Death Star sequence of *Star Wars* where the camera follows a Tie Fighter as it pursues and X-Wing above the surface of the battle station.

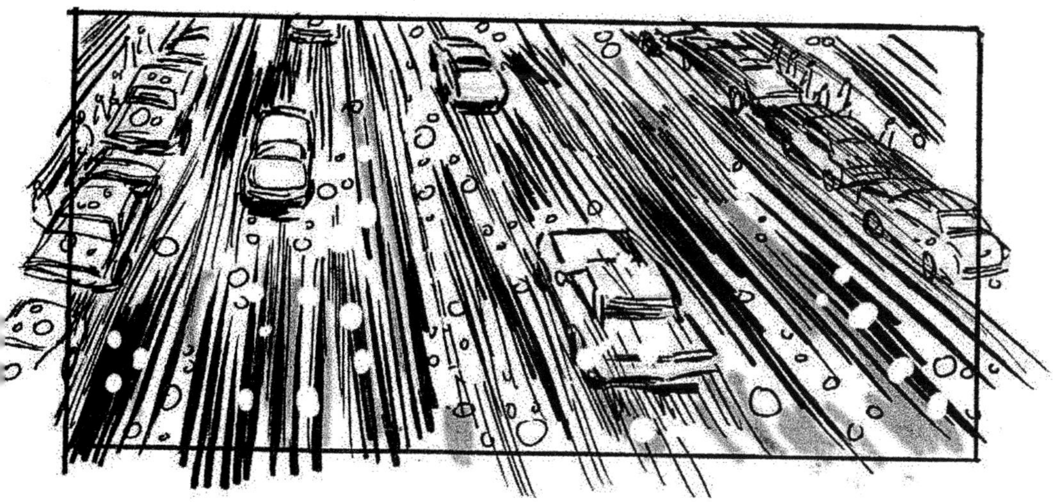

work, that the details of the scene in the final cut of the movie reflects the story-boards I created based on John's shot list.

During preproduction, John also had me work on storyboards for a video game collaboration with Snoop Dogg called *Fear & Respect*. To work the video game into my schedule, I would work on the *Four Brothers* boards during the day hours

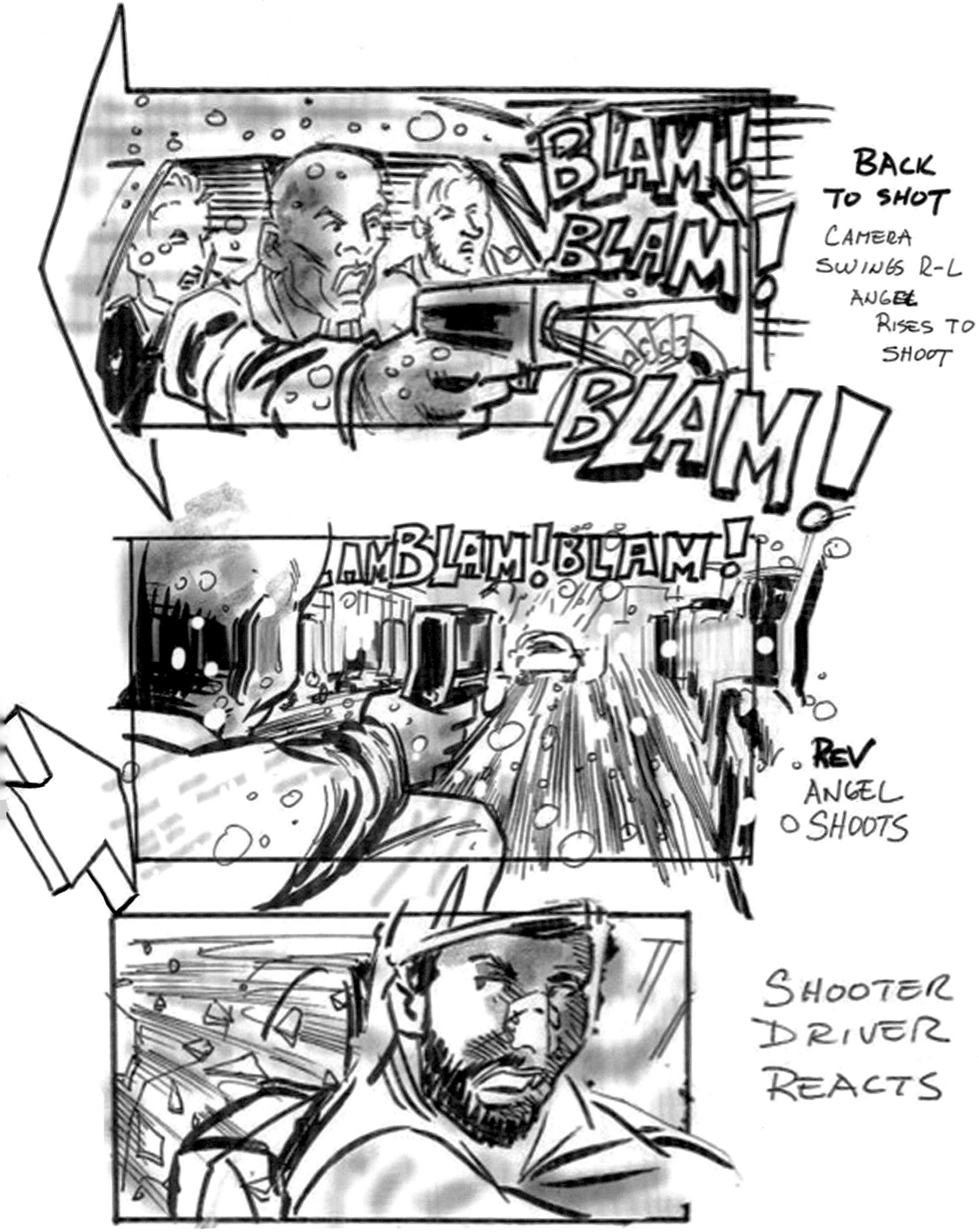
BLAM! BLAM!
BACK TO SHOT
CAMERA SWINGS R-L
ANGEL RISES TO SHOOT
BLAM!
BLAM! BLAM!
REV
ANGEL SHOOTS
SHOOTER
DRIVER
REACTS

and then storyboard for the video game at night. This is what is called "double-dipping" — when artists work on two projects at once. A lot of storyboard artists have to do this, occasionally. John gave me a shot list for the video game and I went to work. I had a bit of freedom to do some things and John was pleased with what I was creating. There was no way I could do all of the full boards on *Fear & Respect* simultaneously while working on *Four Brothers*, so I laid the boards out and had new-to-the-game storyboard artist Todd Harris do tighter pencils on a lot of them. When an artist double-dips, it's quite hard to maintain the quality and quantity of the work over a prolonged period of time without someone to assist.

John took me to Paris with him on a business trip for the video game meeting to meet the people of Ubisoft Entertainment, one of the biggest gaming companies in the world. It was a quick trip of a couple of days but we had a great meeting and I was able to contribute some ideas about video game and how it could work as a more entertaining entity. Being in Paris for the first time was amazing and as a tourist I took in a few sites on our limited time there. John and I met up with his friend and former Miss France, Sonia Rolland as well as another colleague, French storyboard and concept artist, Sylvain Despretz who was Ridley Scott's go-to artist. Sylvain is also amazingly talented and loved meeting John. I had long wanted to meet Sylvain. He was Black and French and my wife was working on a *Savoy* magazine article on Black storyboard artists and wanted to include him in the article which did not materialize because the he lived in France. The company that was eventually interested in John's game idea was Midway Games, but that too, never materialized. Midway had a regime change and F*ear & Respect* was never released. John and Snoop did present some video game footage at the 2004 Spike Video Game Awards show.

While on the movie, Mark Wahlberg came by the office wearing a Red Sox hat. The Yankees had crushed the hopes of the Red Sox in 2003 in the championship with a series ending homerun by Aaron Boone, but the Sox got revenge in 2004 with an epic come-from-behind win when the Yankees choked up a three-games-to-none lead. As a self-respecting New Yorker and Yankees fan, I couldn't not give Wahlberg some ribbing. He took it well and said what happened in the future between the clubs didn't matter.

The Red Sox finally won a title. Yea. Whatever, Mark Wahlberg. Whatever. It's a Yankees world and you're just in it, man.

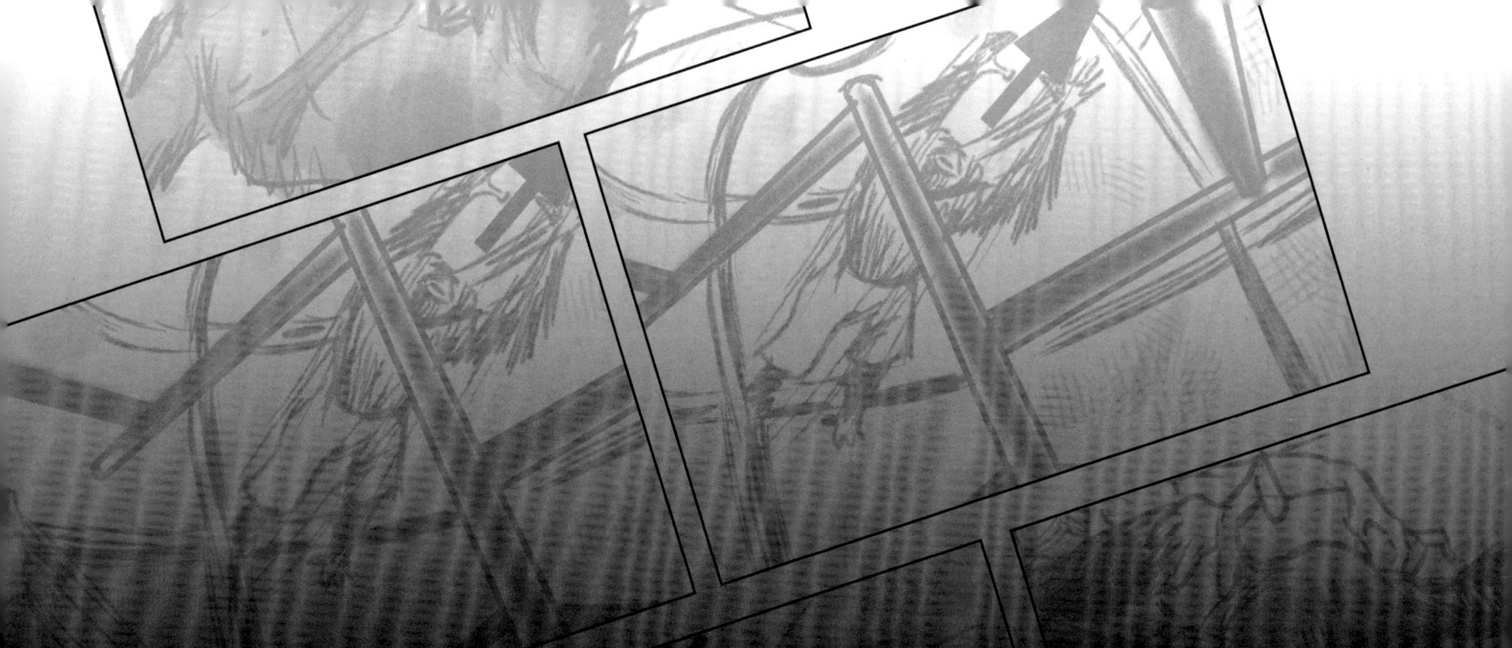

STORYBOARDS AND STORIES OF 15 SELECT FILMS AND TELEVISION SHOWS

HARD DAY'S WORK

Chapter 11

RISE OF THE PLANET OF THE APES

MY NEW LEVEL

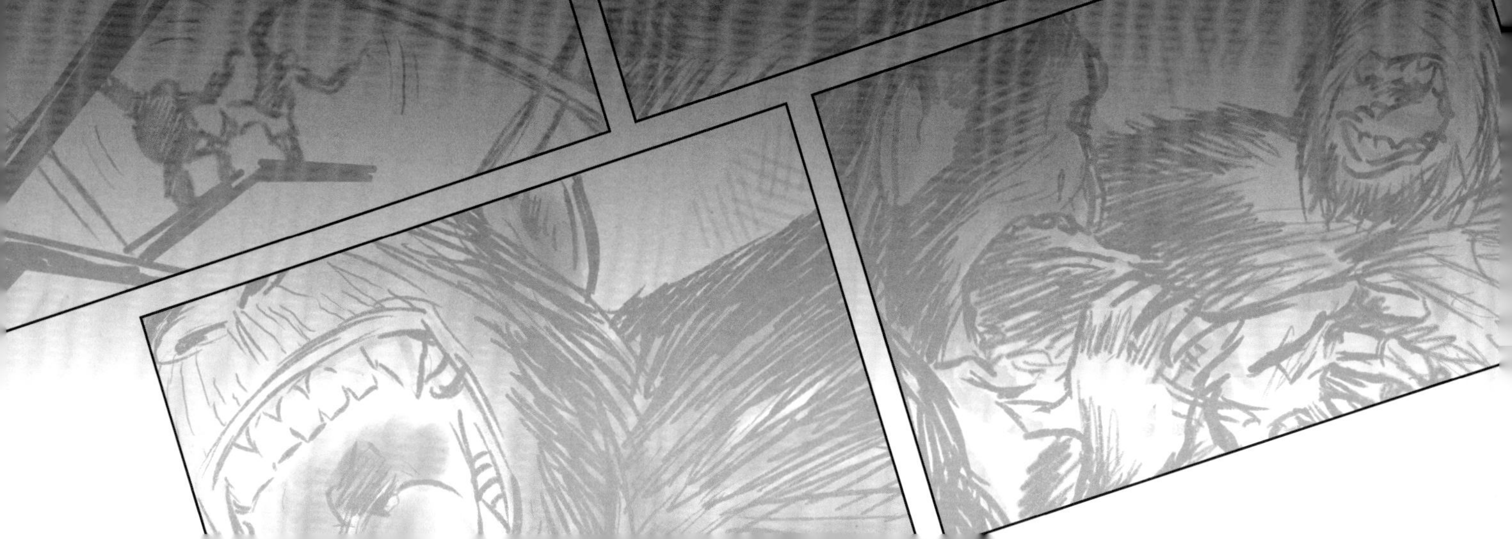

Rise of the Planet of the Apes... my new level

In early 2010, I really needed a job. The entertainment business was slow and as a freelance artist in film and television, too often we live a feast or famine existence. Fox was attempting another reboot of the *Planet of the Apes* franchise with a new film called *Rise of the Planet of the Apes*. This film was to be a modern day take on how the apes came to prominence before the start of the original sixties franchise.

English director Rupert Wyatt was making his American cinematic debut after his film *The Escapist*, a dramatic thriller that brought him to the attention of studio heads. I was called in for a meeting due to the work I had done a couple of years earlier for Fox Studios on John Singleton's then-aborted project *The A-Team* film, so I was now a known hire at the Fox Studios. On a bright sunny morning I had a good initial interview with Rupert. My first impression was that Rupert was calm, methodical and polite. I thought that I had a pretty good shot at landing the job but my hopes were dashed a day or so later when I heard Rupert had chosen another storyboard artist, Tim Burgard. I was disappointed because I needed the job and was a fan of the original "Apes" films. However a week later I got the call. Rupert needed a second storyboard artist on the film. For this film, there was the need of a lot of visual effects (VFX) work to be executed. There were a number of action sequences and all of the apes were to be CGI rather than men and women in makeup as in the original film. All of the CGI sequences needed to be storyboarded so that Rupert, the visual effects team, the stunt team and whomever else would be in total sync. Each individual VFX shot is an added cost to the film budget so filmmakers use storyboards to align the shots needed so as to keep a tally for the film's ledger and bottom line.

I was given the film script and I devoured it. The new screenplay was written by the married team of Rick Jaffa and Amanda Silver. The writing was refreshingly intelligent and engaging. The quality of the work on the page was a stunning blueprint to serve as a springboard for an even better finished film.

Rupert wanted his storyboard artists to be fully present and work in the office, which is my preferred way to work. He wanted to be able to routinely call for brief meetings in the office when he was available so as to oversee the work we were creating. For the direction given on my storyboard scene renderings in our first meeting, Rupert guided me with one very important visual note: a great portion of the film's shots would be done from a low angle view. The reason: Caesar, the lead chimpanzee character would crawl on all fours when he ran and he would actually be lower to the ground than a human, thus the shots from a low angle would work for the film's ape characters. With the modern technology of VFX, Caesar and the other chimps would now move and execute their bodies and facial expressions in the manner of actual chimps. Rupert also stressed that in order to save on the film budget and to create a variation of the visuals, some shots would be filmed from the point of view of the CGI character of the surrounding humans and environment. This would allow for CGI free shots that would keep the VFX budget down. The final design for the adult Caesar chimpanzee character was still being worked on while the film was still in preproduction, but the concept team gave me a their most recent version of the character design as reference for my drawings.

Rupert was very thorough and as well prepared of a director as I have known. We went over my first scene piece by piece. There were certain shots that Rupert knew he wanted while other shots he trusted me to create. As

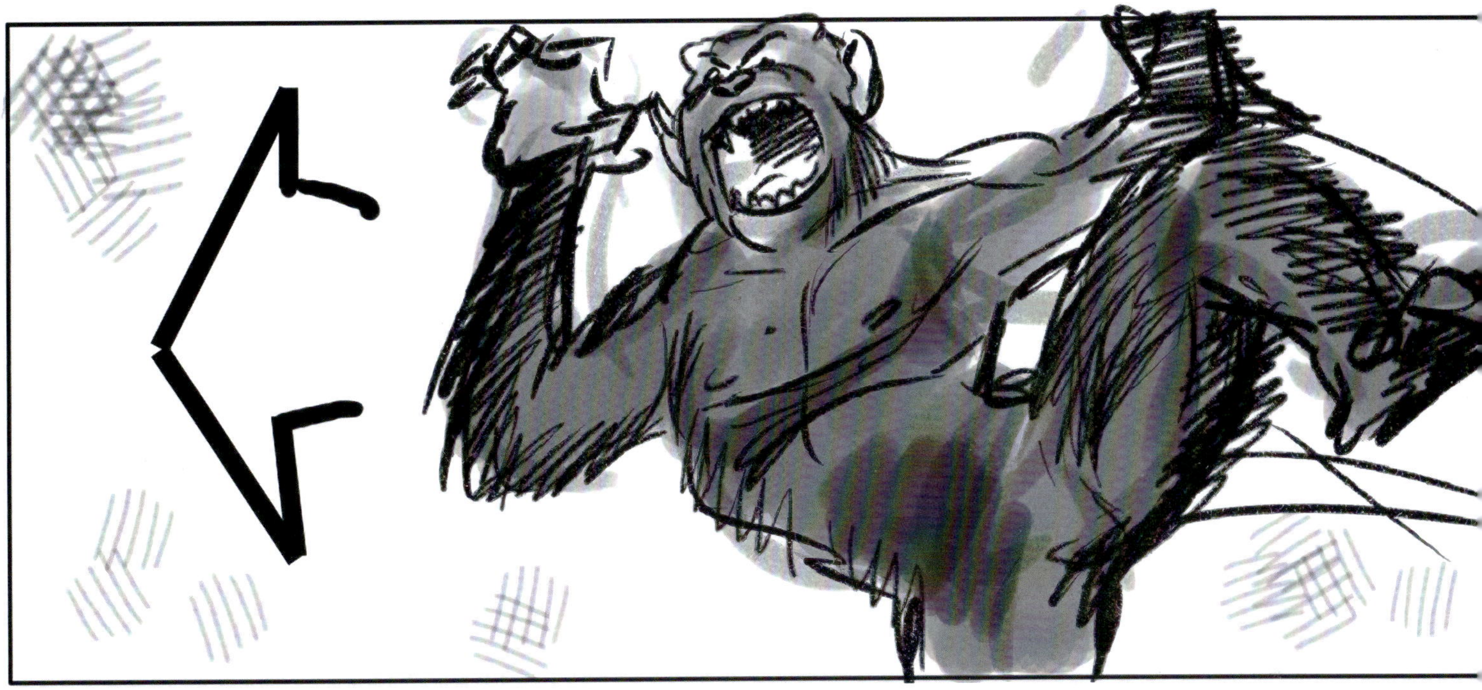

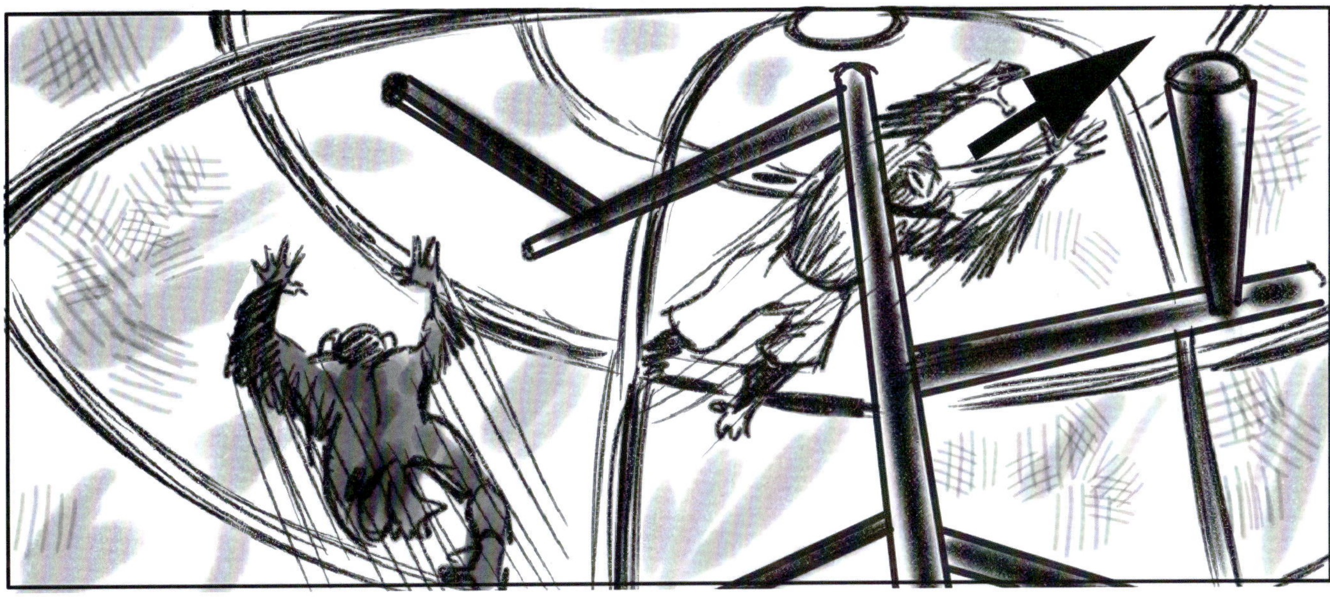

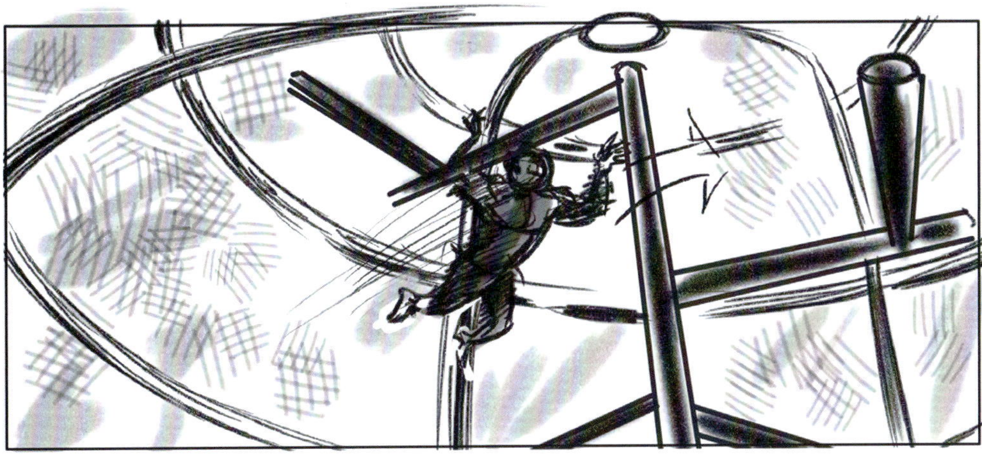

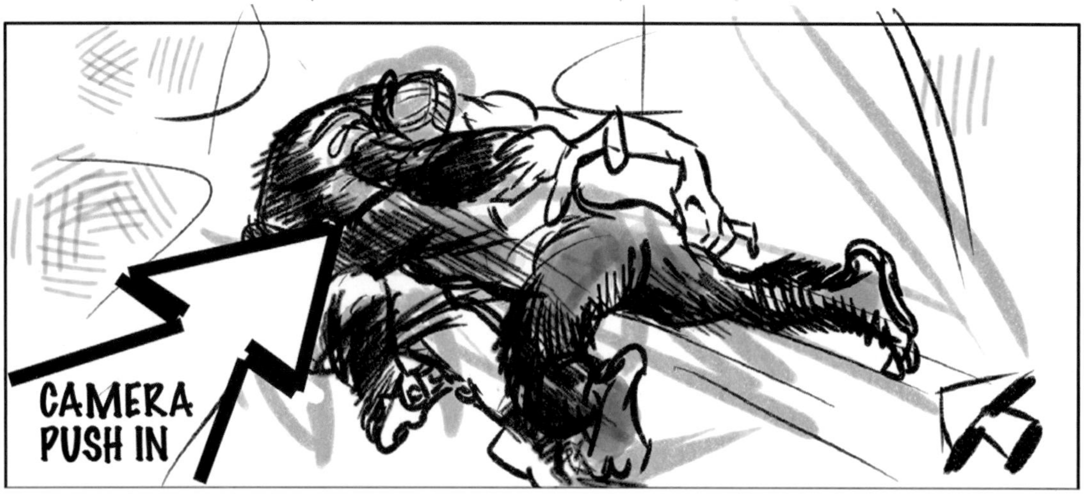
CAMERA
PUSH IN

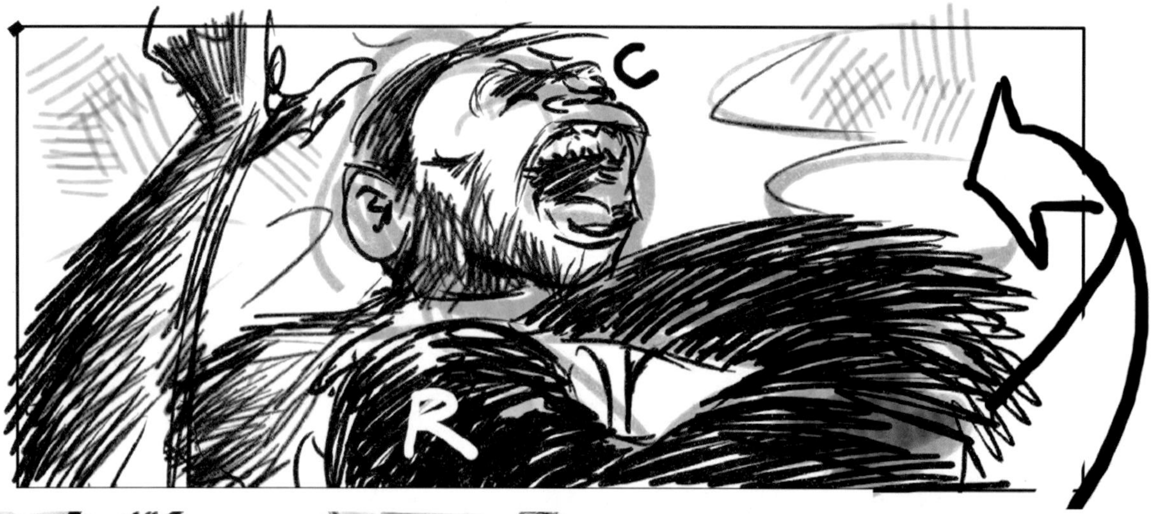
C
R

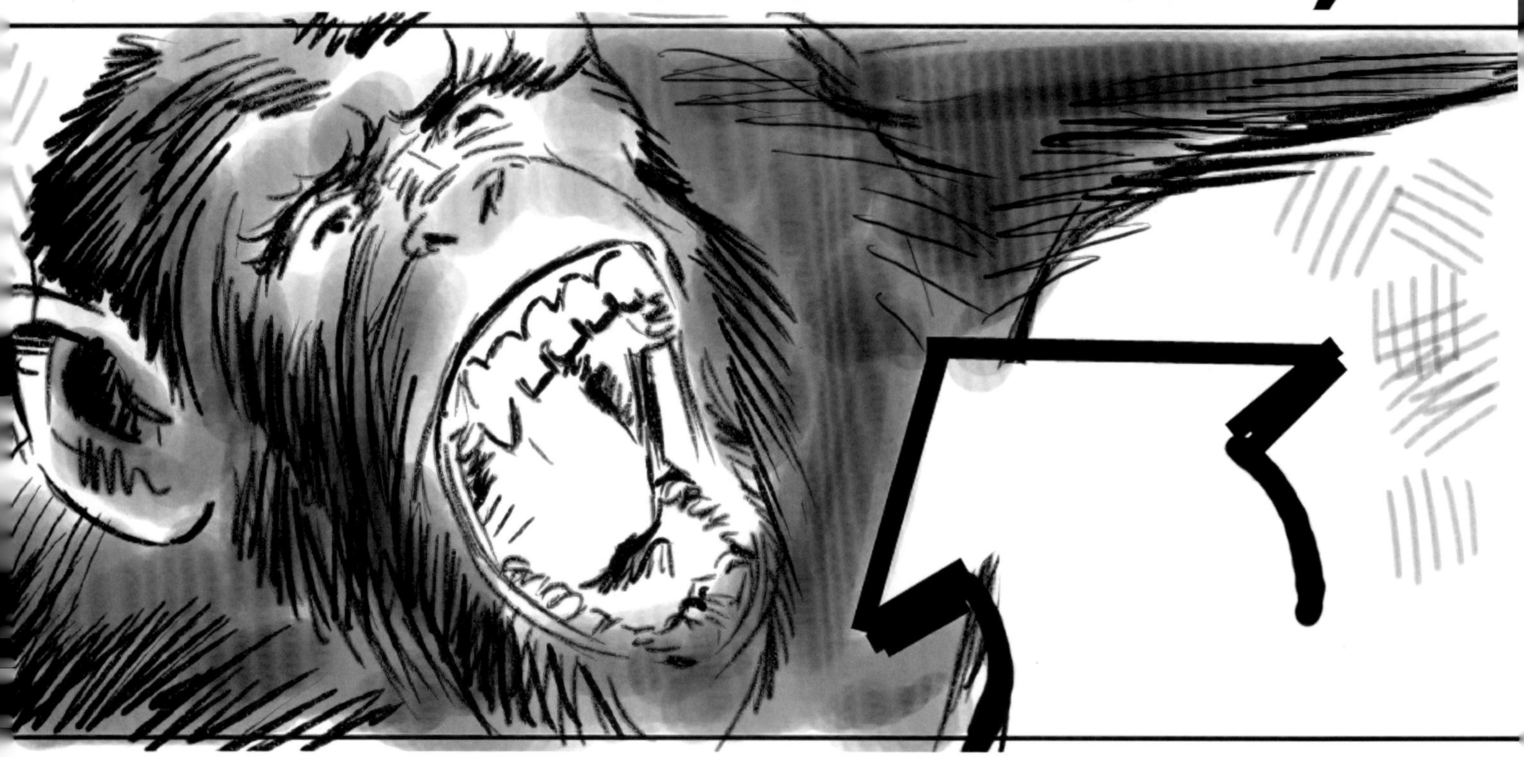

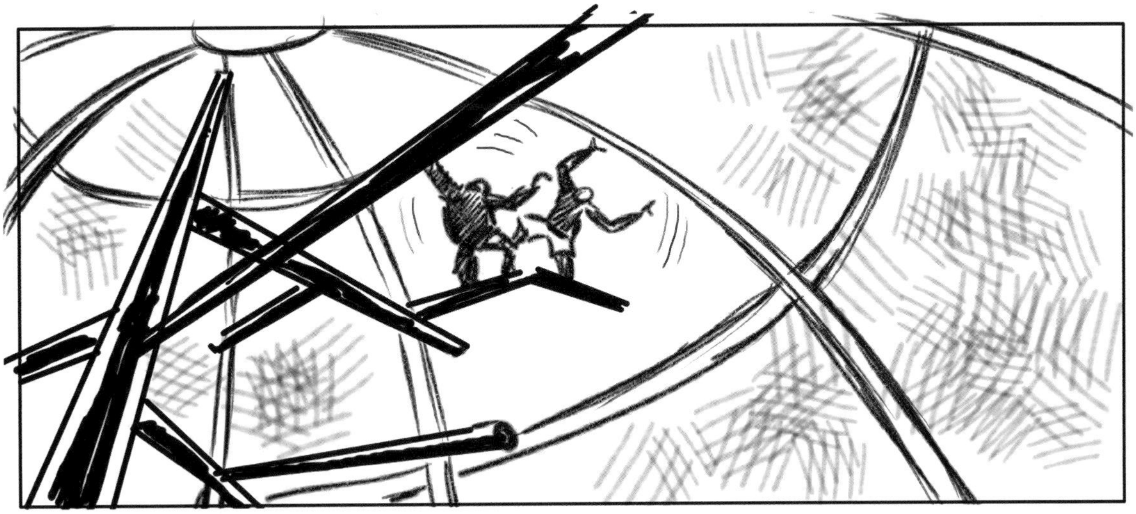

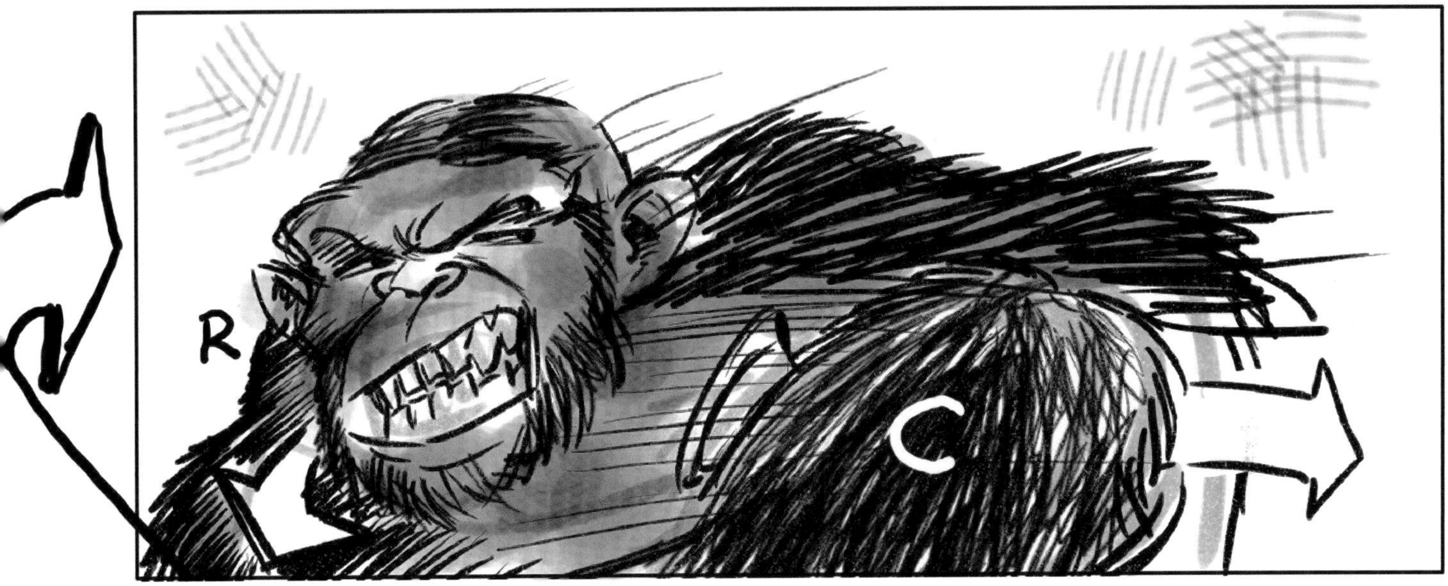
R
C

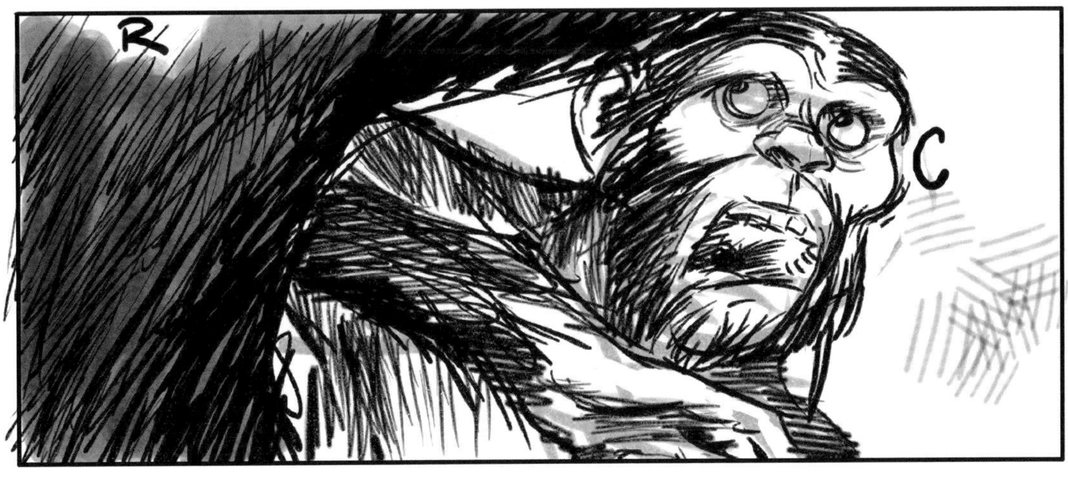
R
C

with all talented directors, Rupert wanted me to know the full intent of the scene and his point of view on the visuals. This first scene I storyboarded was to be of a chimpanzee named Bright Eyes (an homage to the nickname Charleston Heston's "Taylor" had in the original film) escaping captivity in a lab, which leads to a wild chase in a building complex with a tragic end. There weren't any sets built yet but Rupert had a firm idea of the location. I worked from his ideas and had the roughs of the storyboards completed early. I strived to keep the images visually stimulating and to follow Rupert's vision. This made the working process simple: I executed his ideas, he liked the work that I came up with, he gave me notes and I moved on to tighten those sets of storyboards.

I had the idea to draw the adversarial character of the powerful executive, "Steven Jacobs" as a Black man. If characters are not already cast and I think the casting could be open, I'll make a diverse racial or gender choice and place that diverse character's image in the storyboards. This effort is to possibly give the director a new idea from the page about the casting the actor for the character. As it turns out, British actor David Oyelowo was later cast. I don't think he was a known actor until he landed that role. I'm not taking credit for his being cast and getting that role, but I was very happy when I saw the movie that my suggestion in the storyboards of placing a Black man in that role just may have played a part in the end result. The Jacobs character was a "villain" but not in the usual way for characters of color. Jacobs was intelligent, successful and rich, but as a villain he was of course greedy and selfish. Similarly, I had drawn a non-gender specific helicopter pilot in *2 Fast 2 Furious* as a woman and they cast the character with an actual female pilot. Again, was it serendipity or the suggestion from my storyboards images? Who knows.

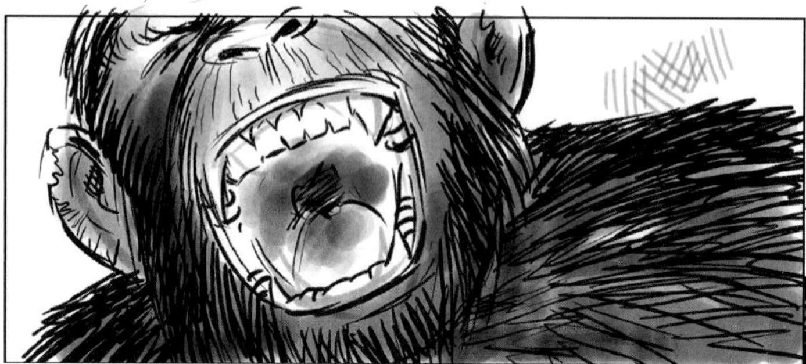

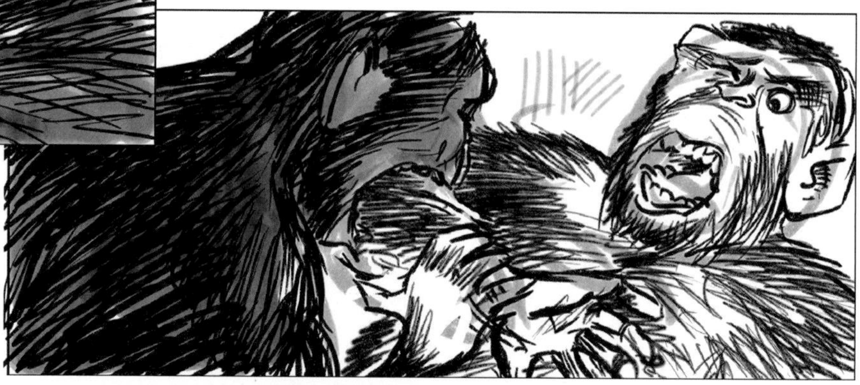

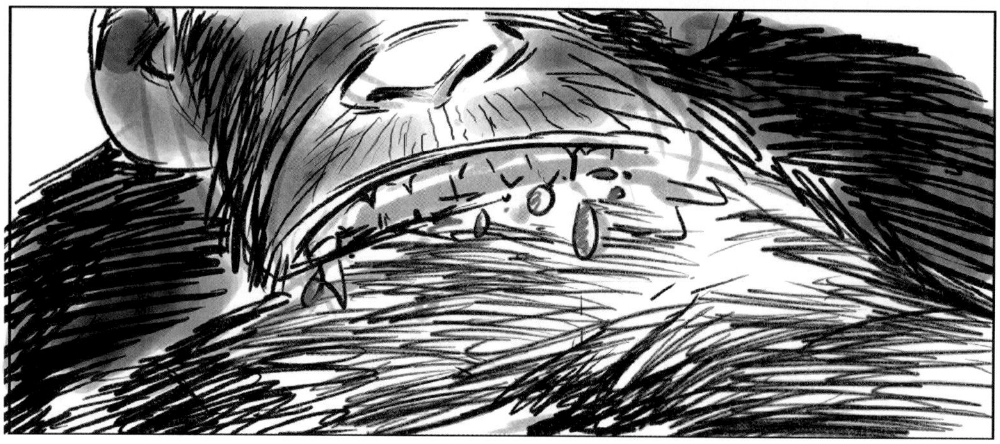

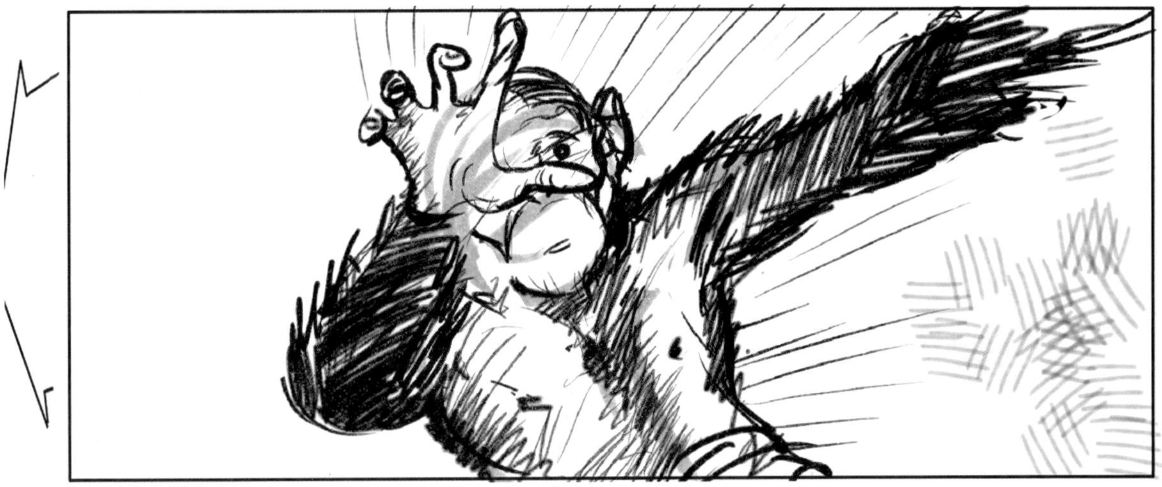

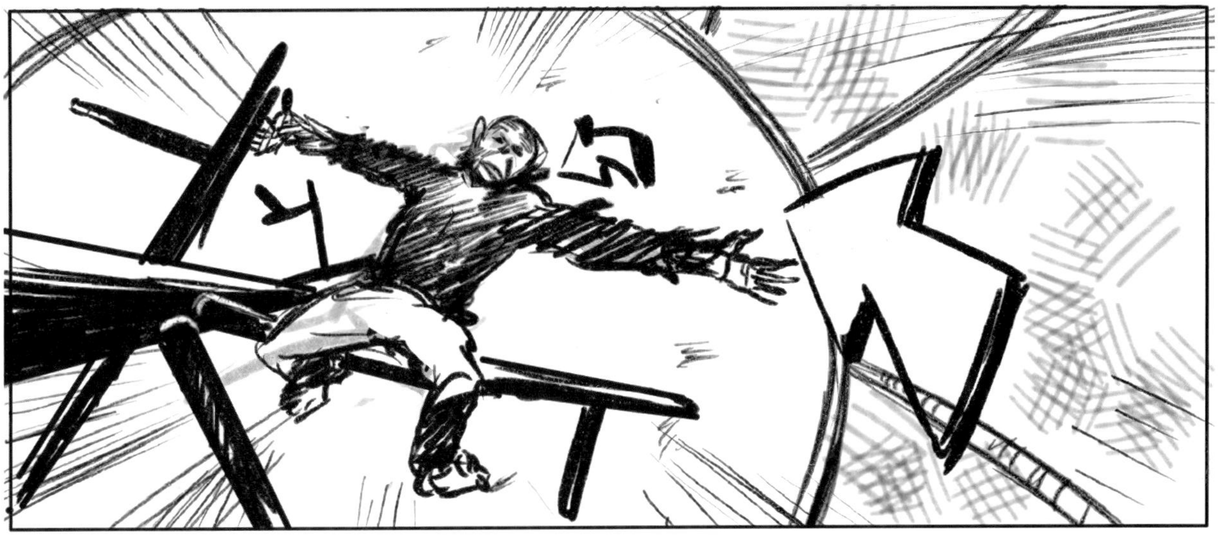

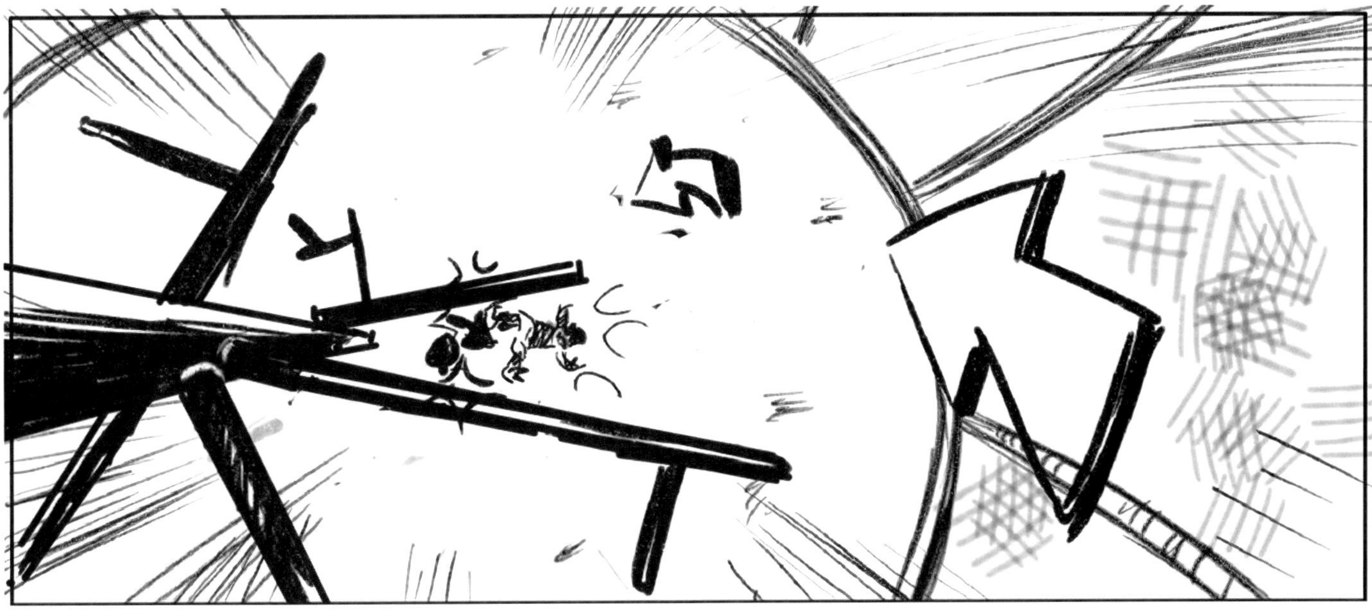

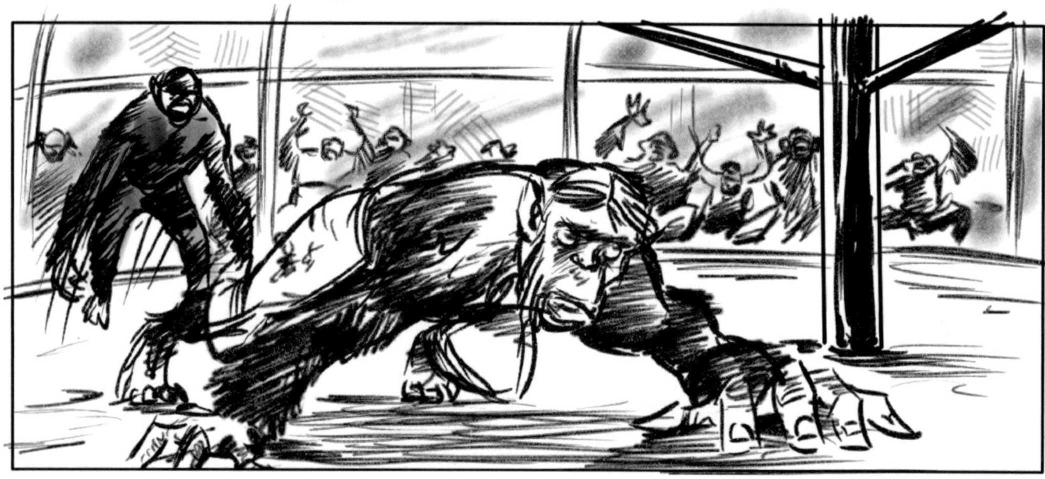

This battle ends when the villainous character "Landon" shoots the chimps with tranquilizers darts. The name Landon was an homage to an ill fated character in the 1968 original.

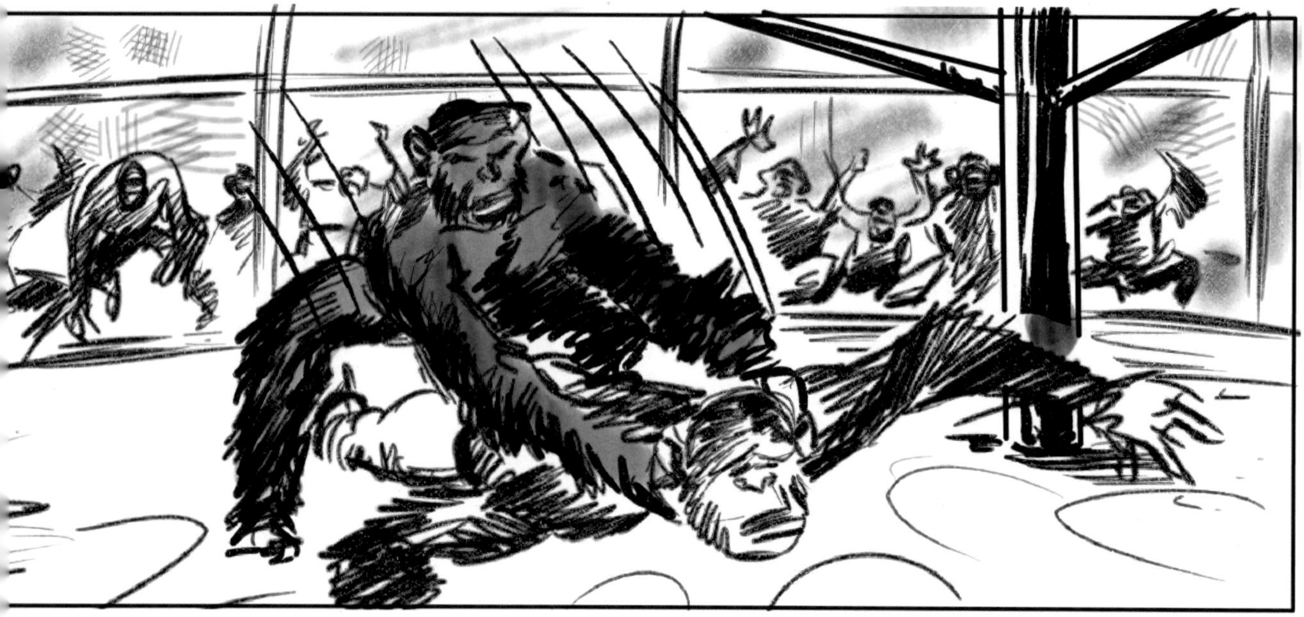

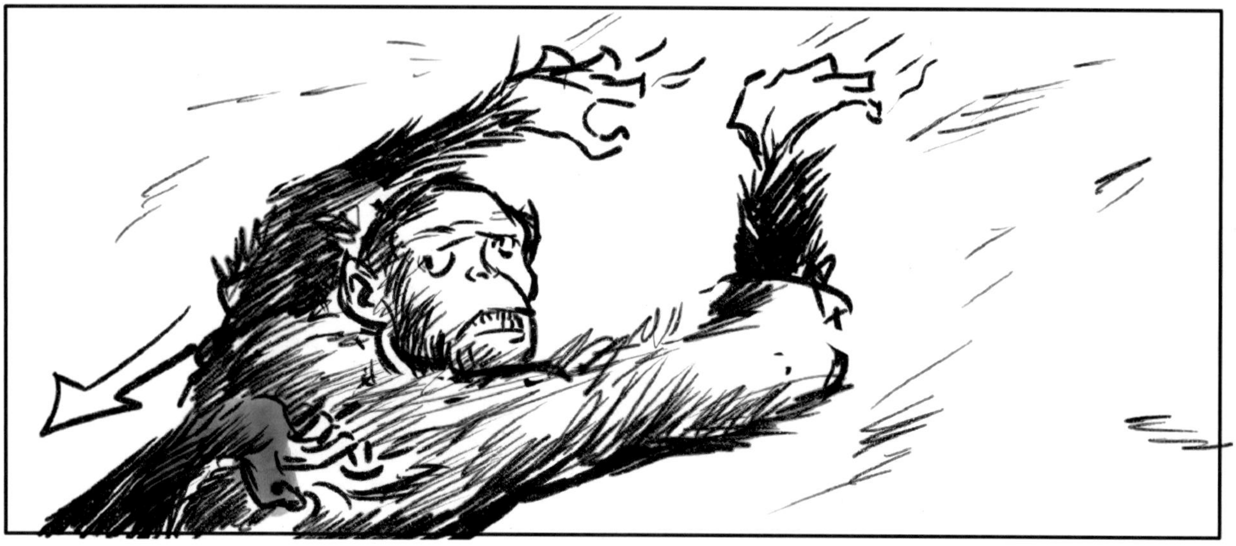

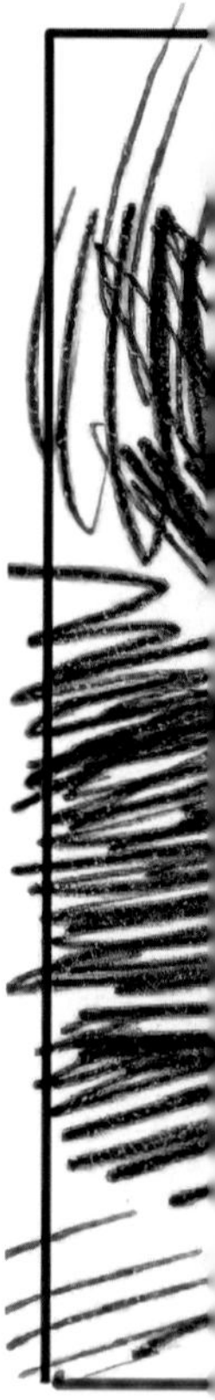

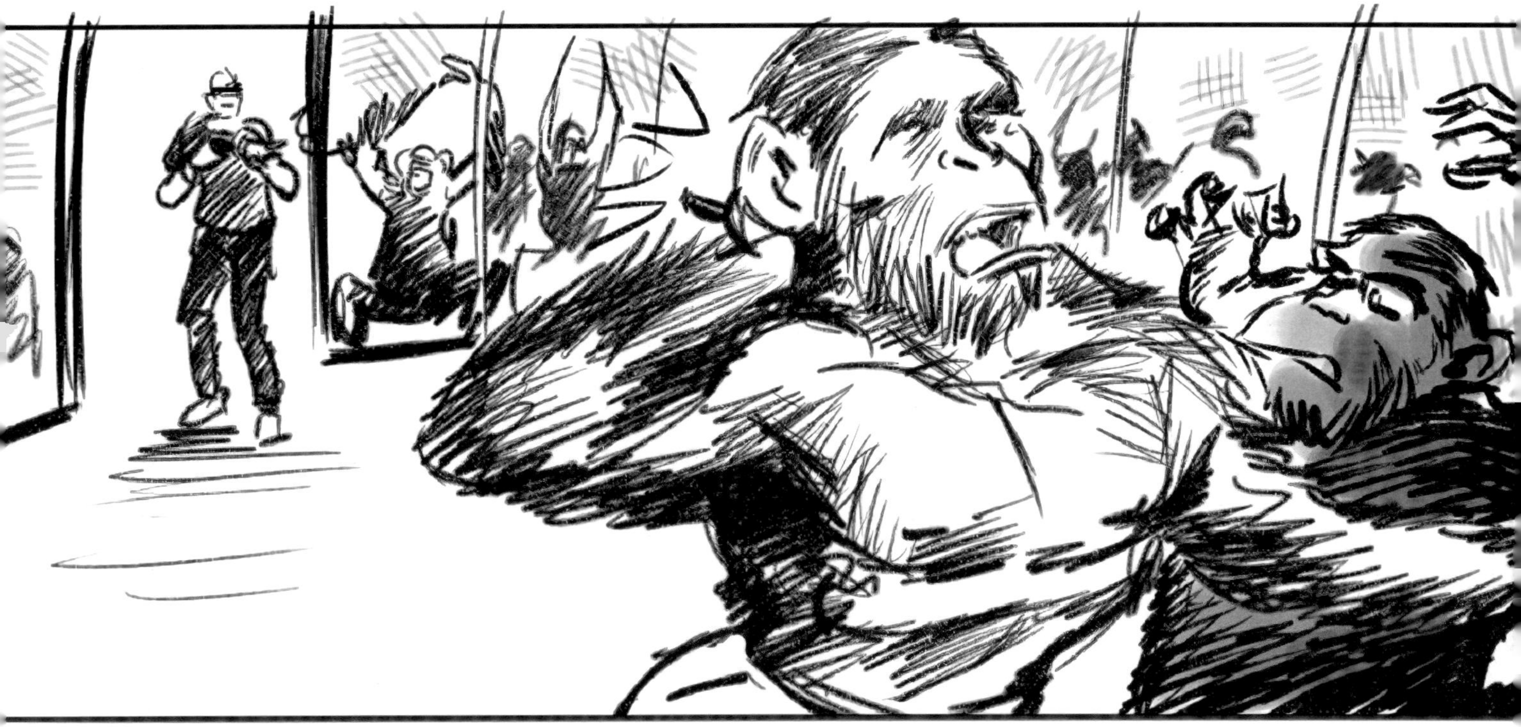

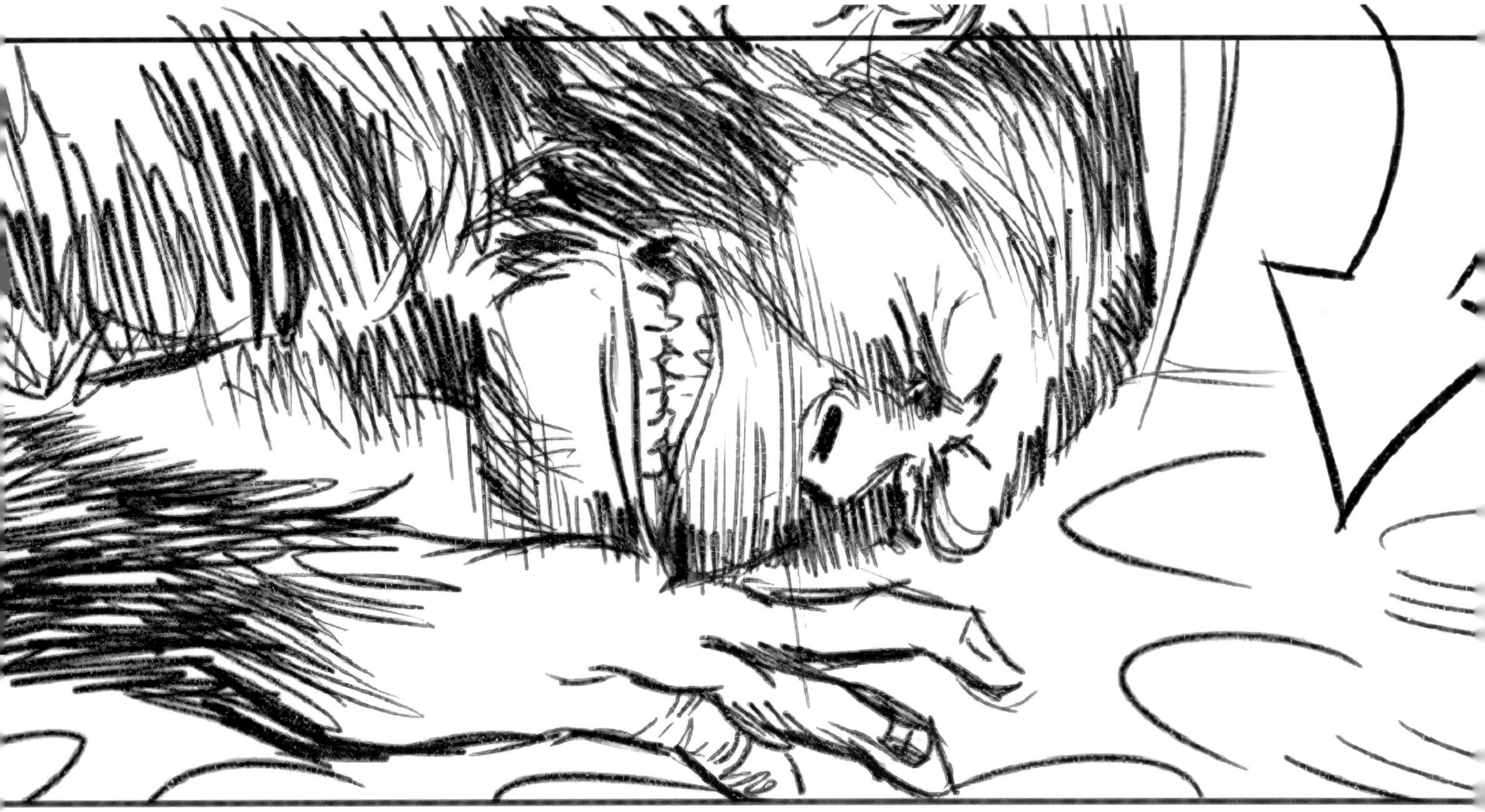

Fox executives came by the office soon afterwards and Rupert showed them some concept designs and storyboards. This type of visit by the executives is routine yet brings ripples of tension to the office. These execs are known as the "suits" and their visits take place particularly when a studio puts a great deal of money into a film's budget. These executives must do their jobs and like any financial representatives, they want to chart the direction of the film's budget and see the proof of where the money invested by the studio is being spent on the film. Once the studio execs left the office, the more calming flow of creative energy of the office returned to normal.

My favorite storyboard scene assignment entailed the super intelligent Caesar being put into a primate shelter with chimpanzees of normal ape intelligence. Caesar tries to make friends with another chimp named Rocket in the way that a human would try to engage another human. Raised with humans, Caesar knows none of the animal hierarchy or behavior and he would pay for it. Rocket savagely attacks Caesar and chases him up and around the artificial trees of the shelter. The fight ends with Caesar crashing to the ground and both he and Rocket being knocked out with tranquilizer darts from an indecent zookeeper named Landon (another homage of a movie-character's name from the original film).

Rupert had the idea to film the climbing movements as shot from Caesar's point of view and to cut in the wide shots of Caesar with Rocket giving chase of him. I worked tenaciously to be as dynamic in the drawings as possible in rendering the action of the scenes but remain loose with the storytelling. Rupert allowed me to set up the opening shots in the scene to build up to the upcoming apes' confrontation. Combined efforts created unison of our ideas on the roughs and Rupert would then add subtle changes. His alterations were the nuances of camera positions and character intent. Rupert was always precise with what he wanted.

With great relief, I was working completely digitally now, so I was able to make quick changes to my work through the wondrous strides and rapid advancements of technology. Our new and glorious world of drawing and inking with ease on a screen had arrived. No more erasing on paper and drawing things completely from scratch when any changes needed to be done.

After that main scene was done, I had a few smaller scenes to complete and then my boards were wrapped. The last thing I remember doing was an interesting assignment Rupert gave of sketching in additional chimps to a digital painting one of the film's conceptual artists had done. I had never done something like that before but thankfully Rupert didn't need me to do anything as illustrative as the original painting. He simply needed simple indications of where to add chimps for the VFX department to do in post.

The following year, Rupert was kind enough to get me two tickets to the red carpet premiere of *Rise Of The Planet Of The Apes*. I took my son, Josh who was sixteen years old at the time. Justin Bieber arrived at the theater and was surrounded by paparazzi as he got out of his limo. Josh thought the affair was fun but even then, he was quite unaffected by "glamour and celebrity" of the moment having been born and raised in the ether of entertainment industry in Los Angeles, particularly with having celebrities, producers, directors and artists who were friends of his parents come to his home, regularly. We both enjoyed the movie immensely though I flushed with an elated sense of satisfaction of having worked on the film and seeing my name in the credits roll. After the film ended, I gave congratulations to Rupert and said hello to actor Andy Serkis whom I had met briefly five years earlier through my friend Bennett Miller, a great director in his own right. Andy was just as nice at the premiere as he had been years earlier. Andy gives his characters so much heart and soul through his amazing skill to act while suited in the motion capture apparatus for the roles of so many great CGI characters that he has played.

Rupert and I went on to work together a few years later on an early attempt to adapt the X-Men character of "Gambit" into a solo movie. It was to star Channing Tatum who was also a producer on the project. It was a fun ride while it lasted. Things didn't work out on the movie and the project has yet to make it into production even after other known directors attached. So goes the movie industry.

Rupert went on to exec produce a television series based on *The Exorcist* but returned to movies with the film *Captive State*. This was a comparatively low budget, twenty-five million dollar sci-fi film that Rupert and his wife, Erica Beeny co-wrote about the repercussions of a worldwide alien invasion. Rupert shot the movie in Chicago but he brought me on early in preproduction to work with him for several weeks. The script encapsulated a hybrid of genres and I was happy to come in to work on the project.

Captive State was had a limited budget so Rupert knew specifically where he wanted to point the camera to avoid having to have too many extras cast in the scenes that would cost more money. He wanted almost everything shot at ground level and seen through the characters' eyes. Rupert said that he wanted it to have the feeling of classic show, *The Wire*. A then unknown actor, Jonathan Majors was cast as one of the leads. Jonathan's career has launched since then and will now be known as the time traveling MCU villain, Kang the Conqueror.

We were so early in preproduction on *Captive State* that the aliens, spaceships or technology specifications to include in the movie had not yet been designed. But as Rupert was always prepared, he gave me a good approximation of what he wanted the aliens and their technology to look like. The two of us would meet several times a week at his office for about three weeks. After I was done on the film a year or so later, I saw a rough cut. Rupert had named two of the lead sibling characters played by Black actors, Jonathan Majors and Ashton Sanders with the last name of "Drummond". It was also a great coincidence that their father had already been named "John," which is the name of my late father and my older brother. I felt a great sense of gratitude and honor that Rupert chose my last name as a character name for his film. What terrific gesture of how Rupert felt about me. The long gestating *Captive State* was released theatrically in 2019 after two years' time.

I had rarely been as delighted with a movie I had worked on from start to finish as I was with the work experience and final print of this film. *Rise Of The Planet Of The Apes* was a great experience in preproduction stage with the finished product being a staggering revelation. And I knew that I had entered a new level as an artist.

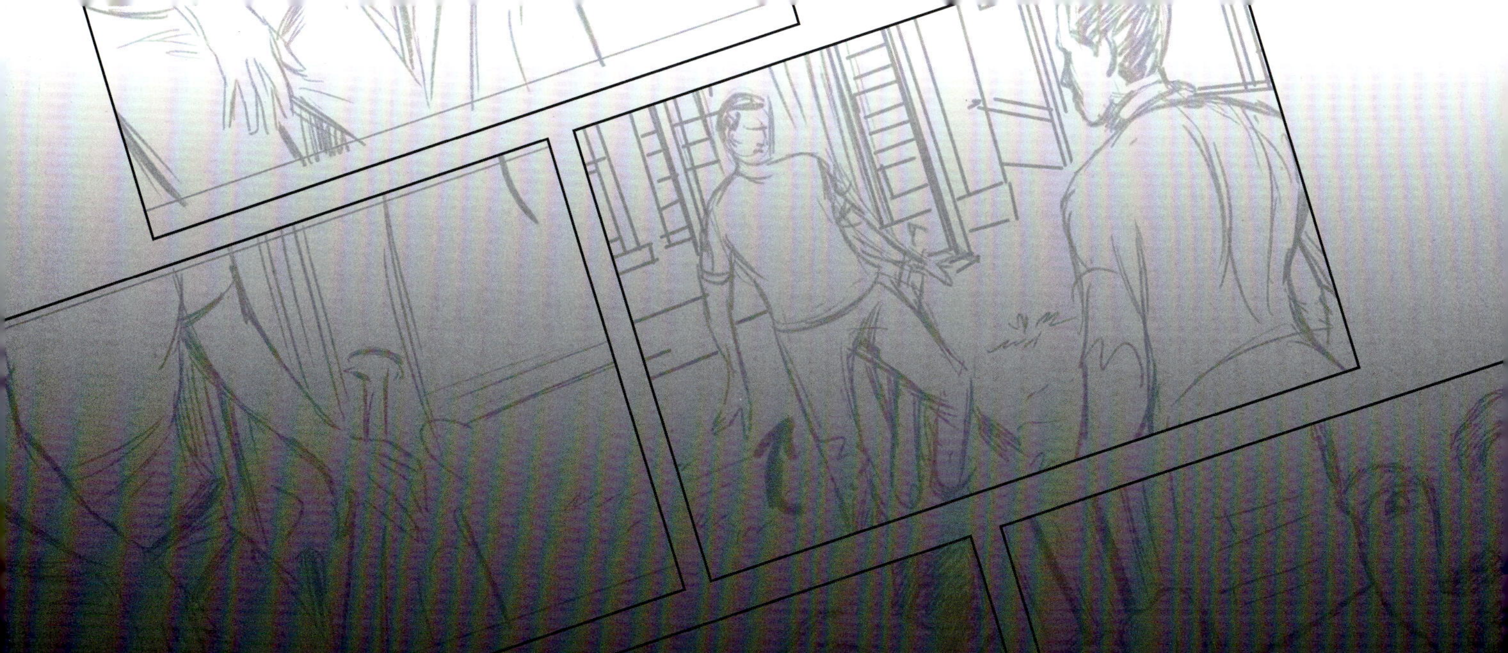

STORYBOARDS AND STORIES OF 15 SELECT FILMS AND TELEVISION SHOWS

HARD DAY'S WORK

Chapter 12

FENCES

STAY ANOTHER WEEK, AGAIN

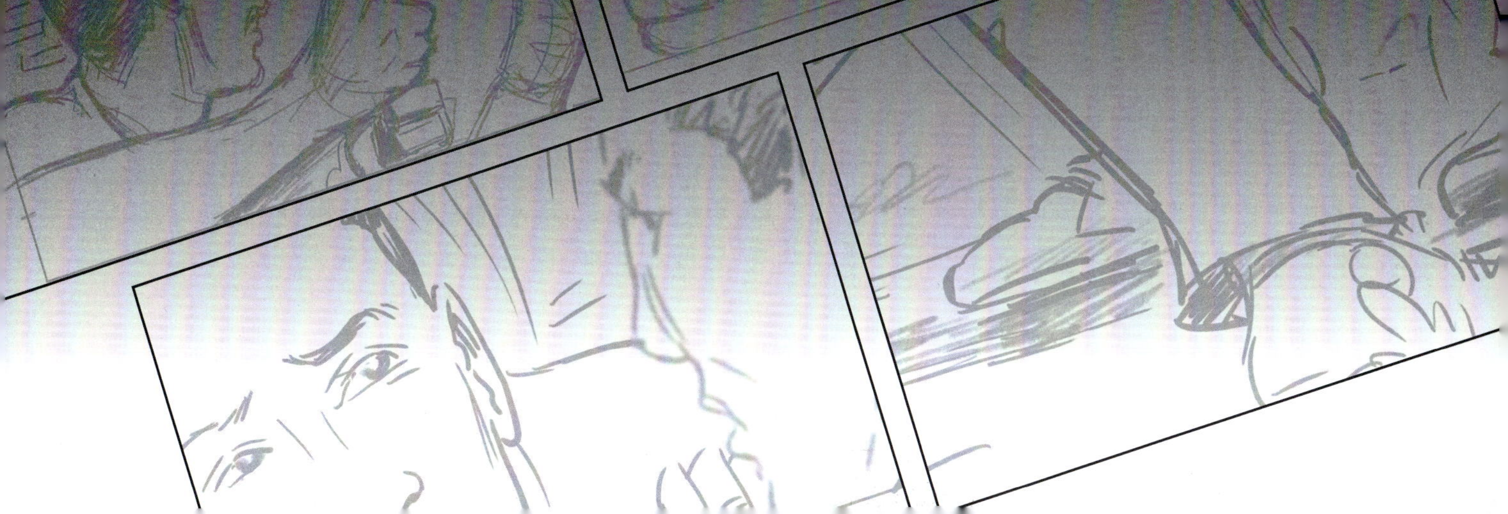

Fences... stay another week, again

About a decade after *Antwone Fisher*, I was contacted by Todd Black to see if I was available to storyboard for Denzel Washington on his second directorial effort, *The Great Debaters*. Working on *Debaters* would have been a few weeks of work but I had just started on the Adam Sandler film, *You Don't Mess with the Zohan* and that job required a great amount of storyboards. Even when you prefer working with one director over the other, the more weeks of work you have the more money you make. I was disappointed that I couldn't work with Denzel not knowing when that opportunity would happen again. But that opportunity came around again in early 2016 when I received an email inquiry from Todd requesting my availability. The film would be an adaptation of the legendary August Wilson play, *Fences*.

My colleague and buddy, Jim Magdaleno had been working for more than six months on *The Magnificent Seven* film remake that starred Denzel, directed by Antoine Fuqua. Jim has been the storyboard artist of choice for Antoine for nearly a dozen projects. During that time, Jim told me that there were early conversations floating around set that Denzel was ready to direct again. I joked with Jim, telling him that as a director, "Denzel is MINE." I became quite territorial. I refused to let one of the most brilliant actors in the history of film slip by me and have any other storyboard artist working with him but myself.

When I got the call, I was elated that Denzel and Todd remembered the amicable working relationship we had on *Antwone Fisher*. Todd and I had always stayed in touch. Also, it made it easier for me in this situation in that there were not a lot of local storyboard artists on location in Pittsburgh where the film was to be shot. Once again I was informed that it would be "only be a few weeks of work" in total on this film and that I would be flown out to Pittsburgh where the play was written and is set. I was originally scheduled to work with Denzel on location for a couple of weeks and then released to return to LA soon afterwards to finish the remainder of the film remotely.

Like a kid going off to summer camp, I said goodbye to my wife and son and flew to Pittsburgh. I hadn't been there since working on John Singleton's *Abduction* years earlier. I never had time to really see the sights of Pittsburgh while on *Abduction* so I hoped that things would be different this time around. The universe would be answering my hopes soon.

August Wilson's *Fences* is the story of Troy Maxon, a middle-aged Black man in his fifties who had the ability and talent to play major league baseball. But because of the time period where major league baseball had not been fully integrated with Black players as well as his past incarceration for murder, Troy never got the opportunity to manifest his dreams of playing baseball as a career choice before his youthful talents expired with age. This misfortune in his life sours Troy and it permeates other aspects of his life in how he treats his loving wife, "Rose" and carries over to his disconnect and downright parental cruelty to his two sons, "Lyons" and "Cory".

Playwright August Wilson was born in Pittsburgh and wrote ten plays covering one hundred years of the city's history. Wilson saw the plight of Black people in the city firsthand. A child of a Black woman and white German man who abandoned them, August and his siblings were left mostly alone while his mother cleaned white peoples' houses for income. To be Black in Pittsburgh was to know a kind of hardship that white citizens would never know. Even in the present day, a Black person's income, life expectancy, and educational opportunities are well below their white counterparts who live in the same city.

I arrived in Pittsburgh in the evening and I was at the nearby production office the next morning. My hotel was a straight line of about a mile from the office, so I even walked some days. I also brought some comic books with me keeping in mind that I could likely be far away from a local comic bookstore in Pittsburgh. Reading a good comic is one of the most relaxing things I do.

65-4

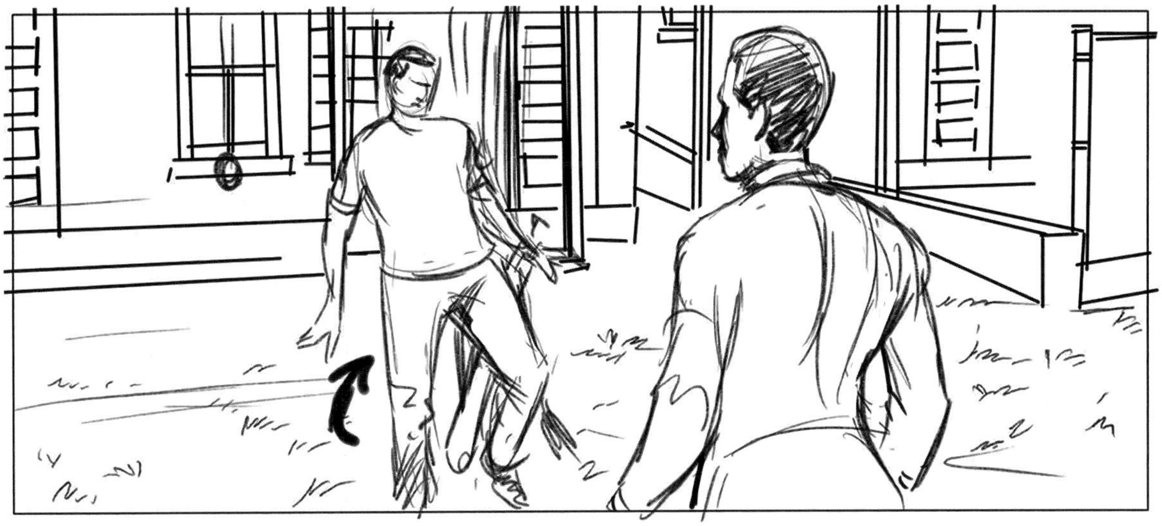

CORY STUMBLES BACK TO THE TREE.

65-5

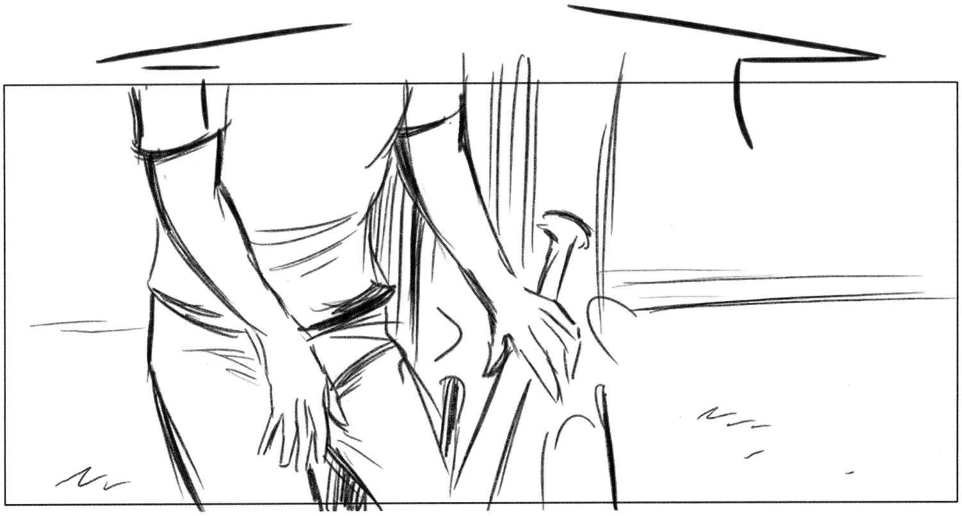

INSERT - CORY GRABS THE BAT.

65-5A

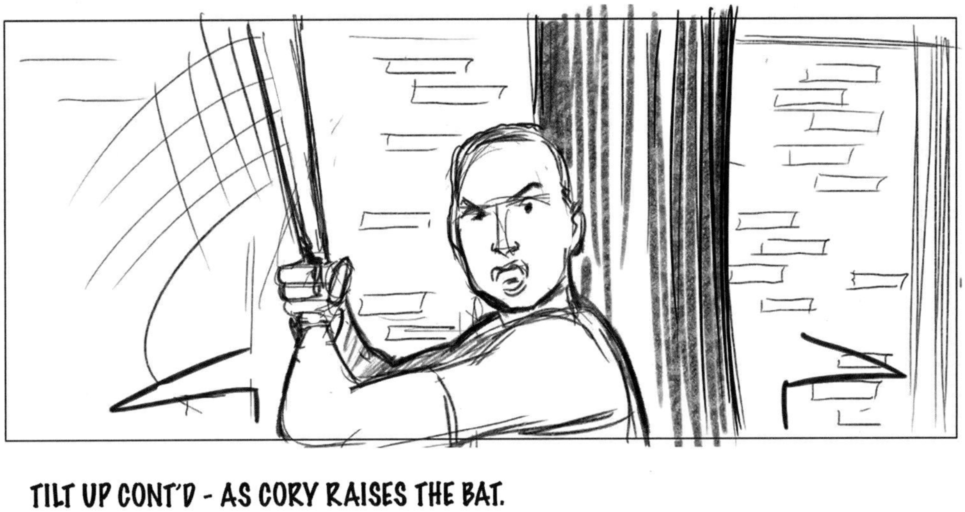

TILT UP CONT'D - AS CORY RAISES THE BAT.

70-8

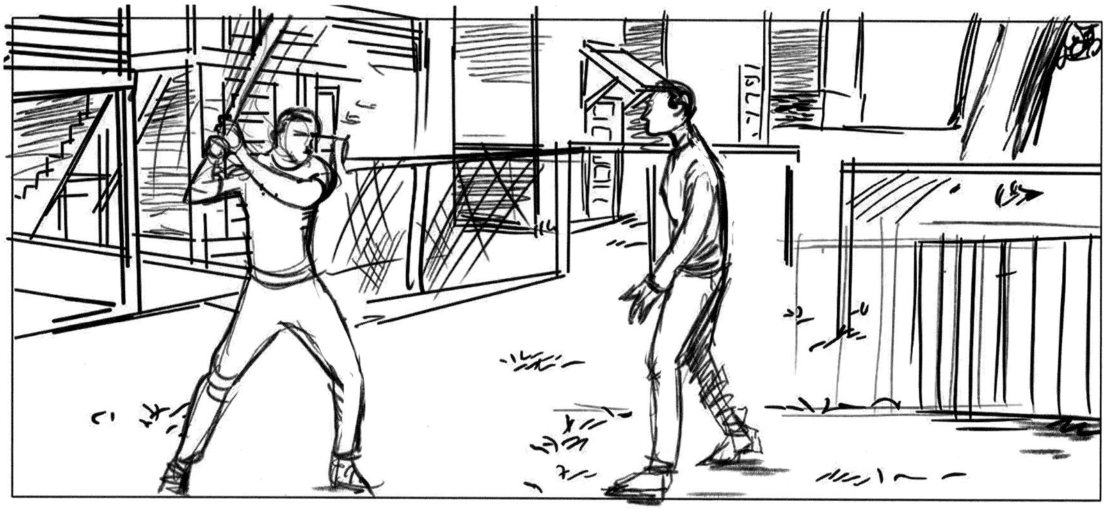

WIDE OF THE SCENE.

70-9

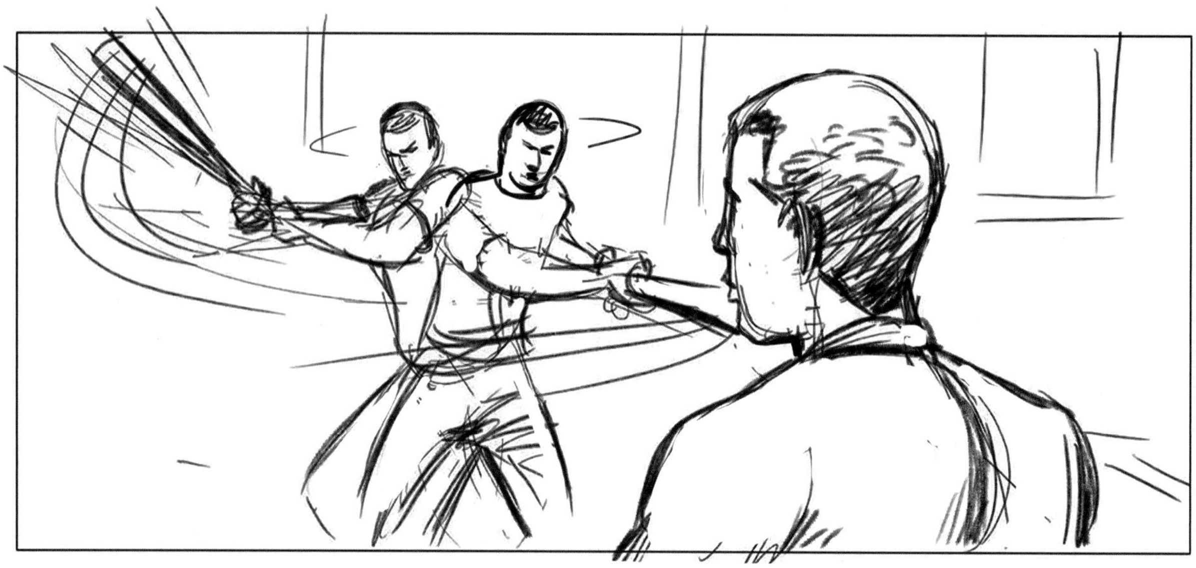

OVER TROY AS CORY SWINGS.

70-10

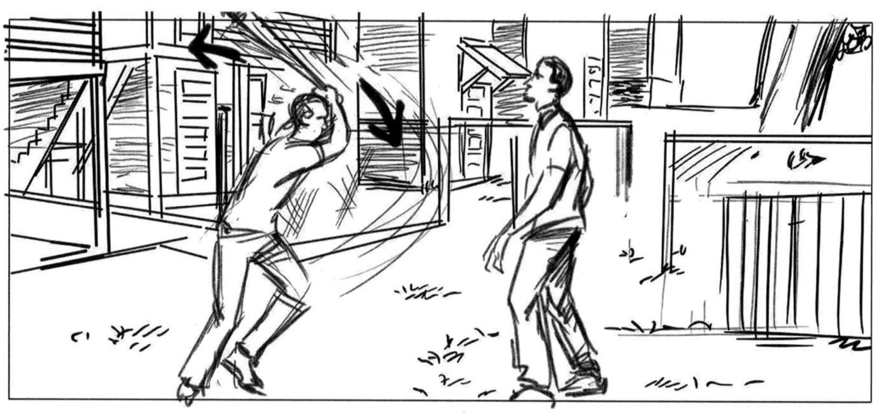

BACK TO SHOT.

70-11

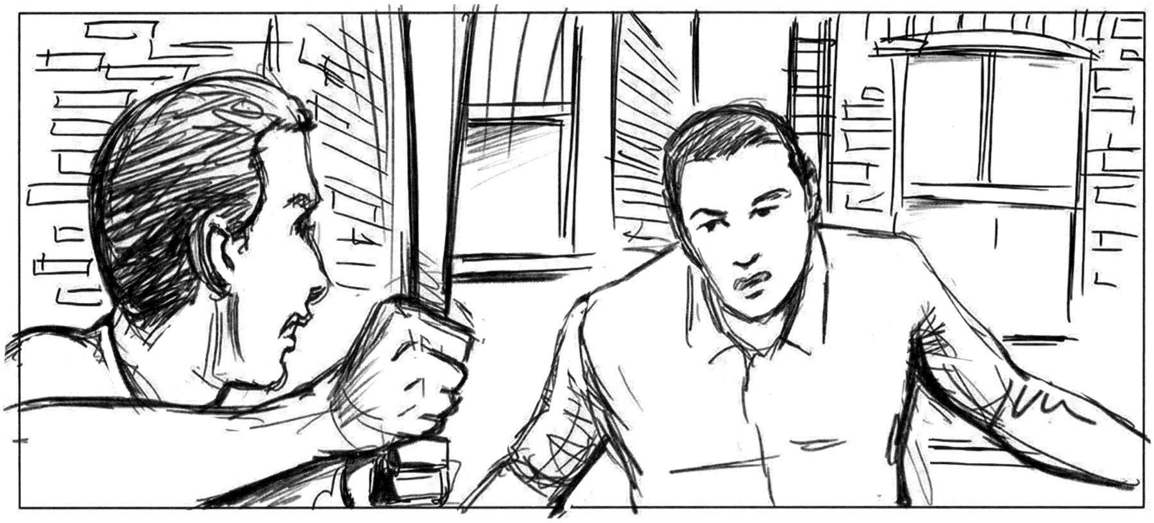

OVER CORY TO TROY, WHO OFFERS HIS HEAD.

70-12

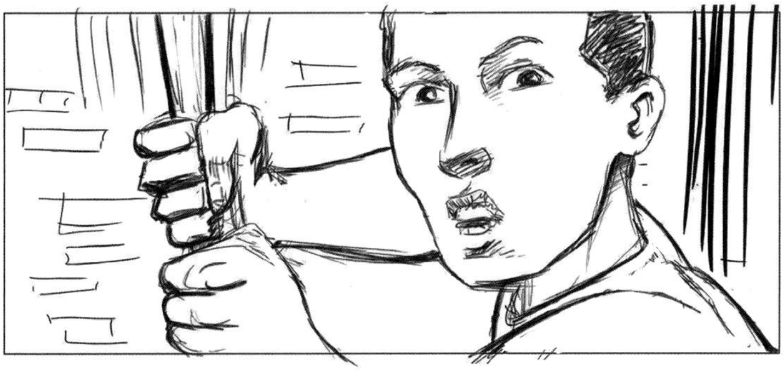

CORY.

"It was super helpful to be able to watch Denzel rehearse this scene with Jovan Adepo who played Cory, along with stunt coordinator Clay Fontenot. I took photos for reference.

70-13

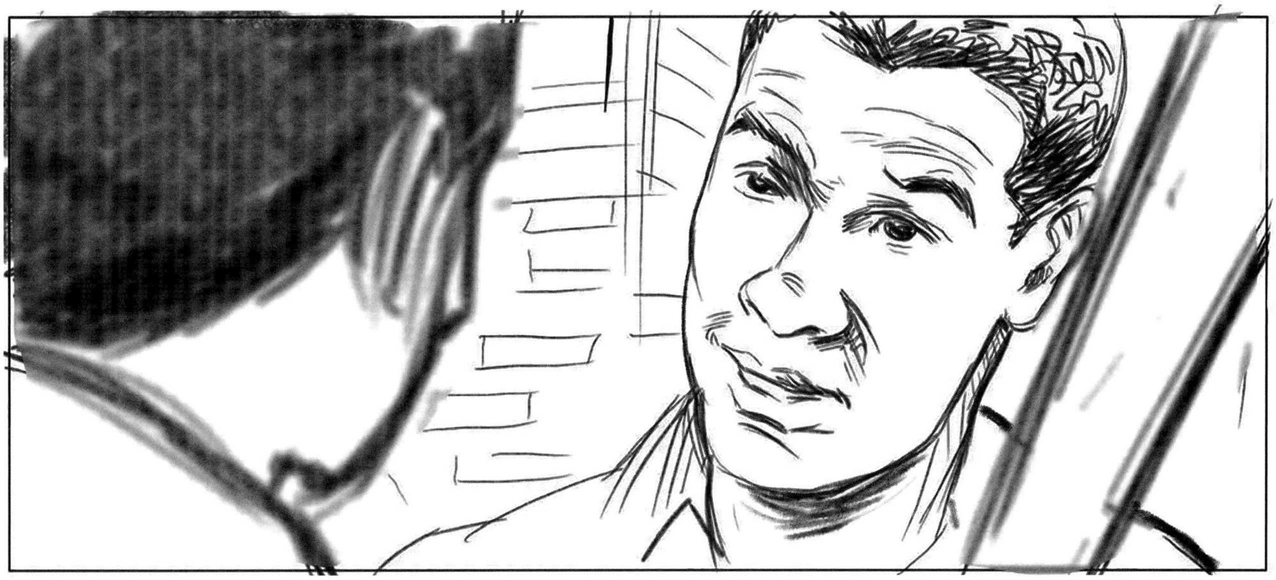

TROY

A notable trait about Pittsburgh is that since some of the blocks are narrow, vehicles are allowed to park the wheels of the passenger side of the car actually on the sidewalk. Having lived in the transit-fueled metropolis of New York and now living in Los Angeles where cars are like an artery of your life where getting parking tickets is always a threat, this seemed a very noticeable yet curious allowance to me.

When you are placed in another city for a job, the first thing you want to know is "how late places stay open?" and "where are the good places to eat?". When I worked on *Pride*, a 2007 movie that was filmed in New Orleans it was perfect that the restaurants stayed open late.

70-14

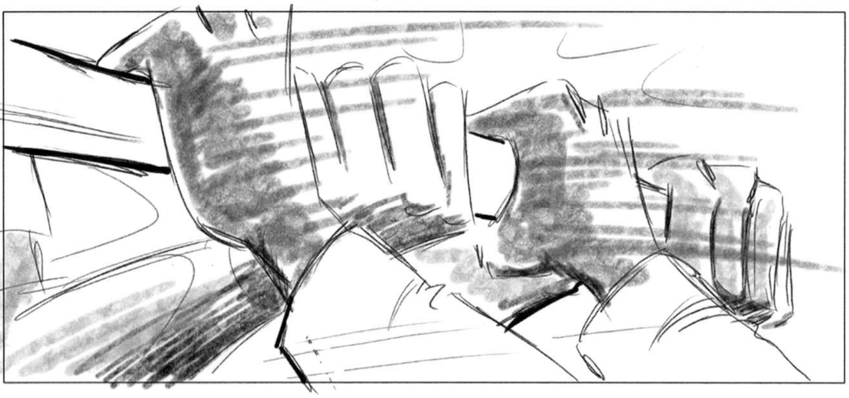

INSERT ON TROY CLOSING THE GAP. GRABS THE BAT.

70-15

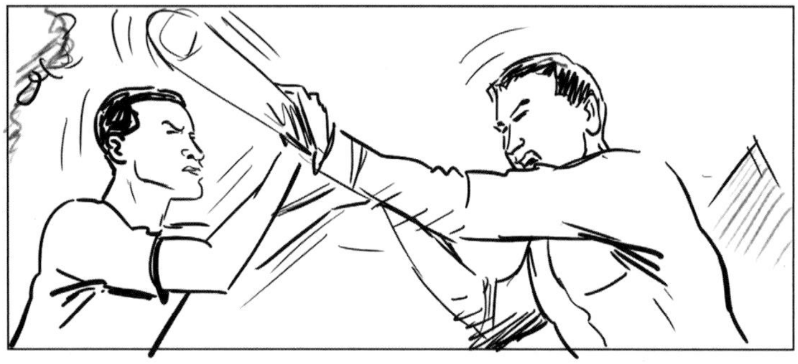

LOW ANGLE.

70-16

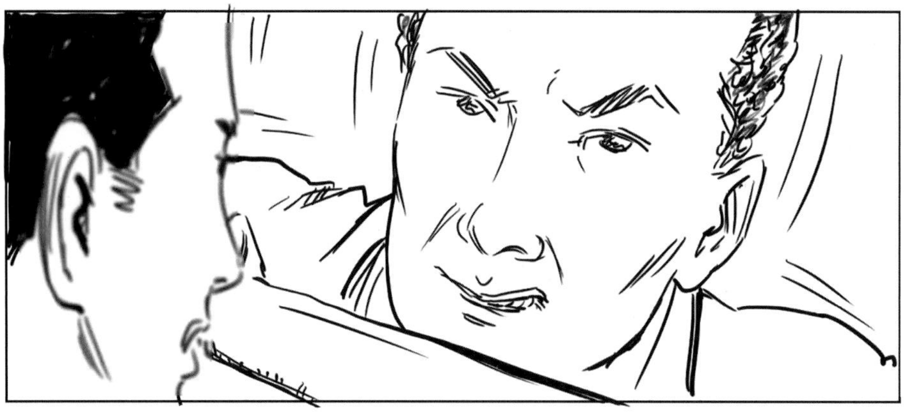

OTS CORY TO TROY.

I had already sent my large Cintiq monitor by FedEx ahead of my arrival so it was waiting for me at the office. I was given a very nice office of my own sandwiched comfortably between the offices of Todd and Denzel. The last time I had seen Denzel, who was as polished and dapper as ever was briefly at church in Los Angeles. When we finally met at the production office we greeted each other with the joy of a family reunion. His hair was now gray in preparation for the role of Troy Maxon. Troy is a character in turmoil and Denzel would capture all of that on-screen in total authenticity.

70-17

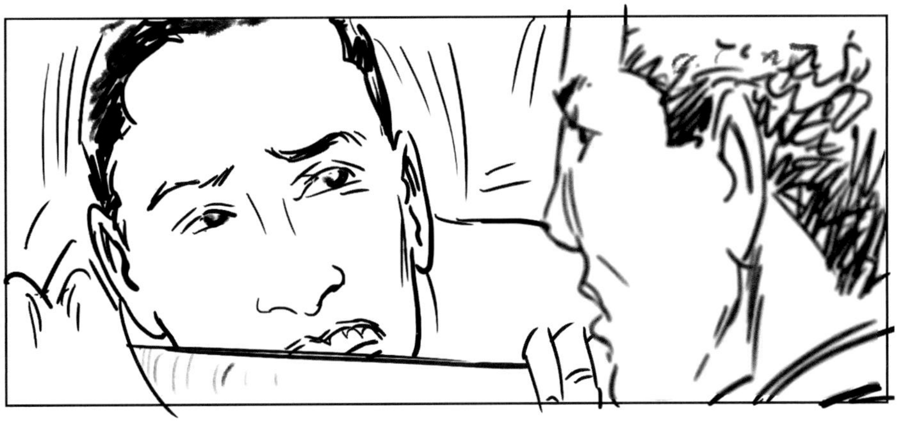

OTS TROY TO CORY

70-18

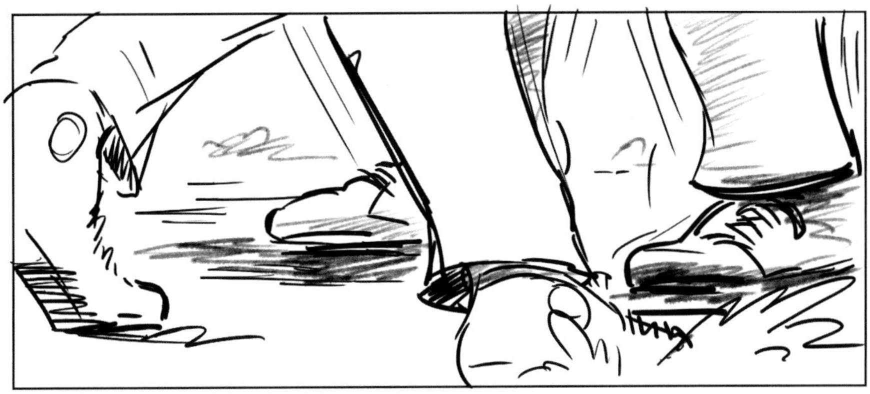

TROY PUSHING CORY BACK.

70-19

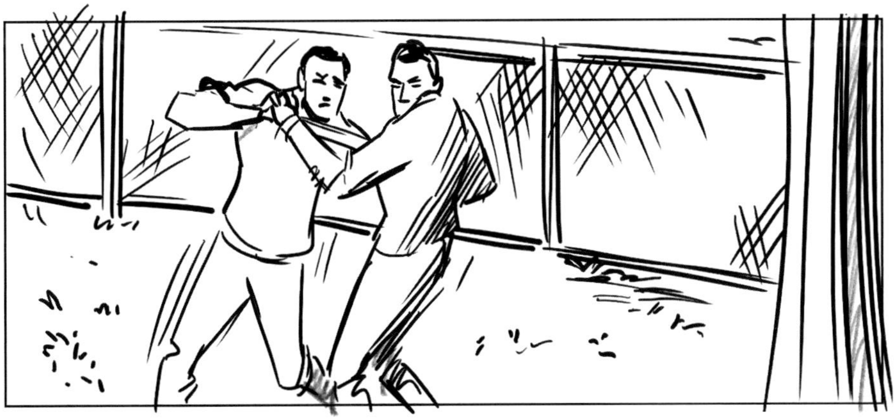

CORY AND TROY FIGHTING OVER CONTROL OF THE BAT.

Denzel often wore his trademark black warm-up pants, jacket and black baseball cap. This time he had on a Pittsburgh Pirates black cap with black emblem instead of his beloved NY Yankees black cap. "D" as I, and other people called him, was going to be in Pittsburgh a long time so he respectful to honor the city and locals by wearing their team logo. I had on a Yankees cap. I was later ribbed with humor by some locals in the office. They guided me to a sports memorabilia store just around the corner, and they had plenty of Pittsburgh team gear. I got a Roberto Clemente "21" cap. I also bought a Steelers cap as a backup. My interest in football is mercurial, so it didn't matter. In support of protesting the horrible reports of police brutality, later like so many other fans skipped watching the NFL for a season in protest to Colin Kaepernick being blacklisted.

Being placed in residence at a first-class hotel in Pittsburgh and being treated by Pittsburgh residents as a welcomed guest on this film allowed me a clear view of the socio-economic disadvantages for most of the Black people of Pittsburgh. While based there for the job,

70-20

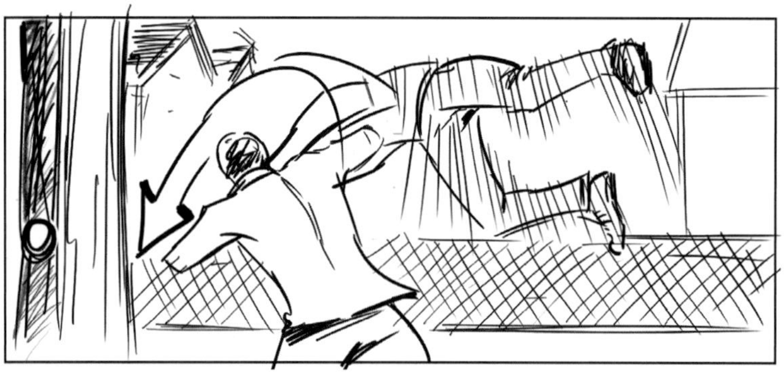

TROY FLIPS CORY.

I learned some of the city's history. A Black community that was a migration point of landing for Black people in the early 1900's, the area called The Hill District, is where August Wilson was born. This community is the place of origin of *Fences*. In fact, The Hill District was home to the earliest inhabitants who were former slaves of Haitian descent during the late 1800's.

70-21

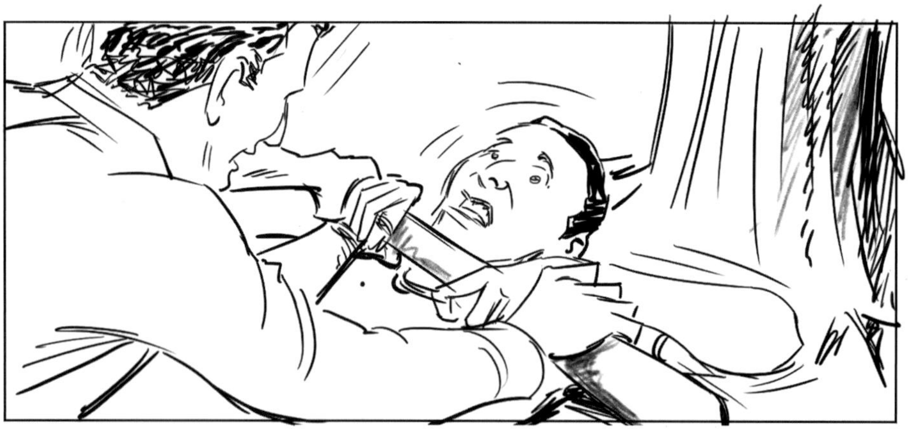

TROY PRESSES THE BAT OVER CORY'S NECK.

As with a lot cities in America with governmentally enforced institution of racism by what is called "red-lining", the Hill District was the only place Blacks were allowed to live in Pittsburgh. The residents built the neighborhood as best they could and by their own growth and tenacity, the Hill became well known for Jazz music. With this history infused into August Wilson's writing, Troy's oldest son, a wayward jazz musician Lyons, finds illegal means to make money and survive due to the blue

70-22

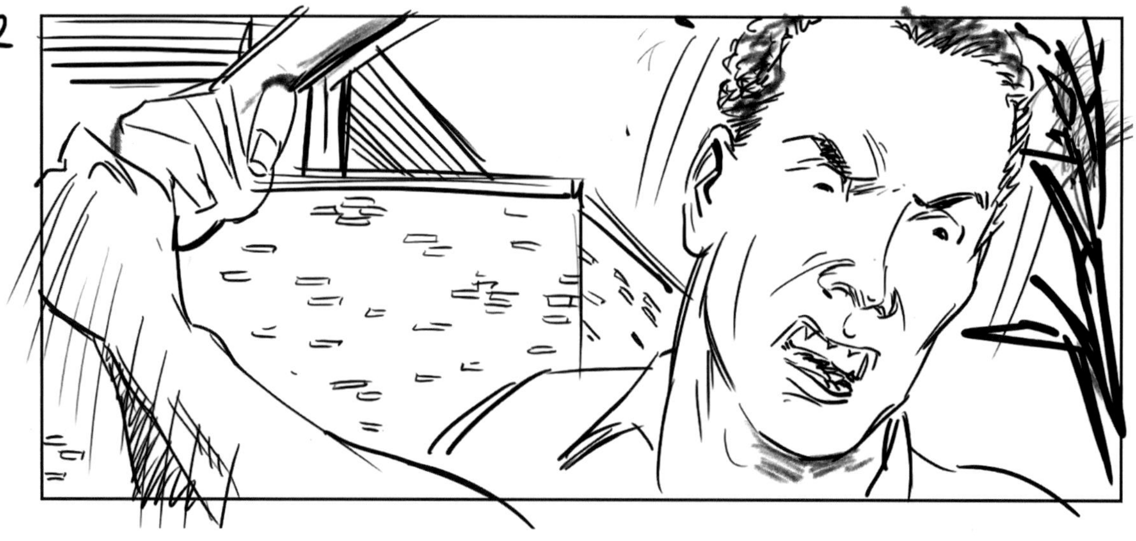

TROY RAISES THE BAT, READY TO STRIKE CORY.

collar low-paying service jobs and lack of better opportunities for work for Black people in Pittsburgh. At the time of the play, in 1957, the Hill District was in a steep economic decline. In 1956, one year before *Fences* is set, eight thousand Black residents and four hundred businesses were razed and disbanded, with some relocated to develop the area long held by Black people to build the Civic Arena which became the stadium for the Pittsburgh Penguins. This act by enforced law at the pen of politicians and government officials of the brutal demolition of Black homes and communities would repeat itself in cities all across America.

The Troy Maxon character is a worker at the sanitation department earning a frail salary and is barely able to care for his family. There aren't any Black truck drivers in sanitation work at this time period so Troy and his best friend, "Bono" are relegated to standing at the back of the truck on a narrow lift facing the opening of the mechanical lid where garbage is placed and compressed. They have to steady themselves on the back of a jerky sanitation truck somewhat dangerously by a holding on to a bolted handle. When the truck stops, the two men step off the lift of the truck, pick up and dump the trashcans into the garbage truck compressor and repeat. You can only imagine the smell of garbage that real garbage workers endured all day, every day. Troy and Bono, and Black men particularly who worked these job positions during that time were never permitted to enter the interior cab of the garbage truck during their entire workday run because they only hired white men as drivers to drive the sanitation trucks during that time period. Imagine being told you can only drive a garbage truck if you are white...*a garbage truck*.

Support of Black issues and concerns also comes in the form of hires for economic and career advancement. As I mentioned earlier when there is a Black director, that director can often be the position to demand more people of color hired in on the crew and/or simply bring in their own qualified people. Sharen Davis, costumes; Jono Oliver, 1st AD; Curtis Fuqua, Denzel's driver; Clay Fontenot, stunt coordinator; myself and others—all of us came on as Denzel's hires. One terrific hire was his talented daughter, Katia who worked as an associate producer on the show.

The first important thing I was able to do on the film was to see the interior and exterior of the location of the actual house where most of the movie would be filmed. The house that was found for the shoot was in the Hill District and was in ill repair. Construction and rebuilding work was done on the house to bring it up to safety standards by the art and construction departments while also maintaining it with a structure that looked as a home inhabited during the fifties. This film was after all, a period piece. The windows needed to be refurbished, the interiors repainted and a back porch had to be constructed and built for the scenes that were shot in the back of the house. This back porch was an important feature in the Broadway play and needed be in the film to reflect the importance of the scenes in *Fences* as written by Mr. Wilson. As a physical presence and a metaphor for Troy's life, the actual "fence" as referenced in the title of the play and film was constructed in the backyard beyond the newly added porch.

Again, scouting the locations for a film can be an extremely important visual asset and can offer a "feel" of the location to invoke into the storyboards. A scene was set in Pittsburgh's City Hall so while on a scout, I took my own camera for reference photos to get my own camera angles for the storyboards. The other location that we visited was the sanitation building and alley that the character of Troy Maxon worked. Denzel was always fully immersed in the scout trips. He would often say what the characters would be doing in each scene and what their mental states might be. By being present on a location prior to shooting, Denzel and the DP, Charlotte Bruus Christensen would discuss what the optimum shooting angles could be and I would take photographs from those exact angles to duplicate their vision into the storyboards as much as possible.

I roughed out a few scenes for Denzel and he was good with what I drew. It was early in the film and "D" as many of us call him, likes having storyboards. This worked out great for both of us because the storyboards I created energized his creative process.

By this time I was near the end of my initial work. The original plan as set by the production office was for me go back to Los Angeles and work remotely to wrap up whatever ongoing boards that were needed for Denzel. I was invited to watch the table read of the cast read-through and there was no way I would pass up seeing Denzel do a live read through of a script! Viola Davis played his wife as she did in the Broadway production of the play. It was a "full house" brimming with excitement. It was amazing to see all of these great professionals work with a stellar supporting cast of Mykelti Williamson, Russell Hornsby, newcomers Jovan Adepo and Saniyya Sidney. At the end of the reading, Denzel came up to me and said, "Stay another week." This became a regular and happy occurrence between us each week. I made the first of many calls to my wife saying I was staying longer than we first thought.

One of the most dynamic scenes we worked on was a proposed flashback sequence. We find out that Troy, as a thirteen-year-old boy suffered a savage beating by his own father after a thwarted romantic tryst between young Troy and a teenaged girl. For the location of this scene, the scout van took us outside of the city to a house in a farming community. The location was to be set there for the scene of young Troy with the teenaged girl that would spiral into a nightmare as Troy would see his father bitterly approaching in the clearing. With this fresh in my mind I drew the scene immediately to capture the essence of the fear and emotion that the location scout had emitted so as to give the work the feel from the page that was needed for the shoot. Weeks later, Denzel was preparing to shoot the flashback sequence of Troy's childhood incident while his grown sons listened. I sent him a couple of ways I thought Troy's recount could be shot while being cinematically riveting.

With time to reflect on these scene elements the next day, I recalled the famous Indianapolis scene from, *Jaws*. This classic scene starts with Brody, Quint, and Hooper engaging in a joke that leads into Quint revealing a personal horror. Quint's capsized WWII ship *The Indianapolis* was assigned on a secret mission so undetectable that the shipmates in the wreckage were left floating in the waters for more than 72 hours, leaving them as food for hundreds of sharks that circled and killed his shipmates. This experience haunts Quint and shapes him into the person he has become. The scene starts with cuts between the triumvirate but proceeds with a slow camera push-in on Robert Shaw's character Quint as he tells his story. I thought this approach would be a strong moment for older Troy to parallel young Troy's incident along that changed his life. Denzel loved the Jaws clip idea that I offered. Using my suggestion, the final version of the retelling of young Troy's story by Denzel's immense talent is so magnificent that no flashback scenes were needed.

Being kept on the film for more time meant I was able to watch the incredible cast in rehearsals. Denzel, Viola, and the cast rehearsed in this space for weeks until the house was safe and ready for the actors to enter. The house used for the film was still under construction so the art department built a scale replica of the house that was placed as a set piece in the basement of a large church. The two floors of the house were laid out by the inch, side by side with the rooms and halls of the house also marked by masking tape to the very inch. Another adjoining area of the layout was taped-off in the basement to represent the backyard of the house. The art department was very helpful with supplying me with reference photographs of Pittsburgh homes that existed in the 1950's. They had done months of research and it paid off nicely with the information that I could pull from.

What was incredible was that Denzel hired a "second team" of stand-ins consisting of young actors. He would let them do a scene to work out the camera blocking and then let the main cast come in when the scene was cinematically prepared. This allowed Denzel to actually teach the understudies as they did their jobs. It was inspiring to watch him mentor these talented young actors.

Denzel needed me remain on the film for more weeks. Travel coordinator, Kim Finoche would set up a departure flight for me only to have me say "guess what, I'm not going." It became a funny routine for us as the weeks went on. Kim would look at me with mock annoyance and then break into a smile that I was staying.

Fences did not have what one could consider "stunts," but there was one scene that fell into that category. In the movie, Troy and his son Cory have a verbal confrontation that turns physical and scary. Years of pent-up emotions have come to a boil and Cory confronts his bigger and tougher father with the same baseball bat that Troy used to practice swings with in the backyard. The fight is quick as Troy disarms Cory and then momentarily chokes him with the bat. Troy's symbol of his lost youth used as the instrument of destruction of his own son.

In rehearsal, stunt coordinator Clay Fontenot worked out the basic choreography with Jovan Adepo. As the director of the film and its' star, Denzel had to maneuver from both sides of the camera in order to figure out the main character beats and movements with Clay, who then stood in for Denzel as Clay and Jovan acted out the fight scene. The trickiest move in the fight was Troy grabbing the bat from Cory and then flipping him. Troy was originally going to start choking Cory with the bat from behind but this was changed. Clay came up with the idea that Troy would be on top of Cory as he choked him and would look in his son's eyes and stop himself before he went too far. Stunt people are filmmakers in their own right and often make valuable character contributions to scenes. I took an abundance of photos of the choreography and went to work. Having a shot-by-shot approximation of the fight was helpful to Denzel.

Continuing on the film, I decided to create smaller, cleaner character scenes for Denzel, rather than scenes with layered storytelling. One scene was the opening featuring Troy carrying on his duties as a sanitation worker early in the film as he rides on the back of the truck with his best friend and partner, Bono. When this scene was shot, Denzel and actor Stephen McKinley Henderson (Bono) were safely strapped on to the cinematic sanitation truck for their dialogue shots. But in the wide shots Clay Fontenot doubled for Denzel and Stephen's position on the truck was doubled by a stuntman to maintain the safety of the actors. Stephen had been one of August Wilson's favorite actors to use in his productions such as *Jitney, King Hedley II, Ma Rainey's Black Bottom* and of course, opposite Denzel in the Broadway revival of *Fences*.

Another non-storyboard assignment I had was to add illustrative detail to a vintage Army promotional illustration that would be seen in the movie. I would be working with the show's graphic designer, Christina Myal on bringing this to pass. The original illustration was great but it needed some additional lighting highlights and shadows to pop more for the screen. I accomplished all this in photoshop. My time in Pittsburgh had moved swiftly. By the time we got to May, Mother's Day was coming up. I had spoken to Betty that I would be home in days to celebrate it with her. It was on a Sunday meeting with Denzel at the main house that he said, "I need you to stay three more weeks." That was an incredible thing to hear. It wasn't the week-to-week extension, but a hard count at three more weeks. I felt incredibly honored that Denzel would ask this so I made an equal commitment.

My extended weeks offer of continued work was almost comedic because I had just told Betty I'd be home. On the spot, I said, "D, I'd love to stay and I thank you so much. I just told my wife that I was going to be coming home, so help a broth'a out when I call her." Denzel basically said, "Let's put her on the phone." What came next was the use of charm and star-swagger. Betty prides herself on being an industry professional, unfazed by actors, herself being a seasoned Screen Actor's Guild member as well as a Writers Guild member. I called her up and said, "Baby, hey, a friend of mine needs to ask you for a favor..." And I passed Denzel my cell. He sat back on the bench on the movie house's porch and calmly chatted. D looked like any of the confident, easygoing characters he's played in countless films. When he gave my phone back to me with a little confident smile, I knew things were good. With that minor issue with my wife fully taken care of, Denzel felt free to storyboard almost every scene in the film.

As we would continue to chat about scenes on the stoop a passersby would notice Denzel and stop to ask for an autograph. One such car had several older women in it. They stopped and called out to him. Denzel walked over and kindly said hello. When they asked for an autograph, he said, "I can't give you that" because he was still working and focused, "but I'll give you a hug." Denzel then politely hugged the driver and then walked over to the other side and hugged the other two women, who were in fact elderly. It was another special moment to witness with him.

Work weeks ended but the work continued. Weekends have a special relaxed air when most of the crew is not around. What I really cherished most were the Sunday meetings with Denzel. I had a private working time with a respectful and respected generational brilliant artist. It was comparable with the one-on-one meetings I would get with Ron Howard. Denzel and I spent time working on one of the later scenes in the film where Troy finally snaps after his mistress has died in the hospital giving birth to their child. In a fit of rage, Troy yells out his window to tempt death and challenges the wrath of God. Denzel and I went over basic blocking for the pivotal and powerful scene...and I took in every moment.

My time on the show was finally winding down. Thankfully, my wife and son were able to visit me for a weekend. They were a breath of fresh air for me since I had been living in a hotel residence. I managed a visit to the set but positioned them at a respectable distance. Denzel didn't like people on set that didn't have to be on set, including crewmembers. He only wanted camera personnel, ADs, and any crew that were absolutely necessary to the day's work. Having folks stand and watch did not appeal to his work ethic as an actor or director and he was in a weighty position as both.

Denzel and I worked out some basic blocking and camera placement for the dialogue scenes of the funeral scene of the movie where after seven years his character Troy has died. A funeral procession with dozens of extras was storyboarded and filmed but it was never used. What was used in its' place to end the movie was the Maxon family coming together with "Gabriel" , Troy's brother in the backyard. Gabriel is trying to blow his horn so that Troy's spirit can reach Saint Peter and the "pearly gates." The scene came out pretty close to the storyboards but a notable occurrence truly added to the film: the film production office was able to schedule the demolition of the house next door with the urban planning office of Pittsburgh. When the final scenes happen in the lapse of seven years, the house next-door to the Maxon house is no longer there because it was demolished during a break in the shooting schedule. This was a great way to show how the area changes with the passage of time in the film. The fence in Fences that Troy referenced during most of the film was built in the span of the seven years' lapse and is in full display and now adjacent to an empty lot.

In another amazing occurrence just before Gabriel finally manages to blow his horn to set Troy's spirit free, *the backyard gate closed all by it self. This actually happened on set.* No rigs, no special effects or wired handling by an off-camera crew personnel. The metaphor could then be that Troy's spirit is involved somehow in his own earthly release in that he is leaving the house on his final sojourn to go to heaven. It's a wonderful thought.

When I left the production office for the last time, I left a sign saying "Straight Outta Storyboards." People got a kick out of it even if they didn't know that I was actually one of two board artists that worked on *Straight Outta Compton*.

The sad part in the week was that Muhammad Ali had just died days earlier. Like so many Americans and people worldwide, I loved Ali. But in my case, I used to do an Ali impression in high school and I did one all the way until his passing. As a huge boxing fan, Ali had a big effect on me. Even Bruce Lee idolized him and used a lot of his footwork in his own training and certainly in his film fights. As a Black man, Ali was the proud brother who said "NO" to white male authority when he stood up against being drafted into the Vietnam war. He did not pander. Ali would tell opponents Black and white that he was going to beat them and he would tell them in what round that it was going to happen.

I was soon on the plane and leaving my Pittsburgh experience. It was an amazing experience that I can never forget. Once again, I worked with Denzel Washington, one of the greatest actors of all time. And I had worked one of the best and certainly the nicest producers in the business, Todd Black. Additionally, I met a lot of great new people. It was almost meditative to be in location long enough where I had started to figure the city out and appreciate its' offerings—if only just a little.

Fences has remained one of my most revered work experiences, ever.

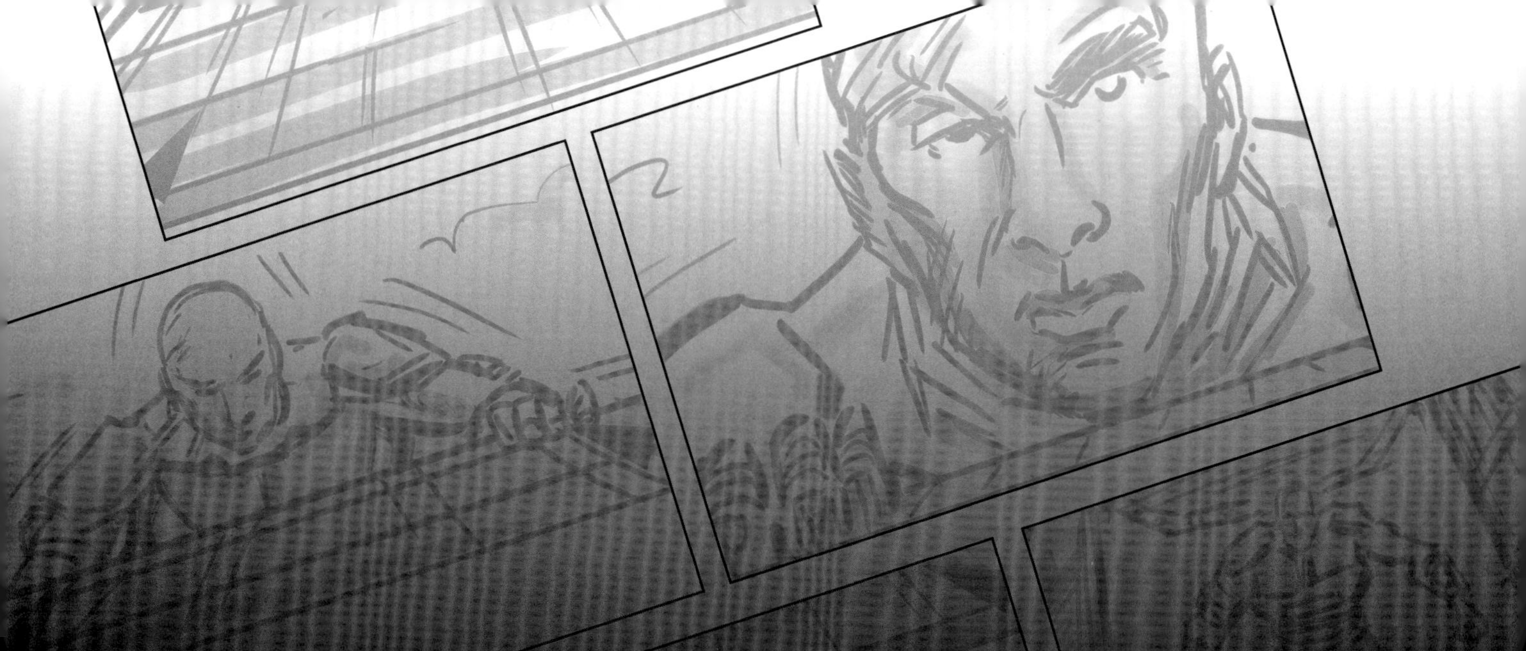

STORYBOARDS AND STORIES OF 15 SELECT FILMS AND TELEVISION SHOWS

HARD DAY'S WORK

Chapter 13

MARVEL'S AGENTS OF S.H.I.E.L.D.

ENTER THE UNIVERSE

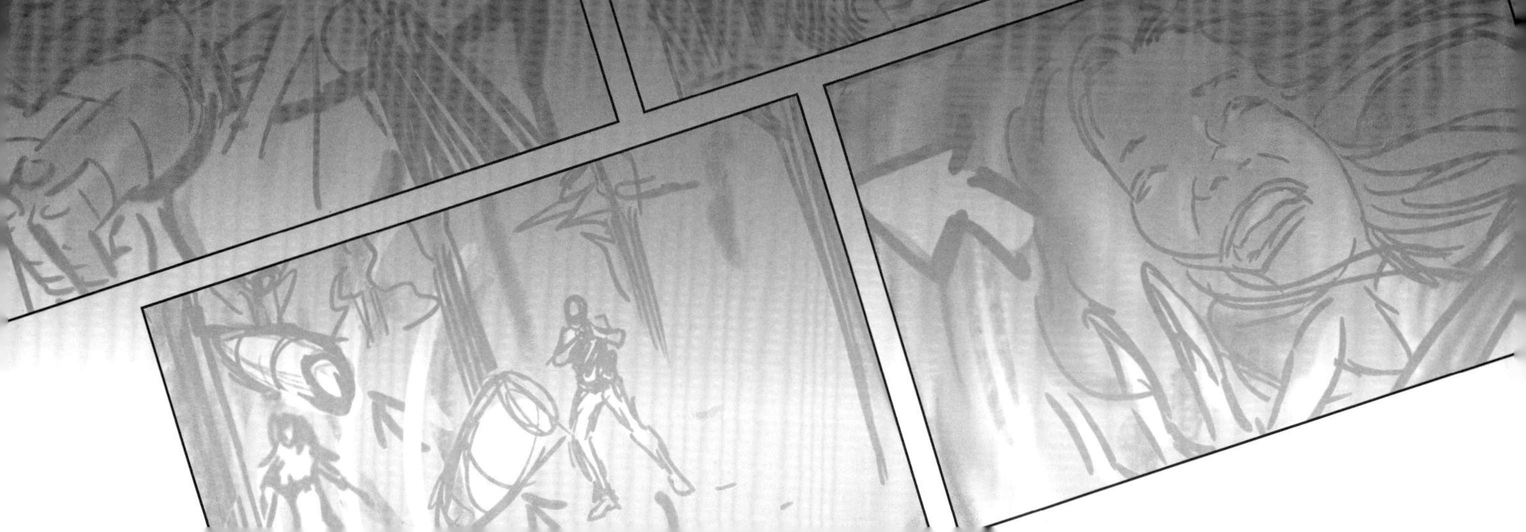

Marvel's Agents of S.H.I.E.L.D. ... enter the universe

Anyone who knows me knows that on par with my love of martial arts is my love of comic books. I've read comic books since I was a child and my love for them has sustained over the years. Only in recent years have I deliberately reduced my actual purchases of comics due to the huge price increases and certainly the dwindling space in on my book shelves to further build out my already extensive collection.

My connection to *Marvel's Agents of S.H.I.E.L.D.* began with the Clark Gregg, the show's star and established actor of stage and screen. Clark had plans to direct an independent feature that he also wrote entitled *Trust Me*. It was about a struggling talent agent who tries to save his career through signing an upcoming child star. I was contacted sometime in early 2012 to work with Clark who was now at his career apex having played agent Phil Coulson of *S.H.I.E.L.D* in several of the Marvel movie releases and most notably *The Avengers*, where his character had a death scene which galvanizes the team. Clark and I met at a nice little restaurant in North Hollywood. He was as humble, self-effacing and as chilled out as can be. Clark was a working actor in a good place in his life.

Clark was ready to direct his second feature film on the heels of having already done the movie *Choke* starring Sam Rockwell. For this initial meeting, Clark just wanted to meet me while he was still waiting for the film's financing to finalize. After all of about twenty minutes into the meeting, we parted ways and that was it. I went on with life as if nothing happened with the project. Many months later, I got the call that *Trust Me* was funded and ready to go. It was very low budget so my pay would be minimal. As a perk, I did receive an Avengers poster from Clark with half of the main cast signing it as an additional "thank you".

It was on a visit to the set of *Trust Me* when I learned of something quite stupendous: Clark and I were alone when he told me that he was in meetings regarding his Phil Coulson character's return in a new television show co-created by Joss Whedon. I believe my first response was, "Isn't Phil dead?" Clark told me that Joss had figured out how to bring the character back to life and that he was excited about it. Clark trusted me to keep my mouth shut because this was confidential information he had shared with me privately. I felt honored to be trusted by Clark with such a thrilling bit of insider information.

When Marvel's *Agents of S.H.I.E.L.D.* pilot was being shot, I had not been hired to work on the show at this point but Clark kindly invited my son Josh and I to visit the set. I had met Josh Whedon earlier but I never saw him work before. In fact, his brother Jed Whedon who was the co-creator of this new television series is married to Maurissa Tancharoen, the other co-creator—who is the older sister of my long time friend, Kevin Tancharoen whom I affectionately call "Lil Brother." I had known Kevin since he was a twenty-year-old fledging director hired to work on a dance-oriented young adult project. Kevin was already an accomplished dancer in his own right. He was only fifteen years old when he worked professionally as a choreographer for Britney Spears.

Sometime later, I got a call from a friend and storyboard artist Robin Richesson. *Agents of S.H.I.E.L.D.* was picked up for a full series run by the network and Robin had been contacted to storyboard the second episode. Robin was working out of town on a movie and couldn't take the job so she wanted to pass the opportunity on to me. To say that I was "happy" to take that gig is an understatement. Later, I got a pleasant call from Maurissa. She stated that she

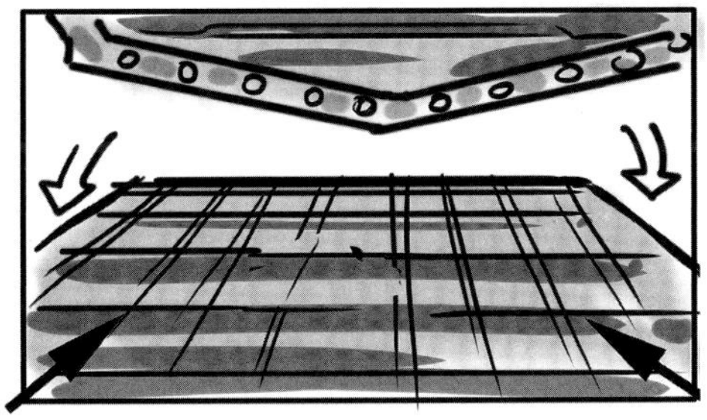

11

BACK TO THE RAMP DOOR.

PUSH IN.

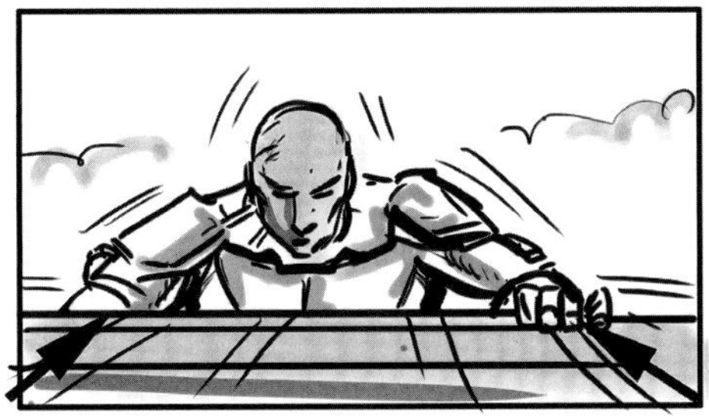

11A

PUSH IN CONT'D

AS WE REVEAL DEATHLOK.

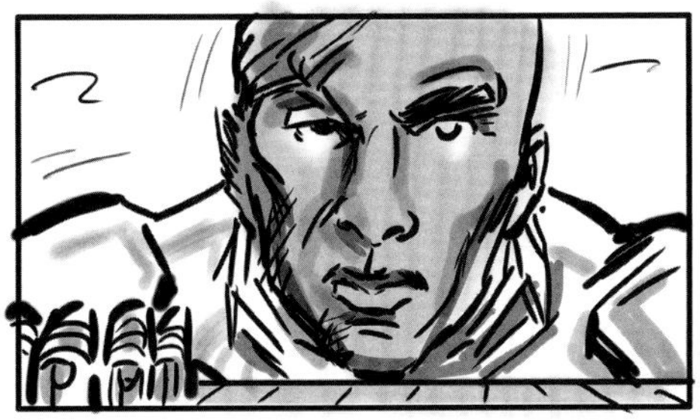

12

CLOSE ON DEATHLOK.

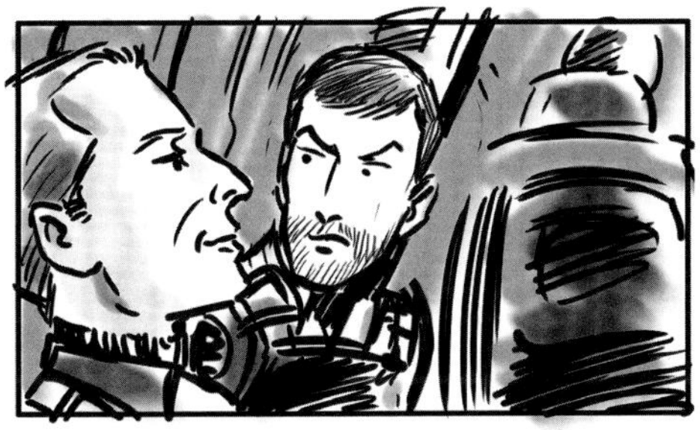

13

HUNTER TURNS TO COULSON.

COULSON "BACK-UP."

This was one of the few times I was able to draw a character who was even close to being in a super-hero costume. I was used to drawing a lot of people in suit and ties and at most, black stealth suits when I drew May or Daisy.

spoke to her brother Kevin on what I was like to work with. Kevin told his sister, "Warren's great!" I was touched, to say the least, by my young friend's sentiment. And as this industry goes, just like that I was in business working on a Marvel television series.

When I came into the production office in Culver Studios—which is thankfully close to my house—I was already floating on a cloud. I had been in the industry twenty years and yet, I was back to that first-day-of-school feeling. The production office was decked out with some very cool Marvel brand items and I knew I was "home." Everyone was friendly—from Kyle Hiemenz, the office production coordinator down to every production assistant. Genre shows often get code names because there are obsessive fans looking to unveil and release all kinds of secrets involving plots, actors, photos, etc. The codename for Marvel's *Agents of S.H.I.E.L.D.* was simply "Ragtag" because the show's cast was a "rag tag" group of seasoned agents who are paired with a cyber hacker and two brainy scientists who were new to the field.

I was again called in to work with second episode director, David Straiton. David is a super experienced pro who knew his craft and always kept his sense of humor. We quickly went over the basics of the show in terms of the characters and then we went over the logistics of "The Bus" which was the large aerial transport ship that served as the *S.H.I.E.L.D.* characters' base of operations for the series. The scenes that I worked on had a big action sequence on The Bus as well as action scenes that had to be shot around a South American temple. I was also introduced to some of the technical devices created for the show that the *S.H.I.E.L.D.* agents' characters would be using in the show.

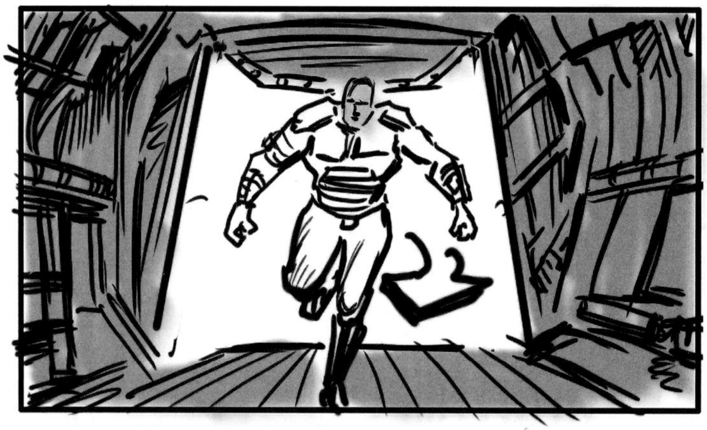

14

ON DEATHLOK CHARGING.

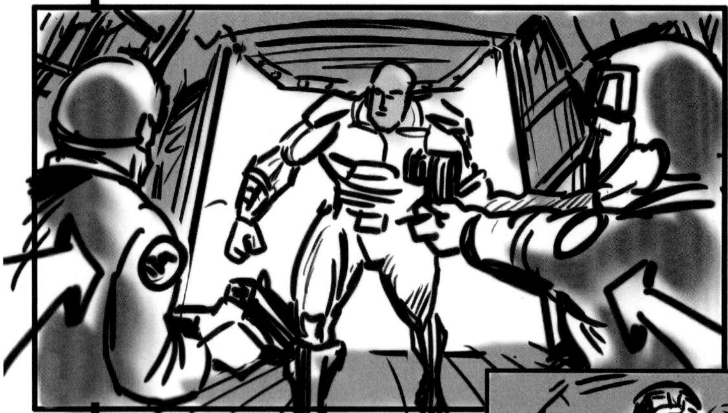

14A

SHOT CONT'D

AS THE AGENTS ENTER THEIR OWN POV.

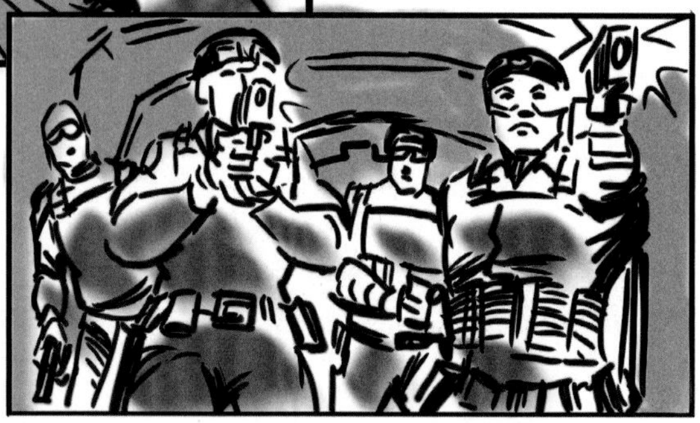

15

THE AGENTS FIRING.

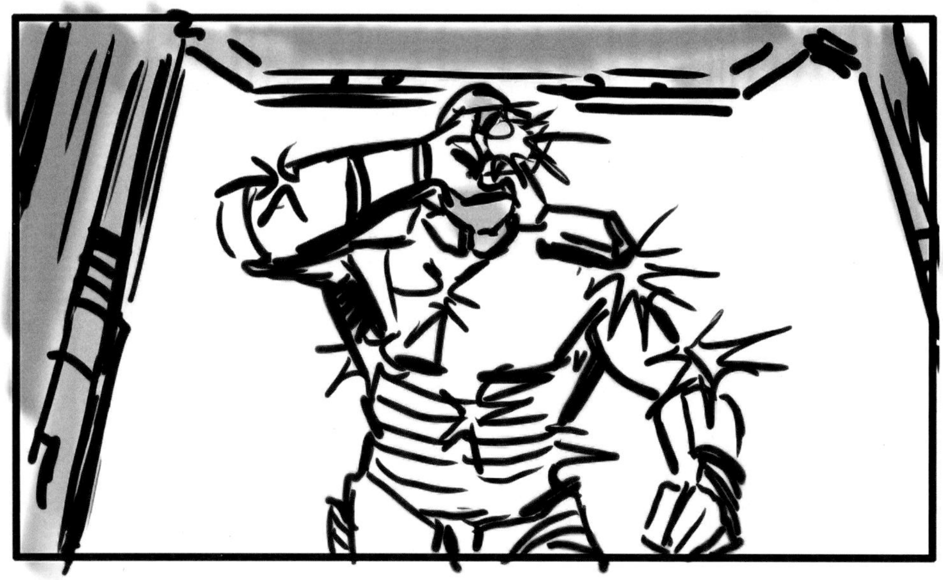

16

BULLETS BOUNCING OFF DEATHLOK.

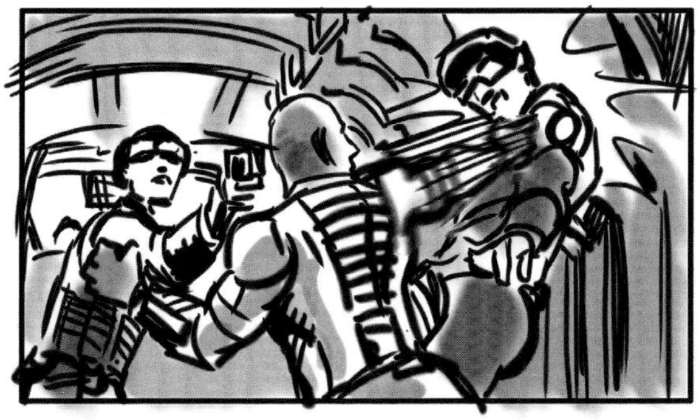

17

REVERSE AS
DEATHLOK HITS AGENT#1

AGENT#2 READIES TO
FIRE.

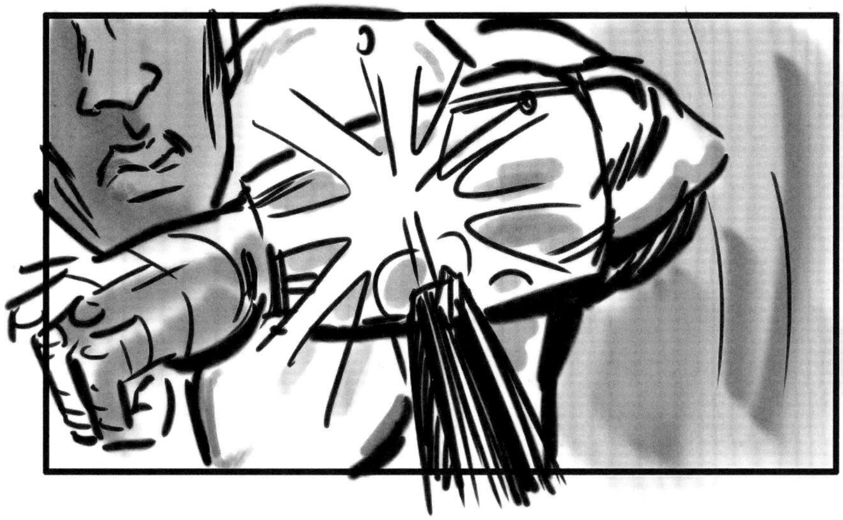

18

CLOSE AS DEATHLOK
USES HIS ARMORED FOREARM
TO BLOCK GUNFIRE FROM
AGENT#2.

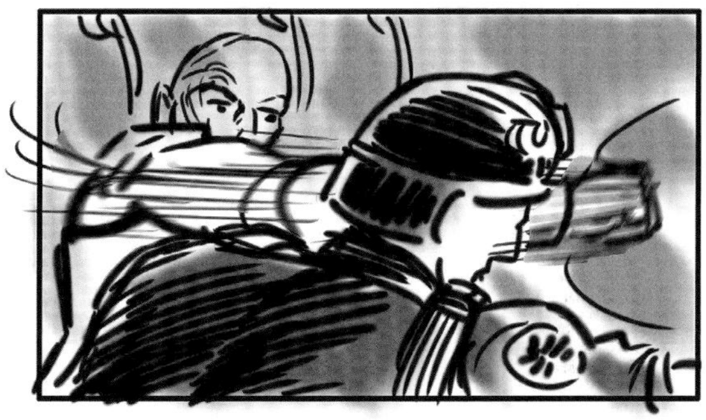

19

WIDER

DEATHLOK HITS
AGENT#2.

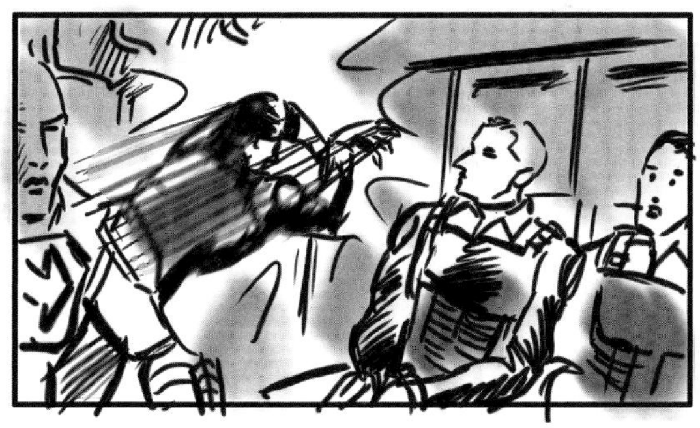

19A

SHOT CONT'D AS

AGENT#2 HITS THE WALL
AND DEATHLOK ADVANCES.

When it rains it pours, even in show business. At the same time I was working on *S.H.I.E.L.D.* I got a call to work with writer/director Dan Gilroy who needed a stunt sequence worked out for a film called *Night-crawler.* The film is a thriller starring Jake Gyllenhaal, who usually played offbeat heroes but was now cast as a ruthless sociopath. I met with Dan and stunt coordinator, Mike Smith. We went over an intense driving chase sequence that would take place in the last section of the movie. I took note of the precise shot-by-shot description from Dan and went home to sketch the work and get it done. My schedule at this point was full and as a professional I always insist on completing and delivering my work in a timely manner or I don't take

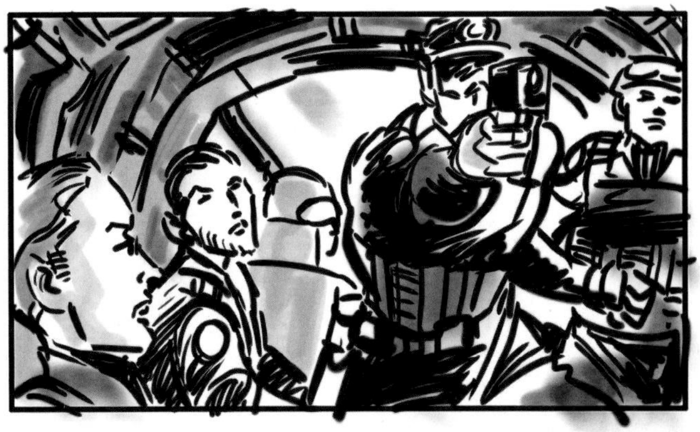

20

AGENT#3 GETS READY TO FIRE ON DEATHLOK.

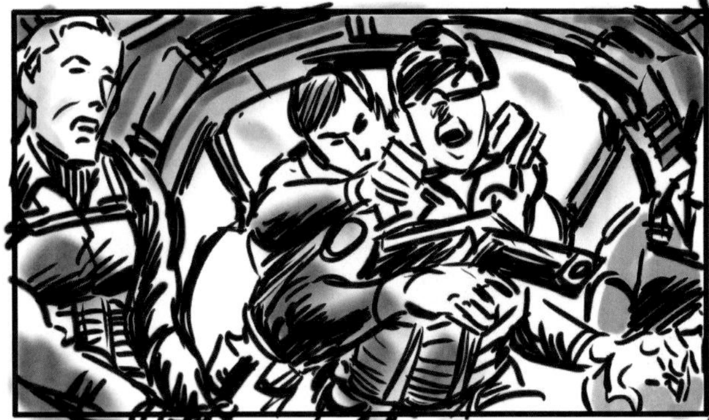

20A

HUNTER WRAPS HIS CUFFED HANDS AROUND AGENT#3.

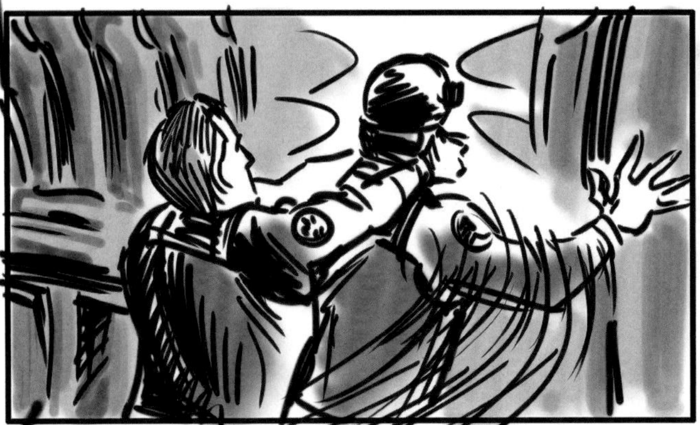

20B

SHOT CONT'D

CAMERA MOVES WITH HUNTER AS HE SPINS AGENT#3 AND SLAMS HIM INTO THE WALL.

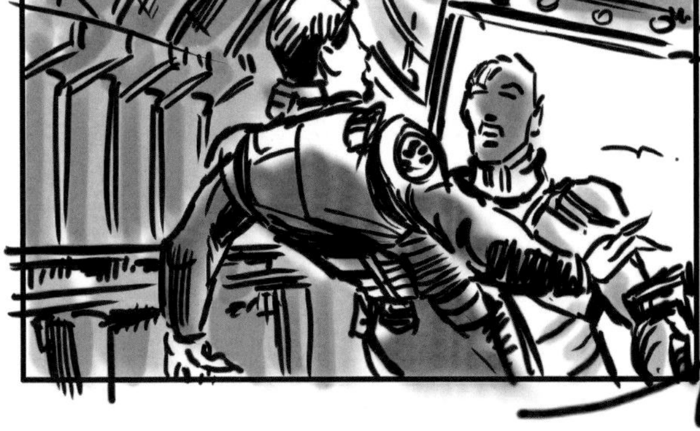

21

DEATHLOK GRABS SHIELD LEADER.

CAMERA PANS SLIGHTLY.

the job. I soon got another call from *Agents of S.H.I.E.L.D.* to do another sequence on the second episode. Dan wanted me back to do more detailed work on the *Nightcrawler* car chase scene but I had to politely tell production that I had a previous commitment. I was super worried that I could have put Dan in a bind, but I also knew that I couldn't do both jobs at the same time because I couldn't double dip this time and provide the best possible work to both directors. In the years to come, I have established a very

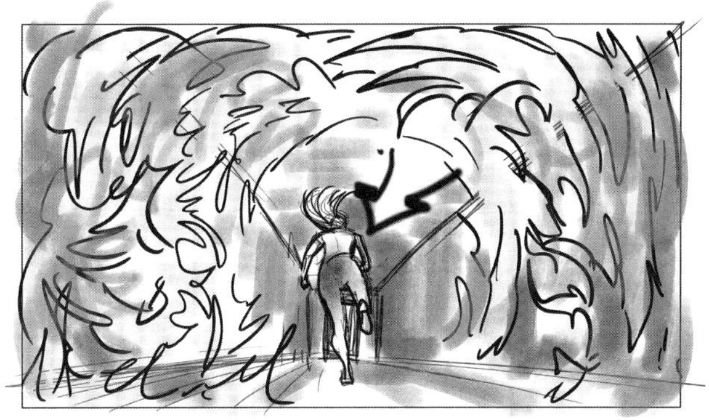

9-5A

SHOT CONT'D

THE FIRE GROWS BEHIND YO-YO AS SHE RUNS DOWN THE HALLWAY.

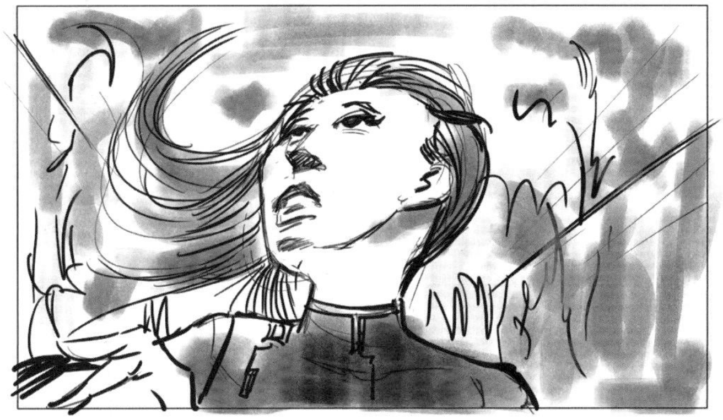

9-6

YO-YO LOOKING AROUND AT THE FIRE ENVELOPING THE HALLWAY.

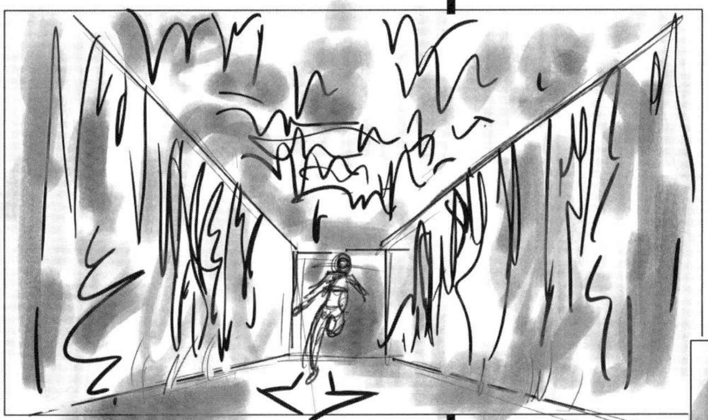

9-7

BACK TO SHOT AS YO-YO NOW RUNS TOWARDS CAMERA WITH THE HALL-WAY ON FIRE.

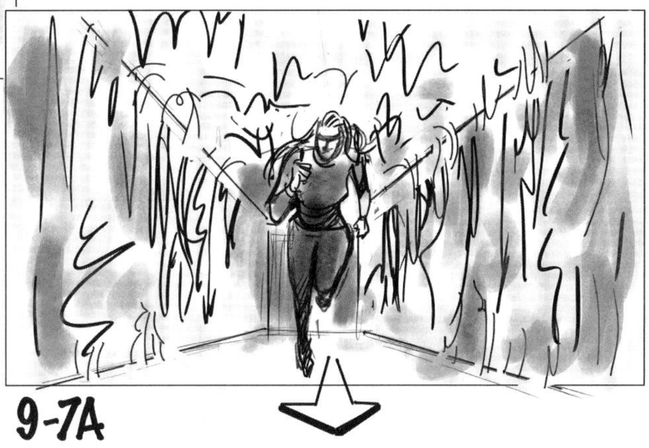

9-7A

SHOT CONT'D

The frames of Yo-Yo running through fire were originally in color.

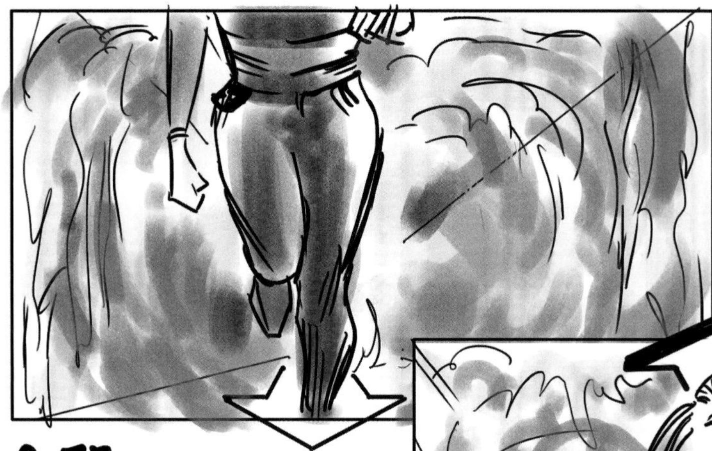

SHOT CONT'D

9-7B

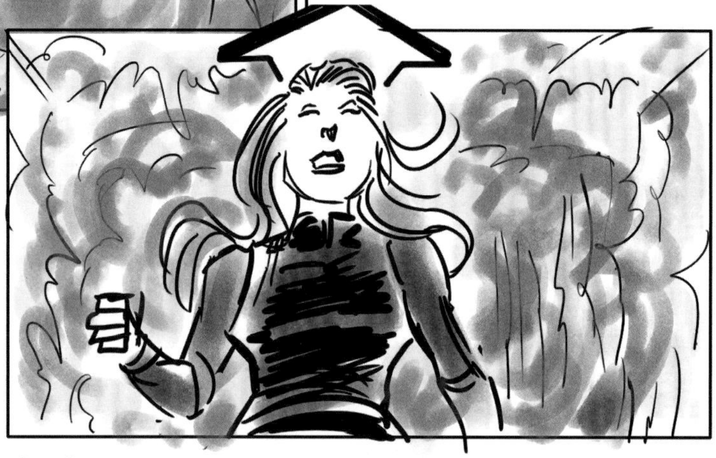

NEW SHOT ON YO-YO RUNNING THROUGH THE HALLWAY.

9-8

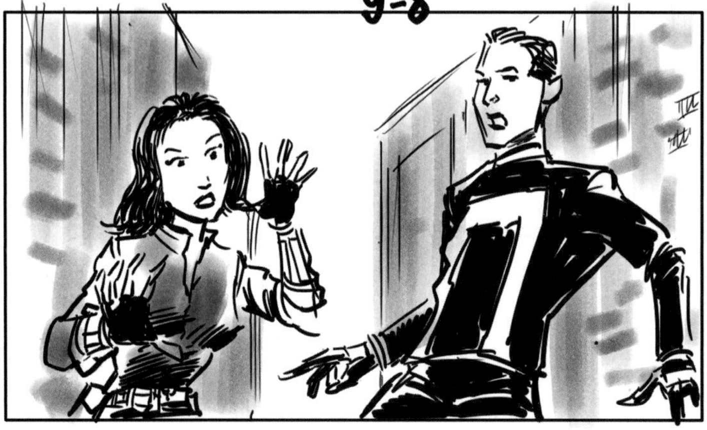

DAISY AND ROBBIE SEE WHAT HAS HAPPENED.

9-9

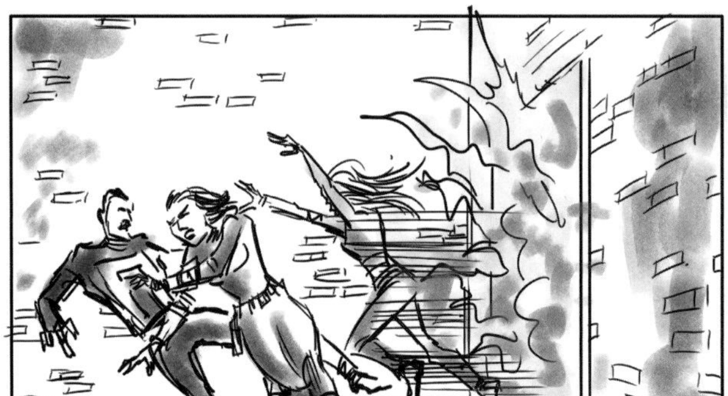

PROFILE ON THE ALLEY AS YO-YO IS BLASTED OUT OF THE EXIT WITH A FIREBALL. DAISY AND ROBBIE GO DOWN AS WELL.

9-10

small circle of talented artists who assist me with tightening my roughs when I get overloaded, but this wasn't the case then.

Even today with a well-planned work schedule, jobs can overlap. It's part of the beast. Dan Gilroy was pleased enough to have called me back on his next two movies and we have had amazing working sessions. He's always super prepared and professional with a great mind for detail.

The *Agents of S.H.I.E.L.D.* episode work wrapped and I was on my way to the rest of the season. The first season was a lot of work. I boarded

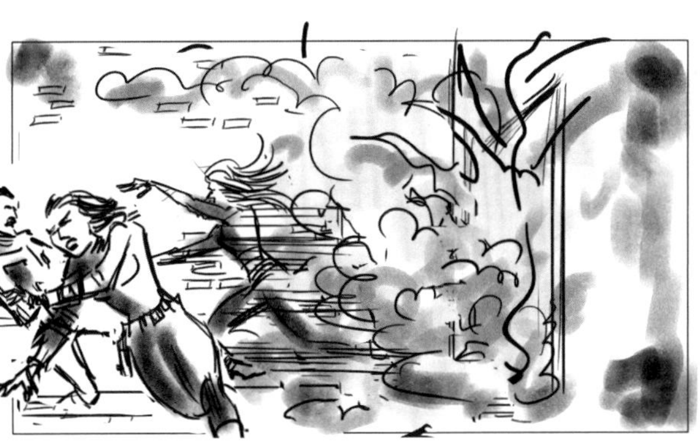

SHOT CONT'D

THE FIREBALL EXPLODES

9-10A

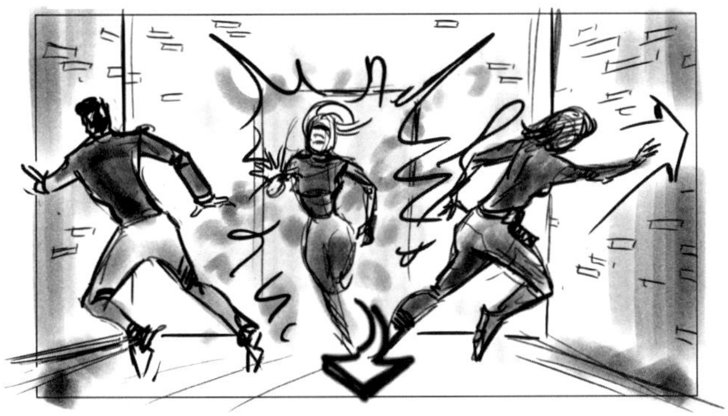

FRONTAL ON THE SAME

9-11

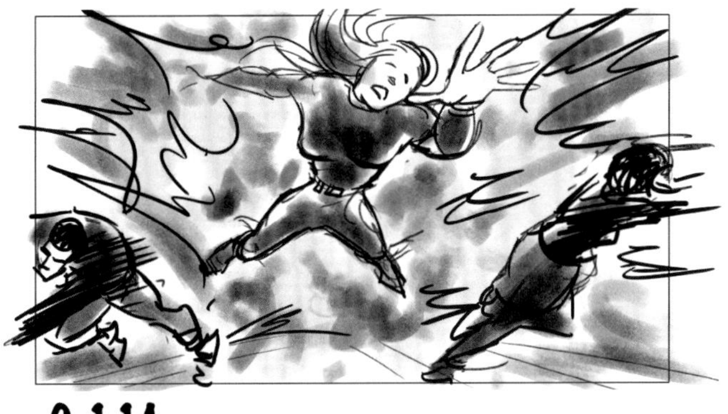

9-11A

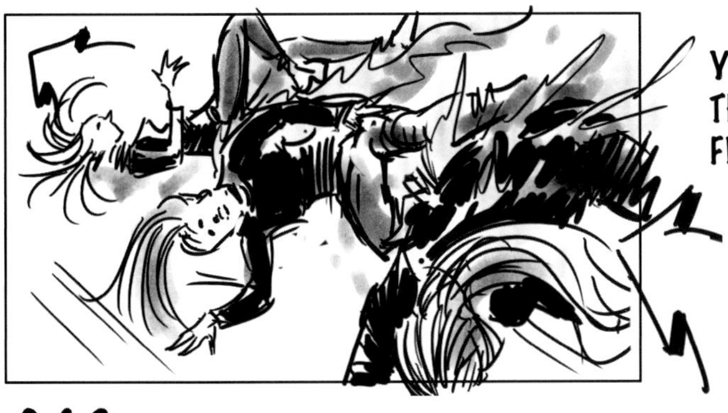

YO-YO ROLLS THROUGH FRAME ON FIRE.

9-12

eleven of the twenty-two series episodes. I was integrated to be part of a trusted team that made sure episodes are done to the highest level. The directors in that first run were truly amazing. Director Roxann Dawson started as actor and had in fact started directing while being cast member "Lt. B'Elanna Torres" on *Star Trek: Voyager*. As a lifelong Trekkie it was cool to work with Roxann, who was always on point in our meetings. Leonard Nimoy was the first *Star Trek* actor to move into directing and it has since become an established tradition for cast members to direct episodes on the various Trek spin-offs. I had previously worked on the television series *Burn Notice* with actor turned director Jonathan Frakes who portrayed "Commander Will Riker" on *Star Trek: The Next Generation*. We had to work remotely on that show via Skype since *Burn Notice* was fully shot in Florida. Jonathan and I finally met in person and we worked together for several weeks while he was developing another project. I was happy when I found out that Jonathan was hired to direct on *Agents* and

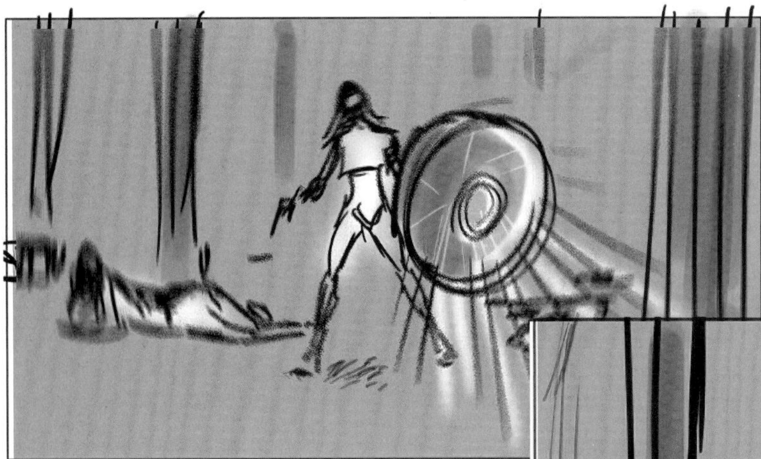

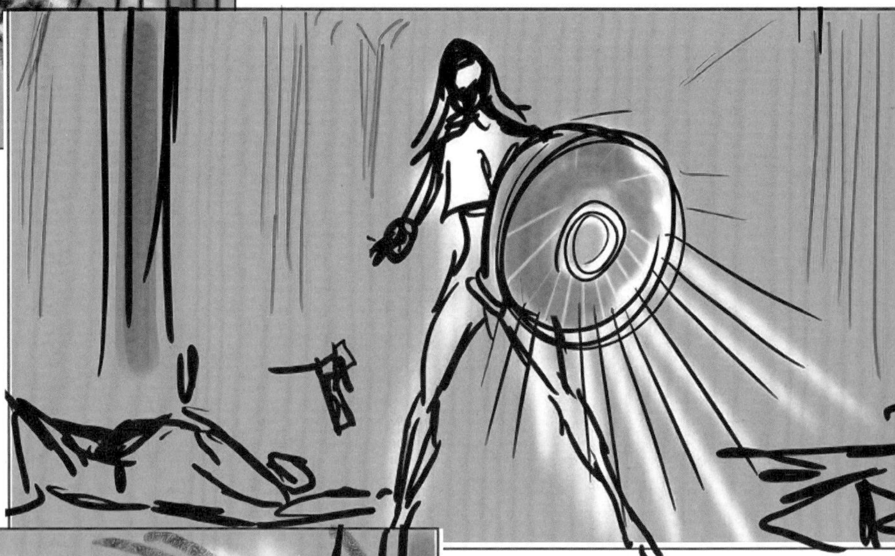

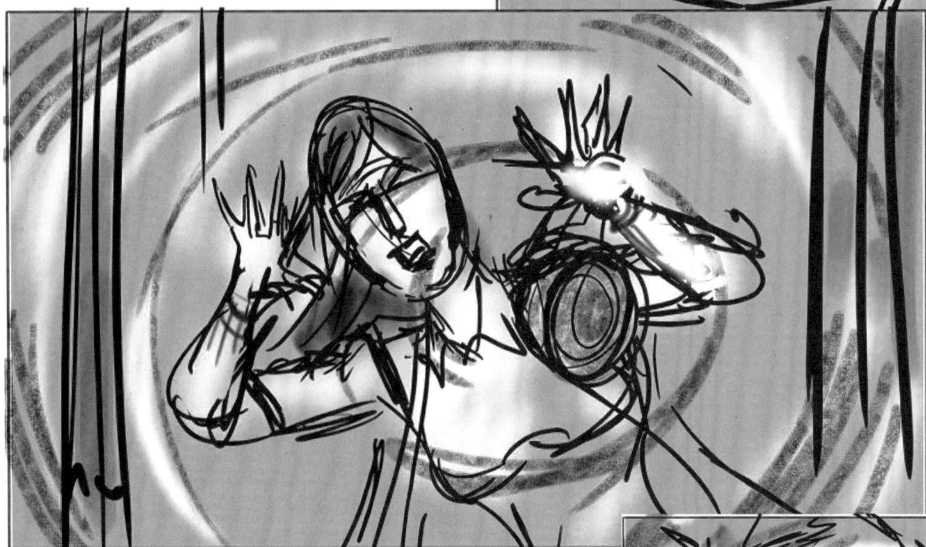

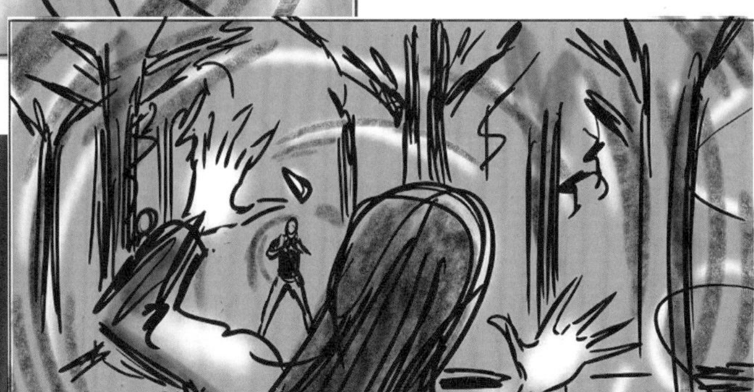

This was a big VFX sequence where Daisy deflects bullets mid-air and then while defending herself lets loose with her quaking powers and wipes out part of a forest.

had requested me to work with him. Jonathan establishes a great work environment on all the television shows we have worked on together. He's a legitimately kind human being with a great sense of humor. I'll never forget the joy in my son Josh's eyes when Jonathan let me bring him to the *Agents of S.H.I.E.L.D.* set when his episode was being filmed.

Being a regular hire as a part of the Marvel Universe was a terrific blessing. As a writer, I also had a chance to consistently read the Marvel series' television scripts to see how certain characters were being developed. I believe the show runners and writers did a daring thing by turning the heroic "Grant Ward" character played by Brett Dalton into a villain in a surprise ending in season one. While reading that particular script of *S.H.I.E.L.D.* versus the criminal faction called "Centipede" (who were secretly the villainous organization of "Hydra") I didn't even notice that the script's final pages had not been included. We had been deliberately given a false ending to that episode so as not to give away the actual ending. The device for secrecy worked. When the episode aired, I audibly gasped as Ward kills the heroic "Agent Victoria Hand" in the last scene. I never saw it coming and was as surprised as any other viewer even though I worked on the episode. This episode was aired during a period when Marvel closely tied the television show to the events in the film, *Captain America: The Winter Soldier* as a cross-pollination of the *S.H.I.E.L.D.* organization that had been infiltrated by Hydra. On the show, Ward was revealed as the Hydra "Trojan horse" and his character went from being the show's *Dudley Do-Right* to being a cold-blooded murderer and a more nuanced character.

Ward's Hydra mentor was played by the late Bill Paxton. Bill was extremely friendly on the day I happened to meet him on set through an introduction by the episode's director, Milan Cheylov. Bill stuck out his hand and with that famous Texas grin, and said, "Hi, I'm Bill." He invited me to sit next to him at video village and for the next few minutes we talked about storyboards and comic books! Bill was a true fan of both mediums and was a director himself, having helmed the movies *Frailty* and *The Greatest Game Ever Played*. Later, Above The Rim producer Jim Brubaker hired me on a project that cast Bill as the lead and would have been directed by Dan Ireland. Sadly, the project never got into production and both Bill and Dan passed away within the next couple of years. This was a great loss and sadness for so many who adored them both. Bill and Dan were both gems as human beings.

Season one ended with a big episode where I was reunited with Samuel L. Jackson. Sam was guest starring as Nick Fury as a cross over with the Marvel films. I had not seen Sam in years though we had kept tabs on each other through his lovely and talented wife, actress and director LaTanya Richardson Jackson whom I would meet at church from time to time. When Sam and I saw each other on set, he gave me a big hug. I assume some of the crewmembers were like, "Who the hell is this storyboard guy?!" Sam and I caught up and got right back into talking about comic books and Kung Fu movies. Sam is the best, ever. I consider Sam to be a kind spirit and not only a great friend but my true brother. He is indeed, one of a kind. And you do not want to be on the wrong side of Samuel L. Jackson, I promise you!

My work in season two was cut down a bit and this would be the trend going forward. The budget for a show of this type is often reduced as time goes on and *Agents* was no exception. The show's directors became more experienced and production would only call me in for storyboards to use for either specific visual effect shots or prolonged action sequences with camera moves and blocking that needed to be worked out. Garry Brown, the show's line producer was also the second unit director and he was excellent at his job. Garry, along with the stunt coordinator Tanner Gill knew how to break down shots and often didn't need to use storyboards. The two people that kept me employed on the series more than anyone were directors Vincent Misiano, a fellow New Yorker and Yankee fan as well Kevin Tancharoen who later joined the show's list of regular directors.

Vincent was old school, straight-to-the-point and a great tactician. In television the director's job isn't to run the show or to be an artist allowed to "interpret" the material by their individual vision. Television is the medium of writers/producers, and it's their vision that is established from the onset of the pilot that is adhered to for the entirety of the

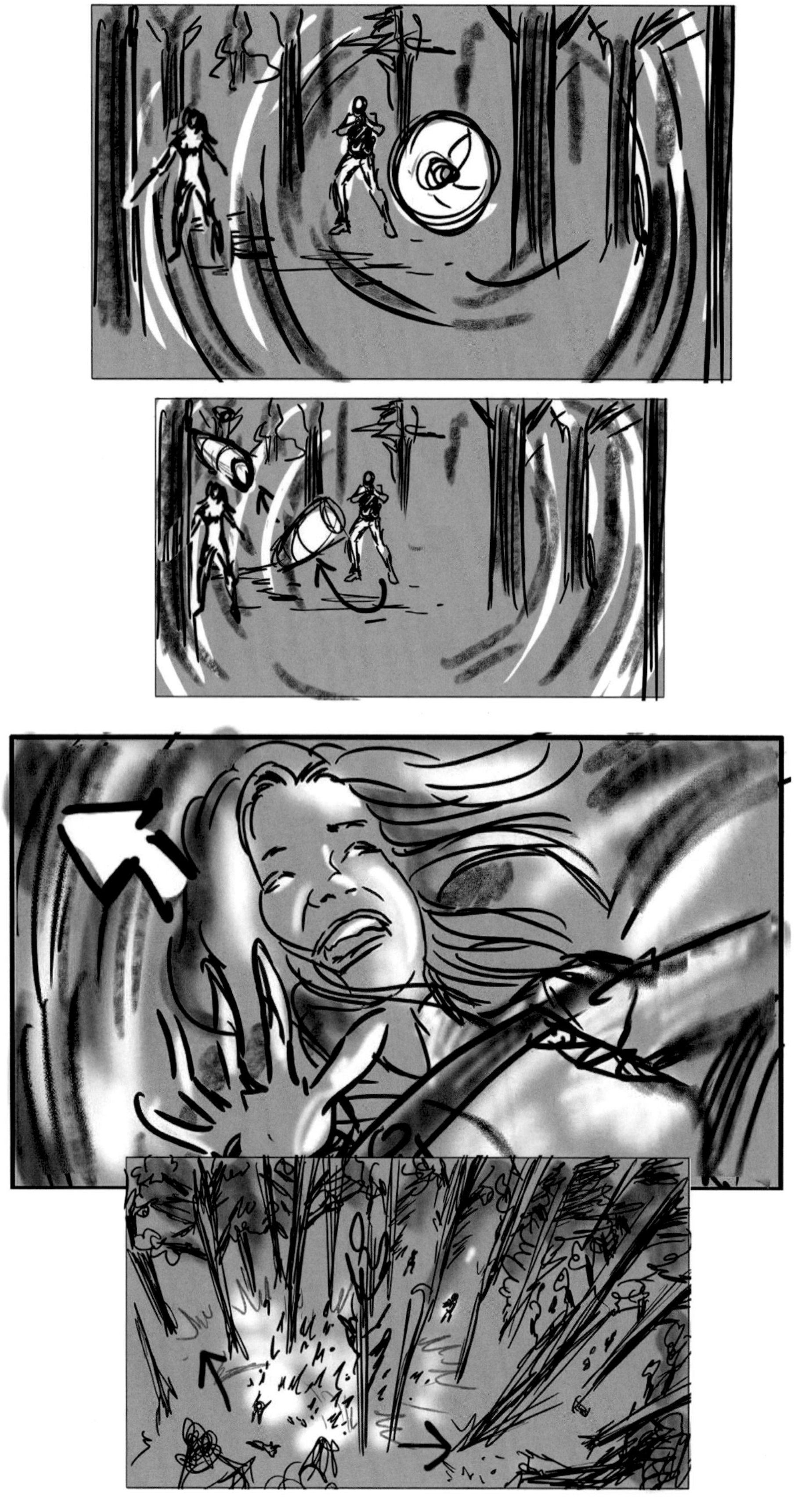

run of the show. As it was explained to me, television directors in the purest terms are asked not to "crash the plane." They have to know the show's characters, visual style and deliver everything on time. Routinely, there will be another director hired for the next episode and the formula of the show cannot change. The best TV directors stick to the formula that has already been set but sometimes add something extra. They will come up with creative ways to shoot and stay within the show's parameters and still bring the best out of everyone. Most television directors don't use a visual style separate from the show's established style, but they do know how to make their episode look good within the set structure. Vincent and I had very detailed meetings as I would with the other series directors. And as time went on, he would trust me to be more creative. I would do a thumbnail pass with the basic blocking and email it to him, while he would sometimes set a follow-up meeting for any needed changes.

When I eventually worked with Kevin, I must admit I had a great sense of pride in his growth in the success he was having as a director on a major television series under the Marvel banner. Knowing him since he was twenty years old, I was witness to his growth as a person and certainly as a director. Kevin had an old soul and seemed as though in those early days that he was a forty-year-old in a twenty-year-old body. I remember on his first episode how calm and relaxed

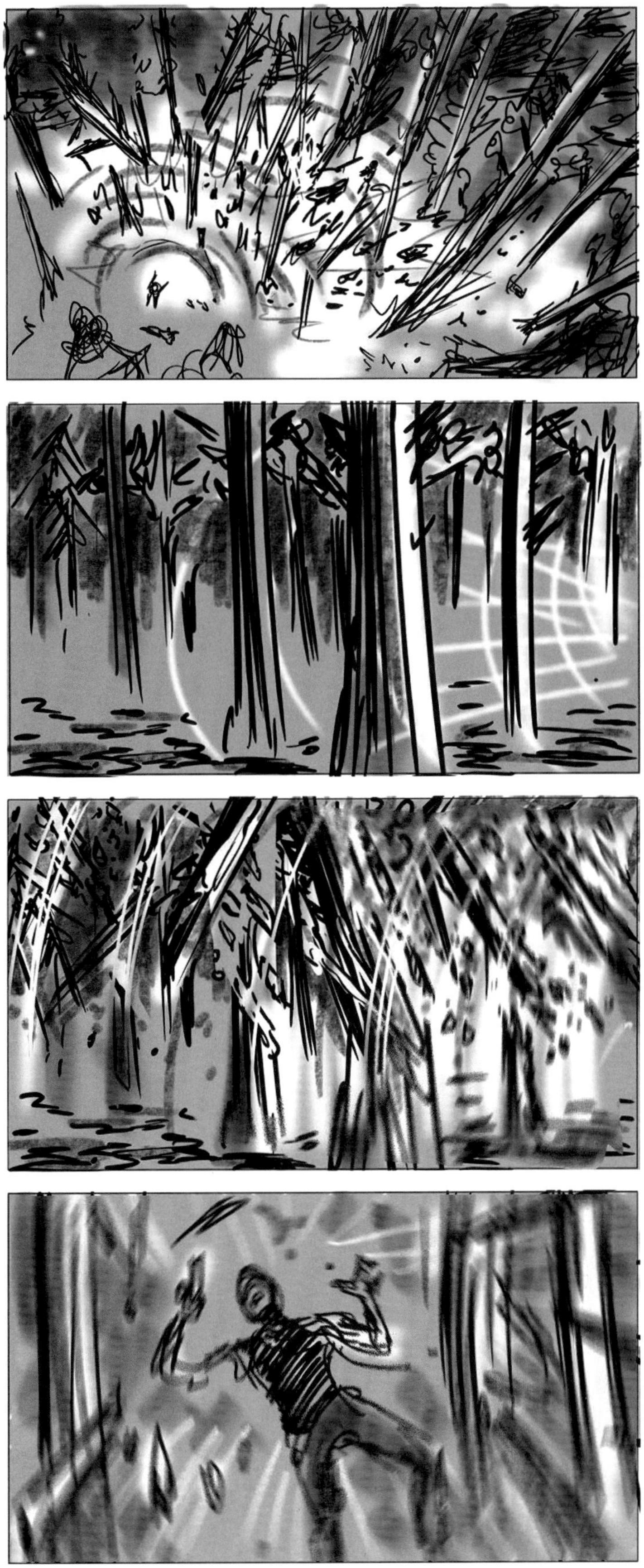

More visual effects specific frames with input from VFX supervisor Mark Kolpak.

he was while working with such a large crew. His sister and brother-in-law were the show runners, his father Tommy Tancharoen was now on his son's show and hired on as the transportation coordinator, so there was an amazing family affair every time Kevin helmed an episode.

Sometimes, my work on *Agents* would only take a day or two. But I was allowed to do more detailed work in some sequences that were more visual effects and action oriented than others. Those sequences took a number of days to complete. There was one scene in one series episode that was shootout fight scene on a "Quinjet" ship with the character of "Deathlok" so I layered in a terrific bit of comic book polish on those storyboards.

I created some of my best work on the season two episode where the new character named Antoine Triplett aka "Trip" was turned to stone by a mysterious mist. Series regular character "Skye" was revealed as a member of a race called "The Inhumans". Not knowing she has new destructive super powers with "earthquake" effects, Skye accidentally "quakes" Trip's stone body apart. The art department executed a detailed vision for an underground cavern set that was magnificent. Episode director, Michael Zinberg and I charted strategically through the action choreography leading up to Trip's death and Skye's new power reveal.

In the next episode, I storyboarded another FX sequence. The Skye character's power erupts in a ballistic manner of hellacious fury. The visual effects department, led by Mark Kolpak did some incredible post-production work on this sequence.

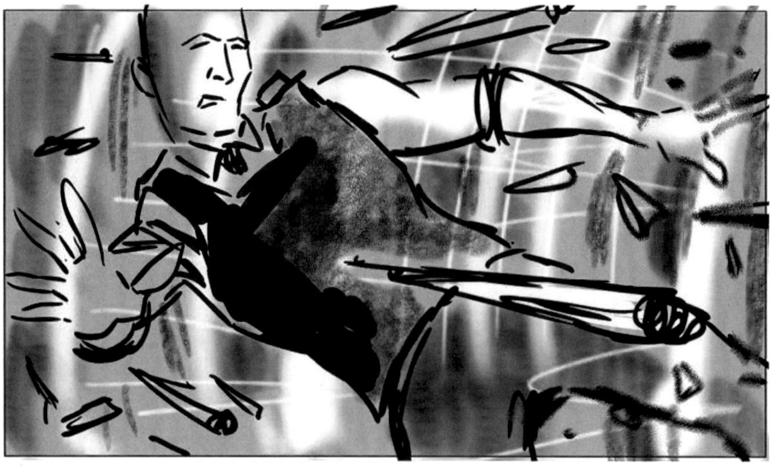

A following episode paired me with another returning *S.H.I.E.L.D.* director, Jesse Bochco, the son of the late television legend Steven Bochco. These storyboards are probably my favorite in terms of the detail I was able to invest into the work. In the scene I drew, Skye is attacked by hostile *S.H.I.E.L.D.* forces so she lets her powers explode and ultimately destroys a chunk of a forest.

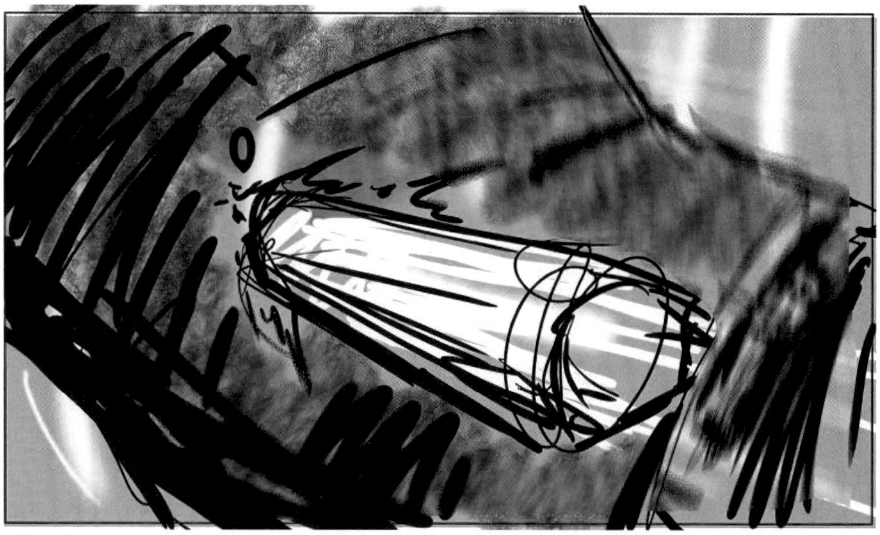

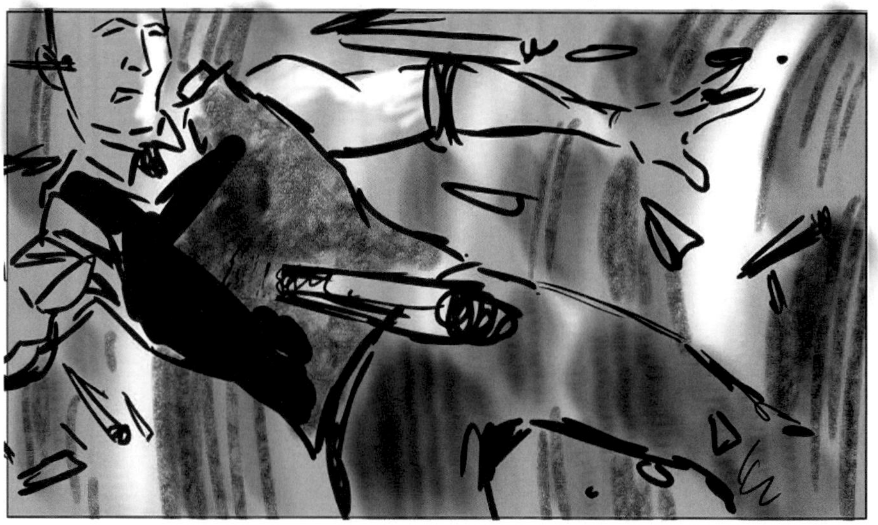

As the series continued I was again working with Vincent Misiano, which was always great. I received the designs for the new "Ghost Rider" character that was being introduced on the show. Vincent and I had great fun doing a car chase where the Robbie Reyes' (Ghost Rider's alter ego) car transforms into the flaming Ghost Rider car while "Daisy" — formally known as "Skye" —clings to the top of Ghost Rider's car. We had location photos as our guide to enable us to break down the shooting sequence, shot-by-shot. I was unable to get the visual effects department's designs for the show's version of

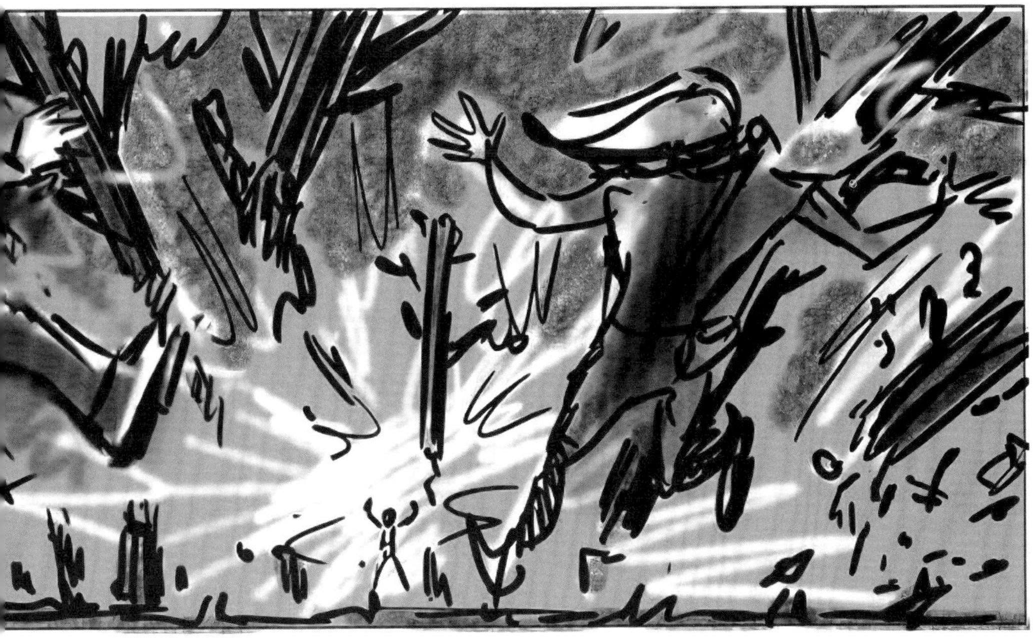

I met Clark and the episode's writer/producer, Brent Fletcher on the arena set which was located on the *Agents of S.H.I.E.L.D.*'s Culver Studios lot. Clark's episode featured a spectacular fight scene that featured Daisy facing off against a villainous Kree warrior named "Sinara", with all of the action set in a futuristic battle arena. Clark broke down the sequence from start to finish, including when each character would use what particular powers and where on the massive set both actors would be. Daisy uses her "quaking" powers and Sinara was armed with two small metal balls that she could hurl telekinetically at an opponent with dangerous results. Both characters are gifted fighters and that added another fantastic visual element. Clark gave me permission to video record the meeting so there would be no loss of notes by verbal discussion. After getting some photos of Sinara's clothing from the art department, I had everything I needed to start working on the boards. I finished the assignment within a few days. When I saw the final fight that aired in the episode, it was very close to what Clark and I had laid out in the storyboards.

As season five continued, the series had a diminished use of storyboards. What I did take advantage of was asking my friend, director Kevin Tancharoen, if I could "shadow" him while he directed his episode which was the next to last show of the season. Traditionally, shadowing a director would entail being with the director virtually every inch of the way from preproduction including the scouting, internal meetings that lead up to the shooting and the final edit. I attended an edit session, a production meeting and a "tone" meeting. In a tone meeting, the director and show runner discuss the details of how they will shoot the style of

Ghost Rider so I drew the character on a combination of the Robbie Reyes and Johnny Blaze comic book versions. Mark Kolpack and his VFX crew did in excellent job in realizing the Ghost Rider's flaming head on a TV budget and made him look quite cinematic.

I only had one scene to board in one particular episode that detailed the character of Daisy evading LMD (Life Model Decoy) Mack in a room full of dormant Daisy LMDs. I had the visual effects department's art of multiple Daisy LMD's to work from as character guides. It was a few days of work and my time on the show was waning. I had one big action scene at the end of the episode when Vincent gave me free reign to layout the storyboard panels without our usual detailed shot-by-shot break down meeting. Vincent was pleased with my storytelling, offered a few notes and the final work was soon completed. I finished strong with the season finale. And with that, season four was a wrap for me.

I worked on one episode in season five with Clark Gregg as director. That episode for me was poetic since Clark was the first to whisper the comings of this new Marvel series to my ears.

the episode while talking through the script scene by scene. Jed Whedon was in the meeting and I was amazed at how he and Kevin gave thorough attention to every aspect of the preparation of the episode. My time shadowing Kevin was cut short since Jed was prepping his episode and needed me to create those storyboards because the scenes for his episode were very specific and detailed.

The closest scene that I storyboarded as an actual superhero fight on the entire series was Jed's season finale. Jed wrote and directed the episode, which pitted Daisy against the show's incarnation of Marvel Comics villain, "Graviton". This television version of Graviton was a former "frenemy" of the team. "General Glenn Talbot", who due to untold stress and torture, gets superpowers and becomes Graviton. Jed acted out the battle scene in his office while I took notes. I also brought a few of my poseable foot-long model figures so Jed and I were like two kids playing with dolls for a few moments. Having model cars, model planes and figurines of humans and animals are extremely helpful in working out a scene. This enables me with the ability to produce an angle on the figure that I like then take a photo of the models as a reference for storyboards.

I worked on one episode in season six with relatively new director Jennifer Phang. I created a simple scene involving VFX that took place on the *S.H.I.E.L.D.* airplane. That was the last scene I ever drew on the show. The remaining episodes didn't need any boards the rest of season six and season seven continued without the call for storyboards.

I visited the *Agents* set on the last episode. Josh had already visited the show's set several times since *S.H.I.E.L.D.* began. But this time, along with my son Josh I also brought along Maasai Singleton, the son of my close friend, John. Both Joshua and Maasai were children together and played video games while visiting each other's homes. It warmed my heart to see the two of them together as young adults and they have since become even greater personal and show business friends. At that time, Maasai and his siblings had been dealing with the recent passing of their father. Maasai had told me that *Agents* was one of his favorite shows so I wanted to invite him along to enjoy some time on the set since the shooting of the final episode was a special moment in Marvel television history.

I was quite melancholy when *Agents* finally ended. The show had run for seven seasons. Even with the last two seasons slated with thirteen episodes instead of a full twenty-two, *Agents of S.H.I.E.L.D.* lasted much longer than many had thought it would.

I went to the last hour of shooting and the wrap party with a resolve that the show had run its course. Two scenes were being shot at once on separate soundstages: one scene with Kevin directing while Garry Brown directed a scene on another soundstage.

In a somber but elated moment the entire crew, actors and staff had gathered on set to watch Kevin direct his last scene of the final episode. When he finally yelled, "Cut," there was an emotional release of hugs, smiles and yes, tears. After both scenes wrapped everyone gathered on the stage where the wrap party was being held. The cast and crew were in a good mood. It was that "happy melancholy" that a graduation from a favorite school gives you. Marvel Television President, Jeph Loeb made a great speech—as he always did at season ending parties—and it united everyone for the evening.

The *Agents of S.H.I.E.L.D.* cast and crew had always been a family. And I was happy to have been invited into this wonderful family and considered an important part of it.

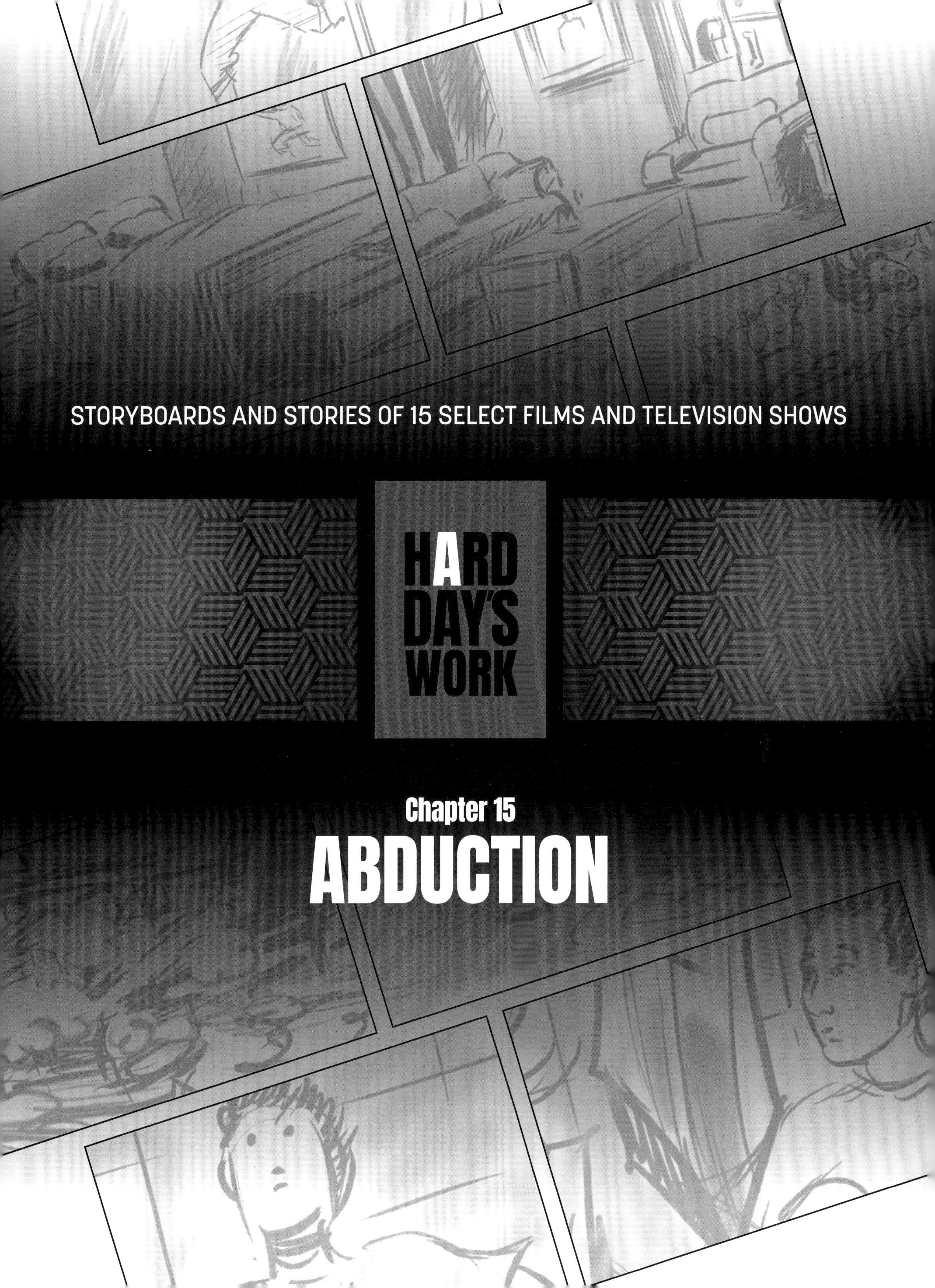

STORYBOARDS AND STORIES OF 15 SELECT FILMS AND TELEVISION SHOWS

HARD DAY'S WORK

Chapter 15

ABDUCTION

Abduction

In 2010, I worked on John Singleton's action thriller, *Abduction*. *Abduction* is about a teenager named "Nathan", played by Taylor Lautner. Nathan discovers his parents are not his biological parents but covert agents who were hired to raise and protect him. There is a crucial sequence in which his fake parents are killed by assassins and the teenager must deal with the surviving assassin. The sequence ends with Nathan and his girlfriend Karen having to escape his house due a bomb set by an assassin that is about to explode. The teenagers make it to the backyard pool just before the entire house goes up in a massive explosion. The remains of the house then crash into the pool where the teenagers are hiding.

ABDUCTION - 2011 - DIRECTOR - JOHN SINGLETON

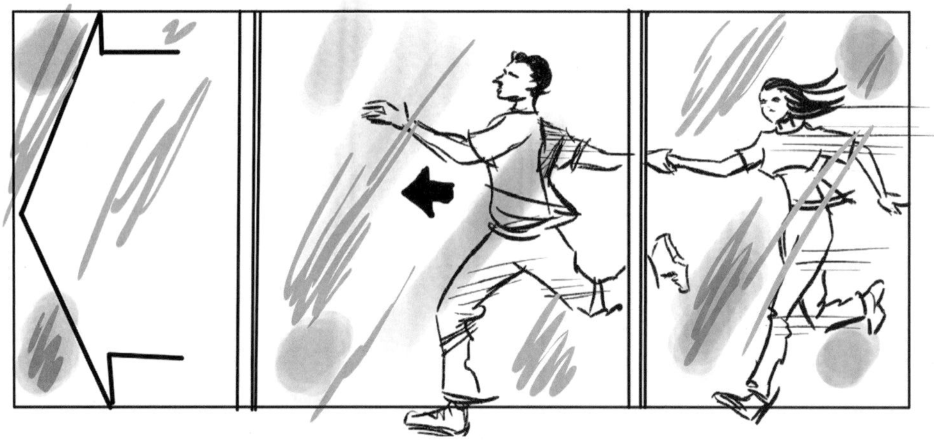

1

TRACK R-L ALONG THE HALLWAY WITH NATHAN AND KAREN RUNNING.

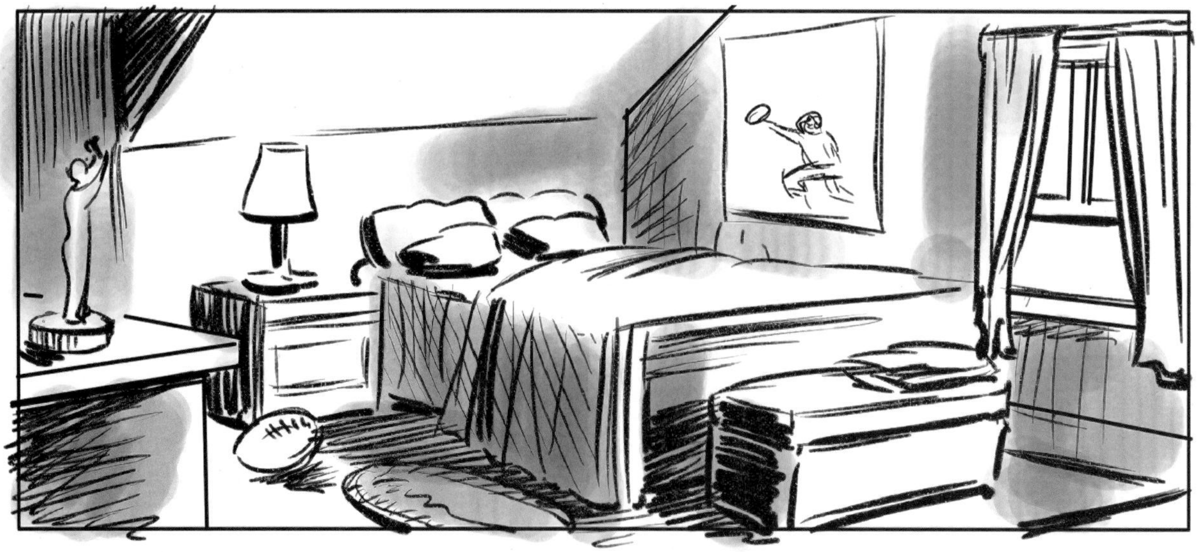

2

CUT TO
NATHAN'S BEDROOM.

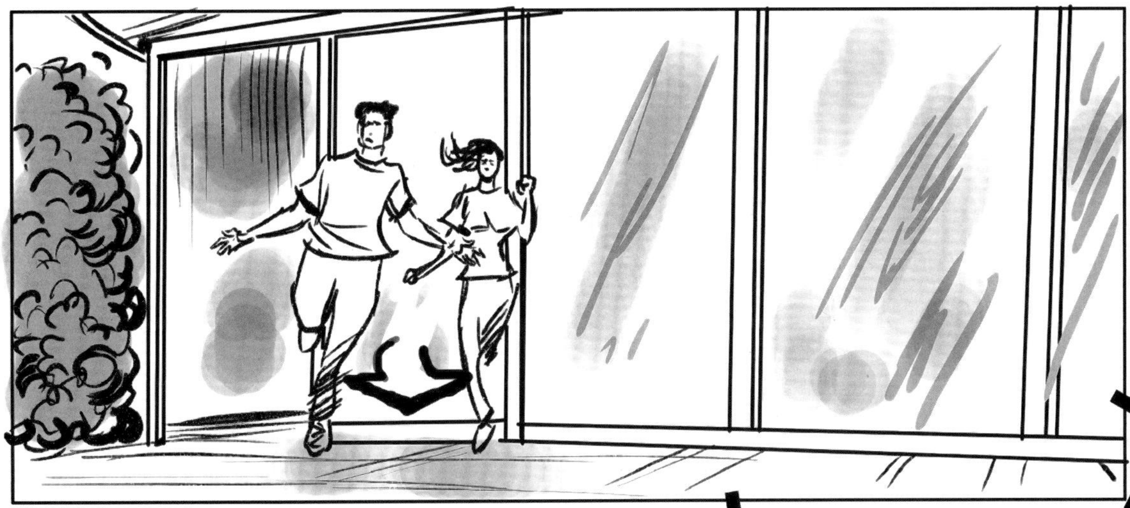

3

BACK TO NATHAN AND KAREN RUNNING.
THEY'VE MADE IT OUTSIDE.
TRACK BACK WITH THEM.

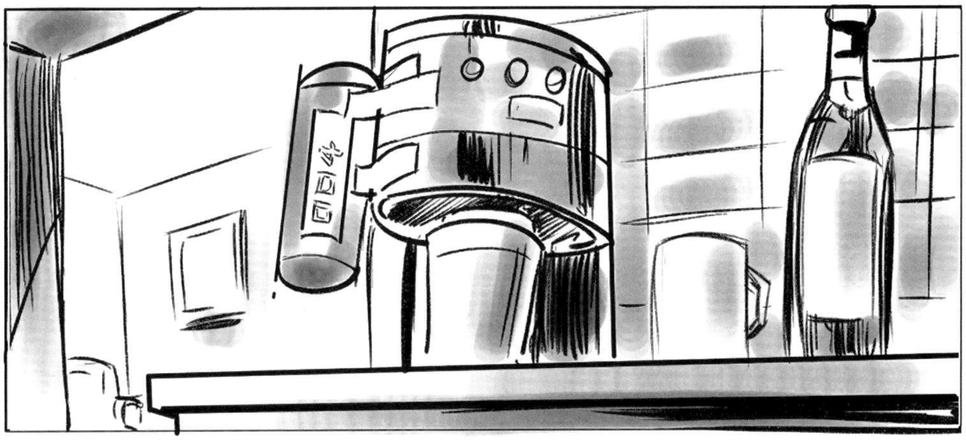

4

TO THE BOMB TICKING DOWN.

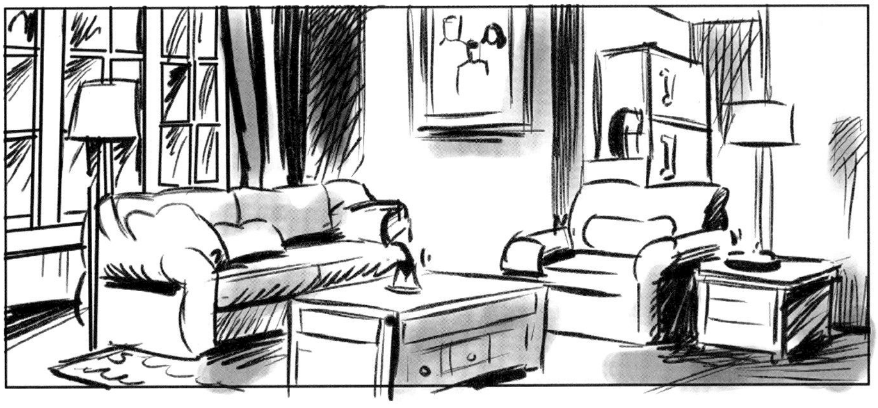

5

THE FAMILY LIVING ROOM.

6

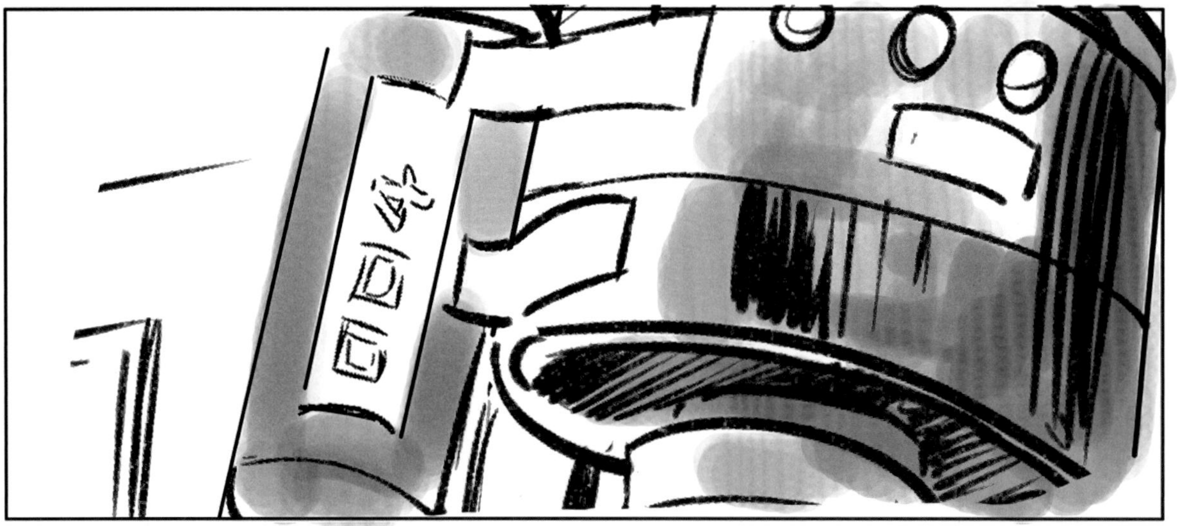

CLOSER ON THE BOMB TICKING DOWN FURTHER.

7

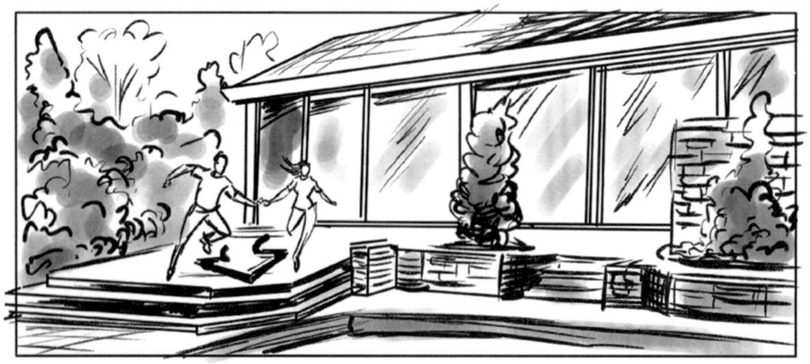

WIDER SHOT ON NATHAN AND KAREN RUNNING FROM THE HOUSE.

8

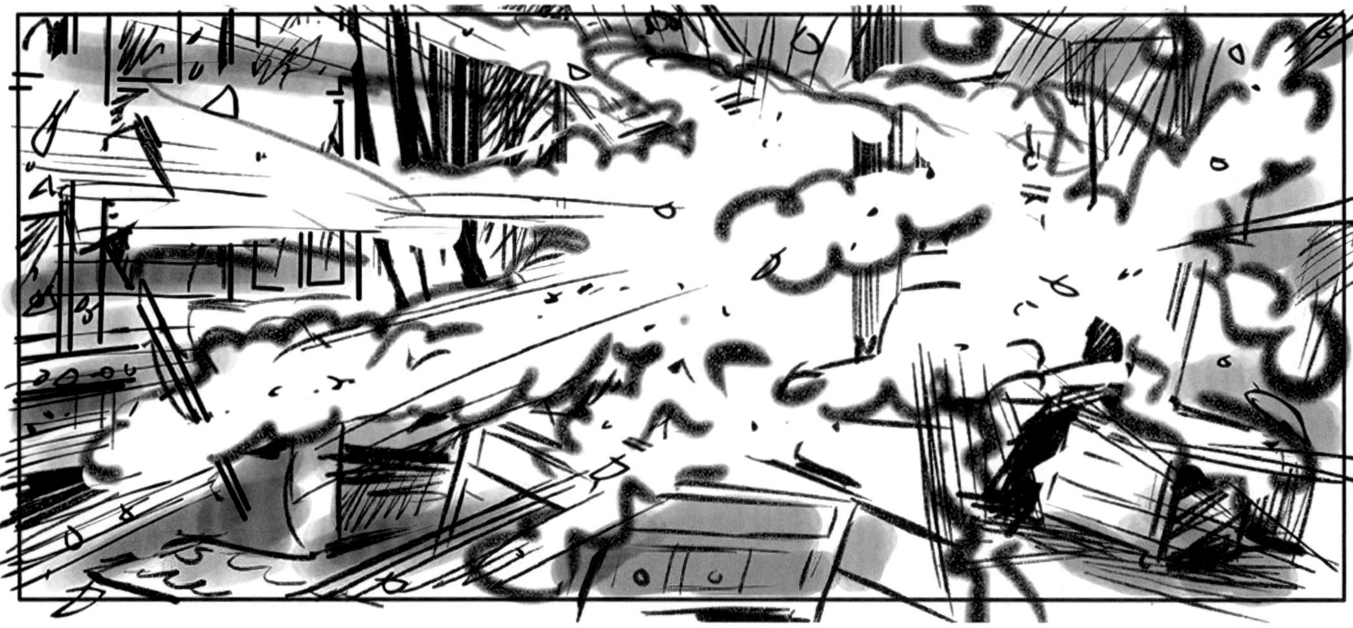

THE LIVING ROOM EXPLODES.

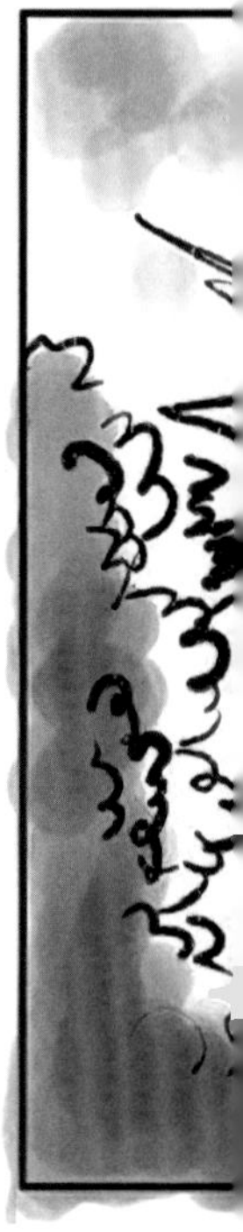

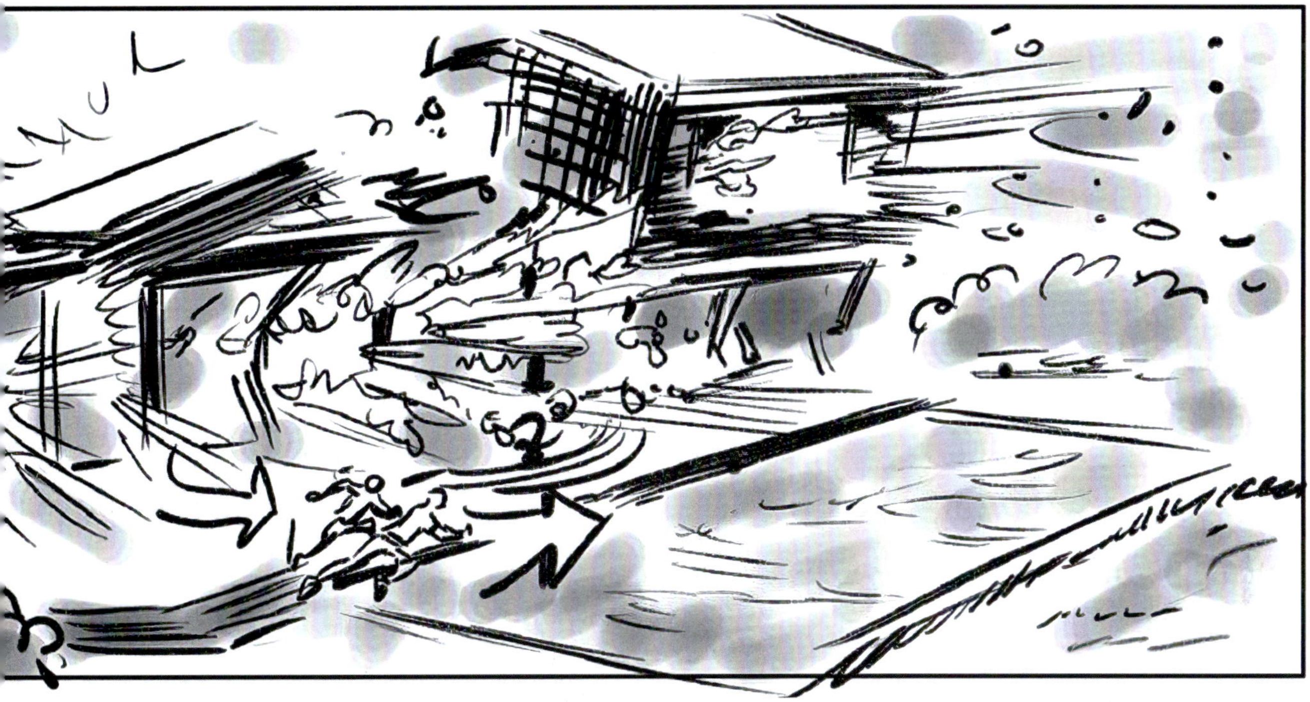

9

HIGH/WIDE ON THE HOUSE EXPLODING.

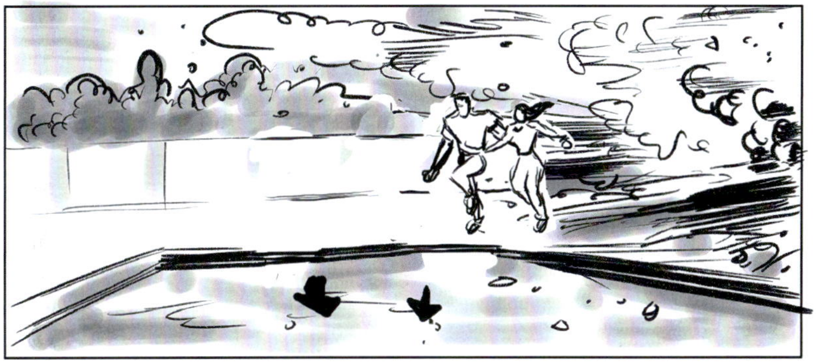

10

NATHAN AND KAREN RUNNING NEAR THE POOL.

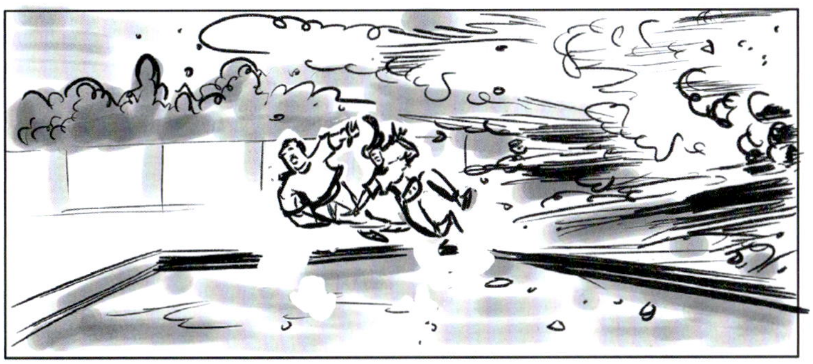

10

NATHAN AND KAREN GET BLOWN INTO THE POOL BY THE EXPLOSION.
(ACTORS WILL BE RATCHETED)

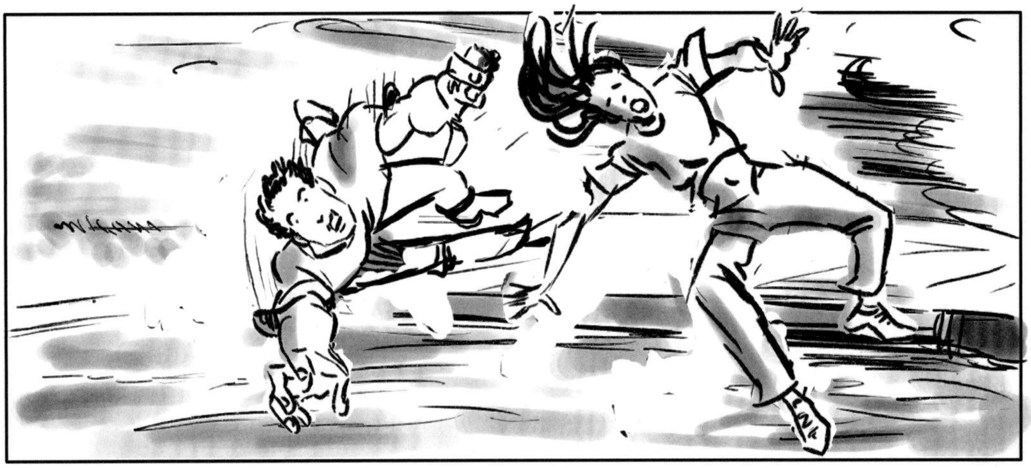

11

CLOSER ON SAME.

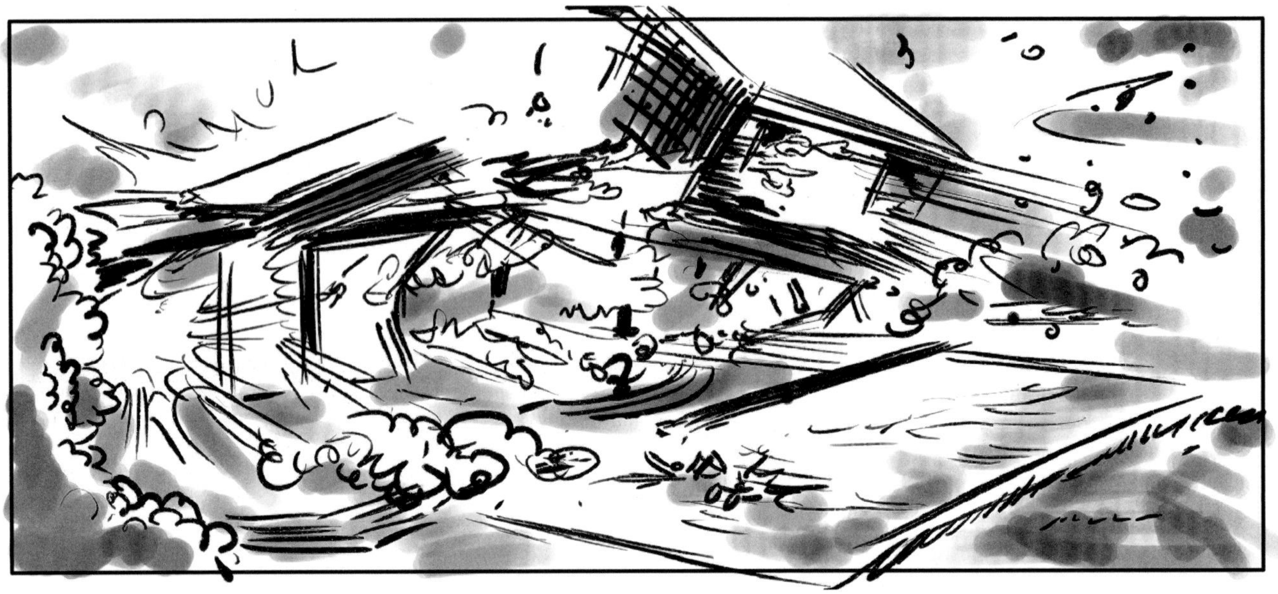

12

WIDE/HIGH OF THE HOUSE EXPODING AND THE TWO DIVING INTO THE POOL.

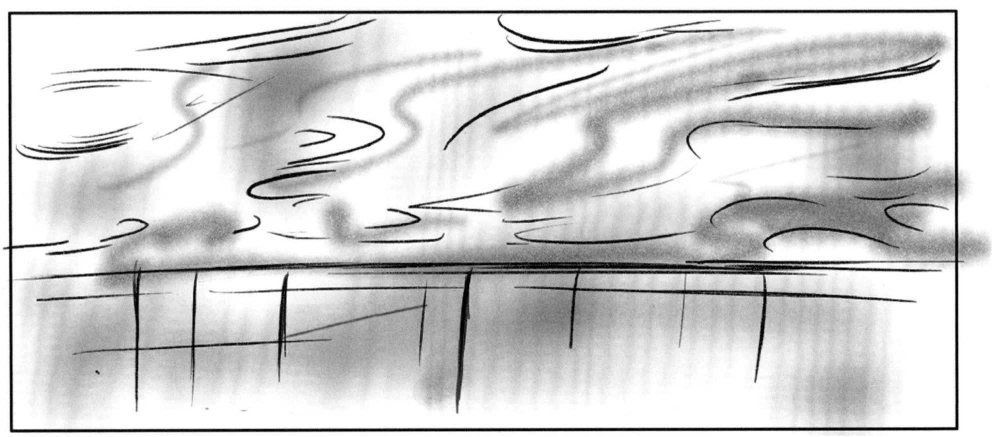

13

UNDER THE POOL SURFACE.

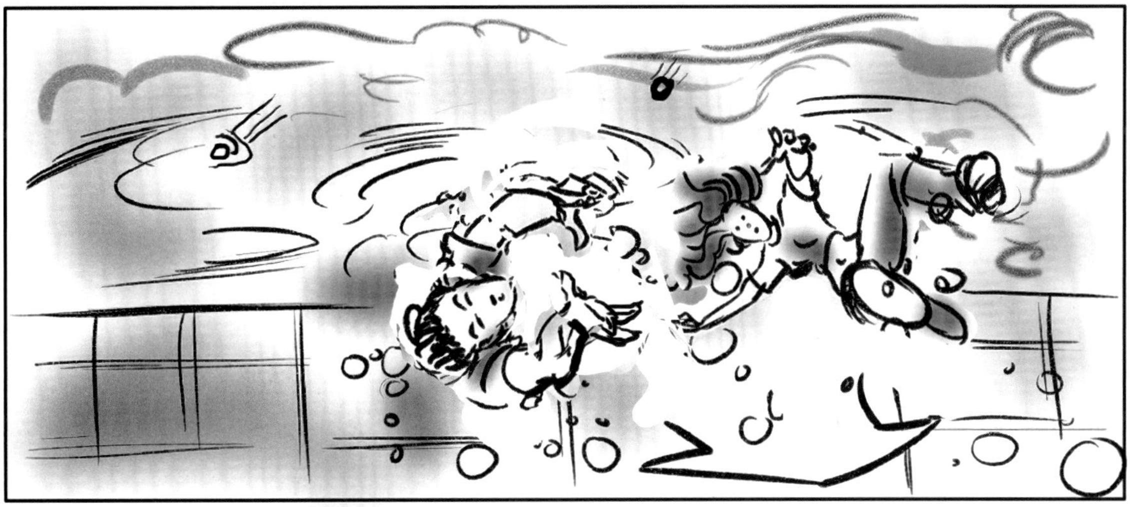

13A

NATHAN AND KAREN BREAKING UNDERNEATH THE SURFACE

These *Abduction* storyboards allowed me to do my cleanest work with the most detail in my early digital storyboard era.

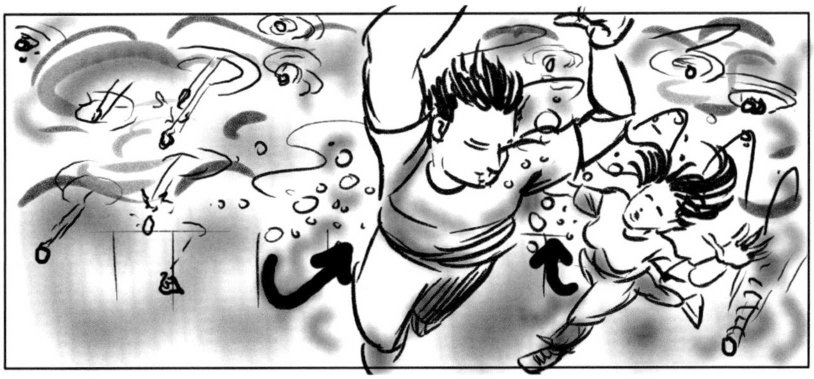

13B

THE TWO CONTINUE TO SWIM TOWARD AND PAST CAMERA.
BURNING EMBERS PIERCE THE SURFACE. THERE IS A LIGHT FLASH FROM THE BLAST.

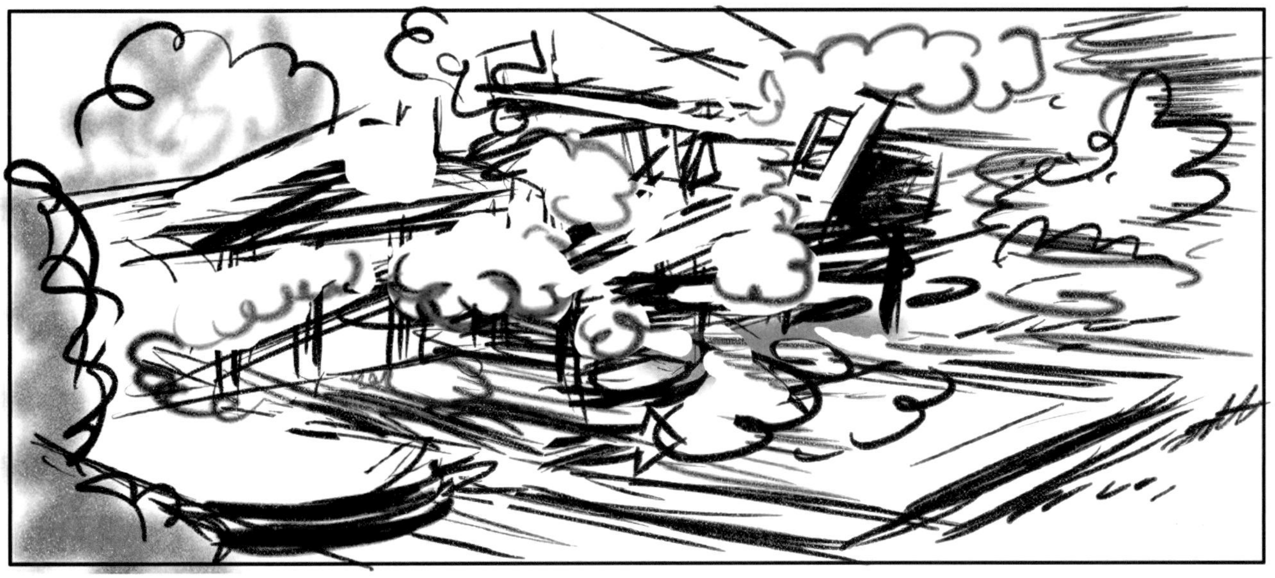

14

BACK TO THE HOUSE GOING UP.

15

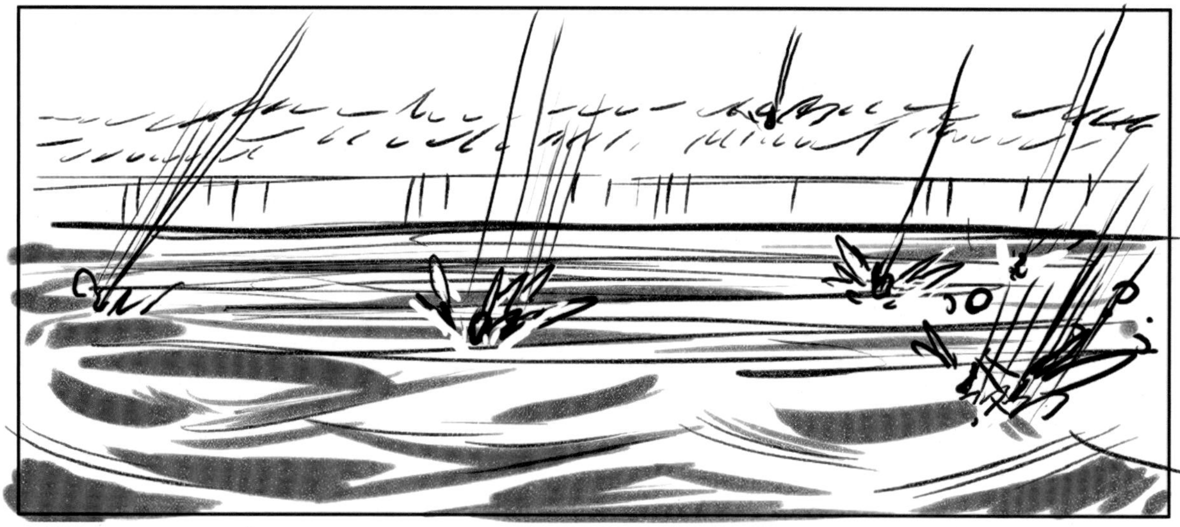

JUST OVER THE SURFACE OF THEPOOK, LOOKING ACROSS.

15A

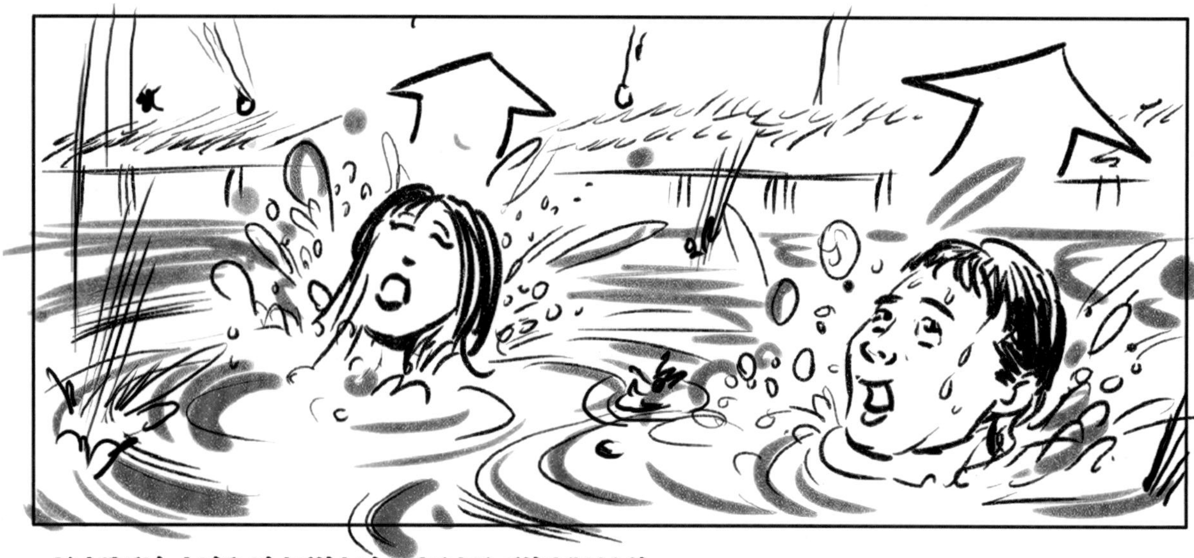

KAREN AND NATHAN BREAK THROUGH.

16

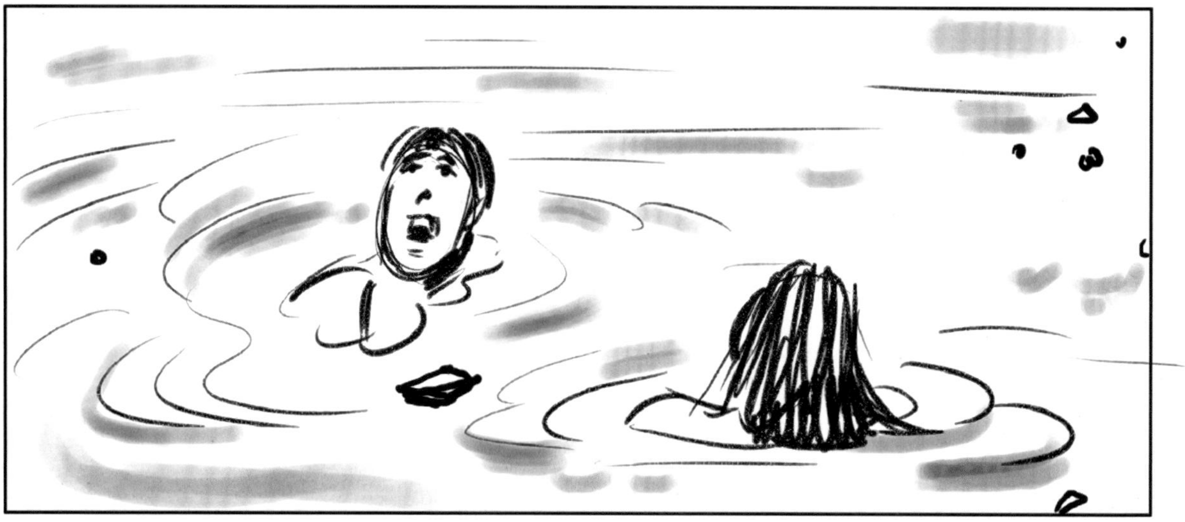

OVER THE POOL.

16A

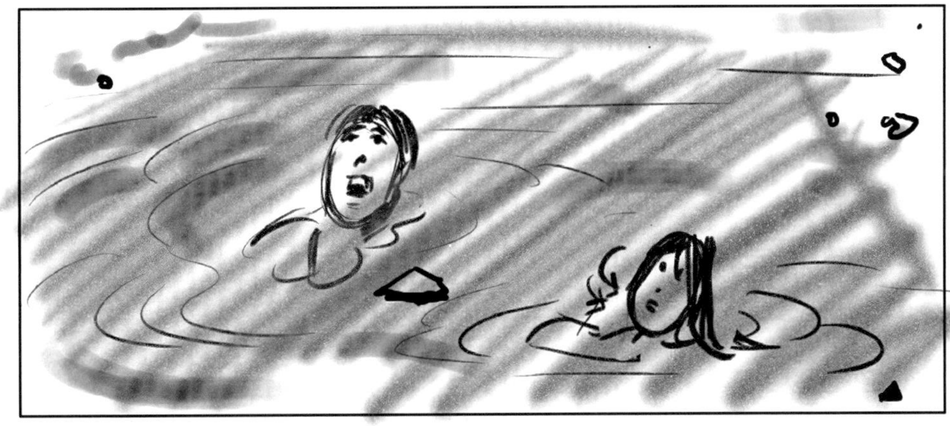

A DANGEROUS SHADOW DESCENDS ON THE TWO.

17

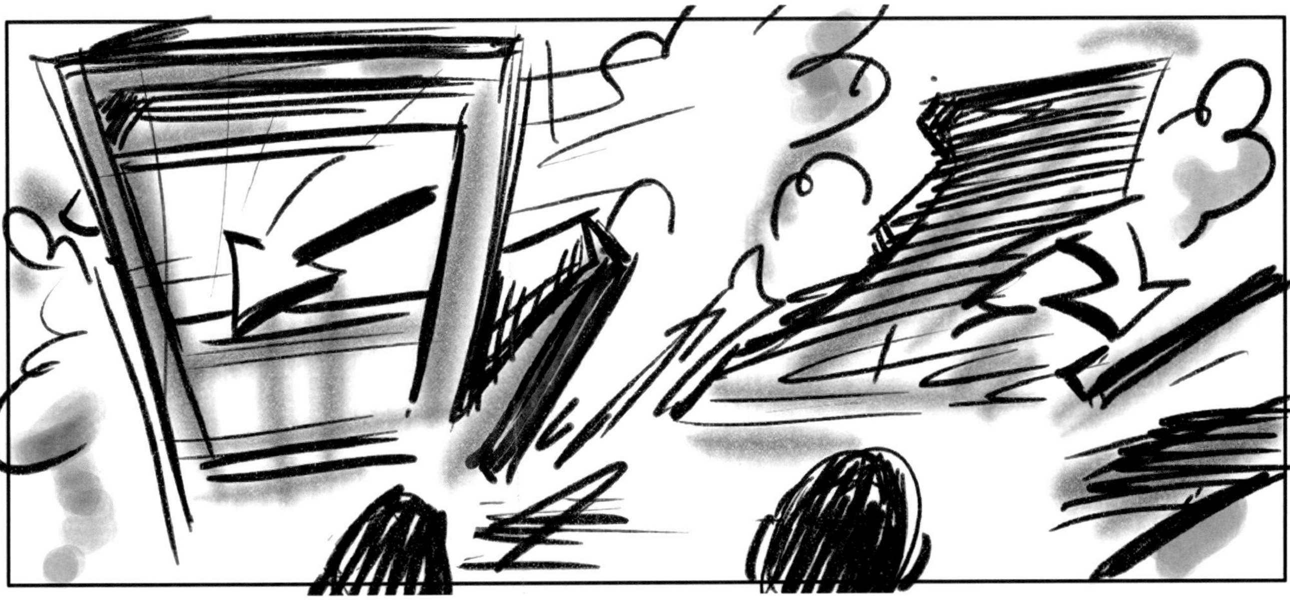

LOW REVERSE AS WE SEE THE BACK FACADE FALLING ON THEM.

18

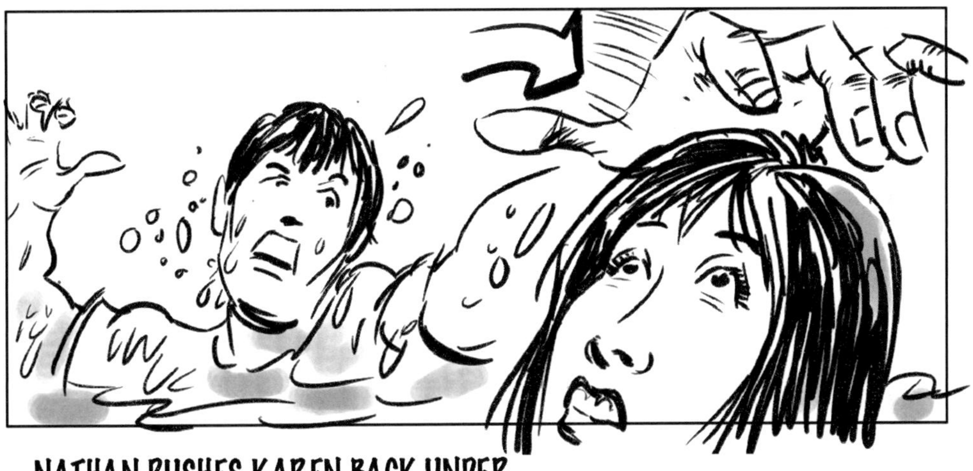

NATHAN PUSHES KAREN BACK UNDER.

19

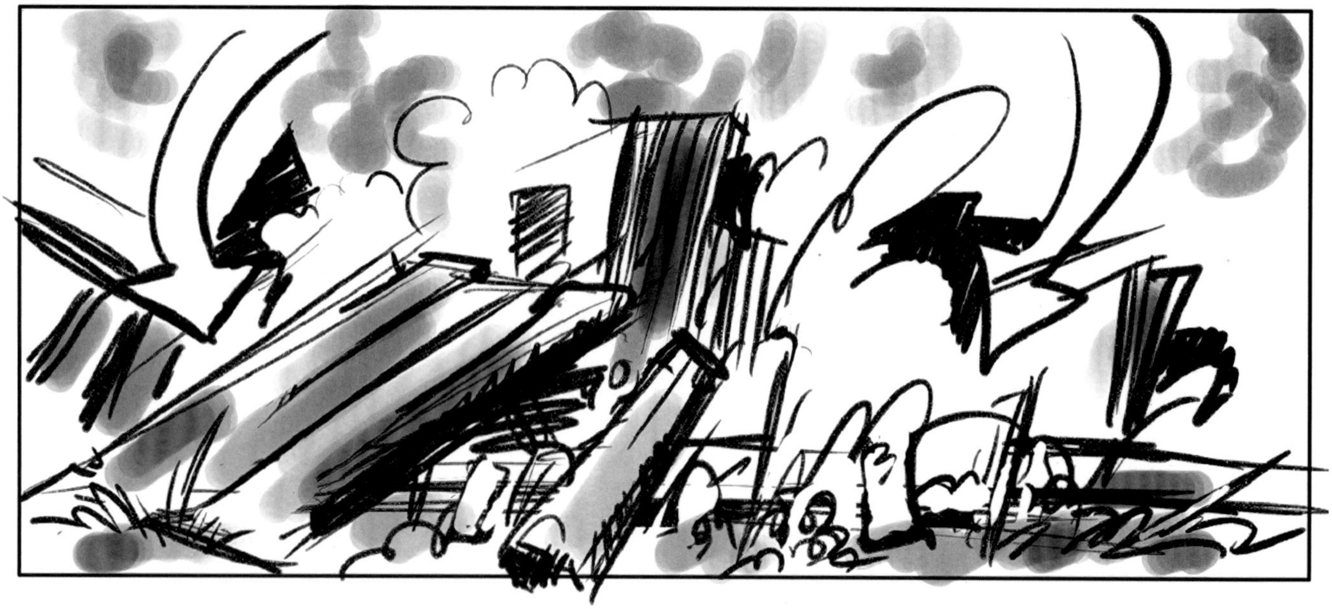

WIDE ON THE FACADE CRASHING DOWN ON THE POOL.

20

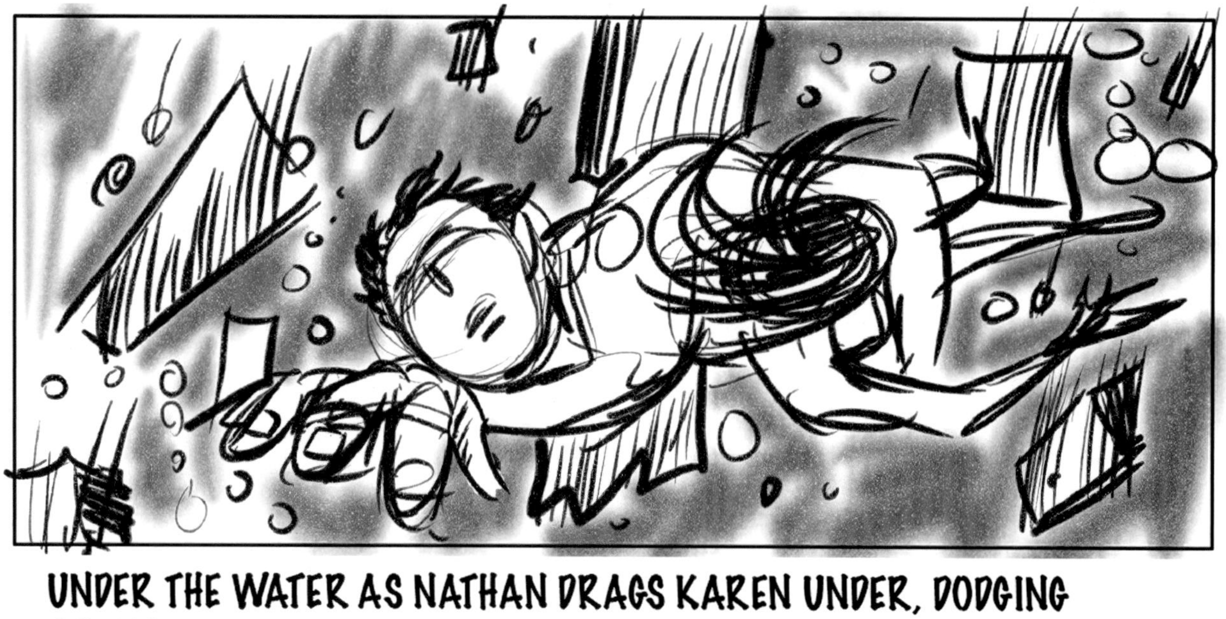

UNDER THE WATER AS NATHAN DRAGS KAREN UNDER, DODGING DEBRIS.

21

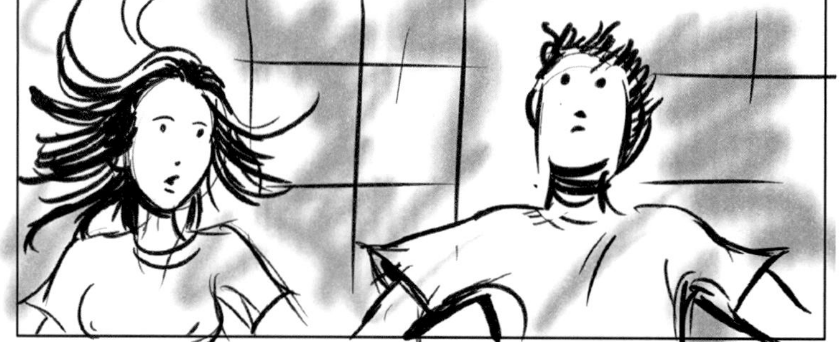

ON THE TWO UNDERWATER BY THE WALL.

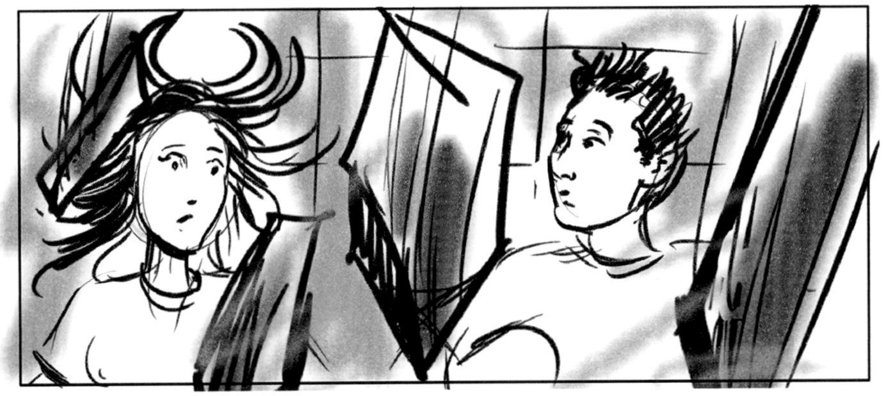

21A

SECONDS LATER, DEBRIS BEGIN FALLING PAST THEM.

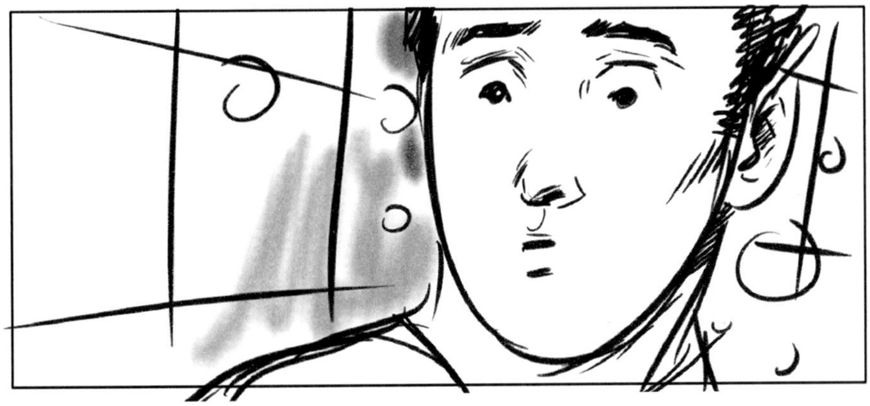

22

NATHAN LOOKS TO KAREN.

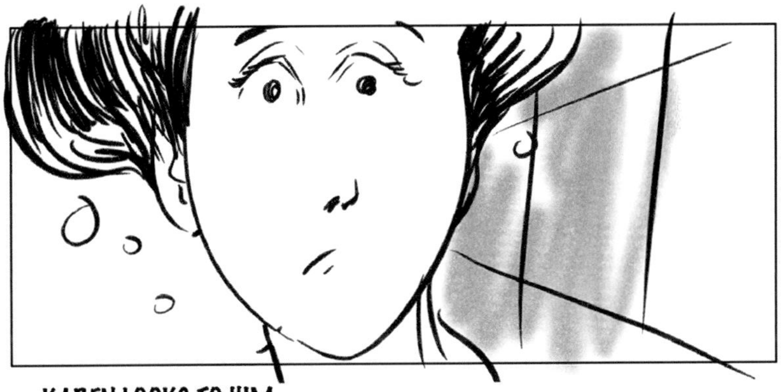

23

KAREN LOOKS TO HIM.

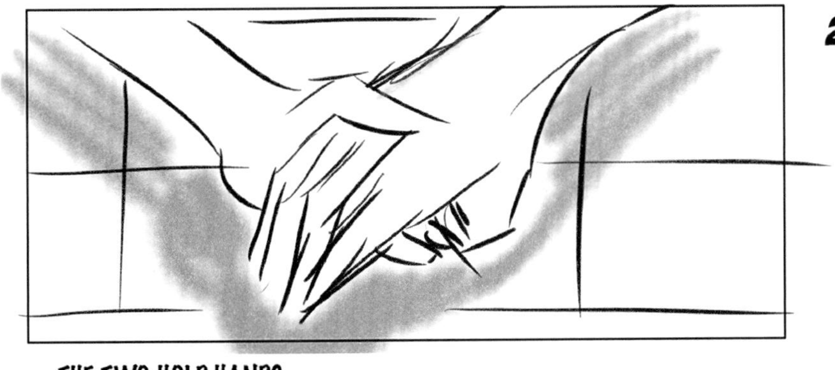

24

THE TWO HOLD HANDS.

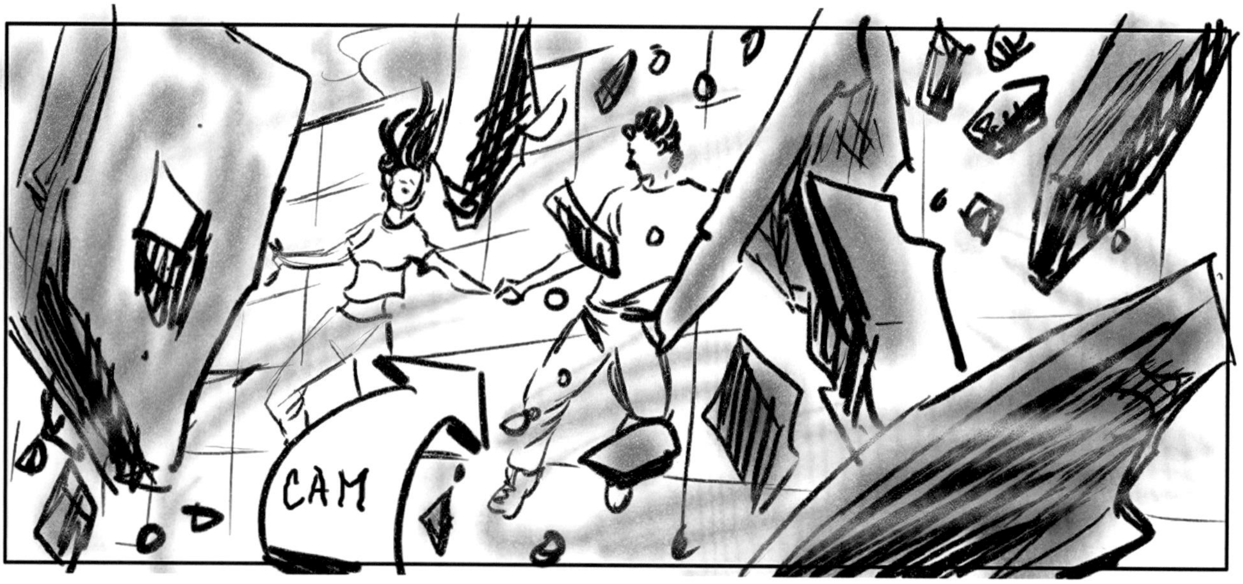

25

CAMERA PUSHES TOWARD THEM THROUGH DEBRIS.

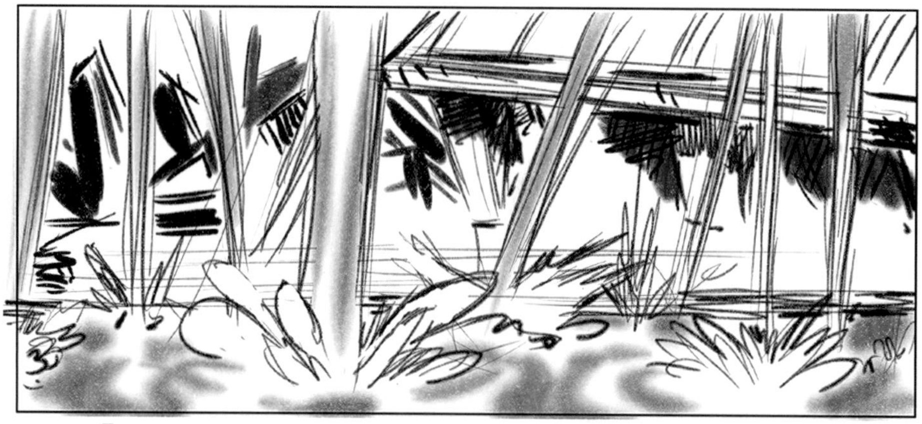

25-1

EMBERS AND DEBRIS HIT THE THE POOL.
CAMERA DIPS BENEATH THE POOL SURFACE.

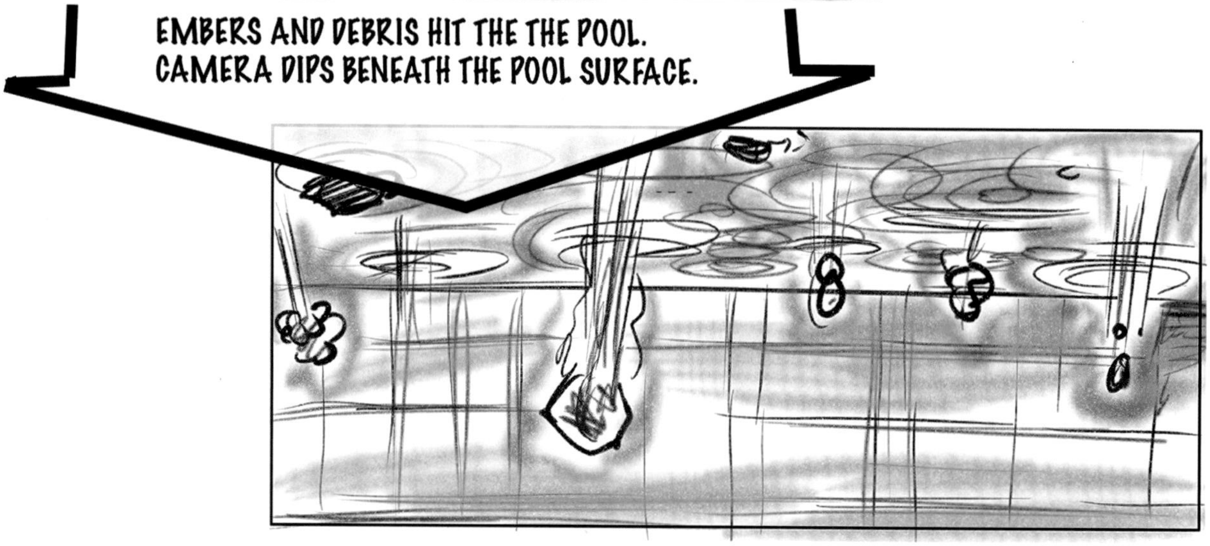

25-1A

SHOT CONT'D WE GO BENEATH THE SURFACE AND SEE EMBERS AND DEBRIS.

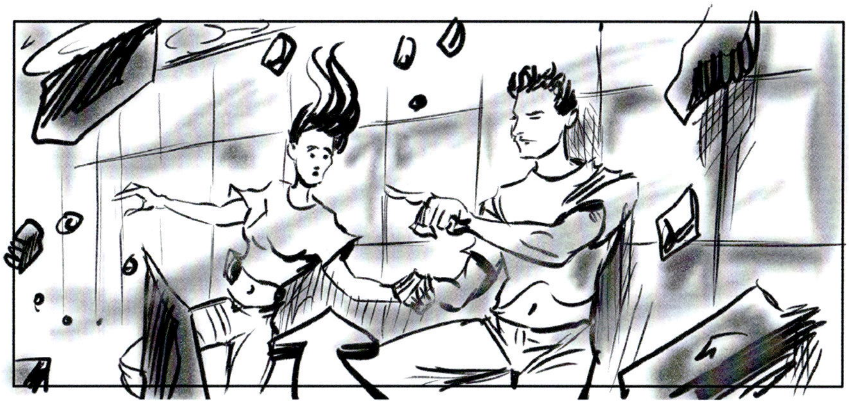

25A

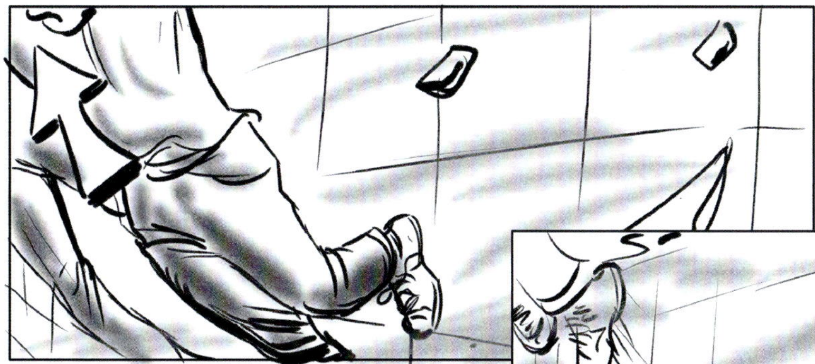

25B

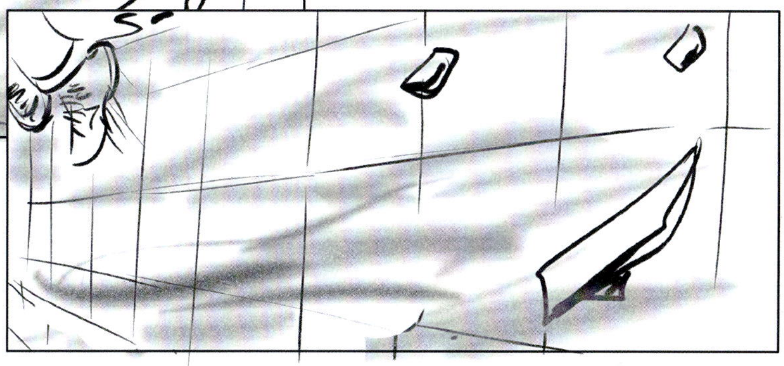

25C

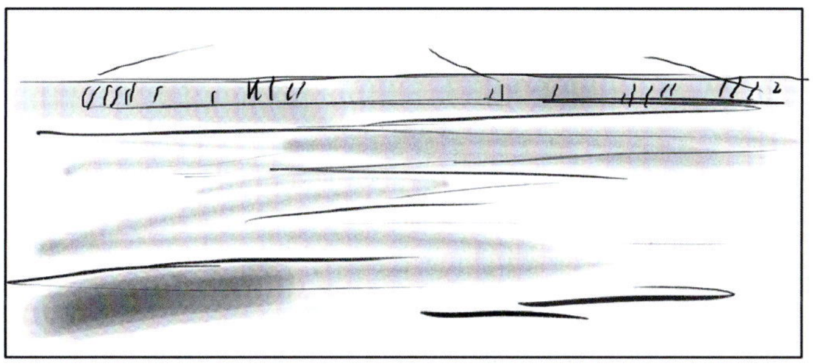

27

OVER THE POOL.

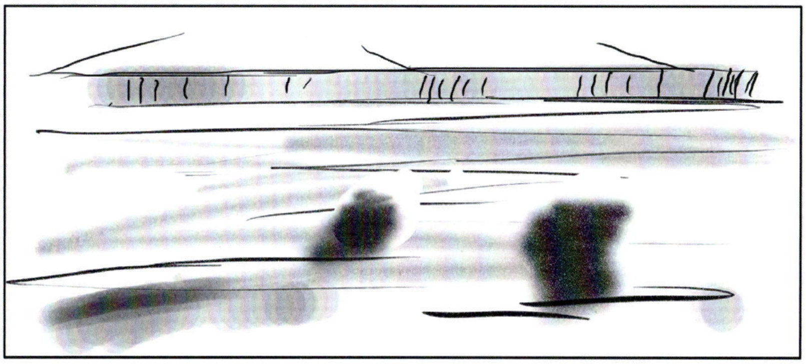

27A

WE SEE SHADOWS RISE.

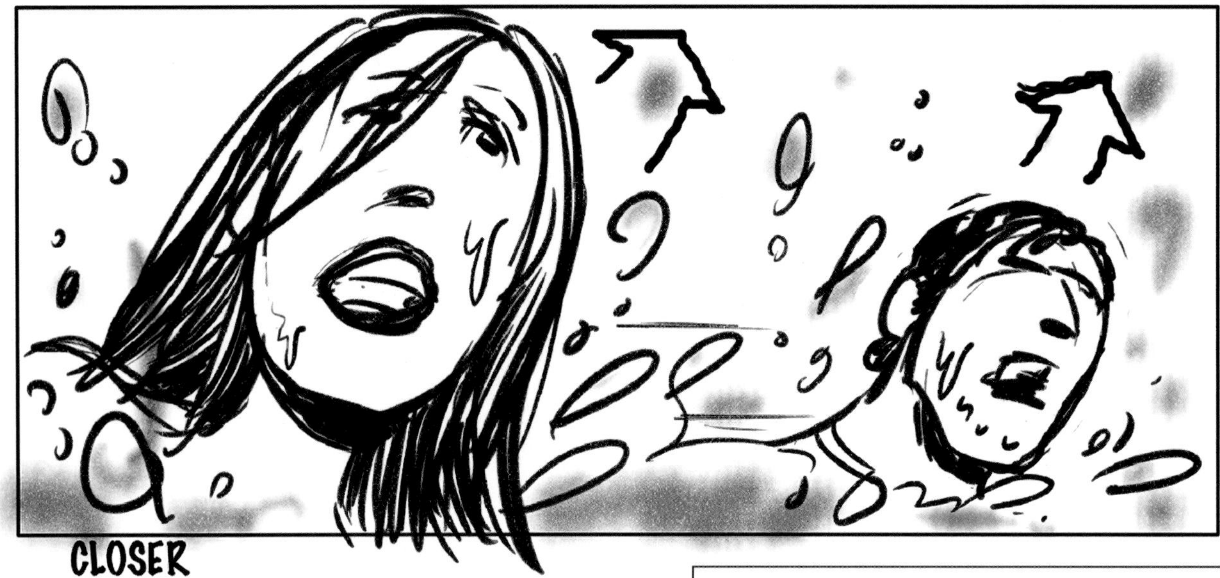

28

CLOSER
AS KAREN AND NATHAN COME UP.

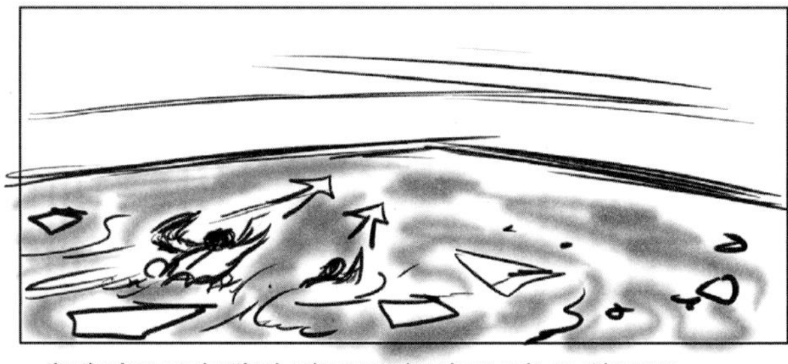

29

HIGH WIDE OF NATHAN AND KAREN SWIMMING TO THE EDGE.

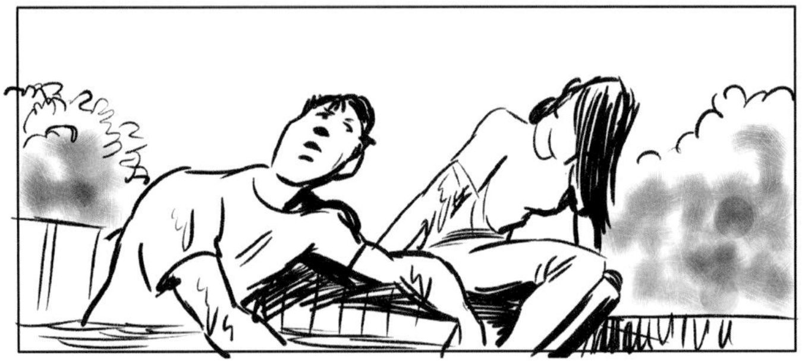

30

NATHAN AND KAREN.

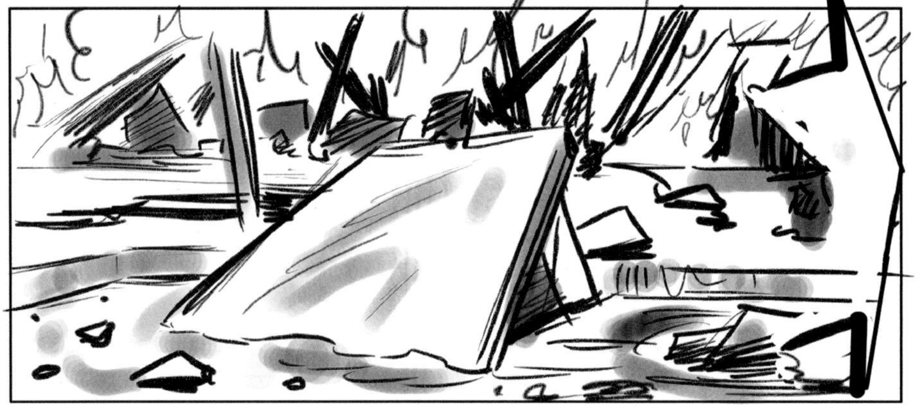

31

NEW SHOT
TRACK L-R VIEWING THE HOUSE IN A MEDIUM, MOVING ACROSS THE POOL.

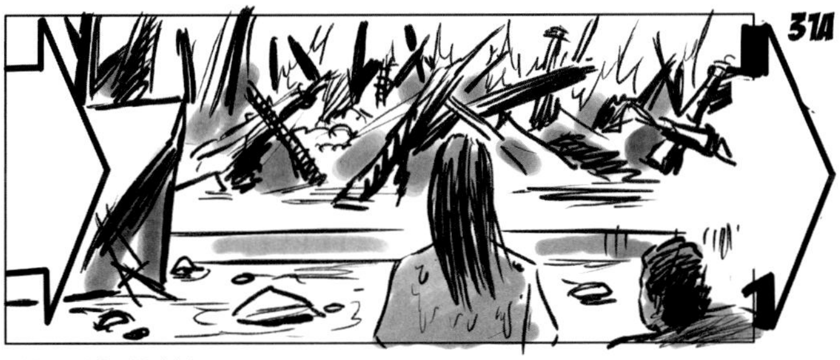

31A

TRACKING CONT'D

REVEAL KAREN AND NATHAN

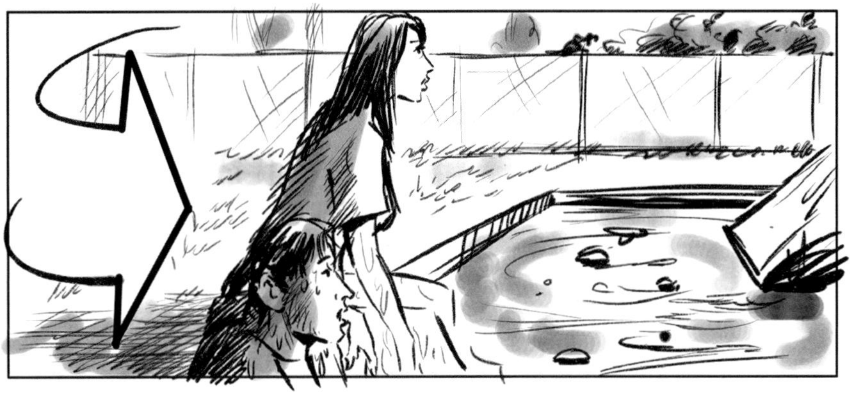

31B

SHOT CONTINUES AROUND NATHAN

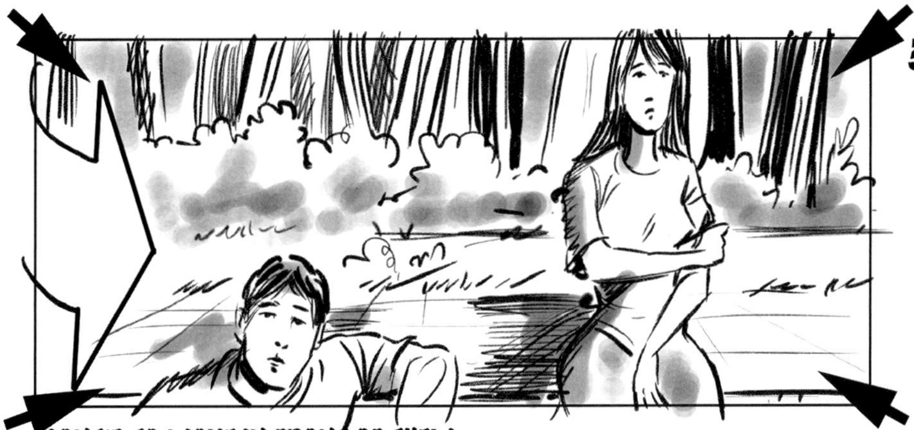

31C

CONT'D TO MOVE IN FRONT OF THEM.
PUSH IN.

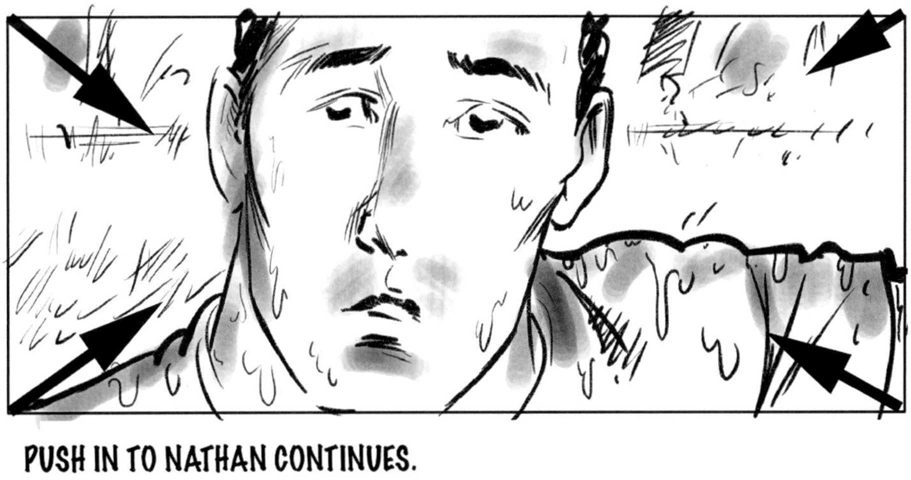

31D

PUSH IN TO NATHAN CONTINUES.

32

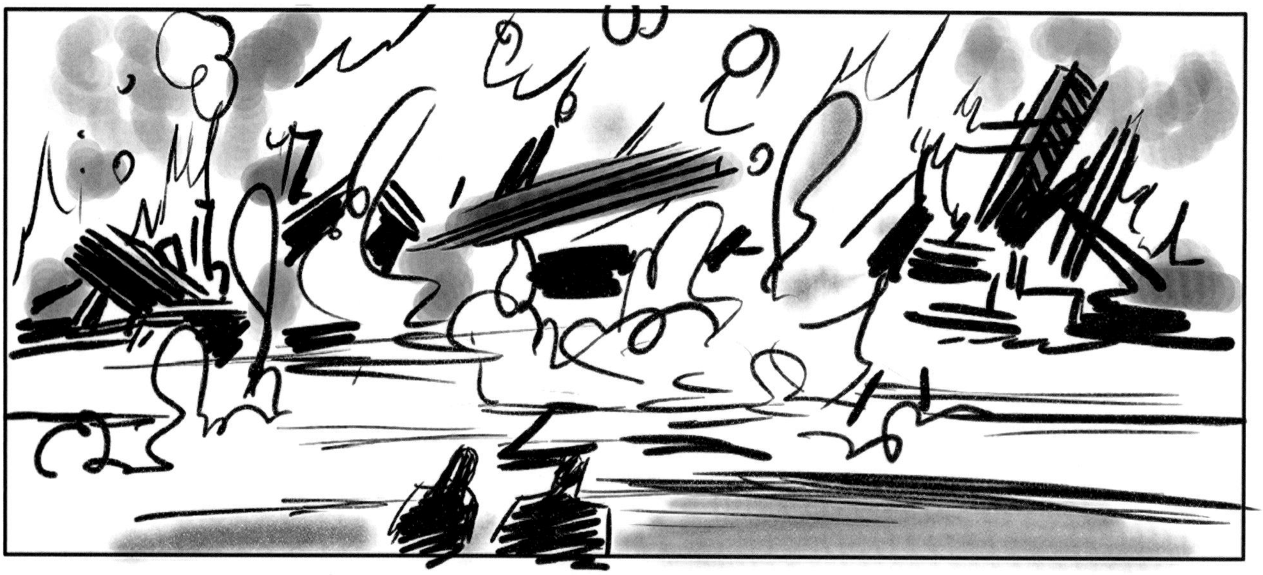

WIDE REAR OF THE HOUSE WITH NATAHN AND KAREN IN MID-GROUND.

33

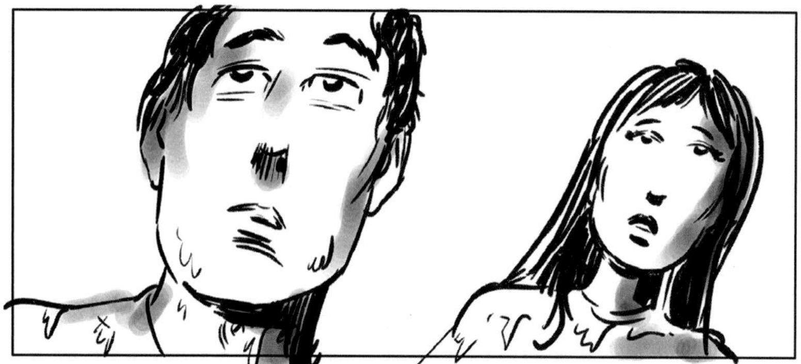

NATHAN AND KAREN LOOKING AT THE HOUSE BURN.
THE FIRE REFLECTS OFF THEIR FACES.

34

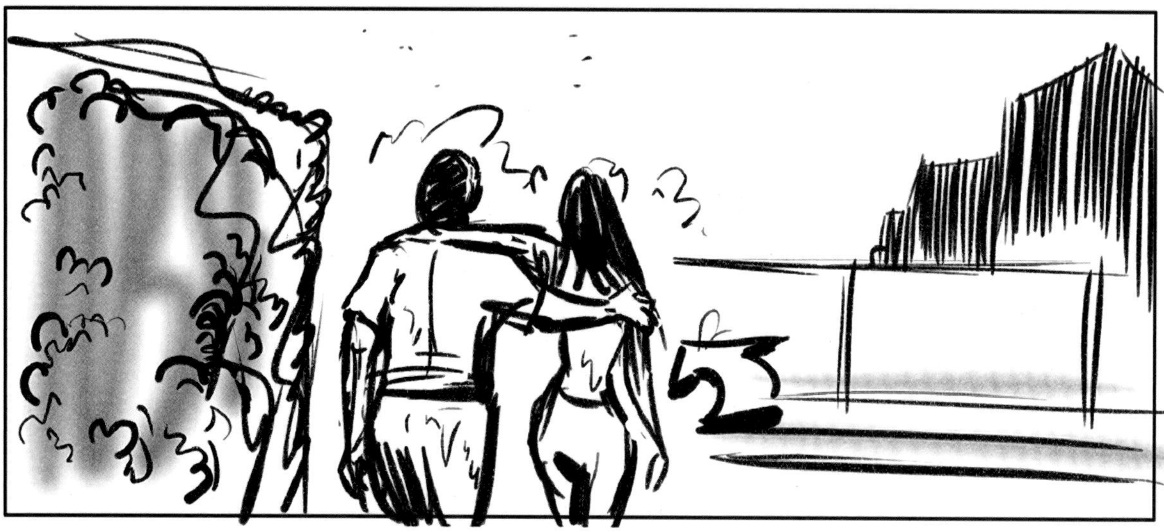

REAR ON NATHAN AND KAREN LEAVING THE PROPERTY.

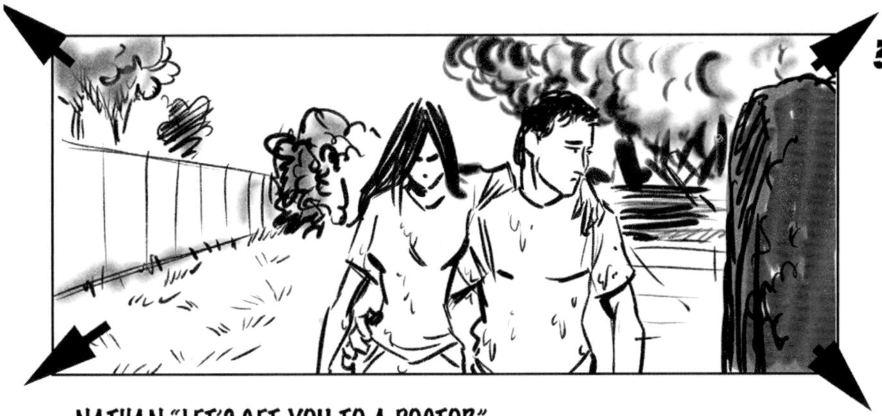

35

NATHAN "LET'S GET YOU TO A DOCTOR"
WE PULL BACK FROM SHOT.

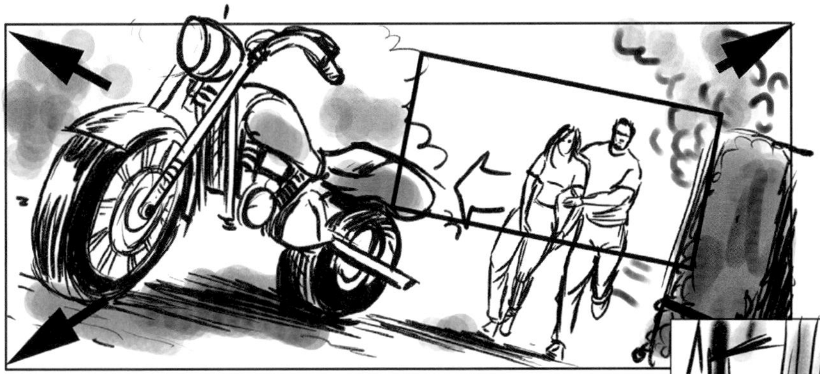

35A

PULL CONTINUED, REVEALING NATHAN'S MOTORCYCLE.

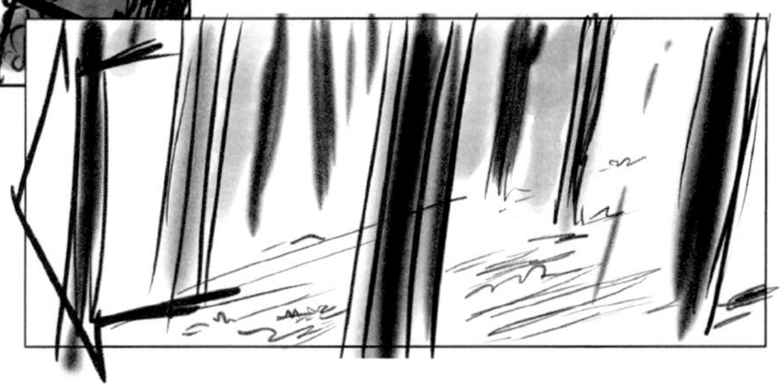

36

TRACKING R-L DOWN A HILLS THROUGH WOODS.

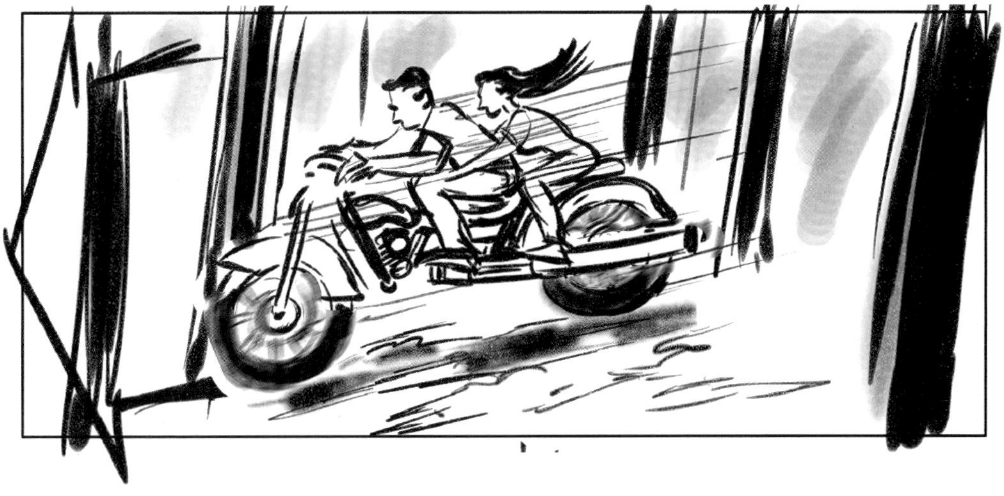

36A

SHOT CONT'D
AS THE MOTORCYCLE ZOOMS INTO THE SHOT.

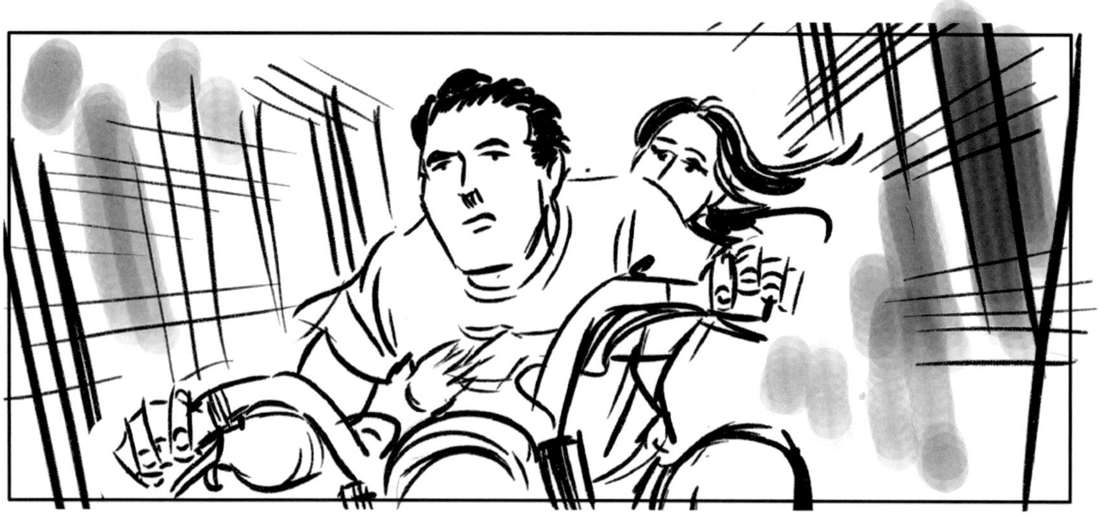

37

FRONT ON NATHAN AND KAREN.

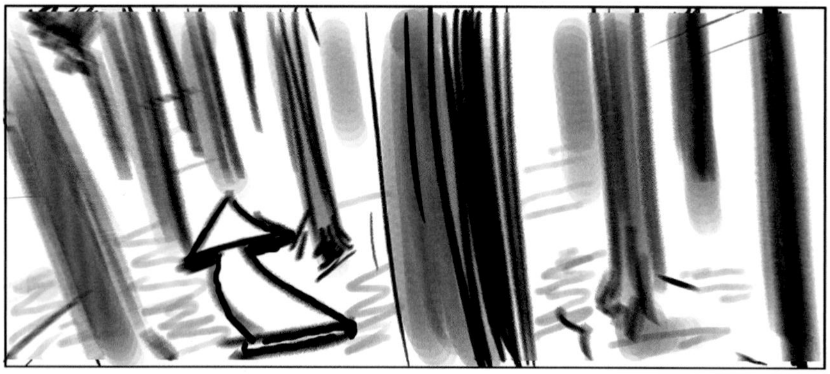

38

LOW /POV SHOT ZOOMING THROUGH THE FOREST.

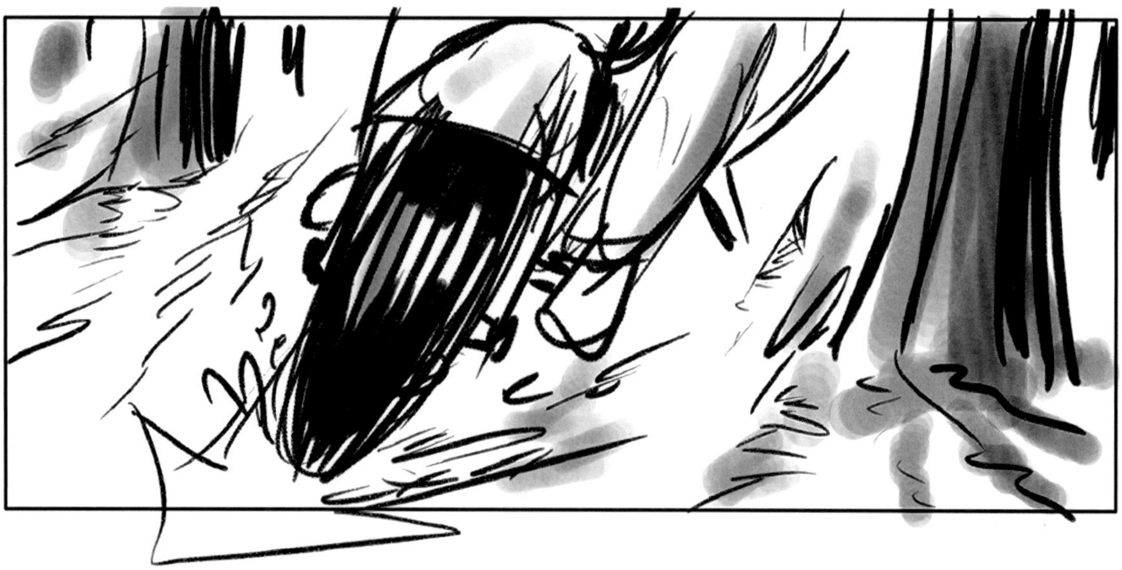

39

FRONT ON THE MOTORCYCLE AS IT BANKS SCREEN LEFT

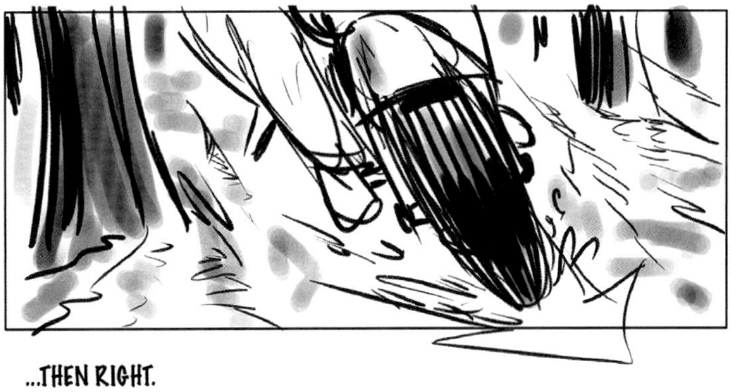

40

...THEN RIGHT.

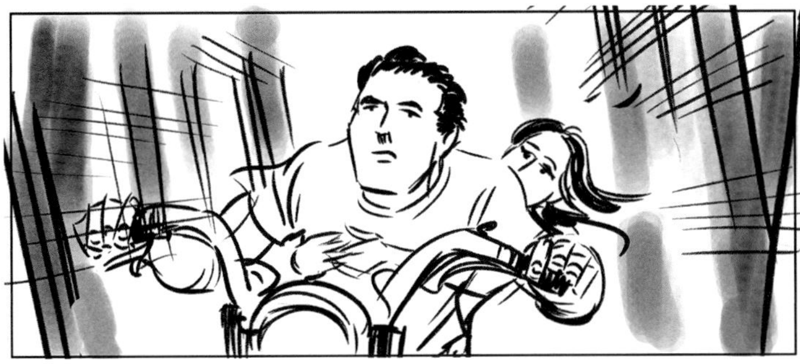

41

BACK TO FRONTAL.

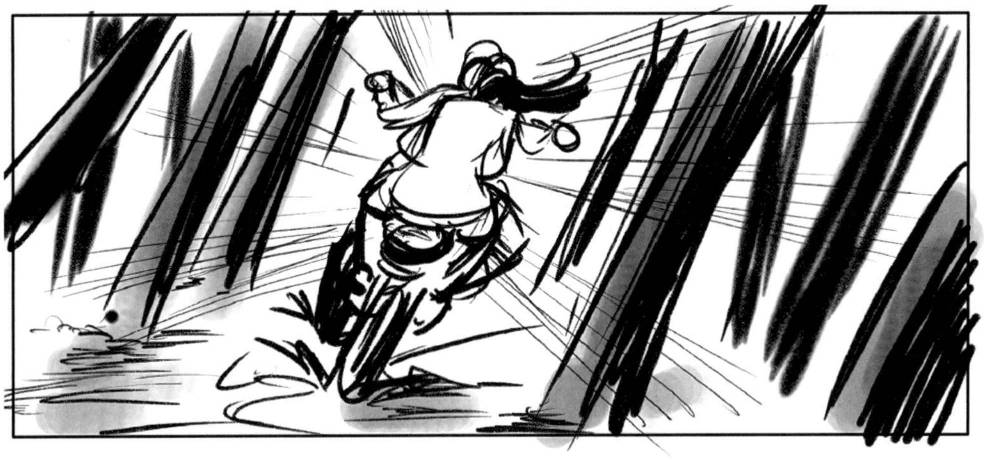

42

REAR MS OF THEM GOING DOWN THE HILL.

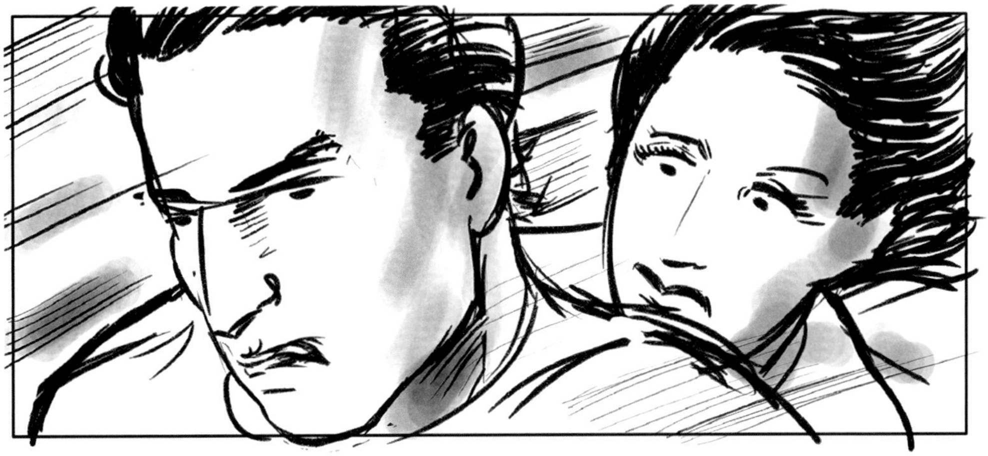

43

CLOSE.

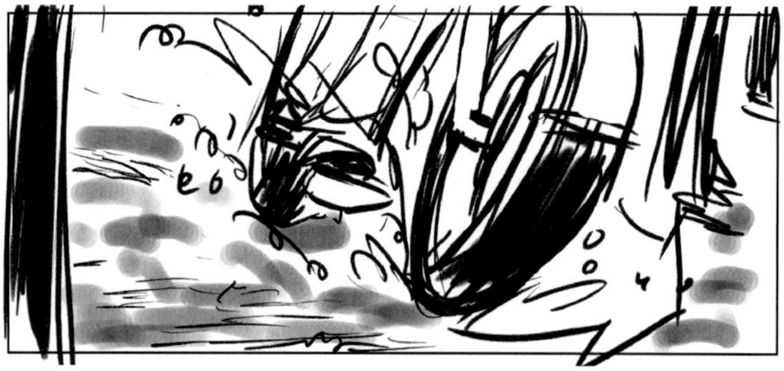

44

THE CYCLE BANKS.

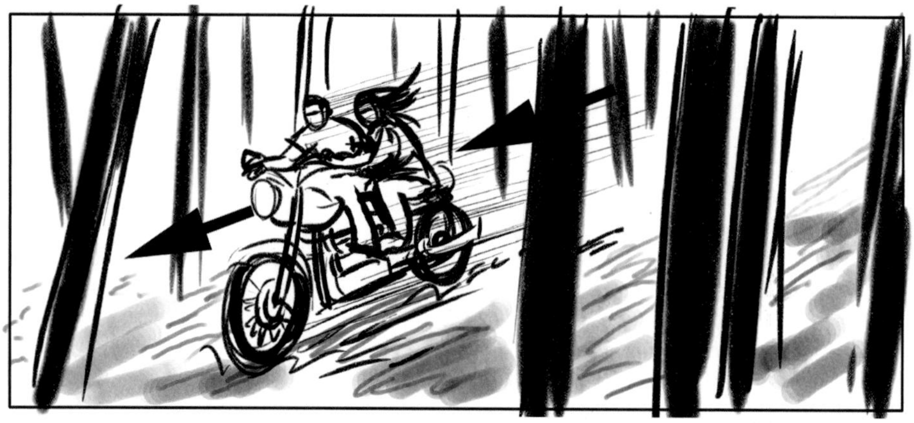

45

WIDE

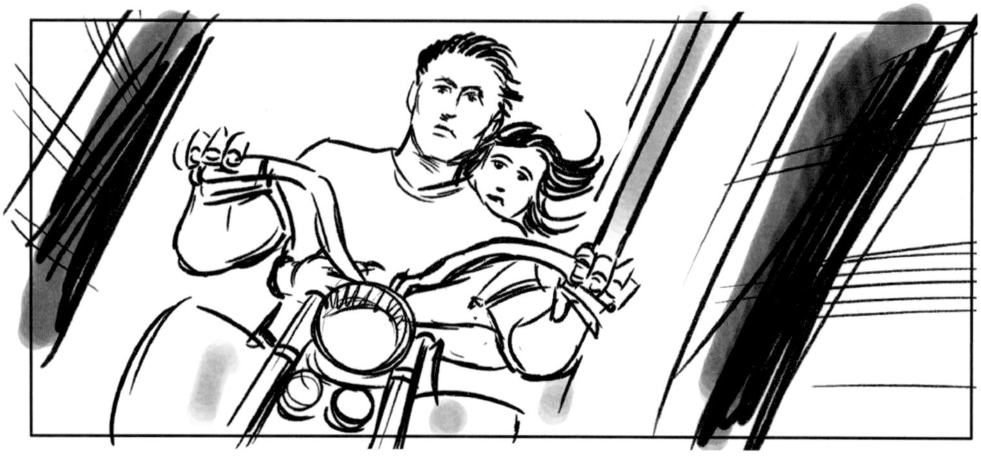

46

CLOSE.

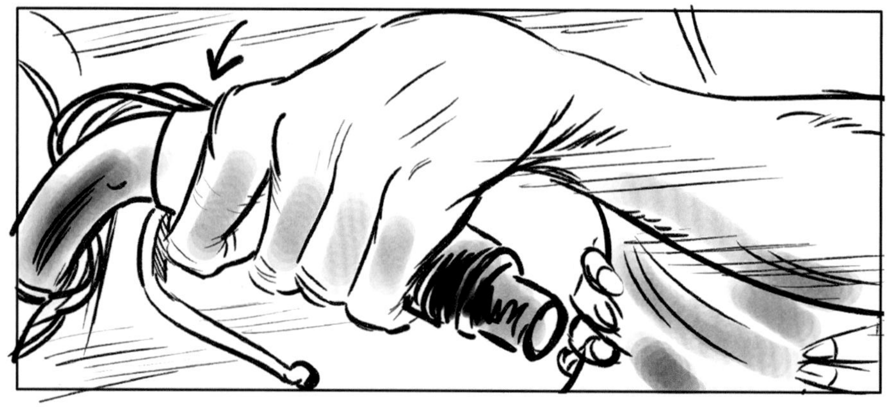

47

NATHAN HITS THE GAS.

48

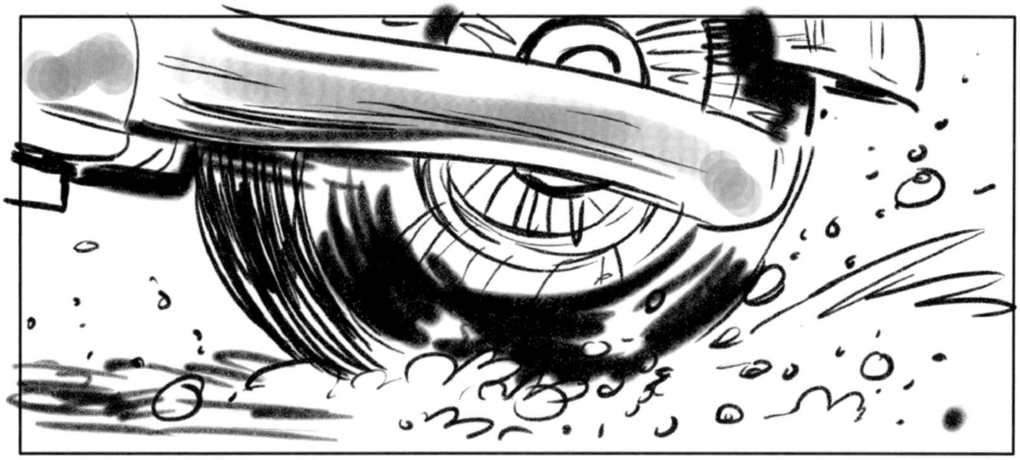

THE BACK WHEEL SPITS DIRT AS IT SHOOTS OFF. THE GROUND.

49

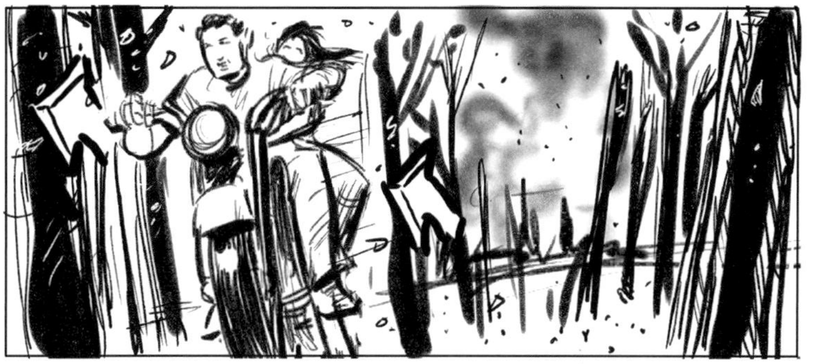

SLO-MO SHOT OF THE BIKE LEAPING AND DESCENDING TOWARD CAMERA.

49A

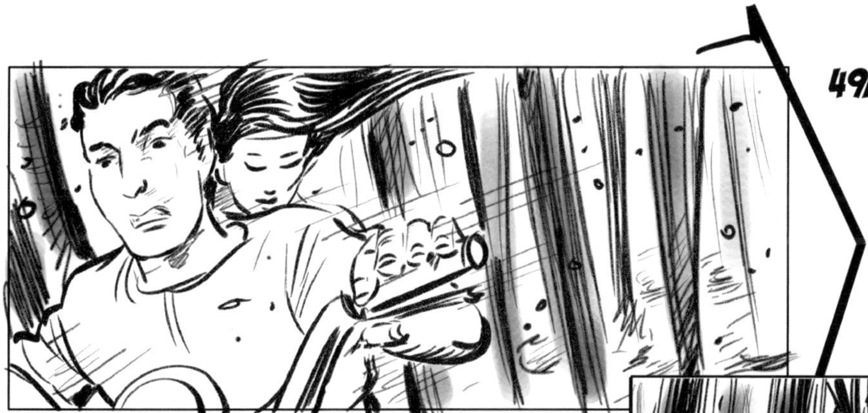

SHOT CONTINUED (SLO-MO) AS NATHAN AND KAREN PAST CAMERA.

CAMERA DRIFTS UP PAST CAMERA.

49B

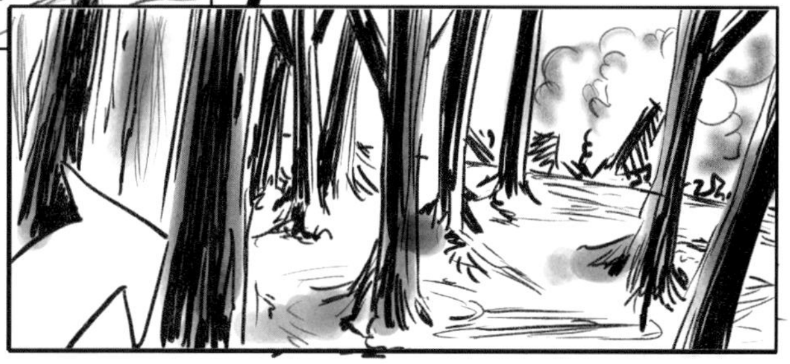

SHOT CONT'D TO VIEW THE BURNING HOUSE.

50

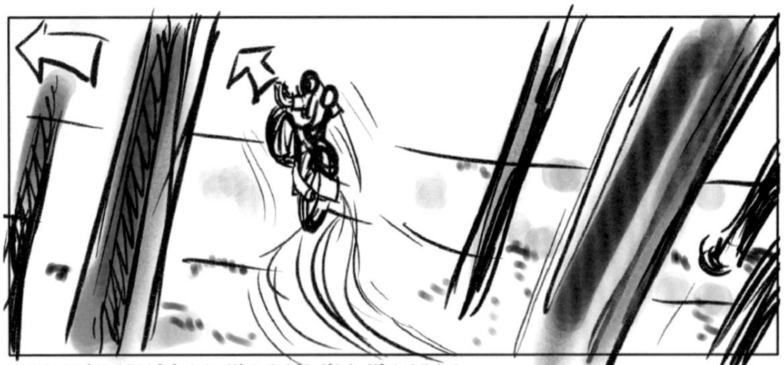

LOOKING DOWN AS THE TWO HIT THE ROAD.

50-1

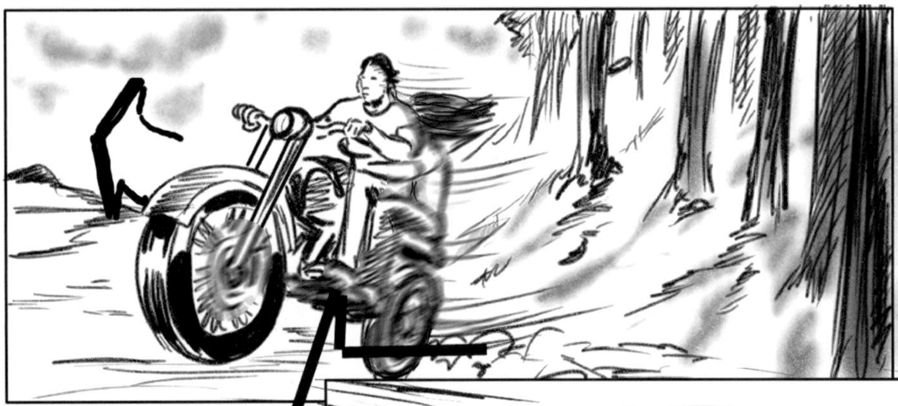

51

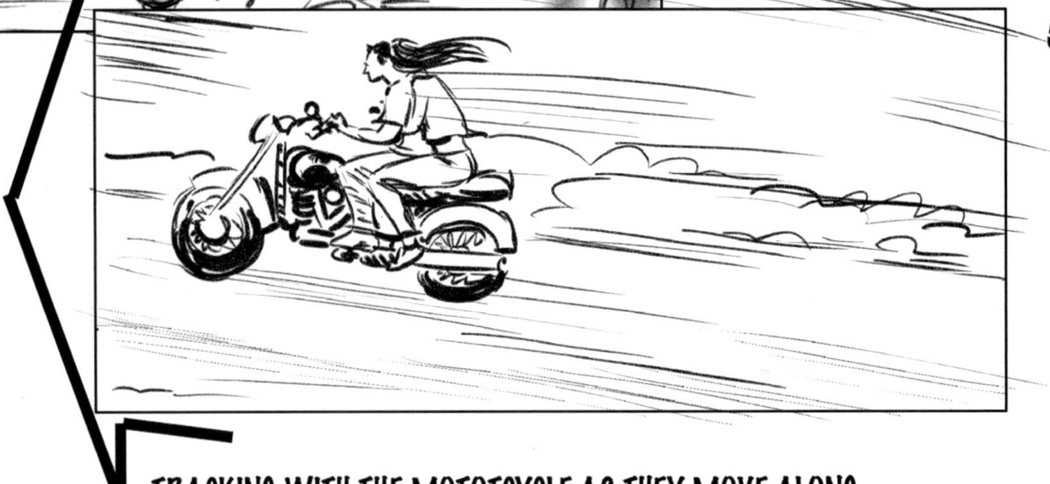

TRACKING WITH THE MOTOTCYCLE AS THEY MOVE ALONG.

52

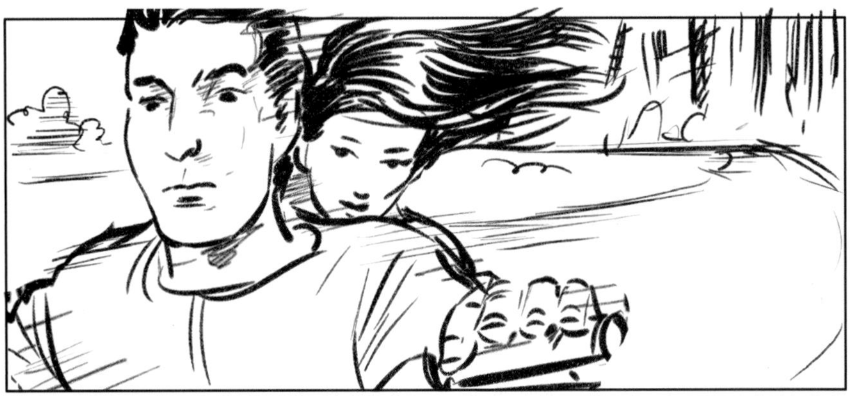

TRACKING/CLOSE ON THE DUO.

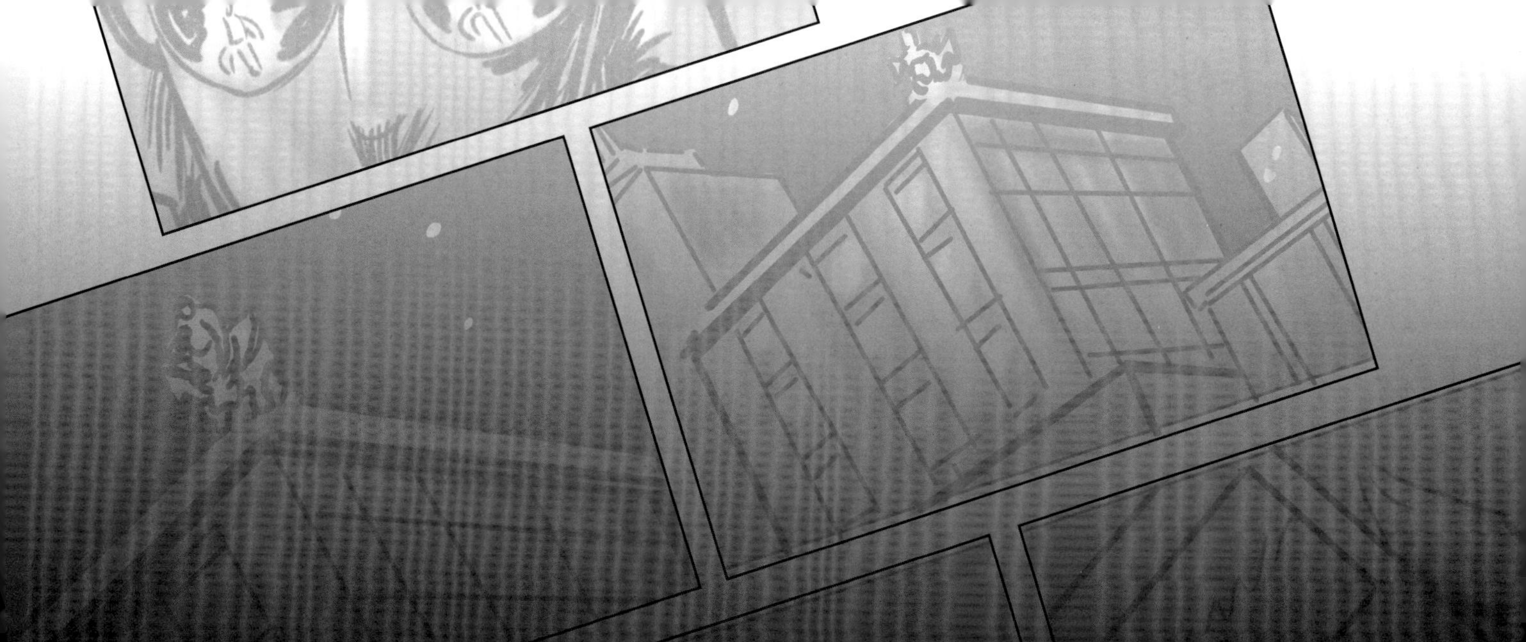

STORYBOARDS AND STORIES OF 15 SELECT FILMS AND TELEVISION SHOWS

HARD DAY'S WORK

Chapter 16

THE AMAZING SPIDER-MAN

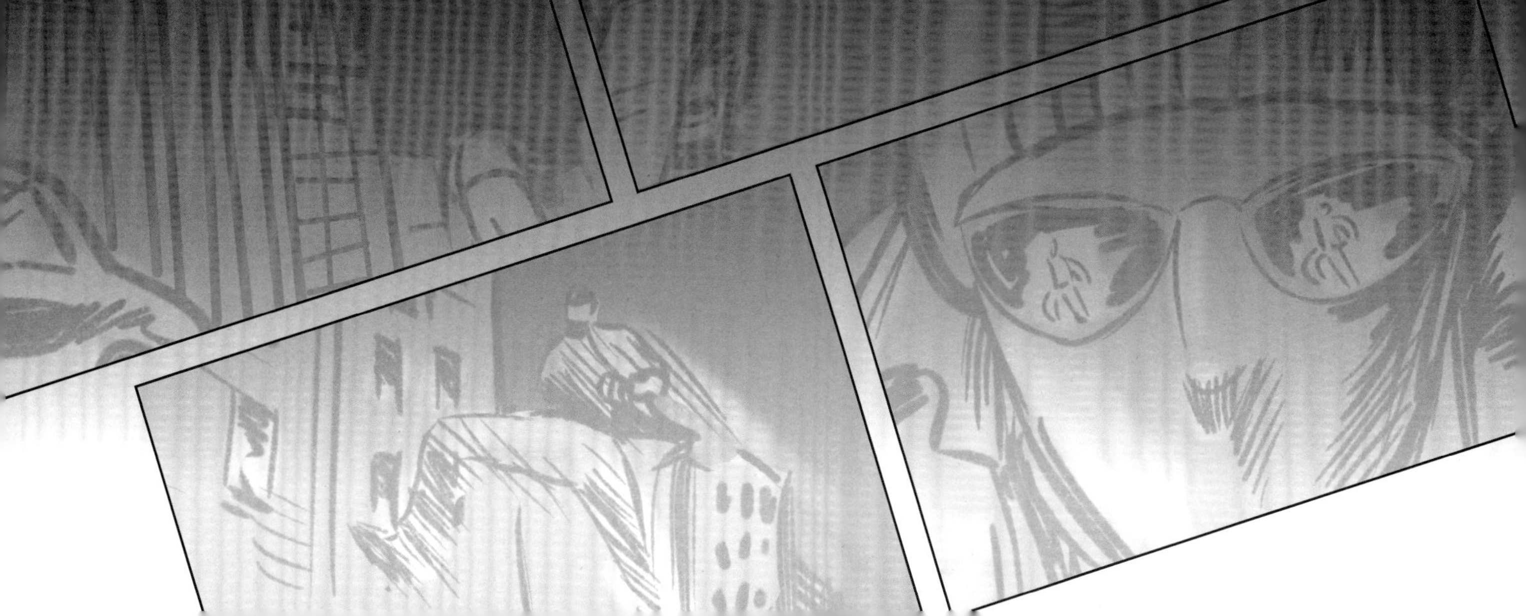

The Amazing Spider-Man

In 2010, I was approached by the production designer, the late Michael Riva the opportunity to work on the Spider-Man reboot, *The Amazing Spider-Man*, to be directed by Marc Webb. I couldn't take the job as I was working on *Abduction* with John Singleton. In 2011, when *The Amazing Spider-Man* production called me to see if I was available to work with Marc storyboards for reshoots, I was ready to go. In one of our meetings, Marc described a scene where Spider-Man (before he has his complete costume) would patrol the city looking for his Uncle Ben's killer. At this point in the story, Spider-Man can only identify the suspect by a unique tattoo on the killer's wrist. Marc and I went over the scene shot by shot, and it was a lot of fun. Ultimately, this scene was never shot, but other scenes I worked on are in the final cut of the movie.

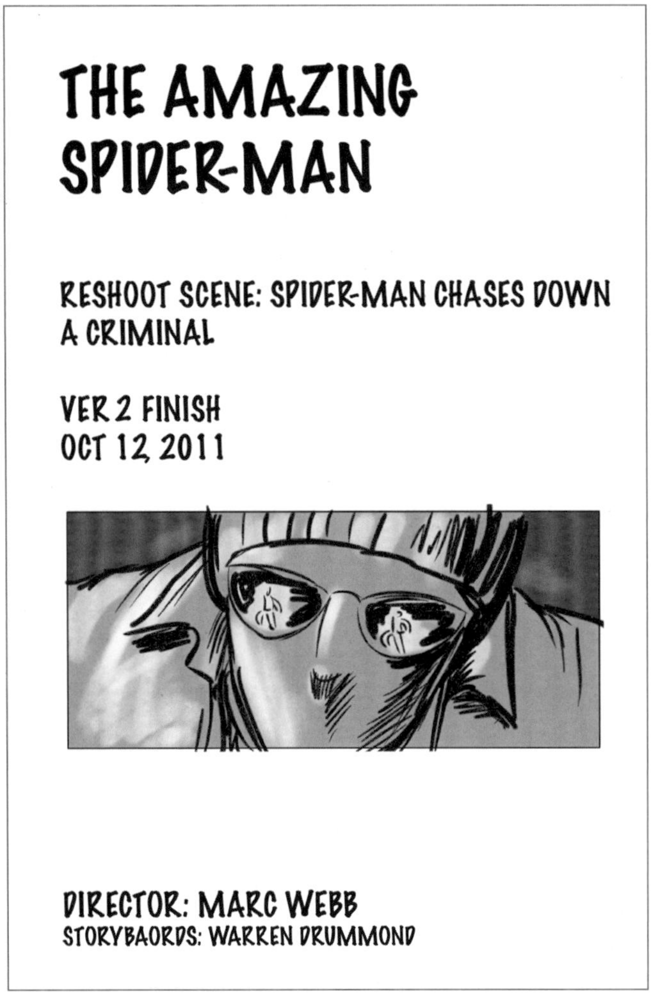

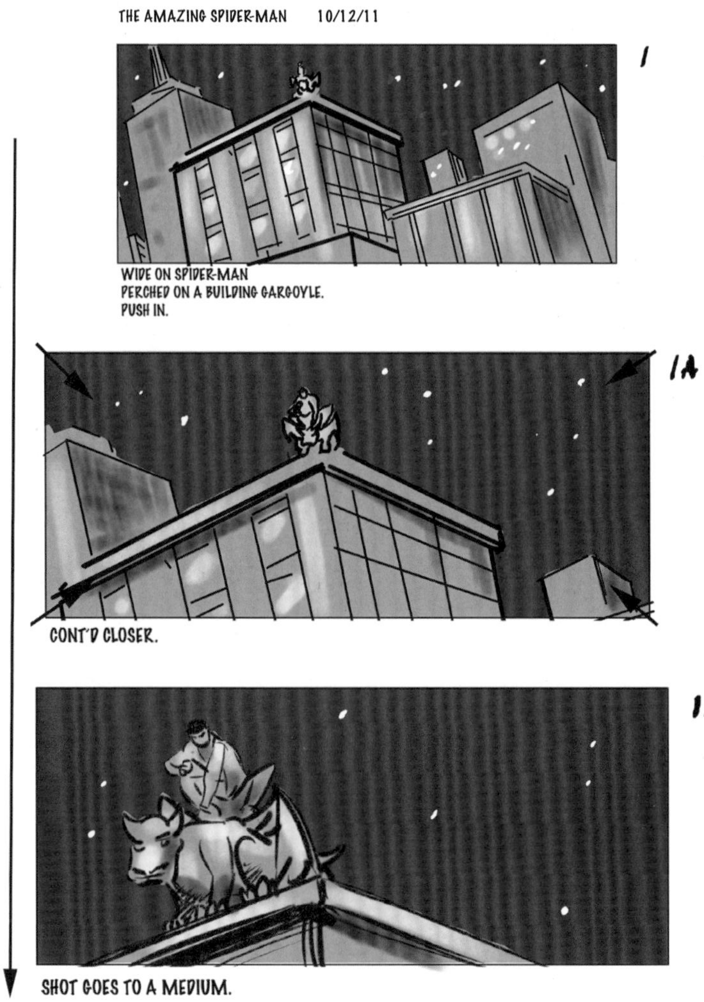

THE AMAZING SPIDER-MAN 10/12/11

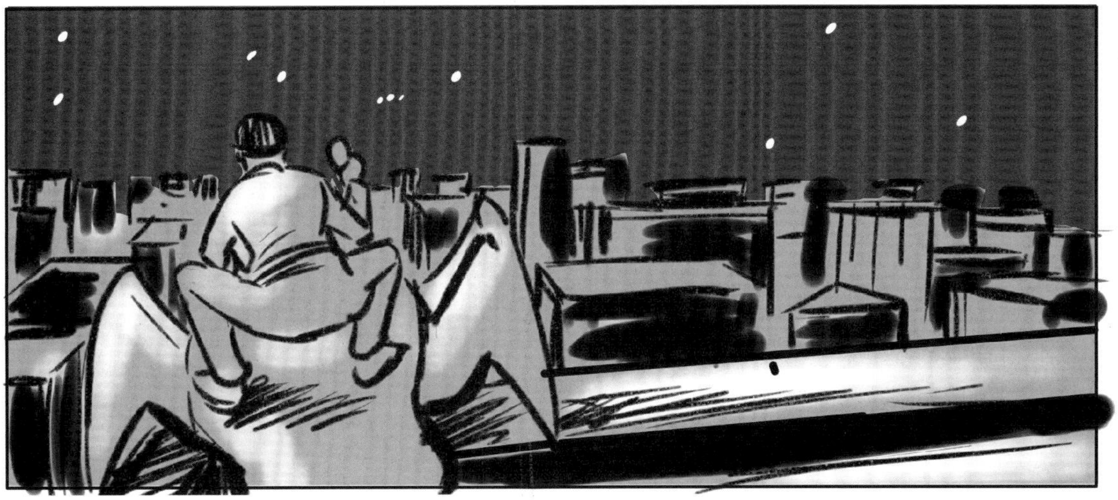

2

REAR ON SPIDER-MAN
HE HAS HIS
MODIFIED IPOD

With all of these Spider-poses, I wish I was able to draw the classic costume, but in this version of the screenplay, Peter had not created his super-hero costume as of yet.

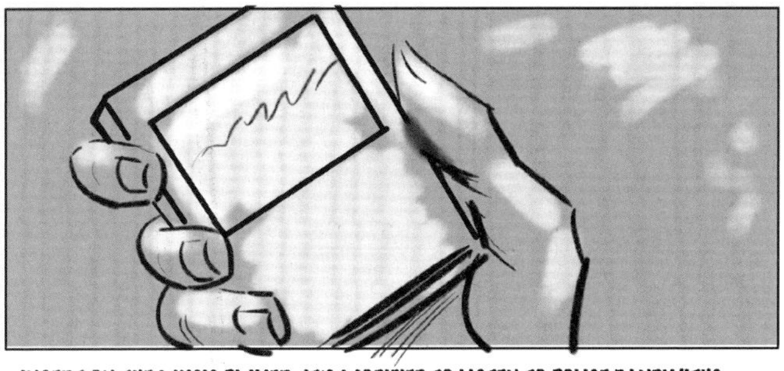

3

INSERT ON THE MUSIC PLAYER. IT'S MODIFIED TO LISTEN TO POLICE BANDWITHS.

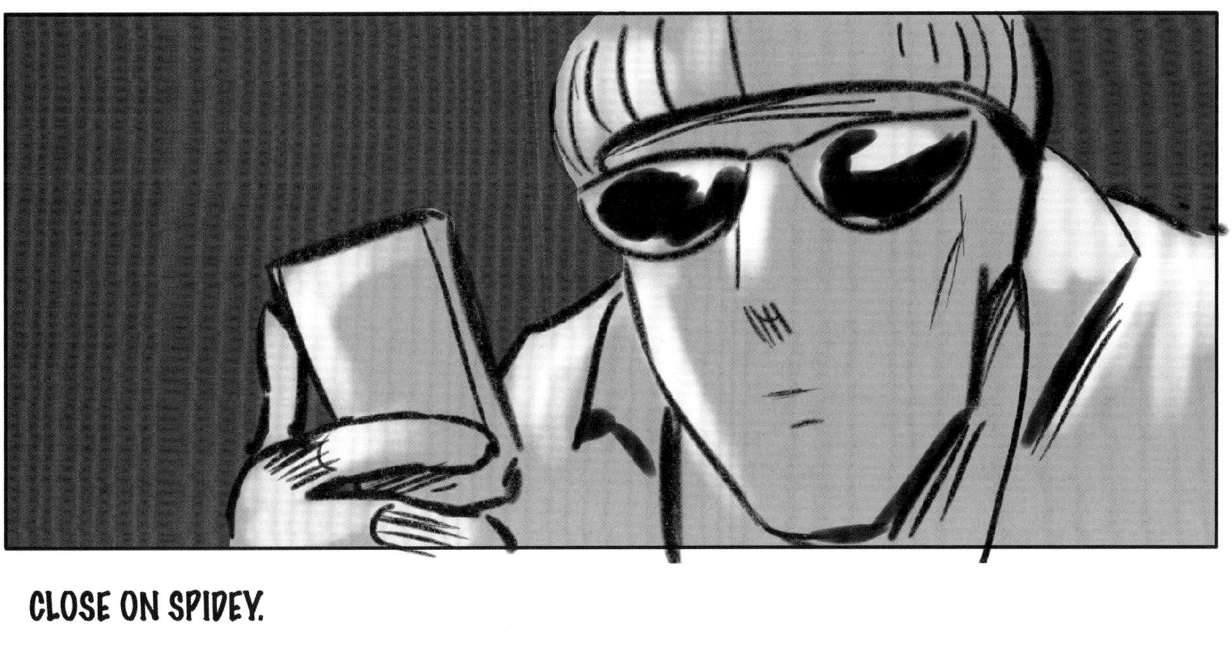

4

CLOSE ON SPIDEY.

THE AMAZING SPIDER-MAN 10/12/11

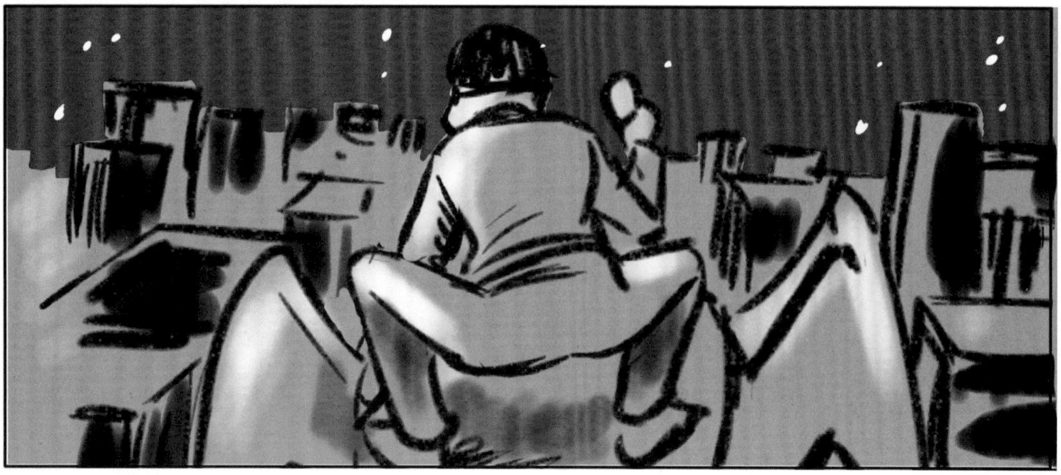

5

BACK TO SHOT
AS SPIDER-MAN KNOWS WHERE HE HAS TO GO. (LEAVE'S FRAME?)

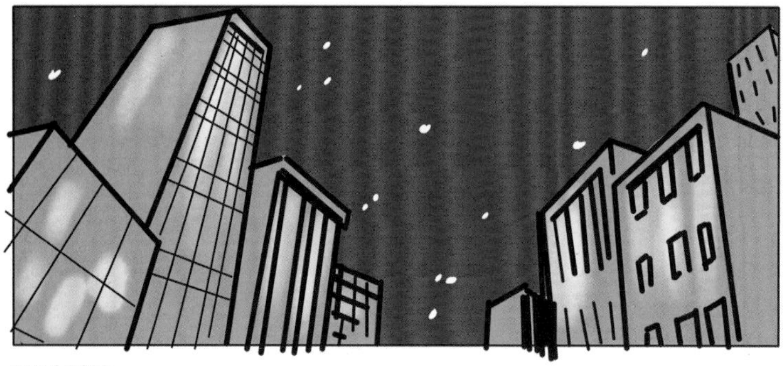

6

NEW SHOT
LOW ON CITY

WE TILT DOWN

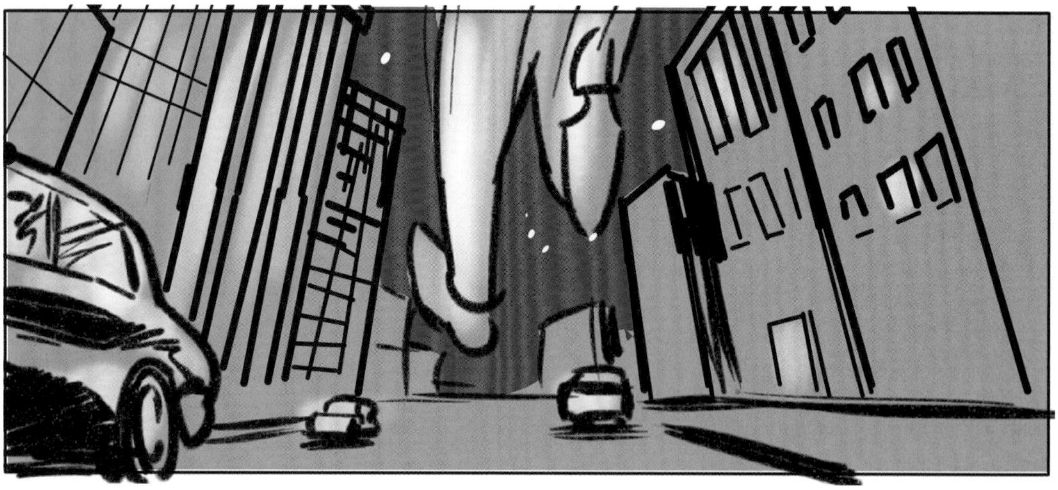

6A

SHOT CONTINUES AS
CRIMINAL LEAPS DOWN OVER CAMERA.

THE AMAZING SPIDER-MAN 10/12/11

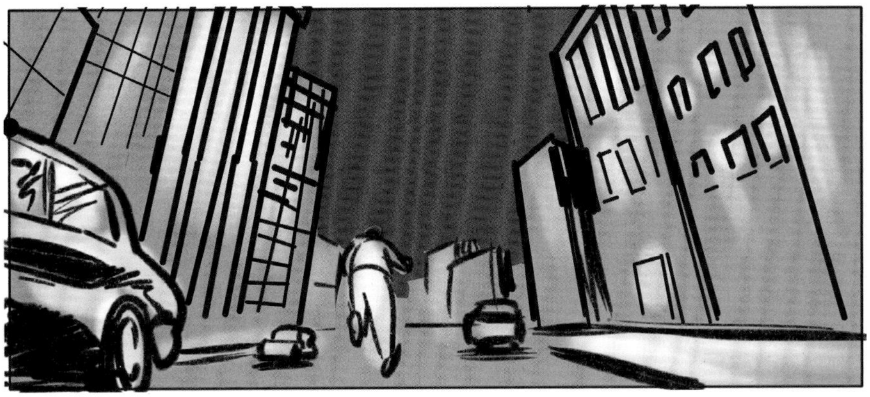

6B

SHOT CONT'D
AS HE RUNS INTO THE DISTANCE.

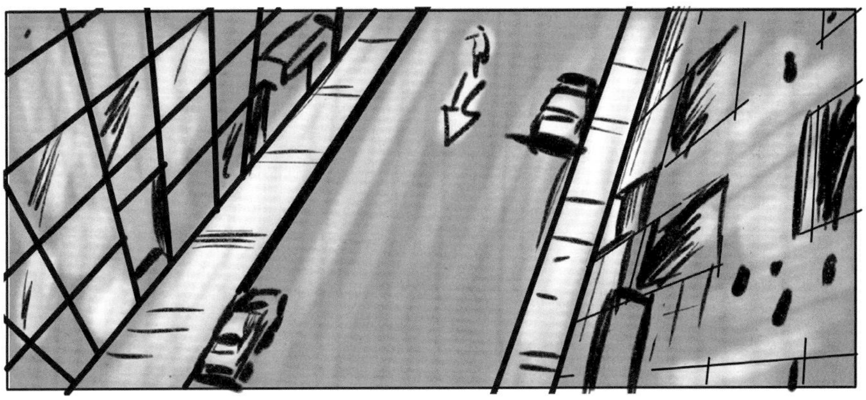

7

NEW HIGH SHOT
PAN DOWN
CRIMINAL IS RUNNING TOWARD US. HE WILL PASS UNDERNEATH.

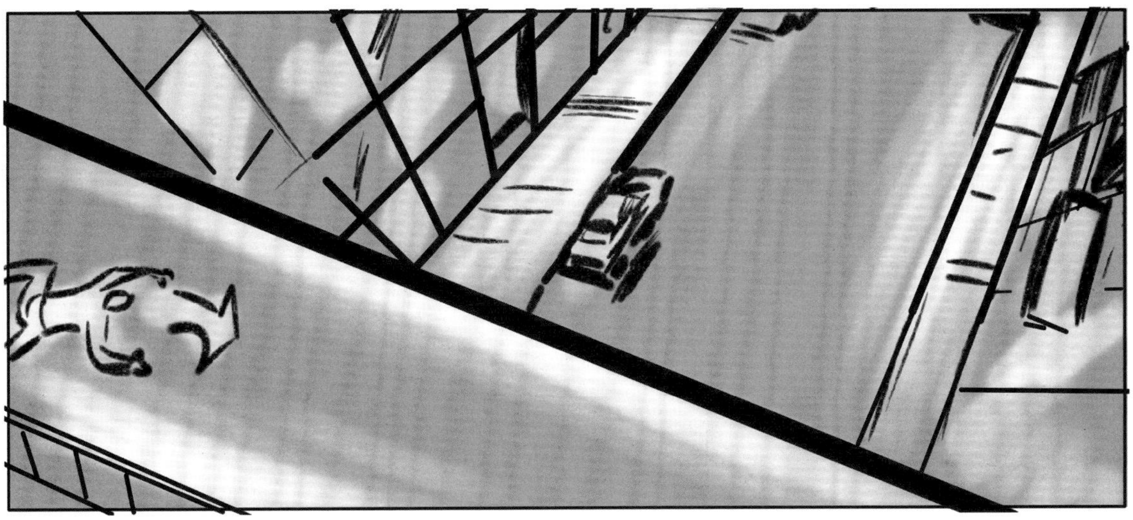

7A

WE REVEAL A BUILDING OVERPASS ON WHICH SPIDER-MAN IS CRAWLING ACROSS THE TOP.

THE AMAZING SPIDER-MAN 10/12/11

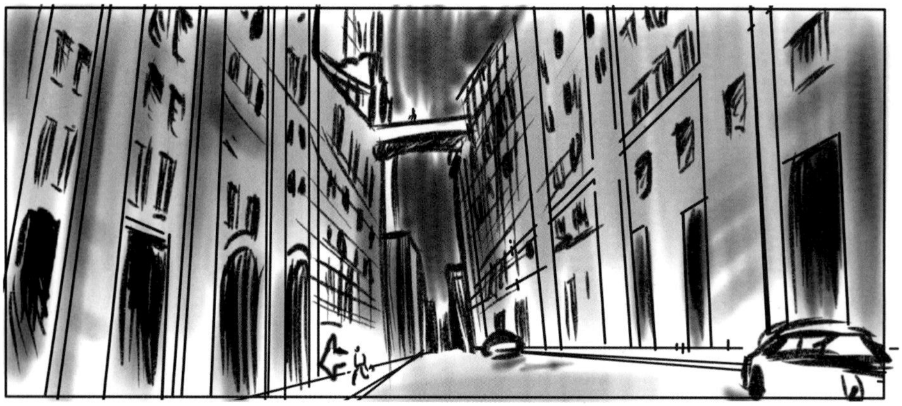

7A-1

SUPER WIDE OF SCENE

THE CRIMINAL RUNS ON THE SIDEWALK AS SPIDER-MAN IS PERCHED ON THE OVERPASS HIGH IN THE B.G.

THE AMAZING SPIDER-MAN 10/12/11

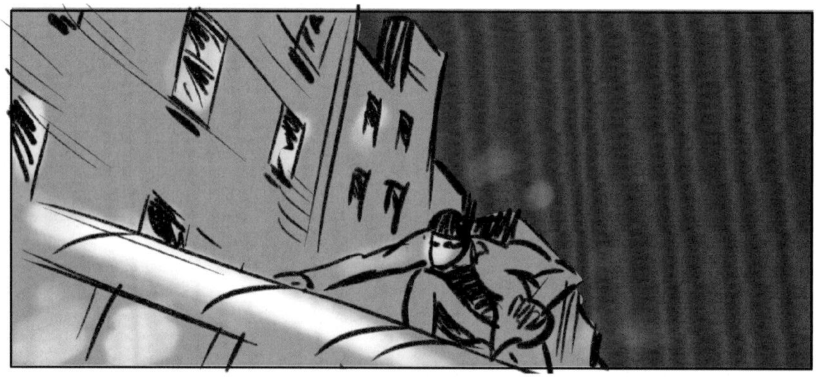

8

SPIDEY CRAWLS TOWARD THE EDGE OF THE BUILDING OVERPASS.

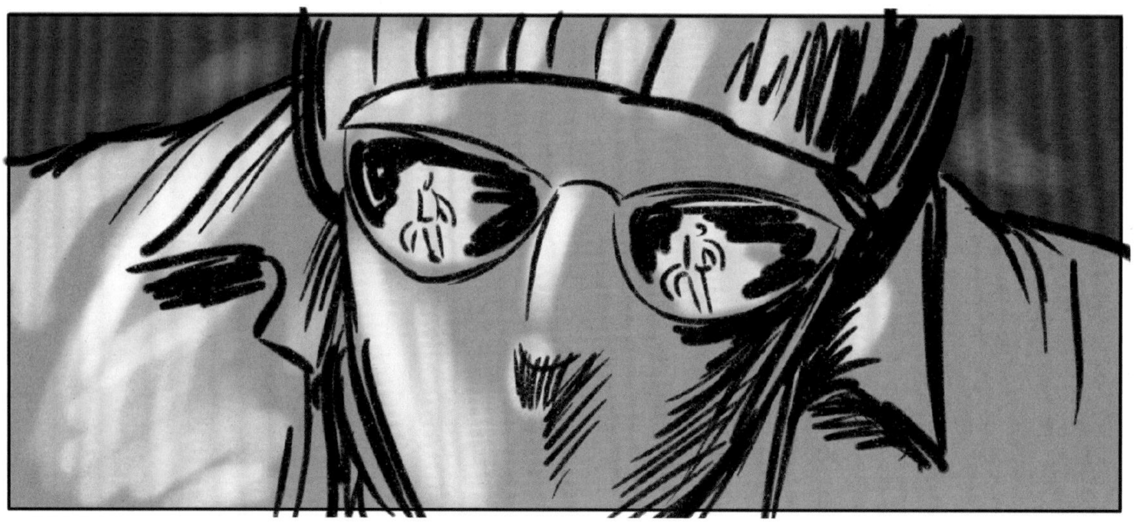

9

CLOSE

THE CRIMINAL IS REFLECTED IN HIS GLASSES.

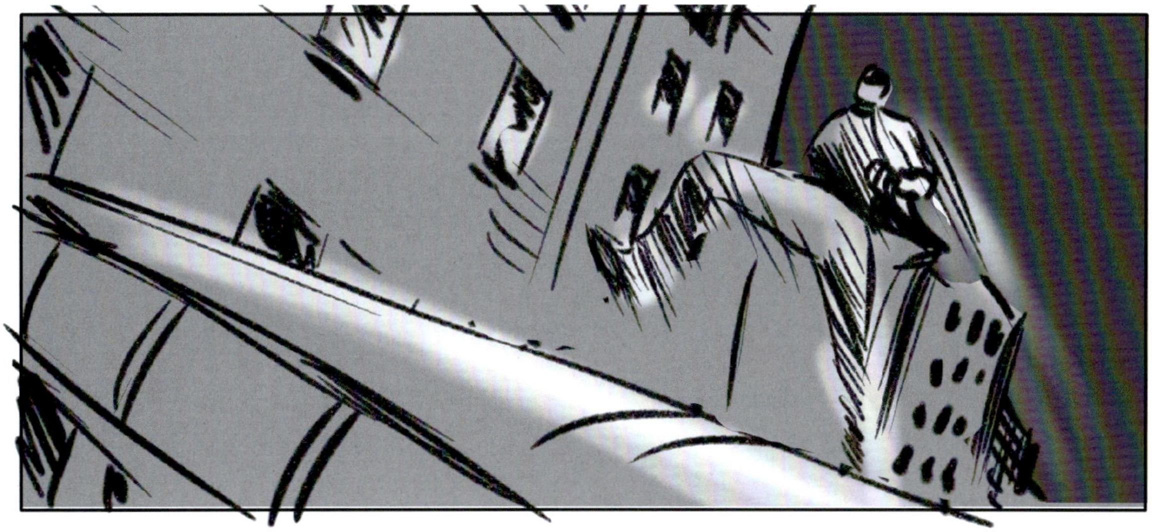

10

SPIDER-MAN LEAPS OFF.

THE AMAZING SPIDER-MAN 10/12/11

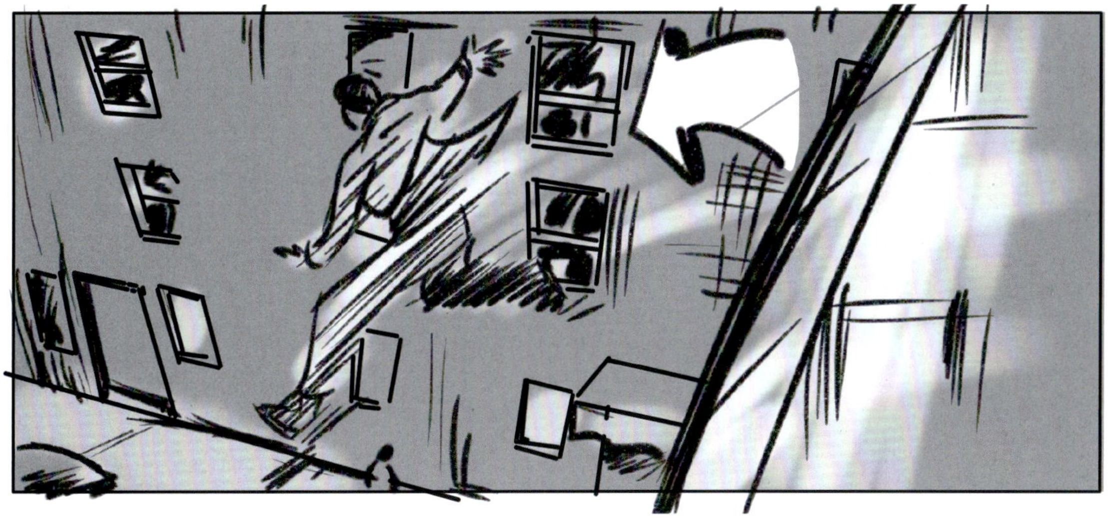

11

DOWN ANGLE
PANNING SLIGHTLY R-L AS SPIDER-MAN FALLS.

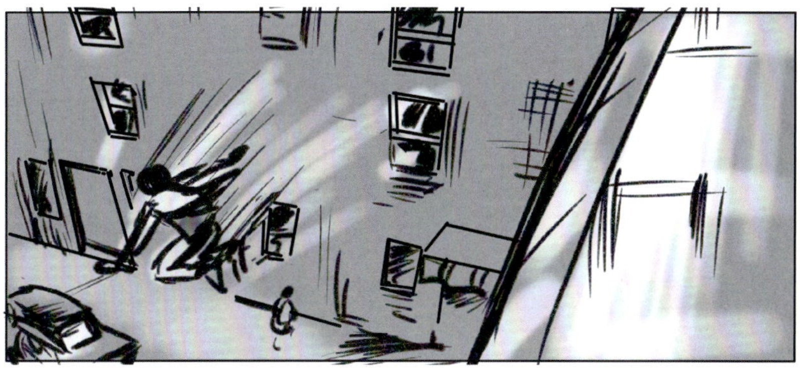

11A

SHOT CONT'D

12

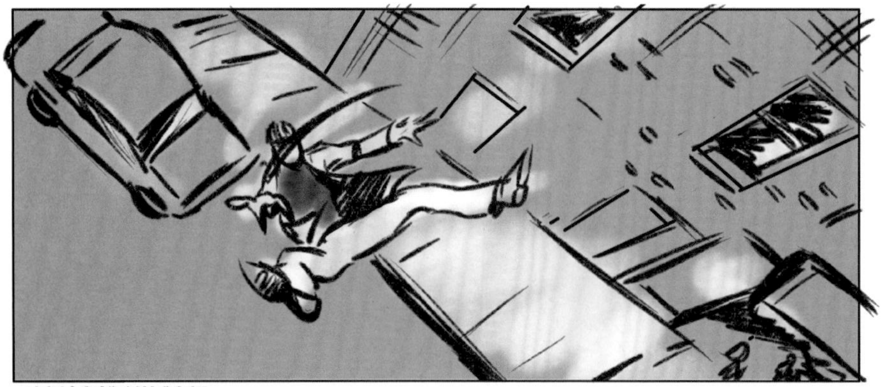

NEW SHOT/CLOSER
SPIDER-MAN FIRES HIS WEB-SHOOTER.

THE AMAZING SPIDER-MAN 10/12/11

13

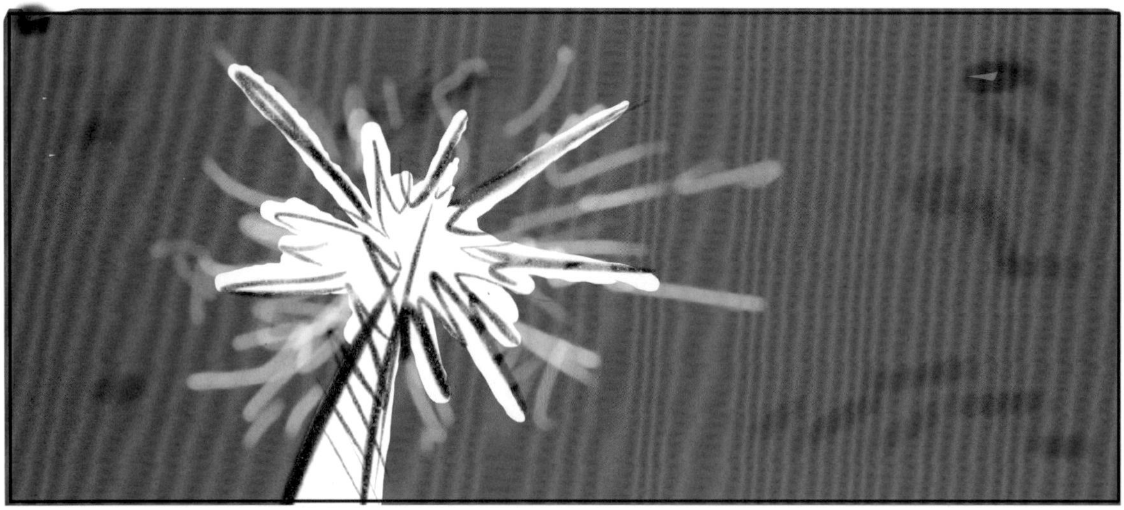

INSERT ON
THE WEB HITTING THE UNDERSIDE OF THE OVERPASS.

14

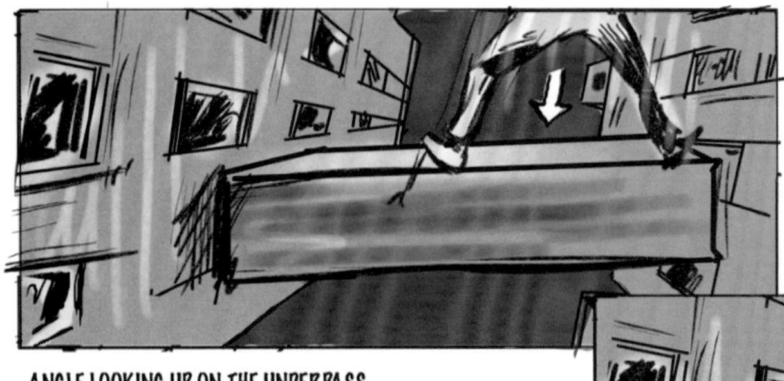

ANGLE LOOKING UP ON THE UNDERPASS
AS SPIDER-MAN SWINGS THROUGH THE FRAME.

14A

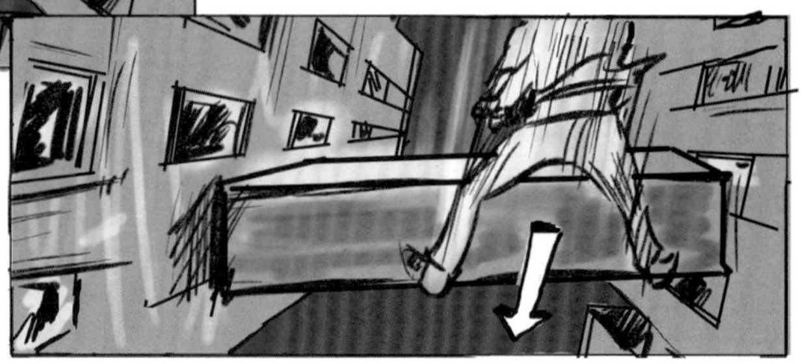

SHOT CONT'D

THE AMAZING SPIDER-MAN 10/12/11

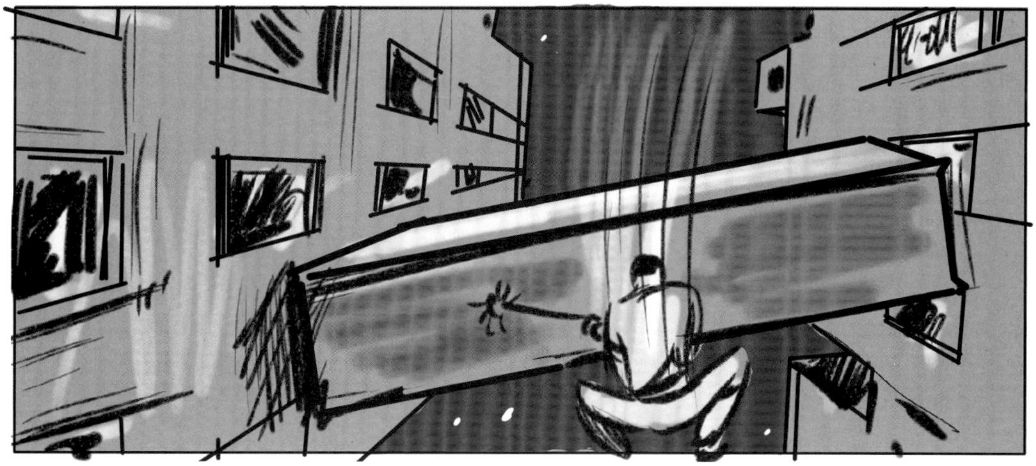

14B

SWING CONT'D

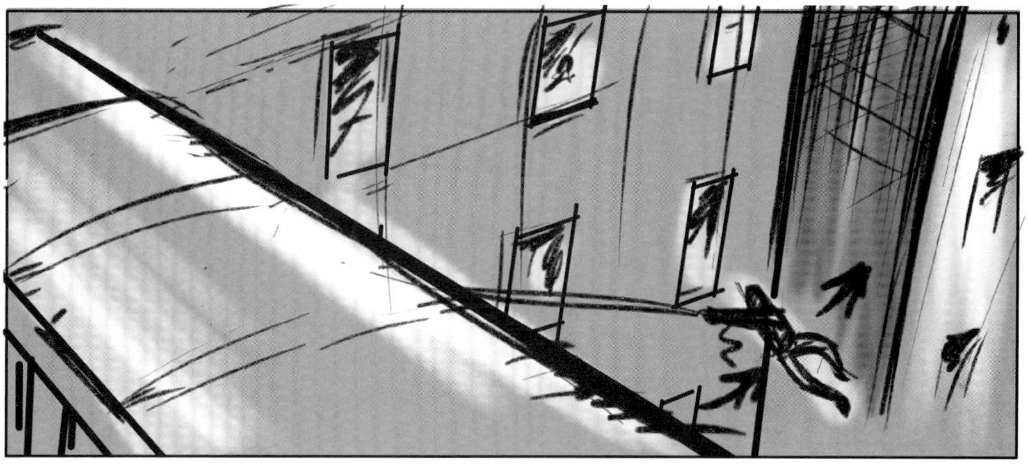

15

SPIDEY COMES OUT ON THE OTHER SIDE OF THE OVERPASS.

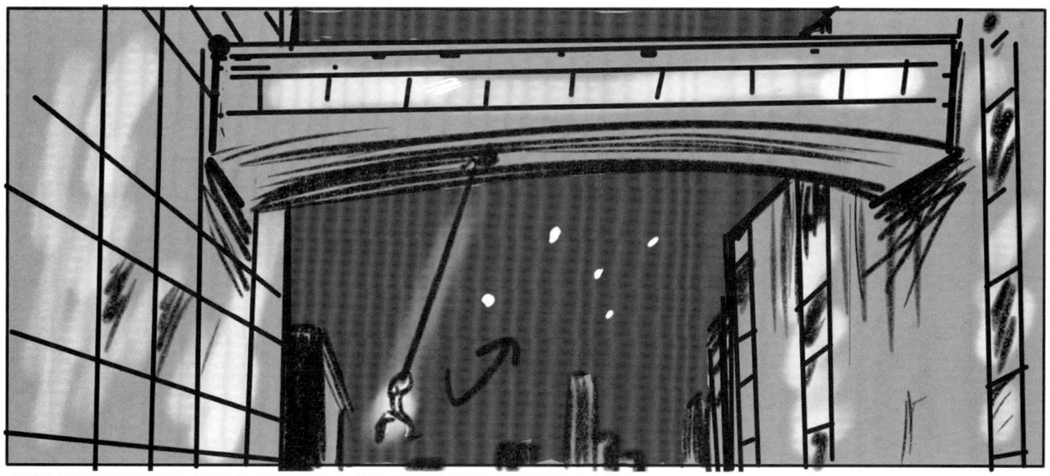

16

ANGLE FROM OTHER SIDE AS HE SWINGS TOWARD US.

THE AMAZING SPIDER-MAN 10/12/11

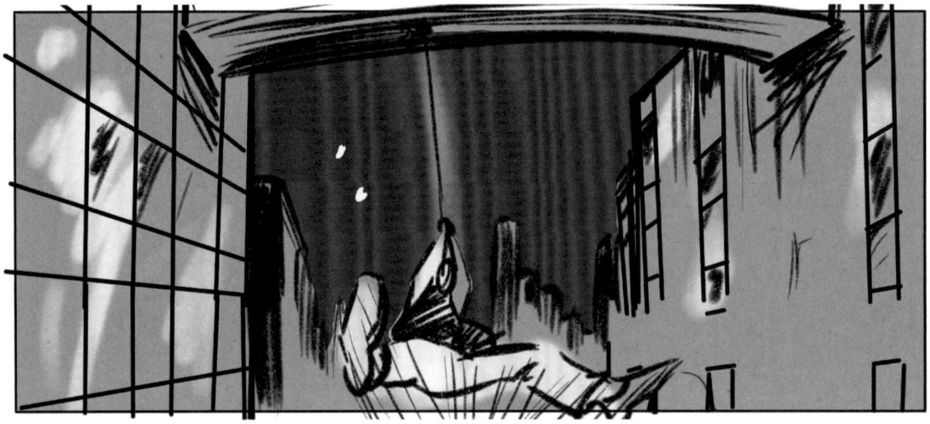

16A

SHOT CONT'D

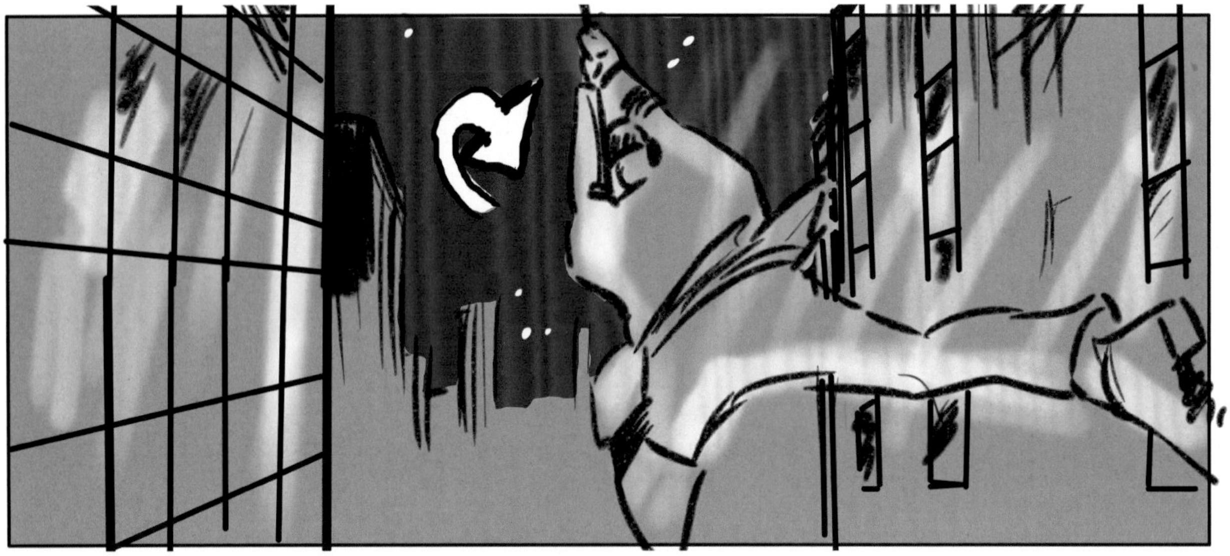

16B

SHOT CONT'D (TILTING DOWN) AS SPIDER-MAN STARTS TO LOWER HIMSELF AS HE SWINGS BACK THE OTHER WAY.

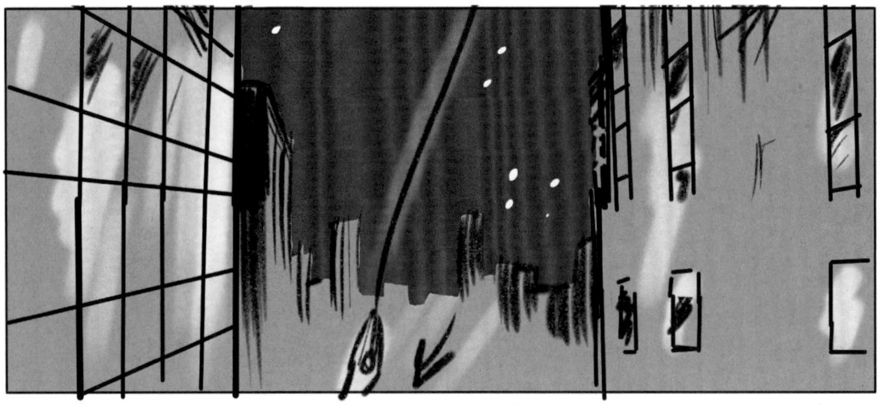

16C

SPIDER-MAN GETS LOWER STILL. CORKSCREWS HIS WAY DOWN.

THE AMAZING SPIDER-MAN 10/12/11

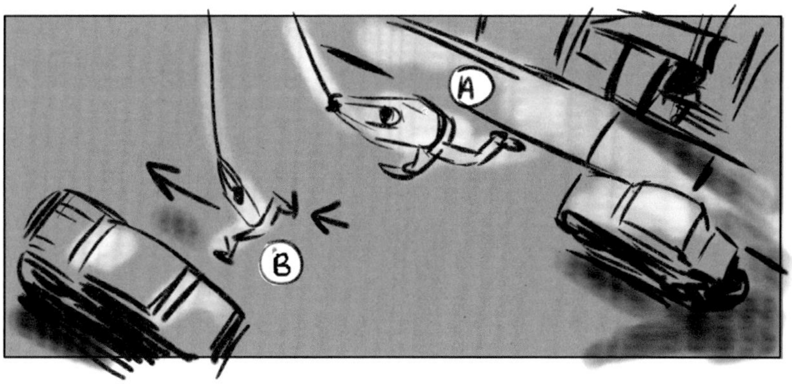

17

DOWN SHOT OF SPIDER-MAN GETTING CLOSER TO THE STREET.

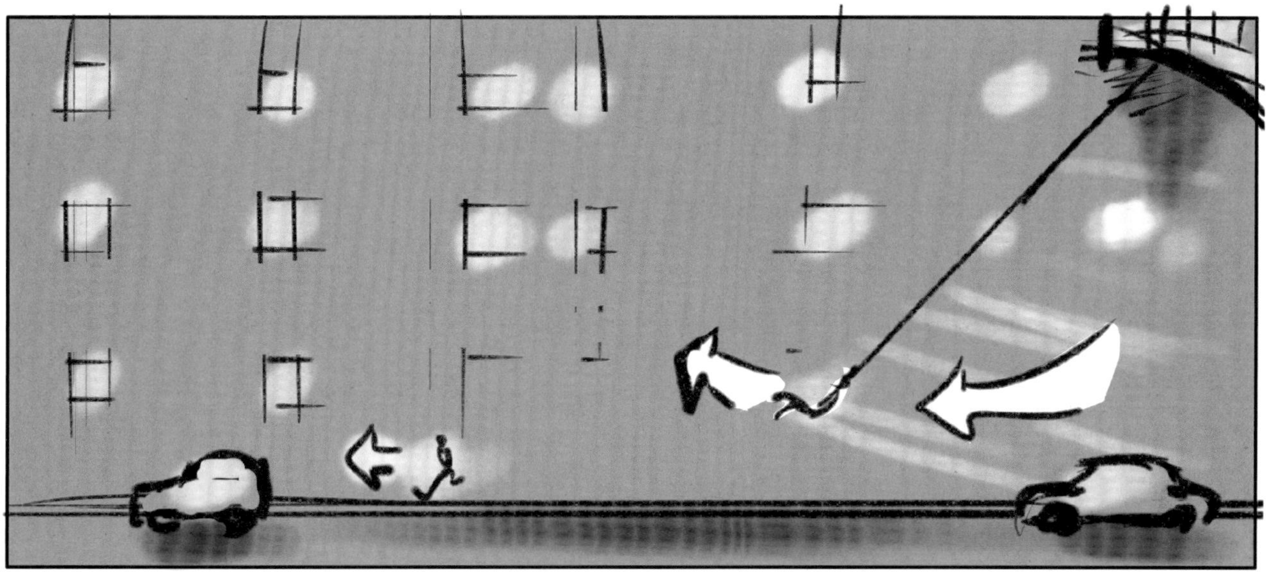

18

WIDE PROFILE SHOT ON SPIDER-MAN, THE OVERPASS AND THE CRIMINAL TO ESTABLISH GEOGRAPHY.

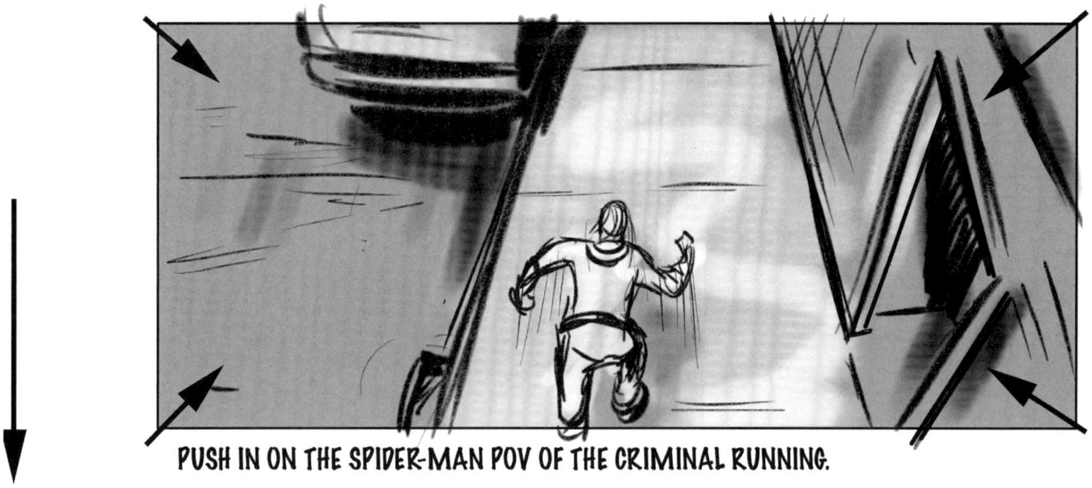

19

PUSH IN ON THE SPIDER-MAN POV OF THE CRIMINAL RUNNING.

THE AMAZING SPIDER-MAN 10/12/11

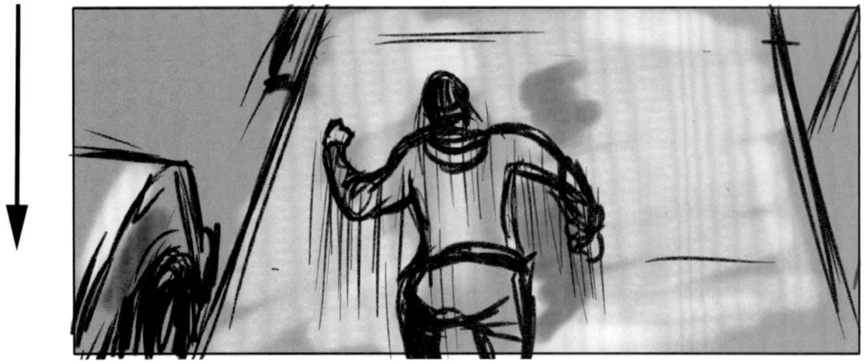

19A

CLOSER

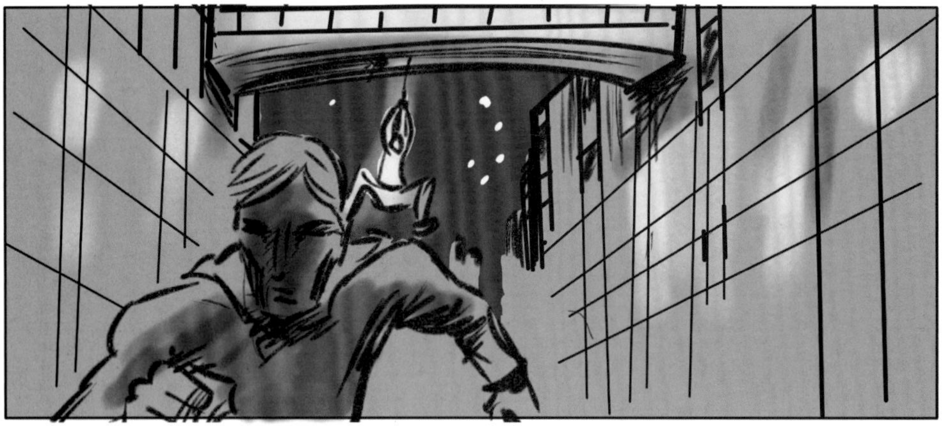

20

REVERSE AS
WE TRACK WITH THE CRIMINAL AS SPIDER-MAN SWINGS BEHIND HIM.

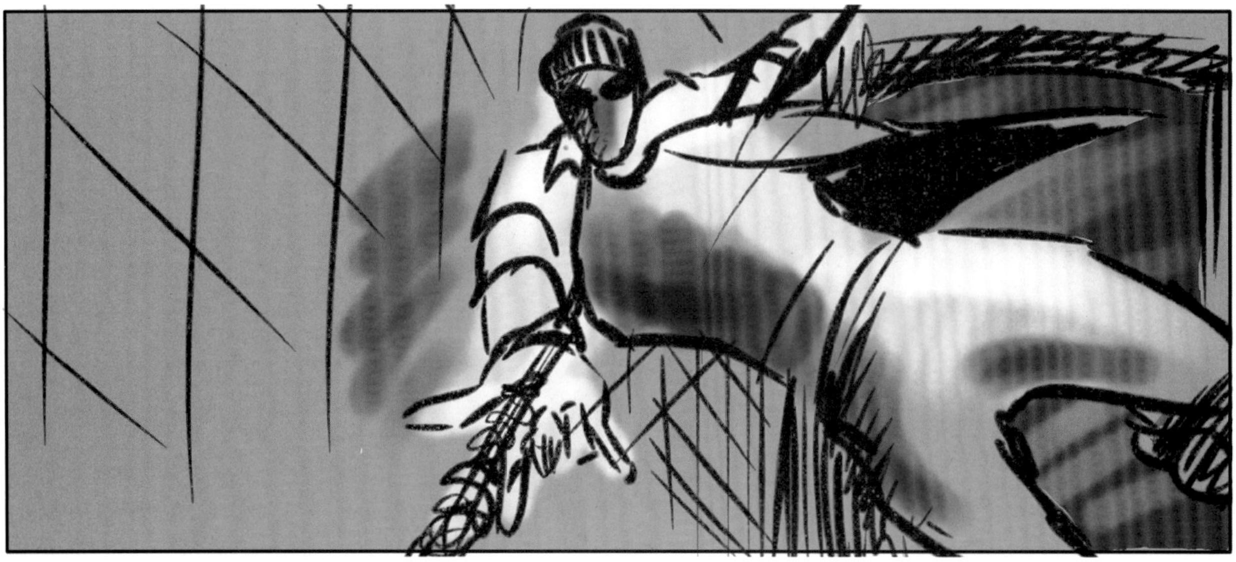

21

SPIDER-MAN SHOOTS A WEB.

THE AMAZING SPIDER-MAN 10/12/11

22

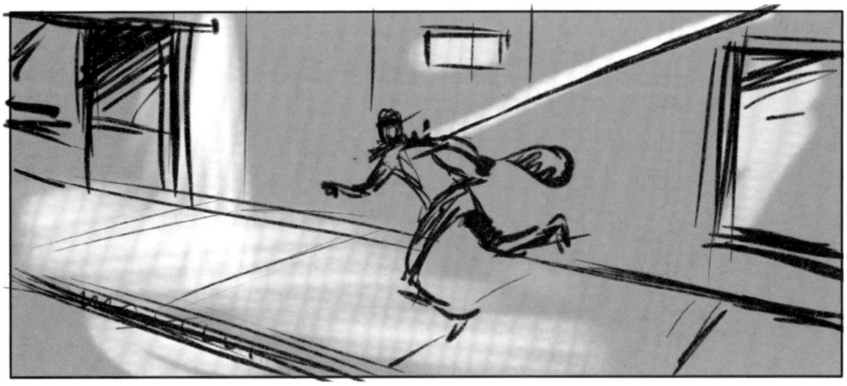

NEW ANGLE AS THE CRIMINAL IS HIT BY A WEB.

23

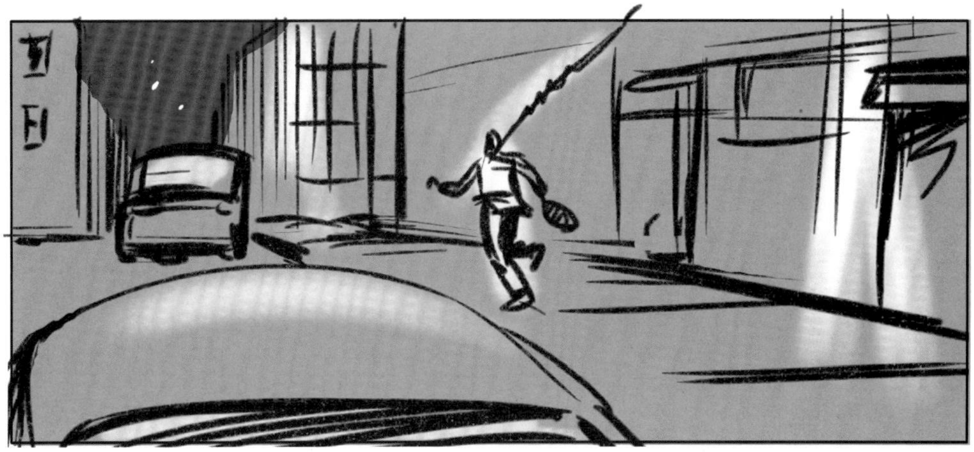

LOWER ANGLE AS HE CONTINUES TO RUN.

23A

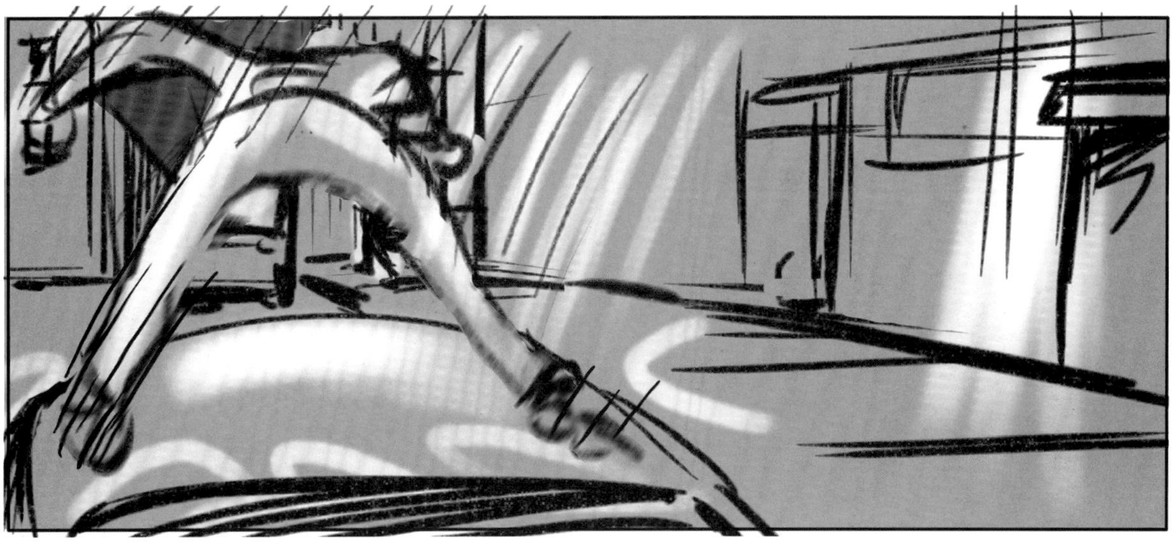

SHOT CONT'D AS SPIDEY LANDS ON A CAR IN FG.

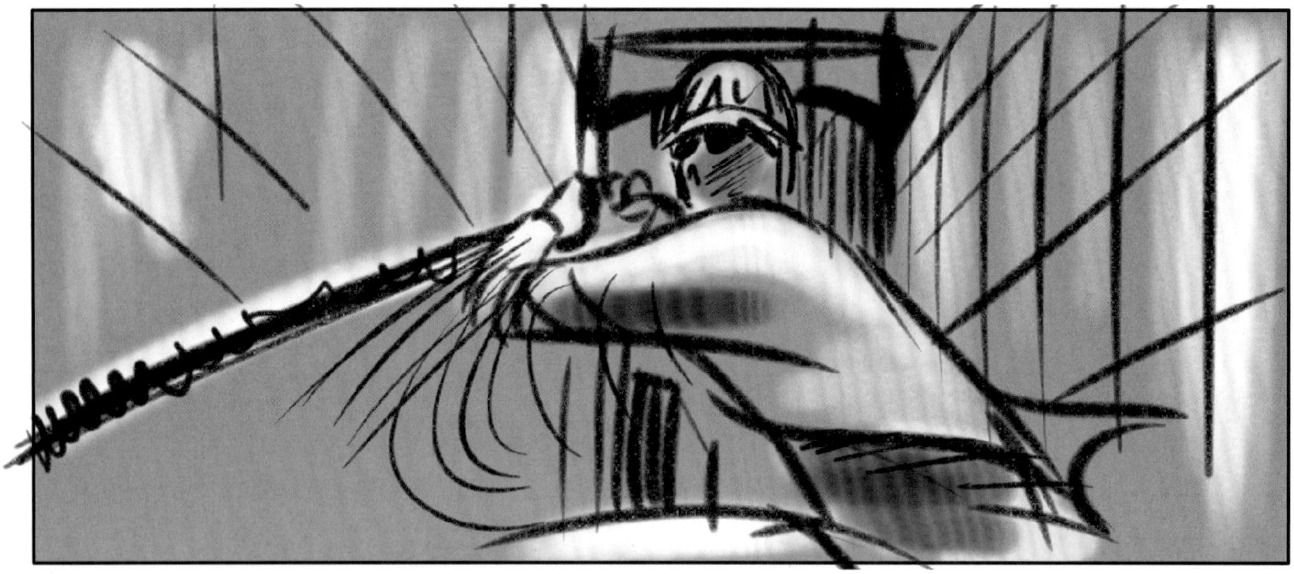

24

SPIDER-MAN JERKS THE WEB.

THE AMAZING SPIDER-MAN 10/12/11

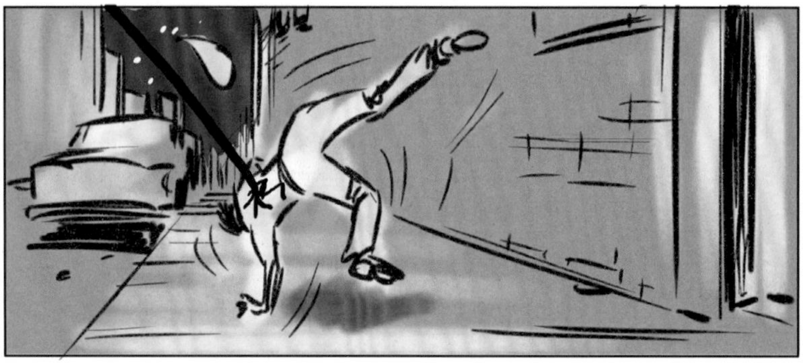

25

THE CRIMINAL IS KNOCKED OFF HIS FEET.

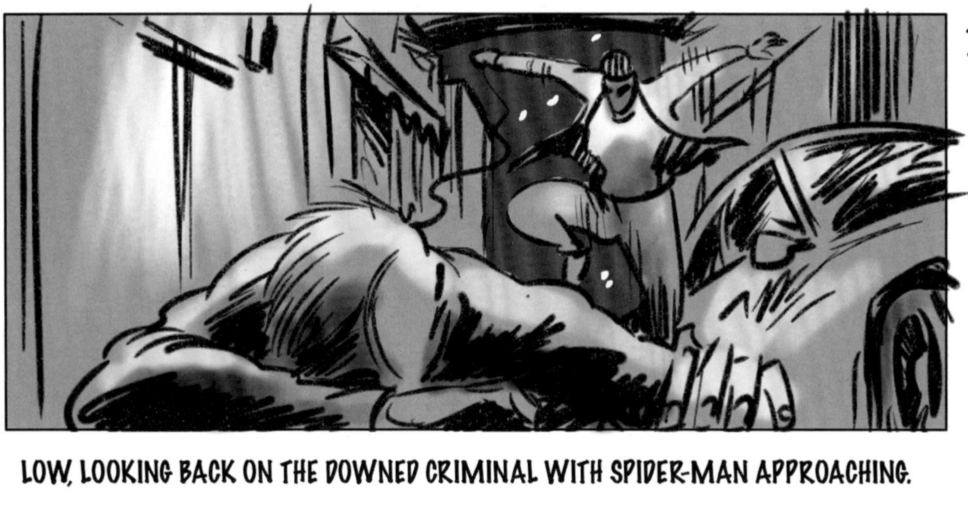

26

LOW, LOOKING BACK ON THE DOWNED CRIMINAL WITH SPIDER-MAN APPROACHING.

26A

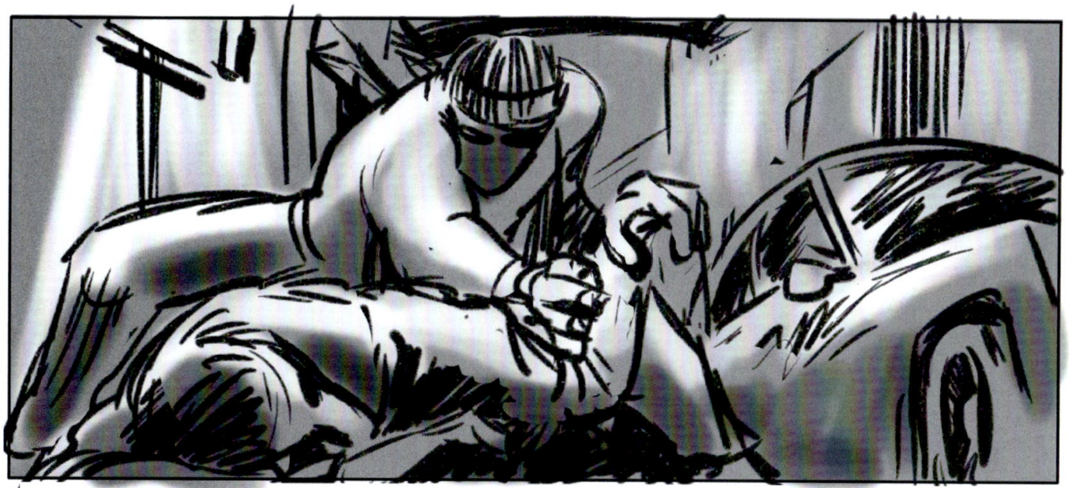

SHOT CONTINUED AS SPIDER-MAN GRABS THE MAN'S LEFT WRIST.

27

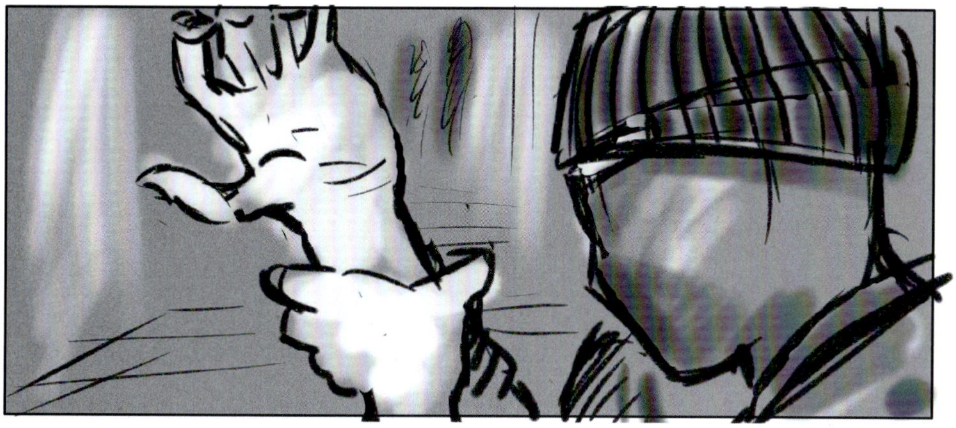

CLOSE
AS SPIDEY LOOKS AT THE BARE WRIST.
NO TATTOO.

The scene would have ended with Peter checking the criminal's wrist for Uncle Ben's killer's tattoo. The wrists would always be clean.

28

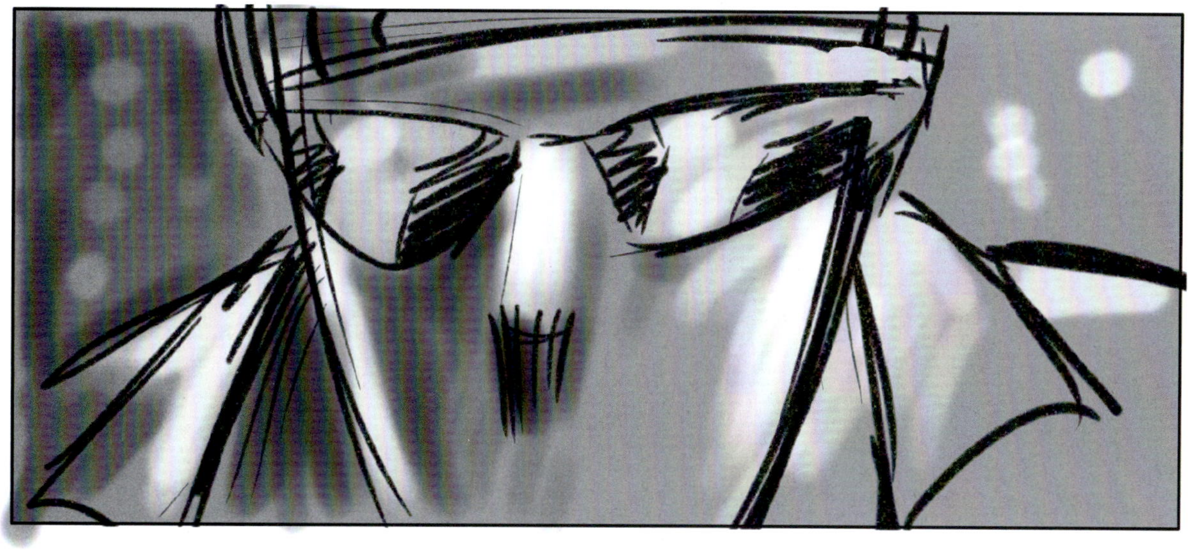

INTENSE CLOSE SHOT ON THE DISAPPOINTED SPIDER-MAN.

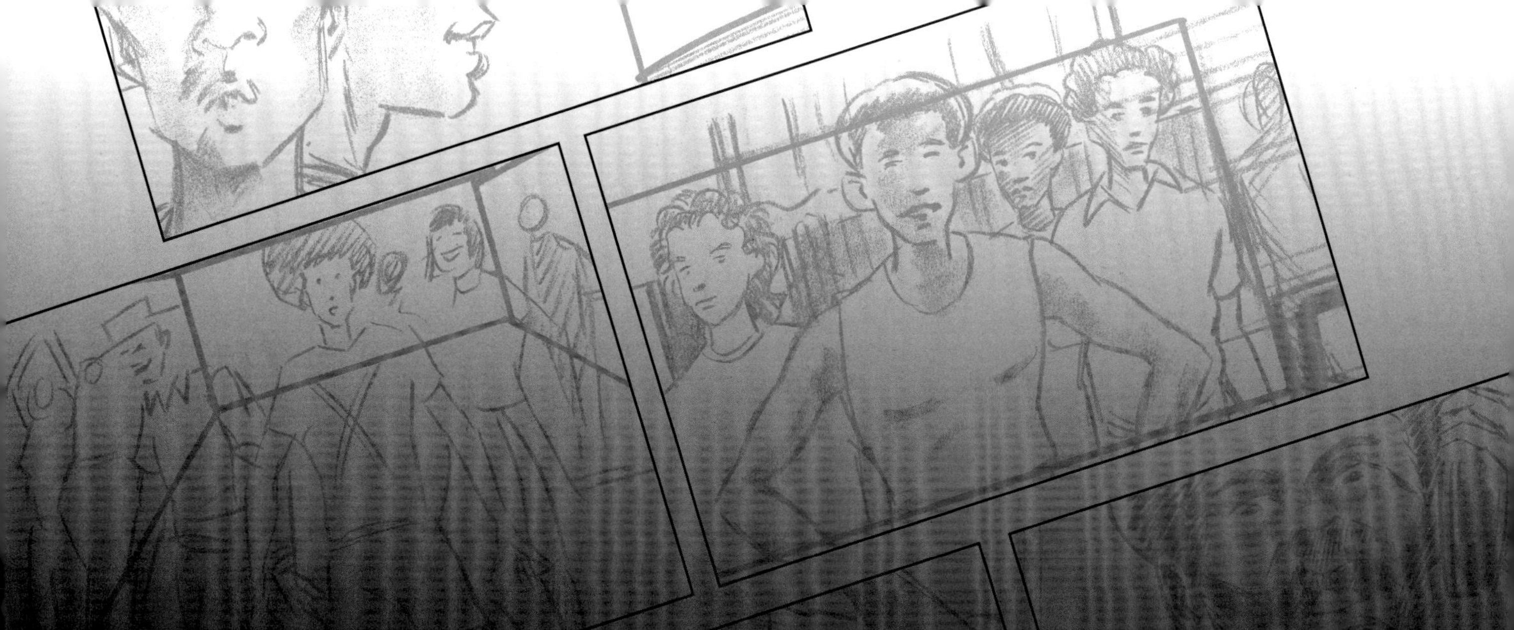

STORYBOARDS AND STORIES OF 15 SELECT FILMS AND TELEVISION SHOWS

HARD DAY'S WORK

Chapter 17

ROLL BOUNCE

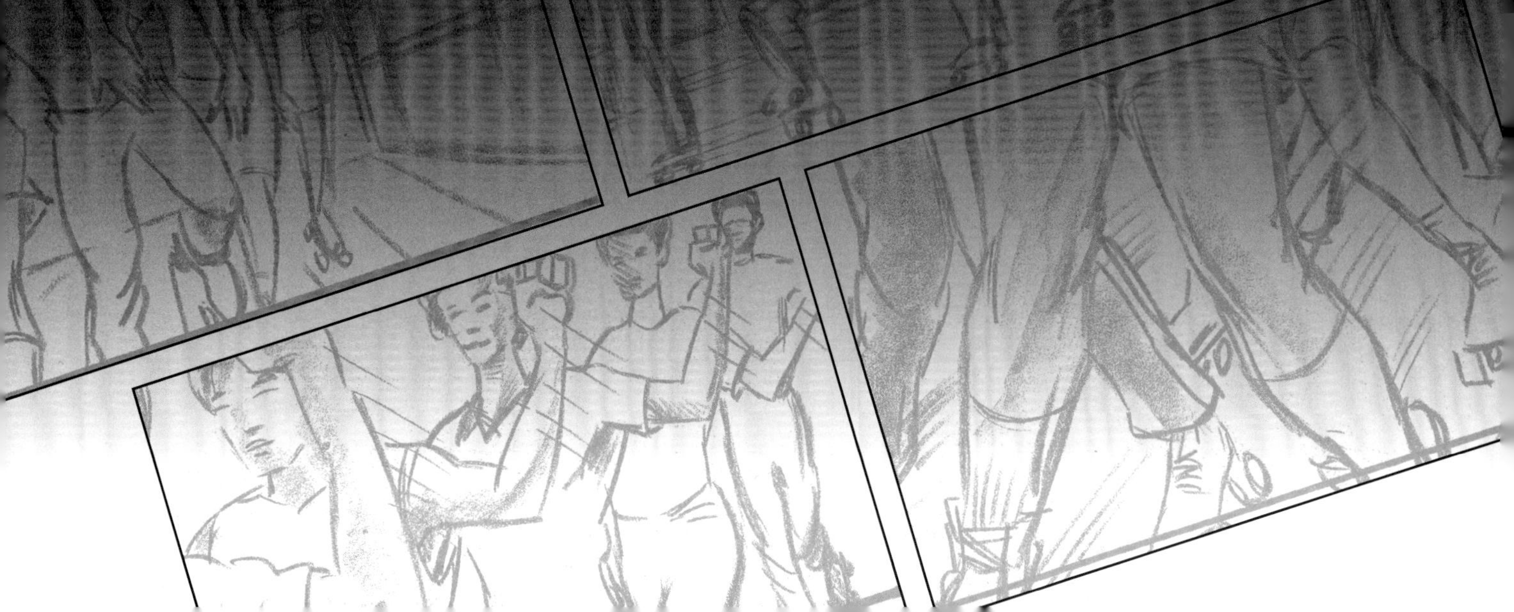

Roll Bounce

In 2004 I teamed up with my frequent collaborator director Malcolm Lee on *Roll Bounce*. It was a sweet natured coming of age comedy-drama set in 1978 Chicago. *Roll Bounce* begins with main character "X Smith" and his friends at their local roller-skating rink. The rink's DJ gets the participants energized as he plays Parliament's "Flashlight" followed by "Bounce, Rock, Skate, Roll" by Vaughan Mason & Crew. After doing choreographed roller-skating routines, X and his friends, slap the behind of a teenaged girl their age, severely annoying her. Note, this was a 2004 film depicting behavior in the seventies, so I am not condoning this to ever be done in real life. Malcolm and I have gone on to do several great projects together including Roscoe Jenkins and the huge hit comedy, Girls Trip.

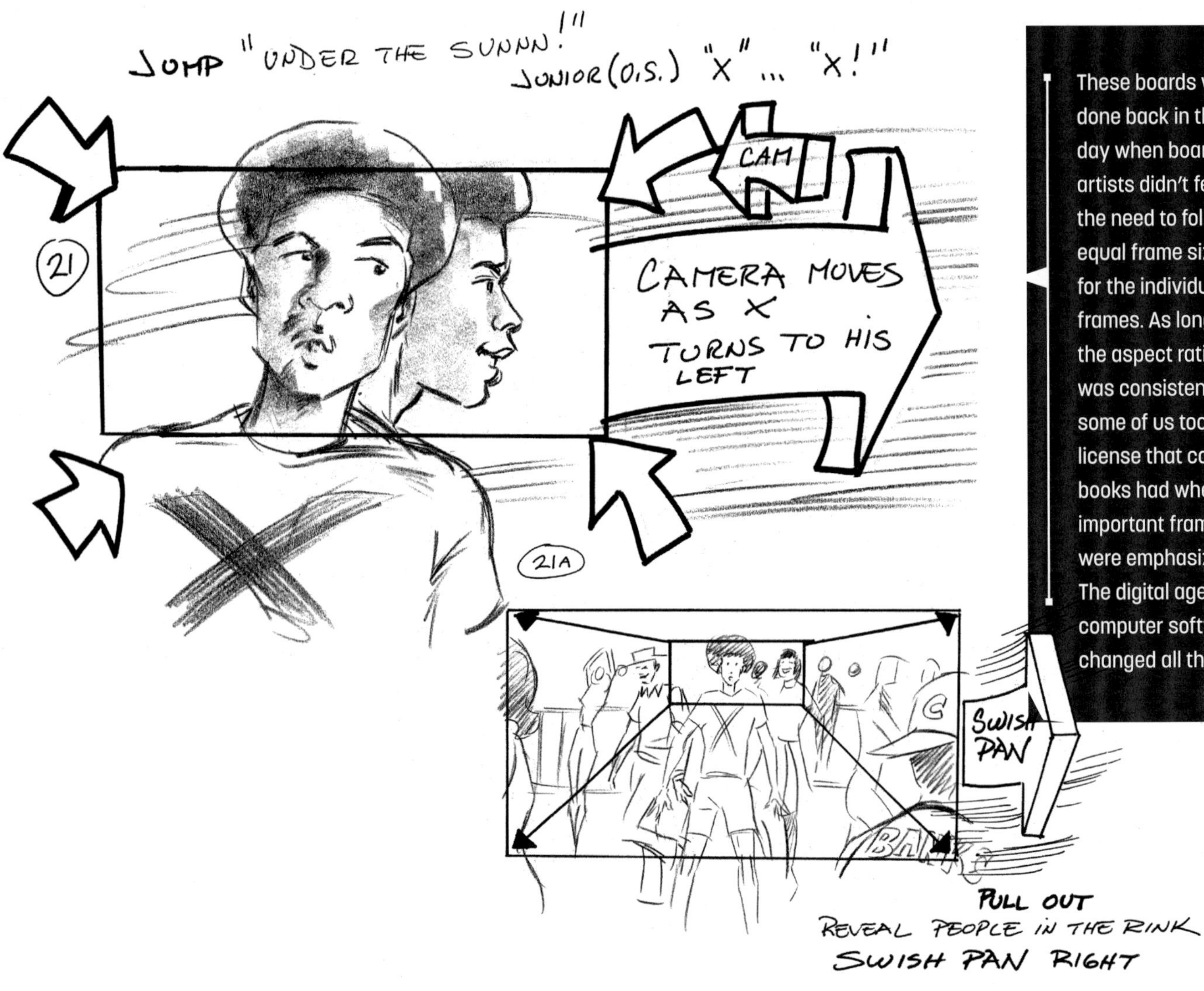

These boards were done back in the day when board artists didn't feel the need to follow equal frame sizes for the individual frames. As long as the aspect ratio was consistent, some of us took the license that comic books had where important frames were emphasized. The digital age and computer software changed all that.

SWISH CONT'D
THEN
PUSH IN

21B

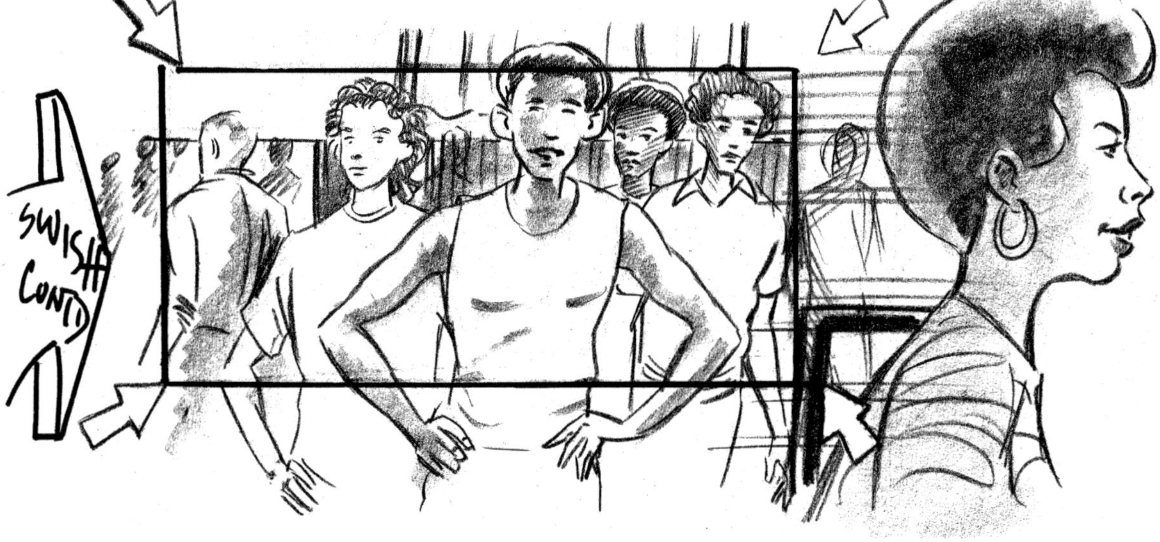

MIKE, JUNIOR, BOO, NAPS
JUNIOR "HEY! STOP PLAYING AROUND, MAN"

22

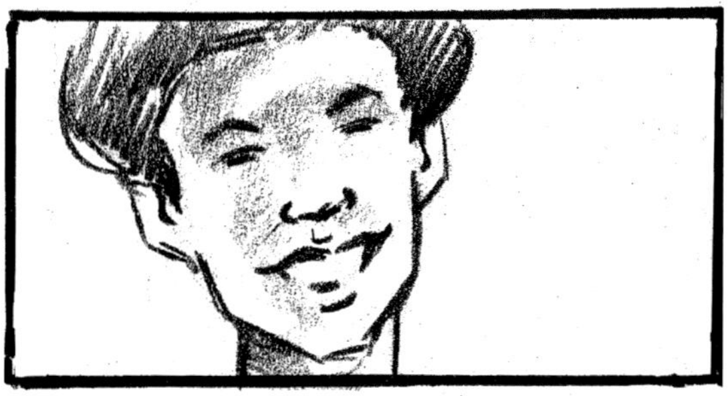

"YEAH ... YEAH.
LET'S GO."

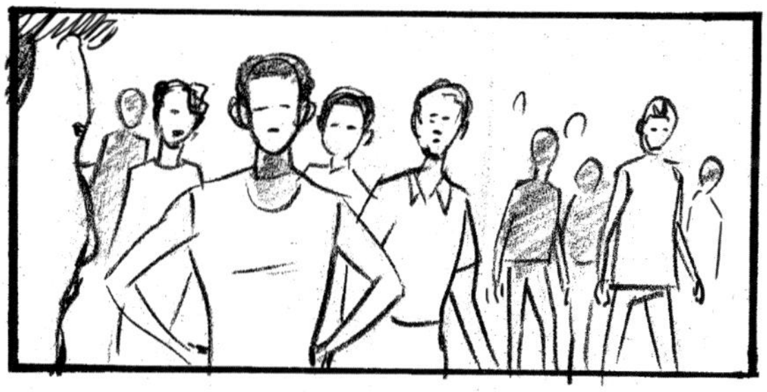

23

23A

X MOVES
OVER TO THE
GROUP

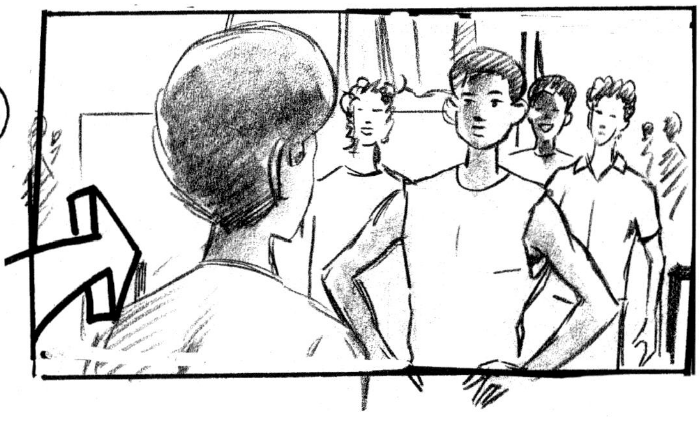

24

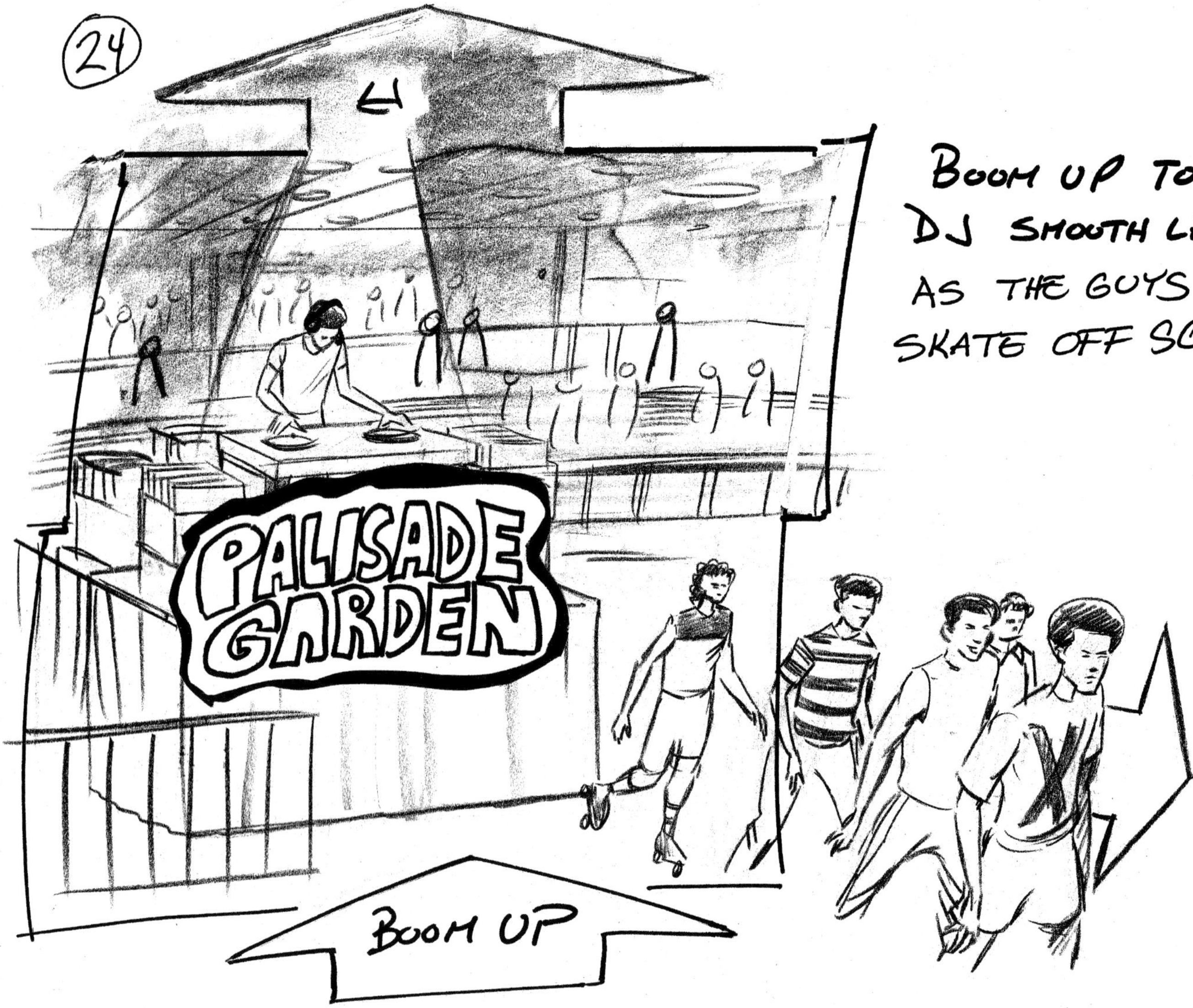

BOOM UP TO DJ SMOUTH LEE AS THE GUYS SKATE OFF SCREEN

25

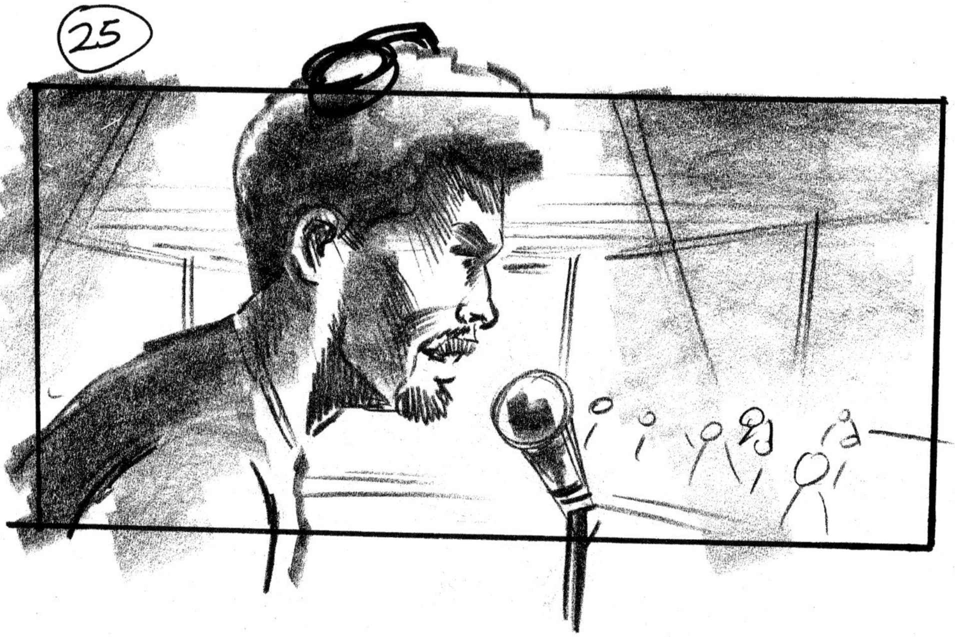

DJ "ATTENTION, ALL YOU WALLFLOWERS AND SEAT WARMERS..."

(26)

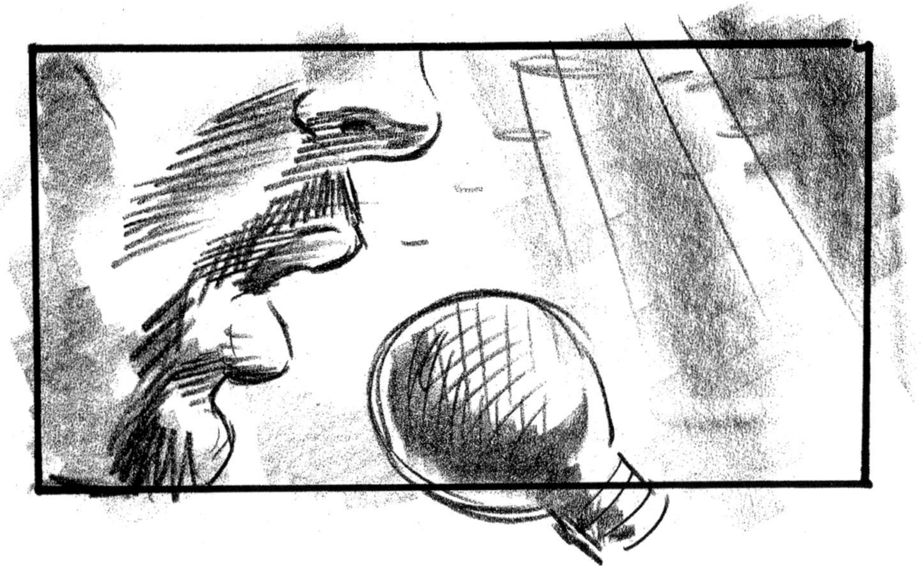

DJ SMOOTH CONTINUES "THE GARDEN'S WILL BE CLOSING..."

CROWD REACTIONS?

(27)

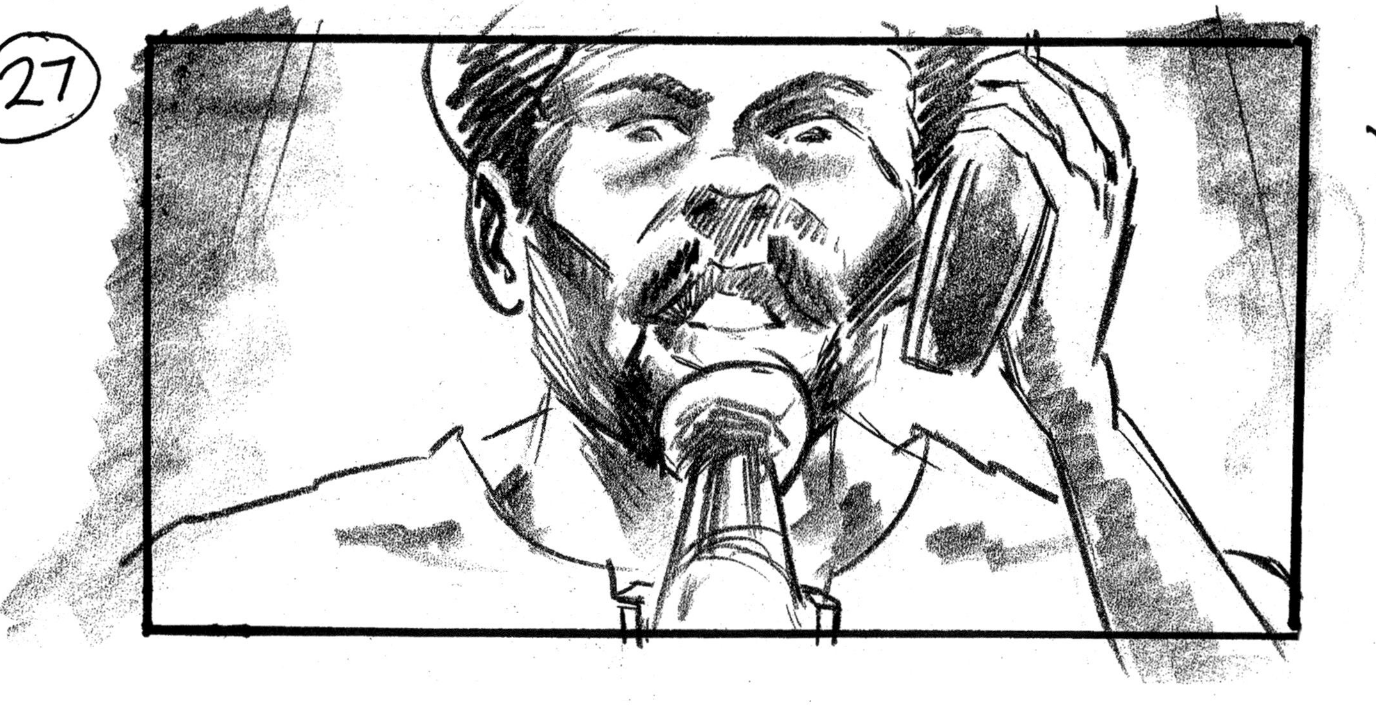

DJ

33

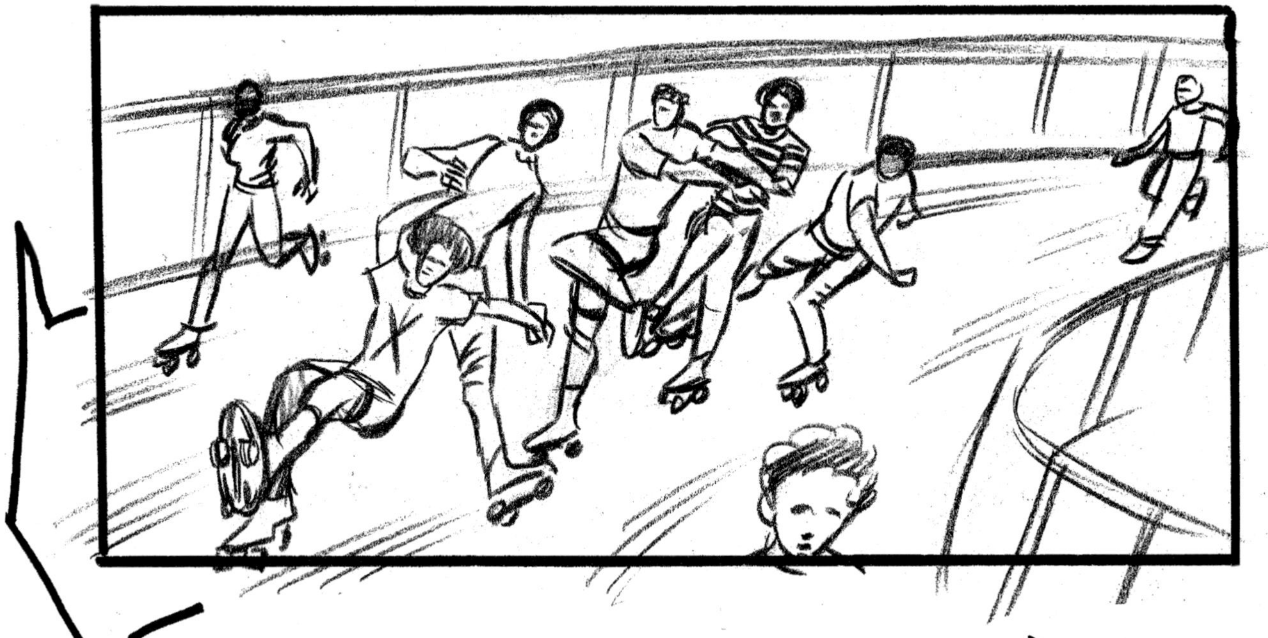

.. AND THE GUYS DOING MOVES

CAMERA PANS

33A

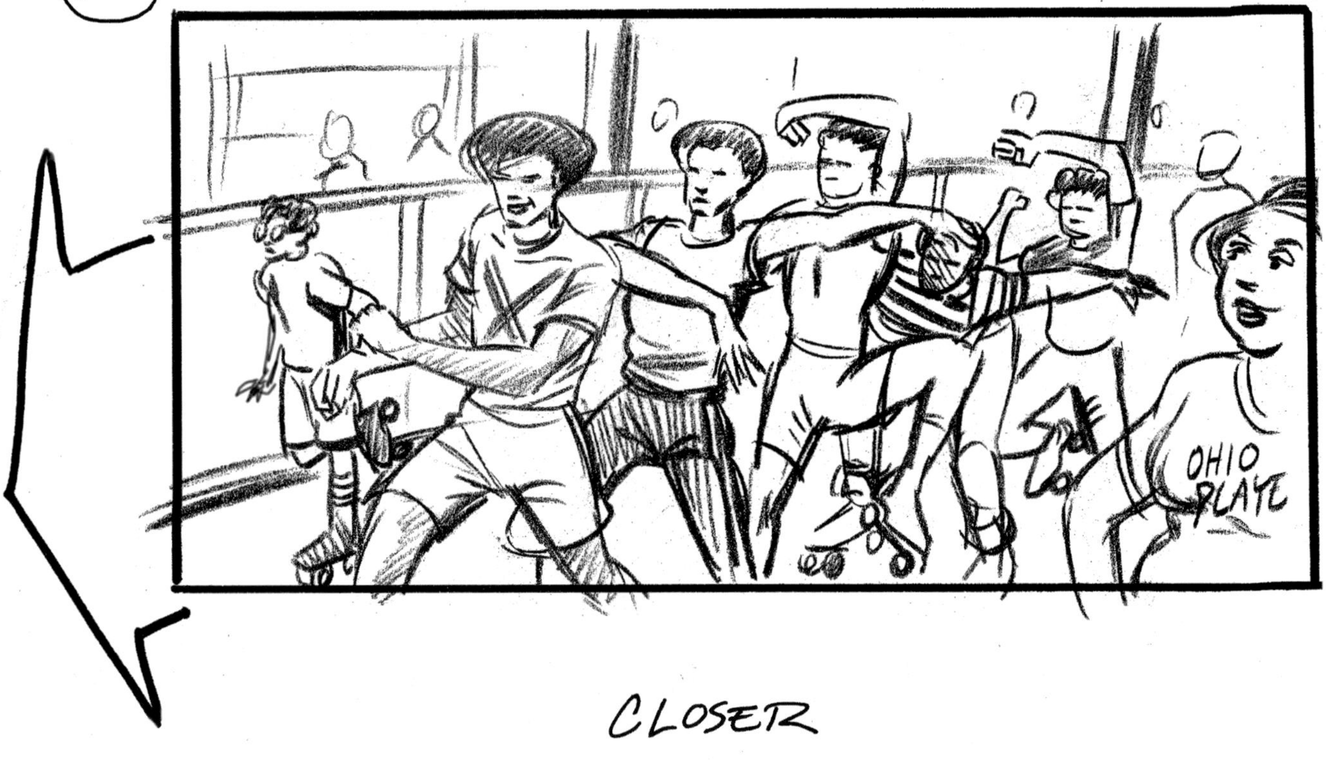

CLOSER

FREE STYLING

(34)

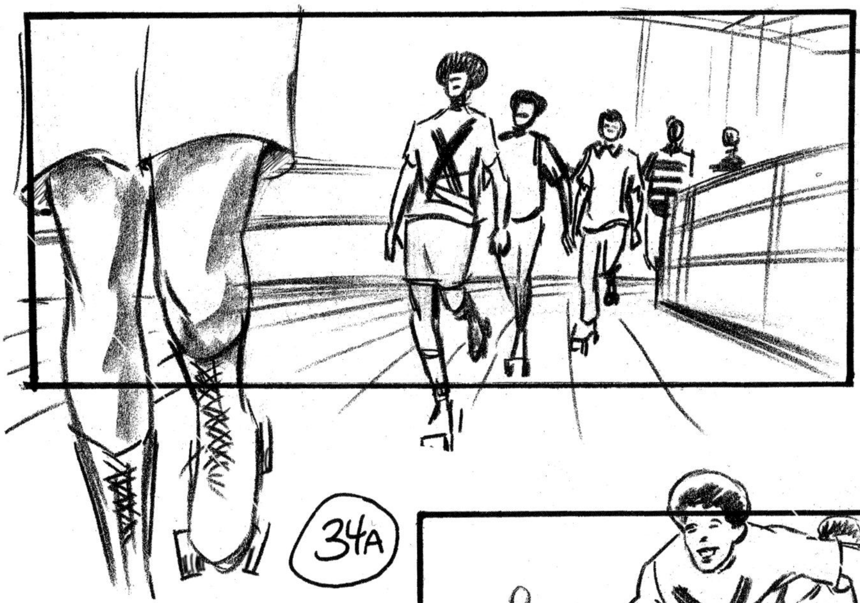

X AND GUYS COMING AROUND THE CORNER

(34A)

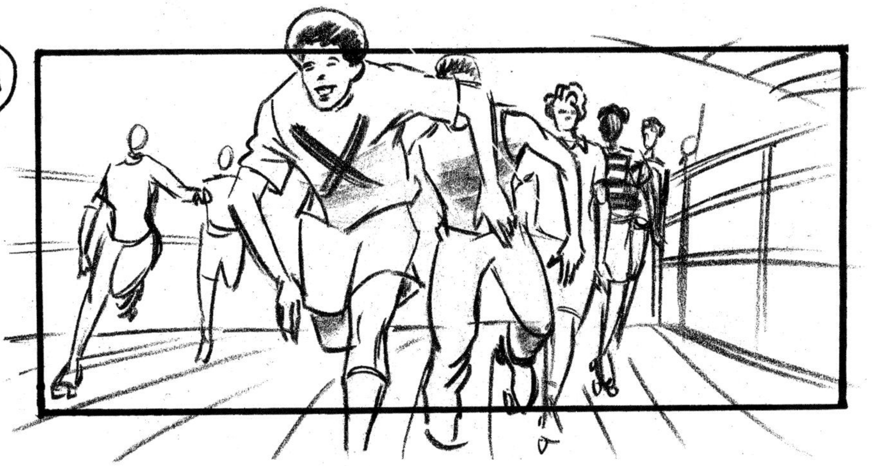

(35)

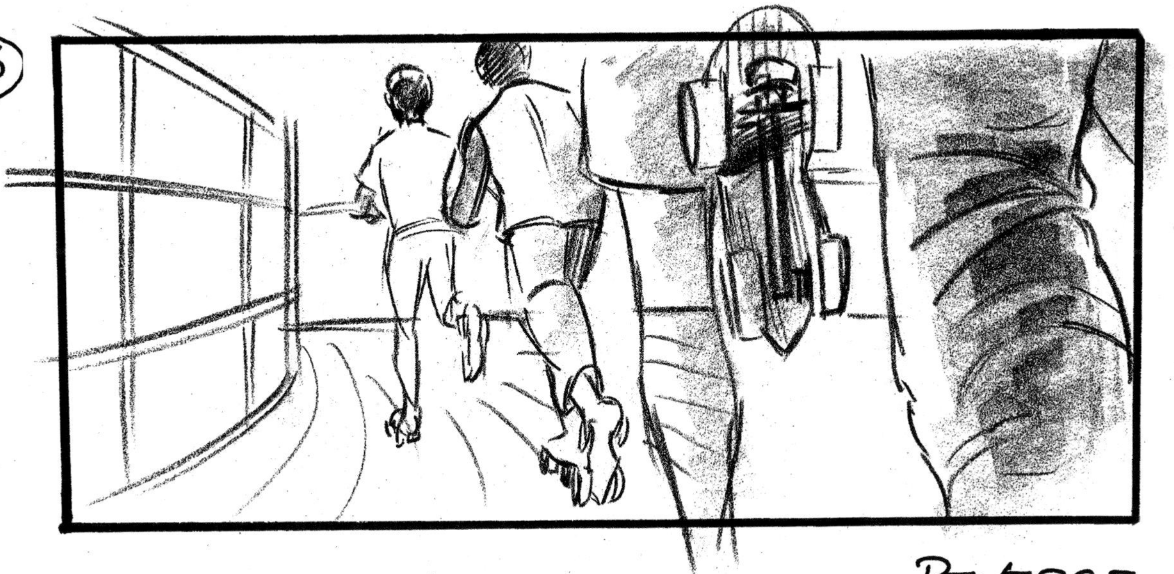

REVERSE

36

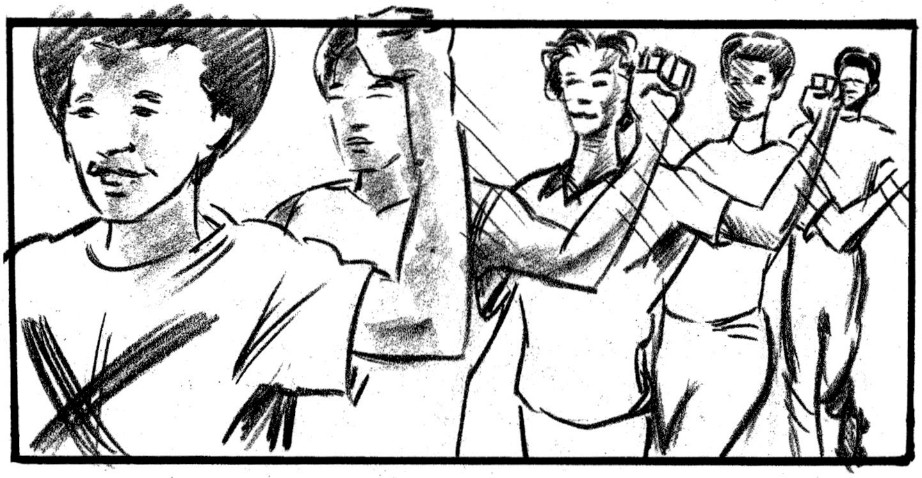

MOVES

37

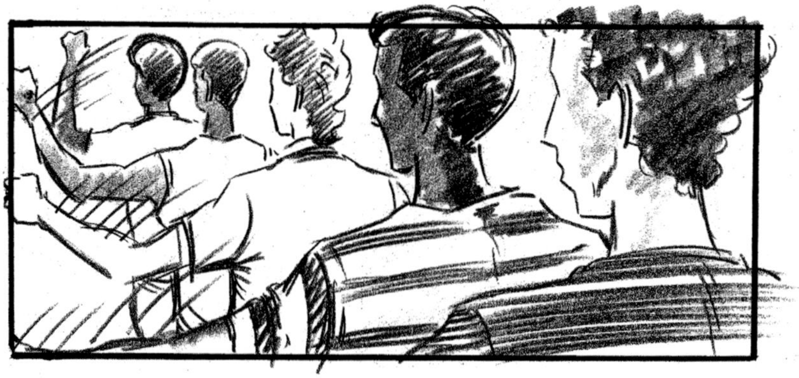

REVERSE

38

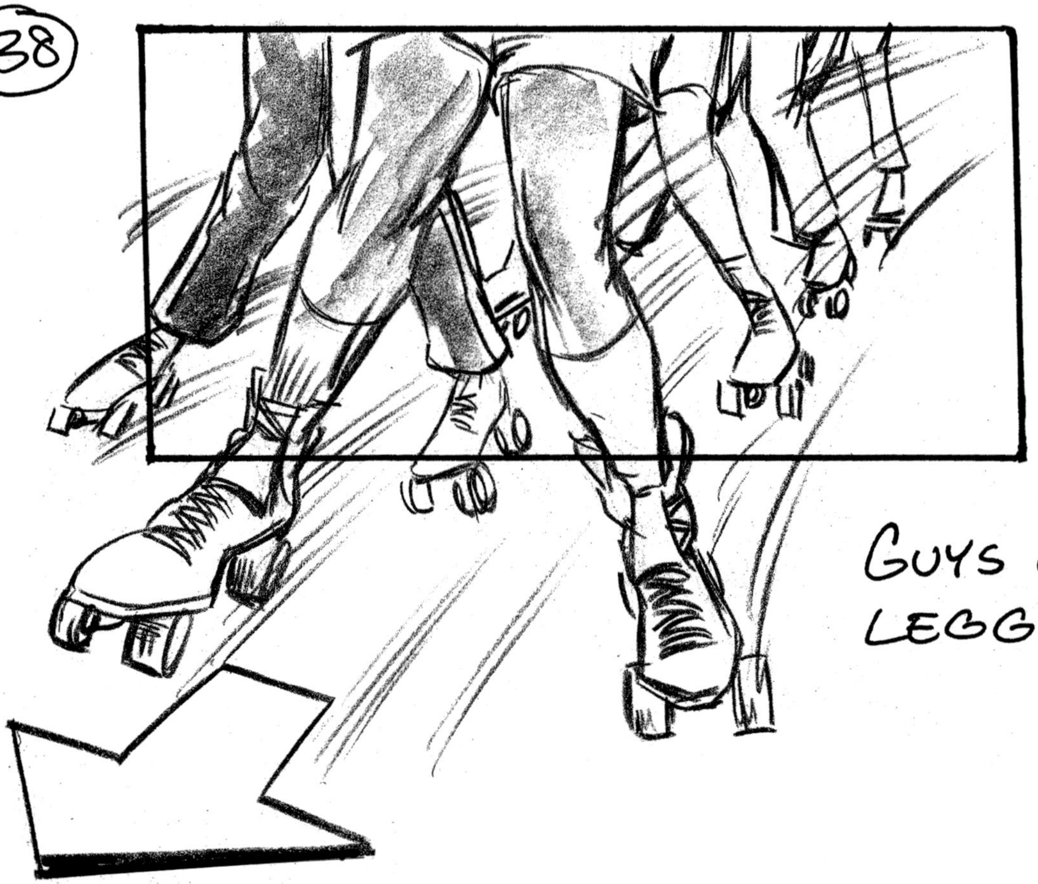

GUYS CRAZY
LEGGING

39

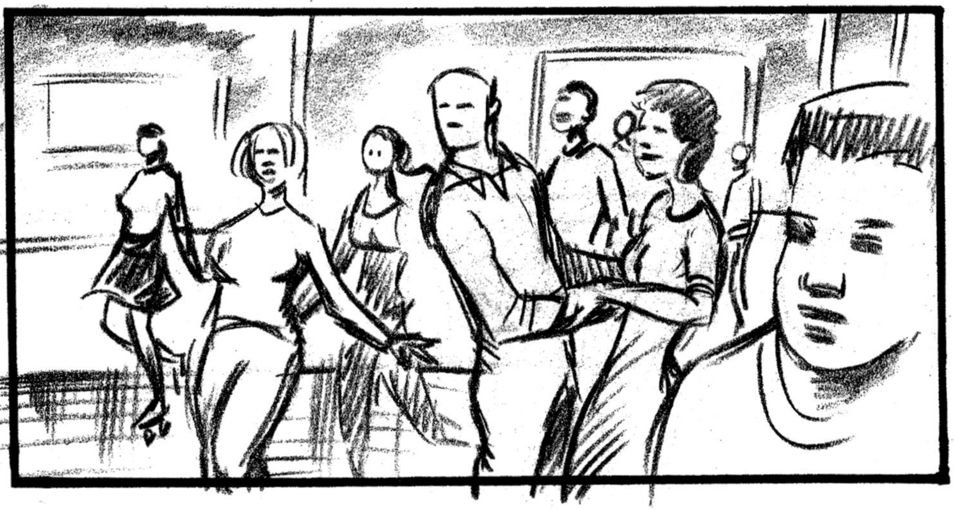

PEOPLE NOTICE

40

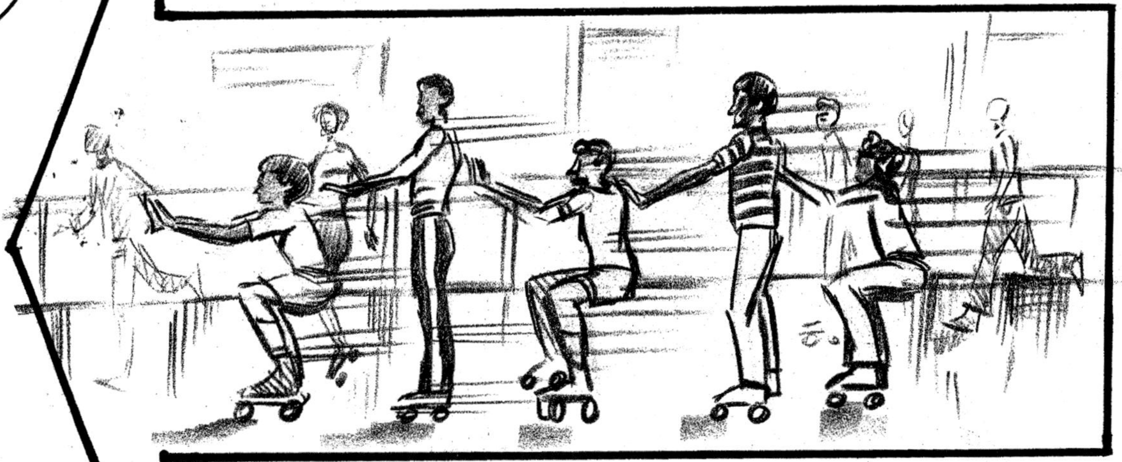

X + GANG

41

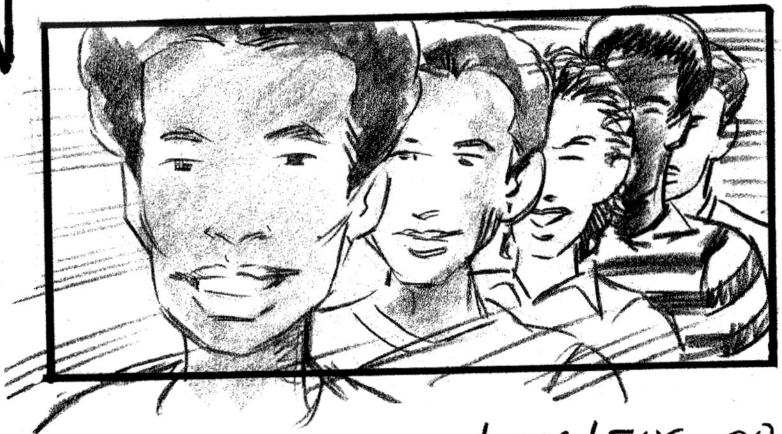

LONG LENS ON
X AND GUYS.

Some of my compositions ended up pretty close to how Malcolm Lee ended up shooting them. He's a lot of fun to work with and gives me plenty of creative room.

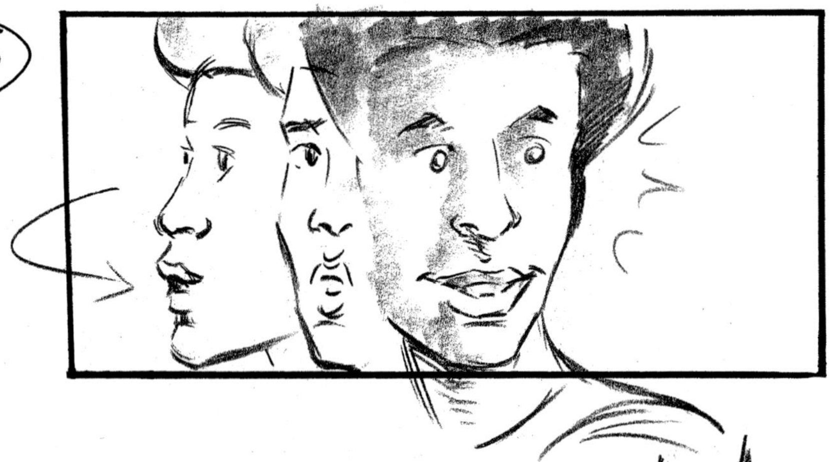

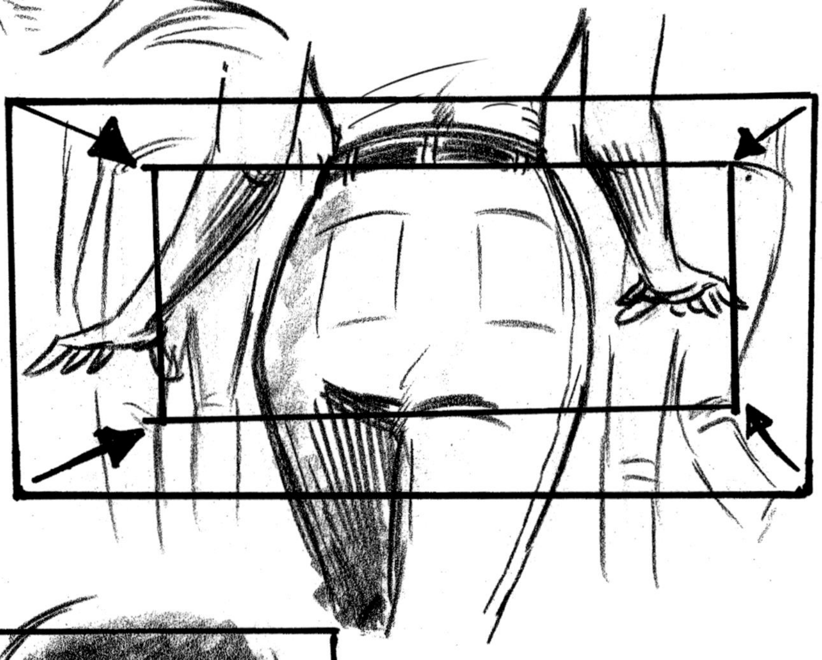

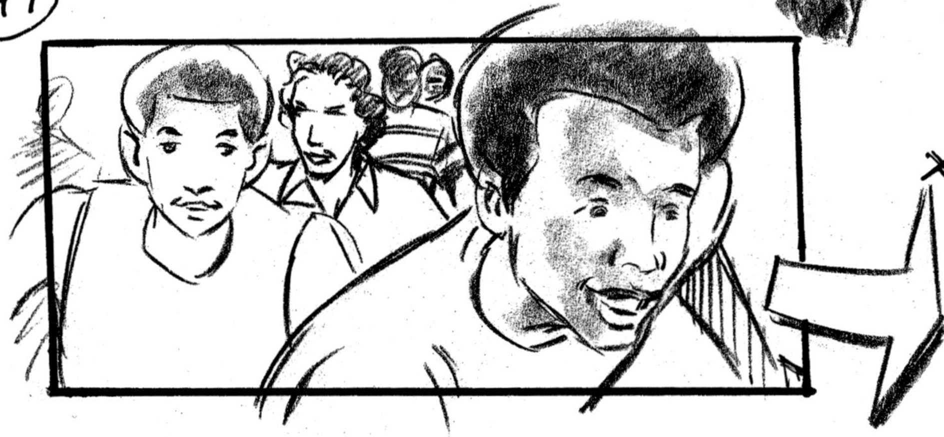

(48)

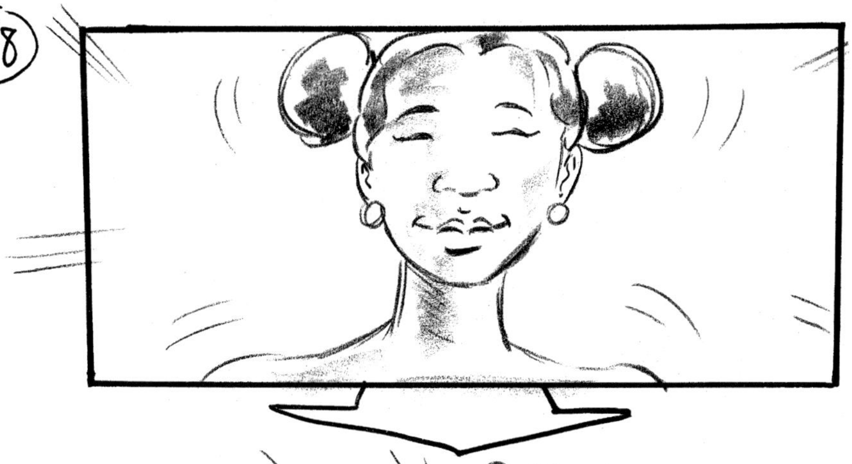

MOVING SHOT

ON THE GIRL HAVING A GOOD TIME IN HER OWN GROOVE.

(49)

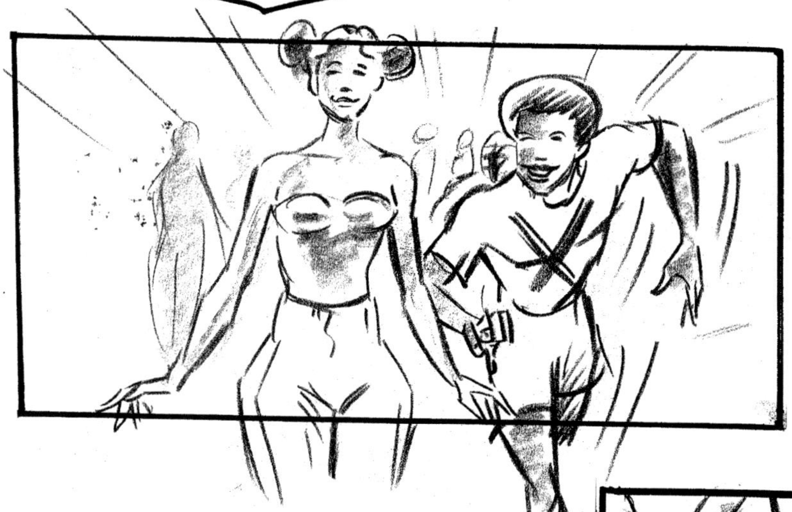

WIDER

X COMES UP BEHIND HER

(50)

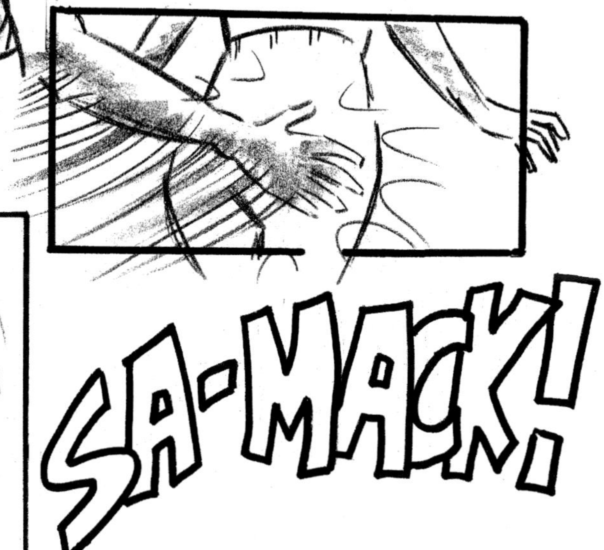

(51)

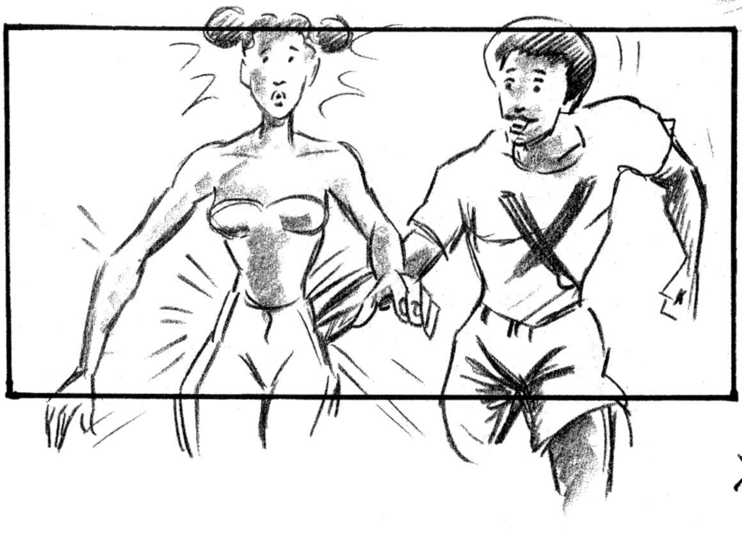

X SMACKS HER BUTT.

52

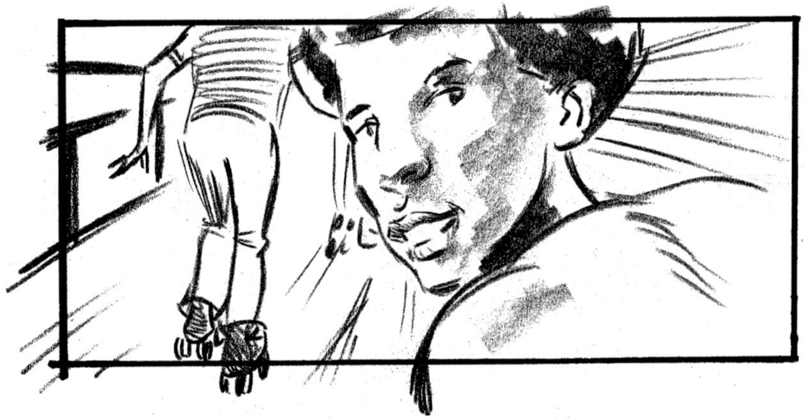

X LOOKS BACK

53

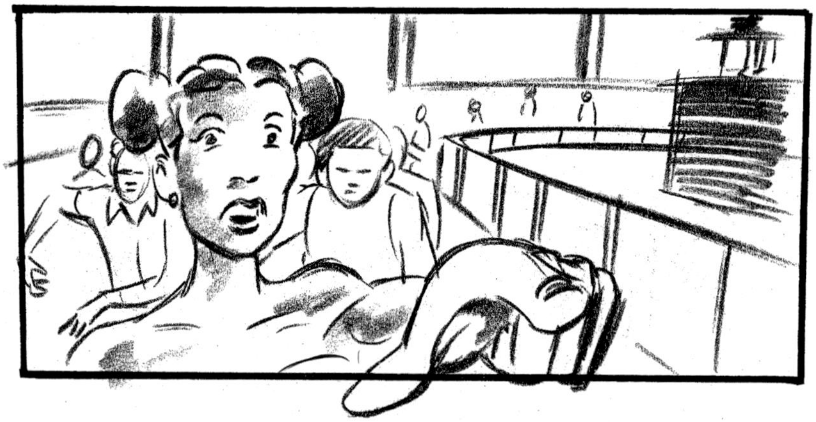

GIRL" BOY!

HIT MY BUTT AGAIN AND SEE WHAT HAPPENS!"

54

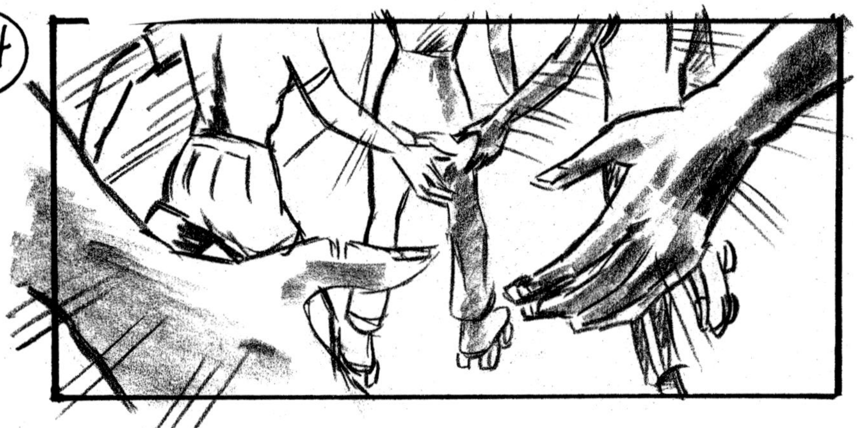

GUYS COME BEHIND HER

55

HIGH ON THE SAME

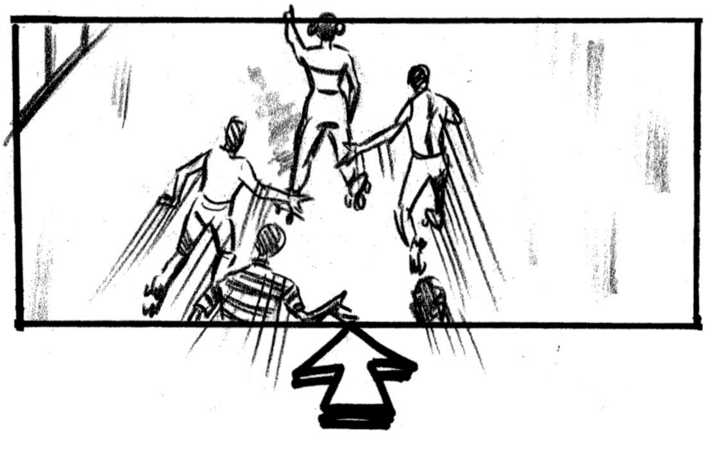

56

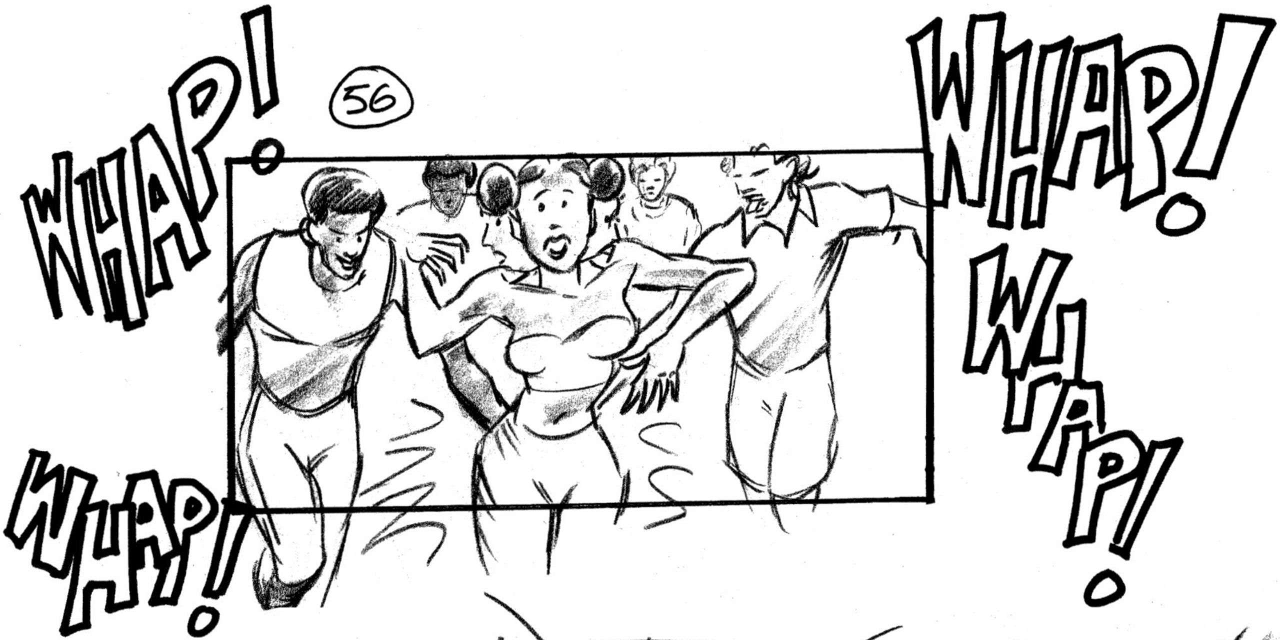

57

JUNIOR AND THE OTHERS TAG IT

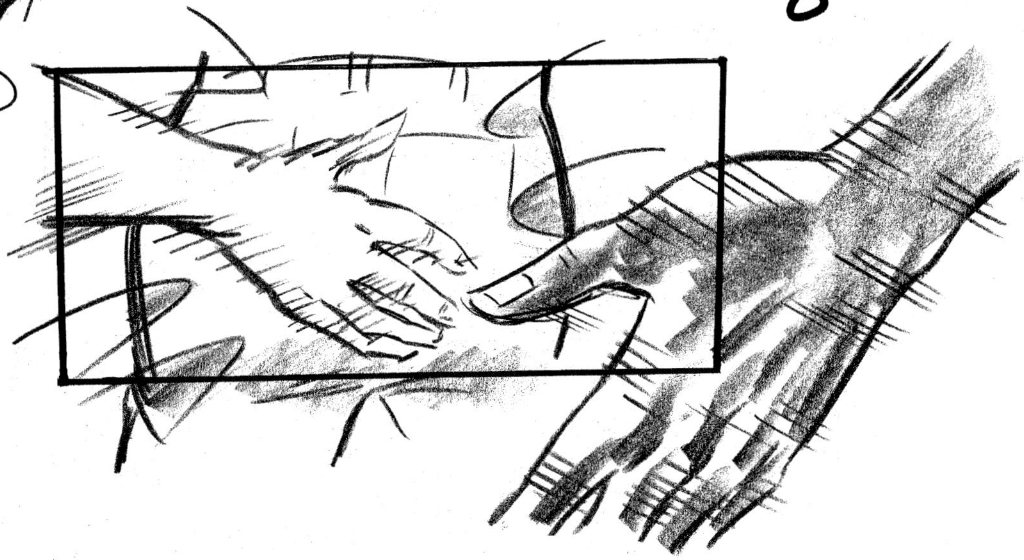

58

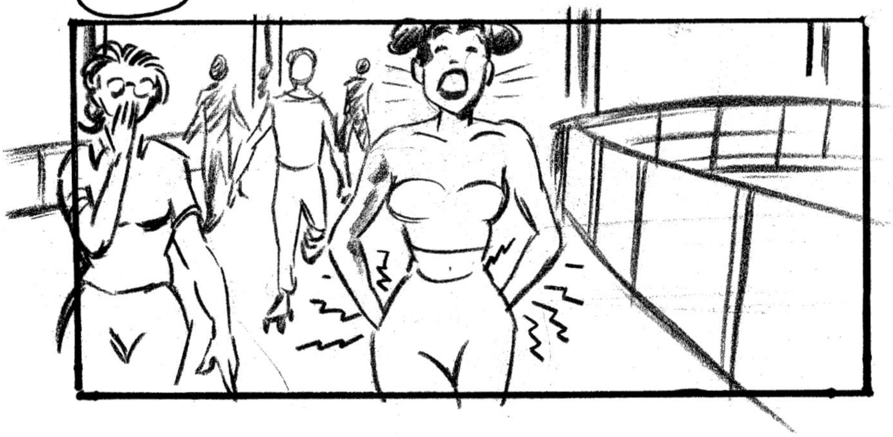

GIRL "MAKE ME SICK"

STORYBOARDS AND STORIES OF 15 SELECT FILMS AND TELEVISION SHOWS

HARD DAY'S WORK

Chapter 18

FREE GUY

Free Guy

Unlike some other more cut-throat jobs, storyboard artists try to help one another. When a storyboard artist gets a job offer but is already on gig, we'll often pass the job off to a colleague who is looking for work. I got the job on *Free Guy* due to storyboard artist Todd Harris (who used to assist me a decade earlier) being contacted to work on the film but being unavailable. Todd then recommended me to lead *Free Guy* board artist Will Groebe, who then showed my work to director Shawn Levy. Upon being hired by Shawn, I found him to be a very collaborative filmmaker who wanted the storyboard artists very involved in group pitch sessions. These are a few finished frames that came out of massive final sequence of *Free Guy*. Ryan Reynold's character of "Guy" finds out he is not a real human, but a computer simulation in a video game. Guy makes his escape to a digital island which holds the possible salvation for his video game world which the villain is trying to delete.

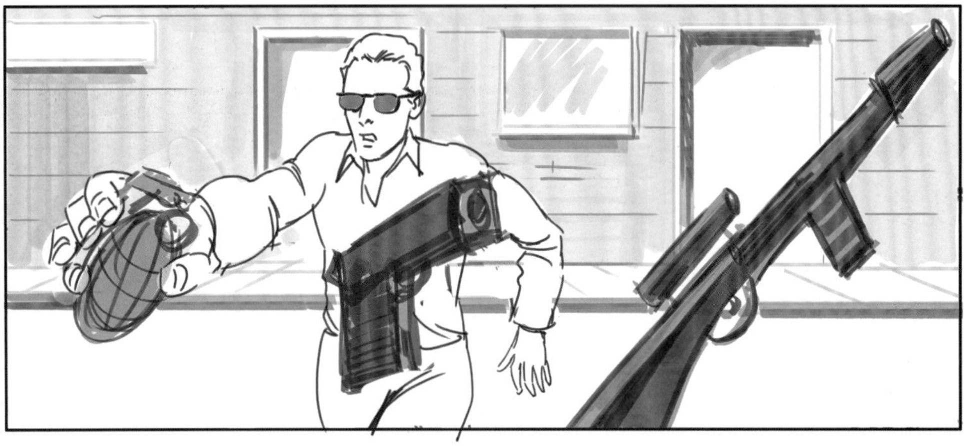

This was a fun sequence to work on as Guy starts to figure out how to access weapons from his video game universe.

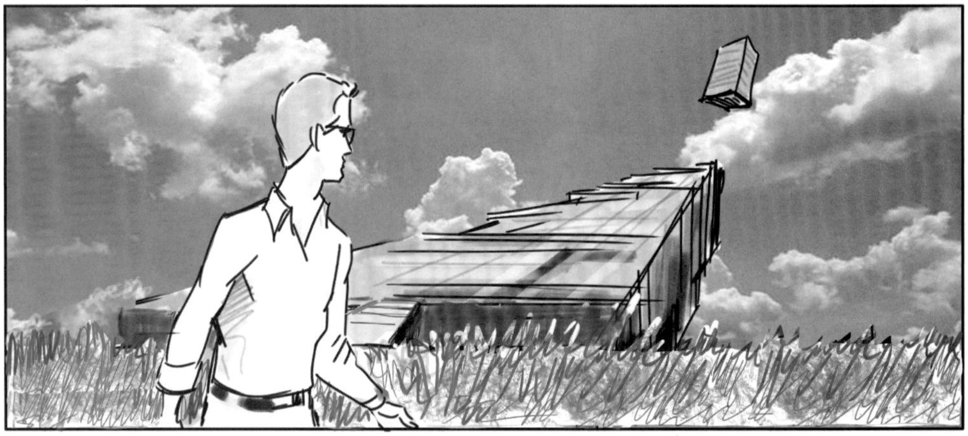

These next few frames are after the video game universe is being erased and Guy has to get to . . .

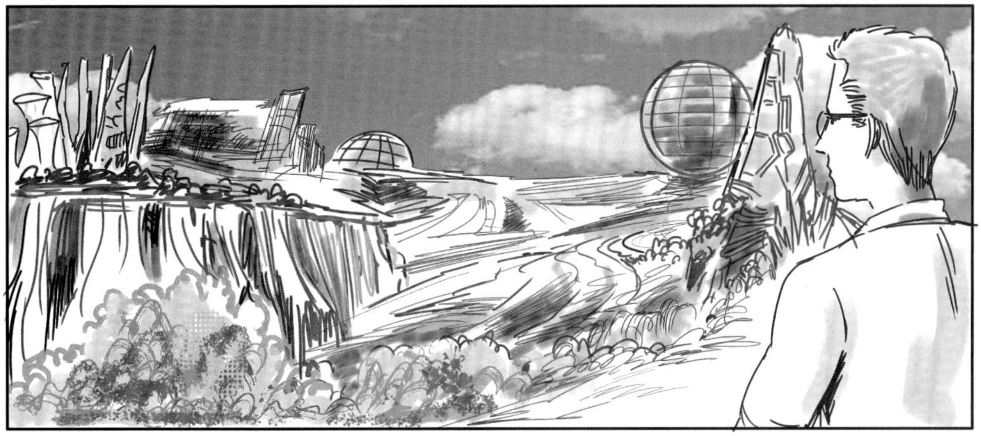

I was working off digital paintings from the concept team when I was drawing the mystical island in the movie that contains remnants of the Life Itself source code.

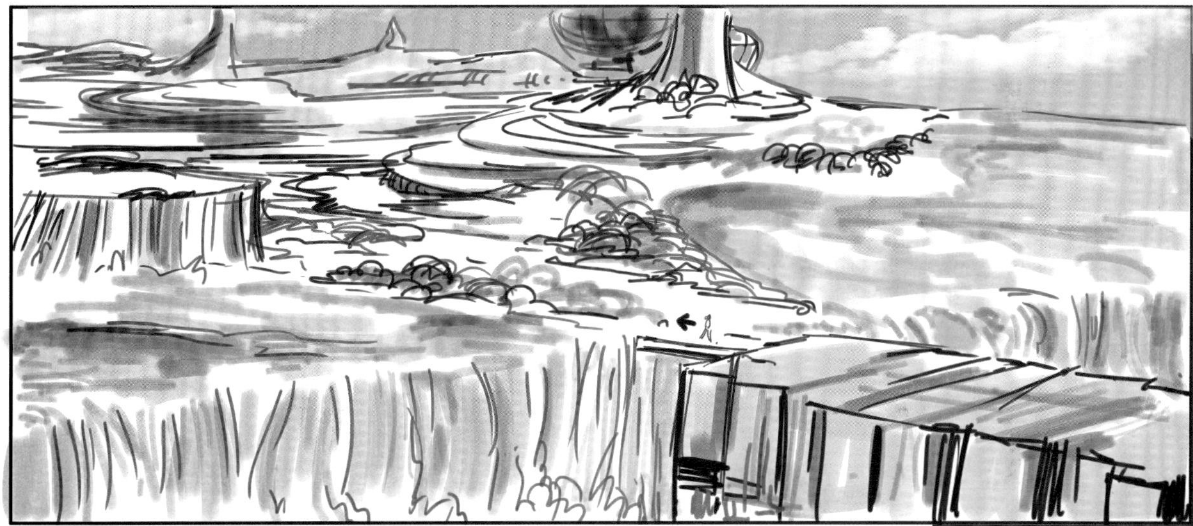

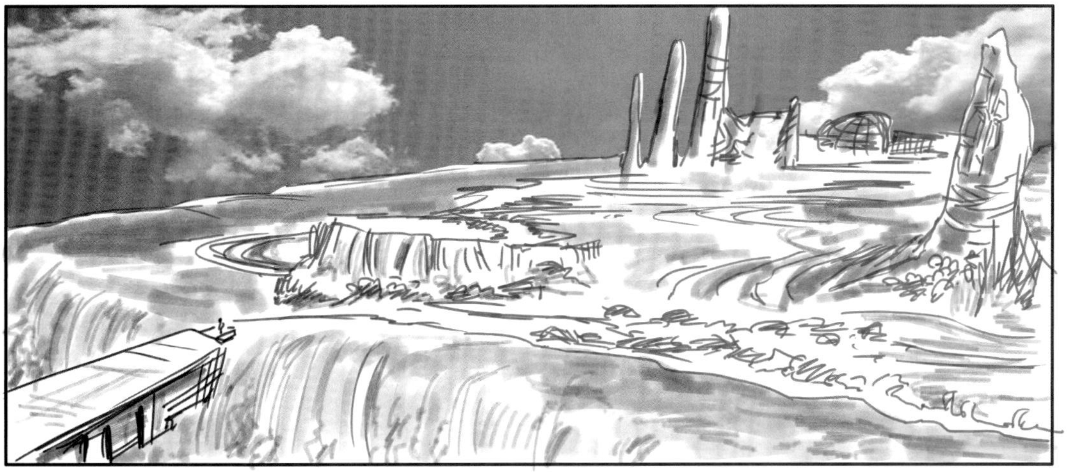

These two drawings were originally in color.

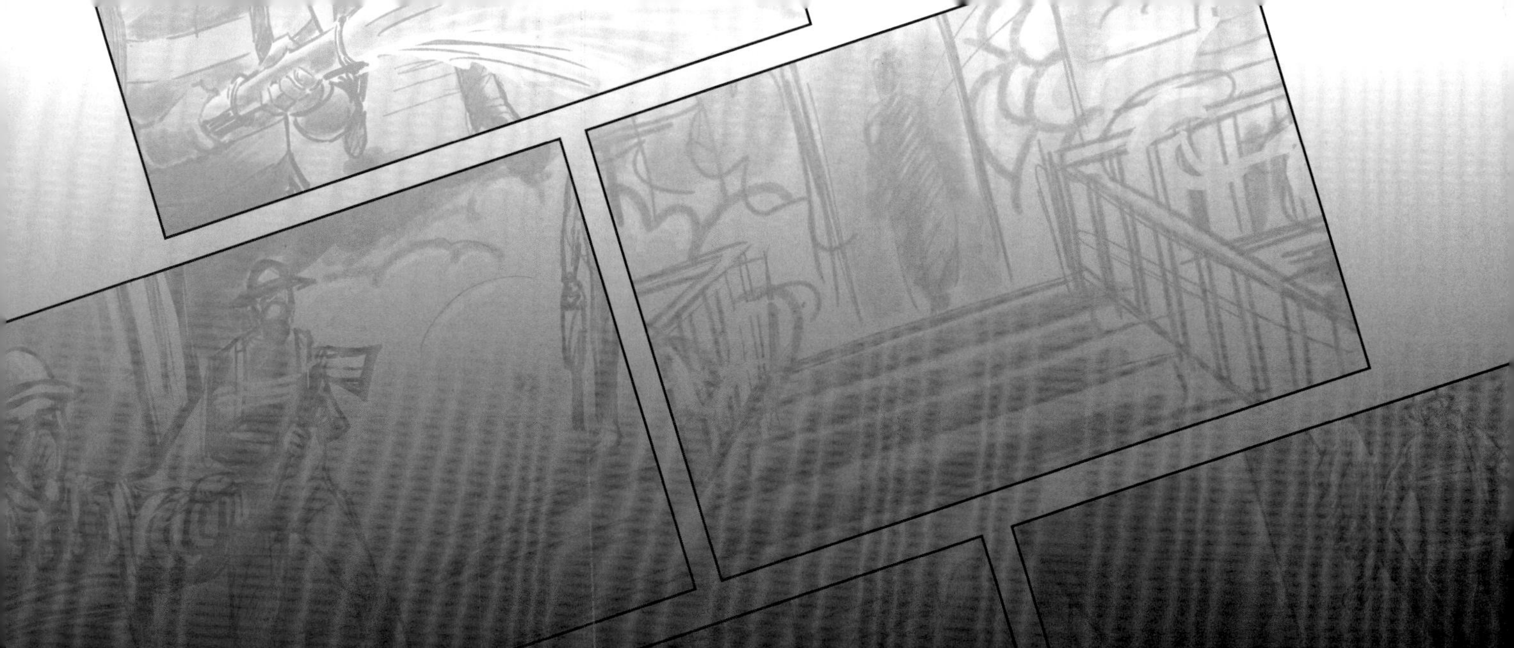

STORYBOARDS AND STORIES OF 15 SELECT FILMS AND TELEVISION SHOWS

HARD DAY'S WORK

Chapter 19

HALLOWEEN KILLS

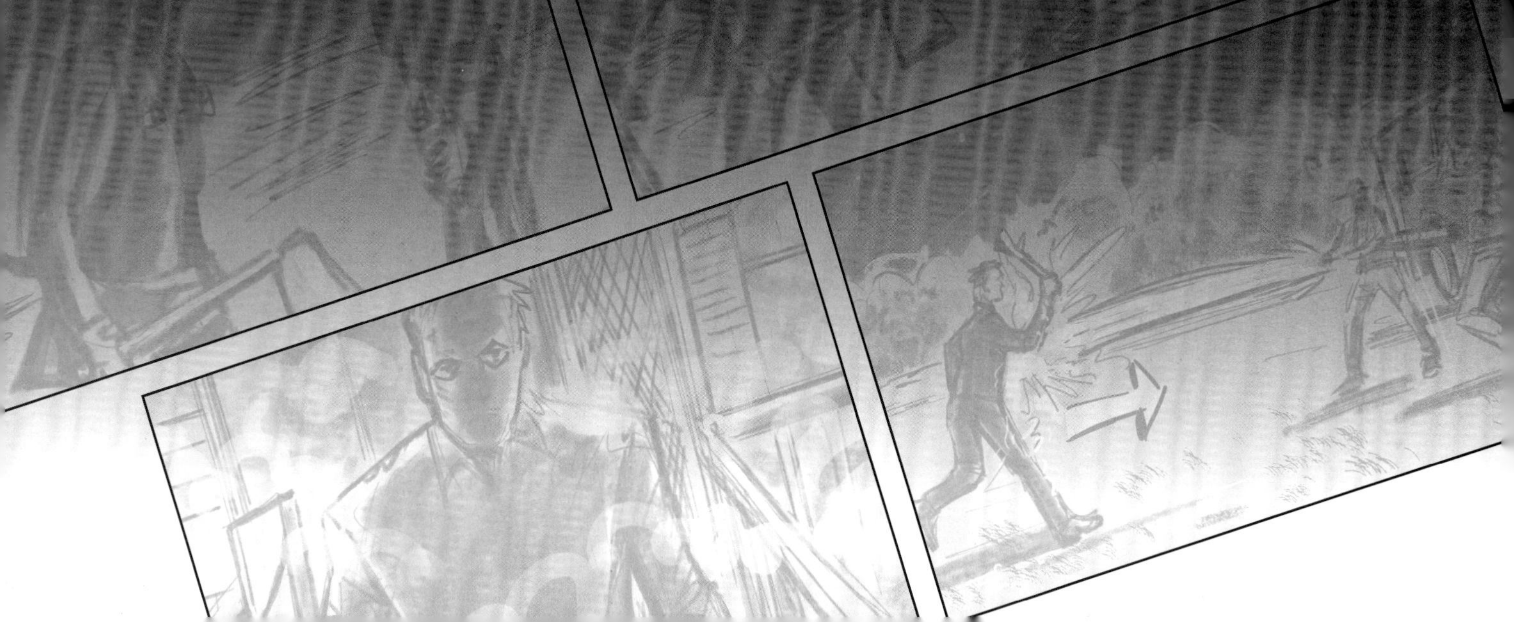

Halloween Kills

Director David Gordon Green and I had a lot of fun collaborating on the 2018 reboot of *Halloween* and so getting back together a year later on *Halloween Kills* was seamless. This scene depicts Michael Myers emerging from Laurie Strode's home which is ablaze. Myers emerges from the fire engulfed house armed only with a Halligan bar he has taken from a fireman he's just killed inside the house. The remaining members of the Haddonfield Fire Department have superior numbers but don't stand a chance against Myers, who decimates them quickly. The scene wasn't overly choreographed, but I did have to cinematically illustrate the main shots based on David Gordon Green's firm concepts on how he wanted to shoot.

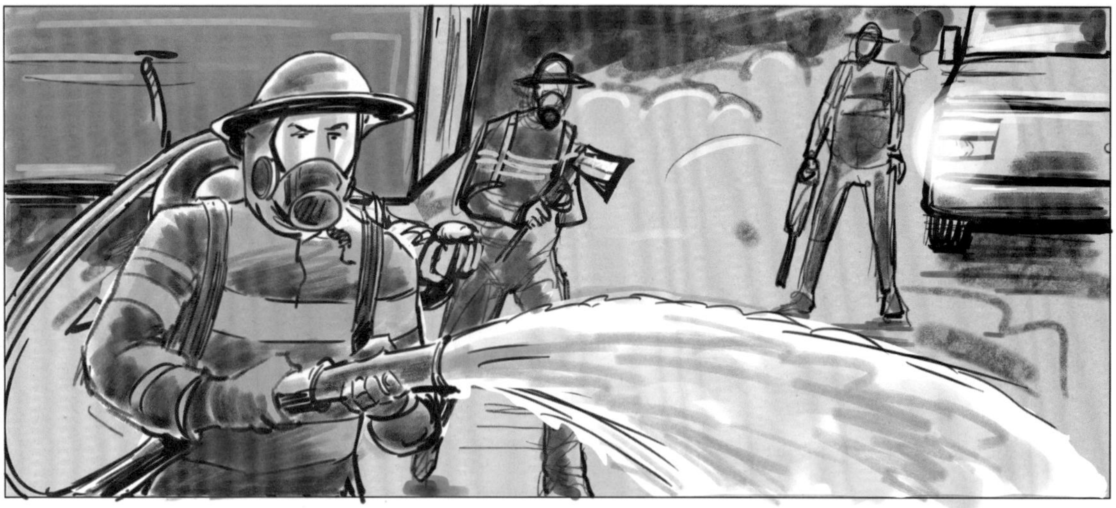

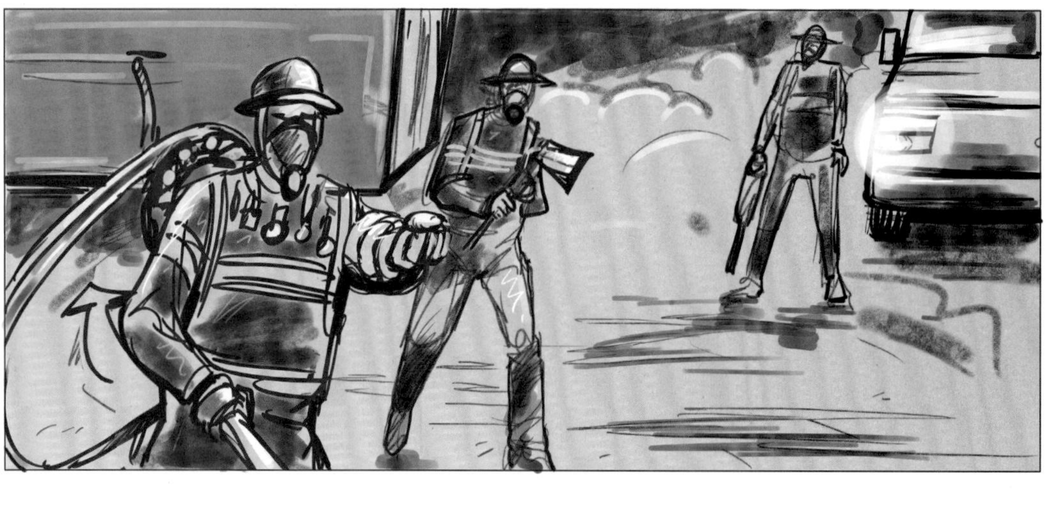

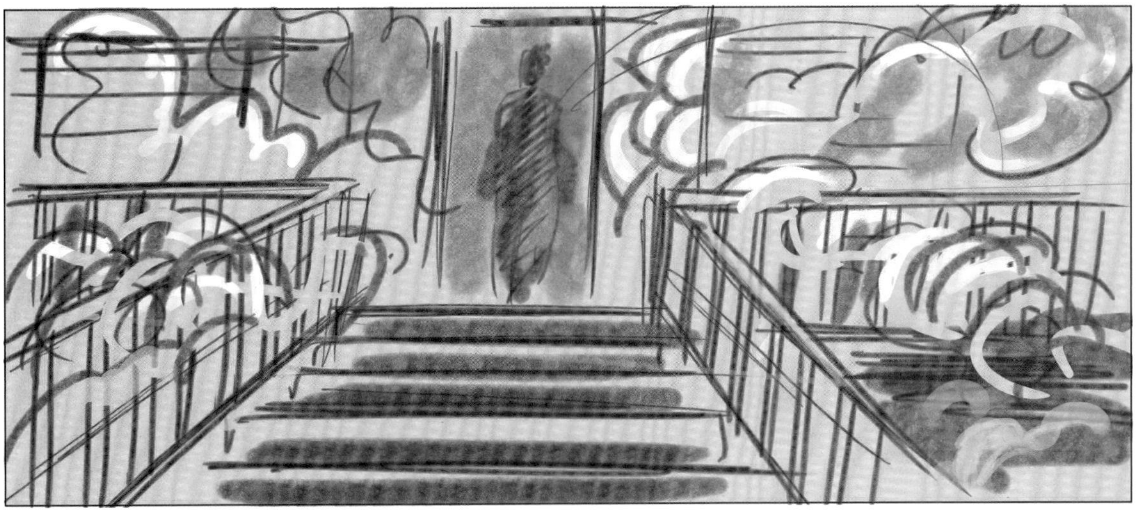

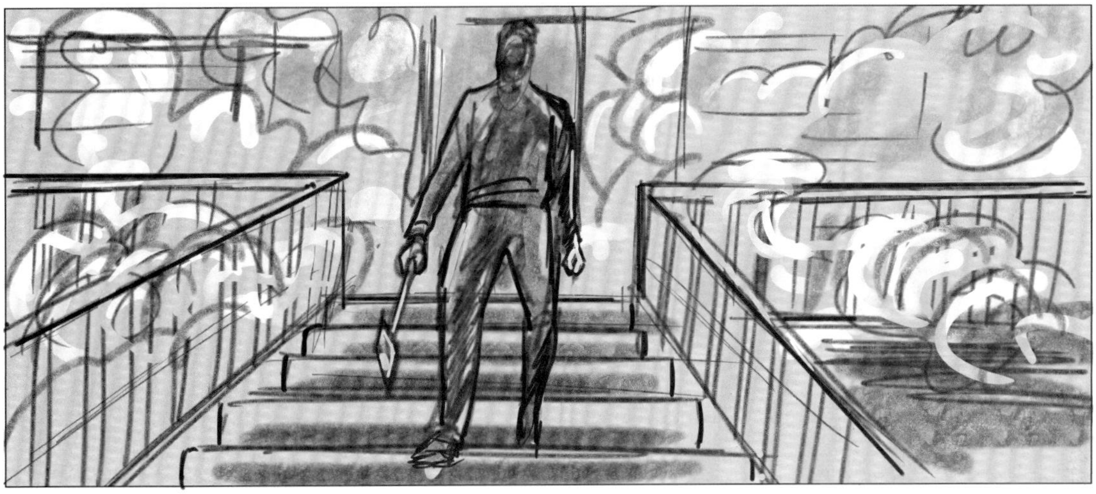

This continuous shot of Michael Myers descending the front steps needed to be dramatic. Myers is being reintroduced in this scene and I wanted the feeling of pure evil being unleashed from hell.

This frame of Michael Myers with the halligan tool of a fireman he's killed inside the house lets up know that the rest of the firemen are in for it. David Gordon Green and I both had this shot in mind.

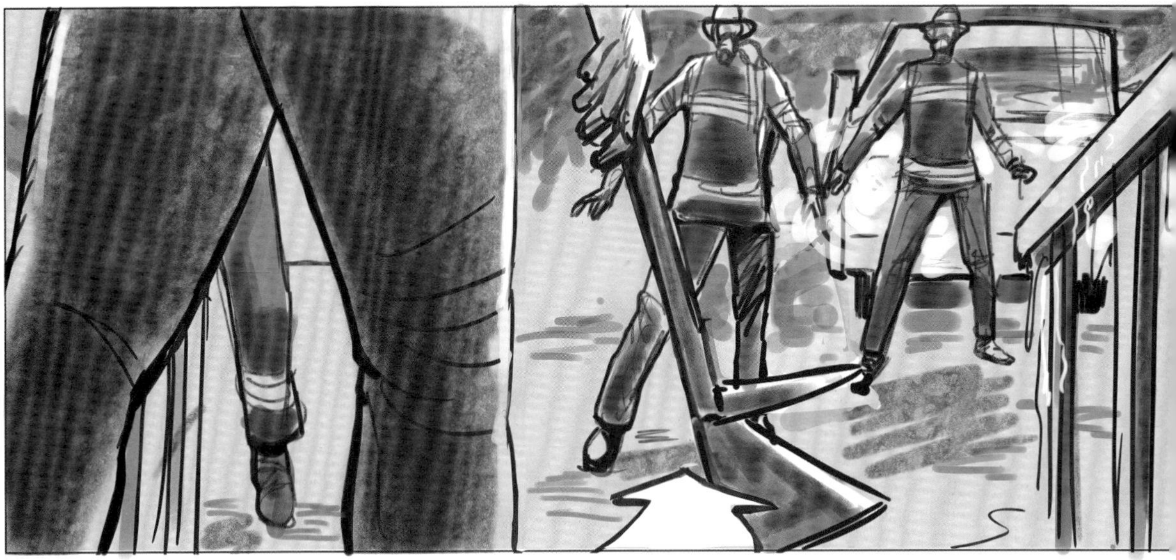

Multiple frames from one locked down angle can say a lot. David wanted some confusion in the firemen thinking "now what?" They have weapons but these aren't fighters.

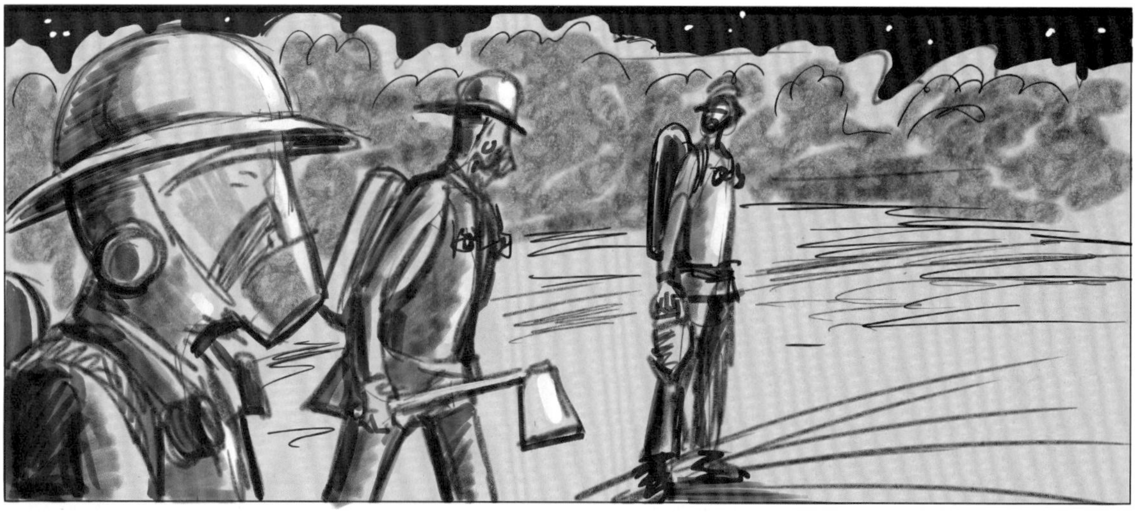

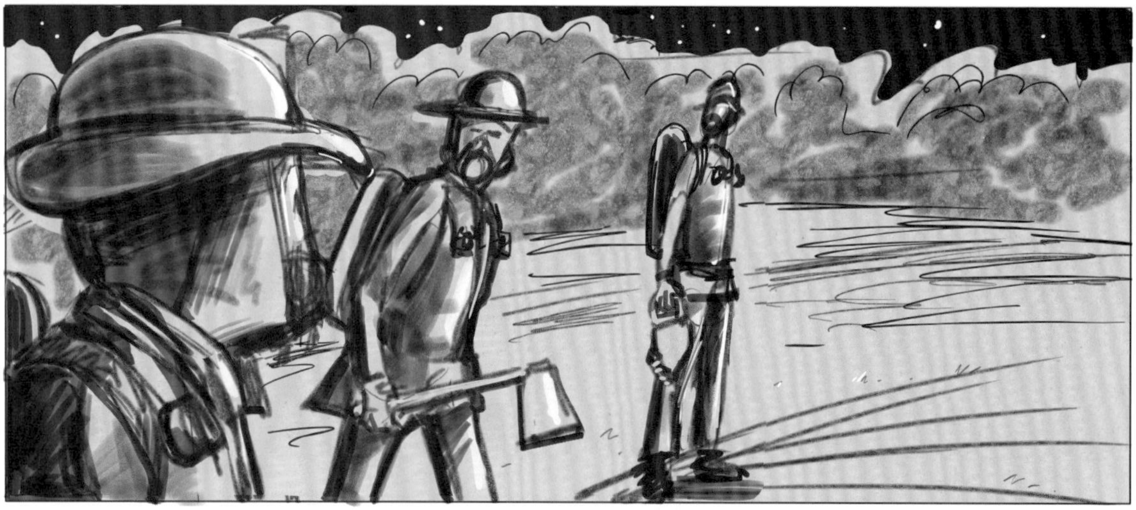

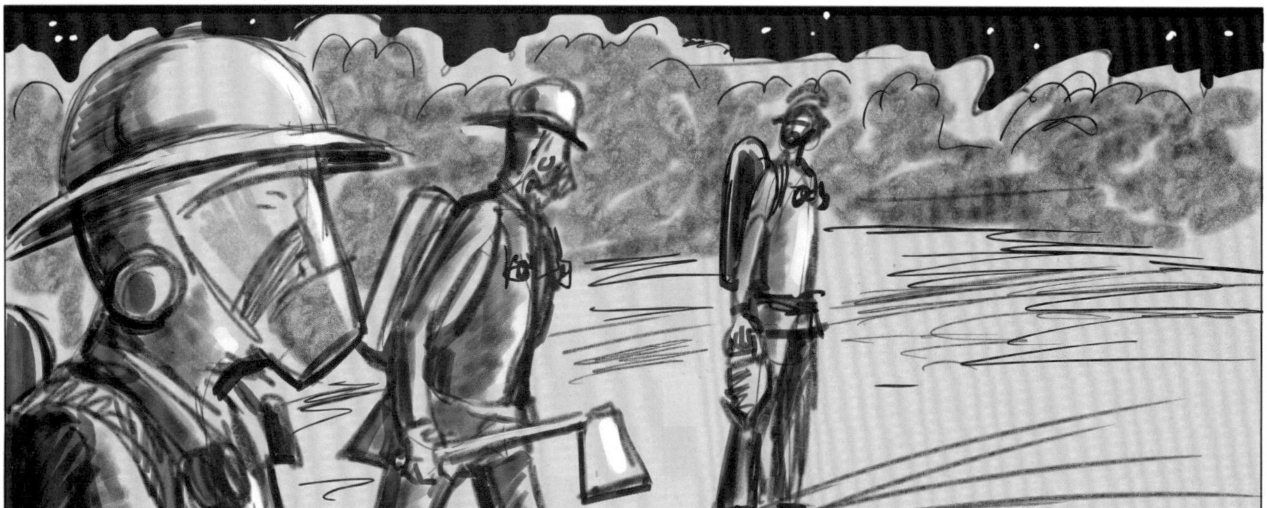

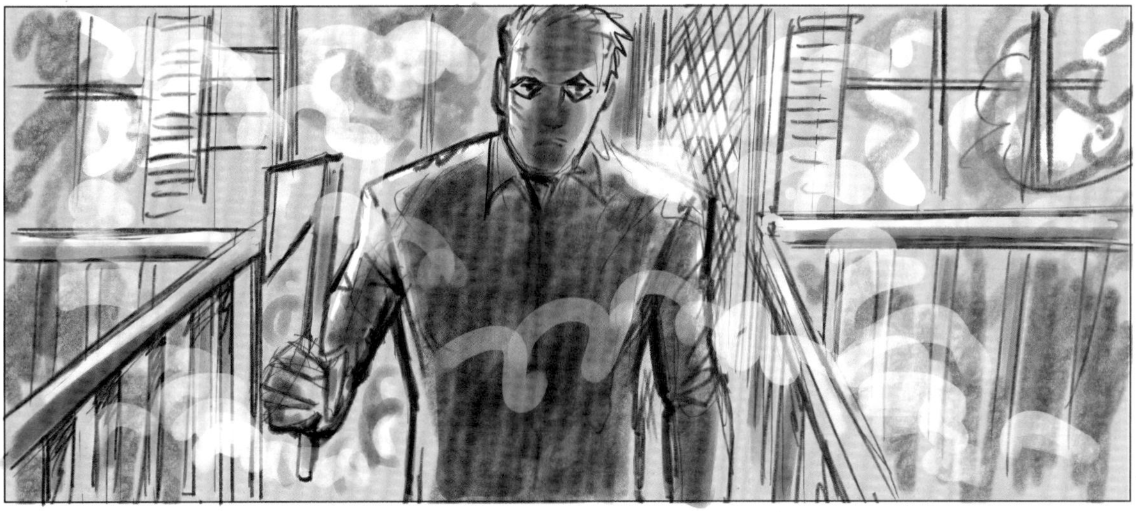

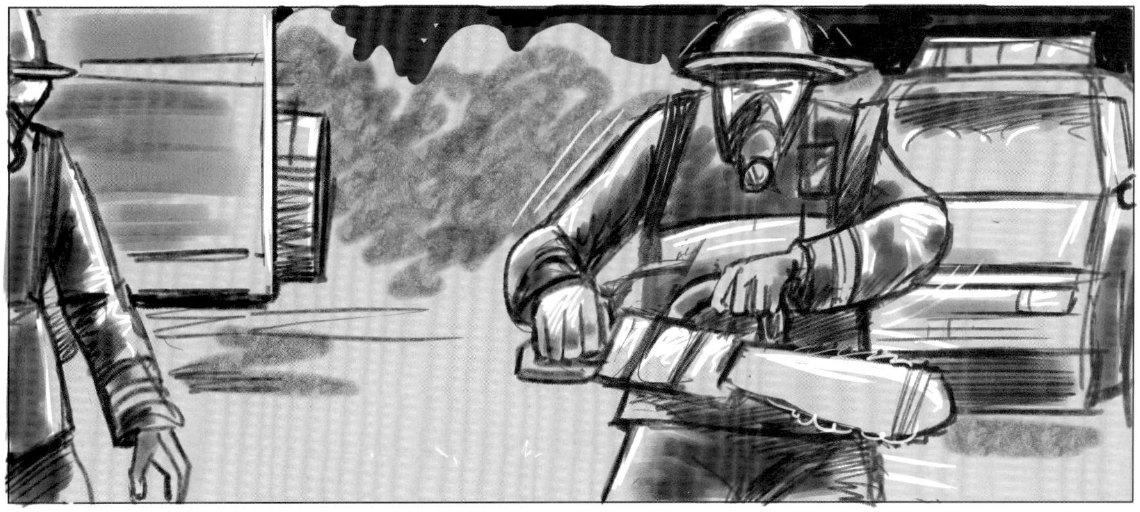

David wanted this panning shot going across the firemen where they display their tools turned weapons.

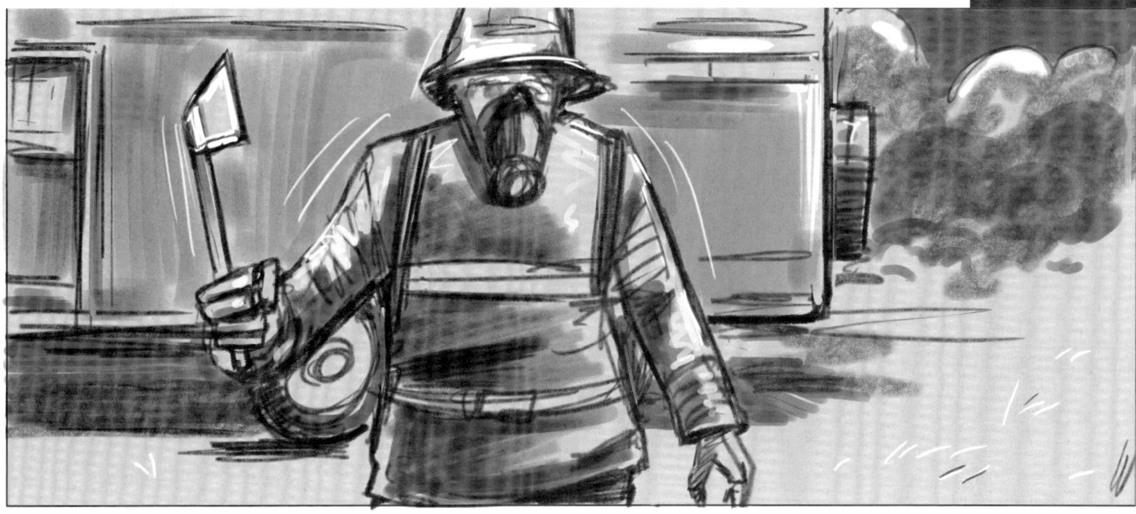

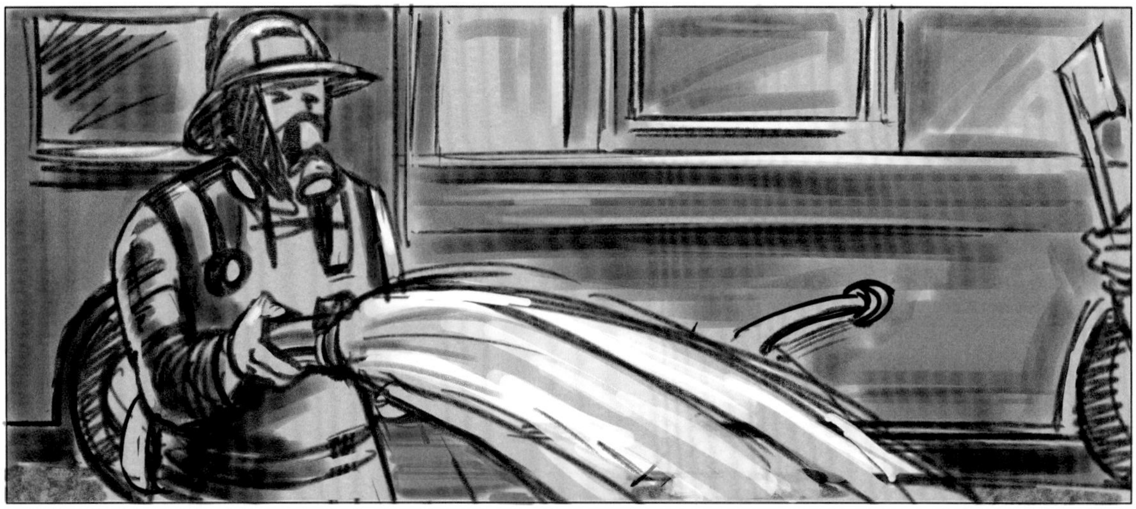

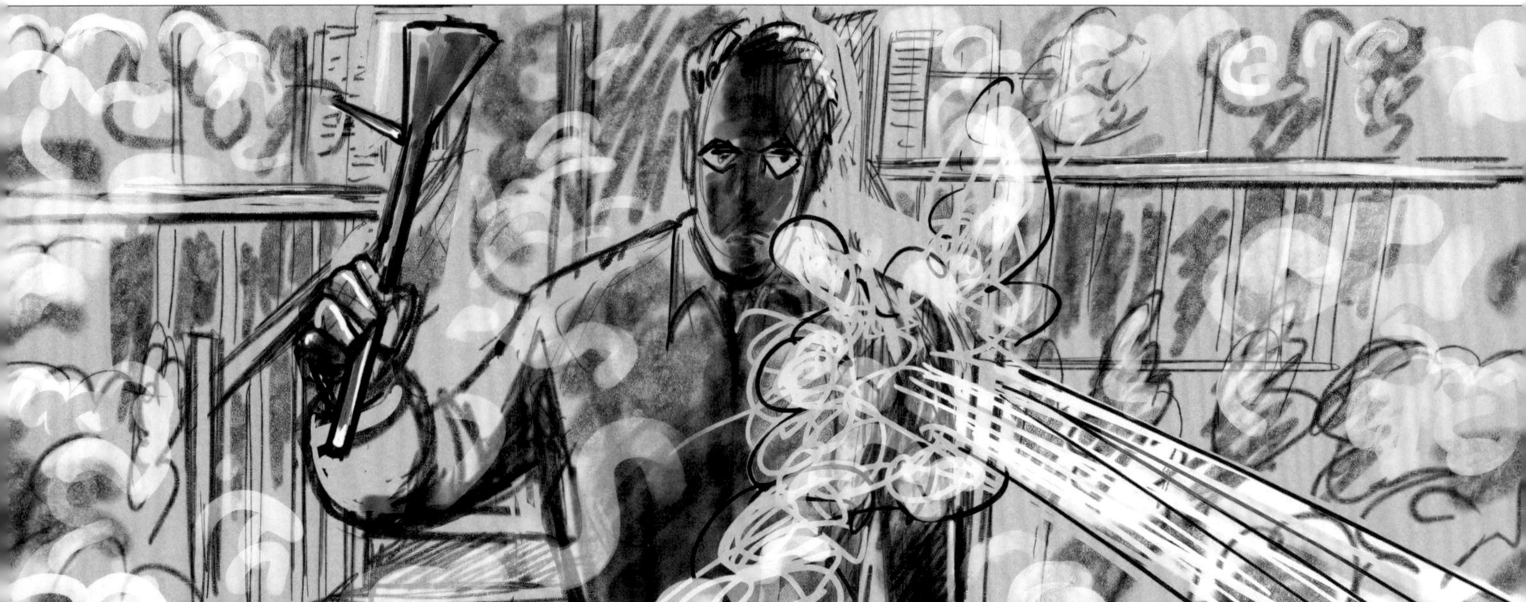

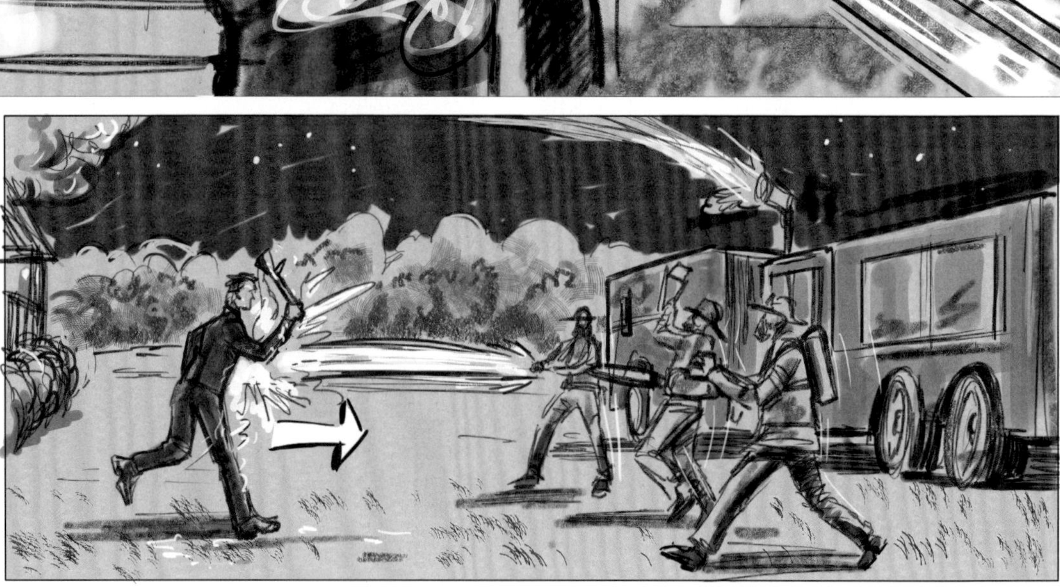

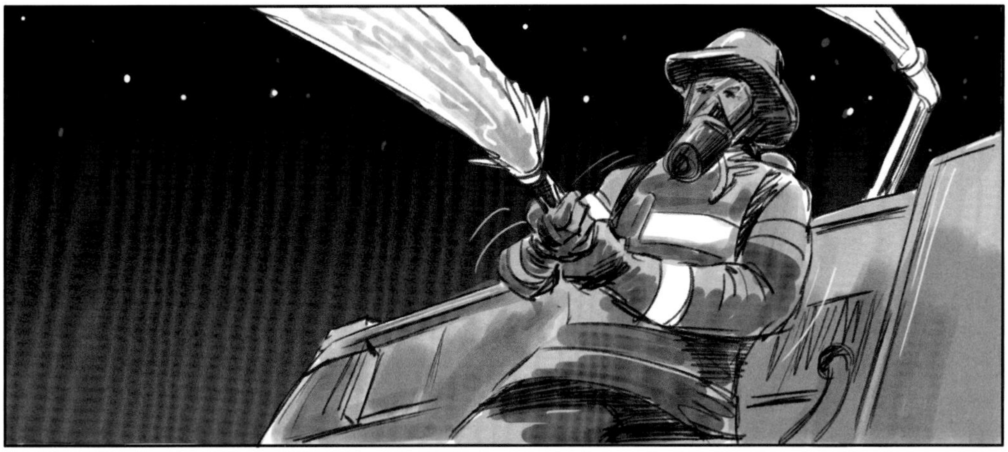

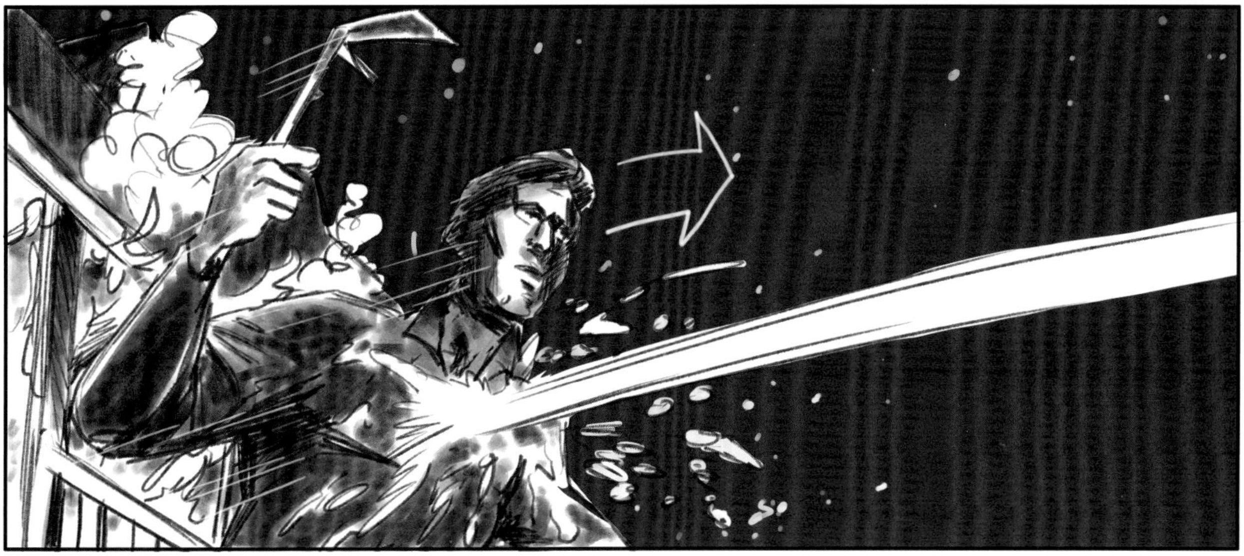

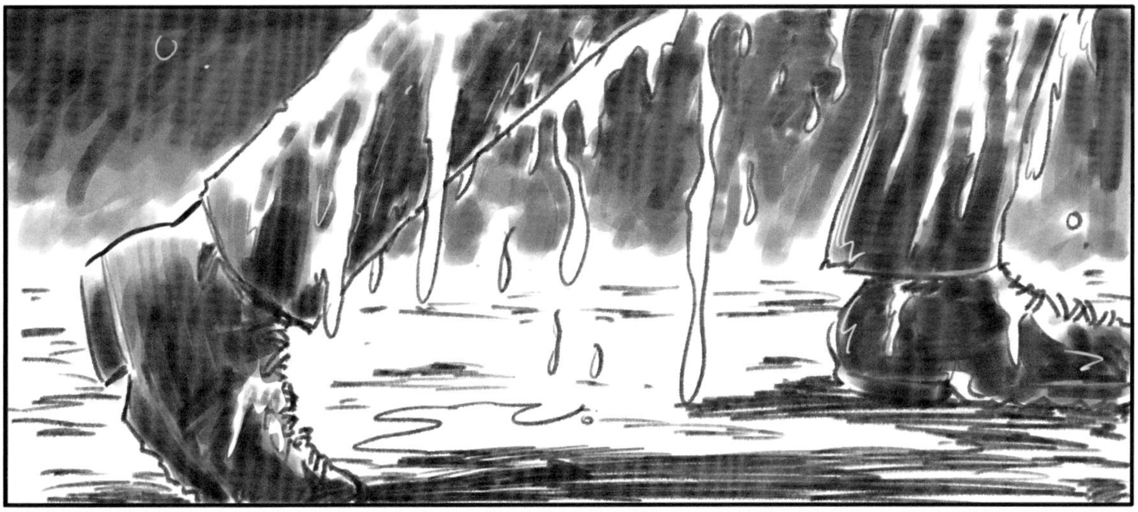

David wanted to show Michael Myers walking through a high pressure firehouse like it was nothing.

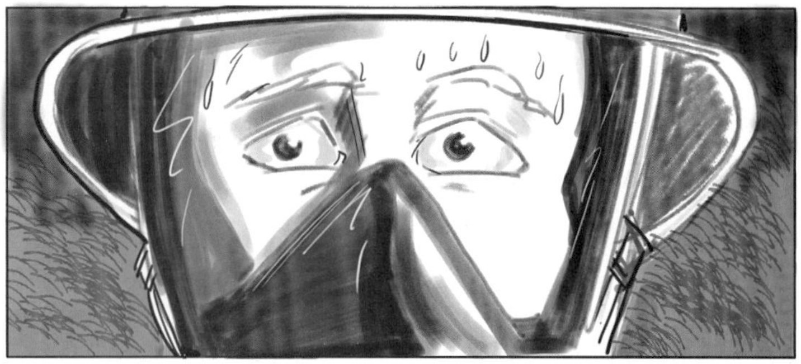

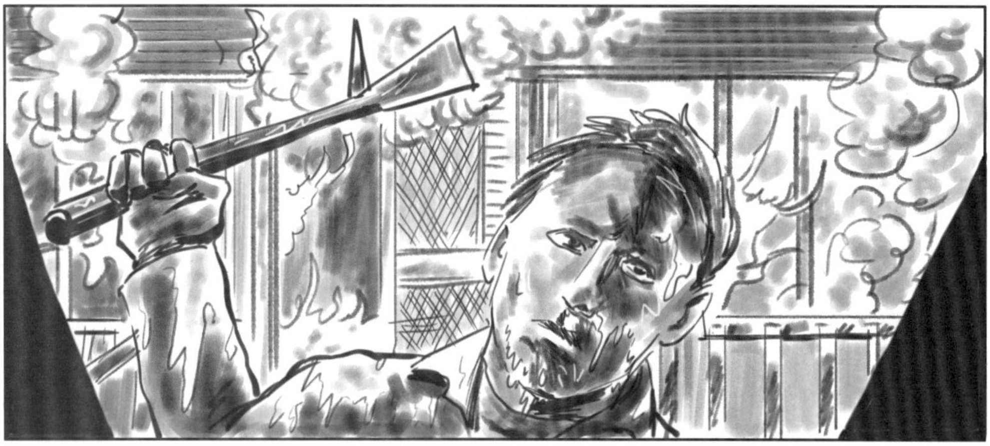

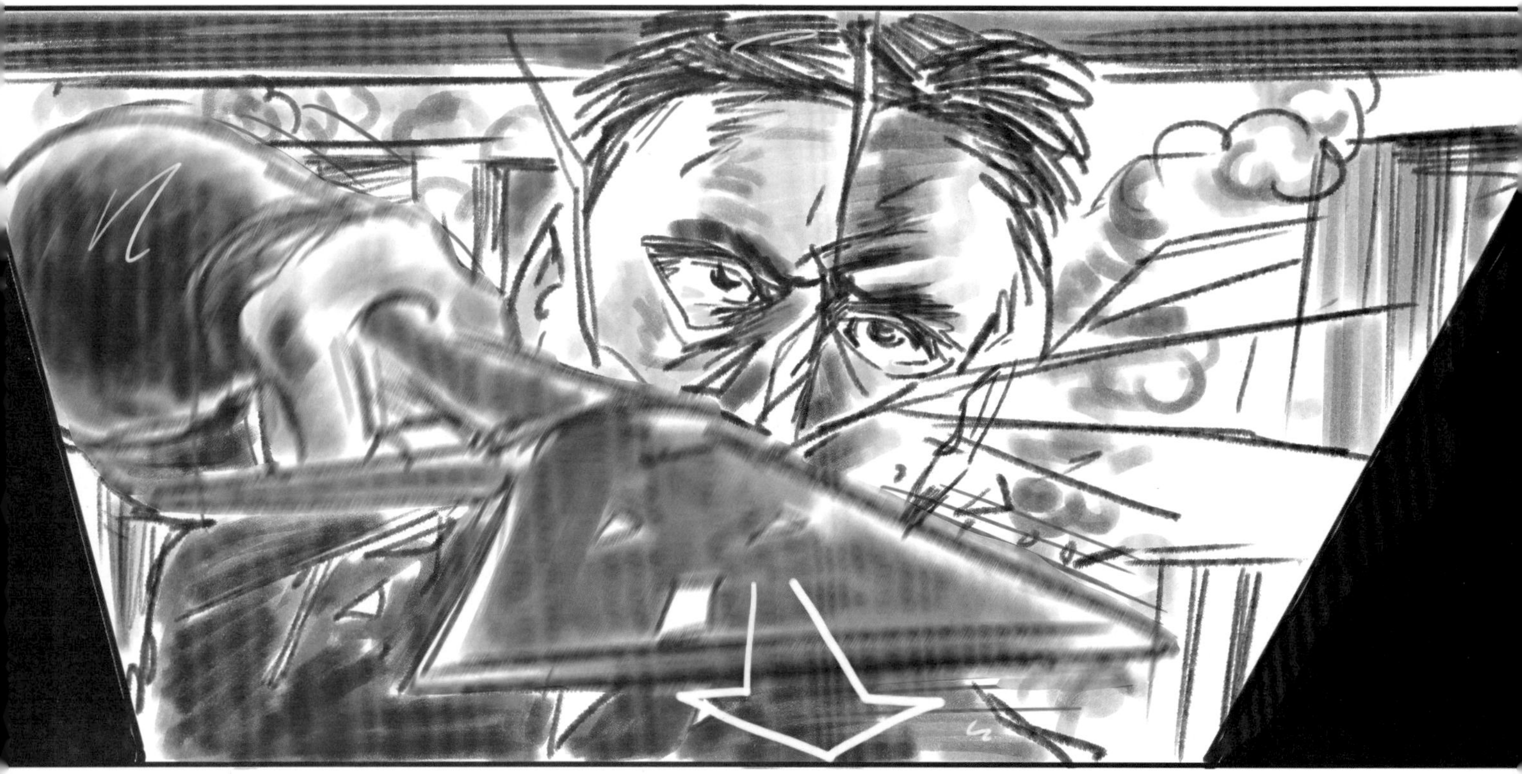

The point of view shots were David Gordon Green's idea. In the original board, I colored the blood red.

I added a splash of color in the original storyboards as the splattering blood was done in a strong red, so it would stand out for David Gordon Green.

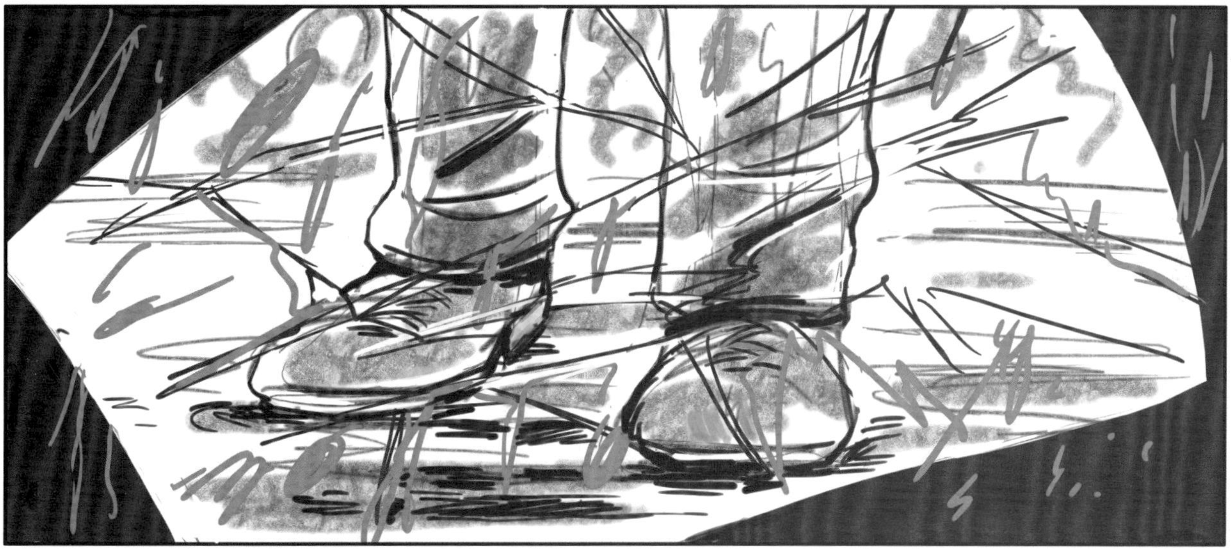

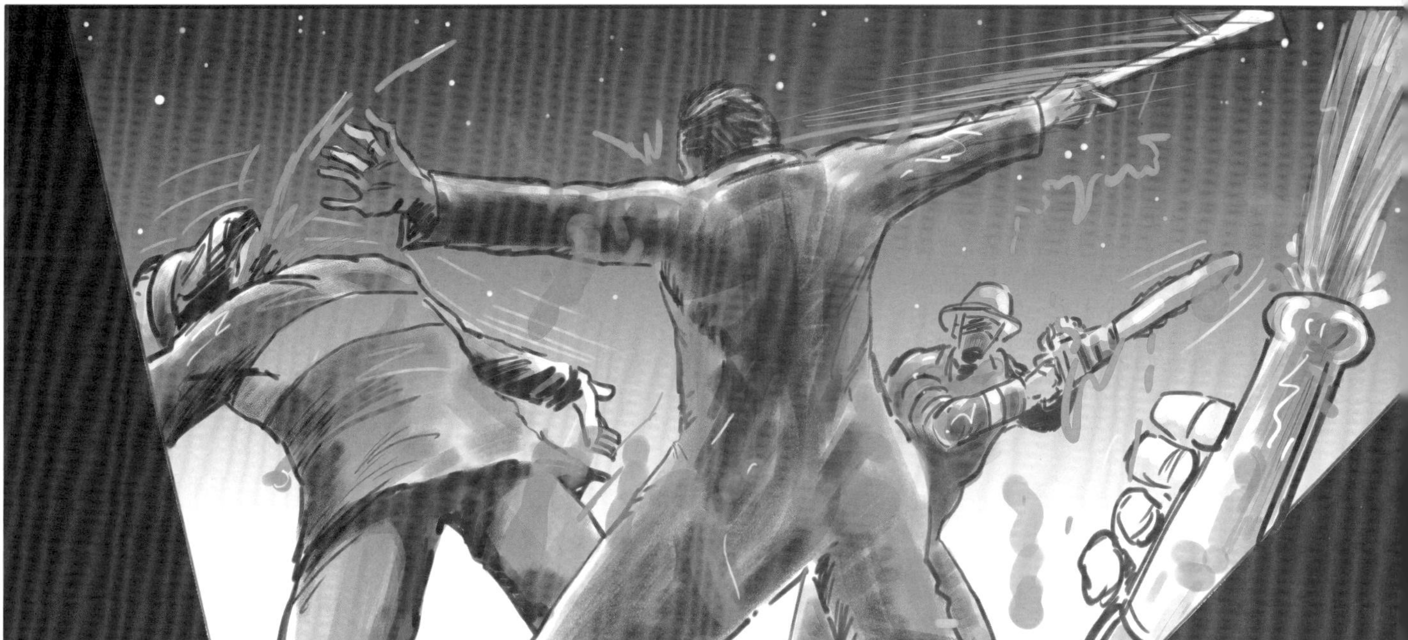

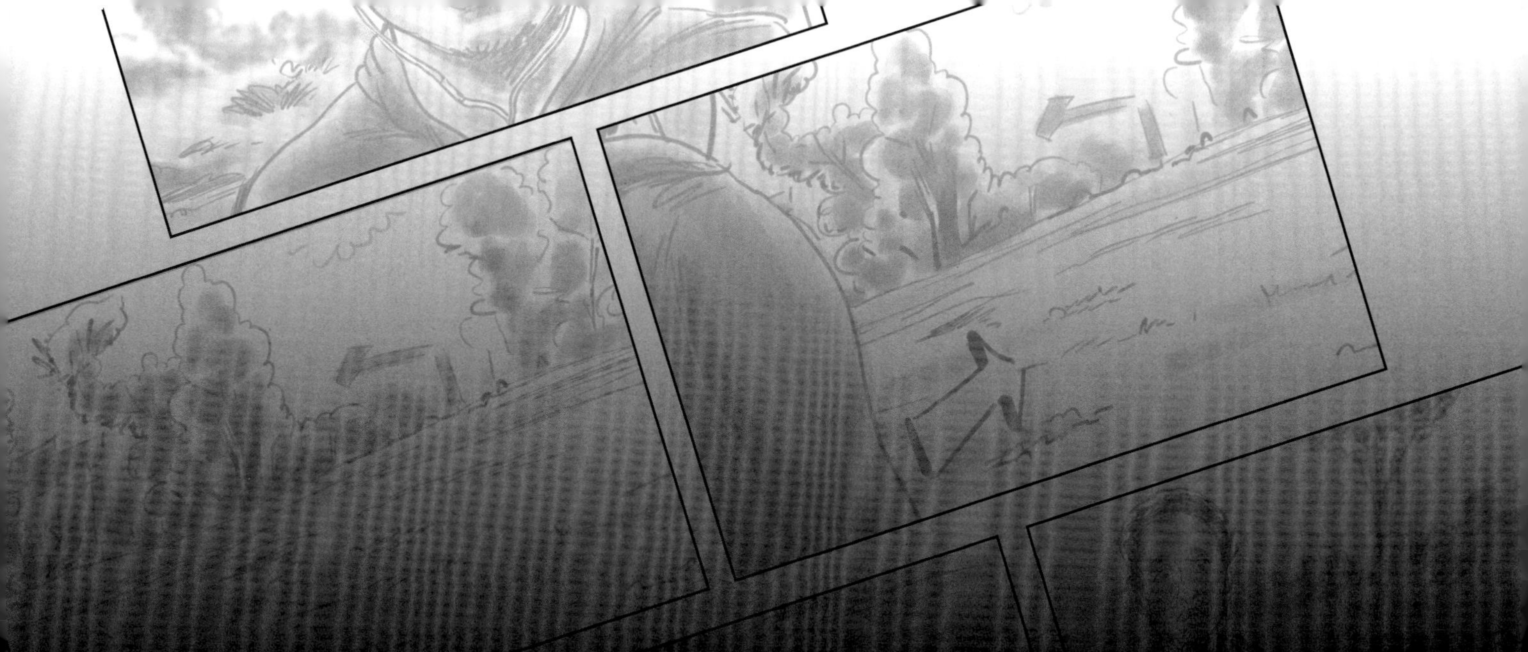

STORYBOARDS AND STORIES OF 15 SELECT FILMS AND TELEVISION SHOWS

Chapter 20

UNKNOWN CALLER

HELLO, DIRECTOR

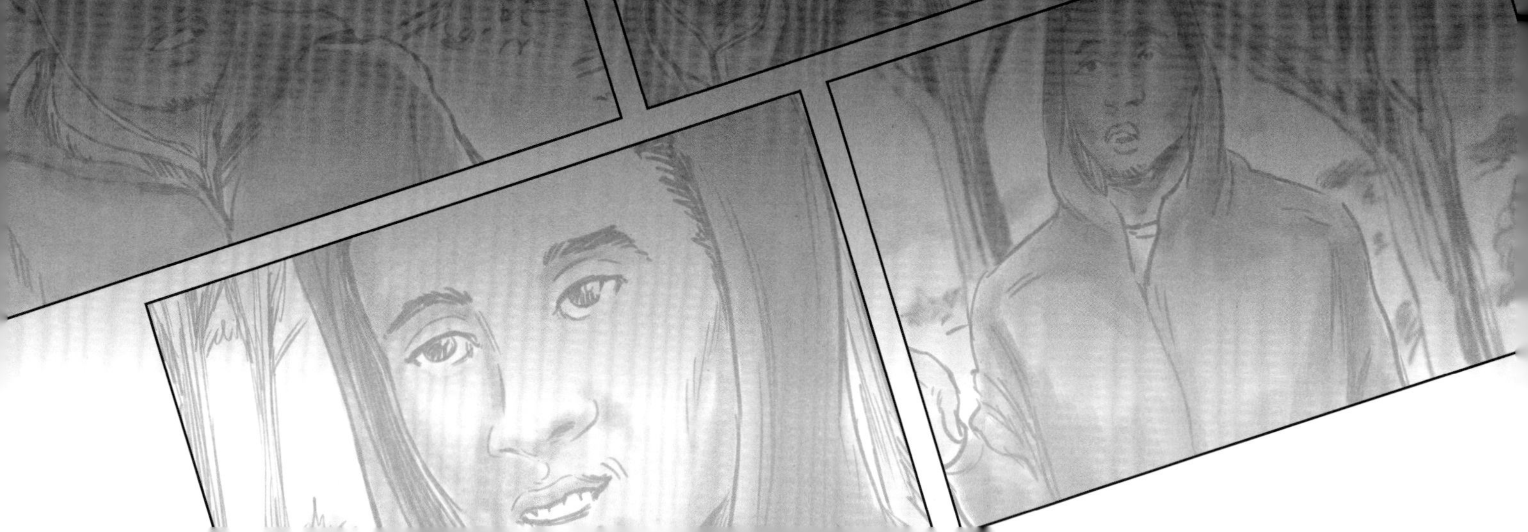

Unknown Caller... Hello, director

So, about this directing thing...

As I may have stated, since I was a kid I envisioned the name of Steven Spielberg and the term "wunderkind". I had imagined having some great success as a screenwriter or comic book artist by the time I was in my mid-twenties. Well, that certainly didn't happen and certainly not for my lack of belief, but for the steely reality of proximity and opportunity. With the severe limits of the film industry in New York during that time period and the lack of opportunities just after graduating from School of Visual Arts, it took me long enough just to be able to stand on my own two feet as an employed freelance artist. But as I grew as a professional creative in the film industry, I did start thinking about directing.

Life comes full circle. My son Josh, a creative mind and a film student at the University of California at Santa Barbara on a full academic scholarship was developing ideas for a short film to showcase his writing and acting talents. Like most twenty-year olds with fantastical imaginations, Josh's initial ideas were quite big, having to do with a vampire infested post-apocalyptic world. Betty was the first to steer him away from that as it would be too expensive, guiding him with the lesson that "simple is best" to get his start with a smaller, more character driven concept. I explained to Josh that his story idea wouldn't show off his acting because it was an action piece rather than a dramatic one. Also, as he wasn't aiming to be a director yet, so it wasn't feasible to do a subject that would demand such a deep

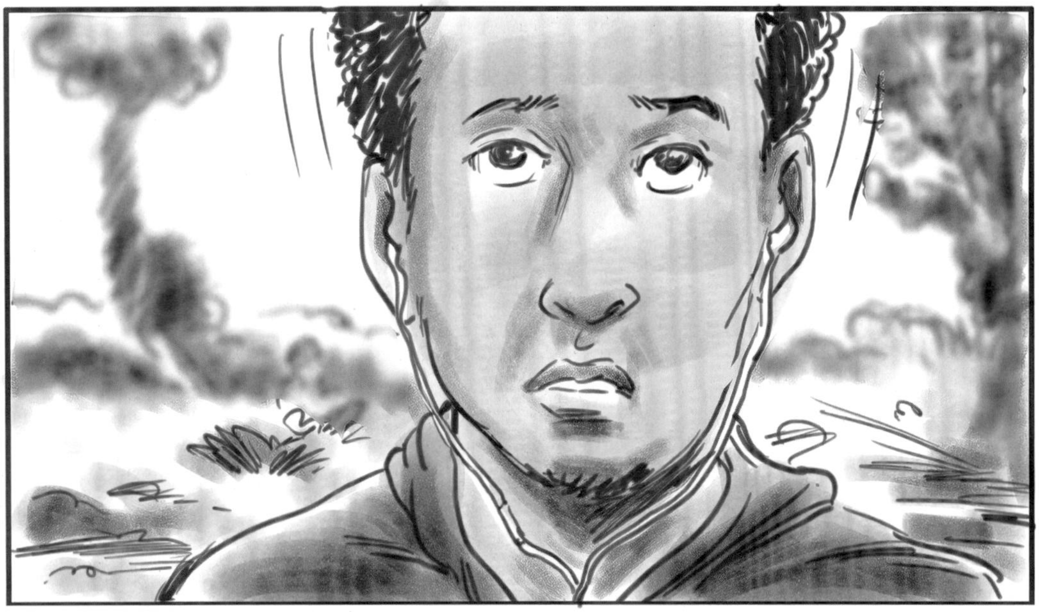

LOOKS STRAIGHT INTO CAMERA.

87

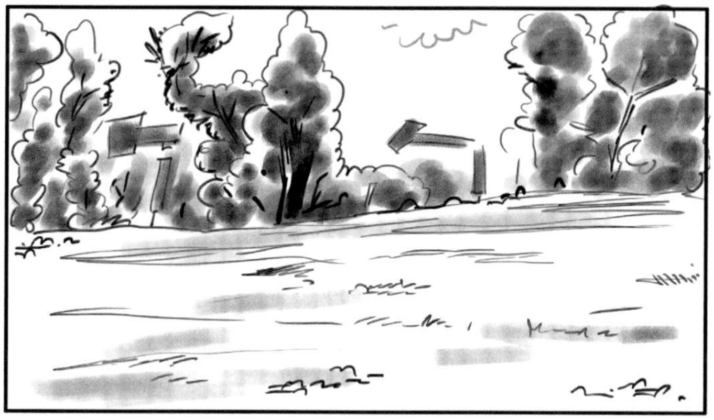

88

MICHAEL POV

THE HOODED FIGURE IS IN THE B.G. BY THE DERRICK.

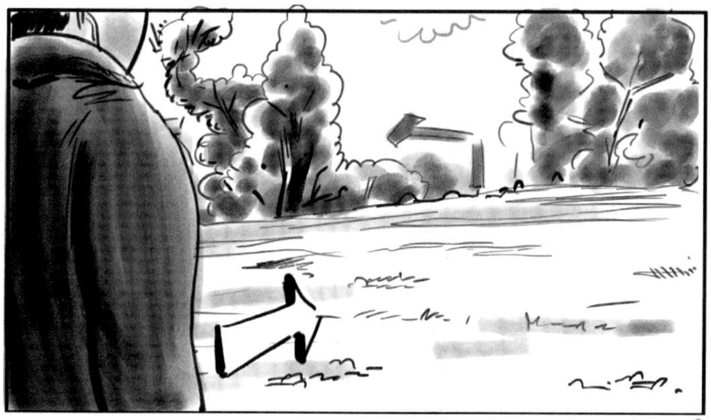

88-A

MICHAEL WALKS INTO HIS OWN POV SHOT.

> Even as the director and storyboard artist, everything isn't copied shot for shot. Fresh ideas and on set situations led me to create some new shots in the short."

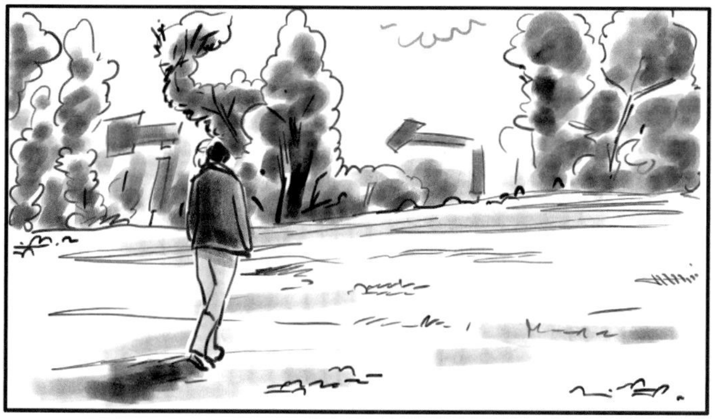

88-B

CONT'D

dive into makeup, VFX, stunts and camera work. The short film that helped to reset a new story idea in Josh's mind was the short film *Multi-Facial* that was self-produced by a young, muscular actor I knew from NYC named Mark Vincent. Mark later changed his name to Vin Diesel. He wrote, directed and starred in a simple but effective film about an actor of mixed race and how hard it was for him to fit into any certain racial casting slot when he auditioned. The film showed Vin's acting abilities and that is what Steven Spielberg saw when he later cast him in *Saving Private Ryan*.

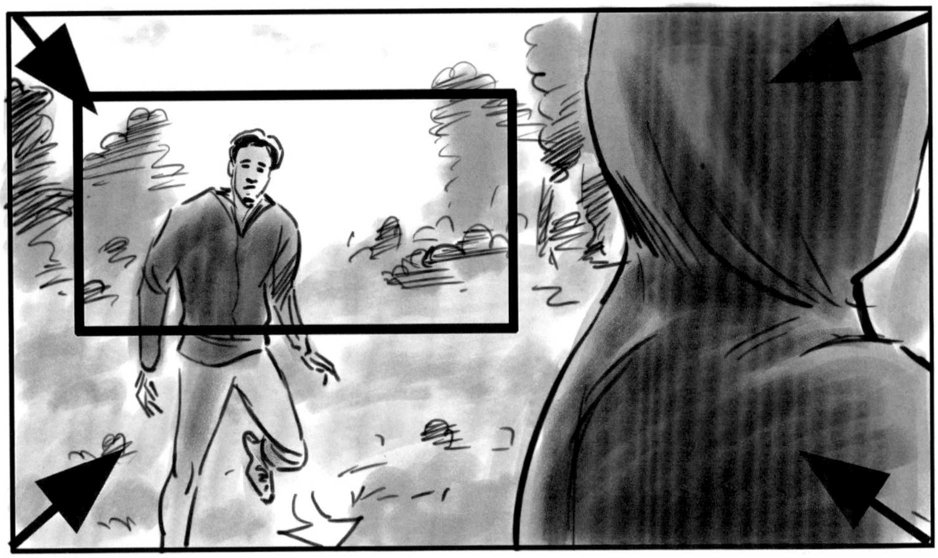

OTS HOODED FIGURE

MICHAEL WALKS TOWARD CAMERA.

89

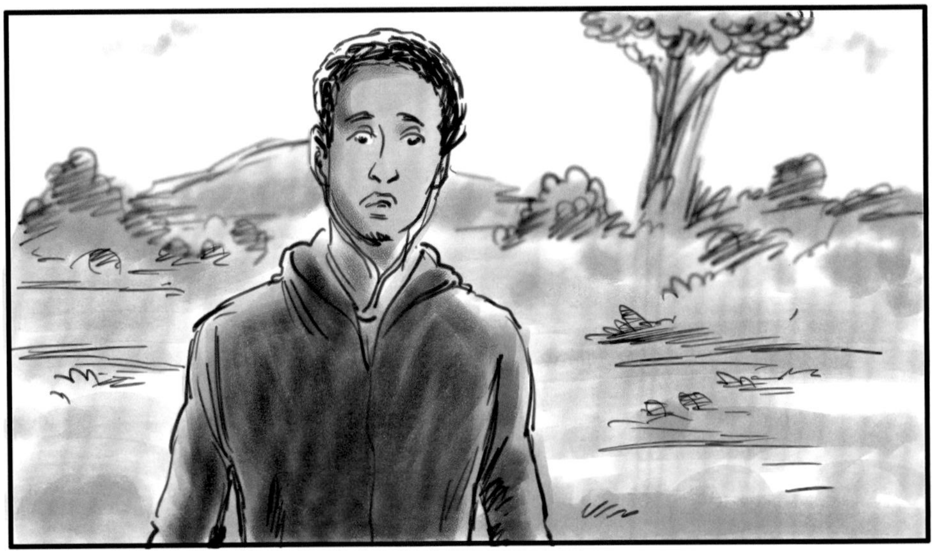

MICHAEL "WHAT'S UP?! HIDING BEHIND ALLA THAT..."

89-A

Josh went "back in the lab" and came back with *Unknown Caller*, a tight, short film script about a young man plagued by a series of cell phone calls from a mysterious and unknown caller. When Josh, Betty and I were at the table conversing with Josh on how proud we were of him with his new script writing achievement, Betty looked me in the eyes and said strongly, "And you're going to direct it!" There was no debate in her eyes. Betty basically called my bluff, forcing me forward. She knew if I wanted to direct anything

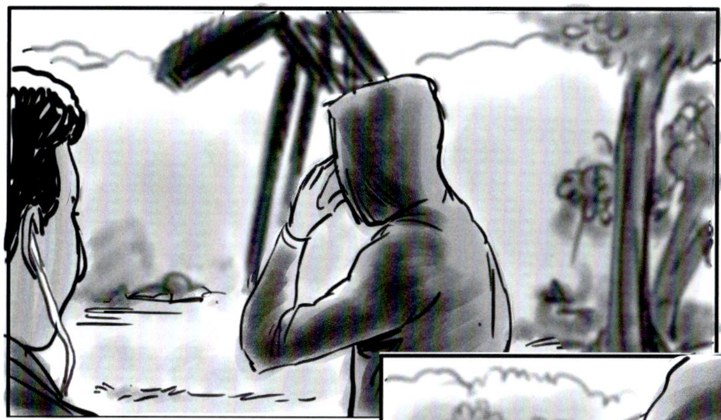

REPEAT MICHAEL DIALOGUE

90

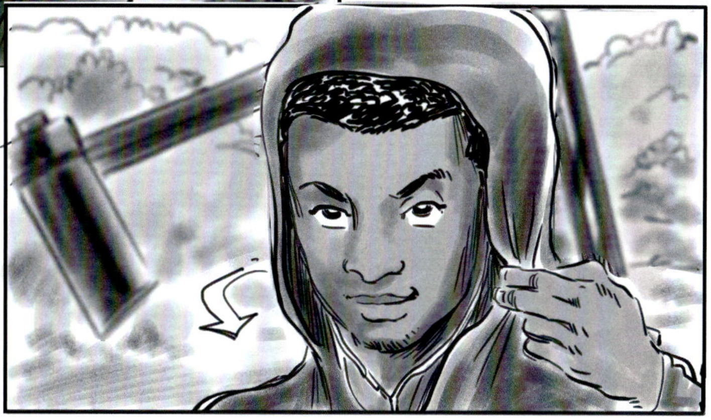

CUT TO

DOPPELGANGER REVEALED AS MICHAEL.

MICHAEL DOPPELGANGER "HI, MIKE."

91

This reveal came off as planned.

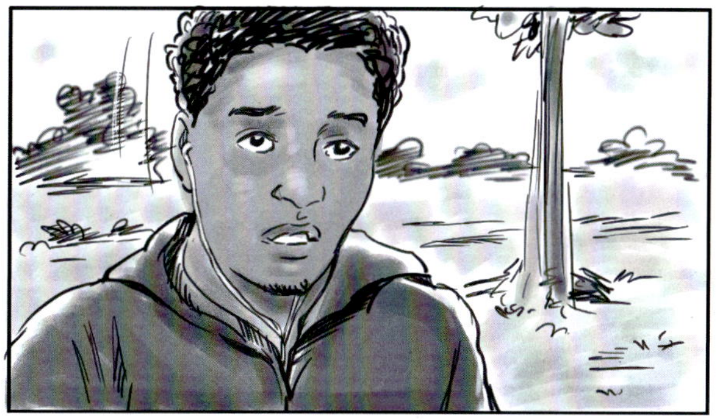

MICHAEL "WHAT..."

92

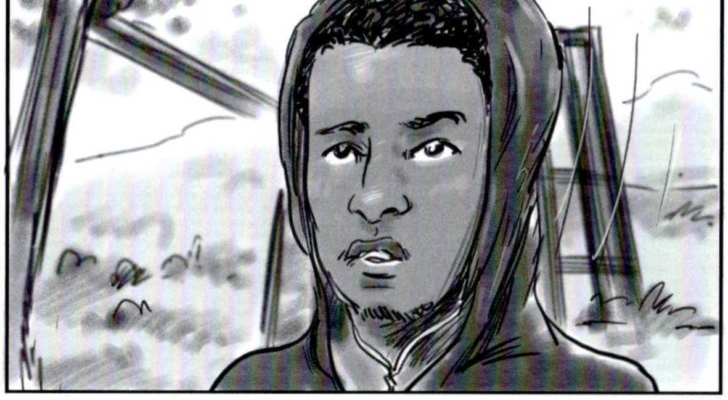

MICHAEL DOPPELGANGER "NO NEED TO BE ANGRY. YOU WANT TO TALK, RIGHT?"

93

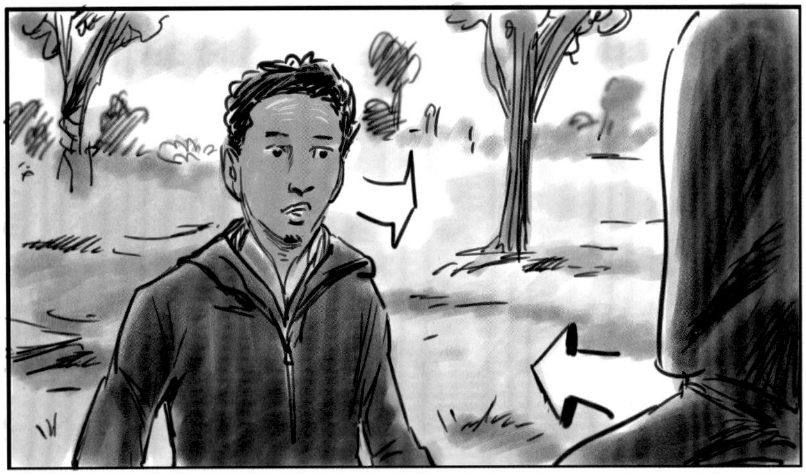

94

REPEAT DIALOGUE.

MICHAEL "WHY HAVE YOU BEEN..."

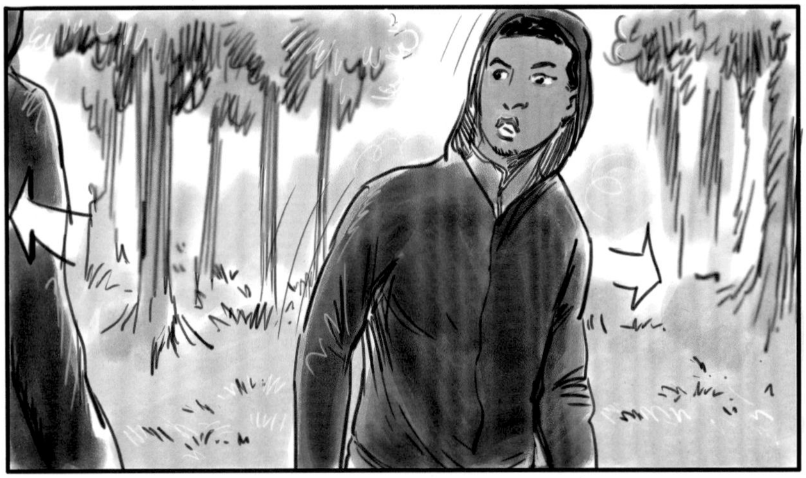

95

MICHAEL DOPPELGANGER 'I NEVER CALLED YOU ONCE..."

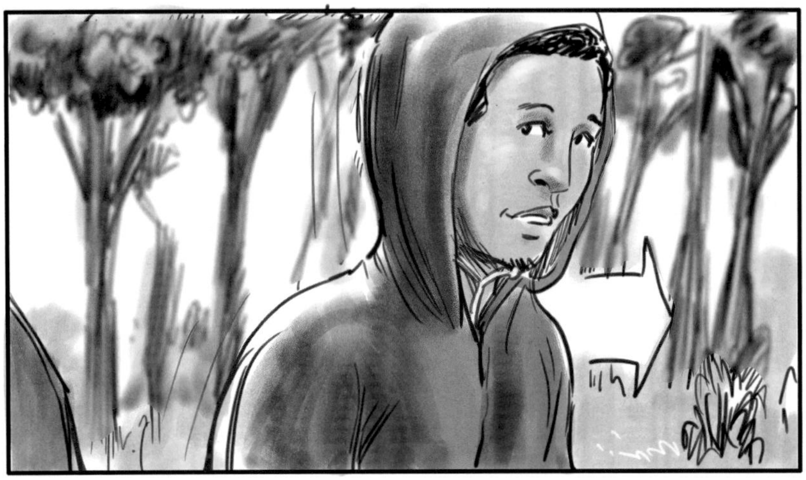

96

A BIT CLOSER. LOWER.

MICHAEL DOPPELGANGER SPEAKS.

in the future I needed to start with Joshua's short film. I figured now was the time, so I of course agreed. In all honesty I did hesitate for a moment as the offer (well, demand) came across the table like a dart. It was put up or shut up time and the creative gauntlet had been thrown down at my feet. My first course of action was to break the script down into sections and then to storyboard it.

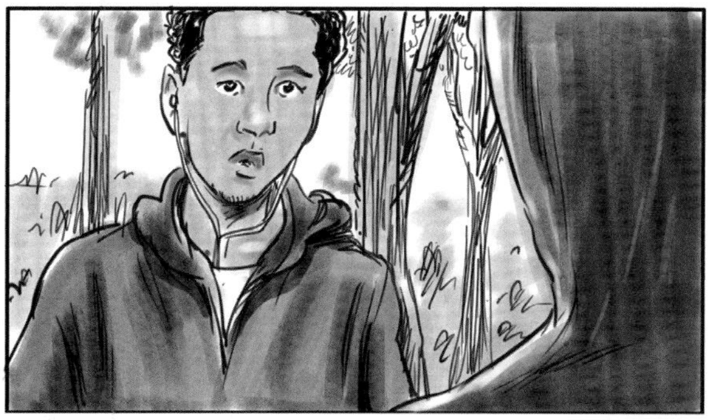

97

THEY STOP MOVING.

ON MICHAEL AS HIS DOPPELGANGER TALKS.

MICHAEL DOPPELGANGER "THE OTHER PHONE CALLS WERE FROM NADESKA..."

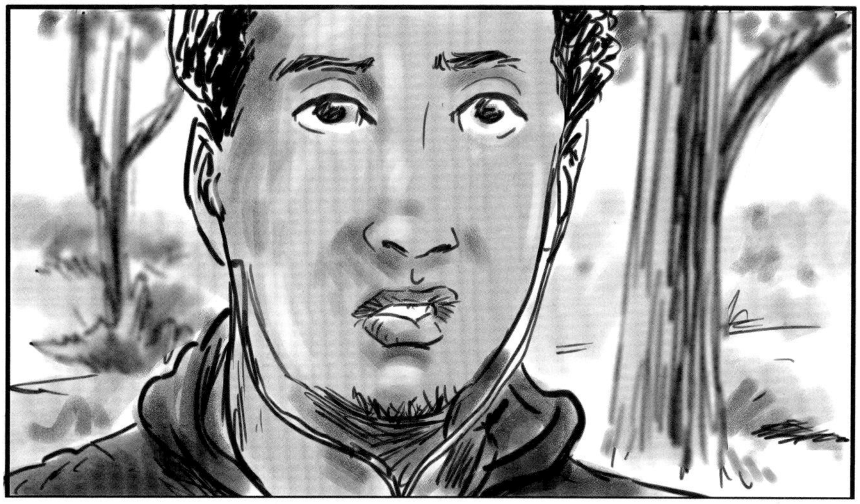

98

MICHAEL REACTION SHOTS.

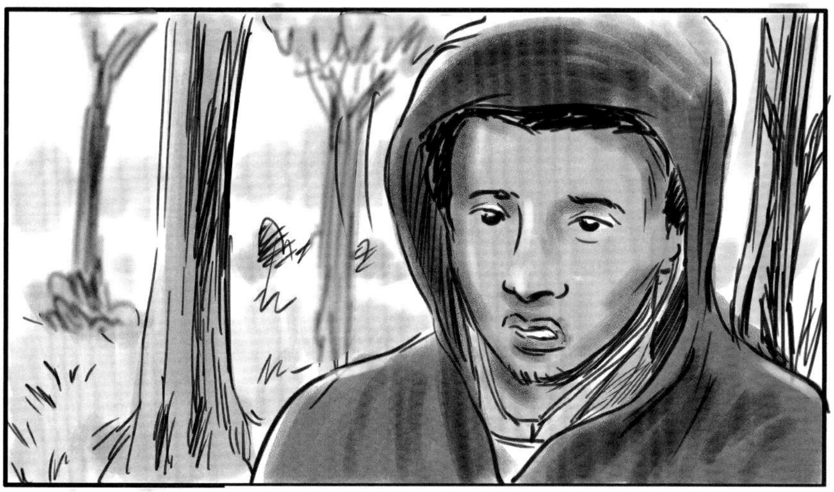

99

MICHAEL DOPPELGANGER "YOU WOULD LIVE LIFE EASIER..."

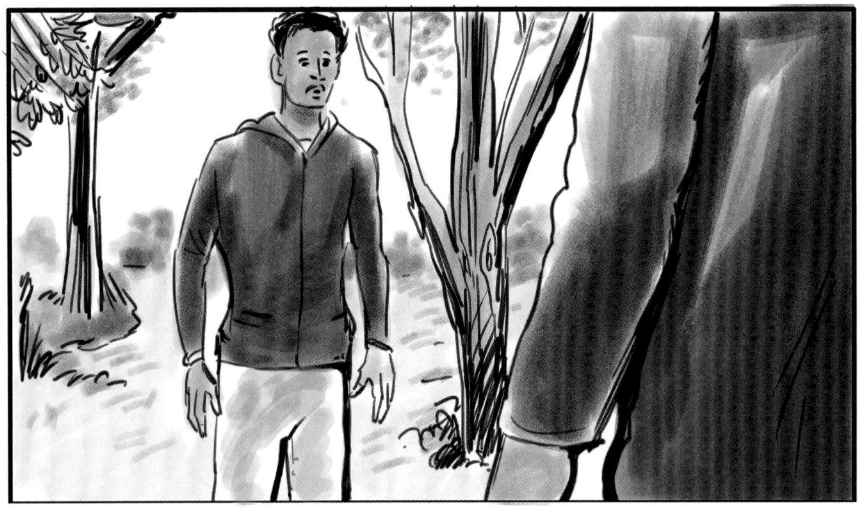

LOW OVER

MICHAEL DOPPELGANGER TO MICHAEL.

100

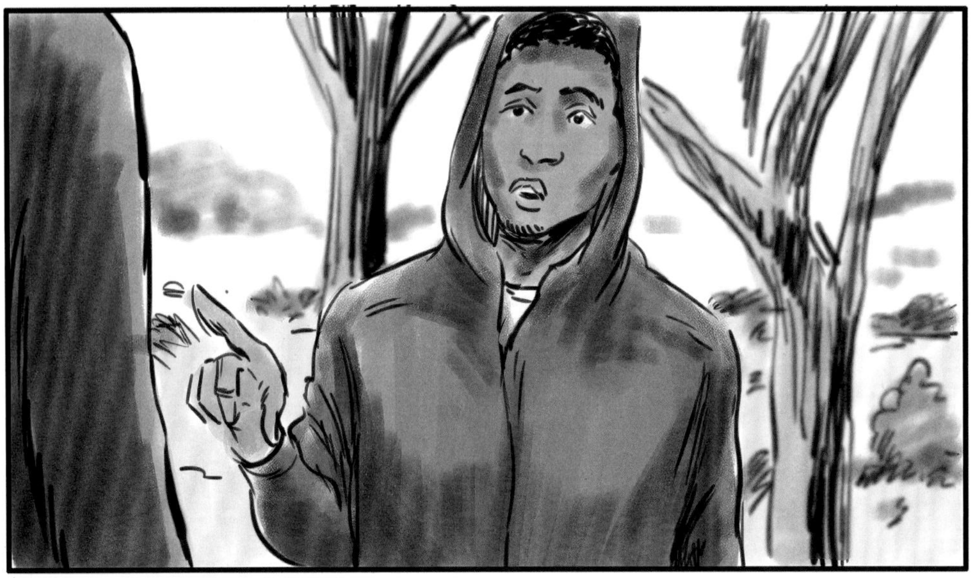

OTS MICHAEL TO DOPPELGANGER.

M.D. "YOU SHOULD TRY IT. STEP BY STEP."

101

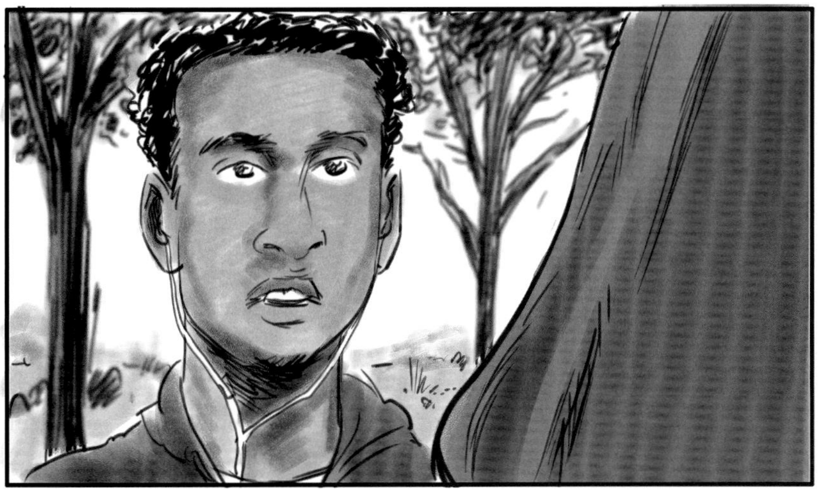

LONG LENS

REPEAT M.D.
DIALOGUE
OTS TO MICHAEL.

102

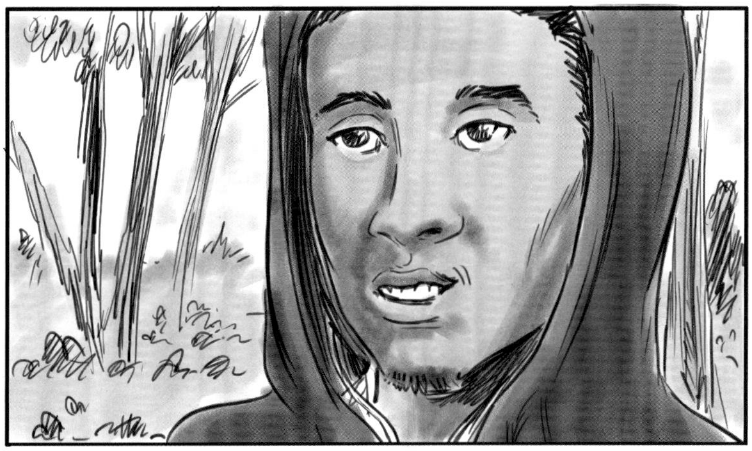

M.D. DIALOGUE

CLOSE UP COVERAGE.

> I must say I am quite proud of how my son, Josh performed this scene."

103

Josh and I did a location scout of the beautiful, spacious nearby grounds of Pan Pacific Park where Betty and I had taken him to play since he was a toddler. We found some nice spots to possibly film and I also took some photos of Josh in these same spots to try to work out some cinematic angles. Josh had to play the lead character as well as his doppelganger character. As a conceptual device, I took photos of Josh with and without a hoodie then melded some of these in Photoshop so he would appear to be his own duplicate.

We then had to hire a crew. Fortunately, our friend and neighbor Karl Hahn was in fact a DP and readily agreed to do the job. Josh was away at college while we handled the pre-production details. When he came back for winter break we dove into the project with full abandon. Josh, Karl and I scouted another location at Kenneth Hahn Park which was more picturesque and was only a few miles away. Kenneth Hahn Park had very photogenic paths and even had a running brook with a small bridge. The park was next to an oil field with moving diesel pumps that would have made a great backdrop for a dramatic scene.

As the lead character's romantic interest was cast with a young actress named Toi'ya Leatherwood whom Josh and I had met at an event a few months earlier. Karl called in a few crew personnel including a gaffer, second unit DP, his assistant, a focus puller and a camera operator. We already had a great sound person, Tom Hopper whom Betty had used on other shoots. Besides his talent, Tom was always in a good mood and was great to be around.

Karl's apartment served as the character's home and that diminished our costs on the budget for an apartment location. We scouted his apartment and figured out angles. We only needed the living room to shoot in and it looked great. The front window was edged with had a balcony window that gave the room a lovely glow from natural daylight.

A Wednesday evening rehearsal was set up for the Thursday morning shoot. Karl sat talking on his phone with a stressed look on his face: his camera rental deal fell through. We were to shoot the next morning and we had no camera! I went into a quiet panic of figuring how to work things out. But then I realized that with twenty-five years in the business I had a long list of awesome colleagues and friends. So I made some calls. One of the calls was to Kyle Newacheck, who had co-created the Comedy Central hit, *Workaholics*. Kyle is the epitome of "chilled out with good vibes." We did a Netflix movie called *Game Over, Man*! and got along so famously that we remained as friends. Kyle generously told me that I could borrow an entire camera package from him at no cost. He set me up with everything for free—the camera, lenses, a camera stand and all the works. Kyle even had his assistant Brendin pick up the equipment from his house and drive it over to deliver it personally to Karl's the next day. Kyle saved the day like a superhero and our short film would not have happened without him. We missed our Thursday shoot day but by Friday morning we were on set and rolling.

The shoot got off to an auspicious start when we were shooting in Kenneth Hahn Park and were told after a few minutes by an attendant that we needed permits to shoot. It was an open public park and we were in the very early morning hours with no other people around so we had not considered that a permit would even be necessary. Karl went rogue and grabbed some more footage in as I tried to negotiate with the park attendant. When negotiations and pleading failed, our crew packed up and went to Pan Pacific Park. I had to make sure that I kept my energy buoyant and positive so that the sudden change didn't wreck the mood of the shoot. Once we got there, everything went smoothly. As the script had two park exterior scenes, the plan was to shoot both scenes that day and shoot the interior and basketball scene the next day, with a third day handy for pick up shots. We shot additional scenes of Josh jogging in the park and then reversed angles to get scenes with him as his nemesis/doppelganger. A friend and young actor, Keith Mills stood in for the reverse shots as the doppelganger's over-the-shoulder shots. Since Keith and Josh did not resemble each other we made sure that the doppelganger wore a hoodie so the shots from behind were indistinguishable for the coverage. Wardrobe can be a very helpful and effective device when used strategically.
After shooting one side facing Josh, we then flipped angles with Josh playing himself as his own hoodie- wearing doppelganger character.

I was really settling in and relaxing around the small crew. I remembered what commercial director Bryan Buckley told me almost twenty years earlier, that seventy-five percent of directing is problem solving. One can argue with casting being a major part as well, but I found myself constantly figuring things out and having to circumvent minor issues. I have to admit there was a freedom to having something in your head and that everyone must follow your lead and give it their all to make it happen. But I must also add that I listened to my crewmembers for any good advice. Everyone was good at their job as experienced and thorough professionals.

Sunset was upon us and we were losing light. We pressed forward to complete shots at the end of the day. There were shots I had devised in my head and storyboarded but executing those shots in a timely matter was another matter. We had to shoot coverage of Josh and Keith over a few angles to wrap the day. While all this was going on, Betty officiated as park patrol to keep stragglers out of the shot as well as taking care of Josh's makeup and costume maintenance. To her credit, she handled the producing of the film and juggled about eight other positions on this low budget endeavor.

The park sequences were wrapped and it was on to the basketball sequences that we were able to shoot in our backyard. We had previously considered doing it in a park court or on another location but filming in our own backyard was free, comfortable and gave us control and access to bathrooms and kitchen for cast and crew breaks. Always seek the path of least resistance when on a budget.

As the day went on, fading daylight was the enemy of the moment. Since we were shooting in January when sunset hit around five o'clock. I got a minimum amount of shots done before everything went dark. Karl's assistant DP, Darryl Walthall had taken over in this sequence and did a great job. We got what we could with the tail end of the shoot in near dark. All of the lighting issues for the basketball scene were fixed in post-production. This is the magic of movies. When the shoot was done, I was a happy camper. We wrapped up and took the equipment back to Karl's apartment in preparation for the interior shoot the next morning.

Saturday was a blur. Shooting in Karl's apartment just two doors down the street was a godsend. We had controlled lighting and the sound and no unwanted stragglers passing through our shots as we dealt with in the park. There were shots that I had mapped out in the storyboards that were able to work perfectly, and others that were not used because of a time constraint. One thing to be aware of when filming: as soon as you think you have a lot of time – you don't. There is always some unforeseen incident to through you off track. The monkey in the wrench was that our lead actress Toi'ya had a noon audition. Getting our shoot schedule pushed back a day collided with her schedule – so I wasn't able to get half of her coverage. Betty helped out by reading Toi'ya's lines off camera to Josh for his close ups. Kyle's assistant, Brendin had to pick up the camera pack at the end of the day so we would not have equipment for a needed Sunday shoot to finish up and do coverage. Most of the other crew was not available for a Sunday shoot. Since we not had to use Karl's personal camera with built-in sound it would pick up every sound being made on the set. In addition, the sound had an "echo" feel to it in Karl's apartment. Still, we made it through with Betty once again reading Toi'ya's lines to Josh as well as providing an off camera eye line for him to act to while on camera.

When we finished shooting we took the footage to my friend, editor Michael D. Schultz. Mike was a total pro with two Emmy's to show for it. His assistant editor, Stephanie Willis completed the edit. Stephanie and I hit it off right away and she had great instincts. She lived a few miles away so travel wasn't an issue. We realized the basketball footage we had wasn't nearly enough. We only had a couple of shots when we needed many more to complete the sequence. We needed coverage. For the reshoot, most of the extra cast could not make it. Keith was able to return as did Josh's grade school friend, Jaxon. Karl wasn't available so Darryl Walthall came back to shoot this second unit footage. The "crew" was just Darryl and his assistant, Chadwick Williams who proved to be a great addition.

What director Bryan Buckley said continues to come to pass. Problem solving. I had to solve the problem that now I only had half the ball players I had in the original shoot. I figured what I had to do was to shoot everyone as close as possible. This would hide the lack of additional ballers. I also had to step into the scene to make it seem as though there were more basketball players. I added myself to the shot as I ran from right to left and back again while extremely close to the camera to give the sense that there were other players just outside of camera view. The trick was that as an older man, I couldn't let my face be seen with a young group of twenty-year olds. The camera would only pick up my legs, waist and maybe a flailing arm to give a sense of on-court action and movement.

The big issue was that the new coverage footage of the basketball scene that Darryl shot had a totally different color grade than what Karl shot because they used two different cameras.

The next step for the short was to have it "color timed." Basically, the film (actually video) was in the stage where the color, saturation, blacks, etc. would be raised up from the comparative drab colors of the original footage. Michael Schultz recommended Von Thomas, who was the "colorist" for the shows *The Conners* as well as *The Ranch*. Over a series of meetings, Von would manipulate the colors to bring them to a proper viewing standard. I got to see the inner workings as he went scene by scene, adding color and tone to the movie. Sometimes Von had to select only part of a frame to manipulate the color when something didn't look right. His scene detailing was quite precise. After the colorist's duties were complete, the last major bit of business was the final sound. My good friend Bobbi Banks, a major ADR sound supervisor—and also part of the Singleton crew—recommended Kenneth L. Johnson. Kenneth had won three Emmy Awards as a sound designer.

Our team, Betty, Josh, and I went to see Kenneth and his sound design studio in Burbank. Kenneth could not have been nicer. What was impressive and sad at the same time was that Kenneth was the only Black sound supervisor who owned his own studio. After walking in, we saw that the studio was spacious and cozy. Kenneth made every sound in our short as crisp and radiant as possible. He added singing birds to the opening scene where there were none. There were a few too many F-bombs in the short, so Kenneth put Josh in a sound booth so Josh could dub in a substitute word. As Josh is also a rapper who produces his own songs he was able to do several dubs effortlessly.

Other details were in the basketball game of how much sound would be Josh's music versus the sound of the basketball dribbling itself. The reshoots done in DP Karl's apartment had a hollow sound because we didn't have mics for Josh. Kenneth was able to make the sound much fuller so that it matched the rest of the short. The movie went back to Michael Schultz for some touch-ups as well as having the credits added and with that, we had completed our son's first short film.

What ever you create, you've got to make some noise about it. Next up was the public relations, marketing of festivals and contests. That proved to be a task all by itself. We had to decide which local ones we could attend, as well as which out-of-state contests and festivals were worth it as submitting cost money and if we got in, there would be significant travel involved. We made it into a few local festivals and several on the east coast. Film festivals are a rewarding experience. It was a nice feeling to see our work blown up on a big screen in front of an audience.

Overall, I came to see that *Unknown Caller* was an invaluable learning lesson rather than a film that would win awards or get me work. Each win, lesson or mistake, large or small, informed me of what I could do in the future. Again, I had to give thanks to Betty for having the confidence that I could do it. And…adding a little note of threat in her sincere tone of love and support.

On a sad note, Karl Hahn, who was the cinematographer of *Unknown Caller* and a good friend of the family, passed away in 2022. We cherish his memory and are grateful for his friendship and fine work.

STORYBOARDS AND STORIES OF 15 SELECT FILMS AND TELEVISION SHOWS

HARD DAY'S WORK

Chapter 14

A PERSONAL NOTE

A FEW OLD THINGS, A FEW GOOD PEOPLE AND A LITTLE OF WHAT I'VE LEARNED.

A Personal Note on: a few old things, a few good people and a little of what I've learned.

It's now been a few years since the shoot of *Unknown Caller* as well as the idea of this book. The three biggest changes have certainly been the passing of my mother Ruth Drummond Ruffin, John Singleton and certainly how Covid 19 has changed the very way we work and live.

I am grateful that Mom was able to see me become successful in the film industry. She saw my childhood dreams and talent becoming one and my growth as an artist as well as becoming a husband and father.

John was my sounding board as I was often his. He was my greatest connection, friendship, and relationship in the film industry. Even when we were not working together, John was like family and a brother in every way. I wish I could have given John and Mom copies of this book but they were there for my journey.

By the time you read this book, Covid will be a horrible memory for us all. To say that Covid flipped the world upside down would be an understatement. When Covid shut the industry down the first time, I was working on the seventh season of the great Comedy Central show, *Drunk History*, which has since been canceled. I had gotten along fantastically with its creators Derek Waters and Jeremy Konner and enjoyed coming in to meet with them as well in addition to Christina Sahakian the fantastic production supervisor, who got me on the show. I even included in a "Making Of Drunk History" documentary that was being shot at their production office while I was working there. What was funny is that Derek and Jeremy had only just started using storyboards after six seasons when they hired me. I strictly remember being told on Friday, March 13, 2020, that the show would take a few weeks off, as this "new Covid thing" had spread to the United States from Europe and China. The thought was things would return to normal after a relatively short period. In hindsight, that belief was laughable and naïve to say the least.

Drunk History never got back into production and I spend the next couple of months at home without work. I certainly worried about the daily safety of my wife, son and the world in general. As months passed, people slowly started to figure things out. Productions came back but only under extreme and careful work conditions. Features and television shows no longer had fully staffed production offices. As many crew members as possible were asked to work out of their homes. Throughout my career, I worked both at home and at production offices, but now I was working exclusively in home my home office. In the spring of 2020, I got a call to work with first time directors/actor Channing Tatum and his producing partner Reid Carolin on their feature, *Dog*. This project was a godsend as it got me back on my feet. Channing and Reid were going to co-direct, and so I began regular Zoom meetings with them both. Their very capable assistant Garret Levitz handled all the small details deftly. Channing was just as laid-back as he was during the *Gambit* film—that never was—and Reid was as warm as a person as can be. It was a month of peace and a regular income that I sorely needed.

Things really got back to "the new normal" when I landed a job on the streaming series *Ms. Marvel* for Marvel Studios. It was my first job in the cinematic MCU under Kevin Feige after many fun years of storyboarding for the separate company Marvel Television on various shows. *Ms Marvel* would follow a format of six episodes with three sets of directors doing two episodes each.

I first worked with the first directing team of Adil El Arbi and Bilall Fallah and their cinematographer Robrecht Heyvaert, followed by director Meera Menon and her cinematographer Carmen Cabrera and finally with director Sharmeen Obaid-Chinoy and her cinematographer Jules O'Loughlin.

The through-line with the three director-DP teams is that I would start working more with the directors and inevitably, they would get pulled away into production details and I would then work almost exclusively with the DPs. These cinematographers would set up shots with the directors first or work out the storytelling with me. Either way, I was always treated like a collaborator and was allowed to come up with fresh ideas myself.

My tenure on *Ms. Marvel* lasted for an amazing six months duration. I followed that with my third cinematic partnership with Denzel Washington when he directed *A Journal for Jordan*. This project was the true-life story of the romance and relationship between NY Times writer Dana Canedy and First Sergeant Charles Monroe King. Michael B. Jordan stars as the lead of the late Sargeant King. As the show was filming, Michael B. was in development on *Creed III*, which he directed as well. I had helped Denzel on his first film, *Antwone Fisher* and he knew the value that storyboards could bring, especially if you were new to directing. As professionals know, being behind the camera is totally different than being in front of it. One day, Denzel called me from the set saying, "Warren, this is D. Remember that kid I was telling you about?" Denzel proceeded to put me on the phone with Michael B., whom I had met briefly about six years earlier. Michael B. was cordial, but I knew he was taken by surprise with the hand-off of the phone conversation and put on the spot. Looking back, it was an impromptu adult play date. Months later, Michael B.'s business partner, Elizabeth Raposo contacted me and I proceeded to work with them intermittently in the following spring and summer on a few scenes as well as some detailed conceptual storyboards. *Creed III* moved into preproduction in Atlanta and they hired other storyboard artists. I wanted to get back on the show, but it wasn't in the cards. More than a year later while promoting *Creed III*'s release, it was my turn to be taken by surprise when Michael B. actually recounted our initial phone call with Denzel while he was a guest on *Jimmy Kimmel Live*. And Michael B. quoted the actual "Warren, this is D". And hell yea, I used that clip for some publicity!

While in preproduction on *A Journal for Jordan*, Denzel and I would meet at the Bel Air Hotel every few weeks in the late summer of 2020 up into the early months of 2021. I was still finishing work on *Ms. Marvel* but there was no way I was turning down Denzel. I told him of my schedule and he trusted me enough to know I could get his work done in the evenings and weekends.

Our meetings were during the pre-vaccination days so Denzel made sure that the two of us kept a healthy distance from each other, even though we met on his suite's outside patio and wore masks. At sixty-five, Denzel wasn't playing around with Covid, and I did not blame him. If I was handing him a piece of paper or got too close, he would tease me with "keep that Covid away from me!"

Denzel did a great show of friendship that I won't forget. During a meeting, I told him that I recently found out from my sister Linda that our mother had a crush on him. Mom had never revealed this to me. The only other celebrity crush that I knew she had was for the late singer, Billy Eckstine, but that was many decades earlier. I also told D that it was possible that his mother and mine could have known each other as they were both ninety-seven or so and had grown up in Harlem. I further explained to Denzel that my mother's ninety-seventh birthday had just passed days earlier. Denzel said, "Let's call her!" I whipped out my phone and video-chatted Linda as Mom was living with Linda and her family by this time. When she answered the call, I told my sister that a "friend of mine" wanted to talk to Mom. As I handed Denzel the phone, Linda saw him on the screen and was understandably in momentary shock. It was after all, Denzel freaking Washington! Linda went to Mom and gave her the phone. As Mom was hard of hearing, Linda put the earbuds in Mom's ears so she would hear clearly.

An important fact is that my mother was dealing with a little dementia at this point. Her long-term memory was better for sure but once when she was having one of "those days" she mistook me for one of her long passed brothers. To be truthful her dementia took some getting used to. When I visited her in New York, she would usually know me and we'd have a chat, but she certainly wasn't the same person I grew up with. I had to accepted the change in her and continued to love her as I always had.

Well, as soon as my sister gave Mom the phone and she saw Denzel's face, Mom's face lit up and she said with a smile, "I know who you are." While I have heard of miracles, I witnessed one right there! Mom was suddenly twenty years younger and sharp as a tack. Denzel asked her what Harlem blocks she grew up on, and Mom went into details on her high school and college. Mom answered Denzel's questions like she was a *Jeopardy* champion. There was no hesitation at all in her voice. Mom was just a woman talking to "her man," Denzel. When the two ended their chat and we hung up, I told D that Mom hadn't been that clear of mind in *years*. It was then that I told him the ability to reach a dementia sufferer was to now be called "The Denzel Effect." After that display of kindness, anyone is going to get a mouthful from me if they ever step to Denzel.

As 2021 pulled to a close, I saw some interesting possibilities. In 2019, I began what I hope to be a great relationship with the talented and ever professional director, Reinaldo Marcus Green, on a Will Smith vehicle *King Richard*. "Rei" as he is known, is from the Bronx so we got along as native New Yorkers. *King Richard* would go on to receive several 2021 Academy Award nominations and a win for star Will Smith that shall be remembered for a few reasons to say the least. Near the end of 2019, Rei interviewed me at a little café in Santa Monica. Once we finally sat down and chatted, I think I impressed Rei with the fact that I had a healthy knowledge of tennis since I had watched the game avidly since college due to my brother John. Two Black men from New York City were vibing on doing a Will Smith movie together. I was also elated that actress Saniyya Sidney, whom I had the chance to know on *Fences*, was cast as a young Venus Williams. This would also not be the typical Will Smith film as he couldn't rely on his usual effortless charm. The real Richard Williams had rather jagged teeth and a country Louisiana accent, so Will would have to challenge himself as an actor.

Rei, myself and cinematographer Robert Elswit—who I worked with on *Roman J. Israel, Esq.*—would meet in Venice and go over the scenes they wanted to attack. Robert is a great and experienced DP so I often sat back and let he and

MY QUICK RULES FOR ASPIRING STORYBOARD ARTISTS

- Have dynamic storytelling.
- Never keep your client waiting.
- Work on your speed.
- Have a positive attitude in a production office.
- Put the hours in. Don't be the last one in the office and the first to leave. Keep these same hours even if you work at home.
- Don't burn yourself out. Take short breaks as you work.
- Take good notes when meeting to your clients! If they don't mind you taking video of the meeting, even better as you can go back to listen to details.
- The director and producer are not your friend, unless they happen to actually **be** your friend.
- Say "thank you." Treat everyone with the same respect. From the person who hired you to craft service. That chicken wing didn't cook itself.
- My favorite quote by Bruce Lee is, "Absorb what is useful. Discard what is not. Add what is essentially your own." I apply this daily, as I have learned and continue to learn from many other artists but sooner or later, I have to put any reference away and just do my thing.

Peace.
Warren T. Drummond

Rei work things out first and then chime in and give my own ideas. It was a totally pleasant experience working with the tandem. After some Covid shutdowns, *King Richard* was shot, and I was asked back a year later to storyboard for a two-day reshoot. I was allowed to see a cut of the movie, and I was amazed with what I saw. But alas, upon *King Richard*'s official release, the studio didn't give me screen credit. It's an unfortunate thing that happens all too often in the industry.

Looking forward, it's my time to seize control of my career and do the two things that have eluded me, selling my scripts and getting directing assignments. So much has changed since I started in the industry. When I worked on *Above The Rim*, there were so few projects with Black casts being sold, let alone Black directors and writers being able to tell our own stories as well. Black directors are now being hired to helm big comedy and science fiction films. There are also Black creatives who create, run, and sometimes star in their own television shows. The internet and streaming "changed the game" as my wife Betty likes to say.

I must start doing everything right now. I can't waffle or hesitate. There are legends like Jimi Hendrix and Bruce Lee who died just as they were exploding worldwide. Even Chadwick Boseman, who was just coming into his own at forty-three. None of these people will be forgotten because of what they did in the time they were on Earth.

My son Josh is grown into manhood and is moving to make his own mark early. As I am writing this, he has released four music videos (and directed three of them) as hip hop artist, Josh D. King. "D" is for Drummond, and he rightfully sees himself as a King.

Betty and I gave Josh a good foundation to learn and grow in the entertainment industry. Betty has so much in her own creative coffers and is about to make her mark with a novel, a television series based on that novel in addition to an animated series based on *I'm a Brilliant Little Black Boy!*, which she and Josh wrote and published in 2016. Betty saw their children's book and said, "This should be an animated series! Let's do it!" So she, Josh and I developed it into series. Betty always says "have the goal and the *how to* will follow."

Now is the time for me be truly fulfilled as an artist and creator. If I can inspire anyone reading this, hopefully it's to use your talents and abilities to the upmost. Don't settle, because life isn't a dress rehearsal.

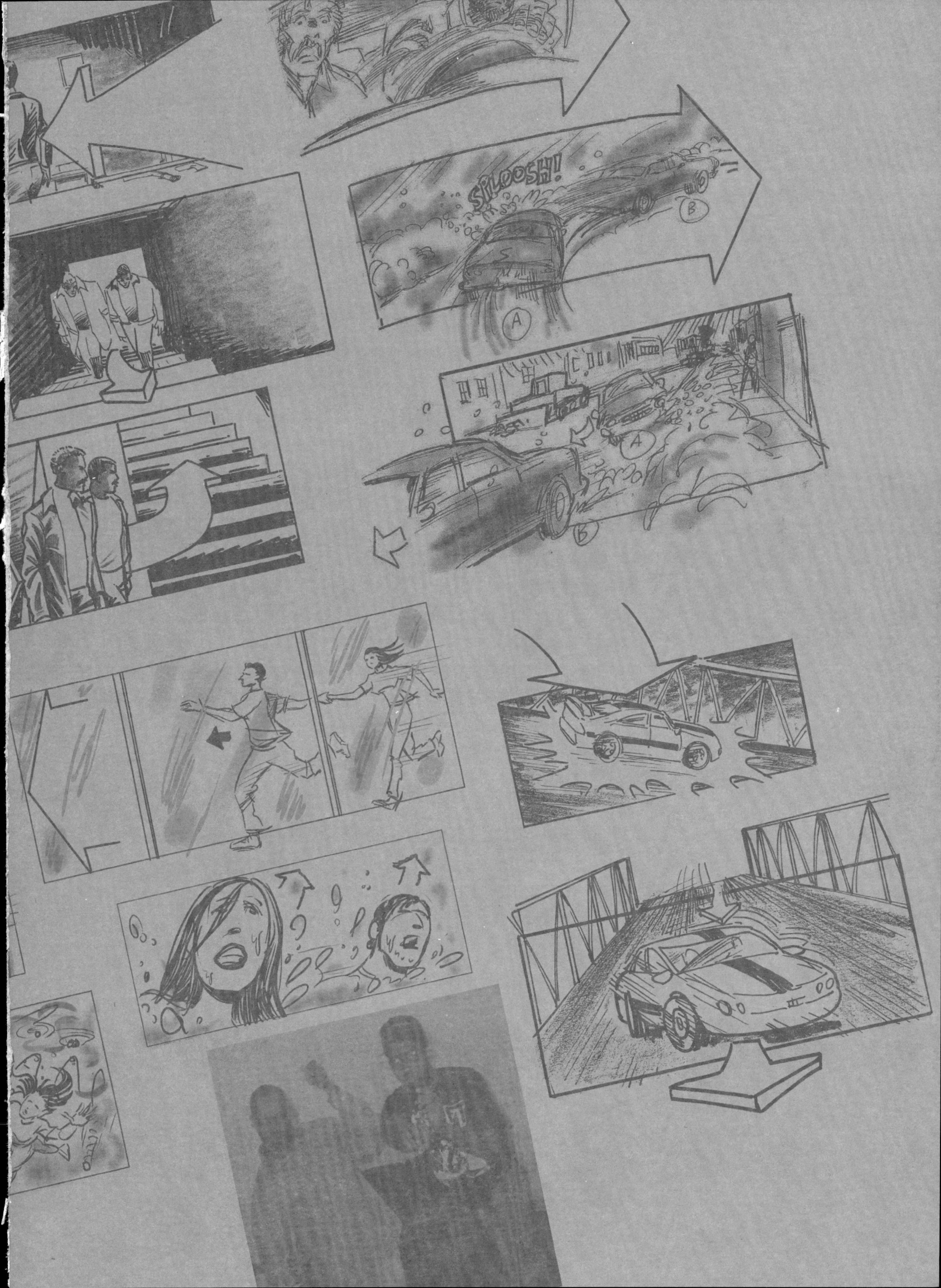
SPLOOSH!

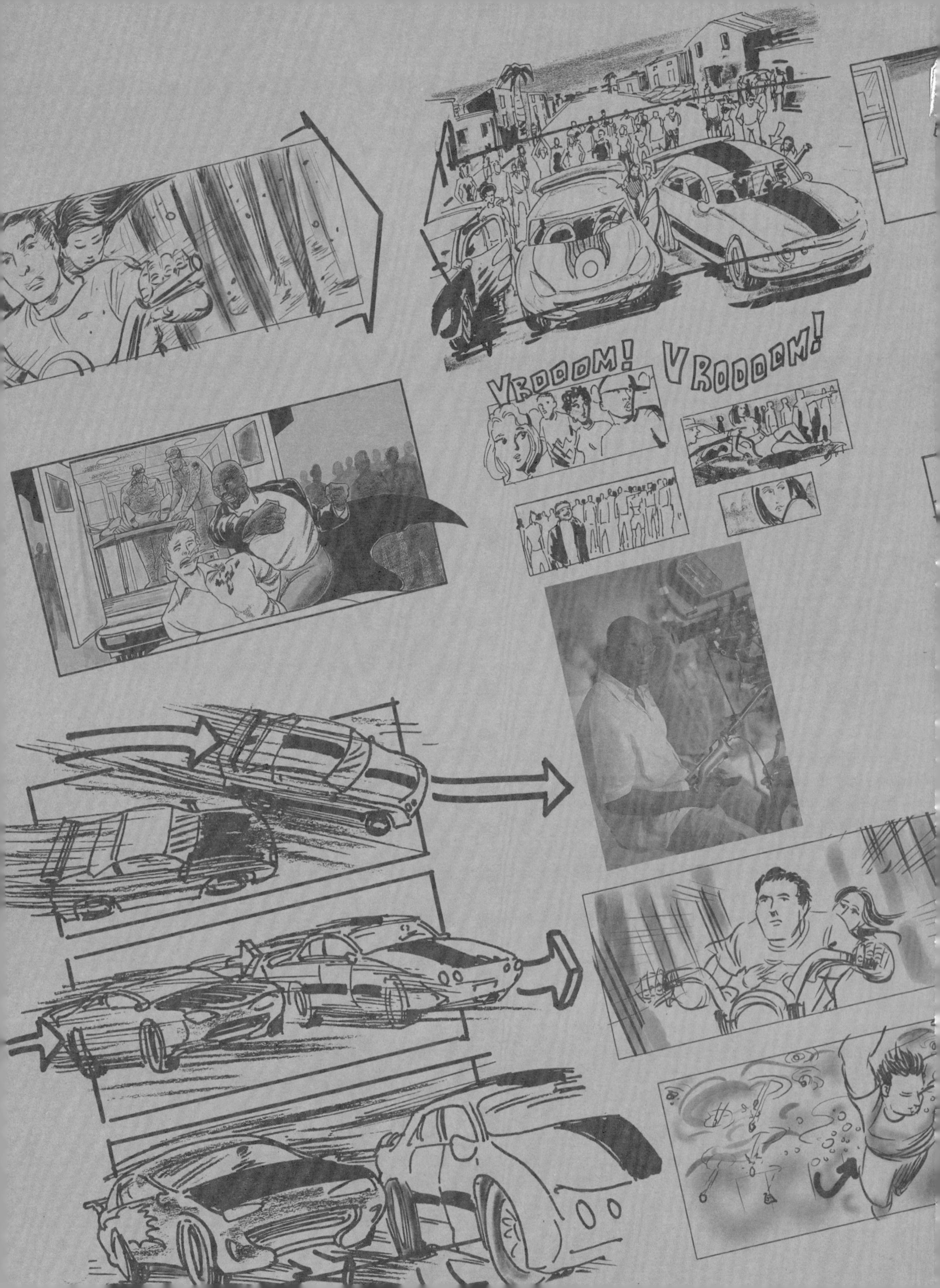
VROOOM!
VROOOOM!